THE ENCYCLOPEDIA OF

SUICIDE

Second Edition

THE ENCYCLOPEDIA OF

SUICIDE

Second Edition

Glen Evans

Norman L. Farberow, Ph.D.

Kennedy Associates

Foreword by

Alan L. Berman, Ph.D.
Executive Director,
American Association of Suicidology

Facts On File, Inc.

The Encyclopedia of Suicide, Second Edition

Facts On File, Inc.
132 West 31st Street
New York NY 10001

Library of Congress Cataloging-in-Publication Data

Evans, Glen
    The encyclopedia of suicide / Glen Evans, Norman L. Farberow.—2nd ed.
        p. cm.
    Includes bibliographical references and index.
    ISBN 0-8160-4525-9
    1. Suicide—Dictionaries. 2. Suicide—United States—Dictionaries. 3. Suicide—United States—Statistics.
    4. Suicide victims—Services for—United States—Directories. 5. Suicide victims—Services for—
    Canada—Directories. I. Farberow, Norman L. II. Title. III. Series.
        HV6545 .E87 2003
        362.28'03—dc21   2002027166

Text and cover design by Cathy Rincon

Printed in the United States of America

VB FOF 10 9 8 7 6 5 4 3 2 1

This book is printed on acid-free paper.

The man who kills a man kills a man.
The man who kills himself kills all men.
As far as he is concerned, he wipes out the world.

—G. K. Chesterton

The great tragedy of life is not death,
but what dies inside of us while we live.

—Norman Cousins

That life is worth living is the most
necessary of assumptions, and were it not
assumed, the most impossible of conclusions.

—George Santayana

CONTENTS

FOREWORD

Why an encyclopedia of suicide? What is it that the average teenager or young or older adult needs to know about suicide? The answers to these questions are both simple and complex.

In the decade 1990–99, more than 300,000 people in the United States took their own life. In the same decade, an estimated 8 million worldwide died by their own hand.

Each and every year, suicide accounts for far more deaths than both homicide and AIDS and HIV-related diseases in the United States and far more than are caused by wars around the world. In China, the most populous country in the world, suicide is the leading cause of death.

Each year in the United States, almost 20 percent of high school students consider suicide—and almost half that number report that they made an actual suicide attempt. Across all ages, more than 650,000 people in the United States receive emergency medical care each year after trying to take their own life.

Suicide and suicidal behaviors know no boundaries. They are tragic outcomes to problems affecting the young and the old, the rich and the poor, males and females, whites and blacks and Native Americans. They are tragedies that, for the most part, need not happen.

Suicides leave family members and friends, classmates and teachers, coworkers and neighbors emotionally wounded—some for many, many years. Suicides rob our society of poten-tially productive lives and cost this country an estimated $11 billion annually. Suicides represent our collective failure to observe and help our fellow human in distress.

Suicide, although ultimately a very private act, is a serious *public* health problem. It is significant enough for our nation's chief physician—the U.S. Surgeon General—to have issued a *National Strategy for Suicide Prevention* in 2001. It is significant enough for the Institute of Medicine to have issued in 2002 a report entitled *Reducing Suicide: A National Imperative*. Note the word *imperative*.

These reports remind us that we know enough to approach suicide as a preventable problem. With information such as the reader will find in this volume, and the willingness to partner with those who have the tools to help, suicide prevention is everyone's business.

Suicide is a complicated subject; as the French novelist and playwright Albert Camus (1913–60) wrote, it is "the only truly serious philosophical problem." It is the province of public health and mental health, of biology and sociology, of psychology and religion. We have no single unifying theory of why a person takes his or her own life, and yet we have a treasure trove of empirical studies to help us reasonably understand the many answers to that question.

There is no one type of suicidal person, yet across cultures and personality types we know much to describe risk for and protection from the urge to self-harm. This volume is a starting point for the reader to explore the complexity of suicide and better understand what is known. In turn, we trust that this understanding will promote an investment of energy to make the difference in the life of a potential suicide.

—Alan Berman, Ph.D.
Executive Director,
American Association of Suicidology

PREFACE

Suicide is a tragic and potentially preventable public health problem that is currently the eighth leading cause of death in the United States. About 11 of every 100,000 Americans commit suicide each year, and about half a million others are treated in hospital emergency rooms as a result of attempted suicide.

Many Americans believe that urban violence and murder are the country's most pressing problems, but what most people do not realize is that while it may seem that the pages of newspapers are filled with murder stories, in fact there are 50 percent more deaths by suicide than by homicide. The very old and the very young are most at risk.

In May 2002, Surgeon General David Satcher launched a national campaign to combat this problem, seeking to create suicide-prevention programs in schools, on the job, in prisons, old-age facilities, and community service groups.

This book has been designed as a guide and reference to a wide range of terms related to suicide and to additional information and addresses of organizations that deal with this topic. *It is not a substitute for prompt assessment and treatment by experts trained in crisis management, depression, and the diagnosis of suicidal thoughts or behavior.*

In this new, revised edition, we have tried to present the latest information in the field, based on the newest research and statistics. Readers will learn the latest developments in a range of topics, including suicide and the law, physician-assisted suicide, and the right to die. All state-by-state and international statistics on suicide have been completely updated.

In addition, the book discusses the latest research into the alleged link between certain drugs and suicidal behavior, such as Prozac and Accutane. Most of the biographies of famous individuals throughout history who committed suicide have been expanded and enlarged, and recent suicides by well-known individuals (such as Kurt Cobain and Vince Foster) have been added. Other all-new topics include

- gender differences in suicide
- suicide bombers
- ethnicity and suicide
- mass suicide
- different types of suicide (such as gestured suicide, love pact suicide, penacide, agenerative suicide, altruistic suicide, and so on)
- suicide by cop
- specific jobs and suicide
- murder-suicide
- new organizations
- psychological tests, such as Suicidal Ideation Questionnaire
- school violence and suicide

In addition to the all-new entries, almost every entry has been revised and extensively updated to include the newest information on statistics, publications, and events in the field of suicidology. Likewise, appendixes have been completely updated, including all addresses and phone numbers for organizations, together with new Internet websites.

Information in this book comes from the most up-to-date sources available and includes the most recent research in the field of suicidology. A bibliography has been provided for readers who seek additional sources of information. All entries are cross-referenced, and appendices provide additional information.

Incidences of suspected or threatened suicidal attempts should *never* be ignored, because it is not true that suicidal thoughts are simply threats or cries for attention. A suicidal threat is a medical emergency and should be promptly referred to mental health professionals, crisis hotlines, or crisis counselors.

—Carol Turkington
Kennedy Associates
Cumru, Pennsylvania

ACKNOWLEDGMENTS

No book is written or revised in a vacuum, and there are many groups and individuals to thank who provided invaluable help during the revision of this book.

Thanks to the staffs of the American Association of Suicidology, the American Psychological Association, the American Psychiatric Association, Profnet, the Hemlock Society, the National Institutes of Health, the Centers for Disease Control and Prevention, the National Library of Medicine, the American Foundation for Suicide Prevention, the American Sociological Association, the Association for Death Education and Counseling, the Center for Suicide Research and Prevention, the Center for Thanatology Research and Education, Compassionate Friends, CONTACT USA, Dying with Dignity, Lifekeepers Foundation, the National Alliance for the Mentally Ill, San Francisco Suicide Prevention Center, SA/VE, and SOLO.

Thanks also to Lanny Berman; my agents, Bert Holtje and Gene Brissie; my editor, James Chambers, for patient editing; and Sarah Fogarty, for handling details so well.

INTRODUCTION:
The History of Suicide

Suicide has been a part of human history since recorded time. It is not universal, for there are some places throughout the world where suicide does not occur, but such places are quite rare.

The word *suicide* is of relatively recent origin. It does not appear in the Old Testament, nor in early Christian writings, nor even in the text of John Donne's *Biathanatos* (1644), one of the earliest English-language works defending suicide. Although the word seems to come from the Latin, there was no original single Latin word for the act; the Romans always used phrases to express the thought. The expressions used most often were *sibi mortem consciscere* ("to procure his own death"), *vim sibi inferre* ("to cause violence to himself"), or *sua manu cadere* ("to fall by his own hand").

The word *suicide* first appeared in 1662, when Edward Philips, in his *New World of Words*, called suicide "a barbarous word, more appropriately derived from *sus*, a sow, than from the pronoun *sui*, as if it were a swinish part for a man to kill himself." The *Oxford English Dictionary*, however, states that suicide was first used in English in 1651, derived from the modern Latin word *suicidium*, which in turn had been produced by combining the Latin pronoun for "self" and the verb "to kill." Almost a hundred years later, in 1752, the word appeared in France, in the *Dictionnaire de Trevoux*.

At one time, it was thought that suicide was a by-product of civilization and therefore unknown in primitive societies. To some extent this belief was influenced by the notion of the "happy savage" advanced by philosopher Jean-Jacques Rousseau (1712–78). Reliable evidence, however, indicates that suicide has existed in numerous primitive tribes around the globe. In 1894, suicide was reported among the North and South American Indians, Bedouins, people of the Caucasus, Indians, Melanesians, Micronesians, Polynesians, and Indonesians. For example, there were two ways the Trobriand Islanders killed themselves: by jumping from the top of a palm tree and by taking fatal poison from the gallbladder of a globe fish. Others reported a relatively high suicide rate in Tikopia, a Polynesian community in the western Pacific; in the Maria and other aboriginal tribes of central India; the American Indians; the Netsilik Eskimos of Greenland; and different rates of suicide among the Africans.

On the other hand, researchers have found that suicide was unknown among the Yahgans of Tierra del Fuego, the Andaman Islanders, and various Australian aborigine tribes.

Attitudes toward suicide have varied a great deal, usually reflecting the psychocultural history of the society in which suicide has occurred. Those societies that strongly condemned suicide most often associated the act with superstition and magic and reacted to it with horror and antagonism. Taboos on suicide were developed in order to ward off the evils that were thought to accompany self-inflicted death or to keep the spirit of the person who committed suicide in prison so that it could not return to haunt the living.

Suicide usually took two forms: social or individual. Social suicide was generally the self-destruction of an individual demanded by a society as a price for being a member of that society. For example, sacrificing one's life for another is a practice found in some Eskimo tribes in which the old and sick were expected to sacrifice themselves to help ensure the survival of their group. In some primitive cultures, suicide was also a way of expressing anger and revenge in a rigidly prescribed way; for example, when a Trobriander was accused of violating a tribal taboo he could climb to the top of a palm tree, name his accuser, and then jump head first from the tree. Individual suicide, on the other hand, usually occurred as a way of preserving honor, expiation of cowardice, termination of pain, preservation of chastity, escaping from personal disgrace by falling into the hands of an enemy, or intense despair from separation or loss of loved ones.

Suicide in Ancient Times

In ancient Egypt the attitude toward suicide was neutral, inasmuch as death was seen as merely a passage from one form of existence to another and suicide as a humane method of escaping from intolerable hardship and injustice. The dead were considered abstract coequals with the living and with the gods and thus had the same physical and emotional needs.

The first known writing about suicide was found in an Egyptian papyrus entitled *A Dispute over Suicide* (also known as *The Dialogue of a Misanthrope with His Own Soul*), written by an unidentified writer during Egypt's First Intermediate Period (2280–2000 B.C.). In one papyrus, a dialogue occurs between the soul and the self in which the man, tired of life, tries to convince his soul to accompany him into death. Many of the arguments address the question of whether a person has a right to take his or her life under any circumstance, reflecting the conflict between individual freedom and social responsibility. The soul hesitates, afraid the man will be deprived of a proper funeral if he commits suicide, destroying the soul's chances for a blissful afterlife. The soul argues that death is accompanied by separation and grief, but the suicidal man contends that death for him would be a cure and a vacation.

Ambivalence toward the choice between life and death is the central theme of this discourse. The soul argues that death is no respecter of social position, but the suicidal self is motivated by other forces: the dishonor of his name, the loss of personal worth, the injustice and depravity of society, the reversal of value and honor, the absence of the good, the severance of friendship, a general mistrust of the world, and a fantasy with death. In death he expects to achieve the triumph of immortality and to be a god who will punish the unjust. The soul's advice, however, is to cling to life, to assume religious responsibilities and to approach death gradually in old age.

The Egyptians allowed a person condemned to death to take his own life (execution by suicide). Later, the Romans also followed this practice. Further evidence of the acceptance and tolerance of suicide by the Egyptians is reported by L. D. Hankoff, who points out that among the 42 questions concerning sinful acts ritualistically asked of a dead person as a Negative Confession or a Declaration of Innocence, there was no question indicating a prohibition against suicide, even though there were questions about violence, bloodshed, and vicious or cruel acts.

Among the ancient Hebrews suicide was infrequent, apparently for several reasons. The Hebrews maintained a strong attachment to life and a positive attitude toward the world, which, according to their teachings, God had made good especially for them, His chosen people. Therefore humans should not find fault with God's work; those who did commit suicide were usually considered insane or temporarily deranged. As a result, sanctions were not usually imposed against suicide; the bodies of suicide victims were not desecrated and they were not refused major funeral rights.

Nevertheless, suicide was clearly prohibited by Judaism, which underscored the sacredness of life as well as the dignity of humans and the value of the individual. It was considered an affront to God to end one's life. Life was to be preserved, except when a person was guilty of murder, sexual immorality, or idolatry. To commit suicide even under the most trying circumstances was to give up hope in God. The value of life, however, was not absolute; life could be sacrificed for the sake of goodness, morality, and God. Exceptions to the prohibition of suicide were made specifically for extreme conditions, such as when a Jew was forced to betray his faith, when he had committed a grave sin, or when he faced capture and disgrace in war.

The Old Testament and related books neither condemn nor condone suicide. The Old Testament matter-of-factly relates seven instances of self-destructive behavior: Abimelech's skull was crushed by a stone thrown from a tower, reportedly by a woman, and he had one of his soldiers kill him with his sword so that it could not be said he had been slain by a woman (Judges 9:54). When Samson's hair grew long again, and his strength returned, he pulled down the pillars of a Philistine temple, crushing to death himself as well as the multitude gathered there to mock and taunt him (Judges 16:28–31). Ahitophel, foreseeing military defeat with his coconspirator Absalom in the revolt against King David, hanged himself (II Samuel 17:23). Saul, the first king of Israel, led his army in a battle against the Philistines on Mount Gilboa. Against overwhelming odds Saul fought as long as he could and then killed himself only after three of his sons had been killed and he had been severely wounded. Seeing his sovereign dead, Saul's armor bearer also fell on his sword and died with

him. Saul took his own life so as not to fall into the hands of his enemies, who would have tortured him and desecrated God (I Samuel 31:4; II Samuel 1:6; I Chronicles 10:4). Zimri killed himself by burning the king's house over him when the city of Tirzah in which he was besieged was captured and he became aware of the hopelessness of the situation (I Kings 16:18). Razis, a patriotic elder of Jerusalem, also chose to commit suicide rather than be slain by his enemies (II Maccabees 14:46).

The New Testament also neither specifically prohibits suicide nor condemns suicidal behavior. The suicides of Judas Iscariot (Matthew 17:5), who hangs himself after betraying Jesus, and the suicide attempt of Paul's jailer (Acts 16:27) are reported factually and briefly.

The deaths of Saul and his armor bearer was related to one of the most important Hebrew taboos of that era—a strong prohibition against human bloodshed. Suicide was abhorrent to the ancient Hebrews because it exposed the community to the possibilities of uncontrolled bloodshed and an unattended corpse. Saul's suicide was a breach of the suicide prohibition and therefore required much justification, such as the inevitability of his death and the degradation that would have followed had he lived as a captive of the Philistines. The Old Testament states that he was beheaded by the Philistines and his body hung on the wall of the city. The Jews of a nearby town are reported to have courageously taken the body down in the middle of the night and carried it back to their town for a dignified burial under a sacred tree. Before the burial they burned the body as an act of reverence and as a way of undoing the illegal spilling of Saul's blood.

The Torah does not explicitly forbid suicide. It is only in the accumulated body of rabbinical literature that prohibitions against suicides and the exceptions to them are provided. The example of Saul is explained as a taking of one's own life in order to avoid the greater sin of profaning God's name. Suicides were permissible if committed to prevent dishonor to God's name.

There was some question concerning burial rituals for ancient Jews who committed suicide. Burial was generally accompanied by an elaborate set of ritual acts. The specific rule was that there would be no rending of clothes and no eulogizing in the case of a suicide. However, the general rule was that the public should participate in funeral rites out of respect for the living rather than for the dead and should say the mourner's blessing. For all practical purposes, suicides have been treated as individuals who destroyed themselves unwillfully, so the honors and rights have usually been granted.

However, suicide during war was acceptable for ancient Jews. For example, Josephus, born Joseph Ben Matthias, was originally a priest and a general in the army of the Jews. He was captured by the Romans and lived the rest of his life as a Roman citizen in a time when great change was taking place in the lives of the Jewish people. He wrote the history of the time in four books, *The Jewish War, Antiquities of the Jews, His Life* and *Against Apion.*

Josephus was involved in a mass suicide when he commanded a detachment of Jewish troops at Jotopata in A.D. 68. Surrounded by the Roman army led by Vespasian, his soldiers wanted to kill themselves to avoid surrender. Josephus argued against it, insisting that "for those who have laid mad hands upon themselves, the darker regions of the netherworld receives their souls, and God, their father, visits upon their posterity the outrageous acts of the parents. That is why this crime, so hateful to God, is punished also by the sagest of legislators. With us it is ordained that the body of a suicide should be exposed, unburied until sunset. . . ." He was, however, accused of cowardice and threatened with death. Josephus finally agreed that this was a situation in which they were defending the Torah and sanctifying the holy name, and therefore even suicide was justified. He proposed the usual solution in such circumstances—"that they commit mutual slaughter by lot"—and they agreed. "By chance or by the

providence of God" he and one soldier remained as the last survivors, and Josephus was able to persuade the soldier to surrender with him to the Romans.

The most spectacular mass suicide occurred in A.D. 74 and was reported by Josephus. Pursued by the Romans, a group of Zealots and their families led by Eleazar Ben Jair took refuge on a high plateau at Masada. By this time, the Second Temple had been destroyed by the Romans, and belief in the hereafter among the Jews had become widespread. After three years of siege Ben Jair realized their stores were low and that they could not hold out much longer. Eleazar called his troops and the people together, reminded his troops of their promise never to become slaves of the Romans, and persuaded them to die by their own hand. He argued that "death affords our souls their liberty and sends them to their own place of purity where they are to be insensible to all sorts of miseries." The soldiers then killed their wives and children and followed this by killing each other—a total of 960 people. Even the battle-hardened Roman veterans were reported to have been awed by the discipline, pride, and contempt for life shown by the people. The only survivors were two women and five children who had hidden in a cave.

In his books Josephus lists a number of individual suicides, some of them concerned with Herod and members of his family. For example, he reports the suicide of Herod's younger brother, Phasael, who had been captured by King Antigones. Phasael, thinking Herod to be dead, had killed himself by hitting his head against a large rock while he was in chains awaiting execution. A year later, Herod conquered Antigones and executed him in revenge for Phasael's death. The suicides described by Josephus ranged all the way from Abimelech, in 1200 B.C., through the mass suicide by the Jews at Masada in A.D. 74. He also described two suicide attempts by Herod, one in 41 B.C. by sword and the second in 4 B.C. by knife.

The Greeks and Romans

The attitude toward suicide among the Greeks and the Romans varied widely over time. Plato condemned suicide in general, although he outlined a few exceptions, but Aristotle condemned suicide as an act of cowardice and an offense against the state. The Epicureans and Stoics considered it a reasonable expression of human freedom, but their beliefs remained unusual throughout that period.

Honor and its various aspects were important concerns among the Greeks and Romans. Suicide was considered an appropriate solution to dishonor during the period of Homer. One of the first examples is of Jocasta, the mother of Oedipus, who was unaware that he was her son, and married him after he had unknowingly killed his own father. Another example is that of Ajax, the Greater, who was able to retrieve the body of Achilles after the latter had been killed by Paris, the Trojan, with an arrow to his only vulnerable spot, his heel. However, the armor of Achilles was given to Odysseus rather than to Ajax, who felt so dishonored as a result that he killed himself.

Suicide to maintain one's honor was highly approved. One example is that of Charondas, a prominent citizen who helped write the laws in Catania, a Greek colony in Sicily. One of the laws he formulated was that no man who was armed was to enter the town assembly, on pain of death. When he inadvertently entered without removing his dagger and realized what he had done, he drew it and used it to kill himself.

Suicides of honor, to avoid capture and humiliation, were common in the wars among the Greeks and Romans. For example, Demosthenes, who took poison when he was about to be captured by the leader of the Macedonians; Vulteius and all his troops killed themselves when they were surrounded by soldiers of Pompey and escape was impossible; and many of Otho's soldiers killed themselves when they learned that their emperor had killed himself rather than continue further slaughter of his men in his war against Vitellius.

Many suicides during the Roman Republic were of the heroic type. Among the more famous are those of P. Decius Mus, 337 B.C., who raced ahead of his troops to certain death in a battle near Vesuvius; Decius the Younger, son of Mus, who also invited his death in 295 B.C., in a fight against the Gauls; and Cato the Younger of Utica, who killed himself in Africa when his troops were defeated by Caesar. Another heroic suicide was that of Regulus, the consul who was captured by the Carthaginians and sent back to Rome to propose peace. He gave his pledge to return no matter what happened. When in Rome, however, he argued strongly against peace and then returned to Carthage knowing that he would be killed.

Unrequited love and the death of a loved one were also considered reasonable cause for suicide. Dido was queen of Carthage when Aeneas landed there on his flight from Troy. Dido fell in love with him and killed herself when he continued on his journey. The Aegean Sea is named after the father of Theseus who forgot to raise the white sail that indicated victory as he returned from his voyage to slay the Minotaur in Crete. When Aegeus saw the black sail he assumed his son was dead and drowned himself in the sea, which from then on bore his name. Another story involving loss of love is that of the suicide of Hero, whose lover, Leander, used to swim the Dardanelles nightly from Abydos to the Hellespont, where she lived. One night, however, the wind blew out the light that Hero set out to guide Leander and he drowned. When Leander's body washed ashore the next morning, Hero was beside herself with grief—and drowned herself as well.

Greek history also relates heroic mass suicides of some Greek soldiers after they were captured. Thucydides recounts two incidents, both taking place at Corcyra two years apart, in 427 B.C. and 425 B.C. The first involved 50 men, who, taken prisoner and condemned to death, escaped execution by killing one another or hanging themselves. Two years later, when another group was again taken prisoner in large numbers, the prisoners realized their fellow men were being taken out and executed, so they killed themselves by thrusting arrows into their throats or by hanging themselves.

According to historians, the period between the seventh and fourth centuries B.C. was filled with pessimism and disenchantment with life; a number of philosophers, such as Theognis of Megara, Sophocles, Euripides, Herodotus, and Democritus, advocated suicide, stating that it was "best to leave this world as quickly as possible." It was at this time, in 403 B.C., that hemlock was introduced. Although not readily available, it was given to Socrates as a special favor. The possibility of a quick and painless death may have been a major reason that the 70-year-old Socrates made the decision to end his own life. Later, when the Greek senate was convinced that any committed crime deserved death, the individual who wished to commit suicide was allowed to do so by choosing to drink hemlock.

Despite his choice of suicide, Socrates is known to have disapproved of ending one's life before God had decided it was time to die. "Man is situated in this life as if he were on a post or station which he must not quit without leave; because the gods exert a providential care over us on which account we are a part (as it were) of their property and possessions; and because we should think it unjust and punishable (if it were in our power to punish) for any slave of our own to kill himself without our permission."

Seneca, in *Epistles* and *De Ira*, defended suicide as a last buffer against intolerable suffering. "The eternal law has done nothing better than this, that it has given us only one entrance into life, but a thousand ways of escape out of it," he wrote. "Does life please you? Live on. Does it not? Go from whence you came." Also, "Wherever you look there is the end of evils. You see that yawning precipice—there you may descend to liberty. You see that sea, that river, that well —liberty sits at the bottom. . . . Do you seek the way to freedom? You may find it in every vein of your body."

Epictetus, a noted Greek Stoic philosopher, stated "live as long as it is agreeable; if the game does not please you, go; if you stay, do not complain." However, he urged restraint and felt a person should have good reason before committing suicide.

In general, the Romans did not encourage suicide, and the government officially opposed it. Nevertheless, there was a permissive attitude toward it, and in some of the municipal senates, free poison containing hemlock was supplied to anyone who could give valid reasons for wanting to commit suicide. Suicide was frequent under the first Roman emperors, with whole families sometimes committing suicide in public. Most often these were families under threat of prosecution for treason. By committing suicide, a condemned person avoided forfeiture of property. Also, the suicide victim was permitted customary burial, which would have been otherwise denied for those who were executed for a crime. It was not until later that Roman law was changed to forbid suicide committed in order to avoid forfeiture of property. It was still possible, however, for the heirs to bring to trial the question of the guilt of the deceased. If innocence was proved, the heirs were then entitled to the deceased's effects.

Suicide in Rome was also punished primarily when the interests of the state were involved, as when soldiers or slaves killed themselves. If the soldier who committed suicide did so for no adequate reason (sickness or disease would suffice) or to avoid military duty, he was considered guilty of desertion. If the attempt was unsuccessful he was then punished with death. If his act was because of depression, sorrow, or madness, however, his punishment was less severe.

Under Roman law those whose crimes merited execution would have their property officially confiscated and would also be deprived of proper burial. Therefore, when Nero ordered the statesman, dramatist, and philosopher Seneca to commit suicide because he suspected his former teacher of having plotted against him, the order was viewed as a kindness. Nero also caused the death of Seneca's nephew, the poet Lucan, and of Petronius, considered the most witty, elegant, and sophisticated Roman of his time. The fear of dishonor brought on the suicide of Cassius, who ordered his slave to stab him.

One of the more striking suicides was that of Arria, the wife of Caecina Paetus, a senator who was involved in plotting against Emperor Claudius. She is reported to have plunged a sword in her breast to show her husband how and then handed the sword to him, assuring him that it did not hurt.

Lucrece committed suicide after being raped by Sextus Tarquinius, a Roman general who threatened to kill her unless she yielded to him, saying that he would tell everyone he had killed her because he had found her with a slave who was her lover. The next morning Lucrece summoned her family and her husband, told them what had happened, and then killed herself. This story has been immortalized in one of Shakespeare's poems.

Stoicism accepted and, under certain conditions, even recommended suicide. Zeno, the founder of Stoicism, wrote that a wise man could accept suicide if it provided escape from intolerable pain, mutilation, or incurable disease, or if it was for his country's safety or the sake of his friends. Zeno is reported to have taken his own life because, feeling advanced in age, he did not wish to endure the discomfort of a broken toe. Cleanthes, Zeno's successor, is reported to have fasted because of a boil on his gum. When the boil disappeared, Cleanthes decided he had gone so far toward death he might as well go the rest of the way, and he killed himself.

The Middle Ages

Suicide in general was tolerated and even approved in the Roman Empire until Christian views began to influence social and legal attitudes. At the very beginning of the Christian era, however, suicide was highly attractive to many Christians because it offered them martyrdom

and, according to their beliefs, the opportunity to enter heaven. In addition, the church undertook care of the surviving family, thus relieving the suicide victim of any guilt or anxiety about abandoning them. This attitude persisted well into the fourth century.

The early Christians were morbidly obsessed with death. For them, life on earth was important only in preparation for the hereafter, so that men studied how to die rather than how to live. The primary objective became the avoidance of sin, because to engage in sin would result in perpetual punishment. Suicide was committed out of fear of falling before temptation, at times indirectly by provoking nonbelievers to kill them, at other times directly, as by jumping off cliffs in large numbers. According to St. Augustine, the heretical Donatists and Circumcelliones in North Africa killed themselves in vast numbers by leaping from cliffs with "paroxysms of frantic joy . . . till the rocks below were reddened with their blood."

Finally, St. Augustine, in the *City of God*, vigorously condemned suicide, stating that no private person could take upon himself the right to kill a guilty person—this right rested with the church and state; that suicide precluded the possibility of repentance, and that it violated the Sixth Commandment ("Thou shalt not kill"). It was, therefore, a greater sin than the sin one might wish to avoid by killing oneself. St. Augustine had to account for accepted suicides and sacrifices in the Old Testament, such as that by Samson and Abraham's willingness to sacrifice his son, Isaac. His answer was that in such instances divine authority had been granted for the death. St. Augustine's stand against suicide was probably a necessary corollary of the church's teaching about the importance of the hereafter. If a human's life on earth was merely a period of waiting for divine glory, the true believer was naturally tempted to hasten the time when he or she would enter eternal bliss.

In addition to St. Augustine, other early fathers of the church who contributed to the development of the church's attitude toward suicide were St. Cyprian, St. Ambrose, St. Irenaeus, and St. Athanasius.

The first Christian prohibition of suicide is sometimes attributed to the Council of Arles in 452. However, this measure was directed only against the suicide of servants, and it described the suicidal person as being possessed by the devil. The second Council of Orleans, in 533, indirectly expressed disapproval of suicide by allowing the church to receive offerings from those killed in the commission of a crime provided that they had not laid violent hands on themselves. In other words, suicide was regarded as worse than any other crime.

The 15th canon of the Council of Braga in 563 took the decisive step of imposing penalties on all suicide victims and their families by denying them the usual funeral rights with the eucharist and the singing of psalms. The Council of Auxerre in 578 decreed that no oblation would be received from any person who had killed himself, and it also reaffirmed the penalties and the principle of indiscriminate condemnation for suicide. The Antisidor Council in 590 invalidated the offerings of a suicide victim as a means of expiation for sin. The canon of the Council of Braga that denied suicide victims the usual funeral rights was adopted in England by the Council of Hereford in 673, bringing England into line with the practices on the Continent. The Capitula of Theodore, archbishop of Canterbury, decreed that neither mass nor Christian burial was to be performed for suicide victims unless they had been insane, but that prayers and psalms could be offered.

In the seventh century, there were reportedly a number of cases of persons condemned to church penance who could not face the severities involved and attempted to kill themselves in desperation. The 16th Council of Toledo, in 693, punished a person who attempted suicide with exclusion from the fellowship of the church for two months.

The church relaxed its attitude toward suicide briefly and provided in the texts of the Penitentials in 829 that masses and prayers could be said for the insane who committed suicide. In addition, the Council of Troyes (878) modified the strictness of previous legislation and allowed certain rituals for suicidal deaths. In 855, however, the Third Council of Valence denied Christian burial to those who died in tournaments, jousts, and other forbidden contests considered similar to suicidal deaths.

Finally, after King Edgar's canon in 967 accepted the ecclesiastical dictum denying burial rights to suicide victims, the Synod of Nîmes in 1204 reaffirmed all the previous council decisions against suicide and then extended their judgments by refusing people who committed suicide even the right of burial in holy ground. While it did not go so far as to demand punishment for the dead, the severe penalty of depriving burial rights suggested a reemergence of some of the earlier pagan horror against such deaths and the practice of dishonoring the corpses. Bodies were buried at crossroads with a stake through their heart to prevent the soul from wandering. This practice continued as late as 1811 and did not actually stop until 1823, when a suicide victim named Griffith was buried at the crossroads formed by Eaton Street, Grosvenor Place, and King's Road. The following month a statute was passed to abolish the practice.

In France the body of a suicide victim was dragged through the streets head downward and then hanged on a gallows. In England the properties of suicide victims were confiscated until 1870, and, as late as 1882, by law the person had to be buried at night. The service of the Church of England still cannot be used for a suicide victim. However, other Protestant denominations do provide for a service. In Danzig, now a part of Poland (Gdańsk), the body of a suicide victim was not permitted to be taken out through the door but had to be passed through a window, even if a hole had to be knocked in the wall when there was no window.

However, heretics and Jews continued to commit suicide frequently during the Middle Ages. Pogroms were conducted against Jews in England, especially in the early years of Richard the Lionhearted, which triggered a number of instances of mass suicides. At York in 1190, 600 Jews killed themselves to escape oppression. Another group of suicide martyrs was the Albigenses in southern France, 5,000 of whom reportedly were put to death as heretics in 1218. The Albigenses believed in the Catharic heresy that substituted belief in a dualism—God versus Satan—for the belief in the Christian idea of a unitary God. The main tenets of their doctrine favored suicide because they included detachment from worldly concerns, rejection of private property, and abolition of marriage, inasmuch as it led to the perpetuation of the human species. Their favorite methods of suicide were by fire, by jumping, and by the *endura,* a voluntary fast.

Another group in which large numbers of suicides commonly occurred was the Russian Raskolniki, who, early in the 17th century, clung to the old faith in the form of the Russian Orthodox Church. A number of incidents of mass suicide by immolation are reported to have occurred in crowded churches and remote monasteries. Suicide in great numbers was also reported to have occurred among wives of priests after celibacy for the priesthood was decreed in the 11th century. There were also reports of numerous suicides occurring during epidemics, particularly when the Black Plague swept Europe in the 14th century.

In the 13th century, St. Thomas Aquinas formulated an authoritative church position on suicide in his *Summa Theologica.* He set forth three arguments against suicide: self-destruction is contrary to man's natural inclinations; man has no right to deprive society of his presence and activity; and man is God's property and it is up to God, not man, to decide on our life and death.

The years between St. Augustine and St. Thomas Aquinas were filled with continual expressions of rejection of and resistance to suicide, with increasingly harsh edicts both against the corpse of the suicide victim and his surviving family. Dante's *Inferno* appeared early in the 14th century and illustrated the strong element of fear in human's reaction to deliberate self-destruction. In his *Divine Comedy,* Dante described the souls of suicides as being encased in thorny, withered trees on which Harpies fed and inflicted severe wounds, drawing hideous cries of lamentation and pain from the trees.

The Augustinian-Thomistic view regarding suicide still remains essentially the position of the Roman Catholic Church, although today the church acknowledges two kinds of suicide: the illicit act of taking one's life and the licit sacrifice of one's life. In the former, an individual may cause his or her own death by doing something that is self-destructive or by refusing to do something that is necessary for survival; either is an act of self-destruction. In general, Catholic theologians agree that direct suicide is intrinsically evil. It is permissible, however, if it is committed in response to an inspiration from God, an explanation used to justify the deaths of martyrs who have sacrificed their lives in defense of their virtue or their faith. However, current thinking among Catholic theologians is that an individual's faith can be defended by means other than direct self-murder.

Sacrifice is deemed licit when the person does not desire death, or when death is not the specific aim but rather a consequence of an otherwise legitimate action that is performed. The important criterion used in judging the act is that the greater the risk to one's life the greater must be the compensating good to be obtained. Formerly the church denied ecclesiastical burial to a suicide victim unless signs of repentance had been shown before death. However, for many years the church has not applied this rule and generally grants the benefit of the doubt to the victim. It is now assumed that a physical or emotional misfortune has caused a psychic disturbance severe enough to make the person not responsible for the act and therefore incapable of sin.

Eastern Attitudes

Among Asian sacred writings, suicide was viewed with many contradictions, with encouragement in some and vigorous condemnation in others. In Japan, suicide was a way in which warriors could expiate their crimes, apologize for error, escape from disgrace, redeem their friends, or prove their sincerity. In China, suicide was so commonplace that it was accepted as a normal feature of everyday life. The wretchedness of people's lives in the Far East made suicide seem logical, and it was accepted without condemnation.

The Hindu attitude is ambiguous, condemning suicide in most instances but approving it in special cases. Suicide is considered justified when the person has lived a full life or has acquired a high measure of ascetic power. Hinduism institutionalized and sanctioned suttee, a ceremonial sacrifice of widows, which persisted in India for more than 2,000 years. This suicide by self-immolation was demanded of the widow after the death of her husband, and she was highly praised when the tradition was followed and severely condemned when there was a failure to carry it out. Pregnant women and mothers of minors were excused from the traditional requirement. Today suttee is forbidden but may still be practiced in some of the rural provinces of India.

The Brahman doctrine was sympathetic to suicide in that it incorporated denial of the flesh, which the philosophies of the Orient constantly sought to attain. One goal of Asian mysticism was to divorce the body from the soul, extinguishing craving and passion and allowing life's chief purpose to prevail, the acquisition of knowledge. Both Brahmanism and Buddhism are considered religions of resignation and despair.

Islam has condemned suicide with the utmost severity, following the cardinal teaching of Muhammad that the divine will was expressed in different ways and that man must submit himself to it at all times.

The Renaissance and the Reformation

The Renaissance saw the emergence of a radical change in attitudes toward suicide, with a shift toward an awareness of the world and its beauty and a euphoric feeling that life was wonderful. This attitude lasted throughout much of the 14th and 15th centuries. The individual became important as humans became aware that they were the master of their own destiny. Values and religion began to change. Luther became the representative of orthodox Protestantism, with a shift in principles from absolutism and obedience to personal inquiry and personal responsibility. Inevitably, as questions and challenges arose and the Industrial Revolution caused sweeping social and economic disruption, there came a sense of self-consciousness and isolation. A marked increase in melancholy appeared along with recognition of life's transience. Death became an escape from the disappointments of life, and suicide began to appear much more often.

Calvinism appeared in the middle of the 16th century, starting first in Switzerland and sweeping across France (with the Huguenots) to reach England, while Lutheranism became firmly entrenched in Scandinavia. The exaltation of God in John Calvin's theology tended to minimize humans and make them feel even more humble, raising indirectly the question of the value of the individual human. Italy saw a revival of learning and a resurrection of ideas that began to diminish the strong feeling of suicide-horror. Erasmus in his *Praise of Folly* (1509), Sir Thomas More in *Utopia* (1516), and Michel de Montaigne in his *Essais* (1580–88) show the absolute condemnation of suicide disappearing, with suicide justified, albeit under still strictly defined circumstances. Erasmus took the position that God meant death to be an agony in order to keep men from committing suicide. Nevertheless, in one of his books he commends those who voluntarily kill themselves in order to leave a miserable and troublesome world, considering them wiser than those who are unwilling to die and who insist on living longer. Montaigne extolled voluntary death but later came to a more moderate practical position, concluding only that unsupportable pain, or a worse form of dying, were acceptable justifications for suicide.

With the spreading of the Renaissance the economic conditions became more and more oppressive as one realized his or her poverty and lack of a future. *The Anatomy of Melancholy* by Robert Burton (1621) condemned suicide but also pleaded for a charitable attitude towards it, asserting that it was up to God to judge. John Donne wrote *Biathanatos* in 1608, the first defense of suicide in English up to that point, but it was not published until 1644, after Donne's death. Donne, like Burton, felt that the power and the mercy of God were great enough that the sin of suicide could be forgiven. In his words it was "not so naturally a sin that it could never be otherwise and suicide was not incompatible with the laws of God, reason and nature." Burton felt that eternal damnation was not necessarily the punishment for every suicide because of the possible presence of mitigating circumstances, such as madness.

The preoccupation with death that characterized this era resulted in many new editions of the "Danse Macabre" which were illustrated by the presence of a skeleton. Rowlandson, a prominent graphic artist of that time, drew a number of the scenes. In "The Gamester's Exit," for example, a man is shown shooting himself in the head while holding a wine glass aloft in his other hand. In the doorway stands a woman vainly attempting to stop him while on the other side of the table a skeleton watches grimly. Shakespeare also produced psychological studies in depth, with suicide appearing no less than 14 times in his eight tragedies.

John Sym, an English clergyman of this period, identified suicide victims as those who were sick in mind. His textbook (1637) was the first to show a concern for understanding and prevention, listing premonitory signs and giving suggestions on how to protect the suicide victim. Sym divides suicides into direct and indirect, condemning especially the indirect type. Among the premonitory and diagnostic signs of suicide he lists "unusual solitariness, neglect of the necessary duties of a man's calling, change in manifest behavior, a distracted countenance in courage, speaking and talking to and with themselves in solitary places and dumps, reasoning and resolving with themselves about that fact and their motives to it in a perplexed, disturbed manner."

Johannes Neser (1613) wrote that those who committed suicide when sane and with premeditation were damned, while those who killed themselves in a state of madness were not damned because they were mentally deranged and were not responsible. Like Burton, he felt that God could decide whether salvation was appropriate in those cases where the circumstances were unclear.

The Industrial World

Throughout the Renaissance and post-Renaissance periods, suicide had become more and more tolerated by the educated people both on the Continent and in England, but the church still remained powerful in its condemnation of suicide, which it now branded not merely as murder but also as high treason and heresy. An important, additional cultural element was added in this era—the stigma of poverty. Up to this time, being poor had not been associated with any moral position. With the rise of commercialism, the development of the Industrial Revolution, and the appearance of Protestantism, a drastic change in the attitude of society toward the poor appeared. Social relationships began to be evaluated from purely economic standards. Good was now rewarded by prosperity and evil by poverty; economic failure was an indication of sinfulness. Most of the condemnation was directed toward those persons who suffered a decline in their fortune, from prosperity to poverty, and it was this change rather than the fact of poverty itself which accounted for many suicides at that time. The impact of poverty was illustrated in 1732 when Richard Smith and his wife killed their infant daughter, hanged themselves, and left a long letter

xxvi The Encyclopedia of Suicide

addressed to the public describing the hopelessness of poverty and complaining that life was not worth living.

The 18th century saw many additional changes in the attitudes toward suicide, such as opposition against the penalties imposed on suicide. During this period of Enlightenment, prominent French literary giants such as Voltaire, Paul-Henri d'Holbach, Jean-Jacques Rousseau, and Cesare Beccaria condemned the conventional harsh treatment of suicides and encouraged the exercise of empirical observation and critical reason. Voltaire (1766) brought a reasonable approach toward suicide, Rousseau (1761) suggested a romanticized approach, and Charles-Louis de Montesquieu (1721) brought for the first time a criticism of suicide from the point of view of the survivors. He urged a view less prejudiced against suicide in his *Persian Letters* and opposed the traditional Christian attitude toward suicide as sinful.

One of the most significant publications in this period was written by David Hume, a Scottish philosopher, entitled "Essay on Suicide" (1783). Hume argued that if suicide were to be abhorred it had first to be proven a crime against God, neighbor, or self. He argued that suicide was not a crime against God because He gave humans the power to act; therefore, death at one's own hand was as much under His control as if it had proceeded from any other source. Second, suicide was not a breach against neighbor and society, "for a man who retires from life does no harm to society, he only ceases to do good and which, if it is an injury, is of the lower kind." Third, Hume stated that suicide cannot be a crime against self because he believed that no man ever threw away a life while it was still worth keeping.

The discussion on suicide in this era saw some writers attempting to relate it to national character. Suicide was associated particularly with the English, for example, and became known as an English symptom because England's inhabitants showed a characteristic gloominess of temperament. In his book *The English Malady* (1733),

George Cheyne associated suicide in England with inclement weather, rich heavy food, and wealthy and sedentary living in large urban centers.

At about this time (1763), Merian offered one of the important new arguments by separating suicide from morality and approaching it from a medical point of view. He suggested that suicide was not a crime but an emotional illness. The natural extension of this argument was that all suicide victims were mentally ill in some degree and so could not run counter to the law of nature. This rationalization eventually paved the way to the church's verdict of "suicide while of unsound mind," allowing the church to skirt its own laws against suicide.

Bishop Charles Moore continued to be critical of suicide but was not so dogmatic as other ecclesiastical writers, stating that each case of suicide had to be judged on its own merits. In his book *A Full Inquiry into the Subject of Suicide* (1790), he argued that humans did not know the importance of their own lives even if they appeared to be useless and that suicide might be an interference with the design that God has fashioned for each person.

In Germany, Immanuel Kant (1797) argued that human life was sacred and had to be preserved at all costs. He also stated that each individual had a definite place in the great universe according to the laws of nature and that man's ability to reason made suicide inconsistent with the sacredness of human life.

The Romantics

During the last half of the 18th century and the early part of the 19th century, the romantic poets had a great impact on the concept of death. It was in 1770 that Thomas Chatterton at the age of 17 committed suicide by poison, which the romantics took as a vivid example of death by alienation—premature death in a blazing genius. Youth and poetry and death became synonymous, with each glorified in the writings of Novalis and Jean Paul in Germany, René de

Chateaubriand and Alphonse de Lamartine in France, and John Keats and Percy Bysshe Shelley in England. Keats died in 1821 at the age of 25, Shelley the next year at 29, and Lord Byron, two years later, at age 36. Johann Wolfgang von Goethe's *Sorrows of Werther* (1774) was inspired by the suicide of a young diplomat, and set a Europe-wide pattern for the romantic style of suffering. The romantics thought of death and suicide as a supreme dramatic gesture of contempt toward a dull world. Suicide was fashionable and was practiced almost as an elegant sport.

Writings nevertheless continued to appear in the early 1800s against suicide. In France, one of the most prominent efforts was that of Madame de Staël (1814), who wrote that living through pain and crisis made a person better, and thus it was unnecessary to commit suicide. She argued that God never deserted man and that the individual need never feel that he or she was completely alone. Her strongest argument was that suicide was against the moral dignity of humans, an argument directly opposed to that of the Stoics and the Epicureans, who felt that suicide helped preserve dignity and self-concept.

Léon Meynard (1954), a 20th-century French philosopher, reasoned that suicide was caused basically by suffering and was essentially a refusal to submit to it. In order not to kill oneself, one must know how to suffer. Suffering, however, could be understood only in the religious perspective. Meynard felt that the existence of God was the supreme argument against the legitimacy of suicide, and that the purpose of life was not to find happiness but to seek purification through suffering. Suffering needed neither to be accepted nor resigned to, but rather to be used as a means of salvation.

The 1800s

During the 1800s a number of significant changes appeared in society. The old religious and social groupings that had offered the strongest resistance to suicide began to lose their effectiveness. Capitalism introduced incentives for individual and personal gain, making people more interdependent economically but isolating them socially. Material values supplanted religious and social values. Suicide began to be considered a disgrace, supplementing the attitudes of the preceding century, when it had been associated with sin and crime. A strong middle class was growing, consistent with the development of increasingly larger urban centers where industry and business could interact. Along with this new middle class came the need for the family to maintain social status within the community, making suicide something to be hidden and denied. This was especially true for the upper class, as suicide became more frequently associated with insanity.

An increasing number of scientists investigated suicide from medical and sociological points of view. One of the earliest works was by Osiander (1813) who attributed suicide to mental illness, blaming such things as diseases in the head, congestion of blood in the brain, weakening of the brain by repeated intoxication, epileptic attacks, progressive inflammation in the small intestine, cardiac aneurysm, swelling of the abdominal glands, persistent constipation, and defects in the sexual organs. Osiander's study of melancholic persons led him to conclude they hanged themselves to avoid the sensation of blood sinking from the brain on account of suspended aerial electricity.

Jean-Pierre Falret's (1822) contribution was significant in that he was one of the first to use statistical data on suicide, albeit not very extensively and with very few conclusions. Falret attributed suicide to four major causes: (1) predisposing, such as heredity, temperament, climate; (2) accidental direct, such as passions and worries at home; (3) accidental indirect, such as bodily pain, disease, and state of health; and (4) civilization and religious fanaticism. He equated suicide and insanity, considering the former to be a special form of insanity.

A number of investigators of this period searched for suicide's relationship to psychosis and pathoanatomical signs. Did suicide automatically mean the subject was insane? Were there neurological lesions or anatomical defects that "explained" suicide? The consideration of suicide as a special form of insanity served as a stimulus for all kinds of medical observations into the connection between a suicide's behavior and anatomical lesions found in autopsy. Clinical pathologists in France pursued this course earnestly in the first half of the 19th century.

Jean-Étienne-Dominique Esquirol, in his chapter on suicide in his book *Mental Illness* (1838), refused to accept the doctrine that suicide was a mental disease in itself, but insisted, rather, that it was a consequence of other illnesses and only a symptom of insanity. He proposed that suicide might depend on hereditary factors. While he urged that the individual disposition be observed very closely, he did offer some general observations: Men committed suicide more often than women, and the number of suicides was greatest in the spring. However, he did not believe in the influence of climate.

Alexandre-Jacques-François Brierre de Boismont studied 4,500 suicides in the Seine Department over a period of 10 years and also reported data gathered from 265 persons who either made a suicide attempt or planned one. For de Boismont, suicide causes fell into two types, predisposing and determinant. In the former could be found demographic variables, such as civil status, age, sex, religion, marital status, and others. Thus, he confirmed that older people committed suicide more often than younger people and that men killed themselves in a ratio of three to one over women. He denied strongly that all suicides were insane but did indicate that an attempt at suicide was often the first indication of insanity, even where mental illness had not been suspected before. Among the behavioral and social causes, he identified such items as trouble at home and with the family, intense worry, poverty and misery, and inebriation. Among somatic diseases he found pulmonary conditions were most frequent, followed by blindness and then cancer. He was one of the first to mention pellagra as a disease that often seemed to lead to suicide. A number of investigations seeking to pinpoint this relationship followed. Social disorganization and alienation also were identified as strong contributors to suicide.

Lisle (*Du suicide*, 1856) also used statistics in dividing the causes into two major groups, predisposing and immediate. Like Brierre de Boismont he opposed characterizing suicide as a mental disease, although suicide was often due to mental illness. He found insanity, monomania, and brain fever in only about one out of every four cases of suicide.

Adolph Wagner (1864), using suicide statistics, agreed that insanity could not be equated with suicide, but he did conclude that it was by far the most common cause for suicide, occurring in about one-third of all the cases. He also concluded that suicide was 100 times more common in mentally ill individuals than in mentally healthy persons.

Siljestrom (1875) studied the increase in suicides from 1730 to 1870 in Sweden and concluded the increase was due to the political, social, and industrial states of transition through which society had passed during that time.

During this period the German philosopher Arthur Schopenhauer expressed the pessimism of the era in his writing ("Parerga and Paralipomena," 1851). While often considered an advocate of suicide he actually was strongly against it. He felt that moral freedom, the highest ethical ideal, could be obtained only by denying the will to live. Suicide, however, was not such a denial. For Schopenhauer the denial lay in shunning the joys, not the sorrows of life. He felt the suicidal person had the will to live but was dissatisfied with the conditions under which he was forced to live.

Another important work of this period is that of Enrico (Henry) Morselli (1881). Analyzing data from Italy, he concluded that suicide was primarily a result of the struggle for life and nature's evolutionary process, by which weak-brained individuals were sorted out by insanity and voluntary death. Other unhappy results included misery, disease, prostitution, and insanity. That men committed suicide more often than women and adults more often than children merely illustrated the struggle of life that led to suicide. To reduce suicide one needed to reduce the number of people, which could be accomplished only by birth control. In Morselli's opinion the progress of civilization and Protestantism, which refused all external worship in favor of free discussion and individual thought, were the most powerful factors in increasing the number of suicides.

Thomas G. Masaryk, in *Suicide and the Meaning of Civilization* (1881), also stressed the difficulty in determining the boundary between normal and abnormal mental life. He felt that civilization and the state of semi-culture were responsible for the increasing suicide frequency in almost every country. The causes of suicide lay in both the biological and social constitution of humans. Suicide could not be explained only in terms of mental illness but must be looked for in the moral disorder of modern societies. Since religion was the source of morality, the increasing secularization that characterized contemporary societies meant a loss of faith. Like Morselli, Masaryk felt that Protestantism stimulated the development of free inquiry, which in turn fostered a much higher degree of individualism than the Catholic Church. The Protestant was more easily left open to doubt and to despair, which essentially was a consequence of a decline in religious belief rather than the result of Protestant theology. Masaryk urged that what was needed was to revive the moral meaning that came from belief in a superior being. Thus, the moral crisis of modern civilization could only be resolved through a religious revival, not a reversion to the repressive control that the church had exerted in previous ages. Eugen Rehfisch (1893) also saw suicide as the final link in a chain of pathological states, with civilization the underlying cause for "mental degeneration." Alcoholism was also important in suicide, he felt.

Two of the most important events in the history of suicide studies occurred near the end of the 19th century. The first was the publication of Emile Durkheim's *Le Suicide* in 1897. Durkheim based his work on an extensive evaluation of suicide statistics in France. He concluded that suicide was a collective phenomenon that was specifically influenced by factors characterizing the society in which it appeared. The basic factors were regulation and integration, with varying degrees of each of these factors, and their interaction, producing characteristic forms of suicide. Durkheim's basic concepts are illustrated by examples of societies that fell at the opposite extremes of each concept. Thus, at one extreme of regulation a society characterized by chaos, confusion, and loss of traditional values and mores would produce "anomic" suicides. At the other extreme of regulation would be found "fatalistic" suicides, where expressive and repressive constraints would produce an extreme feeling of lack of freedom and choice. At one extreme of the integration concept would be found "egoistic" suicides where the person felt alienated and separated from the institutions and traditions that were significant in the society. At the other extreme of integration would be "altruistic" suicide, in which an overidentification with the values or the causes of a society might produce a too-ready willingness to sacrifice one's life in a burst of patriotism or martyrdom. Durkheim's writings have stimulated a host of sociological-statistical investigations up through the present time.

The second most important event in 1897 was the publication of the essay "Is Life Worth Living?" by William James. James concluded that humans did not commit suicide because of religious faith, but rather because faith itself was lacking. It was faith that helped humans to believe, even in deep depression, that life was still worth living. Faith leads to religion, which essentially postulates the existence of an unseen order in a universe beyond our comprehension.

Early 20th Century

The interest in medical investigations in suicide that had begun in the last half of the 19th century continued strongly into the 20th. Autopsies were used as a primary source of data as investigators looked for relationships between suicide and physiological or neurological conditions.

Researchers in the early 20th century found essentially organic changes in three-fourths of the suicides on which autopsies were conducted; others concluded that an anatomically visible cause was related to such motives as alcoholism, financial distress, somatic disease, morality, or conflict with society. On the other hand, some researchers did not see anything related to mental status in one study of 923 suicides; changes in the central nervous system were present in only 13 percent.

A number of other investigators in the early 1900s explored suicide from the socio-statistical point of view. One of the most prominent was Maurice Halbwachs (1930), who collected statistics in France on both attempted suicide and committed suicide and found the ratio to be 164 to 100, respectively. This is in marked contrast to the more recent studies in the United States, which found a ratio of 8 to 1 for the total population (Shneidman and Farberow, 1957) and as high as 50 to 1 and 100 to 1 in adolescents and youth. Halbwachs felt that every person is anxious at the time that he commits suicide and may actually be in a state caused by anxiety or be so emotionally distressed that his state looks psychopathological. Every suicide is thus the result of both organic and social factors.

Ruth Cavan (*Suicide*, 1928; reprint 1965) and Louis Israel Dublin and Bessie Bunzel (*To Be or Not to Be*, 1933) conducted extensive sociological analysis of data on suicide, affirming that the elderly, on the basis of rate, showed the greatest tendency to suicide in comparison to any of the other groups. Dublin and Bunzel also were able to point out that nationalities in the United States frequently showed the same rates as the populations in their respective homelands.

The most significant development in the early part of the 20th century in terms of exploring motivations and stimulating investigations of

suicide dynamics was the growth of the psychoanalysis movement in psychiatry under the leadership of its founder, Sigmund Freud. Freud's approach was a radically new conceptualization of the workings of the mind, with the concept of levels of functioning ranging from conscious through unconscious (id, ego, and superego), and with remarkable insights into the variety of defenses and coping mechanisms, the failures of which may lead to severe neurosis and psychosis. Freud approached suicide first from his studies of melancholia and depression, and his first theory of suicide was developed from the dynamics that characterized the two states. He used his earlier theoretical concept of introjection, in which any person in an intimate relationship with another incorporates parts of that person into his own personality, with that person becoming a "part of the self." Inevitably, all intimate relationships also develop ambivalent or contradictory feelings toward the person, evidenced by fluctuating feelings of like and dislike, love and hate. Freud thought that suicide occurred with the loss of the love object or with the experience of extreme frustration from the loved one. The rage against that introjected but lost or frustrating person is retroflexed against the self and the acting out of that rage may result in death or serious injury.

Freud was not completely satisfied with his theory, because there were many suicides to whom this formulation did not seem to apply. In 1922, in *Beyond the Pleasure Principle*, Freud developed his more complicated theory in which suicide became an expression of the death instinct. Freud postulated two basic instincts in man, the life instinct (Eros) and the death instinct (Thanatos) and saw these in continuous conflict with each other throughout any person's life. Under conditions of extreme stress and/or emotional distress, regression occurred within the individual, more primitive ego states emerged, and the potential for self-destructive behavior was markedly increased.

Karl Menninger (1938) extended Freud's concept of the death instinct even further, hypothesizing three elements that could be found in all self-destructive behavior: (1) the wish to kill, emerging from primary aggressiveness; (2) the wish to be killed, modified from primary aggressive impulses; and (3) the wish to die, derived from primary aggressiveness and other sophisticated motives. Menninger was the first to categorize and relate to suicide the more indirect forms of self-destruction that did not end in immediate death but came out in life-threatening, life-injurious activities. Some he called "chronic suicide," such as addictive behavior and asceticism; some were "focal suicides," in which the focus is on a part, organ, or system of the body, such as in polysurgery or purposive accidents; and some were "organic suicides," in which parts of the body are used in illnesses against the health and well-being of the person.

Other psychoanalytic formulations appeared as some of Freud's disciples and colleagues broke away and developed their own theories. Alfred Adler (1937) related the pathology derived from a person's striving to overcome his innate inferiority, coming to a loss of self-esteem and then attempting to hurt others by hurting himself. Carl Jung considered the self-destructive act to be an effort at rebirth and a way of escaping intolerable conditions of the present (Klopfer, 1961).

Henry Stack Sullivan (Green, 1961) postulated that the subject evaluates himself in terms of the reactions of significant others toward him. The early integration of hostile appraisals of significant others leads to an incorporated concept of negative self frequently expressed in hostile attitudes toward others. When his situation becomes unbearable the individual transfers the "bad me" into a "not me" and redirects his hostile attitude, which has been toward other people, against the self. Karen Horney (De Rosis, 1961) considered suicide to be a "performance failure" arising from the individual's inability to meet the standards expected by society. Gregory Zilboorg (1936) felt that suicide was a way of paradoxically "living by killing oneself," of thwarting outside forces

that made living impossible—while maintaining the ego, rather than destroying it, by making and carrying out one's own decision to kill oneself.

Hans W. Gruhle (1940) attributed about 15 to 20 percent of the suicides to psychosis and felt that the role of alcoholism was overestimated. Among the factors he listed as most closely linked to suicide were social factors, such as financial distress, increasing population density, job and home, aging, marital status, or childlessness, and psychiatric factors, such as alcoholism or mental illness. Factors that helped prevent suicide included decreasing density of the population, a rural occupation, youth, marriage, children, and general circumstances in which emotional stimulation was experienced.

Serin (1926) initiated a procedure that was the forerunner of the psychological autopsy method, later developed by Theodore Curphey, Norman Farberow, Edwin S. Shneidman, and Robert Litman (1961). Serin sent specially trained assistants to obtain information from relatives, neighbors, and others, to inquire about the lifestyle and attitudes of the suicide in the days preceding his death.

While the above investigators were evaluating deaths by suicide a number of studies were also focusing on attempted suicides. Among these Gaupt (1910) analyzed all the cases of attempted suicide brought to a psychiatric clinic in Munich during the period of his study and found that one-third were "insane," about one-fourth were drunk, and one-fourth were psychopaths. Stelzner (1906) studied women treated at a psychiatric clinic in Berlin and found psychiatric symptoms in 84 percent of the cases. East (1913), in the first English study on attempted suicide, found alcoholism more prevalent and more of a factor in attempted suicide. He felt this contrasted with completed suicide where mental illness was more prevalent. Wassermeyer (1913) found a high occurrence of alcoholism in attempted suicides. He anticipated Erwin Stengel (1971) in his cautions that suicide and attempted suicide could not be directly compared to each other because of the differences in the populations. Schneider (1933 and 1934) found only 12 percent of his attempted suicides could be called mentally ill and that suicide was more likely to be a primitive reaction, an escape, or nonlethal communication.

Suicide and Civil Law

In early history civil and religious law were so intertwined that it was practically impossible to differentiate between them. This was especially true in Christianity, which was the source of increasingly severe attitudes of condemnation that governed the civil attitudes and were incorporated into civil regulations toward suicides.

Preceding Christianity, in Athenian and Greek law the body was denied burial rights and the hand of the suicide was chopped off and buried separately. Theban law also deprived the suicide of funeral rights. Roman law, on the other hand, contained no penalties against suicide and no prohibitions relating to burial and funeral rights. Roman law, with its practical and economic approach, condemned suicide especially when committed by criminals, soldiers, and slaves. The soldier was condemned because it was considered desertion, and if he was unsuccessful in his attempt he was killed afterward. The slave was condemned because he was depriving his master of his services.

In English law the ecclesiastical denial of burial rights became a civil punishment when it was adopted by King Edgar in A.D. 967. Along with this the custom of dishonoring and degrading the corpse became incorporated as part of the law and the suicide's goods were forfeited to his lord unless it was the result of an act of madness or illness.

Suicide in the middle of the 13th century was punished by forfeiture of goods and land unless, as stated by English juridical writer Henry de Bracton (Samuel E. Thorne, 1968), the suicide resulted from "weariness of life or impatience of pain," which then limited the loss to goods only. In the 14th century it was declared that the intentional taking of one's own life was a felony,

and in 1551, under Spain's Charles I, the Holy Roman emperor Charles V, a law was passed that confiscated the property, both goods and land, of anyone who committed suicide while under a charge of felony.

Attempted suicide was identified as a crime and written into the statutes of English law in 1854. It continued as such until 1961, when the law was repealed. Before 1916, imprisonment was the normal punishment for attempted suicide; in 1916, attempted suicides were no longer punished but instead were placed in the charge of relatives and friends. However, criminal statistics show that although the policy of both police and courts was lenient, a considerable number of persons were sent to prison for attempted suicide. From 1946 to 1955, 5,794 attempted suicide cases were tried by the courts and 5,447 were found guilty. Of these, 308 were sentenced to imprisonment without the option of a fine.

The practice of forfeiture of the goods of a suicide to his lord was already known to Danes before they came to England. The fact of suicide was considered equivalent to a confession of guilt for the crime of which he had been accused. In England, the goods went to the Crown instead of to the local lord. During the 18th century the Crown limited forfeiture of goods, in cases where suicide was committed, to conviction of a felony. Later, even that was waived when the forfeiture act was abolished in 1870, giving legal effect to an already established practice.

British jurist William Blackstone (1723–80) declared the suicide to be guilty of a double offense—the first was spiritual in evading the prerogative of the Almighty and rushing into his presence before called for, and the second was temporal and against the king who had an interest in the preservation of all of his subjects.

In France, the corpse of the suicide victim was subjected to the same kind of degradation as in England. The French criminal ordinance of August 1670 required the body of a suicide to be dragged through the streets and then thrown into a sewer or onto the town dump. In the early 18th century the law required that the body of a person who committed suicide be buried under the gallows. The attitude toward suicide fluctuated along with French politics. Suicides and the survivors of successful suicides were punished when the liberal legislation of the Napoleonic code was overthrown. When liberty and democratic government reappeared the rights of the suicide also reappeared and were respected.

In many countries, the imposition of penalties varied according to the social rank of the suicide victim and his family, as well as the circumstances of the suicidal act. Physical illness and mental and emotional disease were not punished in Prussia while poverty, dishonor, despair, and debt were.

In many middle European countries, secular law continues to hold attempted suicide a crime. However, this usually results only in registration of suicide attempts. Registration of attempted suicide has been abolished in other European countries such as Germany, Italy, Switzerland, and the Scandinavian countries.

In the United States, following English law, Massachusetts passed a status in 1660 that the body of a suicide was to be buried at the crossroads of a highway. Again following English law, this was repealed in 1823. The view that suicide was a felony was also incorporated into the laws of the individual states. As recently as 1969, seven U.S. states still had suicide as a crime on their books, but currently there is no state that considers suicide or suicide attempts a crime. Physician-assisted suicide is legal in only one state (Oregon).

ENTRIES A–Z

abuse, alcohol See ABUSE, SUBSTANCE.

abuse, child Adults who suffered abuse during their childhood are more likely than their peers to attempt suicide decades later, according to federal health officials. Researchers found that individuals with at least one type of harmful childhood experience were two to five times more likely to attempt suicide.

For example, those who reported being emotionally abused as a child were five times more likely to report a suicide attempt. People who experience several traumatic events may be 30 to 50 times as likely to attempt suicide at some point in their life (either in childhood or adulthood) as those with a more carefree past. Indeed, researchers discovered that adverse childhood experiences have serious long-term consequences, such as suicide attempts.

In one recent study, researchers evaluated more than 17,000 healthy adults who visited a primary care clinic in California between 1995 and 1997. The adults were asked to report whether they had experienced eight various harmful experiences as a child, including sexual, emotional, or physical abuse, parental separation or divorce, witnessing domestic violence, and living with family members who were substance abusers, mentally ill, or criminals.

The investigators found that 3.8 percent of the adults reported they had attempted suicide at some point in their lives, with women three times more likely than men to attempt suicide. Two-thirds of the adults who had attempted suicide had experienced at least one of the negative experiences during childhood.

Only 1.1 percent of adults who reported no negative childhood experiences attempted suicide, whereas 35 percent of adults who reported seven or more negative childhood experiences had tried to kill themselves.

Experts believe that early exposure to child abuse may disrupt the proper development of communication pathways within the brain, affecting subsequent mental health. Children of abusive parents generally do not completely understand the problems that cause such conduct, and are confused about their responsibility for their parents' behavior. As a result, children subjected to mental, emotional, or physical abuse run a high risk of developing a variety of problems later in life.

abuse, drug See DRUG ABUSE.

abuse, substance Substance abuse is frequently associated with suicide, and anyone who abuses drugs or alcohol could be at risk. For instance, high school students who view themselves negatively, who are depressed, or who find little meaning in their lives are more likely to consider suicide and to abuse drugs. Almost half of the teenagers who complete suicide are under the influence of drugs or alcohol shortly before their death; that figure soars to 75 percent of those teens who attempt suicide unsuccessfully.

While no cause-and-effect relationship between the use of alcohol or other substances has been established in research to date, the use of such substances often is a contributing factor, and the research does indicate several possible explanations. First, substance abuse may lessen inhibitions and impair the judgment of someone contemplating suicide, making the act of suicide more likely. Second, the use of substances by family members or the individual may aggravate other risk factors for suicide, such as depression or other mental illnesses. Indeed, those who abuse drugs or alcohol often do so as a result of underlying feelings of hopelessness, anxiety, or depression. If substance abuse fails to relieve the negative emotions, the abuser may turn to suicide as a way to "fix" the problem.

Among the warning signs of suicide, substance abuse is second only to depression as a distress signal.

Experts note that even if suicidal thoughts never occur to the substance abuser, that person is committing suicide just as surely as the individual who puts a gun to his head.

"Chronic suicides" are those people who say they do not want to kill themselves, but because of crippling feelings of dejection and worthlessness, they opt to kill themselves indirectly and slowly.

Between 31 percent and 75 percent of heavy substance abusers have had suicidal thoughts, and are four times more likely to complete suicide. Among all those who complete suicide, 70 percent have used drugs frequently, 50 percent had alcohol in their blood, and 75 percent fit the criteria for drug or alcohol use disorder.

See also DRUG ABUSE.

Academy of Certified Social Workers A professional association of health care workers who hold a minimum of a baccalaureate degree in social work. The ACSW was established in 1960 by the National Association of Social Workers to provide certification of competence by social workers. A social worker applies for membership in ACSW to support high standards of social work and to demonstrate commitment to ethical and competent practice. Potential members must also belong to the National Association of Social Workers; must have a master's degree from a graduate school of social work

accredited by the Council on Social Work Education, and have accumulated at least two full-time years (or 3,000 hours) of postgraduate social work experience. An exam is also given to determine certification.

For address, see Appendix I.

accident prone Authorities speculate that many "accident-prone" individuals are actually suicide attempters. For example, fatal auto accidents account for about 37 percent of all deaths in the 15- to 24-year-old group. Some of these crashes may be suicides listed as accidents, especially single-passenger, single-car accidents. Forensic experts speculate that an estimated 25 percent of these "accidents" are deliberate. In addition, "accidental" poisonings are sometimes suicide attempts in reality. However, the concept of death is known to be very different for the five-year-old and the 14-year-old.

See also AUTOCIDE.

Accutane and suicide The acne medication isotretinoin (Accutane) has been linked to a possible increased risk of suicide in a few patients taking the drug. Some reports noted the appearance of depression following Accutane use, including some cases in which symptoms resolved and then re-emerged when the medication was stopped and restarted.

However, neither the government nor the manufacturer has found proof of a solid link between the drug and suicide or depression. In response to fears about a possible relationship between Accutane and suicide, researchers in Great Britain and Canada studied the drug's risk of suicide in comparison with antibiotics. In the study, 7,195 patients taking Accutane were compared to a control group of 13,700 acne patients who were treated with antibiotics. All were followed for at least 12 months after stopping their medication. Neither the British nor Canadian groups found any differences between subjects treated with Accutane or antibiotics, and there were no differences between either groups in terms of suicide. A separate study actually found a reduction in anxiety and depression in patients with severe acne who had used Accutane.

Despite the fact that thousands of patients take Accutane without experiencing depression or suicide, the U.S. Food and Drug Administration (FDA) required a new warning label about suicide, depression, and psychosis, after accumulating more than a dozen reports linking recurrence of psychiatric symptoms with restarting of medication. This was in addition to 12 reports since 1989 of patients on the medication who completed suicide.

Many suicide experts believe that any link between Accutane and suicide is related to the fact that teens, the largest age group using the drug, have a higher incidence of depression than most—especially those teens with severe, recalcitrant acne for which Accutane is indicated. In this case, experts say, the suicides were probably caused by reaction to the underlying skin disease for which the drug is taken—not by the drug itself.

The revised FDA label warns of the seriousness and persistence of depression and of the possible occurrence of suicide. It warns that discontinuing Accutane might not be enough to stop the symptoms and that further evaluation and treatment may be necessary.

acting out   Term used by professionals to describe the use of behavior instead of words to express emotional conflicts. Attempters may "act out" and show aggressive, hostile, defiant behavior. Others exhibit passive patterns that include withdrawal, melancholy, and uncommunicative behavior. Sometimes attempters will switch from wild, impulsive, loud behavior to quiet, gloomy, uncommunicative demeanor. Some suicidal people are hyperactive, while others seem depressed.

See also DISTRESS SIGNALS.

acute suicides   Suicidal cases with a triggering factor as opposed to those where suicide just

seems to happen—if not today, then some other day.

See also CHRONIC SUICIDES.

adolescent suicide   See TEENAGE SUICIDE.

adoption   Although most adopted teenagers do not try to kill themselves, studies do suggest that adopted teenagers are at higher risk for attempted suicide than their peers who live with their biological parents.

In one Ohio study, almost 8 percent of the adopted teens reported suicide attempts within the previous year compared with only 3 percent of nonadopted teens. Researchers from the University of Cincinnati Medical Center in Cincinnati, Ohio, used data from a national survey of adolescent health to identify 214 adopted and 6,363 nonadopted teens. The teens completed questionnaires and interviews at home and in school, and the parents of the teens were asked to complete separate questionnaires. Teens were asked questions about their general and emotional health, including questions about self-image, depressive symptoms, and whether they had attempted suicide during the past year. Teens also revealed whether they smoked, drank alcohol, used drugs, or had sex. The survey also asked teens to answer questions about their school performance, and both teens and parents were asked to respond to questions about family relationships.

In the Ohio study, teens who attempted suicide were more likely to be girls, and were more than four times as likely as teens who didn't attempt suicide to have received mental health counseling in the past year. In addition, teens who attempted suicide were more likely to report risky behaviors, including using cigarettes, alcohol, and marijuana, to have had sex, and to be aggressive and impulsive.

In addition to adoption, depression, recent mental health counseling, female gender, cigarette use, delinquency, low self-image, and aggression were all factors that increased a teen's likelihood of attempting suicide. Teens who perceived themselves as highly connected to their families were less likely to have attempted suicide regardless of whether they were adopted or not.

adults and suicide   Risk factors for suicide rise as adults age from 30 to 65, although the biggest spike is among elderly adults over age 65. In men between ages 25 and 64, 23.6 per 100,000 complete suicide, whereas women do so at a rate of 6.0 per 100,000.

Many adults cannot negotiate the adjustments necessary in midlife, such as dealing with unfulfilled dreams and plans from youth, coping with the aging process, reaching a job plateau, facing divorce, or experiencing unresolved developmental issues. Suicides by women are highest in this age group, partially due to mothering and nurturing disconnections, such as children leaving home and menopause.

Male executives and midlife males in crisis or burnout are also more likely to commit suicide, as well as middle-aged alcoholics or drug abusers, and those who may be acutely depressed or mentally ill. Often the warning signs for these adults are not noticeable, since they are not in institutions or schools where they would be easily observed.

Treatment

Interventions for midlife adults primarily focus on treatment for specific disorders (especially depression). A combination of antidepressants and supportive psychotherapy can often lessen the suicide risk for these adults. Substance abuse treatment is also a very important component of treatment. In addition, adults must receive support in negotiating life stages, and clear up any developmental issues that may block progress. Resolving financial and job worries and marital difficulties through counseling can also help prevent adult suicides.

See also CHILDREN AND SUICIDE; ELDER SUICIDE; TEENAGE SUICIDE.

Africa   It is very difficult to generate an overall suicide rate for the entire continent of Africa.

With so many different nations representing such varied cultures and subcultures, comparability of even regional suicide rates in Africa are questionable. An overview of suicide, however, makes it clear that the rate of suicide is in direct relationship with changes in social controls and different emphasis on the value of the individual in comparison with the state. Where control is greatest, the suicide rate is lower; where individuals are more free, the rate is higher.

Anthropological studies among African tribes reveal that the frequency of suicide was comparable with that of European countries having moderate to low suicide rates, and that suicide among them was considered evil. In certain tribes, physical contact with the body of a person who has committed suicide is thought to trigger illness or suicide among relatives. The tree on which a person hanged himself is quickly felled or burned; ancestors are placated by sacrifices; and the spot where the suicide took place is believed to be haunted by evil spirits. In some regions, suicide is a source of dread in the community.

In one primitive tribe described by BRONISLAW MALINOWSKI in "Suicide: A Chapter in Comparative Ethics," an individual accused of a transgression of a tribal taboo would climb to the top of a palm tree, declare his hurt at the charge, name his accuser, and then plunge head first to his death.

Without doubt, attitudes toward suicide in Africa, as elsewhere in the world, differ among various tribal societies and countries, and were irrevocably tied to ideologies concerning death and afterlife, as well as the values and/or rules of the different social structures.

African Americans and suicide   Historically, African Americans have had much lower rates of suicides compared to white Americans. However, beginning in the 1980s, the suicide rate for African-American boys began to rise at a much faster rate than their white contemporaries. From 1980 to 1995, suicidal behavior among both black and white boys increased dramatically—but especially among blacks, as the gap between rates for black and white boys narrowed.

Scientists from the Centers for Disease Control and Prevention in Atlanta say that from 1980 to 1995, the suicide rate for blacks between 10 and 19 jumped 114 percent, from 2.1 to 4.5 per 100,000 people. The scientists say a total of 3,030 black youths killed themselves in that period. The rates of suicide among black children, between the ages of 10 and 14, skyrocketed by 233 percent, compared to whites of the same age group, whose rate of suicide increased about 126 percent. The biggest jump was among young black men living in the South.

However, suicide rates for both black and white girls are much lower and have decreased or remained the same over the period.

While in 1980 the suicide rate among white youths was 157 percent higher than the rate among black youths, by 1995 the suicide rate among white youths was only 42 percent higher than the rate among black youths.

Moreover, the peak age for suicide in African-American men continues to be in the 20s, while for white men the risk of suicide rises each year beyond the 20s. Firearm-related suicides accounted for 96 percent of the increase in the suicide rate among black children and teens, with the largest percentage increase in the suicide rate among black teens recorded in the South, followed by the Midwest.

Experts believe the increasing suicide rate among all youths include the breakdown of the family, easier access to alcohol and illicit drugs, and easier access to lethal suicide methods. Experts believe that loss of a loved one and weakening family and community ties are contributing factors in black suicide.

The situations for black youth continues to grow worse judged by factors correlated with suicide rates. Thus, rates of unemployment, delinquency, substance abuse, and teenage pregnancy are higher. In addition, the exposure of black youths to poverty, poor educational opportunities, and discrimination may have negatively influenced their expectations about the future and, consequently, enhanced their tendency to consider suicide.

Scientists predicted as long ago as the 1930s that the rate of suicide among African Americans was going to rise as they moved into the white American culture. Children of upwardly mobile black families may feel as if they are trapped between the poor black community and the middle class, and that they are not accepted by either. This type of social limbo, experts suspect, may be in part a cause of the rising suicide rate.

age-adjusted suicide rates The practice of weighting suicide rates by a population standard to allow for comparisons across time and among risk groups. The U.S. 1999 mortality data is calculated using figures from the 2000 census, whereas previous years have been calculated using 1940 census data. For this reason, comparisons between 1999 and earlier U.S. mortality data should be made carefully.

age and suicide While there is a common perception that suicide rates are highest among the young, in fact it is the elderly (particularly older white men) who have the highest suicide rate. Among white men 65 and older, risk goes up with age; white men 85 and older have a suicide rate that is six times that of the overall national rate.

See also CHILDREN AND SUICIDE; ELDER SUICIDE; TEENAGE SUICIDE.

agenerative suicide Suicide triggered by personal alienation.

aggression Aggressive behavior toward others is often evident in suicidal behavior, especially in a homicide followed by suicide, and in the significant incidence of suicide among prisoners who committed violent crimes. In these cases, the suicide appears to be directed at other, significant persons the victim has known.

aggressive behavior   Forceful physical, verbal, or symbolic behavior is recognized as a general distress signal that, along with other cues, may predict suicidal behavior. In some cases, suicidal adolescents show wildly hostile behavior, such as threatening a teacher with a knife, terrorizing brothers or sisters, stealing a neighbor's car and narrowly missing smaller children at play, running away from home, and even displaying serious violence against parents. Teenagers who fit the aggressive pattern often abuse alcohol and drugs. Psychiatrists believe wild behavior is sometimes a coverup to mask the suicidal person's painful, depressive feelings.

agitation   Extreme restlessness common in individuals during a suicidal crisis.
See also AKATHISIA.

Ahitophel   The Old Testament counselor to King David, who supported Absalom in his revolt against the king. When Ahitophel realized that Absalom would be defeated, "he saddled his ass, and went off home to his own city. And he set his house in order and hanged himself."
This ALTRUISTIC SUICIDE is an example of suicide as a means of escaping political or military defeat, a common occurrence within select societies and at certain periods of history.
See also MASADA.

akathisia   Extreme restlessness and agitation that occurs as an adverse effect of some psychotropic medications. Akathisia has been implicated in suicidal thoughts and behavior of some patients taking these medications.

Albania   According to statistics from the World Health Organization, the suicide rate of Albania in 1998 was a fairly low 4.95 per 100,000. This represents a suicide rate among male Albanians of 6.3 per 100,000, and a rate among Albanian women of 3.6.

alcoholism and suicide   Although many cases of suicide occur as a result of alcoholism, the vast majority of alcoholics do not take their own lives. Alcoholism is a factor in about 30 percent of all completed suicides, and approximately 7 percent of those with alcohol dependence will die by suicide. About half of all people who kill themselves were intoxicated at the time.
Alcoholics kill themselves in reaction to events in their environment: Of the alcoholics who complete suicide, one-third experience the loss of a close relationship within the prior six weeks, and one-third expect to sustain an equally severe interpersonal loss.
Seven risk factors commonly predict suicide among alcoholics:

- continued substance abuse right up to the end of their lives
- communicating suicidal thoughts to others, often over a long period of time
- major depression
- no spouse, family, or friends offering social support
- unemployment
- serious medical problems
- living alone.

While each of these seven risk factors is important, they are also cumulative; that is, the more factors an alcoholic has, the greater the suicide risk. An alcoholic with at least three risk factors is considered to be highly at risk for suicide. Of all seven risk factors, continued drinking (found in 95 percent of alcoholic suicides) is the most important risk factor, driving all the others.
While alcohol reduces tension and anxiety, it also dulls the senses, reduces inhibitions, and clouds judgment. As the alcoholic drinks more, the person's physiological problems worsen.

Appetite and energy levels decline; sleep often becomes restless and troubled. Insomnia follows. Then irritability and depression increase, heightening the desire to drink more. Consciously or unconsciously, the alcohol abuser seeks relief from depression and irritability through alcohol. Indeed, the urge to drink is so strong that 96 percent of alcoholics who commit suicide continue their substance abuse up to the end of their lives. Because alcoholism often causes deep feelings of remorse during dry periods, alcoholics are suicide-prone even when sober.

A number of recent national surveys have helped shed light on the relationship between alcohol and other drug use and suicidal behavior. A review of minimum-age drinking laws and suicides among youths age 18 to 20 found that lower minimum-age drinking laws were associated with higher youth suicide rates. In a large study following adults who drink alcohol, suicide thoughts were reported among persons with depression. In another survey, persons who reported that they had made a suicide attempt during their lifetime were more likely to have had a depressive disorder, and many also had an alcohol and/or substance abuse disorder. In a study of all nontraffic injury deaths associated with alcohol intoxication, more than 20 percent were suicides.

In studies that examine risk factors among people who have completed suicide, substance use and abuse occurs more frequently among youth and adults, compared to older persons. For particular groups at risk, such as American Indians and Alaskan Natives, depression and alcohol use and abuse are the most common risk factors for completed suicide.

Alcohol and substance abuse problems contribute to suicidal behavior in several ways. Persons who are dependent on substances often have a number of other risk factors for suicide. In addition to being depressed, they are also likely to have social and financial problems. Substance use and abuse can be common among persons prone to be impulsive, and among persons who engage in many types of high-risk behaviors that result in self-harm.

Serotonin and Suicide

Scientists studying suicide have also discovered a link between alcoholics and low levels of a brain chemical called serotonin. Serotonin is a neurotransmitter important in the experience of emotion; in low levels, it has been linked to depression. Recent studies also reveal that alcoholics also have a lower number of serotonin receptors in the brain. Experts aren't sure whether the shortage is genetic or developmental and so help predispose someone to alcoholism—or it may just be another of alcohol's many toxic effects. Whatever the cause, it seems that alcoholics lack the ability to compensate for weak serotonin signals, which could help explain why suicide rates in this group are astonishingly high.

Alcoholics at Risk

Federal studies of alcoholics who attempt suicide have found that attempters have more mental health problems than alcoholics who do not try to commit suicide. There were significantly higher rates of psychiatric disorders among alcoholic suicide attempters as compared to non-attempters. Major depression, drug abuse, antisocial personality, panic disorder, generalized anxiety disorder, and phobias were about twice as likely to be found among alcoholic attempters. In addition, alcoholic attempters were more likely to have multiple psychiatric disorders; 66 percent of attempters had two or more of these diagnoses, as compared to 29 percent of alcoholics who did not attempt suicide.

Alcoholic suicide attempters also tend to be more hostile, more fearful, more impulsive, and deviant. These findings suggest that alcoholic suicide attempters experience a combination of mental problems and a lack of restraint over their behavior that may lead to destructive behavior toward themselves and others.

It did not appear that a family history of alcoholism had much effect on whether or not an alcoholic tried to commit suicide, but suicide attempters did report more episodes of drunkenness before age 15. Attempters also reported a significantly higher rate of receiving counseling for alcoholism.

Alcoholic suicide attempters were more likely to be divorced, separated, or widowed, and less likely to be married; they also were more likely to be unemployed and have lower levels of income.

There were no differences between the two groups with regard to racial or ethnic status, age, the level of education, or intellectual performance.

A combination of violence and depression is a warning sign of potential suicide among alcoholics. Furthermore, a person who has attempted suicide in the past is more likely to try again.

Treatment

Fortunately, there are a number of effective prevention efforts that reduce risk for substance abuse in youth, and there are effective treatments for alcohol and substance use problems. Researchers are currently testing treatments specifically for persons with substance abuse problems who are also suicidal, or who have attempted suicide in the past. Treatment programs for alcoholics that include measures aimed at preventing suicides would probably reduce the suicide rate.

Depression, found in nearly three-quarters of alcoholics who commit suicide, is highly treatable with antidepressants and cognitive behavioral therapy. Sobriety, social support, medication, and psychotherapy can reduce suicides among alcoholics.

Alcoholic clients who shows signs of suicidal tendencies benefit from extra time and care during sessions, and longer follow-up care or booster sessions to help decrease the risk of suicide or suicide attempts. Counseling sessions should be doubled or tripled for those clients at high risk for suicide to enable clients to work on self-control strategies and more constructive coping strategies.

alcohol myopia   A theory in which many of alcohol's social and stress-reducing effects are explained as a consequence of alcohol's narrowing of perceptual and thought functions. This effect on a person's thought processes may be associated with a propensity to complete suicide.

Basically, alcohol myopia occurs when people are intoxicated and cannot absorb as much information from the social context as they can when sober. The information they use to guide their responses is increasingly limited in proportion to the amount of alcohol consumed.

As inebriation increases, they begin to focus on small parts of the situation, one at a time, because the ability to perceive the situation as a whole is impaired. This results in unstable, fluctuating perceptions and reactions, depending on which narrow aspect of the surroundings they are paying attention to. This is why there is an increased risk of misunderstandings and misinterpretations when someone is drunk, which can in some contexts lead to aggressive responses or suicide attempts.

alliance for safety   A joint plan between clinician and client with the shared goal of preventing a suicide.

altruistic suicide   Suicide as self-sacrifice, as a result of social bonds that are too strong or smothering. Altruistic suicide can also be considered as an act of duty when individuals feel they are a burden on society at large or when they cannot cope with the demands of a society. Self-sacrifice is the defining trait, where individuals are so integrated into social groups that they lose sight of their individuality and become willing to sacrifice themselves to the group's interests, even if that sacrifice is their own life. The most common cases of altruistic suicide occur among members of the military.

"Altruistic suicide" was the idea of sociologist ÉMILE DURKHEIM, who wrote in *Le Suicide* that suicide was more understandable when considered as a reaction to society. He believed that self-destruction could be traced to the social conditions of the suicide attempter.

Durkheim, whose work is still widely quoted as a landmark of sociological research in suicide, believed there were four types of suicide: egoistic, anomic, altruistic, and fatalistic.

See also ANOMIC SUICIDE; EGOISTIC SUICIDE.

Alvarez, Alfred (1929–   ) English writer and critic who wrote THE SAVAGE GOD: A STUDY OF SUICIDE, in which Alvarez dispels the notion held by many people that suicide is either a terrifying aberration or something to be ignored altogether. He documents and explores man's changing attitudes toward suicide, from primitive societies through the Greek and Roman cultures and the suicidal martyrdom of the early Christian church, to the attitude of the late 19th century and the gradual shift in the responsibility of suicide from the individual society.

In his book, Alvarez discusses various theories of suicide, and explores the minds and emotional states of Dante, Cowper, Donne, and others. The author includes a personal memoir of the young American poet SYLVIA PLATH and discusses why she, and so many artists in the 20th century, chose to commit suicide. From there, the author enters into the closed world of the suicidal person, providing readers with his own personal view of suicide, and chronicles with startling candor his attempt on his own life.

ambivalence The coexistence of opposing feelings such as love and hate, respect and contempt, or sadness and joy, toward the same person or thing. It is perhaps the single most important psychological concept in the understanding of suicide. Ambivalence can be seen in the person who wants to commit suicide but doesn't want to, who simultaneously wishes to die even while fantasizing rescue. The ambivalence is so strong that often suicide victims have been found dead, the telephone clutched in their hand.

American Association of Suicidology (AAS) A nonprofit organization whose goal is to understand and prevent suicide. Founded in 1968 by Edwin S. Shneidman, PhD, AAS promotes research, and offers public awareness programs, and training for professionals and volunteers. In addition, the association serves as a national clearinghouse for information on suicide.

Members include mental health professionals, researchers, suicide prevention and crisis intervention centers, school districts, crisis center volunteers, survivors of suicide, and others who have an interest in suicide prevention.

A primary objective of AAS is to help suicide and crisis intervention centers throughout the United States and Canada provide quality services. The AAS has developed standards for certification of these centers that are described in the AAS Certification Standards Manual for Crisis Intervention Programs.

The AAS, publishes quarterly a journal, *Suicide and Life-Threatening Behavior,* and *Newslink,* a quarterly newsletter. In addition, AAS produces a number of suicide prevention pamphlets for the public as well as a *Directory of Suicide Prevention and Crisis Intervention Agencies in the U.S.*

The AAS holds an annual conference every spring; state and regional groups affiliated with the AAS conduct periodic meetings and workshops.

AAS also produced public service announcements and releases on suicide prevention.

Involvement in suicide prevention legislative efforts also is a priority of AAS. Members often consult on potential or pending legislation at both the federal and state levels; many have provided expert testimony for congressional committees and subcommittees.

The AAS presents yearly awards to outstanding contributors in the field of suicidology. The group assists and encourages survivor activities by maintaining information on survivor groups and lists of books, films, newsletters, and pamphlets that focus on survivor concerns.

For contact information, see Appendix I.

American Foundation for Suicide Prevention, The   A nonprofit group dedicated to advancing the understanding of suicide and how to prevent it. The foundation's activities include research support, providing information about depression and suicide, educating professionals about suicide, and publicizing the magnitude of the problems of depression and suicide and the need for research, prevention, and treatment. The group also supports programs for suicide survivor treatment, research, and education, and maintains local chapters throughout the world.

The foundation was begun in 1987 by a group of suicide experts together with business and community leaders and survivors of suicide. The early members believed only a combined effort would make it possible to fund the research necessary for progress in the prevention of suicide. Since then, the foundation's institutional grants helped begin important centers for suicide research at major medical centers throughout the country, such as Columbia, Einstein, Harvard, Western Psychiatric in Pittsburgh, the University of Texas Medical Branch at Galveston, and Emory University.

The group also holds educational conferences and offers postdoctoral fellowships and young investigator awards for young scientists interested in suicide research. The foundation also supports workshops for survivor group leaders, conferences on survivor problems, regional survivor group directories, and maintains a special 800 number for referrals to these groups. The group also maintains a relationship with more than 300 "survivors of suicide" groups around the country.

In addition, AFSP's National Suicide Data Bank is accumulating information about completed suicide that has been heretofore unavailable.

For contact information, see Appendix I.

American Indians   See NATIVE AMERICANS.

American Medical Association (AMA)   This organization of physicians and surgeons sponsors a special committee to study suicide. The AMA also provides advisory, interpretive, and referral information on medicine, health care, and science. Statistics, clipping services, brochures/pamphlets, library searches, placement on mailing lists, and a newsletter are available through the AMA, and they also will supply a publications list. AMA publishes the prestigious *Journal of the American Medical Association* (JAMA).

For contact information, see Appendix I.

American Psychiatric Association   The professional medical society that represents U.S. and Canadian psychiatrists. The association's goals are to improve treatment, rehabilitation, and care of the mentally ill, to promote research, to advance standards of all psychiatric services and facilities, and to educate other medical professionals and scientists as well as the general public. The association provides advisory, analytical, bibliographical, historical, how-to, interpretive, referral, and technical information on psychiatric care, psychiatric insurance, and mental illness. Publications include advance and post-convention articles and news releases each May concerning annual meetings and scientific proceedings; more than 400 individual papers on a wide range of topics, including suicide, are available each year. Also, periodic news releases are furnished throughout the year concerning new studies published in the APA journals.

For contact information, see Appendix I.

American Psychological Association (APA)   Based in Washington, D.C., the APA is a scientific and professional organization that represents psychology in the United States. With more than 155,000 members, the APA is the largest association of psychologists worldwide.

Psychology is the study of the mind and behavior. The discipline embraces all aspects of the human experience, from the functions of the brain to the actions of nations, from child development to care for the aged. In every conceivable setting from scientific research centers to mental health care services, the understanding of behavior is the enterprise of psychologists.

For contact information, see Appendix I.

amputation metaphor   An analogy in loss commonly used by grieving parents who describe the loss of a child in ways similar to loss of a limb.

Anatomy of Melancholy, The   The first major text in the history of Western cognitive science written by ROBERT BURTON (1577–1640), provides the first modern interpretation of suicide. At the time Burton was writing, early 17th-century physicians were relying on the authority of the great Greek and Arabian physicians such as Galen and Hippocrates. Because there was no new scientific knowledge on which to generalize about suicide and psychology, Burton focused on all previous thinkers about cognition. Burton assimilated these previous thinkers to produce a model of human consciousness brought together by a set of conceptual divisions of the human psyche and body.

One of the major documents of modern European civilization, Burton's astounding compendium surveys melancholy in all its forms. Lewellyn Powys called it "the greatest work of prose of the greatest period of English prose-writing," while celebrated surgeon William Osler believed it was the greatest of medical treatises.

anniversaries   Survivors of suicide often find that each year, on the anniversary of the suicide, they experience renewed grief, anger, anxiety, loneliness, and depression. As with a loss by "natural" death, a process is started within the survivor's psyche that psychiatrists call the "anniversary reaction." Psychiatrists and other counselors suggest these emotions be discussed by survivors with qualified clinicians who can assist them in working through their traumatic loss. Otherwise, the pain can be needlessly prolonged.

anniversary trigger   The idea that people tend to die (or commit suicide) near key dates in their lives.

anomic suicide   Suicide triggered by a disrupted relationship or insufficient regulation in society (*anomie* means "lawlessness"). The term describes one of the four types of suicide as outlined by sociologist ÉMILE DURKHEIM. (The others are egoistic, altruistic, and fatalistic suicides.)

A society is regulated to the extent that it controls the motivations of its members. When a society undergoes rapid changes and regulations are in a state of flux, an individual may be unable to adjust to the lack of definitive rules or customs. Psychologically, the individual may no longer be able to adjust, or to feel that he or she belongs to a group. An example of such a situation might be a long-term employee who suddenly loses a job, or a man whose wife dies after 45 years of marriage.

Anomic suicide was of particular interest to Durkheim, and he divided it further into four categories: acute and chronic economic anomie, and acute and chronic domestic anomie. Each involved an imbalance of means and needs, in which a person's means were unable to fulfill needs.

In suicide due to acute economic anomie, there are sporadic decreases in the ability of traditional institutions such as religion or social systems to regulate and fulfill social needs.

Suicide linked to chronic economic anomie involves a long-term relaxation of social regulation. Durkheim identified this type of suicide with the ongoing industrial revolution, which eroded traditional social regulators and often failed to replace them. Industrial goals of wealth and property were not enough to provide happiness, as was demonstrated by higher suicide rates among the wealthy than among the poor.

Suicide caused by acute domestic anomie involves sudden changes in interpersonal relationships, leading to an inability to adapt—and therefore higher suicide rates. Widowhood is a prime example of this type of anomie.

Suicide due to chronic domestic anomie refers to the way marriage as an institution regulated the sexual and behavioral means-needs balance among men and women. Bachelors tended to commit suicide at higher rates than married men because of a lack of regulation and established goals and expectations. On the other hand, marriage has traditionally served to constrict the lives of women by further limiting their already diminished opportunities and goals. Unmarried women, therefore, do not experience chronic domestic anomie nearly as often as do unmarried men.

See also ALTRUISTIC SUICIDE; EGOISTIC SUICIDE.

anorexia nervosa   A disorder characterized by severe and prolonged refusal to eat, resulting in major weight loss and physical debilitation. It is usually associated with an intense fear of becoming obese and is most frequently found in girls and young women. Bulimia is often associated with this condition. Experts believe most individuals with anorexia nervosa are potentially suicidal. In essence, they are literally starving themselves to the point of self-destruction. People with anorexia tend to suffer with a profound sense of inadequacy, low self-esteem, and self-hatred. This malady affects teenage females for the most part (an estimated one-half million in the United States alone); 15 percent of those with severe cases of anorexia nervosa die.

antidepressants   A major classification of drugs developed to improve mood medically in severely depressed patients.

antidepressants and suicide   Increased use of antidepressants are linked to a decreasing U.S. suicide rate, according to at least one study. From 1995 to 1998, prescriptions for newer antidepressants such as Prozac rose 41 percent, while the age-adjusted national suicide rate dipped about 6 percent. However, there is no

clear cause-and-effect evidence to support this.

While the data are preliminary, scientists believe the link could be real, since depression or related illness is often seen in people who commit suicide. Changes in unemployment did not appear to explain the altered suicide rates. Suicide took 30,575 American lives in 1998, for an age-adjusted rate of 10.43 per 100,000 population, down from 11.11 in 1995, according to federal data.

See also PROZAC AND SUICIDE.

Antisthenes (440–ca. 360 B.C.)   Greek philosopher who founded the Cynic School of Philosophers at Athens; he advocated a simple, austere life. After the death of his beloved teacher, SOCRATES, in 339 B.C., Antisthenes established a school called Cynosarges—hence his followers bore the name "Cynics"—although others argue that his followers were called Cynics because of the gloomy habits of the school. Indeed, the older Antisthenes got, the gloomier he became, until he was a worry to his friends and the object of ridicule to his enemies. He taught that pleasure and desire were evil, and so he wore only a coarse cloak, did not cut his beard, and carried a sack and staff like a wandering beggar. This was meant to express his opposition to the increasing luxury of the age in favor of simplicity in life and manners. Indeed, Antisthenes appears to have been carried to excess in his virtuous zeal against luxury.

In one story, perhaps tired of his continual gloom, his friend DIOGENES offered Antisthenes a dagger, saying: "Perhaps you have need of this, friend?" Antisthenes replied, "I thank you, but unfortunately, the will to live is part of the world's evil, as it is part of our nature."

Antisuicide Bureau   The first crisis center established by the SALVATION ARMY in 1906.

Antony, Mark (Marcus Antonius) (ca. 83 B.C.–30 B.C.)   Roman statesman and soldier who served under Julius Caesar in Gaul. After

Caesar's assassination in 44 B.C., Antony met and fell in love with CLEOPATRA. Ignoring his second wife, Octavia, he settled in Alexandria and ruled from there in a luxurious court until Octavian, his wife's brother, deprived him of power. In the ensuing civil war, Octavian's forces triumphed at Actium in 31 B.C., and Antony fled to Alexandria, where he and Cleopatra committed suicide upon his brother-in-law's approach.

See also ALTRUISTIC SUICIDE.

anxious suicidality   The combination of suicidal thoughts and severe anxiety in children.

Apaches, White Mountain   Suicide and homicide among the White Mountain Apaches (who live on a reservation in the central mountain region of Arizona) are closely related. In certain situations, the Apaches appear to believe the only options open to an individual are self-destruction or murder. The rise in female suicides among the Apaches is part of this suicide-homicide system.

The Apache suicide rate is between 50 and 133 per 100,000. During the 1930s, the male to female rate of suicide was four to one, but by the 1960s, it had developed to six male suicides to every female suicide.

April suicides   The spring months of March, April, and May have consistently shown the highest suicide rate, 4 percent to 6 percent higher than the average for the rest of the year. Contrary to popular myths, the suicide rate during the Christmas season is below average.

See also HOLIDAYS AND SUICIDE.

Aquinas, Saint Thomas (1225–1274)   Brilliant Dominican priest and philosopher of the 13th century who was one of the greatest Christian philosophers to ever live. Called the *Doctor Angelicus* (the Angelic Doctor), he is best known for writing the *Summa theologica* and the *Summa contra Gentiles.*

In *Summa theologica,* St. Thomas formulated the authoritative church position on suicide, writing that suicide was absolutely wrong and unnatural. He believed that every man was a member of some community, and suicide was therefore antisocial. Since life was a gift of God, he reasoned, it was not up to man to throw that gift away. For St. Thomas, all life was merely preparation for the eternal. He stressed the sacredness of human life and absolute submission to God. St. Thomas was one of the greatest and most influential theologians of all time.

He was canonized in 1323 and declared Doctor of the Church by Pope Pius V.

Argentina   Suicide in Argentina has slowly decreased from a 1960s rate of 10 per 100,000 to 6.4 per 100,000 in 1996. As in most countries of the world, men commit suicide at a far higher rate than do women; 9.9 per 100,000 compared to 3.0 for women.

The age group most at risk for suicide in Argentina, as in many other countries, is the elderly—specifically, men over 75 have an extremely high rate of 42.4 deaths per 100,000, soaring far beyond the rate for women of the same age: just 7.7 per 100,000. This continues a trend begun during the 1960s of suicide occurring predominantly among older Argentinians.

According to police files, apparent reasons for suicide among Argentinians include weariness of life, physical suffering, mental alienation, family disgust, lack of resources, and love contradictions.

Aristotle (384–322 B.C.)   Greek philosopher who described suicide as a failure in courage. "To run away from trouble is a form of cowardice," he wrote in *Ethics,* "and, while it is true that the suicide braves death, he does it not for some noble object, but to escape ill." Aristotle believed the attainment of the human form to be of great moral significance; therefore, destroying human life at any stage was morally offensive. In committing suicide, Aristotle believed a person was also committing an offense by robbing the state of civic and economic contributions.

Armenia   One of the lowest suicide rates in Europe is found in Armenia, which listed a rate of just 1.8 suicides per 100,000 people in 1999. This breaks down to 2.7 per 100,000 among Armenian men, and 0.9 for women.

Arria (d. A.D. 42)   The wife of Roman senator Cecina Paetus, who was accused of being involved in a plot against the emperor and ordered to commit suicide. When Paetus hesitated, Arria snatched the dagger from her husband, stabbed herself, then handed the weapon back with the words, "Paete, non dolet" (Paetus, it does not hurt).

See also COMPULSORY SUICIDE.

art, literature, and suicide   In art and literature, attitudes toward suicide remain as ambivalent and divided today as they were in ancient Greece and Rome. There have been apologists for suicide in both cultural fields. Eminent artists and writers have over the years proclaimed man's right to self-destruction, whereas many others have condemned suicide with equal conviction.

JOHN DONNE's *BIATHANATOS* (subtitled "A Declaration of that Paradoxe, or Thesis, that Self-Homicide is Not So Naturally Sinne, that It May Never Be Otherwise") was a classic example of what was then a new look at an old practice. Through the years, many other writers—both inside and outside the Church—explored the endless possibilities of the topic. MONTAIGNE, in his famous *ESSAIS,* calls death "a very secure haven, never to be feared and often to be sought." Romantic suicide has long been used by playwrights and poets; Shakespeare's *ROMEO AND JULIET* is a popular example.

Interestingly, Donne's thesis, written early in the 17th century, was not published until 1646, 15 years after the poet-chaplain's death. Born a Catholic, Donne later took Anglican orders, rec-

ognized his thesis as a "misinterpretable" subject, and asked the person to whom he had entrusted the original manuscript to "publish it not, yet burn it not; and between those, do what you will with it."

DAVID HUME's essay, "ON SUICIDE," was also published posthumously in 1777, a year after his death. The essay, immediately suppressed, is today considered a convincing argument against the moral prejudice that many still hold against suicide. Hume's view was that at the worst, one does not harm society by suicide, but merely ceases to do good. He also believes, that one who is tired of life often is a burden on society—and hinders the work of others.

Perhaps ALBERT CAMUS summed up neatly the ambivalence and division among artists and writers over the years with regard to suicide: "What is called a reason for living is also an excellent reason for dying."

assisted suicide   The completion of suicide by a terminally ill or suffering person with the help of a doctor or other clinician, but in such a way that the person technically dies by his own hand. For example, a person who dies by swallowing pills supplied by a doctor for the purpose of causing death would be considered an assisted suicide. Oregon, Belgium, and the Netherlands are the three jurisdictions in the world where laws specifically permit assisted suicide.

There is a difference between assisted suicide and EUTHANASIA. If another person performs the last act that intentionally causes a patient's death, euthanasia has occurred. Giving a patient a lethal injection or putting a plastic bag over a person's head would be considered euthanasia. Assisted suicide indicates that the person who dies actually performs the last act, and only gets "assistance" from a second person. Therefore, a patient who pushes a switch to trigger a fatal injection after the doctor has inserted an intravenous needle into the patient's vein would be committing an assisted suicide.

Assisted suicide remains extremely controversial in the United States and in many countries around the world because it reverses the physician's usual approach to patients. Some patients desire an assisted suicide if they believe adequate relief is not possible. Others may request earlier death to exercise autonomy and to end their lives on their own terms. Proponents argue that terminally ill patients should have the right to end their suffering, and that involving another person (such as a doctor) makes the suicide easier and less risky. Critics worry that assisted suicide might lead to abuse, exploitation, and erosion of care for vulnerable people.

Numerous attempts by other states to pass laws legalizing assisted suicide have failed. In November 1998, Michigan voters defeated an initiative that would have legalized assisted suicide by a vote of 71 percent. In January 2000, an attempt to legalize assisted suicide in the California Assembly (AB 1592) failed, and on November 7, 2000, voters in Maine also rejected the proposed "Maine Death with Dignity Act." This law was virtually identical to the assisted suicide law that passed in Oregon in 1994.

The frequency of physician-assisted suicide for the terminally ill is unknown, but, based on anecdotal evidence, is probably both substantial and increasing.

While it is against the law in all states except Oregon to assist another person to commit suicide, it is not against the law to give general information to people on ways to kill themselves.

In April 2002, Europe's leading human rights court rejected an appeal by a terminally ill and paralyzed British woman who wanted her husband to help end her life. She died a month later.

Diane Pretty, 43, suffered from a motor neuron disease that left her paralyzed and confined to a wheelchair. She brought her case to the European court after Britain's highest appeals court ruled in November 2001 that her husband could not be guaranteed immunity from prosecution if he helped her die. Suicide is legal in Britain as it is in the United States, but in Britain

helping someone else commit suicide is a crime punishable by up to 14 years in prison. A seven-judge panel of the European Court of Human Rights in Strasbourg, France, sided unanimously with British authorities.

In their ruling, the judges rejected her lawyers' claims that British laws infringed on portions of the European Convention on Human Rights guaranteeing the right to life, prohibiting inhuman or degrading treatment and protecting respect for private life. The court said any change to the law would seriously undermine the protection of life which Britain's Suicide Act was intended to safeguard.

The court's judgment was considered a test case for Europe, where the Netherlands became the first country to fully legalize euthanasia on April 1, 2002. Belgium approved a similar law a month later. Legislation is expected to be enacted soon in Switzerland, France, Germany, and Sweden.

This has not always been the case. In English common law—the system of legal tradition inherited by the United States from Britain—suicide was at one time a felony. It was called *Felo de se*—the felony of self-murder. Under the law, property of a person who committed suicide was forfeited and burial was "ignominious."

Moreover, anyone who assisted a suicide and was present when the suicidal act was initiated was considered to be guilty of murder. If the person assisting was not present, he or she was still considered an "accessory before the fact" and was considered guilty of murder or manslaughter. In certain jurisdictions, however, the one assisting sometimes escaped punishment because the person who committed suicide, being deceased, could not be convicted and thus, the accessory could not be tried.

In the past 100 years, most common law provisions have been abolished in the United States. The English Suicide Act of 1961 legalized suicide in that country but still made aiding and abetting suicide a criminal offense.

If suicide is no longer a crime in the United States, aiding a suicide remains a potentially serious offense. In a 1920 case in Michigan, *People v. Roberts,* a husband who had prepared a poison and placed it within his wife's reach was convicted of first degree murder and given a life sentence. The man had done as his wife requested (she suffered from an incurable and physically incapacitating affliction). The decision was upheld in appellate court.

Today, there remains real risk of criminal prosecution for anyone who assists a suicide, even for humanitarian and compassionate reasons—and even at the victim's request. However, prosecution under criminal law does not begin until police or other law enforcement officials believe that a crime has been committed and they can identify those responsible. If no one knows a crime has occurred, no charges are filed. If, for instance, a terminally ill person's death is declared "natural" by the attending physician because no one knew another person helped in the suicidal act, then no charges would be filed and no prosecution would begin. This undoubtedly happens more than the public generally realizes.

Should there be some question or suspicion as to final cause of death, authorities may order an autopsy. A family can usually refuse to give permission for the autopsy, if they do not, in their refusal, arouse suspicion of "foul play." Should that happen, officials will probably order that the autopsy be performed.

Whether or not criminal proceedings are started is within the discretion and judgment of the prosecutor, usually the district attorney. A number of factors affect the prosecutor's decision, such as: if a death causes considerable public attention; if public attention is generated by a particularly vocal group opposed to the act of suicide; if there appears to be a likelihood of significant financial gain or other selfish motive on the part of the person assisting the suicide; or, if the person helping happens to be a total stranger to the suicide victim.

Once it has been determined to prosecute, a request by the victim for help in the suicide is almost certain not to be considered a valid legal defense. The risks for aiding and abetting in the suicidal act are both real and serious. Still, there is considerable room for argument under certain circumstances (such as providing information only to a terminally ill patient about the deadliness of various drugs). Then the focus in a criminal case usually becomes one of *intent* of the person to *cause*—or assist in—the death. In today's society, information about drugs is fairly common knowledge. Thus, the closer the person who assists is to a terminally ill person (and the more specific the response to a request for help in the suicide act), the more likely the chance of criminal prosecution.

In addition, the laws of conspiracy (an agreement among two or more people to commit a criminal act and some action by at least one of them toward further preparation) form a separate basis for prosecution.

Therefore, even for advocates of euthanasia who support the option of active voluntary "self-deliverance" for the terminally ill, the risk of criminal charges is real and serious for those who would help someone commit suicide.

All this concerns only criminal law. Of concern to professionals such as physicians, psychologists, psychiatrists, nurses, social workers, and attorneys is the potential jeopardy to their license should their participation in assisting another's self-destruction become known. The revocation or suspension of professional licenses comes under administrative law, which is complicated and involves a formal administrative proceeding, the accused professional's procedural rights of due process, a list of charges, and the right to an impartial hearing on the charges, with opportunity to cross-examine adverse witnesses and produce evidence refuting the charges. Clearly, this involved process is but one important reason why professional people are generally very reluctant to offer or provide active assistance even to tragic victims of painful terminal illnesses.

Finally, in contrast to criminal law, there is civil law which involves one citizen or more bringing a lawsuit against another, alleging injuries to themselves or one of their recognized "interests." A typical case in civil law might be one concerning alleged direct bodily injury to the plaintiff (the one bringing a lawsuit) as a result of medical malpractice (against the defendant physician).

The required elements for having grounds to file a civil suit include: liability, damages, and causation. In the context of those who have chosen to assist a suicide, there are at least three potential areas of "exposure" to civil litigation: (1) dissent by survivors (some family member learns of the helper's role and actively disagrees with actions taken); (2) unsuccessful attempt (perhaps brought about by the potential suicide himself against the helper who either withdrew or who inadvertently botched the suicide attempt); (3) wrong person dies (when someone other than the suicide, perhaps a child, comes into possession of the drug(s), ingests them, and fatal results are misdirected).

It is clear there are legal risks for anyone who might agree to assist someone in suicide. That is why the voluntary euthanasia groups (BRITISH VOLUNTARY EUTHANASIA SOCIETY, THE HEMLOCK SOCIETY, and CONCERNS FOR DYING) advise followers always to proceed with great care and caution when considering help to a terminally ill patient in "self-deliverance."

Assisting a person whose personal choice is suicide is not to be confused with "mercy killing." Whereas voluntary self-destruction involves personal decision and self-control, mercy killing is the *unrequested* taking of another's life in order to save that person further suffering. Mercy killing is usually an act of desperation and despair, and often the life-taker is near emotional collapse caused by the stress that comes from caring for and watching someone terminally ill. Pushed to such limits, the life-taker at some point feels compelled to hasten death—by whatever means—because no one else will.

Mercy killers are usually confronted with the criminal charge of murder or manslaughter. Up until the 1960s, "mercy killers" in Western society often were sentenced to death, later commuted to life imprisonment. In the United States, in the past 10 years, there have been several cases where juries refused to indict or convict "mercy killers," though all evidence weighed against such a decision.

In March 1986, the American Medical Association decided that it would be ethical for their members to withhold "all means of life-prolonging medical treatment," including food and water, from patients who are in irreversible comas. The AMA's judicial council, meeting in New Orleans, decided unanimously that withholding treatment in such cases, even when death is not imminent, would be ethically appropriate. The council made clear its decision does not oblige any physician to stop therapy, and that each case should be decided individually.

At present, there are an estimated 10,000 people who are in irreversible comas in institutions in the United States, according to *The New York Times*. In such cases, doctors in the past have often refused to withhold or withdraw treatments (such as respirators or artificial feeding), citing ethical standards and fear of criminal prosecution or malpractice suits—despite the requests of family members and the previously expressed wishes of the patients to have such treatments withdrawn.

The opinion of AMA's judicial council has no legal standing, although it is an indication of a shift of social opinion. Today, an estimated 80 percent of the 5,500 Americans who die each day are wired and incubated and in institutions.

The crux of AMA's policy lies in the stipulation that the patient need not be terminally ill for halting treatment to be acceptable. Such decisions to remove life-support systems will probably be difficult for many doctors. The recent AMA decision is but one more cautious step in the evolution of a social policy in the complex, delicate and shadowy area of dying and death.

Association for Death Education and Counseling   The oldest interdisciplinary organization in the field of dying, DEATH EDUCATION, and

bereavement. Members of this nonprofit organization include educators, counselors, nurses, physicians, hospital and hospice personnel, mental health professionals, clergy, funeral directors, social workers, philosophers, psychologists, sociologists, physical and recreational therapists, and volunteers. ADEC works to promote and share research, theories, and practice in dying, death, and bereavement.

The group was formed in 1976, when a group of interested educators and clinicians organized the Forum for Death Education and Counseling, eventually changing the name to the Association for Death Education and Counseling (ADEC).

For contact information, see Appendix I.

attempted suicide   A suicidal act that is not fatal, possibly because the self-destructive intention was slight, vague, or ambiguous. Most people who try to kill themselves are ambivalent about their wish to die, and the attempt may be a plea for help that fails because of a stronger wish to live. There may be as many as 20 attempted suicides to every one that is completed; the ratio is higher in women and youth, and lower in men and the elderly.

Each year, at least 300,000 Americans survive a suicide attempt. Most have injuries minor enough to need no more than emergency room treatment, but about 116,000 people are hospitalized; of these, most are eventually discharged alive. The average hospital stay is 10 days.

Without knowledge of proper dosages and methods, suicide attempts may be bungled, leaving the victim worse off than before. For example, some suicide attempts by gunshot leave the person alive but brain-damaged; drug overdoses that are not fatal may have the same effect. About 17 percent of attempted suicides (about 19,000 Americans) are permanently disabled or unable to work.

Risk factors for attempted suicide in adults include depression, alcohol abuse, cocaine use, and separation or divorce. Risk factors for attempted suicide in youth include depression, alcohol or other drug use disorder, physical or sexual abuse, and aggressive or disruptive behaviors. Most suicide attempts are expressions of extreme distress, and are not just harmless bids for attention. For this reason, a suicidal person should never be left alone and needs immediate mental health treatment.

Treatment

Many people who attempt suicide are admitted to a hospital emergency department in a coma. After an overdose of a potentially lethal drug has been confirmed, the drug should be removed from the patient, so as to prevent absorption and expedite excretion. Treatment of symptoms to keep the patient alive should be started; and any known antidote should be given if the specific drug can be identified.

Every person with a life-threatening self-injury should be hospitalized to treat the physical injury and also to get a psychiatric assessment. Although most patients are well enough to be discharged as soon as the physical injury is treated, they should always be given follow-up care. Psychiatric assessment should be performed as soon as possible for all patients who attempt suicide.

After the attempt, the patient may deny any problems, because the severe depression that led to the suicidal act may be followed by a short-lived mood elevation. Nevertheless, the risk of another suicide at a later date is high unless the patient's problems are resolved.

The patient needs a secure, strong source of help, which begins when the physician provides sympathetic attention and expresses concern, commitment, and understanding of the patient's troubled feelings. Although only 10 percent to 15 percent of attempters go on to kill themselves, it is estimated that between 30 percent and 40 percent of suicides make at least one nonfatal attempt.

It is believed that most suicide attempts, for whatever reasons, are essentially a cry for help. However, it is sometimes hard to tell whether an attempt is genuine or a dramatic gesture toward self-destruction. For instance, there are reported cases where the person took a small number of sleeping pills and called a physician. On the other hand, a suicide attempt that turns deadly is the last in a long series of cries for help. Yet another myth that persists today, despite statistics to the contrary, is that once a person tries to kill himself and fails, the pain and shame will prevent a second attempt.

In the United States, the ratio of suicide is about three men to one woman, although women usually make two-thirds of the unsuccessful attempts at suicide. In most countries, attempted suicide is no longer a punishable offense, though it is still frowned upon by many segments of society and causes guilt feelings to those closely involved.

The peak age for suicides lies between 55 and 64; for attempted suicides, between 24 and 44. Nine out of 10 teenage suicide attempts take place in the home, between the hours of 3 P.M. and midnight, when parents are home.

The more lethal and violent methods (guns, explosives, hanging) are used less often in the nonfatal attempts than in the successful suicidal acts.

attitudes Suicide and suicidal behavior have been a part of human culture since ancient man first realized he could kill himself. Still, the act of self-destruction is often considered taboo, an act that stigmatizes not only the victims but the survivors as well. The word *suicide,* however, is a relatively recent term, first used in 1651 and taken from the Latin *sui,* "of oneself," and *cide,* "a killing"—literally, to kill oneself.

Attitudes concerning suicide and those who try it have varied widely in societies and the groups within those societies over the centuries. These attitudes run the spectrum of feelings and emotions from revulsion, condemnation and total disapproval, to pity, benign acceptance, and reluctant recognition of the right to die voluntarily under certain circumstances.

Through the years, philosophers have pondered the problem: PLATO strongly condemned

suicide, together with Virgil, Cicero, and Ovid. IMMANUEL KANT called suicide "an insult to humanity." The Roman Stoics accepted the option of suicide, as did the EPICUREANS, who considered that one's destiny was a matter of individual choice. Cato, Pliny, and Seneca all considered suicide to be acceptable.

On the whole, however, society began to take a hostile attitude toward self-destruction or unnatural deaths.

Suicide became taboo as superstitions and myths were created to discuss the act. The law began to deal with suicide in punishing terms, even going so far as to enact statutes against the suicide's survivors, and as a deterrent for future offenders. In ENGLAND, suicide attempters were imprisoned until 1916; then, instead of prison, the suicidal person was placed in custody of relatives or friends. In fact, not until 1961 did the British Parliament abolish the criminality of suicide and declare that the act of self-destruction was not "a species of felony."

Today legal restrictions have been abolished in most countries. As research in mental health increased and improved, legislation changed (if only gradually). In India, attempted suicide is still an indictable offense. For many years, nine states in the United States still considered attempted suicide a misdemeanor or felony. But even in those states (Alabama, Kentucky, New Jersey, South Carolina, North Carolina, North Dakota, Oklahoma, South Dakota, and Washington) such laws were seldom enforced.

The world's various religions have profoundly influenced the American legal position on suicide, because laws in America are based on English common law, which in turn was impacted by religion.

The three denominations of modern Judaism consider the act of suicide a crime against God, but an act that can sometimes be explained, understood, and forgiven. But in Judaism, as in other religions, there has never been universal agreement.

After the birth of Christ, suicide was commonplace in Greece and Rome. Early Christians seemed to accept the attitudes prevailing at the time. The Apostles did not denounce suicide, and the New Testament mentioned the matter only indirectly, in the report of Judas's suicide. For centuries, church leaders did not condemn suicide.

Then Augustine denounced suicide as a sin that precluded the possibility of repentance, calling the act "a form of homicide, and thus a violation of the DECALOGUE ARTICLE, 'Thou shalt not kill.'" The earliest institutional disapproval didn't come until 533, however, with the Second Council of Orleans. Suicide, it was determined, became the most serious and heinous of transgressions. In 563, the Fifteenth Canon of the Council of Braga denied funeral rites of the Eucharist and the singing of psalms to anyone who committed suicide. The Council of Hereford of 673 withheld burial rites to those who died of self-destruction. In 1284, the Synod of Nimes refused self-murderers even the quiet interment in holy ground.

SAINT THOMAS AQUINAS refined and elaborated on Augustine's concept, opposing suicide on the basis of three postulates. His opposition was predicated on the sacredness of human life and absolute submission to God.

The philosophical and religious stances have changed over time and brought new attitudes regarding suicide. JOHN DONNE, dean of St. Paul's Cathedral, London, reacted against the Church's view of suicide. He admitted it was contrary to the law of self-preservation, but saw it as neither a violation of the law nor against reason. His position was supported in time by secular writers and philosophers, including DAVID HUME, Montesquieu, Voltaire, and JEAN-JACQUES ROUSSEAU.

Among other religions, Brahmanism tolerates suicide, whereas the attitude of Buddhism is ambiguous, although it encourages suicide in the service of religion and country. Hindus consider suicide an ultimate death, thus leading to an earthbound, ghostly existence. In Japan, compulsory hara-kiri was declared illegal in 1868, though voluntary hara-kiri occurs occasionally even today.

In modern times, Dietrich Bonhoeffer considered suicide a sin because it represented a denial of God. Yet he suspended that judgment for prisoners of war, for the obvious reasons. Perhaps Bishop John Robinson best sums it up: "Truth finds expression in different ages. Times change and even Christians change with them." Overall, it appears that society's attitude toward suicidal behavior is less moralistic and punitive than it was a generation ago. Increasingly, suicide is recognized not only as a philosophical, religious, legal, and cultural question, but also as a psychosociobiological problem. This may be another reason why there is a greater readiness today to understand rather than condemn.

Augustine of Hippo, Saint (354–430)

North African theologian and one of the outstanding theologians of the Catholic Church. Son of Saint Monica, a Christian, Augustine had been influenced by the pagan philosophers until his conversion. After a dissolute youth, he returned to his native town following his baptism at age 32 on Easter Sunday, 387. He was ordained in 391, and then was consecrated a bishop of Hippo in 396. His *City of God* and *Confessions* are among the greatest Christian documents. In *Confessions*, Augustine recounts how even his youthful insincerity was reflected in prayers for repentance: "Da mihi castitateur et continentiam, sed noli modo" (Give me chastity and continence, but not yet.)

Augustine's denouncement of suicide as a sin greatly influenced thinking at the time. He espoused four arguments to justify the Church's antisuicide position: (1) no private individual may assume the right to kill a guilty person; (2) the suicide who takes his own life has killed a man; (3) the truly noble soul will bear all suffering from which the effort to escape is an admission of weakness; and, (4) the suicide dies the worst of sinners because he is not only running away from the fear of temptation, but also any possibilities of absolution.

Australia The suicide rate in Australia has risen from a low of 12.7 per 100,000 in the 1960s to a high in 1977 of 14.3 per 100,000. Within the Australian island continent, suicide rates have varied, and will probably continue to vary, among the five continental states (Queensland, New South Wales, Victoria, South Australia, and West Australia).

Unlike many other industrialized countries in which the age group with the highest suicide rate tends to be older citizens, in Australia men age 25 to 31 have the highest rate (31 per 100,000). Australian women age 45 to 54 have the highest suicide rate—7.7 per 100,000, still far below the men's rate.

Austria This country has a relatively high incidence of suicide, unlike other such predominantly Catholic countries as Ireland, Italy, and Spain. The suicide rate, which peaked in the 1930s and then dropped, rose and then dropped again, from 22.8 per 100,000 in 1965 to 24.8 in 1978, then back down to 19.5 in 1998.

Suicide among Austrian men has been rising from 14.9 per 100,000 in 1965 to 17.2 in 1978 to 28.7 in 1999. Although the suicide rate for Austrian women is much lower than for men, it has risen from 7.8 in 1965 to 10.3 in 1999.

In one study, researchers concluded that the Viennese seemed socially alienated and isolated, and in poor communication with spouses, relatives, and close friends. Alcohol was a serious problem for about one-third of the suicides in the study.

authoritarianism Favoring blind submission to authority. Historically, authoritarian cultures have produced a very high suicide rate. Some experts believe that this type of culture affects a person's self-concept. For example, in the past, the highly authoritarian Japanese culture produced a very high suicide rate in that country, according to sociologists Mamoru Iga and Kichinosuke Tatai. When an authoritarian society produces intense desires for success, the person

who fails in performing to role expectations is often morally condemned.

autocide Suicides disguised as automobile accidents. Forensic experts and highway transportation safety officials say that auto fatalities (which, in any given year, account for about 37 percent of deaths in the 15- to 24-year-old group) are accidents that are probably deliberate in roughly one-fourth of reported cases. Although some reports indicate emotional stress may be present, the conditions of the road, traffic flow, weather, and status of the car are pointed out most of the time as the cause in auto accidents. These fatalities probably represent the biggest block of suicides disguised as accidents. If these "autocides" are added to known suicides, argue authorities, they would make suicide the number one killer in the 15-to-24 age group.

autoerotic asphyxiation Also known as sexual hanging, this is a type of abnormal sexual behavior in which a person tries to restrict the supply of oxygen to the brain (usually with a rope around the neck) while masturbating to orgasm. The most common practitioners are teenage boys.

People who engage in this practice do not intend to kill themselves; instead, they are simply seeking sexual gratification by blocking the flow of oxygen to the brain. Experts estimate that between 500 to 1,000 deaths a year are the result of autoerotic asphyxiation. However, the actual incidence is likely underreported. Teenage victims are most often found by parents or other relatives who, because of the graphic, highly emotional, and often shocking circumstances under which the victims are found, may clean up or change the death scene. In addition, emergency personnel and police investigators often don't understand the signs of this behavior, so autoerotic asphyxiation cases are often officially reported as an intentional teen suicide. It may often be easier for relatives to handle teen suicide resulting from depression or drug abuse than from this form of sexual behavior. Denial and repression on behalf of parents and relatives likely contribute to the underreporting of AEA cases.

Conservative estimates suggest AEA may make up as many as 6.5 percent of adolescent suicides and at least 31 percent of all adolescent hangings. Therefore, up to 4,379 teens and young adults may have taken their lives in the past decade through the practice of autoerotic asphyxia.

Warning Signs

The most obvious warning sign is any type of trauma to the neck area, such as abrasions or rope burns, any sign of black and blue marks, blood clots, or pressure marks. In addition, any kind of padded ropes, belts, knotted sheets, pillows, towels, or underclothes that are hidden in a special place may be another warning sign.

Possible personality traits include:

• risk-taking behavior
• experimental behavior
• impulsive behavior
• thrill seeking

A person who practices AEA is not necessarily disturbed or perverted. Typically, these are not adolescents who have problems in school, give their parents trouble, or don't have friends. Instead, they are usually normal, well-adjusted teenagers who tend to come from a middle-class background, appear happy, and are generally very intelligent, are popular, and have a good relationship with parents. The FBI estimates that 500 to 1,000 deaths of this nature occur every year in the United States.

auto-euthanasia   Euphemism for suicide involving a suffering person.

autopsy, psychological   See PSYCHOLOGICAL AUTOPSY.

Azerbaijan   Although most of the countries of eastern Europe show alarmingly high suicide rates, the rate for Azerbaijan is extraordinarily low—a mere .65 per 100,000. Such an abnormally low rate may indicate irregularities in reporting of statistics, experts suggest. In 1999, Azerbaijan reported 1.1 suicides per 100,000 men, and 0.2 for women.

Baechler, Jean (1937–) French moral philosopher and author of *Suicides*, who described the suicidal motive of transfiguration. As an example, Baechler describes a pair of young people who drove off the cliffs in a car. The couple left a letter in which they explained that they killed themselves 'to preserve their love.'" This report was evidently sufficient for Jean Baechler to classify the case as a suicide of "transfiguration," which he defined as one undertaken by the suicide victim(s) to achieve a state infinitely more desirable.

Most suicidologists are skeptical of young couple SUICIDE PACTS as transfiguration, because motives often involve anger, coercion, and revenge. In cases like this, as in most others, suicide notes are designed to conceal—not reveal—motivation.

Bahamas Life in the idyllic islands appears to be linked to a low suicide rate, because the overall rate of suicide per 100,000 in 1995 was just 1.1. This is broken down into 1.1 suicides per 100,000 among Bahaman men, with no reported suicides at all for women.

Baldwin, James (1924–1987) American author who explored the racial significance of suicide in his novel *Another Country*. For homosexual African Americans who are also suicidal, the rage and bitterness caused by rejection may either be expressed in their homosexual relationships or by depression and suicide, according to Baldwin.

Balzac, Honoré de (1799–1850) French novelist who agreed with the Romantic dogma that the intense, true life of feeling does not—in fact, cannot—survive into middle age. Balzac wrote in *La Peau de Chagrin*: "To kill the emotions and so live on to old age, or to accept the martyrdom of our passions and die young, is our fate."

Barbados Islands typically reveal very low suicide rates, and Barbados in 1995 reported a rate of 6.65 per 100,000 citizens—9.6 per 100,000 for men, and 3.7 for women.

barbiturates Any one of a class of drugs that act as central nervous system depressants, inducing drowsiness and muscular relaxation. They can make an already depressed person even more depressed. The drugs slow a person's movements, thoughts, feelings, and recollections. By interfering with chemical messengers in the brain, the drugs also slow the activity of nerves that control breathing and heart action, creating effects ranging from relaxation to coma and death.

Barbiturates mixed with alcohol claimed the lives of rock star Jimi Hendrix, actress Marilyn Monroe, radical guru Abbie Hoffman, American Conservatory Theater founder William Ball, and Jeanine Deckers, the "Singing Nun," who killed herself with 150 pills and a shot of cognac.

Each year more than 15,000 deaths caused by barbiturate poisoning, often combined with alcohol, are reported in the United States. Almost certainly a high percentage are suicides, but exact figures are impossible to obtain.

When they were created in the late 1800s to cure insomnia, barbiturates were heralded as "continuous sleep therapy" and welcomed as an improvement over traditional substances such as alcohol and opiates. Since then, several thousand kinds of barbiturates have been synthesized. There are several different categories, based on how quickly they are broken down chemically in the liver and eliminated: ultra-fast, short-acting, and long-acting. It is the short-acting barbiturates that are the choice for most suicides.

These drugs—pentobarbital (Nembutal), amobarbital (Amytal), secobarbital (Seconal), and a secobarbital-amobarbital mixture known as Tuinal—are the type commonly known as "sleeping pills," taking 20 to 45 minutes to work. The intoxicating effect lasts four to five hours.

Suicidologists believe most coroners and/or medical examiners in other countries, and in some areas of the United States, appear to be more inclined to give an accident verdict or declare the cause of death "undetermined" in cases of narcotic poisoning than in other cases of self-inflicted death.

Suicidal individuals are considerably more prone to be violent or substance abusers. People *do* kill themselves by a simple overdose of barbiturates; mixing them with alcohol (the organ most immediately affected by alcohol is the brain) produces a synergistic effect that only enhances the possibility of lethality.

See also ABUSE, SUBSTANCE; ALCOHOLISM AND SUICIDE.

Barnard, Christiaan (1923–2001)
Internationally acclaimed physician recognized for his pioneering work in heart transplant surgery. Barnard was a strong advocate of euthanasia and candidly supported a doctor's right to participate in euthanasia as a humane and compassionate end to human suffering.

Baxter, John Clifford (1958–2002)
A former senior executive of the bankrupt energy giant Enron, the biggest corporate failure in U.S. history, who committed suicide by firing a gun to the head. His body and a suicide note were found in his car in his hometown of Sugar Land, Texas, a suburb of Houston.

Sources suggest that he could not stand the pain of the Enron scandal, and was depressed that he might have to testify about the role his colleagues had played in the collapse of the giant corporation. He is said to have questioned the company's accounting practices before his resignation as the firm's vice chairman and chief strategy officer in May 2001. Two days before he died, he broke down in tears as he discussed the firm's collapse with a business colleague.

Befrienders International
Nonprofit volunteer organization that works for suicide prevention in 41 countries. Befrienders International develops volunteers to try to prevent some of the 1 million suicides around the world, and provides information about suicide, including the world's most comprehensive online directory of emotional first aid helplines.

Befrienders International involves a network of 357 "befriending centers" around the world run by trained volunteers offering a service that is free, nonjudgmental, and completely confidential. People are befriended by telephone, in face-to-face meetings, by letter, and by email.

Founded in 1974, Befrienders International coordinates and develops the work of its member centers around the world, advises new centers and is involved in new approaches toward suicide prevention. The most exciting of these is Reaching Young Europe, a program that teaches coping skills to six-year-olds. U.S. centers are known as the Samaritans.

For contact information, see Appendix I.

Belarus
Suicide rates have risen in Belarus since 1990, and suicide rates are higher in rural than in urban areas. The regional distribution of suicide rates suggests a north-south variation

that may be a result of ethnic and cultural differences between the regions. As of 1999, the suicide rate nationwide was 35.5 per 100,000; this breaks down to an astounding 61.1 per 100,000 for men and 10 per 100,000 for women.

Belgium   The third country to approve physician-assisted suicide for terminally ill adults who are suffering unbearable pain. The new law, passed on May 17, 2002, sets out strict safeguards to protect the vulnerable, after research showed assisted dying was going on anyway in an unregulated way. The law has overwhelming public and parliamentary support. More than 72 percent of Belgians support the new law.

The law stipulates that prospective patients must be over age 18, suffering from an incurable illness, and have made repeated requests for help to die. They must be of sound mind and in constant suffering, and at least one month must elapse after a patient has made a written request for help to die before medical assistance is given. All assisted deaths must be reported to a national committee.

The Belgian law was passed in response to research showing that vulnerable people were not protected by the law. Nonvoluntary euthanasia (when a doctor deliberately hastens the death of an incompetent patient) was shown to be five times as common in Belgium as it is in countries that regulate physician-assisted suicide. Belgian rates of nonvoluntary euthanasia (3.2 percent) dwarfed the incidence of nonvoluntary euthanasia in the Netherlands, where assisted dying is regulated (0.7 percent).

Bell Jar, The   A brilliant novel about a gifted young woman's mental breakdown beginning during a summer internship as a junior editor at a magazine in New York City in the early 1950s.

Written by poet SYLVIA PLATH, the book was published in 1963 only weeks before Plath killed herself. The book is based largely on Plath's own suicide attempt in the summer of 1953, and her subsequent treatment at McLean Hospital in Belmont, Massachusetts. It represents a culmination of Plath's attempts to describe her experience of mental illness and treatment and is considered to be one of the best-told tales of a woman's descent into insanity.

bereavement groups   There are a number of self-help organizations for families and friends struggling to come to terms with the loss of loved ones due to suicide. Such groups try to help families, friends, and close associates of the victim deal with the death.

Surviving loved ones of suicide are too often forced to carry the stigma for years, if not for life. All too often, suicide of a family member or close friend is never completely forgotten and forgiven.

Berryman, John (1914–1972)   American poet who was born John Smith in McAlester, Oklahoma, whose major theme was mourning. He wrote of poetic mourning for the suicide of his father, the premature deaths of friends, and his own prevalent suicidal despair.

Berryman received an undergraduate degree from Columbia College in 1936 and attended Cambridge University on a fellowship. He went on to teach at Harvard and Princeton, and from 1955 until his death he was a professor at the University of Minnesota.

His early work was published in *Five Young American Poets* in 1940. *Poems* (1942) and *The Dispossessed* (1948) reveal great technical control. However, it was not until he published *Homage to Mistress Bradstreet* in 1956 that he won widespread recognition as a boldly original poet. This was followed by *77 Dream Songs,* which was published in 1964 and awarded a Pulitzer Prize. In succeeding years Berryman added to the sequence, until there were nearly 400 collected as *The Dream Songs.*

Unfortunately, however, Berryman never recovered from the childhood shock of his father's suicide. Prone to emotional instability and alcoholism throughout his life, he died by throwing himself off a bridge in Minneapolis.

Bettelheim, Bruno (1903–1990) American developmental psychologist who was born in Austria and received his doctoral degree in 1938 from the University of Vienna. Dr. Bettelheim was imprisoned in the concentration camps at Dachau and Buchenwald during the Nazi occupation of Austria. After immigrating to the United States in 1939, he published an influential essay on the psychology of concentration camp prisoners. A professor of psychology at the University of Chicago from 1944 to 1973, he directed a Chicago school for children with emotional problems.

In his book *The Uses of Enchantment: The Meaning and Importance of Fairy Tales*, Bettelheim discusses the power that fairy tales and myths have over children, contending that children love these stories because they embody their strongest hopes and fears.

One prevalent fear that is virtually universal in fairy tales is fear of being separated from parents. Many suicidologists believe that the "typical" suicidal adolescent is likely to be a teenager who early in life was literally separated from vital relationships or who never truly experienced a trusting family relationship.

The young person who hasn't had sufficient nurturing to develop a sense of self has nothing when he separates from his parents. Of course, not every person separated early in life from his parents becomes suicidal. Other vital relationships may occur that help blunt the impact of such separation.

As an adult, Bettelheim was plagued by fits of depression and haunted by the memory that his father had died of syphilis. In 1990 he committed suicide at the age of 86, an act that surprised many, given the optimistic tone of many of his books.

Biathanatos The first defense of suicide written in English by poet JOHN DONNE in 1608. It was originally circulated in manuscript form and only published posthumously, in 1644. In his work, Donne proposed to demonstrate that suicide is not incompatible with the laws of God, reason and nature. Moreover, inherent in the condition and dignity of being a man is the right to end one's life. As Donne expressed it, "methinks I have the keys of my prison in mine own hand, and no remedy presents itself so soone to my heart, as mine own sword."

Biathanatos was the model of thought on the subject of suicide for almost a century and a half. During that period, Rationalists such as Voltaire and Hume openly and persistently attacked suicide taboos and superstitions and the primitive punishments for suicide. This led to legal changes in the prosecution of suicide attempters.

biblical suicides There are a number of suicides reported in the Old Testament of the Bible, and they are presented either neutrally or as appropriate, under the circumstances. Neither the Old or the New Testaments of the Bible prohibit suicide.

Examples include:

- Abimelech (Judges 9:54), dying of a skull fracture during a siege, ordered his armor-bearer to kill him to avoid the embarrassment of having been killed by a woman (she threw a millstone at him).

- Samson (Judges 16:26–31) killed himself to avoid being "made sport of" by the Philistines, after his capture and haircut, taking his tormentors with him.

- Saul (1 Samuel 31:3–6), wounded and defeated in battle with the Philistines, asked his armor-bearer to kill him. When the aide hesitated, Saul fell on his own sword. The armor-bearer then did likewise.

- AHITOPHEL (2 Samuel 17:1, 23), plotted to overthrow King David. When the plan failed, he hanged himself and was buried in his father's sepulchre, in contrast to the Christian

Church's long history of refusing burial in hallowed ground to suicides.

- ZIMRI (1 Kings 16:18) usurped the throne of Israel; when he failed, he burned down the palace around himself.

biological aspects of suicide   See NEUROBIOLOGY OF SUICIDE.

bipolar disorder   The medical term for manic depression. Bipolar disorder is a neurobiological brain disorder involving extremes in mood, one of the three major mood disorders. (The other two are depression and schizoaffective disorder.)

If untreated, the rate of suicide and associated accidental injury among bipolar patients is at least five to 30 times higher than that of the general population. About 1 percent of the world's population is thought to have some form of bipolar disorder, from mild to severe, and approximately one in five people with bipolar disorder eventually complete suicide. Moreover, between 20 percent and 50 percent of people with bipolar disorder attempt suicide at least once.

Patients with bipolar disorder are far more likely to complete suicide than individuals in any other psychiatric or health risk group, yet this risk is often underemphasized. For a person with bipolar disorder, suicidal thoughts and plans may occur during depression or mania.

Symptoms

Most people with bipolar disorder have extreme cycles of depression and mania only once every few years. Rapid cyclers go through four or more episodes of mania and depression per year. Ultra-rapid cyclers have episodes shorter than a week. Ultradian cyclers have distinct and dramatic moods shifts within a 24-hour period.

Some people have mild symptoms of mania (hypomanias), while others have wild manias. Some people have depressions that are deep and long-lasting, while others experience only brief episodes of depressions. Still others have a "physical" depression or physical pain, with no obvious emotions at all. Occasionally, a person with bipolar disorder may have accompanying psychotic problems such as delusions or hallucinations.

When mania and depression occur at the same time, doctors refer to this condition as a "mixed state."

Treatment

Treatment with effective medications and regular counseling discussions about coping with the illness reduces the risk of suicide. While there is no cure for bipolar disorder, it may be managed with medication (usually lithium and Depakote) and psychotherapy. Supportive family therapy is also often recommended. However, finding the right medication is not always easy; what works for one person may not work for another. Sometimes a combination of medications is required, including a mixture of antipsychotics, benzodiazepines, antidepressants, thyroid supplements, and sleeping aids.

birthdays and suicide   While there are some instances of suicides on a person's birthday, the incidence of self-destruction does not necessarily correlate with the birthdate. Although a potentially suicidal person may suffer symptoms of loneliness, despair, and loss of self-esteem on such an occasion, suicide rates are instead linked to other factors, such as gender, increasing age, widowhood, single and/or divorced states, childlessness, residence in urban centers, high standard of living, economic crisis, drug and alcohol consumption, history of a broken home in childhood, mental disorder, and physical illness.

As for month of birth and suicide, more suicides take place in the spring than in the winter, with March, April, and May the most common months.

Sometimes suicidal people do attach particular significance to birthdays; for example, if a parent committed suicide on the 40th birthday, the child might feel destined to die before or on that day. If the potential suicide arbitrarily sets the next birthday as the very last day to remain alive, suicide will be attempted either before or on that day.

black Americans   See AFRICAN AMERICANS AND SUICIDE.

bonding   The strong attachment of mother to infant and infant to mother that develops shortly after birth. Many authorities in the suicidology field see a direct correlation between lack of bonding and the development of suicidal tendencies. The infant whose physical and psychological needs are satisfied develops a sense of well-being. Proponents of this theory maintain that the suicidal impulse can therefore be ingrained within the first months of life. For these people, any problem in the child's life may precipitate a suicide try, but the underlying cause frequently can be traced to emotional scars inflicted during infancy.

PLATO believed that the first step is always what matters most, particularly when dealing with children. "That is the time when they are taking shape," he wrote, "and when any impression we choose to make leaves a permanent mark."

Freud, writing some 2,000 years later, made the same point: "The very impressions we have forgotten have nevertheless left the deepest traces in our psychic life, and acted as determinants for our whole future development."

Boyer, Charles (1897–1978)   French singer and actor who completed suicide just two days after his beloved wife died. Unlike so many of his Hollywood contemporaries, Charles Boyer married once and only once.

Boyer was born in the country town of Figeac in southwestern France. Charles was an only child, the son of a self-educated merchant who dealt in farming implements and coal; his mother, Louise, was an amateur musician. Charles was a precocious, introverted child, whose father died

suddenly of a stroke when Charles was only 10 years old. His mother sold the family business and concentrated on raising her son. A year later, Charles discovered the cinema and professional theater. Mme. Boyer tried to pretend that her son's infatuation with dramatics was only a phase, since she hoped he would eventually become a doctor or a lawyer. However, all he wanted was to act. Eventually, Charles left Figeac in 1918 to enroll at the Sorbonne and pursue an acting career in Paris. Soon he was one of the busiest actors in the city, and eventually moved on to success in Hollywood.

During one of his stays in Hollywood, he met a young Fox starlet, Pat Paterson, and three weeks later they married. The marriage would last 44 years, until Pat's death in 1978. During the filming of *Gaslight* (1944), Charles became a father for the first and only time when Pat Boyer gave birth to their son, Michael.

Sadly, tragedy struck in Boyer's later years. His son, Michael, committed suicide at age 21, reportedly over a broken relationship with a young woman he wanted to marry. Then, in 1977, Pat Boyer was diagnosed with cancer and Charles devoted himself to her care. She died on August 23, 1978, and after her funeral, Charles quietly put his affairs in order. On August 25, two days before his 79th birthday, he took a fatal overdose of barbiturates. He was buried alongside his wife in Holy Cross Cemetery in Los Angeles.

Brahmanism and suicide   Among the earliest of the great cultures, Oriental sacred writings contained many contradictions about suicide. Although it was encouraged in some parts, it was vigorously condemned in others. Brahmanism institutionalized and sanctioned suttee, a ceremonial sacrifice of widows that was as common in China as in India. The Brahman doctrine was sympathetic to suicide, for it was consonant with the denial of the flesh, a common objective in philosophies of the Orient.

Brahmanism is the religious and social system of orthodox Hindus, interpreted and enforced by the Brahmans (the highest or priestly caste). Their system of doctrine and religious observances was codified c. 550 B.C., but has long since been simplified or modified in both theology and ritual. It borrowed freely from newer sects of the Vedic religions such as Buddhism and Jainism, to create the philosophical basis for modern Hinduism in the *Bhagavad-Gita* and commentaries on the *Upanishads.*

Brazil   As is typical of many countries in South America, Brazil has a fairly low suicide rate, perhaps related to the strength of the Catholic religion on the continent. As of 1995, the national rate of suicide was 4.2 per 100,000. This breaks down to a rate of 6.6 per 100,000 for men and 1.8 for women. However, indications are that the suicide rate varies widely from different parts of the country, and the reporting rates do not include all parts of the country uniformly.

British Voluntary Euthanasia Society   See EXIT.

broken homes and suicide   Children who are victims of broken homes through either divorce or death may frequently begin to see themselves as either guilty or unloved, and sometimes both. They can become increasingly despairing, angry, anxious, and depressed. The irony is that the more confused, the more depressed they become, the more need they have for the parent or parents who may no longer be there. They grow into adolescence at one and the same time furious with their predicament but feeling guilty. Such children are often are potential suicides.

Many experts in the field of suicidology see broken homes, latchkey children, and the shifting state of the American family as among the several major reasons for the rising suicide rate among children.

Bruce, Lenny (1925–1966)   Noted comedian who died on August 3, 1966, at the age of 41 of acute morphine poisoning in Hollywood. His lifelong involvement with drugs and his lifestyle in general prompted many authorities to classify his behavior as that of a CHRONIC SUICIDE.

Born Leonard Alfred Schneider, Lenny Bruce was a brilliant satirist who created controversy because of his use of "dirty words" in his nightclub comedy act. The satire and black humor of Bruce's largely improvised shows often overstepped the bounds of what was considered respectable in the 1950s and 1960s. Bruce was one of the first performers to usher in a new, more honest, more permissive, and more indulgent brand of American humor.

bloodless means   Methods of suicide that do not involve drawing of blood, such as toxic substances, drowning, hanging, suffocation.

Buddhism   The religious, monastic system, founded c. 500 B.C. by Buddha, the son of a petty raja who ruled over a small community on the southern border of the district now known as Nepal. Buddha's family name was Gotama (in Sanskrit, Gautama), and it was probably by this name that he was known in life; it was only after his death that his disciples gave him the name Buddha ("the enlightened one").

One goal in Oriental mysticism is to divorce the body from the soul so that the soul might occupy itself only with supersensual realities. Buddhism emphasizes that through extinction of craving or passion, life's chief purpose of acquisition of knowledge could be achieved.

Buddhists believe that suicide occurs because of one's lack of tolerance or patience toward stress. Although there is some sanction against suicidal behavior in Buddhist concepts, it is nevertheless accompanied with sympathy, regret, and a feeling of mercy. Buddhists believe human life is stressful and that the individual who kills himself is destined to remain in a hundred-year-hell and cannot expect reincarnation in any form.

Buddhism is based essentially on the doctrines that life is intrinsically full of suffering and stresses self-denial and ascetic disciplines. There are a number of alternative forms of Buddhism, collectively known as Mahayana, that have developed outside of India, generally marked by proliferation of local deities (buddhas, bodhisattvas), and religious observances drawn from local cults. In its various forms, Mahayana now claims almost half a billion adherents, especially in China, Tibet, Korea, Japan, and Mongolia.

bulimia   A serious, potentially life-threatening eating disorder characterized by a secretive cycle of bingeing and purging. Bulimia is a distress signal that may be one of many signs of trouble in suicidal teenagers. Often called the "binge-purge syndrome," bulimia is thought to be a disorder with emotional and physical roots. Although not clearly established, persons with eating disorders have been identified to be at significant increased risk for completed suicide.

Bulimia patients are 95 percent to 98 percent young girls, who are also usually white, single, ambitious, educated, and mid-to-upper class. Girls gorge and then purge in secret, in behavior that some experts believe is potentially suicidal.

Bulimia affects between 1 and 3 percent of middle school and high school girls, and 1 to 4 percent of college-age women. People struggling with bulimia, who often appear to be of average body weight, develop complex schedules or rituals to provide opportunities for binge-and-purge sessions. Many people struggling with bulimia recognize that their behaviors are unusual and perhaps dangerous to their health, but cannot stop.

Warning Signs
Warning signs include:

- self-induced vomiting
- using laxatives to prevent weight gain
- an obsession with gaining weight
- a fascination with food
- rapid consumption of large amounts of food
- extreme guilt over food eaten.

Experts believe that there is a relationship between bulimia and depression. One survey on eating disorders showed 60 percent of the women studied in the project reported feeling depressed most of the time; 20 percent had tried suicide at least once. Bulimics also may experience other serious side effects that range from ulcers to hernias, dehydration, stomach rupture, and disturbance of the blood's chemical balance that could cause heart attacks. The obsession with food is similar to an addiction to alcohol and generally ends in dominating the young person's life.

Treatment
Bulimia is best treated when diagnosed early. Unfortunately, even when family members confront the ill person, or physicians make a diagnosis, individuals with eating disorders may deny that there is a problem. Treatment is vital, and the sooner, the better, because the longer abnormal eating behaviors persist, the harder it is to overcome the disorder and its effects on the body. In some cases, long-term treatment may be required. Families and friends can play an important role in the success of the treatment program.

The complex interaction of emotional and physiological problems in eating disorders calls for a comprehensive treatment plan, involving a variety of experts and approaches. Ideally, the treatment team includes an internist, a nutritionist, a therapist, and someone who understands medications useful in treating these disorders. The combined use of cognitive-behavioral therapy and antidepressant medications such as desipramine, imipramine, and fluoxetine was most helpful. The combination treatment is particularly effective in preventing relapse once medications were discontinued.

bullycide   Suicide in children that is triggered by bullying. The term was coined by writers Neil Marr and Tim Field in their book, *Bullycide: Death at Playtime*. Victims of bullying have increasingly been identified as being at increased risk for depression and suicidal behavior.

burial (for suicides)   Since ancient times, almost all cultures prohibited normal burial for people who committed suicide, although the precise restrictions varied according to time and place. At the Council of Braga in 563, the Catholic Church condemned suicide—a position that was subsequently confirmed by the councils of Auxerre (578) and Antisidor (590) and remained as canon law in 1284, when the Synod of Nimes refused burial in consecrated ground to suicides. The one exception was for the insane.

The *Carolina*, the Criminal Constitution of Charles V of Spain, in 1551 confiscated all property of suicides who took their lives while under accusation of a felony. More severe was the punishment given to a corpse after the suicide. A common practice in England was to bury the suicidal person at a crossroad by night with a stake driven through the heart. The practice was not discontinued until 1823.

TACITUS, the Roman historian and distinguished lawyer, reports on "bog burials," the practice of pinning down the body with a stake. This practice, confirmed by numerous authorities, seems to antedate Christianity among the Germanic peoples of Europe. The purpose was to ensure that the spirit of the dead person would not return to haunt or harm the living.

Attitudes toward the act of suicide remained conservative well into the 18th century. In fact, at that time suicide was equated with murder in many parts of Europe, and the corpse was treated accordingly. For example, in France and England, the suicide's body was dragged through the streets, head downward on a sledge, on which criminals were dragged to their place of execution, and then strung up to hang from public gallows. The French Criminal Ordinance of August 1670 still decreed that the suicide's body be dragged through the streets, and then thrown into a sewer or onto the town dump. Because of spectator reaction against the practice of dragging the corpse, the penalty was not carried out after 1768. Still, burial in consecrated ground was frequently denied to people who committed suicide; in Prussia, early 18th-century law required that a victim of suicide be buried under the gallows.

The degree to which such burial restrictions or penalties were applied varied from time to time and place to place. In general the penalties against the body of a suicide tended to lessen by the latter part of the 17th century, and even the sanction of confiscation was handled more leniently. Important factors in such cases were the social rank of the suicide and the family, as well as the circumstances of the suicidal act.

Between 200 and 500 A.D., an increasing number of suicides was recorded among the Jewish population, partly due to spiritual and social crises, and partly to a growing Roman influence. Now that suicide had become more frequent, it became less accepted. A person who committed suicide forfeited his share of the world to come and was denied burial honors. The Talmud decreed that suicides could not receive a eulogy or public mourning. They were buried apart, in community cemeteries.

There was never universal agreement, however. Various scholars and legal authorities disagreed on the matter, pointing out that extenuating circumstances generally accompanied any suicide. The big question was how to be certain that a death was truly a suicide.

If the act was prompted by madness, some Jewish scholars believed the suicide should be treated as an ordinary deceased person. Some legal experts of the time believed that while suicide was considered a crime against God, it could be explained rationally, understood, and forgiven. This enlightened view has been incorporated into the approach of the three denominations of modern Judaism. The generally accepted custom is to give burial and last rites in a manner similar to any other deceased person.

In most Christian groups today, suicide is recognized not only as an ethical-religious-social sciences question, but also as a major medical problem. Many, if not most groups have revised the harsh religious laws governing suicides. For example, the Anglican Church and the Lutheran

Church do not deny the victim of suicide a Christian burial.

In the Catholic Church, the *Code of Canon Law,* Canon 1240, forbids Christian burial to "persons guilty of deliberate suicide." The late Richard Cardinal Cushing of Boston's archdiocese interpreted this to mean that the element of notoriety must be present in a suicide for the penalty to be incurred. "Hence, no matter how culpable it may have been, if it is not publicly known that the act was fully deliberate, burial is not to be denied," he said. "Ordinarily, there is not too great a difficulty in granting Christian burial to a suicide, since most people these days consider the fact of suicide to be a sign of at least temporary insanity."

In general, Catholic funeral rites for a suicide differ only in a relatively few instances from the rites accorded those who have died a natural death. Exemption from sanctions on the grounds of mental disturbance or "temporary insanity" is more frequently granted than in the past.

See also BURNETT V PEOPLE.

Burnett v People   Leading U.S. case regarding suicide. The 1903 case of *Burnett v People* states: "We have never seen fit to define what character of burial our citizens shall enjoy; we have never regarded the English law as to suicide as applicable to the spirit of our institutions" (*Burnett v People,* 68 N.E. 505 [Sup. Ct. IL, 1905]). The United States *never* adopted the English common law method dealing with suicide or suicide victims, in which suicide was a felony and attempted suicide a misdemeanor. In 1961, both British laws were abolished.

In another famous American case, the 1908 Texas case of *Sanders v State,* it was declared: "Whatever may have been the law in England . . . so far as our law is concerned, the suicide is innocent of criminality" (*Sanders v State,* 112 S.W. 68 [Ct. Crimm App. TX, 1908]).

Burton, Robert (1577–1640)   Oxford-educated author of THE ANATOMY OF MELANCHOLY, first published in 1621. The book is a curious compendium of esoteric knowledge with reference to melancholy: its definition and causes; its various types; the life of man and the institutions of society, all written in a style characterized by high fancy, extravagance, outlandish imagination, whimsy and affectation, and far-fetched figures of speech.

Burton was sympathetic to the idea of suicide. "These unhappy men are born to misery, past all hope of recovery, incurably sick; the longer they live, the worse they are; and death alone must ease them," he wrote. His views were considered courageous for the times.

Robert Burton is said to have hanged himself to fulfill his own astrological prophecies about the date of his death.

business cycle   Some experts believe that suicide rates can be related to economic cycles. In this theory, suicidal behavior is determined by both external and internal forces operating together.

People in high-status categories may experience greater frustration during downswings in business and less frustration during upswings in business than do those in "low-status" categories, according to this theory.

When the stock market crash occurred on October 29, 1929, and stock prices plummeted, a number of businessmen committed suicide as a consequence of their financial losses. These suicides would appear to support the concept of "hope" as the basis of suicide theory. According to this theory, suicide occurs when the individuals's life outlook (for whatever reason or reasons) is one of despairing hopelessness. Whether or not one completes suicide in such a situation depends upon a personality factor experts call "the sense of competence," which is related inversely to the potential for suicide.

calcium channel blockers Drugs to treat high blood pressure that should be considered as a possible cause of depression and suicide. One study of 3,397 outpatients in 152 Swedish municipalities revealed a five-fold greater incidence of suicide among those using calcium channel blockers than among patients using other antihypertensive drugs. No other cardiovascular drugs studied were linked with suicide risk once the research team adjusted the data to account for varying rates of use. For this reason, the researchers conclude that the increased suicide risk was unrelated to cardiovascular disease itself.

Previous research has suggested that the use of calcium channel blockers increases the risk of depression. This effect may constitute a link with risk of suicide.

Researchers suggest that the drugs may trigger depression and suicide because they easily penetrate the blood-brain barrier, where they may be able to interfere with neurons and receptors involved in the regulation of mood.

Although calcium channel blockers were introduced within the past decade and are longer-lasting than other blood pressure medications, they are also significantly more expensive, costing up to 15 times more than some diuretics. The shorter-acting versions have been shown to be dangerous. Now the longer-acting versions are being shown to be ineffective and possibly dangerous as well, so some doctors believe the future does not look very promising for these drugs.

Calcium channel blockers include Norvasc (amlodipine besylate), Vascor (bepridil), Cardizem (diltiazem), Procardia and Adalat (nifedipine), Calan and Isoptin (verapamil), Plendil (felodipine), Dynacirc (isradipine), and Nimotop (nimodipine).

Camus, Albert (1913–1960) French philosopher and one of the most important authors of the 20th century, who wrote of poverty, existentialism, and the horror of human mortality. Although born in extreme poverty, Camus attended the lycée and university in Algiers, where he developed an abiding interest in sports and the theater. His university career was cut short by a severe attack of tuberculosis, an illness from which he suffered periodically throughout his life. After winning a degree in philosophy, he worked at a variety of jobs, including journalism. In the 1930s, he ran a theatrical company, and during World War II was active in the French Resistance.

Author of such well-known works as *The Fall, The Stranger,* and *The Plague,* he addressed the issue of suicide in *The Myth of Sisyphus and Other Essays.* In this work, he stated, "There is but one truly serious philosophical problem, and that is suicide. Judging whether life is or is not worth living amounts to answering the fundamental question of philosophy."

Camus ultimately affirmed the value of life, although he also wrote that "if one denies that there are grounds for suicide, one cannot claim them for murder. One cannot be a part-time nihilist." In his *Notebooks,* Camus determined that "there is only one liberty, to come to terms with death. After which, everything is possible."

Albert Camus won the Nobel Prize in literature in 1957 for his "important literary production, which with clear-sighted earnestness illuminates the problems of the human conscience in our times." He died in a car crash near Sens at the age of 47 on January 4, 1960, as he was returning to Paris from the southern part of France.

Canada   One in seven Canadians has seriously considered suicide, and more than 3,500 Canadians kill themselves each year. Canada's suicide rate of 12.3 is consistently higher than the United States's rate of 11.2 per 100,000. Between 1980 and 1986, Canada's suicide rate ranked 22nd of 62 countries reporting statistics to the World Health Organization.

In 1997, Canadian men committed suicide at a rate of 19.6 per 100,000, compared to the female rate of 5.1. Unlike other countries with a very high suicide rate among elderly citizens, in Canada the group at highest risk for committing suicide was men age 45 to 64 (25.5 per 100,000). Suicide rate among Canadian teens age 15 to 19 was 12.9; the rate for children age 14 and under was 0.9.

Suicide is not illegal in Canada, but attempted suicide was not removed from the country's Criminal Code until 1972. However, counseling suicide (sometimes referred to as "aiding and abetting" suicide) remains a criminal act.

Mental disorders are a factor in more than half of the suicides in Canada. These people typically suffer from an identifiable condition, most often depression or alcohol/drug abuse. Native Canadians and in particular, young Native men, are especially at risk. However, not all native groups have high rates of suicide, and many native communities have suicide rates equal to or lower than the general population.

There are important differences between the methods chosen by men and women. Regional differences in Canada depend in part on the availability of the method. For example, death by firearms is more common in rural areas, where there is increased availability of familiarity with guns. The most common nonfatal suicide attempts in both sexes are drug overdoses and poisonings.

The SUICIDE INFORMATION AND EDUCATION CENTRE (SIEC), one of the world's most extensive resource libraries on all aspects of suicidal behaviors, is located in Canada. SIEC has developed it own bibliographic database and provides literature searches, online access, and document delivery. Publications include monthly newspaper clipping services, a quarterly Current Awareness Bulletin, selected reading lists, and information kits on selected topics.

For contact information, see Appendix I.

Canadian Association for Suicide Prevention (CASP)   A nonprofit Canadian organization that was incorporated in 1985 by a group of professionals interested in reducing the suicide rate and minimizing the harmful consequences of suicidal behavior. The group supports research, holds conferences, and advocates for policy development.

For contact information, see Appendix I.

Canadian Mental Health Association (CMHA)   A professional group that provides a wide range of suicide prevention data and services. The association has branches throughout the country, including the remote Northwest Territories and the Yukon Territory. Though Canada does not have a nationwide system of county mental health clinics as does the United States, it does provide universal health insurance that includes treatment of both physical and mental illness. The CMHA has been instrumental in working closely with groups operating a vast nationwide network of suicide hotlines and distress centers. In Canada, the Salvation Army also operates several suicide prevention agencies. The country has branches of the SAMARITANS and CONTACT USA (in Canada called Tele-Care).

See also Appendix II.

cancer and suicide   Studies indicate that the incidence of suicide in cancer patients can be up to 10 times as common as suicide in the general public. While some studies suggest relatively few cancer patients complete suicide, they are at increased risk for suicide. Men with cancer in particular are clearly at an increased risk of suicide compared to the general population.

Indeed, experts have found that passive suicidal thoughts are relatively common among cancer patients, yet the relationships between suicidal tendency and the desire for a hastened death, requests for PHYSICIAN-ASSISTED SUICIDE, and EUTHANASIA are complex and poorly understood.

Overdosing with analgesics and sedatives is the most common method of suicide in the cancer patient, with most cancer suicides occurring at home. Reports identify a higher incidence of suicide in patients with oral, pharyngeal, and lung cancers, and in HIV-positive patients with Kaposi's sarcoma.

Experts suspect that the actual incidence of suicide in cancer patients is probably underestimated, perhaps because there may be a reluctance to report death by suicide in these circumstances.

General Risk Factors

There are a number of risk factors for suicide in the general cancer patient. These include:

- a history of psychiatric disorders, especially those associated with impulsive behavior (such as borderline personality disorders)
- a family history of suicide
- a history of suicide attempts
- depression
- hopelessness (an even stronger risk factor than depression)
- substance abuse
- recent death of a friend or spouse
- lack of social support

There are also risk factors that are specific to cancer patients. These include:

- having oral, pharyngeal, or lung cancers (often associated with heavy alcohol and tobacco use)
- advanced stage of disease and poor prognosis
- confusion/delirium
- inadequately controlled pain
- problems such as loss of mobility, loss of bowel and bladder control, amputation, sensory loss, paraplegia, inability to eat and to swallow, exhaustion, fatigue.

Treatment

A therapist should carefully assess suicidal cancer patients to determine whether the underlying cause of the suicidal thoughts are due to a depressive illness or an expression of the desire to have ultimate control over intolerable symptoms. Prompt identification and treatment of major depression is essential in lowering the risk for suicide in cancer patients. A 1995 study of advanced cancer patients who expressed a consistent and strong desire for suicide suggested that this wish is, in fact, related to depression. Patients with the desire to die should be carefully assessed and provided with help in treating depression. Whether this desire to die would persist or decrease with improvement in mood disorder has not yet been studied.

The assessment of hopelessness is not straightforward in the patient with advanced disease with no hope of cure, but it is important to understand the underlying reasons for feelings of hopelessness, which may be related to poor symptom management, fears of painful death, or feelings of abandonment.

Treatment with therapy and antidepressants may be helpful in easing a cancer patient's suicidal thoughts. On the other hand, the principle of respecting patient autonomy has been one of the driving forces behind the hospice movement and right-to-die issues that range from honoring living wills to promoting euthanasia. These issues can create a conflict between patient autonomy and the doctor's obligation to keep patient alive.

A 1994 survey suggests that hospice physicians favor vigorous pain control and strongly approve of the right of patients to refuse life support even if life is thereby shortened by this choice. However, these physicians strongly oppose euthanasia or ASSISTED SUICIDE, clearly making a sharp distinction between these two interventions.

carbon monoxide poisoning   Carbon monoxide is a colorless, odorless gas that is used by more than 2,000 Americans each year to commit suicide by intentionally poisoning themselves. Considered to be a "silent killer," carbon monoxide can cause sudden illness and death.

It is found in combustion fumes, such as those produced by cars, small gas-powered engines, stoves, lanterns, burning charcoal and wood, and poorly functioning gas ranges or heating systems. Carbon monoxide from these sources can build up in enclosed or semi-enclosed spaces; people and animals in these areas can be poisoned by breathing it.

Symptoms

The most common symptoms of carbon monoxide poisoning are headache, dizziness, weakness, nausea, vomiting, chest pain, and confusion. High levels of carbon monoxide can cause loss of consciousness and death.

In addition to the effects already mentioned, carbon monoxide exposure can cause long-term psychiatric problems (more likely to occur in older individuals) such as personality changes, dementia, and psychosis.

Diagnosis

Unless suspected, carbon monoxide poisoning can be difficult to diagnose because the symptoms mimic other illnesses. People who are sleeping or intoxicated may die of carbon monoxide poisoning before ever experiencing symptoms.

Cardano, Girolamo (1501–1576)   An Italian mathematician, physician, and astrologer well known throughout Europe for his medical prowess.

His unhappy childhood began after he was born despite attempts to induce an abortion. The illegitimate son of the jurist Fazio Cardano and Chiara Micheri, his early years were marked by frequent illness and unkind treatment by his parents. In 1520, he escaped his family situation by enrolling at the University of Pavia, eventually earning a medical degree from the University of Padua. He set up a medical practice near Padua and married a local woman, Lucia Bandarini, with whom he had two sons and a daughter.

Reflecting on this time in his life in his autobiography, Cardano observed that "enterprises I have undertaken before the full moon have turned out successfully." It is clear that at least this early part of his adult life was happy.

In 1534, Cardano and his family moved to Milan, where he began teaching Greek, astronomy, dialectics, and mathematics, marking the beginning of his active interest in mathematics. In 1539, he began writing mathematical treatises, while maintaining a growing medical practice. In 1543, he accepted the chair of medicine at the University of Pavia, and by 1552 he was traveling as far away as Scotland to treat the archbishop of Edinburgh.

Sadly, by the mid-1500s, his life began to unravel. In 1560, his eldest son was accused of trying to poison his wife while she was recovering from childbirth, and eventually he was beheaded. Calling his son's problems "my supreme, my crowning misfortune," Cardano was forced in disgrace from Milan, ending up as a medical professor at the University of Bologna.

But Cardano's troubles began to multiply. Like many during the Renaissance, Cardano was always a firm believer in astrology, even traveling to England to cast the horoscope of the young King Edward VI. In 1570, he was imprisoned by the Inquisition for the heresy of casting the horoscope of Jesus Christ. An arch-believer in the accuracy of his own craft of astrology, he cast his horoscope and predicted the hour of his death. When the day dawned and found him in excellent health and safe from any harm, Cardano committed suicide that day rather than face the humiliation of having his own horoscope publicly found to be in error.

Cassius Longinus, Gaius (?–42 B.C.)

A Roman general and statesman who, with Marcus Junius Brutus, led the conspiracy against Julius Caesar. An honorable soldier with an admirable amount of capability and power, Cassius was a man ruled by his own ambition and vanity, with an uncontrollable temper and a sharp tongue.

During the civil war between Caesar and Pompey, Cassius commanded a fleet for Pompey. Caesar won the war, but pardoned Cassius and made him praetor (administrator of the courts) in 44 B.C., and promised him a governorship of Syria.

However, Cassius helped murder Caesar later that year, ostensibly to revive the republic. His conspiracy, involving some 60 to 80 prominent men, culminated in Caesar's assassination in the Senate on March 15, 44 B.C. Cassius and his brother-in-law Brutus fled east and raised a large army, but Mark Antony aroused the populace against Caesar's murderers; together with Octavian, MARK ANTONY defeated Cassius and Brutus at Philippi.

While at Philippi, Cassius saw a troop of soldiers approaching and sent his best friend, Titinius, to see if the troop was friend or foe. Due to his nearsightedness, he asked his servant, Pindarus, to stand on a nearby hill and make sure Titinius was safe. When the friendly troop surrounded Titinius to give him a garland to prove they were friends, Pindarus misunderstood and thought they were attacking. When he reported this to Cassius, the great statesman became distraught and asked Pindarus to hold his sword while Cassius ran it into himself. When Titinius returned to camp and found Cassius dead, he

placed the garland over Cassius and took his own life.

Mark Antony later committed suicide himself in Alexandria in 30 B.C.

Cato the Younger (95–46 B.C.)

Born Marcus Porcius Cato Uticensis, Cato the Younger was a great-grandson of Cato the Elder, and was raised by his uncle Marcus Livius Drusus. Cato showed an intense devotion to the principles of the early republic, and was considered the most honest and incorruptible man of ancient times. Called "the conscience of Rome," his Stoicism put him above the graft and bribery typical of the times, but his extreme conservatism and refusal to compromise made him unpopular with some of his colleagues.

As a violent opponent of Julius Caesar, he was eventually exiled to Cyprus, and he and his party supported Pompey after the break with Caesar. He fought on the Pompeian side in the civil war of 49 and governed Utica with great honor.

After Pompey's forces in Africa had been defeated during the civil war by Julius Caesar, Cato fell on his sword in Utica during an unwatched moment, claiming that at last he was free and bidding his people make their peace with Caesar. However, he was discovered by those watching him and a doctor was called to bandage him tightly. Knowing that Caesar's arrival in the city was imminent, Cato ripped through his bandaged abdomen and bled to death, literally taking his life with his own hands rather than surviving to be pardoned by the man he believed would destroy the republic.

He may have killed himself in part to spare the city from attack by Caesar, but his undying hatred of Caesar was probably the main reason behind his particularly violent suicide. It was said he would rather die than give Caesar the pleasure of pardoning him in defeat.

Cato is said to have read PLATO's *Phaedo* twice on the night before he killed himself. The Greek philosopher CLEOMBROTUS is said to have been inspired by the same book to drown himself.

In death, Cato's stubborn determination was praised as the highest example of Roman patriotism, but Caesar appears to have disliked Cato as he disliked few men. When told of Cato's suicide, Caesar is said to have spoken, as if to the living man: "I envy you this death, for you [denied] me the chance to save you."

Austere, humorless, puritanical, and unable to compromise, Cato was a fanatic in defense of liberty and the republic. For his steadfast honesty and courage, he was deeply admired by Americans in the Revolutionary period.

celebrity suicides   Studies done in the past have shown that suicide rates rise after the suicide of a prominent person or celebrity has been heavily publicized. For example, the youth suicide rate went up briefly after 23-year-old actor-comedian FREDDIE PRINZE shot himself to death. Prinze, who skyrocketed to fame as costar of the television series *Chico and the Man*, died in a Los Angeles hospital on January 29, 1977, 36 hours after shooting himself in the head with a revolver. Prinze left a note in his apartment that read: "I cannot go on any longer."

Another and more celebrated case in point is that of actress MARILYN MONROE. In the calendar month after she overdosed on sleeping pills, the suicide rate in the United States rose by 12 percent. Several of the suicides left behind notes that linked their lethal acts to the movie star's presumed suicide.

And although Beatle John Lennon was a murder victim, not a suicide, the youth suicide rate increased noticeably after his death on December 8, 1980.

Studies suggest that sensational media coverage of suicide and other tragic deaths results in an increase in suicide immediately afterward.

Centers for Disease Control and Prevention
One of six agencies of the U.S. Public Health Service responsible for surveillance and control of communicable diseases, occupational safety and health, family planning, birth defects, lead-based paint poisoning, urban rat control, and health education. The Centers deal with programs that include tracking, combating and publicizing epidemic and disease outbreaks, foreign travel (making health recommendations and setting forth requirements), surveillance of international health activities, training of foreign health workers, etc. The CDC will provide references, background materials, and photographs on communicable diseases and other subjects, such as suicide.

Publications include *The Morbidity and Mortality Weekly Report* and *Surveillance Reports.*

Charondas   Lawgiver of Catana, a Greek colony in Sicily, committed suicide after discovering that he had broken one of his own laws. The particular law forbade citizens to carry weapons into the public assembly. Charondas momentarily forgot this, wore his sword into the public meeting one day, and was reproached by a fellow citizen for violating one of his own laws. "By Zeus," said Charondas, "I will confirm it." He then drew his sword and killed himself.

Chatterton, Thomas (1752–1770)   British writer and forger who committed suicide at the age of 17, and who was subsequently transformed by romantic poets of his age into the symbol of the doomed poet.

The son of a poor Bristol schoolmaster, Chatterton was a voracious reader and developed an early interest in antiquities. Chatterton's access to a chest in his uncle's parish church, which contained historical documents, enabled him to obtain scraps of ancient parchment. It was on these scraps that at the age of 12 he began producing manuscript poems that he claimed were the work of a 15th-century Bristol monk and poet, Thomas Rowley. These were hailed as a magnificent find and many antiquaries were taken in.

Initially, Chatterton's audience was limited to local antiquaries who were thrilled to learn of the existence of this early Bristol poet. But soon Chatterton became more ambitious and began to send samples of his work, including some of the Rowley poems, to *Town and Country* magazine. Next, in an effort to impress Horace Walpole, whose gothic novel, *The Castle of Otranto,* the author had claimed to be a translation of a lost manuscript, Chatterton sent Walpole samples of his Rowley poems.

After initially encouraging the young prodigy, when Walpole was advised that the poems were not genuine, he returned them and ended the correspondence, denouncing Chatterton in the process. After this crushing defeat, Chatterton went to London in 1770 to sell his poems to various magazines, but only one of the Rowley poems was ever published during his lifetime (in *Town and Country* magazine in May 1769).

After his rebuke by Walpole, Chatterton turned aside from poetry and began writing political satire and magazine articles, usually writing under pseudonyms. He was moderately successful as a writer, and developed a reputation of some note in literary circles. Despite his achievements, he led the life of a pauper and became severely depressed, dogged by health and financial problems. On the point of starvation, he was too proud to borrow or beg.

Neighbors at Chatterton's lodging house found his body lying on his bed on the afternoon of August 25, 1770. According to a local surgeon, he was "a horrible spectacle, with features distorted, as if from convulsions." He had swallowed arsenic three months before his 18th birthday.

The first published collection of the Rowley poems appeared in 1777, seven years after Chatterton's death, and was greeted with both enthusiasm and skepticism. The poet Thomas Warton, in particular, questioned the authenticity of the Rowley poems and pronounced them forgeries in his *History of English Poetry.*

And so the great debate over Chatterton's work began, eventually becoming a pivotal episode in the history of 18th-century litera-ture. While there were many critics, others believed in the authenticity of the poems, and it was not until the end of the 19th century that experts finally began to accept that Chatterton was undoubtedly the true author of the Rowley poems. An original genius as well as a gifted imitator, Chatterton used 15th-century vocabulary, but his rhythms and his approach to poetry were quite modern. As a result, the Rowley poems were eventually recognized as modern adaptations written in a 15th-century style.

Throughout the controversy, however, even Chatterton's harshest critics nearly all agreed that while he might have been a forger, he was also a genuine poet of enormous talent. The medieval beauty of poems like "Mynstrelles Songe" and "Bristowe Tragedie" revealed Chatterton's poetic genius.

This gifted, rebellious youth later became an icon to the romantic and Pre-Raphaelite poets. Keats dedicated "Endymion" to Chatterton's memory, while Wordsworth dubbed him "the marvelous boy." To Shelley he was one of the "inheritors of unfulfilled renown," and remains today a symbol of the misunderstood poet.

child abuse   See ABUSE, CHILD.

children and suicide   While most people recognize the high incidence of suicide among teenagers, many do not realize that children under age 12 are also capable of killing themselves. Over the last several decades, the suicide rate among young children has increased dramatically. In fact, between 1980 and 1996, the suicide rate among children age 10 to 14 increased by 100 percent. In 2002, suicide was the sixth leading cause of death for five- to 14-year-olds, and the third leading cause of death in preteens (10-to 14-year-olds).

Most suicides in the five-to-14 age group are among those children age 12 to 14; it is fairly rare—but not impossible—for children under the age of 10 to take their own lives. Although official suicide rates are much lower for children under 15, suicidal behavior has been reported even in very young children. The reason why suicide is so rare before puberty is not known, but it is a universal phenomenon found in all countries. A likely explanation is that critical risk factors such as DEPRESSION or exposure to drugs and alcohol are rare in very young children. It is generally accepted that many suicides are unreported or misreported as accidents or death due to undetermined causes (particularly for young children), and that the actual number of suicides may be two to three times greater than official statistics indicate.

In the United States, youth suicide rates (uncorrected for ethnicity) are highest among the western states and Alaska, and lowest in the southern, north-central and northeastern states. Overall, the U.S. suicide rate of children under age 15 is twice the rate for all other countries combined. For suicides involving firearms, the suicide rate in the United States is almost 11 times the rate for all other countries combined.

Methods

Hanging is more common in early adolescence than in later years in all locations. The other most frequent methods by location include firearms (rural), asphyxiation (suburban), and jumping (urban).

Risks

Every child's personality, biological makeup, and environment are unique, and both depression and suicidal thoughts in children are complex issues that involve a myriad of factors.

Some research suggests that there are two general types of suicidal youth. The first group is chronically or severely depressed; their suicidal behavior is often planned. The second type is the child who shows impulsive suicidal behavior consistent with a conduct disorder, and who may or may not be severely depressed. This second type of child often also engages in impulsive aggression directed toward others.

Children are more likely to attempt suicide shortly after a stressful event, such as a disciplinary crisis, a recent disappointment or rejection (such as a dispute with a girlfriend, bad grade, or failure to get a job). In addition, studies show that children exposed to violence, life-threatening events, or traumatic losses are at greater risk for depression and suicide.

Youngsters who complete suicide are somewhat more likely to come from a broken home than are other youngsters of the same ethnic group, although about 50 percent of children who kill themselves live with both biological parents at the time of the death. Many children who complete suicide have had significant communication problems with their parents. Children also may suffer from the effects of social problems such as divorce, poverty, negative peer pressure, drug abuse, and violence.

Depression is also a significant risk for suicide in children. About 5 percent of children in the general population suffer from depression; children under stress, who experience a loss, or who have learning, conduct, or anxiety disorders are also at a higher risk for depression. Despite some similarities, childhood depression differs in important ways from adult depression. Psychotic features do not occur as often in depressed children, and when they occur, auditory hallucinations are more common than delusions. Anxiety symptoms such as fear of separation or reluctance to meet people, and general aches and pains, stomachaches, and headaches, are more common in depressed children than in adults with depression.

A high proportion of children who attempt suicide had a close family member (sibling, parent, aunt, uncle, or grandparent) or friend who attempted or completed suicide. Familial suicide could be a function of imitation or genetics; if genetic, it is not clear whether the inherited risk is related to underlying personality or predisposition to mental illness.

There is good evidence that more than 90 percent of children who complete suicide have a mental disorder. The most common disorders that predispose to suicide are some form of mood disorder and certain forms of anxiety disorder. Although the rate of suicide is much higher among children with SCHIZOPHRENIA, because of its rarity it accounts for very few suicides in this age group.

Gender Differences

Among children age 10 to 14, girls and boys commit suicide in about the same numbers; this changes as they get older; once they reach puberty, teenage boys are far more likely to complete suicide than teenage girls. Controlled studies of completed suicide suggest similar risk factors for both boys and girls, but with marked differences in their relative importance.

Among girls, the most significant risk factor for suicide is being depressed, which in some studies increases the risk of suicide 12-fold. The next most important risk factor is a previous suicide attempt, which increases the risk about threefold. Among boys, a previous suicide attempt is the most potent predictor, increasing the rate more than 30-fold. This is followed by depression (increasing the rate by about 12-fold), disruptive behavior (increasing the rate by twofold), and substance abuse (increasing the rate by just under twofold).

Warning Signs

There are a number of warning signs among children under age 14 that they may be thinking about suicide. While young children may not be able to express their feelings in words, they may provide indirect clues in the form of acting-out or violent behavior, often accompanied by suicidal threats. Among preschool children, those at risk for suicide may have a somber appearance, lacking the bounce of their nondepressed peers. They may be tearful or spontaneously irritable (not just upset) when they do not get their way. They make frequent negative self-statements and are often self-destructive. In elementary school, children at risk may experience disruptive behavior, problems in school, and peer problems, with increased irritability and aggression and suicidal threats. Parents often say that nothing pleases these children, that they hate themselves and everything around them.

Parents should be aware of the following signs of children who may try to kill themselves:

- change in eating and sleeping habits
- withdrawal from friends, family, and regular activities
- violent actions, rebellious behavior, or running away
- drug and alcohol use
- unusual neglect of personal appearance
- marked personality change
- persistent boredom, difficulty concentrating, or a decline in the quality of schoolwork
- frequent complaints about physical symptoms, often related to emotions, such as stomachaches, headaches, fatigue
- loss of interest in favorite activities
- intolerance of praise or rewards
- previous suicide attempts
- depression (helplessness/hopelessness)
- risk-taking behavior (acts of aggression, gunplay, and alcohol/substance abuse)
- self-destructive behavior can occur among children as young as elementary school age, and includes running into traffic, jumping from heights, and scratching, cutting, or marking the body
- changes in physical habits and appearance
- death and suicidal themes in classroom drawings, work samples, journals, or homework

A child who is planning to complete suicide may also complain of being a bad person or give verbal hints such as: "I won't be a problem for you much longer," "Nothing matters," "It's no use," or "I won't see you again." The child may give away favorite possessions or throw away important belongings, become suddenly cheerful after a period of depression, or experience hallucinations or bizarre thoughts.

Treatment

Any child who threatens suicide should always be taken seriously. When a child says, "I want to kill myself," or "I'm going to commit suicide," parents and teachers should always take the statement seriously and seek help from a child psychiatrist, child psychologist, family doctor, or other mental health care worker. Asking children whether they are depressed or thinking about suicide can be helpful, and will not "put thoughts in a child's head." Such a question will provide assurance that someone cares and will give a young child the chance to talk about problems.

Parents or teachers who notice any of the warning signs above should talk to the child about their concerns and seek professional help if the worries persist. With support from family and professional treatment, children who are suicidal can heal.

Prevention

Talking about suicide, depression, and mental health issues is the best way to prevent suicide among children. This may be done in a health class, by the school nurse, school psychologist, guidance counselor, or outside speakers. Education should address the factors that make a person more vulnerable to suicidal thoughts, such as depression, family stress, loss, and drug abuse. "Turn off the TV Week" campaigns can increase family communication, especially if the family continues with the reduced TV viewing. Parents should understand the risk of unsecured firearms in the home.

Peer mediation and peer counseling programs can make help more accessible, although it is critical that a child seek help from an adult if serious behavior or suicidal issues emerge. Many schools have a written protocol for dealing with a student who shows signs of suicidal or other dangerous behavior, as well.

All available evidence indicates that talking to a suicidal child lowers the risk of suicide. The message should be: "Suicide is not an option. Help is available." Parents of a suicidal child should suicide-proof the home, making sure all knives, pills, and guns are inaccessible. Any child who mentions suicide should receive immediate help, and should not be left alone, even if the child denies "meaning it." If necessary, the parents should drive the child to a hospital emergency room to ensure a safe environment until a psychiatric evaluation can be completed.

Teachers should know the school's responsibilities. Schools have been held liable in the courts for not warning parents quickly, or for not adequately supervising a suicidal student. Students should be encouraged to confide in teachers and to let them know if they or someone they know is considering suicide. A suicidal child should not be "sent" to the school psychologist or counselor, but should be escorted by a teacher to a member of the school's crisis team. If a team has not been identified, the teacher should notify the principal, psychologist, counselor, nurse, or social worker.

Chin, Larry Wu Tai (1928–1986) Retired CIA analyst convicted of spying against the United States for the People's Republic of China for 33 years. He was found dead in his jail cell, apparently a suicide.

Chin appeared to have suffocated himself with a plastic trash bag at the Prince William-Manassas Regional Adult Detention Center in suburban Virginia. A convicted spy, Chin was 63 years old and faced two life terms in prison and fines totaling $3.3 million at his sentencing, scheduled less than a month from the day he killed himself.

China China has the world's largest number of suicides (more than 300,000 each year) not just because of its large population. China also has a very high suicide rate per 100,000 population—two to three times higher than that of the

United States. China's suicide rate, which corresponds to about 22 people out of every 100,000, is higher than in affluent Western nations such as the United States, Canada, and Britain, but fewer than in places such as Hungary and Lithuania, where the ratio is between 40 and 50 per 100,000.

While it's clear that suicide is a big problem in China, it is also clear that the Chinese kill themselves for different reasons than do people in the West. While 40 percent of all suicides in the world occur in China, depression there is three to five times less common than in the West, and substance abuse, often viewed as another cause of suicide, is much less common in China than in the West. The Chinese also have emphasized the social dimensions of suicide and have shown that it correlates with social problems.

And while in the West, far more men in urban areas commit suicide, it is the exact opposite in China, where suicide is more common among women; indeed, 50 percent of all suicides among women in the world occur in China. The suicide rate is particularly high among Chinese women age 16 to 26. And since 70 percent of China's 1.2 billion people live in rural areas, it is not surprising that 90 percent of the suicides occur in the countryside.

Women probably always have been at high risk for suicide in Chinese society, where their innate worth is considered to be low. However, their suicide rate today seems to be related to social changes, as well as to continuing social problems. The paternalism in Chinese families has often led to abuse of women (especially young women) in the past, which has been intensified by economic developments of the last two decades that have worsened the situation of rural women. Another factor for the high suicide rate among Chinese women could be the one-child-per-couple policy in China. While this reduces the risk of a population explosion, it can be a major blow to disempowered young women in many rural areas who need to have more sons and grandsons to raise their inferior status in a world still ruled by patriarchal values.

The Chinese government itself addressed the problem of suicide among rural women by suggesting that the country could cut its suicide rate in half by keeping pesticides out of the reach of desperate women in the countryside, according to the official Xinhua news agency.

Oddly enough, both women and men over age 55 are also at increasing risk for suicide, even though Chinese society has always revered the elderly. This may be in part because the elderly Chinese commit suicide rather than become a burden on limited resources for their families.

According to ELISABETH KÜBLER-ROSS, in *Death: The Final Stage of Growth,* the Chinese are not only a practical people, but also fatalistic. She explains, "They believe that death is one of the true certainties in life, that when there is life as a beginning, there is death as an ending."

The people of China have historically believed in immortality, that the dead live on. They burn paper money in order to provide the deceased with spending money in the "other world," and children in years past would sell themselves as slaves so as to give parents a good funeral. When the time came to cover the casket, the living would turn their backs toward the casket, so evil spirits that might hover around the dead would not follow them home. For similar reasons, the Chinese preferred a patient to die in the hospital rather than at home, because the house might be haunted if a family member died at home. To elderly Chinese, the hospital is still the best place to die.

Suicide was common in pre-Communist China—so common, in fact, that 19th-century missionaries were appalled. Deliberate overdoses of opium and drowning were the two most preferred methods because they left the body undisfigured for the afterlife. Committing suicide on an enemy's doorstep was the ultimate revenge because it rendered the house uninhabitable and unrentable. Everyone believed the house would be haunted by the ghost of the suicide.

cholesterol-serotonin hypothesis A theory that suggests a link between suicide and low levels of cholesterol and a brain chemical called serotonin. Serotonin is also believed to be one of the primary biological triggers of DEPRESSION.

Several studies have reported an association between lower cholesterol (and subsequent low serotonin) and increased incidence of violent acts, including suicide. Scientists are clearly divided over this controversial finding. Given the major impetus to prevent cardiovascular disease by using cholesterol-lowering drugs, not surprisingly cardiologists have been particularly alarmed. They dismiss the aggression findings by quoting the results of two large studies of cholesterol-lowering drugs that found no link to accidents or suicide. However, other studies—particularly a large analysis of several coronary disease primary prevention trials—showed that lowering cholesterol via drugs and diet was associated with more suicides, accidents, and violence.

Several studies over the past five decades have reported that low cholesterol is associated with depressed mood. A link between cholesterol-lowering and brain serotonin may have direct relevance for a potential association between low cholesterol and increased likelihood of suicidal acts.

Serotonin is a brain neurotransmitter that is involved in the regulation of mood, appetite, and impulse control; and problems with the serotonin system have been linked to major depression and also with suicidal behavior. Lower levels of serotonin function are associated with an increased likelihood of, and increased severity of, suicidal acts during a depressive episode.

Studies suggest that serotonin in the brain may act as a kind of "restraining" neurotransmitter. In healthy people the serotonin system will discharge to suppress harmful impulses, but people with low levels of serotonin fail to adequately suppress negative impulses.

Antidepressants that boost the level of serotonin in the brain can be very successful in alle-viating depression, and cholesterol appears to directly affect serotonin levels. For example, some studies have shown that lowering and raising cholesterol levels in monkeys significantly lowers and raises serotonin activity. So although lowering cholesterol levels in humans does reduce heart attacks, it may raise the risk of dying from other causes, including suicide.

Recently, European researchers found a genetic mutation that appears to increase a person's odds of committing suicide more than threefold. The gene affects the levels of the chemical serotonin in the brain. The serotonin levels are affected because the mutation reduces the ability of brain cells to absorb serotonin.

It is well known that defects in serotonin uptake can cause depression, eating disorders, and other mental illnesses. These genetic data are consistent with a correlation between low serotonin uptake activity and violent behavior, including violent suicidal behavior.

See also MENTAL ILLNESS.

Christianity Self-destruction was common-place in both Greece and Rome when Christianity was born. Suicide at the time was tolerated and, in some instances, actually encouraged by the Stoics, the Cynics, the Cyrenaics, and the Epicureans. Early Christians seem to have accepted the prevailing attitudes of that era. The Roman emperor Nero began the persecution of the Christians. Because the life of an early Christian in the Roman Empire was intolerable, the Church's promise that death would lead to ever-lasting glory and redemption paved the way for a flood of suicides and martyrdom, which would not abate until a powerful religious figure arose in the fifth century.

In A.D. 413, the man who would become St. Augustine—Augustinus, Bishop of Hippo in Roman Africa—began a comprehensive overview of Christian theology. It was a project that would take 13 years to complete. Encompassing 22 books, *The City of God Against the Pagans* begins in the first book with the subject of self-murder.

Although the Old Testament mentions suicides without adverse comment, Augustine takes the Fifth Commandment ("Thou shalt not kill") at its word. He also criticizes Judas for committing a second crime by hanging himself, even though he was atoning for the earlier crime of betraying Christ. Ultimately, Augustine agrees with Plato's argument that life is a gift of God and bearing suffering, instead of shortening it by suicide, is a measure of the soul's greatness.

Voluntary martyrdom was common among the early Christians, particularly when persecution made life unbearable. Eusebius (ca. A.D. 260–ca. 340), bishop of Caesarea, tells of Christians about to be tortured who committed suicide, "regarding death as a prize snatched from the wickedness of evil men." In fact, there was virtually a pathological element present in the craving for martyrdom as expressed by Ignatius of Antioch in his letters, such as that written to Rome's Christian community. "I beseech you . . ." he wrote, "Suffer me to be eaten by the beasts that I may be found pure bread of Christ. Rather entice the wild beasts that they may become my tomb, and leave no trace of my body, that where I fall asleep I be not burdensome to any. Then shall I be truly a disciple of Jesus Christ, when the world shall not even see my body. Beseech Christ on my behalf, that I may be found a sacrifice through these instruments."

The Christians, then, saw their religion as offering a chance of martyrdom and an opportunity to die as a blood-witness to Jesus Christ. Martyrdom, with its exalted emotionalism, characterized large groups in the Roman Empire between the reigns of NERO and Julian (A.D. 54–363).

The Apostles did not denounce suicide; the New Testament touched on the question of self-destruction only indirectly, in the report of Judas's death. So for several centuries, the leaders of the church did not condemn this widespread practice.

Augustine (see also AUGUSTINE, SAINT) was the first to denounce suicide as a sin. Until then, there had been no official church position against it. Then, in 533, the Second Council of Orleans expressed the initial organizational disapproval of self-destruction. In 563, the Fifteenth Canon of the Council of Braga denied suicides the funeral rites of the Eucharist and the signing of psalms. In 673, the Council of Hereford withheld burial rites to any who committed suicide. And in 1284, the SYNOD OF NIMES refused suicides burial in holy ground.

Saint Thomas Aquinas (see AQUINAS, SAINT THOMAS) opposed suicide on the basis of three postulates, stating a belief that all life was a preparation for the eternal. Aquinas stressed the sacredness of life and absolute submission to God.

Four centuries later, JOHN DONNE, then dean of St. Paul's Cathedral, reacted to the church's existing strict attitudes toward self-destruction. He believed suicide was neither a violation of church law nor against reason. His position was soon supported by such secular philosophers as DAVID HUME, Montesquieu, Voltaire, and JEAN-JACQUES ROUSSEAU. They insisted on greater freedom of the individual against church authorities.

"In modern times," writes Rabbi Grollman in *Suicide*, "Dietrich Bonhoeffer viewed suicide as a sin in that it represented a denial of God." Yet Bonhoeffer, the German Lutheran theologian who was hanged by the Nazis in 1945 at age 39, qualified his position to accommodate prisoners of war who might commit suicide rather than give out classified information that could injure or destroy the lives of others.

Modern-day views and attitudes by Christians toward suicide are just as confused and controversial as were those of earlier times. Even with the arrival and application of sociology, psychology, psychiatry, and anthropology to the problem, Christian attitudes still vary widely. Suicide is no longer a crime in any state, but aiding and abetting a suicide is against existing laws in 25 states. (States having specific laws regarding assisting suicide are: Alaska, Arizona, California, Connecticut, Delaware, Florida, Hawaii, Indiana, Kansas, Maine, Minnesota, Mississippi,

Montana, Nebraska, New Hampshire, New Jersey, New Mexico, New York, Oklahoma, Oregon, Pennsylvania, South Dakota, Texas, Washington, and Wisconsin.) And Christian church authorities of varying faiths continue to regard it as a sin against God. Suicide is still covered up by many, whispered about, and concealed in many instances.

The Christian faith has always extolled the virtue of suffering, with its "ennobling" effects, as DORIS PORTWOOD points out in *Common-Sense Suicide: The Final Right.* Catholic spokesmen continue to often call suffering "the greatest possible source of heroism, purification and redemption." Protestant clergy continue in many cases to cite Job's rejection of suicide, despite his trials, as evidence that the Bible is opposed to self-destruction.

Portwood contends that "The analysis of Christ's death on the cross also is variable." She writes that "many people, within and without the Church, consider Christ's death a premeditated suicide—a deliberate sacrifice that, given his powers, he certainly could have avoided." Others, obviously, consider such an analysis as blasphemy.

There are today a number of "progressive" Christian denominations that distribute study literature on the option of EUTHANASIA. Nor is suicide consistently rejected as an alternative to life by some churchmen, even for themselves. One such instance was the now famous attempted double suicide of Dr. Henry Pitney Van Dusen and his wife in 1975. He had been head of the Union Theological Seminary and enjoyed world recognition. In 1970, Dr. Van Dusen suffered a stroke and lost the speaking facility that played such a key role in his professional life. His wife suffered from arthritis. In late January 1975, they took massive doses of sleeping pills. Mrs. Van Dusen died peacefully, but her husband was hospitalized and lived until mid-February of that year. The famous couple's own simple note said, "Nowadays it is difficult to die," and added, "We feel that this way we are taking will become more usual and acceptable as the years pass."

Today, ethical-religious approaches are counter-balanced with the broader perspectives of the social sciences, according to Grollman. Increasingly, suicide is being recognized not only as a religious question, but as a major medical problem.

chronic suicide   Term coined by Dr. KARL MENNINGER, noted psychiatrist and the best-known proponent of Freud's theory that suicide is aggression turned upon the self. Menninger, in his 1938 book *Man Against Himself,* called "chronic suicides" those individuals who might find the idea of killing themselves to be repugnant, but who nevertheless choose to destroy themselves slowly by way of drugs, alcohol or other methods. Behind their denial syndrome they justify their actions by, in Dr. Menninger's words, "claiming that they are only making life more bearable for themselves."

chronic suicider   A person who attempts repeated acts of suicide.

classification of suicides   The idea that there are different types of suicidal behavior.

ÉMILE DURKHEIM, a 19th-century sociologist, conducted a pioneering study of the sociology of suicide. His detailed work, *Le Suicide,* was published in 1897. Durkheim maintained that suicide was more easily understood and explained as a reaction by the suicide to the peculiarities of society. Durkheim identified four types of suicidal behavior, basically falling at the extremes of two groups. The first is characterized by the extremes of integration, and the second group by extremes of regulation.

At one extreme of the integration concept lie the "egoistic suicides," which occur, according to Durkheim, when a person feels alienated from society and has few binding ties to family, church, business, education, or social groups. The egoistic suicide victim is usually lonely, unmarried, and unemployed. But sometimes it maybe represented by the self-destruction of a teenage runaway who finds herself alone and friendless in a strange town.

"Altruistic suicide" is at the other extreme and is the opposite of egoistic self-destruction. It comes about with people so caught up with a particular cause of the ongoing values of their society that duty takes precedence over their own individual needs. The young Japanese KAMIKAZE PILOTS during World War II are a classic example of altruistic suicides. They sacrificed their lives to crash their planes into Allied warships. The national military authority over the kamikaze pilot was so pronounced that he lost his own personal identity and instead wished to sacrifice his life for his country.

Along the other continuum, that of regulation, at the two extremes are ANOMIC SUICIDES and FATALISTIC SUICIDES. Durkheim never fully developed the concept of fatalistic suicides, which referred to suicides as a result of excessive constraints and repressive regulations in society that limited choice and reduced opportunity.

Durkheim's category of anomic suicides, however, was expounded fully, and referred especially to the confusion and sense of loss when traditional values and mores underwent marked or rapid change. Talcott Parsons, a noted sociologist, writing in *International Encyclopedia of the Social Sciences,* says that in this state of the social system, some or many of its members reach the point where they "consider exertion for success meaningless, not because they lack capacity or opportunity to achieve what is wanted, but because they lack a clear definition of what is desirable. . . . It is a pathology of the collective nominative system."

See also TERRORISM AND SUICIDE.

Cleanthes (331–232 B.C.) Philosopher and successor to ZENO, founder of the STOICS, a philosophical school that taught that pain and pleasure, poverty and riches, and even sickness and health, were equally unimportant, and that sui-

cide was the most logical and desirable of all ways to die. After Zeno hanged himself at age 98—a true Stoic—Cleanthes took over as leader of the Stoic school.

Cleanthes was originally a wrestler, and in this capacity he first visited Athens, where he became acquainted with philosophy. Although poor, he was determined to study with an eminent philosopher, and chose Zeno. For many years Cleanthes was so poor that he was compelled to take notes on Zeno's lectures on shells and bones, since he could not afford to buy better materials. He remained a pupil of Zeno for 19 years.

At the age of 99, Cleanthes developed a boil on his gum, and was advised by a doctor not to eat for two days to allow the boil to heal. After fasting, he decided that since he had come that far on the road toward death, he might as well go all the way, and so he starved himself to death.

Cleombrotus Greek philosopher said to have been inspired by Plato's *Phaedo* to commit suicide by drowning. It was in *Phaedo* that PLATO made SOCRATES repeat the Orphic doctrine—before he drank hemlock—that suicide was not to be tolerated if it seemed like an act of wanton disrespect to the gods. Plato used the simile of the soldier on guard duty who must not desert his post, and also that of man as the property of the gods, who are as angry at our suicides as we would be if our chattels destroyed themselves.

Cleopatra (69–30 B.C.) Queen of Egypt who killed herself, most likely by the bite of an asp. Cleopatra was born in 69 B.C. in Alexandria, Egypt, and inherited the throne when she was 18 upon the death of her father, Ptolemy Auletes. Cleopatra was a strong-willed, brilliant Egyptian queen who dreamed of a greater world empire.

Married to her young brother to fulfill Egyptian law, Cleopatra eventually had liaisons with both Caesar and MARK ANTONY. After Antony was defeated by Octavian during the defense of Alexandria, he was given a false report of Cleopatra's death, and committed suicide by falling on his own sword in 30 B.C.

After Antony's death, Cleopatra was taken to Octavian, where she was told she would be displayed as a slave in the cities she had once ruled. Unable to face this humiliation, Cleopatra had an Egyptian cobra called an asp brought to her, hidden in a basket of figs. The Egyptian religion declared that death by snakebite would secure immortality, which was her dying wish.

clergy and suicide prevention   Members of the clergy have been a valuable resource in the area of suicide prevention. Frequently when a parent or a teacher suspects that a young person is having problems, the pastor, priest, or rabbi is the first person to whom they turn. The potential suicide will often confide in a clergyman or woman before they will anyone else—because they view them as people who understand their futility and anguish, yet won't betray their confidence.

Spread throughout the United States are about 250 suicide prevention and crisis centers that help suicidal people cope with life crises.

Many of the trained volunteers and counselors who work at such centers are members of the clergy. They provide a lifeline for those distraught people who call them on hotlines.

Clergy volunteers take part in the same intensive training program as others to learn how to handle emergency problems they constantly face. They do not attempt long-term therapy, but concentrate only on coping with emergencies and immediate crises. For extended therapy, the clergy volunteers usually refer callers to professional psychiatrists, psychologists, social workers, or other qualified counselors who work with particular centers.

It was the clergy who first developed the idea of a community center to help prevent suicide. In 1906, a center was established in England by members of the SALVATION ARMY. It aimed at treating suicidal people *after* they had tried to kill themselves rather than attempting intervention beforehand. The Salvation Army's antisuicide department exists to this day, though much of its work has been taken over by other organizations in England.

Another major suicide prevention organization started in England in 1953, and now operating centers in 26 countries of the world, is the SAMARITANS. The Reverend CHAD VARAH started the organization in London in 1953 with the notion of "befriending" suicidal people. Today, all of the Samaritan centers, both in the Commonwealth and in the United States, are staffed by volunteers who act as substitute families or close friends to people who come to them, offering love, care, compassion, and companionship. The inspiration for the various Samaritan programs is not spiritual—they gain only their name from the parable of the Good Samaritan—and their approach is always secular, pragmatic, and nonsectarian.

At the time the Samaritans was founded, Chad Varah was rector of St. Stephen Walbrook, one of the City of London's historic churches. An honors degree in philosophy from Oxford University, considerable success as a professional journalist, and the care of a number of Anglican parishes all helped to prepare the Reverend Varah for his work with the Samaritans.

A suicide prevention service network that has a more directly religious orientation is Contact Teleministries USA (see CONTACT USA). The organization boasts more than 100 telephone counseling ministries throughout the United States. They try to listen to and help any suicidal person in distress. Contact Teleministries USA is a Christian ministry whose aim is "sharing the goodness of God's compassionate love with each and every person." They ask their telephone volunteers to "undertake to counsel in accordance with Christian insight." Contact is an American affiliate of Life Line International, a worldwide organization with the same mission (in Canada called Tele-Care).

In Boston, Massachusetts, Father Kenneth B. Murphy organized Rescue, Incorporated, in 1959. The nondenominational agency, located at Boston's City Hospital, uses the volunteer services of over 70 clergymen and women and also the help of medical professionals.

For the person who is threatening suicide, the various suicide prevention and crisis center organizations extend life-saving assistance, compassion, and support.

Pastoral volunteers and counselors who have taken special training in social work, psychology, and suicide prevention techniques can be extremely helpful to the suicidal person, but untrained members of the clergy working at suicide prevention centers do not pass themselves off as substitutes for effective psychotherapists.

Suicide prevention and crisis centers accredited by the American Association of Suicidology (AAS) are listed in Appendix II.

See also SUICIDE PREVENTION ADVOCACY NETWORK.

clues of suicide Most people who seriously intend suicide leave discernible clues to their planned action. At times, the warnings take the form of broad hints; at other times, there are merely subtle changes in behavior. But the suicide decision is seldom impulsive; usually, it is premeditated.

The following are clues or warning signs of a potential suicide:

- Preoccupation with themes of death or expressing suicidal thoughts
- Giving away prized possessions, making a will, or other "final arrangements"
- Changes in sleep patterns (either too much or too little)
- Sudden and extreme changes in eating habits, losing or gaining weight
- Withdrawal from friends and family or other major behavioral changes, accompanied by obvious depression

- Changes in school performance, lowered grades, cutting classes, dropping out of activities
- Personality changes, such as nervousness, outbursts of anger, or apathy about appearance and health
- Use of drugs or alcohol
- Recent suicide of a friend or relative
- Previous suicide attempts

Three-fourths of those who kill themselves have seen a physician within at least four months of the day on which they commit suicide. People who threaten suicide usually mean it, at least unconsciously. They just haven't yet decided on the *how* or *when*. If conditions in that person's life fail to change, he or she will soon set a time and choose the method of self-destruction.

When people are suicidal, there is no single trait by which all of them can be characterized. Always, however, they are disturbed and often they are depressed. The various verbal or behavioral "hints," some obvious, others subtle, should be taken seriously. A suicide attempt, no matter how feeble or unlikely to succeed, is stark testimony of the suicidal state. Suicide attemptors do want attention and, without it, they may well succeed in their next attempt.

Four out of five persons who succeed in taking their lives have previously given clues of their imminent action. Even the vague clues often predict a suicide accurately. Once a person has finally decided to kill himself, he begins to act differently.

Those "different" actions, both verbal and behavioral, become the clues or warning signs of a potential suicide.

Though these clues to suicide are not especially difficult to recognize, it is not that easy to determine just how close the disturbed person may actually be to a suicide attempt. Trained professionals or volunteer staff members of any suicide prevention center or service can predict a suicide with more than chance accuracy.

See also DEATH WISH; EATING HABITS; FRIENDS; IMPULSIVENESS; INSOMNIA; IRRATIONALITY; MOOD SWINGS; RECKLESS DRIVING AS SUICIDE CLUE; WILL, LOSS OF; WITHDRAWAL.

cluster suicides   A chain of completed suicides by people in neighboring geographic areas. Every year, 100 to 200 American youngsters die in suicide clusters, and there are signs that the rate is rising. These estimates do not include clusters of attempted suicides, since there is no registry of suicide attempts.

Still, suicide clusters in general—whether multiple simultaneous suicides or a series of suicides occurring close together in time—may account for no more than 1 percent to 5 percent of all youth suicides. Nevertheless, when a suicide cluster does occur, an extraordinary amount of community effort and resources is temporarily devoted to suicide prevention.

Suicide contagion is not a new phenomenon. Evidence of suicide clusters has been reported in accounts from ancient times through the 20th century. Concern about suicide clusters has deepened after a number of highly publicized suicide outbreaks among teenagers and young adults in recent years, and because of new evidence that a significant number of suicides appear to be associated with suicide stories in the mass media.

Suicide clusters have been reported among psychiatric inpatients, high school and college students, Native Americans, Marine troops, prison inmates, and religious sects, although U.S. suicide clusters occur predominantly among teenagers and young adults. While clusters have included friends or acquaintances in the same school or church, it is not necessary for those who complete suicide in a cluster to have direct contact with one another: sometimes knowledge of the first suicides was obtained through the news media.

Scientists generally agree that prominent media coverage of a suicide increases suicide behavior in those who view the coverage. The magnitude of the increase is related to the attrac-tiveness of the individual whose death is being reported and the amount of publicity given to the story.

Prevention

The CENTERS FOR DISEASE CONTROL developed guidelines for a community response to a suicide cluster. The recommendations include:

- creating a coordinating committee from community: education, public health, mental health, local government, and suicide crisis centers
- responding in a way that minimizes sensationalism and avoids glorifying the suicide victims
- evaluating and counseling close friends of the deceased and suicide attempters who may be at high risk.

In the past, other groups have seen waves of suicides, including Roman circus performers, early Christian church followers, and Viking warriors. Early in 1987, south Florida counted eight elderly murder-suicides. But for a problem that has been around since at least the fourth century B.C., when a series of self-inflicted hangings took place among the young women of the Greek city of Miletus, all evidence points to the youth suicide cluster phenomenon being on a dramatic increase during the 1980s.

Sometimes called the "Werther syndrome," after the 1774 novel *The Sorrows of Young Werther* by JOHANN WOLFGANG VON GOETHE (which resulted in many young men committing suicide in imitation of the book's central character), clustering is thought by some authorities to be triggered by the media. Other experts openly speculate that such TV movies as ABC's "Surviving," might also play a key role in young people's suicidal behavior.

Cobain, Kurt (1967–1994)   Musician, leader of the grunge band Nirvana who took his life at age 27. Cobain was a driving force behind the grunge music scene, but struggled with chronic health problems, depression, and substance abuse.

Born in Aberdeen, Washington, Cobain dropped out of high school and left home in his late teens. He married Courtney Love on February 24, 1992, and shot himself two years later.

cocaine   Cocaine use is associated with a much higher risk of suicidal behavior and suicidal thoughts in depressed people. Cocaine abuse is also one of the top predictors of suicide among teenagers. Moreover, teens having parents with cocaine use disorder were 3.5 times more common among those in the suicide attempter group than among those in the non-attempter group.

Although no statistics are available to indicate a direct correlation between suicide rates and use of the illegal and addictive drug cocaine, authorities do know that drug overdoses in general claim about 7,000 lives in the United States annually. In 1984, the U.S. drug overdose death figure was projected at 6,994, according to federal government sources.

Cocaine leads from a quick high to a crash that most users relieve by taking either heroin or more cocaine—then more and more as tolerance for the drug increases. People have become suicidal during the "down" periods following cocaine use, as they have when "crashing" from other drug use. This is usually a time of extreme depression, and some users have also become suicidal as a result of losing touch with reality and imagining themselves capable of unrealistic feats and immune from all danger.

college students   Suicide is the third leading cause of death among young people. For those of college age, it is the second leading cause (after accidents). In addition, the suicide rate is higher among 19- to 24-year-olds enrolled in college than it is for those who aren't enrolled. Since 1950, the suicide rate among college-age women has more than doubled, while the rate among college-age men has tripled.

Suicide among this age group is extremely difficult to investigate, and because so few college students kill themselves, the small studies that examine the problem can suggest only tentative conclusions. Despite their limitations, however, some of these studies do suggest that certain student groups may have much higher rates of suicide, and that suicide may be more prevalent among students attending some elite schools in the United States, ENGLAND, and JAPAN. For example, foreign students in American and British schools have a much higher suicide rate. In the 1950s, when these studies were done, foreign students had a suicide rate of 80 per 100,000—many times higher than the rate of their nonforeign peers. Researchers suspected that social isolation, which is a particular problem for these foreign students, may have been the cause for their higher rate.

The most common factor among college suicide is mental illness—in particular, mood disorders such as clinical DEPRESSION and BIPOLAR DISORDER. And while suicide is not more frequent in any of the four years of college, it does occur more often with students who take more than four years to earn their degrees, perhaps because this group includes many students whose studies were interrupted by serious depression or other emotional problems.

The impact of mood disorders, which often appear between age 18 and 25, is heightened by drinking—a staple of college life. Many people with depression drink or use drugs to ease their symptoms. But alcohol and drugs more often worsen the pain they were intended to alleviate. Substance abuse undermines the students's willingness to seek out and receive good clinical care and sabotages the effectiveness of treatment. Substance abuse reduces inhibitions and increases risk-taking, reinforcing tendencies toward self-destruction. One recent study of campuses showed more than half the students completing suicide were intoxicated, and a slightly larger number were thought to have a significant substance use problem.

In addition, college students who complete suicide have different personality traits from other students. While most young adults who complete suicide have impulsive, high risk-taking personalities, and abuse drugs and alcohol, college students who kill themselves are usually depressed, quiet, socially isolated young people who do not abuse alcohol or drugs. Many college students feel depressed and rejected by their families, and struggle to be accepted by doing well in school or athletics.

Many suicidal students experience anxiety and insomnia, although these may disappear shortly before the suicidal act, as the plan to complete suicide provides a seeming solution to their psychic pain. When they do go for help, few report their suicidal intentions or get any psychiatric treatment, even though nearly half the suicidal students seek some medical treatment in the months before completing suicide.

Experts suggest that schools should prepare plans in case a suicide does occur on the campus, focusing on outreach to survivors and on preventing suicide contagion by managing the information that is presented to the press and public. As few suicides occur on each campus, however, few schools have prepared such plans for managing the acute disruption in campus life that follows a suicide.

Authorities attribute a number of reasons to the college suicide rate: living away from home for the first time; stress and tension caused by academic pressures; competition for jobs upon graduation; alcohol and/or drug abuse; loss of self-esteem and self-worth; feeling unloved and unwanted; pessimistic outlook concerning the future; sense of failure; alienation; emotional emptiness and/or confusion; lack of self-confidence; and general feeling and attitude of despair and hopelessness.

One study found that in a random sample of 792 college students, 30 percent had entertained suicidal thoughts during an academic year. One study of college freshmen shows 70 percent had actually experienced suicide thought(s) in a given school year.

Common Sense Suicide: The Final Right A nonfiction book by the late DORIS PORTWOOD that is a carefully researched examination of what has been called "the last taboo" in our society: suicide. The book is a thought-provoking statement of the right to suicide for certain members of society. She addressed the audience of which she was herself a member: the aging.

Her theme: Increased longevity has its rewards, but when the penalties get too high, the self-destruct mechanisms built into all living organisms should be freed for people, and it must be our choice what price we, sane and long-living, ought to pay for the time we do or do not linger.

communication of suicidal intent Before their attempted death, suicidal people leave a discernible trail of hints—sometimes subtle, often obvious—of their intentions. Every suicide attempt is a serious cry for help. If the cry is heard and duly acted upon, suicide can usually be prevented. Most obvious communications are the cries of those who threaten, "I'm going to kill myself." They should be taken seriously, as should such angry asides as "I wish I were dead," or "Everyone would be better off without me." All such dejected or rage-filled remarks are real communicative clues to suicide intent. All too seldom are they taken seriously.

> verbal direct: "I will shoot myself if you leave me."
> verbal indirect: "A life without love is a life without meaning."
> behavioral direct: Hoarding pills by a chronically ill, severely disabled person.
> behavioral indirect: Giving away prized possessions, loss of appetite, insomnia.

The indirect communications, both verbal and behavioral, become significant when evaluated in context; that is, they are not in and of themselves a communication of suicidal intent but become so when they occur along with other clues and communications.

In addition, "blocked communication" is a factor in suicide cases. In one study, 90 percent of teenage suicidals admitted they could not talk with their parents. Researchers concluded that the most common factor in the continuing chaos and unhappiness in the young person's life is the lack of parental appreciation or understanding. Indeed, studies show that one of the two factors that indicate serious trouble ahead for suicidal children was poor or disordered parental communication. (The other factor: "overly critical, overly involved or actively hostile parenting style.")

As Dr. Mary Giffin says in *A Cry for Help*, "The child who can talk about his pain—and his plans —to someone who is really listening can usually work out or, at least, work on his problems. The child who can't talk is the child who may commit suicide." Giffin adds, "Remember, teens who need help don't 'grow out of it.' They become adults who need help—if they live that long."

See also CLUES OF SUICIDE.

community-based suicide prevention
Most public health approaches to suicide prevention have included CRISIS HOTLINES, restrictions on access to suicide methods, and media counseling to minimize imitative suicide.

Crisis Hotlines
Although crisis hotlines are available almost everywhere in the United States, research has failed to show that they reduce the incidence of suicide. Perhaps actively suicidal individuals do not call hotlines because they are acutely disturbed, preoccupied, or intent on not being deflected from their intended course of action. In addition, hotlines are often busy, and there may be a long wait before a call is answered, so that callers disconnect. Moreover, the advice a person gets after calling a hotline may be stereotyped, inappropriate, or perceived as unhelpful by the caller.

And while men are at highest risk for committing suicide, gender preferences in seeking help mean that most callers are women.

Method Restriction
Preferred methods for suicide differs among men and women, and among different countries and cultures. In the United States, the most common method for completed suicide is by firearms; it has been suggested that reducing firearms availability will reduce the incidence of suicide. However, an experiment in Great Britain suggests this is unlikely. The favored suicide method there at one time was asphyxiation with coal gas, but this became impossible after the introduction of natural gas. This resulted in a marked but short-lived decline in the suicide rate. Within a decade, however, the suicide rate had returned to previous levels, as suicides were being completed by other means.

Therefore, while reducing access to firearms with gun-security laws reduces accidental deaths from firearms, there is no evidence to date that such laws have a significant impact on suicides attributable to firearms. Any temporary decrease in suicide rate by firearms would probably be reversed as people chose alternative means of killing themselves.

Media Counseling
Even though it appears prudent for reporters and editors to minimize coverage of youth suicide in general and attention to individual suicides, there is as yet no evidence that these guidelines, issued by the CENTERS FOR DISEASE CONTROL AND PREVENTION, are effective in reducing the suicide rate.

community resources
See SUICIDE PREVENTION CENTERS.

Compassionate Friends
A national nonprofit, self-help support organization that offers friendship and understanding to bereaved parents, grandparents, and siblings. There is no religious affiliation, and there are no membership dues or fees. The Compassionate Friends helps families deal with grief after the death of a child of any age, and offers brochures and information,

sponsors an annual conference, and maintains an active website.

The Compassionate Friends was founded in Coventry, England, in 1969, after the deaths of two young boys, Billy Henderson and Kenneth Lawley. Billy and Kenneth had died just three days apart, and a bond was formed between the two sets of parents as they shared the memories and the dreams that had died with Billy and Kenneth. They continued to get together regularly, slowly adding other grieving parents to their group, until they decided to organize as a self-help group and actively begin reaching out to newly bereaved parents in their community. Because the word *compassionate* kept coming up, they called the new organization "The Society of the Compassionate Friends." Word of the organization spread rapidly around the world, via interest generated by TV coverage and the columns of Dear Abby and Ann Landers. The Compassionate Friends was incorporated in the United States as a nonprofit organization in 1978.

There are now Compassionate Friends chapters in every state in the United States—almost 600 altogether—and hundreds of chapters in CANADA, Great Britain, and other countries throughout the world. In the United States, chapters are open to all bereaved parents, siblings, grandparents, and other family members who are grieving the death of a child of any age, from any cause.

competition   It appears that intense competition affects the suicide rate of every age group in many countries, including the United States and particularly in JAPAN, where cultural tradition has come to mean that a family's prestige hinges on a child's academic performance, both grade and career competition is extremely fierce. Tokyo newspapers and other media have recently editorialized about the "annual slaughter of innocents" as that country's children jump off buildings, hang and gas themselves, and leap in front of speeding trains—because of failure to achieve a certain rung on the academic ladder.

Children in Japan do not get a second or third chance; in fact, they must even pass a written examination to enter a "good" kindergarten. The latter is a must to enter into a good primary school which, in turn, becomes a prerequisite for a good high school and ultimately to a good university.

Thus, it isn't surprising that the suicide rate in Japan rises every February as students write their various entrance examinations. Failure to get through "examination hell," so called by the youngsters, means shame for the student *and* his or her family because chances for later-life success are thereby greatly reduced.

Suicide rates for young people run higher in Japan than in the United States, but the rate for young men in the United States has lately surpassed Japan's rate. In 1964, there were 9.2 suicides per 100,000 men in the 15 to 24 age group in the United States. The rate in Japan was 19.2. But in 1977, the Japanese rate was unchanged while the U.S. rate had soared to 21.8. In 1982—the last year for which data are available for both countries—the Japanese rate was 14.5 compared to the higher U.S. rate of 19.8 suicides per 100,000 males in the same 15 to 24 age grouping. Experts see this as an indication that career and grade competition is becoming more intense in America.

Germany also has a high youth suicide rate, as well as educational competition similar to that in Japan. In 1982, the suicide rate for men in the 15 to 24 age group was 20.9; the rate dropped slightly to 19.4 in 1984. For women, age 15 to 24, the 1982 suicide rate per 100,000 was 6.3; that was reduced to 5.2 in 1984.

According to reports for German students under 18, the suicide rate is 50 percent higher than for U.S. students. The country has a punishing system of preselection for higher education, which means that the student who doesn't do well from the start will have no academic future.

Business experts in the United States report that the phenomenon called "winner depression"—a feeling that despite great competitive success, professional accomplishments are somehow inadequate—is appearing with greater frequency in the world of business and commerce. It appears that mergers, acquisitions, the introduction of new technology, plus rising competition from abroad—all are placing new pressure on and causing greater tension for managers and executives. Particularly vulnerable are managers who have lost jobs as a result of corporate restructuring and reorganization.

These same experts see winner depression (which has sometimes led to suicides) cropping up more often in tradition-bound fields where competition is now intense.

Until recently, depression was a taboo subject in the fiercely competitive business world. Today, however, as a result of the victims of winner depression, many firms take a more constructive view. Companies use consulting firms to help staff people experiencing psychological and emotional problems. The consulting services say such employee-assistance programs are effective and have a high recovery rate.

Comprehensive Textbook of Suicidology
An important textbook of the field of suicidology that presents an overview of scientific knowledge about suicide and suicide prevention for professionals. Multidisciplinary and comprehensive, the book provides a solid foundation in theory, research, and clinical applications. The book was written by Ronald W. Maris, Ph.D., of the Center for the Study of Suicide at the University of South Carolina, Alan L. Berman, Ph.D., director of the AMERICAN ASSOCIATION OF SUICIDOLOGY, and Morton M. Silverman, M.D., of the psychiatry department of the University of Chicago.

compulsory suicide A type of suicide performed out of loyalty to a dead master or spouse, or when commanded by the government for disgraced officials.

Compulsory suicide out of loyalty to a dead master or spouse is characterized by SUTTEE in India; and similar behavior was expected of a dead emperor's favorite courtiers in ancient China. Such practices, now largely extinct, most likely developed from the ancient, widespread custom of immolating servants and wives on the grave of a chief or noble.

Self-murder may also be encouraged for the welfare of the group. For example, among preindustrial people, an elderly person who could no longer gather his own food would be expected to kill himself.

Finally, compulsory suicide may be offered to a favored few as an alternative to execution, as among the feudal Japanese gentry, the Greeks (such as SOCRATES), the Roman nobility, and high-ranking military officers such as Erwin Rommel, who had been accused of treason.

In traditional Japanese society, in certain situations suicide was seen as the appropriate moral course of action for a man who otherwise faced the loss of his honor. Compulsory SEPPUKU (also known as hara-kiri) was declared illegal in Japan in 1868. The custom had been reserved for the nobility and members of the military caste, who would plunge a ceremonial knife into the stomach when disgraced. The word *seppuku* is the only Japanese rendering of the Chinese reading of two characters meaning "cutting of the stomach." The same two characters in reverse order can also be pronounced "hara kiri"—and the latter is more common in spoken Japanese.

Self-killing also may be practiced by people who don't really have a code of laws; for example, the Trobriand Islanders hurl themselves ceremonially from the tops of palm trees after a serious public loss of face. In these situations, the line between social pressure and personal motivation blurs.

Today, self-destruction as a military, paramilitary, or political act (although not always compulsory) brings veneration among certain terrorist groups and some Middle Eastern countries, even though in Islam, suicide is the gravest sin, which is expressly forbidden in the Qur'an.

concentration, loss of Loss of concentration is considered one of the several warning signs or distress signals given by potentially suicidal persons. Sometimes the signal is hard to detect at first, but then it grows progressively more apparent.

Any sudden change in a person's personality is usually a warning sign. Ordinary daily tasks become difficult to carry out. There is often lassitude and lack of energy. Even the simplest decisions become difficult to make. With lack of concentration, depression usually begins gradually. The person often talks less, prefers to be alone, and there is a marked decline in the level of interest as well as concentration.

constriction The narrowing of a suicidal person's outlook, thinking, and options.

CONTACT USA A human service organization that operates a network of crisis intervention and telephone helpline centers across the nation. Conceived in 1967 as a response to the growing social issues of a changing nation, CONTACT has evolved into a network of centers in 20 states, exploring new ways in which to serve their individual communities. More than 10,000 volunteers commit their time to serve their community through work at a CONTACT center.

The organization was founded on March 16, 1963, by Rev. Dr. Alan Walker, minister in the Methodist Church, Sydney, Australia. Called Life Line, the original organization operated a unique program designed to train volunteers to be available by telephone to callers 24 hours a day. Two years later, Rev. John Brand of Dallas brought the program to the United States, using his church as the location for the first center. Since the name of Life Line was being used in Texas by a nationally broadcast radio program, CONTACT was chosen as the name of this new ministry.

In autumn 1966, a class of 150 began the six-month training as telephone helpline volunteers; on March 27, 1967, CONTACT Dallas became the first center in the United States. A year later, the Council for Telephone Ministries was formed to develop CONTACT centers throughout the United States. During the next three years, under the leadership of Rev. Ross Whetstone and the support of the United Methodist Church, 36 communities began the process of starting a center.

Today, CONTACT USA has expanded to more than 60 centers in 21 states, with 10,000 volunteers responding annually to 1.2 million callers per year. As the only national network of telephone helpline centers in the United States, CONTACT USA is committed to a vision of reaching all who seek someone to listen.

For contact information, see Appendix I.

contagion The risk arising from exposure to suicidal behavior in a family, peer group, or the media. It results in what is called CLUSTER SUICIDES, where one suicide seems to be the trigger for others, most often among adolescents.

For example, Yukiko Okada, 18, jumped to her death in 1986 from the seventh floor of her recording studio after receiving an award as Japan's best new singer. In the wake of intense media attention, 33 young people (one only nine years old) killed themselves in the next 16 days—21 by jumping from buildings.

Even fictional accounts of suicide may be enough to trigger contagion, as in a claimed spurt of Russian roulette deaths shortly after the release of the film *The Deer Hunter,* which contained a disturbing scene about Russian roulette.

Intervention After a Suicidal Death of a Relative, Friend, or Acquaintance

Studies have shown that the suicide of a relative or friend may increase the risk for childhood or adolescent suicidal behavior. Counseling can help a child realize that suicidal behavior is not an effective coping strategy in dealing with adversity, and may reduce the risk for suicidal behavior in these circumstances. Intervention may also be needed to decrease the child's personal sense of guilt, trauma, and social isolation. This treatment can be given in individual meetings, at group sessions with other teens, or with parents who need help to support the adaptive capacities of their children and adolescents. School professionals sometimes offer programs of this kind and can be invaluable in identifying grieving friends who may need help.

coping mechanisms   The characteristic manner in which individuals deal with their physical and social environment, particularly as they mobilize their resources to handle stress. For example, people with healthy coping mechanisms can deal satisfactorily with the stressors of daily frustrations and even periodic tragedies.

Those who have not acquired and developed healthy coping mechanisms, who do not display "normal" coping behavior, may exhibit totally inappropriate responses to stress (or a combination of stresses) that indicate warning signals or distress clues of potential self-destructive behavior.

See also CLUES OF SUICIDE.

cop suicide   See POLICE SUICIDE.

copycat suicide   Duplications of a suicide due to repeated accounts or depictions of the original suicide on television and other media. The well-publicized suicide serves as a model to the next suicide, and occasionally spreads through a school system, a community, or—in terms of a celebrity suicide wave—across the nation.

See also CLUSTER SUICIDES; CONTAGION.

coroner   An elected official responsible for determining the manner and the cause of death in all cases of suicide. The office of coroner was developed in England at about A.D. 1100 or 1200. Coroners were originally referred to as "crowners," the name given to those persons appointed by the Crown to represent the king's interest in the investigation of violent, unexplained, or suspicious deaths. They were also responsible for disposing of property that became available under the existing laws after a homicide or suicide. The Latin word for crown is *corona*.

The disparity between official suicide rates per 100,000 persons and the actual number of suicide victims exists for a number of reasons. Generally, coroners list suicide as a cause of death only when circumstances unequivocally justify such a determination such as, when a suicide note is left by the victim of sudden death, when the person has a history of suicidal tendencies or has tried suicide before, or when cause of death simply cannot be other than suicide.

When such obvious clues are absent, most coroners admit that they are reluctant to rule the death a suicide. In fact, some coroners or medical examiners indicate that in many small towns and communities, suicide is seldom listed as such on a death certificate. This practice, they contend, is the pragmatic action for a coroner, because life pressures in a small community dictate certain unwritten rules of conduct. Many of these coroners also act as personal physicians for members of the community, and cannot afford to jeopardize their income by antagonizing patient-clients.

Many traffic deaths, especially those involving one person in a single car collision with a stationary object, are suspected "AUTOCIDES," or impulsive, spur-of-the moment suicides. One estimate places such autocide explanations at 75 percent of this type of accident. Authorities who use this interpretive theory have often set the actual number of suicides at twice the official U.S. figure.

Finally, there are also many and varied forms of self-destructive behavior (CHRONIC SUICIDES) that may ultimately end in accidental death or death due to chronic health problems. Chronic suicides are long-term self-destruction by people who consciously or subconsciously have been killing themselves over a period of time. Such cases are never listed as suicides by coroners. Victims of such chronic suicides are more likely to be listed among the nation's mortality statistics for heart disease, cirrhosis of the liver, pneumonia, or "accidental death" due to drug overdose, drowning, automobile accident, fire, falls, poisoning, or accidental gunshot wounds.

Coroners say they generally will consider the following as likely suicide: cut throat, hanging, self-immolation, crushing under a train, and car exhaust poisoning. The following are given the benefit of the doubt by many coroners and/or medical examiners and considered as problematic (unless other unequivocal proof exists): fall from a height, drowning, firearms, poisoning, and even drug overdose.

The question remains how best to assess a dead person's motives.

The chief method used widely today is that of the PSYCHOLOGICAL AUTOPSY. Developed by psychologists Edwin Shneidman and Norman L. Farberow after they began the LOS ANGELES SUICIDE PREVENTION CENTER in 1958, the important research tool is a method to assist coroners and medical examiners to determine the cause of an uncertain death by gathering data on the victim based on psychological status and personality characteristics.

Investigation teams interview relatives and friends, coworkers, teachers, and anyone else who perhaps played a significant role in the deceased's life. The purpose is to reconstruct the final days and weeks of life by gathering facts and opinions about a recently deceased person in an effort to understand the psychological components of death.

Council of Orleans (Second)   Held in A.D., 533 the Council expressed the first institutional disapproval of suicide by the Catholic Church which it determined was the most serious and heinous of transgressions. However, it was not until 563 and the Council of Braga (the Fifteenth Canon) that there was institutional denial for suicides of funeral rites of the Eucharist and the singing of psalms.

See also ATTITUDES.

counseling   Hundreds of suicide prevention and crisis centers, teleministries, and counseling groups indicate nations are well aware of the enormity of the problem of suicide. Today, there are many self-help organizations designed to help all those who are victims of suicide and suicidal behavior. This includes services not only for potential suicides, but counseling for survivors of suicide. An example of the latter type group is LOSS (LOVING OUTREACH TO SURVIVORS OF SUICIDE), sponsored by Catholic Charities, which has autonomous groups in most areas of the country. Such self-help groups have proved valuable for suicide survivors because they offer mutual support. Members are able to talk as well as listen as they learn to live with their tragedy and can see that suicide happens to average people from average families. The sense of shared community and hope that members experience in these self-help groups usually extends beyond the meetings themselves.

Family service agencies are community sponsored and have qualified social workers on staff; in addition, most have at least one psychiatrist who serves as a professional consultant. Sometimes these agencies are denominational, such as the Jewish Children's Bureau and Catholic Charities (sponsors of the LOSS groups for suicide survivors). Lutherans also support several hospitals that provide services similar to those offered by other Family Service Agencies.

The Family Service Association of America, with its chain of member agencies nationwide, offers low-cost individual and family counseling, family life education programs, special groups for teens, and family advocacy activities.

The SAMARITANS, one of the major suicide prevention organizations in England, now has centers in many parts of the world.

See also COMMUNITY RESOURCES; HELP FOR SUICIDAL PEOPLE; PREVENTION (OF SUICIDE).

Craig and Joan   A book by Eliot Asinof that deals with the true story of two New Jersey teenagers who killed themselves in 1969 to protest the Vietnam War. Joan Fox and Craig Badiali, both 17, asphyxiated themselves after leaving behind 24 suicide notes that explained their political protest of the war. Their suicide pact generated a great deal of national publicity.

See also TEENAGE SUICIDES.

Crane, Harold Hart (1899–1932) A prize-winning U.S. poet who produced several volumes of poetry and then killed himself by jumping off a steamship. Hart was born in 1899 in Garrettsville, Ohio, the only child of Grace Edna Hart and Clarence A. Crane, a candymaker and original manufacturer of the Lifesaver, who tried to dissuade him from a career in poetry.

Crane was a high-strung, volatile child who began writing verse in his early teenage years. He never completed his final year of high school, but at the age of 17 persuaded his recently divorced parents to let him live in New York City to prepare for college. He wandered back and forth between Cleveland and New York, briefly working in Cleveland as a cub reporter and as a menial in his father's candy factory, and in New York as a copywriter for mail order catalogs and ad agencies. He lived a nomadic life, in and out of apartments and rooms in New York City and southern Connecticut, where he shared farmhouses with friends. In New York, he associated with the literati of the time, including Allen Tate, Katherine Anne Porter, E. E. Cummings, and Jean Toomer. However, his alcoholism and instability interfered with lasting friendships.

His major poems were published as *White Buildings* (1926), *The Bridge* (1930), and *Collected Poems* (1933), a slim body of intense, sensitive, modernistic poetry. Most of the poems in *The Bridge* were written on the Isle of Pines off the coast of Cuba, where his family owned a vacation cottage. When he was struggling to complete *The Bridge*, Crane sought inspiration by traveling to Europe, but once the book was published, he received instant notoriety and fame.

Upon being awarded a Guggenheim fellowship in 1931 to complete a series of poems about the Aztec, he temporarily settled in Mexico. Yet things did not go well south of the border, where Crane found himself a gay male in a culture that was largely homophobic.

He had discovered he was a homosexual after an affair in 1919 in Akron, when he was working as a clerk in one of his father's candy stores. In the spring of 1924, he met a ship's purser named Emil Opffer, forming an intense emotional relationship. Unfortunately, Crane never found a partner with whom to share his life. After Opffer, his affairs were temporary, anonymous, and sometimes violent.

As he returned to New York from Mexico, years of drink had almost certainly ravaged his physical condition, undermining his ability to control his mental stability. Tormented by a sense of failure after his torturously produced pieces, Crane committed suicide by jumping overboard from the steamer SS *Orizaba* off the coast of Florida on his way home.

crime In America over the past two decades, there has been astonishing rise of almost 300 percent in both suicide rates and homicide rates among young white males age 15 to 19.

The United States now ranks among the highest of countries in the world in both suicide and homicide rates. As a group, people who kill themselves have committed homicide at a much higher rate than has the general population, and persons who have killed others have a much higher suicide rate than has the overall population.

The relation between homicide and suicide in the United States is dramatized by the fact that guns, used in more than 60 percent of the homicides, are used as well in some 55 percent of the suicides. Despite the impersonal nature of certain homicides, in four out of five homicides the victim is a relative, lover, friend, or acquaintance of the murderer.

Murder, like suicide, is for the most part a personal matter: both suicide and homicide usually have destructive consequences to a number of people involved.

Crisis: The Journal of Crisis Intervention and Suicide   A journal published quarterly under the auspices of the INTERNATIONAL ASSOCIATION FOR SUICIDE PREVENTION.

crisis hotlines   Although crisis hotlines are available almost everywhere in the United States, evidence that they reduce rates of completed suicide is unclear. The lack of clear benefit could be related to the fact that actively suicidal individuals do not call hotlines as they are acutely disturbed, preoccupied, or intent on not being deflected from their intended course of action. In addition, hotlines are often busy, and there may be a long wait before a call is answered, so that callers disconnect. Moreover, the advice a person gets after calling a hotline may be stereotyped, inappropriate, or perceived as unhelpful by the caller.

While men are at highest risk for committing suicide, gender preferences in seeking help mean that most callers are women.

crying   Crying is considered a distress signal for the potentially suicidal, especially in cases where the person feels depressed and wants to be alone much of the time. Such persons will often withdraw from family and friends, lose their sense of humor, and may cry for no apparent reason—or for the most trivial reasons. Conversely, when the depression becomes especially severe, potential suicides find themselves incapable of crying even when they want to.

Crying is another clue, warning or distress signal of the overwrought, anxious, unhappy individual who probably exhibits a cluster of clues that may indicate the potentially suicidal. These suicide-prone persons, experts agree, need help immediately.

The help may come from understanding family and friends, from suicide prevention or crisis center personnel, or, as is often necessary, in the form of professional treatment by a trained psychiatrist, psychologist, social worker, or physician aware of and sensitive to such conditions.

See also COMMUNICATION OF SUICIDAL INTENT.

cult suicide   Mass suicide as directed by a religious leader or group. A number of large cult-related suicides have occurred in the past 20 years. These include:

HEAVEN'S GATE   The bodies of 39 young people who were part of a religious cult died in March 1997 in a mansion near San Diego. The victims, who were all between 18 and 24 years old, drank a lethal mixture of phenobarbital and vodka and then settled to die over a three-day period. Twenty-one victims were women; 18 were men. The victims apparently believed their deaths would lead to a rendezvous with a UFO hiding behind Comet Hale-Bopp.

Solar Temple   Members of the Solar Temple believe that ritualized suicide leads to rebirth on a planet called Sirius. In three years, murder-suicides by Temple followers have resulted in 74 deaths in Europe and Canada. The charred bodies of three women and two men were found on March 23, 1997, inside a house in Saint Casimir, Quebec. Two years earlier, in December 1995, 16 Solar Temple members were found dead in a burned house outside Grenoble, in the French Alps. The year before that (October 1994) the burned bodies of 48 Solar Temple members were discovered in a farmhouse and three chalets in Switzerland. At the same time, five bodies, including that of an infant, were found in a chalet north of Montreal.

Branch Davidian   On April 19, 1993, at least 70 Branch Davidian cult members died after a fire and a shootout with police and federal agents ended a 51-day siege of the compound near Waco, Texas. The government called the deaths a mass suicide in fires set by cult members. The sect's leader, David Koresh, who had preached a messianic gospel of sex, freedom, and revolution, had told followers he was Jesus Christ. Koresh died of a gun-shot wound to the head sometime during the blaze.

Vietnamese Suicide In October 1993, 53 hill Vietnamese tribe villagers committed mass suicide with flintlock guns and other primitive weapons in the belief they would go straight to heaven. Officials said they were the victims of a scam by a man who received cash donations for promising a speedy road to paradise.

Mexican Cult In December 1991, Mexican minister Ramon Morales Almazan and 29 followers suffocated after he told them to keep praying and to ignore toxic fumes filling their church.

Tijuana Cult On December 13, 1990, 12 people died in a religious ritual in Tijuana, after drinking fruit punch tainted by industrial alcohol. It was never clearly established if this was a suicide, and authorities speculated the deaths might have been accidental.

Jonestown Massacre Rev. Jim Jones led more than 900 followers to their deaths on November 18, 1978, at Jonestown in Guyana, by drinking a cyanide-laced grape punch. Cult members who refused to swallow the liquid were shot. Jones, who was found dead with a bullet wound in the head, had led the Peoples Temple in San Francisco and moved it to Guyana.

Falun Gong Seven Chinese Falun Gong practitioners tried to kill themselves in Tian'anmen Square in January 2001 by setting themselves on fire. Five practitioners, including a 12-year-old girl, soaked themselves in gasoline and set themselves on fire at around 2:40 P.M. on the eve of China's lunar New Year. One died on the spot, and the four others were injured. Police on duty at the time rushed to the rescue and immediately sent the injured to a local hospital. Two others planning a suicide attempt were found by the police and stopped.

See also MASS SUICIDE.

culture Since the beginning of recorded history and man's discovery that he could kill himself as well as other living creatures, attitudes toward suicide have differed in various societies and cultures, and are generally linked with ideologies of death and afterlife. Cultural attitudes toward suicide seem to be as ambivalent and divided today as in ancient Greece and Rome. In recent times, there have been apologists for suicide even among the clergy. Prestigious philosophers and writers have defended man's right to end his own life, whereas eminent others have decried such a right with equal conviction.

The suicidal acts by terrorists in the Middle East, some of whom are Muslims are undertaken despite the QUR'AN decrying suicide as an act worse than homicide. Shiite Muslims believe that to die in a *Jihad*, or holy war, assures them of a place in Heaven.

The collective representations through which individuals view suicide seem to have changed. Not a few authorities postulate that the "permissiveness" of modern society in general, which reflects a growing tolerance of deviant behavior, may be responsible for the rising suicide and suicide attempt rate. The various world societies appear to be less moralistic and punitive toward suicidal behavior today than a generation ago. Whether or not this societal attitude implies a greater readiness to understand than condemn, a lack of value commitment, or merely general apathy, remains to be seen. Yet the tendency to conceal suicidal acts still prevails in most cultures, even though the reasons for this reaction are not the same as at those times in history when suicide, or even attempted suicide, was considered a crime and a sin.

Suicidal acts will continue to be committed, but the world's various societies and cultures will, it appears certain, view this peculiarly human problem in different ways and for different reasons.

Czech Republic The Czech Republic, together with the other countries of Central Europe, form a geographical region with a high suicide rate, in spite of its predominantly Catholic population. Statistical data indicate, however, that the suicide rate in the area of the former Czechoslovakia has declined during the last 20 years. In 1999, the Czech Republic reported a suicide rate of 15.9 per 100,000 (25.7 for males, 6.2 for females).

The rate of suicides has always been higher in the Czech Republic than in Slovakia, although the rate at the beginning of the 1990s was the lowest of the postwar years. The greatest decline has been noted for the age groups 15 to 24 years and 40 to 59 years. As in most countries, the male suicide rate is much higher than for females, especially in Slovakia, and the difference is still increasing.

In the '60s and '70s, the suicide rate of the capital cities of Prague and Bratislava was much higher than in smaller towns and villages, but these rates are now tending to draw closer.

As high as the suicide rate in Czechoslovakia was in 1983, it was nowhere near the astonishing, world-leading rate in nearby Hungary, with its 45.9 percent rate total per 100,000 population.

Asked about the fact that Hungary has for several years been the world's most suicide-prone nation, Dr. Geza Varady, director of the Institute for Mental Health in Budapest, told an interviewer: "The phenomenon reflects the Hungarian temperament, which is volatile and likes dramatic gestures." Many suicidologists contend that figures such as the World Health Organization statistics do not say as much about national characteristics as they do about the way facts are gathered or covered up in the various reporting nations.

Dada Short-lived European literary and art movement that reflected disillusionment with all conventions and World War I. *Dada* is French baby talk for "anything to do with horses." The two founders of the movement were German poets Richard Huelsenbeck, and Hugo Ball. Dada was representative of the extreme, violent, and self-destructive impulse against *everything*, not simply against the establishment and the bourgeoisie which was the artists' audience, but also against art, even against Dada itself. For the Dada purist, suicide was inevitable.

The movement was a precursor to surrealism and subsequent radical art doctrines. Dada negated all formalism in art and produced "paintings" that were primarily collages made of such materials as newspaper bits, buttons, and photographs.

Its reign began with a suicide, ended with one, and included others in its progress. Like so many of the Dadaists, Dada died by its own hand. Jacques Rigaut, whose suicide in 1929 is thought by many to mark the end of the Dada era, believed that "suicide is a vocation." Other Dadaists who committed suicide included Arthur Craven and Jacques Vaché.

Dante Alighieri (1265–1321) Born in Florence in 1265 into an aristocratic family, Dante was schooled by the Franciscans. Among his teachers was Guido Cavalcanti, a poet of local fame who died in 1300. Dante later began writing love poetry, especially sonnets, at an early age, and devoted much of them to a Florentine woman, Bice, whom he called Beatrice ("the bringer of blessings"). They met for the first time when he was nine, and he grew infatuated with her. She grew impatient with the attention he paid other women, and she eventually married a banker. She died at a young age in 1292.

Perhaps the greatest of Italian poets, his chief work is one of the world's poetic masterpieces (*The Divine Comedy*). For Dante, there appears to have been no recognition or acceptance of extenuating circumstances regarding suicide.

In Canto XIII, Dante writes about the Wood of the Suicides, explaining that when a soul is forced from its body in the violence of suicide, Minos sends it down to the Seventh Circle. The soul, wherever it lands, falls into the ground, sprouts, and grows into a sapling and then a tree. The Harpies feed on the leaves and branches, causing great pain. After Judgment Day, when all sinners' bodies are reunited with their souls, the bodies of the Suicides will hang from the thorns of the trees. Dante, indeed, put suicide in the Seventh Circle of Hell, below the heretics and the murders, to express his moralistic horror of suicide.

daredevils Suicide is the number-three killer of young people; for those of college age, it is the second leading cause of death. Many suicidologists believe that suicide is actually the number-one killer of young people, and that many homicide and accident victims are suicides in disguise.

These CHRONIC SUICIDES include the daredevil who shouts "Look, no hands" as he speeds on his motorcycle on a narrow road; the preteen boy, dressed in Superman cape, who jumps from the roof; or adolescents abusing drugs and alcohol.

Sigmund Freud, pioneer in the study of the unconscious mind, concluded that everyone has a desire to harm or even totally destroy themselves. Some people, because of their unfortunate life circumstances, are driven to suicide openly and consciously. Others seek more subtle means without comprehending why or what they are doing. Fortunately, most persons seem able to perceive the consequences of their self-destructive behavior and change direction. Most people, in fact, control these negative urges or impulses.

But there are still far too many people, especially among the young, who either do not recognize their own self-destructiveness or deny it till it is too late. They are the ones who drive too fast, drink excessively, smoke three packs a day, mix drugs and alcohol, and play Russian roulette with loaded guns. They are the "daredevils."

Some suicide experts suggest this as a possible cause of actor JAMES DEAN's death, at age 24, in a car accident on a lonely California highway. On September 30, 1955, Dean—a heavy drinker and drug user at the time—was driving at a reckless 85 mph in his silver Porsche on Highway 41 at Chalome, near Pasa Robles. He was en route to a sports car race at Salinas when he smashed into another car, and was pronounced dead on arrival at the Pasa Robles Hospital. To compound the tragedy, some grief-stricken fans committed suicide.

See also CELEBRITY SUICIDES.

David of Augsburg (?–1272)

Medieval German mystic born probably at Augsburg, Bavaria, early in the 13th century, who wrote about the emotional and mental problems that could lead to suicide.

He entered the Franciscan Order probably at Ratisbon, where a monastery of this order was located as early as 1226; the Franciscan monastery at Augsburg was not built until 1243. At Ratisbon, David served as master of novices and wrote his celebrated "Formula Novitiorum."

During the medieval period, there was a growing recognition that mental and emotional disorders could lead to suicide. Such states and their potential consequences are often related to the concept of melancholy or *acedia* (spiritual sloth). In his writing, David distinguished among three types of *acedia*, one of which be thought could lead its victim to suicide when oppressed by unreasonable grief. This type of sorrow, David believed, might be triggered from a previous impatience, from frustration, or from an abundance of "melancholic humors" that require a doctor to cure.

Dean, James B. (1931–1955)

An actor killed at age 24 when he was speeding along in his new silver Porsche Spyder sports car and slammed into another auto at an intersection. He died instantly. Some suicide authorities suggest that Dean's death might come under the heading of CHRONIC SUICIDE, a term attributed to Dr. KARL MENNINGER. Menninger interpreted most accidents to be the result of unconscious self-destructive drives. Recent studies indicate that suicidal fantasies and "death wishes" do lie at the root of some traffic and other kinds of accidents. Many others appear to be related to brash, impulsive, spur-of-the-moment behavior—a "daredevil" defiance of fate that Dr. Menninger still considers as self-destructive or "chronic" suicide.

James Dean, born in tiny Fairmont, Indiana, had a reputation as a sullen, unfriendly, moody person to those in power, a man who would not give ground if he thought he was right. His few close friends thought him warm and loyal. In an interview not long before his death, Dean is quoted as saying, "If a choice is in order, I'd rather have people hiss than yawn." At famed Chasen's restaurant, he often accompanied rude requests for service by table-banging and silver-clanging. He reputedly drank heavily and used drugs abusively at times. On the eve of his death, he had attended a party at Malibu, which had ended in a shouting match with another person.

Yet, Dean's sudden death touched off the greatest wave of posthumous hero worship in Hollywood since the untimely death of Rudolph Valentino. Some fans committed suicide. Many of his fans refused to accept his death. Today, more than 40 years after his death, fan mail for Dean keeps arriving, mostly from teenagers across the country who identified with the troubled youngster, the man-boy anti-hero, played by the actor in *Rebel Without a Cause*.

death certificates In the United States, a coroner or medical examiner usually determines whether a death is a suicide, and records that decision on the death certificate. For each death certificate filed in the United States, the certifier must indicate the cause of death and the manner of death as "natural," "accident," "suicide," "homicide," or "undetermined." Laws guiding these decisions differ by state and sometimes by country.

Several factors, including uncertainty about what evidence is necessary and pressures from families or communities, may influence a coroner or medical examiner not to certify a specific death as a suicide. Because the extent to which suicides are underreported or misclassified is unknown, it has not been possible to estimate precisely the number of suicides, identify risk factors, or plan and evaluate preventive interventions. Some suicidologists believe that death certificates do not provide enough (or the right kind of) information to be helpful.

For example, accurate estimates correlating the risk of suicide with religious affiliation cannot be easily obtained, since religion is not recorded on death certificates. And yet, religious affiliation is known to affect a person's risk of suicide.

In addition, suicide statistics are grossly underestimated. In suspected suicide or homicide cases, state laws usually require a medical examiner or coroner to complete the death certificate. Because suicide is particularly subject to inaccurate determination, the incidence of suicide may be conservatively estimated at a minimum of 10 percent. Unfortunately, suicide data are sometimes quoted without either qualification or recognition of the incomplete nature of the death certificate information.

death education Discussion of grief, bereavement counseling, and death as a human experience. Proponents of death education say it is beneficial and long overdue. Critics, on the other hand, claim such courses are often introduced haphazardly by unqualified teachers and point to cases of negative, damaging information affecting young people. In fact, the suicides of former death-education students and the traumatic reactions of others have generated increasing criticism of death education classes.

Conservatives complain that the practice usurps the prerogatives of home and church. In Oklahoma, conservative legislators tried unsuccessfully to introduce a bill that would ban death education altogether. Some critics worry that in the hands of unskilled and overenthusiastic teachers, death education may in fact inspire more anxiety, depression, and fear than it reduces.

Some schools have asked students taking such courses to write their own obituaries, their own epitaphs, or even to visit funeral homes and crematoria. Others have had students lie down in empty coffins, plan their own funeral services, and attend death education classes held in cemeteries.

Serious thanatologists believe that if death education is to become a truly meaningful part of school curricula, it must be standardized and professionalized.

Death of Peregrinis, The An essay written by Greek satirist LUCIAN after he personally witnessed the fiery death by immolation of Peregrinis Proteus, a Cynic philosopher. Peregrinis, who early in his life left home under suspicion of having strangled his wealthy father to get his hands on the family fortune (it was never actually proven), in A.D. 165 ended his restless, wandering life before a large crowd at the Olympic festival by cremating himself on a pyre in the Indian manner. Peregrinis instructed his disciples to establish a cult in his honor after his death; this was done in his native town of Parium, on the Hellespont. It is said that the statue set up in his honor worked miracles and attracted many pilgrims. Just before jumping into the fire, he exclaimed: "Gods of my mother, gods of my father, receive me with favor." The time of Peregrinis was a period when many were filled with contempt for the human condition, felt themselves to be aliens in this world, and asked the question, "What are we here for?" SENECA (ca. 5 B.C.–A.D. 65) in his *Epistles* says that a desire possessed many, a longing for death. EPICTETUS (ca. A.D. 50–120) also noted this death wish among young men and tried to restrain it by urging them not to commit suicide.

death wish   The (often unconscious) desire to end life, almost as a way of approaching life. Suicidal adolescents will often seem to have a "death wish." They amble across busy streets, speed around icy corners on motorbikes, and mix drugs and alcohol without knowledge of their synergistic effect. Other suicidal behavioral hints sometimes include repeated auto accidents, driving bicycles into stationary objects, and picking fights with bigger youngsters and sometimes even with police.

This kind of attitude reflects an abnormal preoccupation with death and usually means the person is trying to send parents or significant others a message.

Almost everyone who seriously intends suicide leaves clues to their imminent action. Sometimes there are broad hints; sometimes only subtle changes in behavior. But the suicide decision is usually not impulsive.

death with dignity   See EUTHANASIA.

Decalogue Article   The Decalogue (Ten Commandments) was the primary source for St. AUGUSTINE's denouncement of the act of suicide. At the time there was no official Catholic Church position on suicide. He asserted that the act could not be condoned, even in the case of a woman whose honor was endangered, because suicide is an act which precluded the possibility of repentance, and it is a form of homicide and thus a violation of the Fifth Commandment, "Thou shalt not kill."

Definition of Suicide   A book that outlines 10 characteristics common in suicide, written by EDWIN SHNEIDMAN, Ph.D., professor of thanatology at the UCLA School of Medicine. Shneidman provides detailed explanations of these "Ten Commandments of Suicide" that together offer an intimate portrait of the suicidal person's emotions, thoughts, internal attitudes, desires, actions, and inner stresses.

The author, cofounder and formerly codirector, with Dr. Norman L. Farberow, of the LOS ANGELES SUICIDE PREVENTION CENTER, uses examples of actual suicide to construct a deeper, clearer understanding of the driving forces behind the act itself.

Definition of Suicide is considered by authorities as both a major theoretical treatment of self-destruction and a practical first-aid manual and guide for preventing suicidal deaths.

"Dejection: An Ode"   Written by Samuel Taylor Coleridge in 1802, this autobiographic poem resulted from his unhappy love for Wordsworth's sister-in-law, Sara Hutchinson. It is an intensely moving confession of his poetic sterility, a recognition of the death of his creativity as a kind of suicide.

Samuel Taylor Coleridge was born in Ottery St. Mary on October 21, 1772, youngest of the ten children of John Coleridge, a minister, and Ann Bowden Coleridge. He was often bullied as a child by Frank, the next youngest, and so Coleridge ran away at age seven.

His brother Luke died in 1790 and his only sister, Ann, in 1791, inspiring Coleridge to write "Monody," one of his first poems, in which he likens himself to Thomas Chatterton. Coleridge was very ill around this time and probably took laudanum for the illness, which triggered a life-long opium addiction.

He went to Cambridge in 1791, poor in spite of some scholarships, and rapidly worked himself into debt with opium, alcohol, and women. Four years later, Coleridge married a woman named Sarah Fricker, but soon afterward he met William Wordsworth, who introduced him to his sister-in-law, Sara Hutchinson. Coleridge fell in love with Sara almost immediately, putting an extra strain on an already troubled marriage.

In 1806, he divorced Sarah, but his paranoia and mood swings, brought on by the continual opium use, were getting worse, and he was hardly capable of sustained work. He was still haunted by his inability to stop using opium, however, and so he moved into the house of an apothecary named James Gillman to help cut back his opium dose. Unfortunately, this did not work, and like all addicts, Coleridge quickly had an alternative supply arranged.

He died peacefully on July 25, 1834, leaving only books and manuscripts behind. His symbolic suicide over many years—his creative death by opium—was to become one of the romantic alternatives for those not lucky enough (in the romantics' eye) to die prematurely.

Demosthenes (384?–322 B.C.) One of the greatest Athenian orators of all time. He based his political career on enmity against the Macedonians, and was ultimately exiled (in 324) on charges of financial corruption brought by the pro-Macedonian faction in Athens. Returning in 323, after the death of Alexander the Great, Demosthenes organized an unsuccessful revolt and took poison from a pen while fleeing Antipater, who captured Athens in 322 B.C.

Demosthenes's end came in the famed temple of Poseidon. In completing suicide, the great Greek orator joined the company of some of the ancient world's most distinguished men.

Denmark High rates of suicide are reported in Denmark, Sweden, and Austria, lower rates occur in the United States, England, and France, and the lowest rates are in Ireland, Italy, and Spain.

According to the most recent suicide figures from the World Health Organization (1996), there were 34.1 suicides in Denmark per 100,000 people—a slight decrease from the year before (35.4), yet significantly higher than a decade earlier (28.6 in 1983).

The suicide rate in 1996 among Danish men was 24.3 per 100,000, and the female rate was 9.8. This represents about an equal number of suicides in 1995 and 1996 among men, but is a decrease among women when compared to a rate of 11.2 in 1995 and 12 in 1994.

By far the highest suicide rate among various Danish age groups is in the over 75 group, with 90 suicides per 100,000. The suicide rate among Danish teenagers is 15.6 per 100,000.

dentists and suicide There is little valid evidence that dentists are more prone to stress-related suicides than the general population, according to an article in the June 2001 issue of the *Journal of the American Dental Association (JADA)*.

Since 1933, both the public and professional media have repeatedly portrayed dentists as being suicide-prone, and this message was repeated casually and accepted without supporting data. There have been few formal attempts over the last two decades to statistically verify this alleged risk on a national basis.

An estimated 31,000 Americans, including health care workers, died in 1996 from self-inflicted injuries, according to the National Center for Health Statistics, but there is no reliable information on the number of suicides by dentists.

For the *JADA* article, researchers evaluated current literature on stress and suicide in health professionals in an effort to verify or refute the widely held belief that dentists and other health care professionals are at higher risk of committing stress-related suicide. They found no consistent statistical evidence available to prove that dentists are suicide-prone, and most reliable data suggest the opposite.

It is unclear whether those dentists who kill themselves do so because of occupational stress, or because of other factors such as malpractice suits, divorce, alcohol abuse, unfulfilled expectations, or DEPRESSION.

The ADA offers a Dentist Well-Being Program to those dentists experiencing personal problems, including alcohol or substance abuse, stress, burnout, and depression.

departing drugs　The term popular among those in the EUTHANASIA movement for lethal medications used to bring about death.

depression　About half of all suicides each year in the United States are said to be victims of depression. Although most people who are depressed do not kill themselves, having major depression does increase a person's suicide risk. The more severe the depression—especially if untreated or inadequately treated—the greater the suicide risk. New data on depression suggest that about 2 percent of those people treated for depression in an outpatient setting will die by suicide, rising to 4 percent for those treated as inpatients. Moreover, those treated for depression as inpatients after having suicidal thoughts or making a suicide attempt are about three times as likely to die by suicide as are those who were treated only as outpatients.

There are also dramatic gender differences when it comes to suicide risk among depressed people. Whereas about 7 percent of men with a history of depression will kill themselves, only 1 percent of depressed women will die by suicide.

It is estimated that about 60 percent of people who complete suicide have had a mood disorder such as major depression or BIPOLAR DISORDER (manic depression), and about nine out of 10 people who kill themselves have at least one mental illnesses. Younger persons who kill themselves often have a substance abuse disorder in addition to being depressed.

However, no one theory can account for the many and varied forms of suicidal behavior. Certainly not all severely depressed persons commit suicide; nor do all those who kill themselves suffer from depression.

Still, depression is a warning sign that should not be ignored, and ranks high on the list of predisposing factors for suicidal behavior. Among the mental disorders, depressive illness carries the highest suicidal risk, since depression is characterized by a feeling of worthlessness and despair and a wish to die.

Since the risk of a severely depressed person committing suicide is so pronounced, it is essential to recognize the signs of depression. Some of the many warning signals depressed people usually exhibit in varying degrees include: sadness, apathy, expression of feeling empty and numb, inability to enjoy anything, pessimism, feelings of hopelessness and worthlessness, guilt and anxiety, indecisiveness, memory and concentration problems, and often, preoccupation with suicidal thoughts. Other warning signs include persistent sadness, withdrawal, headaches, stomachaches, insomnia, fatigue, and, at times, aggressive behavior. There is more often than not a decline in sexual drive as well.

Because the primary risk of depression is suicide, a good diagnosis and effective treatment are critical. At least 80 percent of people who commit suicide never got that treatment. While about 30,000 Americans kill themselves each year, at least 10 times that number make unsuccessful attempts.

Most experts believe that depression does not have one specific cause, but is the result of a collision between genetics, biochemistry, and psychological factors. The biological basis for depression can be found in nerve cells in the part of the brain responsible for human emotions. When levels of certain messenger chemicals called neurotransmitters are too low, communication in the brain slows down. While there are as many as 100 different kinds of neurotransmitters, there are three that seem to be of particular importance in depression—norepinephrine, serotonin, and dopamine. It is clear that these neurotransmitters are related to depression because drugs that boost levels of these chemicals also ease depression.

In addition to biochemical reasons, most cases of depression seem to be triggered by a serious loss or unpleasant experience that pushes a person into depression who may be genetically or psychologically vulnerable. At other times, a depression may appear to occur spontaneously, perhaps triggered by hormonal changes or a physical illness.

Treatment

Fortunately, as many as 90 percent of people with depression can be successfully treated with a combination of antidepressant medication and psychotherapy, usually within three months.

diabetes There have been cases where diabetes victims consistently "forgot" to take their medication and, as a result, became dangerously sick. Complications from such destructive behavior have sometimes led to diabetics' death. In such situations, people seldom think to connect the self-destructive behavior directly to suicide. They are simply, tragically, examples of the kind of "uncounted suicides" described by Dr. KARL MENNINGER as CHRONIC SUICIDE.

dichotomous thinking Increasingly rigid thought processes and loss of ability to see any options to death by a suicidal individual.

Diogenes (?412–323 B.C.) Greek philosopher and principal exponent of the Cynic school of philosophy who believed that the wise man will for reasonable cause make his own exit from life on his country's behalf, or for the sake of his friends, or if he suffers intolerable pain, mutilation, or incurable disease.

It was Diogenes who, seeing that Antisthenes was overcome by a distaste for life, offered a dagger to his friend and said: "Perhaps you have a need of this, friend?" ANTISTHENES replied: "I thank you, but unfortunately, the will to live is also part of the world's evil, as it is part of our nature."

direct and indirect self-destructive behavior (ISDB) Both classifications end in death, but direct suicide death is quick and more obviously what has traditionally been termed "suicide." ISDB is considered a slow form of suicide which hastens death, but is not clearly what is usually meant by the word "suicide." ISDB examples might include: overeating and chronic obesity, smoking, alcoholism or other drug overuse or abuse, risk-taking, accident proneness, and not adhering to behavior regimens that would sustain and/or prolong health and life.

To date, experts have failed in their efforts to come up with a term, definition, or classification that satisfactorily covers the complex grouping of behaviors that have been put forth as "suicidal."

distress centres (Canada) CANADA, like the United States, has a nationwide network of suicide hotlines (called "distress centres" in Canada). Distress centres nearly always have telephone numbers listed on the inside front cover of the local phone book, along with other emergency numbers. If no phone book is available, telephone operators have numbers for crisis services of all kinds, including suicide prevention. In larger population centers of Canada, as in the United States, one can also dial 911 for emergency services.

Canada suicide prevention services are also available to anyone at Salvation Army agencies and at branches of the SAMARITANS and CONTACT (in Canada, called Tele-care). In addition, there are Canadian Mental Health Association (CMHA) branches throughout the country, including the remote Northwest Territories and the Yukon Territory.

The SUICIDE INFORMATION AND EDUCATION CENTRE (SIEC), which is international in scope, has a comprehensive data bank of articles, newspaper and magazine clippings, books, films, cassettes, etc., about suicide.

distress signals   Almost everyone who seriously intends suicide leaves clues to his or her imminent action ranging from broad hints to subtle changes in behavior. But the suicide decision is usually *not* impulsive.

Called risk factors (see RISK OF SUICIDE), early-warning clues or distress signals, these changes of behavior represent very important warning signs to trained suicide prevention authorities.

divorce and suicide   Divorced people are three times as likely to commit suicide as people who are married, according to federal researchers. Moreover, children of divorce are at higher risk for committing suicide when they grow up; adults who reported having had parents who divorced or separated during childhood were also nearly twice as likely to report a later suicide attempts.

Divorce now ranks as the number one factor linked with suicide rates in major U.S. cities, ranking above all other physical, financial, and psychological factors. However, divorced men and women don't commit suicide at the same rate. Divorced and separated men are two and a half times more likely to commit suicide than married men. But divorce doesn't seem to lead more women to commit suicide. The difference could be in the social bonds for men and women. Because women are socialized to have deeper friendships, when a divorce occurs, women tend to have more of a social support network. In addition, men may have trouble coping with divorce because they not only lose the role of husband, but often of

father as well. It is still typical that mothers become the custodial parent, so that generally speaking, men lose the role of being a father in a way that women do not lose the role of being a mother.

Making the problem worse, men often feel as if they're responsible for the failure of a marriage. And typically, men tend to cope more destructively with stress, such as drinking too much.

Divorce statistics also reveal that in one study of 13 European countries conducted by the regional European office of the WORLD HEALTH ORGANIZATION found that divorce was the only factor linked with suicide in every one of the 13 countries. The study showed that factors such as poverty, unemployment, and disability were associated with divorce in some of the countries, but that disruption of the family was the only factor linked with divorce in all 13.

At the same time, the statistics for divorce and for teen suicide are closely related. In the past several decades, both the number of divorces and the number of young suicides have tripled. Indeed, a number of reliable studies indicate that most young suicides are children of divorce. In one study, 71 percent of young suicide attempters came from broken homes.

Another study found that of young attempters, 72 percent had at least one natural parent absent from the home, 84 percent of those with stepparents wanted them to leave, and 58 percent had a parent who had been married more than once.

In another study of young suicide attempters treated over a seven-year period, more than half of the families of the suicide attempters had an absent parent, while in one quarter of these families, *both* parents were absent.

doctor-assisted suicide   See PHYSICIAN-ASSISTED SUICIDE.

doctors   Among the professional disciplines, doctors are twice as likely to kill themselves as the general population. However, the true higher rate of suicide is really among women physicians. For example, in one study, white men over age 25 had a suicide rate of 34.6 per 100,000, which is very close to the suicide rate for men physicians of 35.7. But the general population of women over age 25 shows an 11.4 rate of suicide, whereas women physicians attained a rate of 40.7.

Researchers speculate this may have something to do with the changing roles for women, in addition to the high stress of their jobs and easy access to drugs.

Other studies have identified psychiatry, anesthesiology, and ophthalmology as specialties at greater risk for suicide, with pediatrics the least risk. In some studies, psychiatrists were found to kill themselves twice as often as other specialties.

Risks

Physicians at risk for suicide often send out indirect calls for help to their colleagues, and especially to their own personal physicians.

The following events can signal a higher risk for physicians to commit suicide:

- transition from residency to independent practice
- approach of retirement
- when parents become terminally ill
- when children leave home
- chronic marital problems
- intense competition from younger colleagues
- substance abusers who experience new losses

The AMERICAN MEDICAL ASSOCIATION, the American Medical Student Association, and the AMERICAN PSYCHIATRIC ASSOCIATION all recognize the growing seriousness of this problem and submit that suicide prevention and intervention programs are now urgently needed among physicians. These organizations have established special task forces and committees to deal with the problem of suicide and suicide attempts by member-colleagues.

Donatists The Donatists were a schismatic sect of especially rigorous Christians living in North Africa from the fourth to the seventh centuries, who elevated suicide to a religious experience. The Donatists, named after their bishop Donatus, had split from wider Roman Catholicism in their theology of the church. Donatism was basically a response to alternating periods of persecution and toleration, culminating in the formal legalization of Christianity by Constantine in the fourth century. The Donatists believed that Christians who had given in to persecution were no longer fit to occupy positions of leadership in the church, and could no longer administer sacraments.

As time went on, the Donatists began to believe not only that the clergy needed to be holy and in a state of grace but also that the entire church needed to be holy and in a state of grace—and any member who did not remain holy faced expulsion from the church. At this point the Donatists began to embrace a cult of martyrdom, greeting one another with the wish "may you gain your crown."

The Donatists were so extravagant in their horror of life and so desirous of martyrdom that they inspired their contemporary, ST. AUGUSTINE, to the view " . . . to kill themselves out of respect for martyrdom is their daily sport." JOHN DONNE noted, with no little embarrassment "that those times were affected with a disease of this natural desire of such a death . . . for that age was growne so hungry and ravenous of it [martyrdom], that many were baptized only because they would be burnt, and children taught to vexe and provoke Executioners, that they might be thrown into the fire."

The Donatists didn't care how they perished, so long as their conduct was, in Gibbon's words, "sanctioned by the intention of devoting themselves to the glory of the true faith and the hope of eternal happiness." When all else failed, they would, in the presence of relatives and friends, plunge headlong from some lofty rock, and, writes Gibbon, "many precipices were shown, which had acquired fame by the number of these religious suicides."

During Donatus's lifetime Donatism became the dominant Christian church in North Africa, but it faded in importance by the third generation. Early in the fifth century, St. Augustine rose to power and spent time addressing the problem of Donatism. At Augustine's death, both Catholic and Donatist Christians suffered under the Vandal invaders, which probably encouraged both sects to accept one another more easily. Although Donatism became more popular again in the sixth century, the entire North African Church was weakened and compromised by infighting, and was unable to withstand the attractions of ISLAM in the seventh century, when the Christian church disappeared entirely from western North Africa.

Donne, John (1572–1631)   English poet who entered the Church in 1615 and became dean of St. Paul's in London. As a young man, he was considered the foremost metaphysical poet in Britain, noted for his beautiful, witty love lyrics.

Donne, who was chaplain to King James I, removed suicide from the realm of religion and morality. To him, suicide was the act of a person driven by personal motives. He wrote a defense of suicide as a young man in which he candidly admitted that he had contemplated taking his own life. It was because of such extreme personal revelations that he refused to publish his essay on suicide, BIATHANATOS. Written in 1607 or 1608, the book was not published until 1646, 15 years after his death and nearly 40 years after it was written.

Donne's defense of suicide was one of the first reactions against prevailing Church attitudes. He agreed that self-destruction was contrary to the law of self-preservation, but no more than that. He postulated that suicide

was neither a violation of the law nor against reason.

Other noted secular writers and philosophers (Hume, Montesquieu, Voltaire, and Rousseau) later echoed Donne's position, arguing that suicide was indeed defensible under certain conditions. They wrote notable essays stressing the need for greater freedom of the individual against the ecclesiastical authority.

In the end, suicide for the famed poet-preacher was not a possibility, because Donne's Christian training and devotion were ultimately stronger than his despair.

Dostoevsky, Feodor Mikhailovich (1821–1881)   Russian novelist who became involved with a semirevolutionary group, was arrested and condemned to death, and at the last moment reprieved and sent to Siberia. There he underwent the torments reported in many of his later novels. In his novel *The Possessed* (1871–72), Dostoevsky's graphic treatment of nihilism, the antihero Alexsey Nilich Kirilov kills himself, he says, to show that he is God. Secretly, however, he kills himself because he knows that he is not God. He commits, by shooting himself, what the author calls a "logical suicide," self-destructing triumphantly.

Off and on throughout 1876, Dostoevsky reportedly stewed over the suicide question, pursuing the subject in newspapers, official government reports, and in conversation with friends. In *The Diary of a Writer* he wrote: "It is clear, then, that suicide—when the idea of immortality has been lost—becomes an utter and inevitable necessity for any man who, by his mental development, has even slightly lifted himself above the level of cattle."

But Dostoevsky, in the last analysis, clings to his traditional beliefs in Christianity and its attendant love and charity.

double suicide   A suicide that is completed by spouses, a couple, or by two friends, also known as dyadic death.

Douglas, Jack D., Ph.D.   Author of the well-known sociological study of suicide, *The Social Meanings of Suicide.*

Douglas is also known for outlining the fundamental dimensions of meanings required in the formal definition of suicide. These are:

1. The *initiation* of an act that leads to the death of the initiator.
2. The willing of an *act* that leads to the death of the willer.
3. The willing of self-destruction.
4. The loss of will.
5. The *motivation to be dead (or to die)* which leads to the initiation of an act that leads to the death of the initiator.
6. The *knowledge* of the actor that actions he initiates tend to produce the objective state of death.

drop-in centers   Name given by the Chicago area's North Shore suicide workers to suburban places where young people drop in to listen to music, do their homework, play cards or just talk. The important thing is that staff workers get to know the adolescents and can observe them over a period of time. Drop-in centers provide a source of crisis support for youngsters who lack caring communication and feel alienated from school, their peers, often even their own parents.

drug abuse   One of the strongest risk factors for suicide is drug abuse. The potential for suicide is in everyone; whether or not the potential grows and rises to the surface depends on how well one's individual system of checks and balances continues to function.

While there is no single explanation for suicide, certainly drugs play a key role in many suicide attempts and "completed" suicides. Use of barbiturates has decreased to less than 5 percent of cases, but use of other psychoactive drugs is increasing. Use of salicylates has decreased from less than 20 percent of cases to about 10 percent,

but the use of acetaminophen to commit suicide is increasing. While most people think of acetaminophen as a safe painkiller, in fact an overdose can be very dangerous.

One study of 100 young adults from New York City's Upper East Side who had tried suicide found that each suffered from some form of psychiatric illness, primarily depression. The most frequently given reason for attempting self-destruction was a feeling of utter hopelessness brought about by the threatened or actual loss of an important person in their lives. Some of the group blamed their attempts on alcohol and/or drug abuse; fearful of psychiatric symptoms, they became hopeless and isolated themselves.

Psychiatrist HERBERT HENDIN studied college students abusing drugs as part of a psychoanalytic study he conducted at Columbia University for his book *The Age of Sensation.* He discovered that while some drug abusers mixed the drugs they used, others favored one or another group of drugs depending upon their emotional problems and needs.

LSD and other psychedelic drug abusers wanted to escape feeling emotions. These students grew up feeling rejected and lonely; they didn't allow themselves to get close to others because it might prove too painful.

Amphetamine abusers in the Hendin study were mostly women students. Most of these users wanted desperately to please their parents, to fulfill the goals their parents had set for them. These pleasers ignored their own needs, kept themselves high on amphetamines, so they would have no time left to think about how they felt or what they wanted. Having destroyed their true selves, these young women programmed themselves to be efficient machines. But at times when the programming failed and the machinery broke down, they became openly suicidal.

Until recently, the most despairing, self-destructive drug misusers and abusers have been heroin users, who had usually suffered early and deep hurt in their lives. They abused drugs to prevent further hurt, to dull all feelings, and keep everybody at a safe distance.

At least 1 million people in the United States have tried crack, creating a new wave of cocaine addiction.

Paranoia and extreme agitation caused by the crack "high" have, in many cases, led to violent crime and suicidal behavior. Crack destroys the user's mind and body, causing convulsions, brain seizures, heart attacks, respiratory problems, and severe vitamin deficiencies. Addicts suffer depression and suicidal or homicidal thoughts when they crash.

Despite its relatively low per-unit cost, addicts end up spending thousands of dollars on binges, smoking the contents of vial after vial in crack or "base" houses—not unlike modern-day opium dens—for days on end without food or sleep. Authorities say users will do anything to repeat the brief high, including robbing their parents, relatives, and friends, selling their possessions and their bodies.

Crack, like other addictive drugs—including some over-the-counter prescription drugs—leads all too quickly to serious trouble, from a euphoric high to a startling crash that many people relieve by taking more . . . then more and more. Users gamble with their lives again and again.

Authorities report that thousands of teenagers and other young people (in the 20 to 26 age group) have plunged so deeply into drug abuse that it has cost them their lives. Unfortunately, thousands of others are now living lives where "accidental" death or suicide become daily occurrences. Some experience the agonizing, slow death of mental, emotional, and physical deterioration, while untold numbers die or become crippled or disfigured for life because of highway crashes caused by reckless driving or driving while in a drugged stupor.

drug treatments for suicide prevention
There is very little research on the usefulness of medication for reducing suicidal thoughts or preventing suicide in children and teens. How-

ever, among depressed adults, the newest anti-depressants—SSRIs such as Prozac and Zoloft—have been found to reduce suicidal thoughts and the frequency of suicide attempts in nonde-pressed patients who had previously made at least one suicide attempt.

In a controlled trial of the experimental neu-roleptic drug flupenthixol, researchers noted a significant reduction in suicide-attempt behavior in adults who had made numerous previous attempts. Similar studies have not yet been conducted on teens, although antidepressant studies in depressed teens suggest that these drugs are effective for treating DEPRESSION and for reducing suicidal ideas in this age group.

Because controlled studies of tricyclic antide-pressants have not been found to be helpful in depressed children and adolescents, SSRIs instead are considered to be a first choice in treating depressed suicidal children and adoles-cents. Unlike tricyclics, the newer SSRIs have a lower likelihood of being fatal if taken in over-dose.

In adults with major depressive disorder, con-trolled research suggests that lithium reduces suicide risk, but this has not yet been shown in children and adolescents.

Doctors should be careful about prescribing medications that may reduce self-control, such as benzodiazapines, amphetamines, and pheno-barbital. Also, these drugs are highly lethal if taken in overdose or mixed with alcohol.

druids Priests of the Celtic people who believed that there is another world beyond this one, and they who kill themselves to accompany their dead friends, will live with them there.

This belief is similar to a custom once com-mon among certain African tribes in which warriors and slaves put themselves to death when their king dies, in order to live with him in paradise.

Du Suicide et de la Folie Suicide The first important psychiatric study of suicide written by the French physician Charles-Henri Brierre de Boismont (1798–1881). The book, which was published in 1856, made extensive use of statistics in addi-tion to information obtained by questioning 265 people who either had planned or tried to commit suicide.

After an extensive analysis, de Boismont concluded that not all suicides are due to insanity, although many are caused by mental illness. Other causes he discovered include alcoholism, illness, family problems, love problems, and poverty.

He also discovered a higher proportion of unmarried people, old people, and men among the suicides he studied. He came to believe that suicide was the result of a changing society that led to social disorganization and widespread alienation.

dual suicide   A type of suicide in which two people kill themselves. It usually includes sub-categories such as parent-child suicide, MURDER-SUICIDE, murder-suicide between lovers, suicide after the death of a spouse, and love pact suicide.

See also SUICIDE PACT.

Dublin, Louis I.   Author of *Suicide: A Sociological and Statistical Study, The Facts of Life from Birth to Death,* and with B. Bunzel, *To Be or Not to Be.* ÉMILE DURKHEIM's *Le Suicide* established a model for sociological investigations of suicide; there have been a number of subsequent studies of this genre.

Dublin's work falls within the sociological tradition. He is considered one of the principal demographers of suicide this century, whose valuable summary of suicide rates showed the wide variation in those rates during the period 1900 to 1960.

Dublin noted the inverse association between economic prosperity and suicide and the positive association between depression and suicide. He also suggested that recorded suicide figures in cause-of-death certification

are understated by as much as one-fourth to one-third.

Durkheim, Émile (1858–1917)   French social philosopher and pioneer in social psychology whose monumental book *Le Suicide* (1897), established a model for sociological investigations of suicide. One of the most important and prolific sociologists in the history of the field, Durkheim is credited with making sociology a science by using an empirical methodology in his own studies, especially in regard to his study of suicide rates and issues of European nations.

David Émile Durkheim was born on April 15, 1858, in Epinal, in Lorraine. His mother, Mélanie, was a merchant's daughter, and his father, Moïse, had been rabbi of Epinal since the 1830s. Émile, whose grandfather and great-grandfather had also been rabbis, appeared destined to follow in their footsteps. He was sent for part of his early education to a rabbinical school, but Durkheim soon realized he was not interested in the rabbinate. Indeed, soon after his arrival in Paris, Durkheim abandoned Judaism altogether, although he always remained a part of a close-knit, orthodox Jewish family with roots deep in the Jewish community of Alsace-Lorraine.

An outstanding student at the Collège d'Epinal, Durkheim skipped two years, easily obtaining his baccalauréats in Letters (1874) and Sciences (1875). Intent on becoming a teacher, Durkheim left Epinal for Paris to prepare for admission to the prestigious École Normale Supérieure. However, he was miserable in Paris, worried over his father's illness and his family's financial security. A provincial alone in Paris, his scientific interests did not help him prepare for the study of Latin and rhetoric he needed to be admitted to the école. After failing in his first two attempts at the entrance examination, Durkheim was at last admitted near the end of 1879. Despite constant fears of failure that plagued him throughout his life, Durkheim participated in the political and philosophical debates at the école.

Though ill through much of 1881–82, he passed his exams and began teaching philosophy in 1882. Durkheim was appointed in 1887 as "Chargé d'un Cours de Science Sociale et de Pédagogie" at Bordeaux, and sociology first entered the French university system. This appointment of a young social scientist to the predominantly humanist Faculty of Letters at Bordeaux was not without opposition, and Durkheim made this worse by emphasizing the value of sociology to the more traditional humanist disciplines of philosophy, history, and law.

His groundbreaking 1897 study of suicide focused on the advent of technology and mechanization that he believed was endangering ethical and social structures and triggering suicidal tendencies. Since then, more and more scientific studies of what was once called "self-murder" were completed each year, and today the subject of suicidology is studied at major medical institutions around the world.

Within 10 years of Durkheim's study, the SALVATION ARMY established an anti-suicide bureau and American minister Henry Warren started the National Save-a-Life League. In 1910, SIGMUND FREUD'S VIENNA PSYCHOANALYTICAL SOCIETY held a symposium on suicide, and investigation into suicide took a new turn.

Durkheim, who also is considered a pioneer in the origins of religion, analyzed his French data on suicide and then proposed four kinds of suicide, each emphasizing the strength or weakness of the individual's relationship or ties to society. They are:

- ALTRUISTIC SUICIDES, in which a group's authority over one individual is so strong that the person loses his own identity and wishes to sacrifice his life for the community (such as, soldiers who willingly give their lives for their country).
- EGOISTIC SUICIDES, in which the person has too few ties with the community, with little religious, family, political, or social controls.
- ANOMIC SUICIDES, which occur when the individual simply cannot adjust to social change.
- fatalistic suicides, which result from excessive regulation (such as, among prisoners or slaves).

Durkheim was devastated by the death of his beloved son Andre in World War I, withdrawing into silence and forbidding friends to mention his son's name in his presence. Burying himself in the war effort, he collapsed from a stroke after speaking passionately at a committee meeting. After resting for several months, he began to work on *La Morale;* but on November 15, 1917, he died at the age of 59.

dutiful suicide Suicide understood as a culturally defined obligation.

Dying with Dignity A registered Canadian charitable society whose mission is to make dying with dignity an option available to anyone, to protect patients and doctors alike, to seek legal reform, and to introduce safeguards regarding voluntary EUTHANASIA.

To accomplish these goals, the group provides counseling and advocacy services, and provides Living Wills, powers of attorney for personal care, and other advance health care directives.

For contact information, see Appendix I.

dysphoria Depression accompanied by anxiety: A feeling of malaise or nonspecific illness or general discomfort that often accompanies a hangover or withdrawal.

East, John P. (1931–1986) U.S. Republican senator from North Carolina for five and a half years, who was found dead on the floor of the garage of his home in Greenville, North Carolina. The county medical examiner ruled the death a suicide. Police said the garage was sealed and full of fumes from a running station wagon inside.

East, who had contracted polio in the 1950s and consequently had to use a wheelchair, had many physical problems and was being treated for DEPRESSION, factors that may have contributed to his 1986 suicide by carbon monoxide asphyxiation.

Senator East had announced in 1985 that he would not seek a second term in office because of ill health.

Eastman, George (1854–1932) A brilliant scientist who revolutionized photography with his inventions of dry-rolled film and the hand-held cameras that used it, but who ended his life by his own hand when illness overtook him.

Eastman was born on July 12, 1854, to Maria Kilbourn and George Washington Eastman, the youngest of three children, in Waterville in upstate New York. The house on the old Eastman homestead, where his father was born and where George spent his early years, has since been moved to the Genesee Country Museum in Mumford, New York, outside Rochester.

When George was five years old, his father sold a nursery business and moved the family to Rochester, where the elder Eastman established Eastman Commercial College. Sadly, George's father died suddenly, the college failed, and the family was plunged into poverty. George continued school until he was 14, when he was forced to get a job as a messenger with an insurance firm to support the family. Through his own initiative, he soon took charge of policy filing and even wrote policies. But his income was not enough, so he studied accounting at home in the evenings to get a better job. After five years in the insurance business, he was hired as a junior clerk at the Rochester Savings Bank, tripling his salary.

Planning a vacation to Santo Domingo at age 24, Eastman bought a camera and wet plate to make a record of the trip. The camera, which was as big as a microwave, required a heavy tripod and a tent to protect and develop the glass plates. The paraphernalia required included chemicals, glass tanks, a heavy plate holder, and a jug of water. While Eastman never made it to Santo Domingo, he became fascinated with photography and sought to simplify the complicated process, experimenting at night in his mother's kitchen. By 1880, he had patented not only a dry plate formula, but also a machine for preparing large numbers of the plates. His inventions were phenomenally successful and made him a wealthy man. Thanks to the profits of the company he founded to produce his cameras and film, Eastman Kodak, he was able to contribute $100 million to various educational institutions.

Plagued by progressive disability resulting from a hardening of the cells in the lower spinal cord, Eastman became increasingly frustrated at his inability to maintain an active life. He committed suicide on March 14, 1932, at the age of

77. His suicide note read: "To my friends: My work is done. Why wait?"

eating habits A noticeable, often dramatic, change in a person's eating habits is a warning sign or distress signal of possible suicide. Experts believe most suicidal children will show changes in eating habits that can be one of many early signs of trouble. A few children (almost always girls) will show extreme eating disorders that usually last several years and come to monopolize their lives.

Parents, teachers, friends, and counselors should consider eating disorders, especially anorexia nervosa and bulimia, as urgent warning signs. Experts believe such behavior is really an attempt at slow suicide, rather than an instant attempt with a bullet through the brain or a rope around the neck.

See also ANOREXIA NERVOSA and BULIMIA.

economic class Statistics show that suicide occurs equally among rich and poor alike, and among adults as well as adolescents. Suicide is usually caused by a combination of forces one of which may be economic fluctuations.

Egbert, Archbishop of York (?–766) Eighth century archbishop who made burial allowances to those suicide victims who had mental and emotional disorders. Egbert made an exception for the insane concerning burial in consecrated ground.

See also CHRISTIANITY.

egoistic suicide Suicide committed by people who feel alienated from others and who lack social support. As defined by sociologist ÉMILE DURKHEIM, egoistic suicide is an attempt to annihilate the self because the individual feels extremely alienated from others and from society. According to Durkheim, most suicides are egoistic, committed by those with few community ties. Experts believe that egoistic suicides

occur when a person is not properly integrated into society, but is dependent instead upon personal resources.

egotic suicide A type of suicide triggered by an intrapersonal problem.

Egypt A devout country where suicide is considered by most people to be a mortal sin. As a result, Egypt has a correspondingly low suicide rate, the lowest in the world.

The most recent statistics provided by the World Health Organization were reported in 1987, when the rate was allegedly 0.1 per 100,000 for men. According to the statistics that were reported, not one Egyptian woman committed suicide. These statistics, some experts believe, say less about national character than the way facts are gathered or covered up. While highly industrialized and prosperous countries tend to have comparatively high suicide rates, they also tend to have more sophisticated methods of collecting the information on which statistics are based, and comparatively few prejudices against doing so.

Religion is a factor here, as well, since Muslims are strongly opposed to self-destruction. The QUR'AN, the sacred scripture of the Muslims, decries suicide as an act worse than homicide.

In ancient Egypt, suicide was viewed as a neutral event, because death was merely a passage from one form of existence to another. It was simply a way to avoid disgrace, abandonment, guilt, cowardice, or loss of a loved one.

The oldest known reference to suicide is Egyptian: "Death is before me today, Like the recovery of a sick man . . . Like the longing of a man to see his home again. After many years of captivity . . ." (*Man Disputing over Suicide with his Soul,* Egypt, ca. 2100 B.C.).

Elavil (amitriptyline) The brand name for one of a group of antidepressants called tricyclics.

Before popular antidepressants such as Prozac, the tricyclics were the first line of defense against encroaching DEPRESSION. Today tricyclics are a less popular choice than the new generation of antidepressants, but they are still an important weapon for those patients who do not respond to any other drug.

Cyclic antidepressants work by beefing up the brain's supply of norepinephrine and serotonin levels, chemicals that are abnormally low in many depressed patients. This allows the flow of nerve impulses to return to normal. Unfortunately, cyclics also interfere with a range of other neurotransmitter systems. Used with central nervous system depressants such as alcohol, it can have an addictive effect. Abrupt cessation can result in nausea, headache and malaise, but these withdrawal symptoms are not necessarily indicative of addiction.

Patients who are potentially suicidal should not have access to large quantities of the drug, as severe overdosage can cause convulsions, congestive heart failure, coma, and death.

eldercide   See ELDER SUICIDE.

elder suicide   Completion of suicide by an individual aged 65 or over. While suicide can occur at almost any stage of life, it becomes a much more serious problem in the United States after age 65, when the suicide rate increases abruptly.

About every 83 minutes, one adult over age 65 commits suicide in the United States. The suicide rate for this general age group rose by 9 percent between 1980 and 1992. During that period, there were 74,675 suicides by elderly people. In 1993, suicide rates ranged from 15 per 100,000 population among those 65 to 69 years old, to 24 per 100,000 population for persons 80 to 85 years of age, a rate that is double the overall U.S. rate.

Among elderly Americans, white men are the most likely to die by suicide, especially if they are socially isolated or live alone. In fact, white men are at nearly 10 times the risk for suicide as nonwhite men across the age spectrum, and white men over age 80 have the greatest risk of all age, gender, and racial groups. The suicide rate for this group is six times the current overall rate and three times the rate of African-American men over 80 years old. This high rate among white men over 80 is important because the very elderly age group (85 years and older) is the fastest-growing sub-population of elderly adults in the United States. The widowed, divorced, and recently bereaved are at especially high risk, as are depressed individuals and those who abuse alcohol or drugs. The suicide rates for women peak between the ages of 45 to 64, and do so again after age 75.

Experts suspect that rates are so high for this group because older people are less likely to survive attempts because they are less likely to recuperate. More than 70 percent of older suicide victims have seen their primary care physician within a month of their death, many with a depressive illness that was not detected.

Minimum estimates of suicides among the elderly in the United States range from 6,000 to 10,000 annually, but the actual rate for the elderly is probably a good deal higher, since many deaths from suicide are never investigated, and are reported mistakenly as accidents or deaths from natural causes. Many are committed by isolated, lonely, older people. In some cases, there are no friends or family members who care about the person's cause of death; in other cases, they may be too afraid to ask because of the stigma attached to this kind of death.

Additionally, suicides are often mistaken for natural deaths, especially in cases of medicinal overdosing, because many older people take many medications.

However, the rate for women is relatively under-reported, since they tend to use methods (such as a drug overdose) that leave room for other verdicts. Since American men most often use guns, these deaths are harder to attribute to "natural causes." Nevertheless, that American male suicide rates peak in old age while female rates are at their maximum during middle age is difficult to explain. The unpleasant realities of old age—increasingly poor health, death of a spouse, relegation to a nursing home—fall more frequently on women than men, since women tend to live much longer.

On the other hand, women are generally better than men at maintaining social and family contacts. And men, due to the higher status and more competitive nature of their activities, lose more social standing as they age than do women.

Risk Factors

Risk factors for suicide among the elderly include the presence of a mental illness (especially depression and alcohol abuse), being sick, being socially isolated (especially widows), and having guns in the home. Elderly widowers are a very high-risk group, probably because they are more socially isolated and because of the loss of emotional and social support provided by their wives.

Between 60 and 85 percent of elderly suicides had significant health problems, and in four out of every five cases this was a contributing factor to their decision. On the other hand, nonsuicidal elderly had similar rates of physical illness as the suicidal.

Life events commonly associated with elderly suicide include:

- death of a loved one
- uncontrollable pain
- fear of dying a prolonged death that damages family members emotionally and economically
- loneliness
- major changes in social roles, such as retirement

Most elderly patients who complete suicide visit their doctors within a few months of their death; more than a third consult a physician within the week of their suicide.

Methods

Older adults tend to use highly lethal means to commit suicide. In 1988, nearly eight out of 10 suicides committed by men 65 years and above used a firearm. Hanging and poisoning were the second and third leading causes of suicide in this group.

Suicide Attempts

For the population as a whole, there are about 25 suicide attempts for every suicide completion. For elderly people, the ratio of attempts to completed suicides narrows dramatically to 4:1. This means that an older person who contemplates suicide is more likely to complete the act.

Elderly people often choose lethal methods when attempting suicide, and because they tend to be more frail, they are less likely to recover from a suicide attempt.

Suicide notes left by the elderly tend to show a desire to end their suffering, rather than dwelling on interpersonal relationships, introspection, or punishing themselves or others, which are common themes in younger suicides.

Prevention

Maintaining close family ties with available relatives, involvement in community groups such as volunteer organizations, and access to good medical and mental health care provide substantial protection from suicide by the elderly. Careful monitoring of prescription drugs and observing any signs of substance abuse also help prevent suicide, as do bereavement support groups for the elderly who have lost loved ones.

electroconvulsive treatment (ECT) A form of treatment for DEPRESSION consisting of the application of a weak electric current to the head in order to produce convulsion and unconsciousness. While often effective for severe depression, ECT has caused a great deal of controversy because of its frightening reputation and tendency to trigger memory loss in many patients.

The modern practice of electric shock treatments is less than 65 years old. Because it was cheap and easy, the use of ECT soon spread; by the 1950s it was the primary method of treatment for depression until the discovery of antidepressants led to a substantial decline in its use. Today, about 100,000 people a year are treated with ECT.

In a typical ECT treatment, the patient is given an anesthetic and a muscle relaxant before padded electrodes are applied to one or both of the temples. A controlled electric pulse is delivered to the electrodes until the patient experiences a brain seizure; treatment usually consists of six to 12 episodes (two or three a week). After the treatment, the patient may experience a brief period of confusion, which is later forgotten, and a brief period of amnesia covering the period of time right before the treatment.

While serious depression in teens can lead to suicide, ECT is rarely considered for these younger patients, and there have been no controlled studies for this age group. There is a risk of prolonged seizure in younger patients, who are more susceptible to seizures than are adults.

Likewise, ECT in elderly patients who are depressed and demented is not recommended because the treatment can worsen their condition.

electromagnetic fields   Prolonged exposure to extremely low-frequency electromagnetic fields such as those emitted by large power lines may double the risk of suicide, according to a study from the University of North Carolina. The highest risk of suicide was found among those with the highest levels of exposure, particularly in the year preceding death. The association was even stronger among those whose death occurred before the age of 50.

The health records of all electricians and field technicians at any of the five major electric power companies in the United States between 1950 and 1986 were studied by Dr. David Savitz, professor and chair of the epidemiology department at the University of North Carolina, Chapel Hill. Almost 6,000 from a total of 139,000 workers were selected for detailed study.

Out of the 6,000 workers studied, there were 536 deaths from suicide. These suicide deaths were twice as high among those whose work regularly exposed them to extremely low-frequency (EMF) electromagnetic radiation. Suicide risks were considered for electricians, linemen, and power plant operators, the three most common jobs with increased exposure to magnetic fields among the five utility companies. (Only men were studied because women rarely worked in jobs where they were exposed to EMFs.)

The researchers suggest that electromagnetic fields may reduce the production of melatonin, a hormone that maintains daily circadian rhythms, including the sleep and wake cycle. Reduced levels of melatonin are associated with depression.

What scientists found particularly interesting is that the greater the amount of exposure to EMFs, the greater the likelihood that the worker would commit suicide. Researchers also noted that the younger workers seemed to be more affected by the EMF radiation.

Established risk factors for suicide are history of mental and addictive disorders, abnormalities in the serotonin system, and disrupted family environment. Unfortunately, information about these risk factors was not available from personnel records at the companies.

The authors concluded that there is an association between cumulative exposure to extremely low-frequency electromagnetic fields and suicide, especially among younger workers, and physical impairments among older workers. The study was published in the *Occupational and Environmental Medicine Journal*.

emergency rooms, help in   Suicidal persons who survive a serious attempt are usually rushed by EMS or paramedic teams to a hospital emergency room. Authorities urge parents and relatives to make certain the patient is evaluated and treated (where possible) by a professional therapist.

Parents or relatives cannot rely on the emergency room staff of a hospital to refer a suicidal patient for psychiatric care. There are times when the staff will call in a hospital psychiatrist or psychologist for consultation on an attempted suicide victim. When this happens, the patient is often transferred, after recovering from the attempt, to a psychiatric ward. But a family cannot count on this always happening; emergency room staff personnel are simply too busy (or uninterested) to follow through with psychiatric consultations.

Unfortunately, once the person—and especially the adolescent—checks out of the hospital, statistical studies indicate that the majority fail to seek additional professional assistance. It is up to the suicide attempter's family to make certain he or she receives therapy by a certified professional.

Empire State Building The tallest building in New York City that was for many years the site of many spectacular suicides. The last time a person jumped off the Empire State Building was in 2000, but there have been more than 30 suicides at the 1,250-foot skyscraper since it opened in 1931. Most of those who have leaped to their deaths never made it to the street, landing instead on one of the building's setbacks.

Over time, protective barriers were built higher around the observation platform to prevent suicides. Today the barriers, plus sharp-eyed guards, make the top of the Empire State Building virtually suicide-proof.

employment There is an inverse association between economic prosperity and suicide and the positive association between depression and suicide.

Andrew F. Henry and James F. Short, trying to determine more clearly how economic cycles are related to suicide, analyzed separately the trend in suicide rates for whites and nonwhites, males and women, and young and old persons. Their study showed the rate increased more for high status groups (whites, men, and younger individuals) during economic depressions than for low-status groups. They concluded that the data indicate high-status groups are more sensitive to the frustrations produced by business cycles.

In the United States, other studies show that rates of suicide are highest among laborers, while in Great Britain both professional and laborer groups had higher rates than other occupational groups. Experts caution that occupation may be an important factor in assessing suicide rates not only because of the work involved, but also because of the lifestyle outside of work established by persons in particular occupations.

During rapid rises in the business index, suicides tend to fall. With only slight business index increases, during the final phase of increase, the suicide rate does increase—but primarily among females, particularly among those least involved in the machinations of the economy. Generally, business cycles are more highly correlated with male suicides than with the suicide of women. But the suicide of black women is more closely linked to business fluctuations and employment than is the suicide of black men.

It's clear that suicide rates vary in response to economic conditions. In the United States, for example, rates declined during the prosperous years of World Wars I and II but rose during the Great Depression. After World War II as the country prospered, the rates remained low. European countries in general showed similar trends.

England Suicide in England has for centuries been regarded with significant disfavor. The rising rate of suicide among men in England and Wales observed in the 1970s and '80s has reversed, and the suicide rate for both sexes is now decreasing, according to an analysis of suicide data from the British Office for National Statistics.

Between 1990 and 1997, the suicide rate for men and women decreased in all age groups.

There were also changes in the methods used to commit suicide. Rates of self-poisoning with solids and liquids leveled off for men between these years, and rates fell by 22 percent for women. Poisoning by gases and vapors (including car exhaust fumes) fell by 61 percent in men and 60 percent in women. However, suicides by hanging and strangulation increased in men.

The fitting of catalytic converters onto cars accounted for some of the fall in male suicides, according to Guy McClure, M.D., consultant psychiatrist at the Chelsea and Westminster Hospital in London and author of the study. All gas-powered cars sold in the United Kingdom since December 31, 1992, have had to have converters, which reduce the carbon monoxide content of the exhaust gas.

However, since only 36 percent of cars had converters by 1997, there may be other possible explanations for the fall. Levels of psychosocial stress may have declined in men and women between 1990 and 1997 as the national economy and unemployment statistics improved. A move toward psychiatric care in the community may also have had an impact.

Attempts had been made to limit the availability of certain suicide methods, such as detoxifying domestic gas, reducing the prescribing of barbiturates, and fitting catalytic converters. Recent legislation reducing the number of available paracetamol (Tylenol) pills per packet has been shown to decrease suicide by paracetamol by eight percent in one year after the law passed. Therefore, the rates for hanging may have increased because it is not possible to limit the availability of rope.

The teachings of ST. AUGUSTINE and other early church leaders became incorporated into the laws of the Roman Catholic Church and later the Anglican Church. Suicide was declared an act inspired by the devil, as church councils deemed it a mortal sin. Bodies of suicides were denied Christian burial, and even suicide attempters were excommunicated. Church laws did distinguish, however, between the self-destruction of sane and insane persons, and also excluded young children from the harshly cruel penalties imposed by Anglican Church law.

When a suicide did take place, townspeople often dragged the degraded body through the streets to be spat upon or hanged from public gallows. Sometimes the victim was buried on the spot where he or she had committed suicide; at other times, the body remained unburied in the area of town reserved for public executions. Often the suicide's body was buried at a crossroads with a stake driven through its heart and a stone placed on the face to prevent the dead person's spirit from rising.

In England as recently as 1823, the body of a man who killed himself was dragged through the streets of London and buried at a crossroads. He was the last suicide in England whose body was so mistreated; Parliament passed a law shortly thereafter authorizing private burial of a suicide in a churchyard or in a private burial ground.

In 1961, a new law repealed all previous civil rulings about suicide—rulings that had been based on early Anglican Church doctrine.

Today it is no longer a crime to attempt or successfully to commit suicide in England. Famed poet-preacher JOHN DONNE, who became dean of St. Paul's Cathedral in London, was highly influential in changing public's attitudes by his defense of suicide in the book BIATHANATOS, published in 1644. About 100 years later, Scottish philosopher DAVID HUME argued convincingly against treating suicide as a crime in his short essay "On Suicide." Suicide was regarded at the time as so widely prevalent that many believed the problem constituted a national emergency.

The World Health Organization (WHO) statistics on suicide and self-injury includes Wales's figures with England (Northern Ireland and Scotland are listed separately). Most recent statistics (1997) show a suicide rate per 100,000 population totaling 13.2, a slight drop of .2 since 1996.

The male suicide rate is 10.3 as opposed to the much lower female rate of 2.9. Highest rate for specific age groupings is that for 75+ years of age; for males, it is 16.9 per 100,000 population. Highest female age group rate is the 45–54 category, where the rate is 4.4 per 100,000 population.

English Malady, The

English Malady, The   Book presenting suicide as a medical problem, written by Scottish physician George Cheyne (1671–1743) in 1733. Cheyne opened a practice in London in 1702, where he published a number of medical treatises. In 1715, he argued that life cannot be created from inorganic matter; all living things, he reasoned, "must of necessity have existed from all eternity."

In *The English Malady,* Cheyne wrote that melancholy was caused by "the moist air of these islands, our variable weather, a too-rich diet and overpopulation." Cheyne's text offered a new perspective on the problem of melancholy. He linked suicide to the social conditions that prevailed in England in the early 18th century, rather than to the particular moral attributes of the sufferer of melancholy. The change is subtle but of utmost importance to the history of subjectivity.

According to Cheyne, melancholy was caused by the luxurious lifestyle of wealthier English people of the day. Many later sociological terms for similar states of psychological distress were developments of Cheyne's cultural approach to psychic ailments, such as alienation, chronic boredom, anomie, neurosis, anxiety, disenchantment, depression, nerves, and so on. The full title of the book was: *The English Malady: Or a Treatise of Nervous Diseases of all Kinds, as Spleen, Vapours, Lowness of Spirits, Hypochondriacal, and Hysterical Distempers, Etc.* (London: G. Strahan and J. Leake, 1733).

Enigma of Suicide, The

Enigma of Suicide, The   A deeply compassionate treatment of suicide that examines suicide from the historical, moral, sociological, and psychological angles, written by *Life* magazine writer George Howe Colt. The book includes case histories of adult and adolescent suicides, and clarifies the various motives for completing suicide.

Enlightenment, Period of

Enlightenment, Period of   The mid-18th-century era when new views led to more tolerant attitudes and opinions about suicide. Leaders of the "Enlightenment" included Voltaire, JEAN-JACQUES ROUSSEAU, and DAVID HUME among others. They and their allies condemned the traditional cruel treatment of suicides.

environment

environment   The idea that a person's surroundings can influence a person's desire to commit suicide can be traced to antiquity. Early physicians, writers, and philosophers began to discuss the role of environmental factors such as air, diet, and temperature on both social and medical problems. These discussions became so common and widespread in the 18th century that they led to the opposition of sanctions against suicide, and the development of toleration for such acts.

Henry Morselli, an Italian professor of psychological medicine, was an early researcher of the subject. In his book *Suicide: An Essay on Comparative Moral Statistics* (first published in Milan in 1879, reprinted in 1975 by Arno Press, New York), Morselli studied endless statistics and, among other things, tried to relate "cosmico-natural" influences such as climate, geological formations, and so on to suicide. He also considered biological factors, social conditions of the suicidal person and individual psychological influences.

Many, if not most, of Professor Morselli's conclusions would be challenged today (such as the frequency of suicide in various parts of Italy generally is in a direct ratio with stature, and the inclination to self-destruction increases from south to north as the stature of Italians gradually increases). Yet, if Morselli's correlations seem strange, consider that there was a study in the spring 1977 issue of *Suicide and Life Threatening Behavior* that attempted to correlate the rate of suicides with the moon's position. The only relationship appeared to be a slight increase in the number of suicides during the new moon phase, suggesting perhaps that a small percentage of suicide-prone people are influenced by lunar changes.

It has also been postulated by some authorities that geography may affect people who live in isolated areas, in regions where days are short and the nights long, and/or where climate is gloomy. Northerly countries such as SCANDINAVIA show higher suicide rates than do tropical regions. In the United States, suicide frequencies rise as one travels from east to west (Nevada has the country's highest suicide rate per 100,000 population with Arizona and Alaska close behind).

Others theorize that spring is the deadliest time of year for suicides and winter the least deadly. One researcher notes that people of slight physique tend to commit suicide in early spring, those more stockily built, toward the end of spring. More suicides are said to occur on certain days of the week—Monday is the favored day. Also, suicides are said to prefer certain hours of the day, usually in late afternoon or early evening, presumably when they know other family members are at home.

Some of these environmental correlations obviously play a part in the frequency and motivation of suicidal persons, but other circumstances and statistics vary so greatly that it is impossible to draw any useful conclusions.

Environments in which there is crime, violence, alcohol and/or drug abuse, divorce, or unemployment, appear to make some individuals especially vulnerable.

Epictetus (ca. A.D. 55–ca. 135) Greek philosopher and an eminent exponent of Stoicism who approved of suicide in some cases. Born about A.D. 55 in Phrygia (now central Turkey), as a boy he came to Rome as a slave. While still a slave, he studied with a Stoic teacher. He lived about 400 years after the Stoic school of ZENO was established in Athens. He lived and worked first in Rome, and then as a teacher with his own school in Greece.

The philosophy of Stoicism was among several at the time that accepted and even recommended suicide under certain conditions—particularly as an escape from evil. Epictetus also endorsed suicide in some cases. The principal moral theme of Stoic philosophy is that humans should resign themselves to whatever fate has in store. For some of us, Epictetus suggests, there may be limits to what we can endure in this life and, so, when things become intolerable, we may wish to end our lives. He describes our options by saying:

" . . . Above all, remember that the door stands open. Do not be more fearful than children. But, just as when they are tired of the game they cry, 'I will play no more,' so too when you are in a similar situation, cry, 'I will play no more' and depart. But if you stay, do not cry. . . . Is there smoke in the room? If it is slight, I remain. If it is grievous, I quit it. For you must remember this and hold it fast, that the door stands open." [*Discourses*, Book 1, Ch. 24, 25]

Although Epictetus based his teaching on the works of the early STOICS including thought, logic, and ethics, he emphasized ethics. The role of the Stoic teacher was to encourage his students to live a philosophic life of reason, whose end was happiness. For Stoics, being happy meant living virtuously and according to nature. The task of a Stoic is to live according to nature, which means intelligently responding to one's own needs and duties as a sociable human being, but also wholly accepting one's fate and the fate of the world as coming directly from the divine intelligence.

Epictetus, along with all other philosophers of the Hellenistic period, saw moral philosophy as having the practical purpose of guiding people toward leading better lives. The aim was to live well, to secure happiness. Epictetus encouraged his students to think of life as a festival, arranged for their benefit by God, as something that they can live through joyously, able to put up with any hardships because they have an eye on the larger spectacle that is taking place. Epictetus did not marry, had no children, and lived to an old age.

Epicureans   Adherents of a philosophical school of thought in ancient Greece that taught that pleasure was the goal of life, and could be attained by moderation. Epicureans considered suicide an appropriate escape from the sufferings of this world, especially physical illness and emotional frustration. For the Epicureans, it was better by far to have a few friends with whom to serenely contemplate the universe and with whom to enjoy moderate and secure pleasures.

Expounded by Lucretius, the philosophy was much followed in Rome and during the Renaissance.

Epicureans opposed suicide because self-destruction simply did not fit their concept of the calm life, with its primary quality of joy.

Epicurus (?342–270 B.C.)   Greek philosopher who opposed suicide and whose work was popularized by the Roman poet Titus Lucretius Carus. Epicurus was born on the island of Samos in Ionia, going off at age 19 to Athens to study at the Academy.

Epicurus had little patience with religion, which he considered a form of ignorance, but he said that the gods existed, although they lived far away in space and had nothing to do with people on Earth. (Atheism was still illegal in Athens.) Epicurus believed it was useless to argue over metaphysics, that there was no such thing as a soul that lived after death, that humans arrived at their present condition by means of evolution, and that people have free will.

Virtue for Epicurus was a means to an end—and that end was happiness. He believed it was good to feel pleasure and to avoid pain, although sometimes pain was necessary in order to gain happiness. On the other hand, he believed that sometimes pleasure leads to more suffering than it is worth.

Society is seen as a necessary protection from injustice, and the ultimate happiness is peace. His motto was *lathe biosas* ("live unobtrusively").

epilepsy   Research suggest that patients with epilepsy (especially temporal lobe epilepsy) attempt suicide at a rate about four, five, or seven times as high as that of the general population, depending on the study. The last 10 years of suicidology literature continues to report both higher suicide rates among people with epilepsy, and the fact that many use antiseizure medications to kill themselves.

There is also an increased risk for suicidal behavior in children with epilepsy, who are more likely to complete the attempt. The higher risk for these patients is attributed to their problems with housing, schooling, work, social relationships, psychiatric disturbances, and anticonvulsant drugs. The risk can be lessened by education, watching for psychiatric disturbances, and monitoring their medication level.

Other studies have noted more suicidal thoughts and impulses and higher risk factors for suicide in three samples of epileptics studied in metropolitan Los Angeles, noting a higher prevalence of depression and hostility. Unexpectedly, researchers also found the patient fears about seizures played a significant role in actual suicide attempts, and were the reasons for their suicidal impulses and fantasies.

Furthermore, other studies have found that incarceration suicide among people with epilepsy is especially high, especially among those who are also depressed. Epileptic prisoners tend to be more depressed and suicidal, and to have drinking problems.

Epistles   Seneca, Roman statesman, philosopher, and author, in his famous *Epistles* refers to a desire that seemed to possess many at the time—a morbid longing for death (*affectus qui multos occupavit, libide moriendi*). Seneca was tutor and trusted advisor to Emperor NERO until he fell from Nero's favor and was obliged to commit suicide in A.D. 65.

See also SENECA, LUCIUS ANNAEUS.

equivalents of suicide   Actions such as drinking, smoking, substance abuse and reckless driving that may reflect an unconscious wish to die.

SIGMUND FREUD believed that everyone has a desire to totally destroy themselves. He thought that some people are driven to suicide consciously, whereas others seek more subtle methods without understanding what they are doing. On the other hand, certain people can perceive the consequences of their self-destructive urges and control these negative impulses fairly well, to live normal, happy lives.

Such "suicide equivalents" are sometimes labeled by experts as a partial suicide, a subintentioned suicide, a submeditated suicide, indirect self-destructive behavior or a suicide equivalent, respectively. Authorities such as Norman L. Farberow have long insisted that the definition of who and what constitutes a suicide should include the numberless, diverse group of individuals engaged in life-shortening activities. While these kinds of death are not ruled "suicides," they represent cases where definite, unconscious lethal intention is involved.

See also ABUSE, SUBSTANCE; DAREDEVILS.

equivocal deaths   A death in which the cause is uncertain or unclear. The PSYCHOLOGICAL AUTOPSY procedure often makes possible a decision as to the cause of death. This usually proves therapeutic for grieving survivors.

Erasmus, Desiderius (1466–1536)   Dutch humanist scholar and writer who explains in *Funus* (*The Funeral*) why God meant death to be an agony and explains further that he did this "lest men far and wide commit suicide." Yet Erasmus had said otherwise in his well-known *The Praise of Folly* (1509), wherein he commends those who would voluntarily kill themselves to be rid of a miserable and troublesome world,

considering them, wiser than those who are unwilling to die and want to live longer. His *Encomium Moriae* (*The Praise of Folly*) was a satire on the state of Europe in his time; it became a best seller, sometimes called "*In* Praise of Folly."

Eskimos and suicide   The suicide rate for Alaskan Natives is twice that of the U.S. population, and in western Alaska, the Eskimo suicide rates are even higher. The most common method of suicide among many Alaskan natives is hanging, although other Eskimo groups also use drowning and guns. Motives include illness or old age, unhappy love affairs, and depression.

Certain Eskimo civilizations practiced suicide motivated by social concern. Because these people lived in regions where the food supply was limited, aged members of the group sometimes would deliberately wander off and freeze to death, in order that the others might sustain themselves with whatever food was available.

The Iguliic Eskimos believed that a violent death was a guarantee the individual would end up in paradise, which they called the Land of Day. In contrast, those who died peacefully from natural causes were consigned to eternal claustrophobia in the Narrow Land.

Esprit des lois   Influential book by French writer Charles-Louis de Secondat, baron de la Brède et de Montesquieu, who theorized that the occurrence of suicide among different people was due to climate influence combined with certain cultural factors.

The baron was born in the Château de la Brède near Bordeaux on January 18, 1689. His family was of noble rank; his grandfather was president of the Bordeaux parliament, his father was a member of the royal bodyguard, and his mother, who died when he was age 11, traced her ancestry to an old English family. Young Charles de la Brède, as he was then known, was sent to the Oratorian College at Juilly, where he received a classical education in which religion was not important. When, at 25 he returned home after being called to the bar, he received from his paternal uncle the style and title of Baron de Montesquieu, by which he was afterward known, and became councillor of the Bordeaux parliament.

In *Esprit des lois,* the baron expressed his belief that the English willed themselves to die without reason, seemingly in the midst of happiness, while the Romans committed suicide as a result of their education. Montesquieu concluded that English suicides were the result of a malady caused by the effect of climate on the body and mind. He reasoned, therefore, that suicide should not be punishable. His view reflects the trends of opinion about suicide that had been developing up to his time.

Esquirol, Jean-Etienne-Dominique (1772–1840)

French psychiatrist who described the difference between mental deficiency and insanity, and who believed suicide was almost always triggered by insanity. He outlined his beliefs on suicide, in which genetics and a person's individual disposition played a role, in *Des maladies mentales.* It was the first book to espouse an objective and rational view of mental disorders. He interviewed a number of people who attempted suicide, and worked with many inmates in prisons to develop his theories.

Essais   Michel Eyquem de Montaigne, in his *Essais,* wrote that death is "not a remedy for one malady only, but for all ills. It is a very secure haven, never to be feared and often to be sought. It is all one whether man ends his life or endures it; whether he ends it before it has run its course or whether he waits for it to end; no matter whence the end comes, it is always his own; no matter where the thread snaps, it's the end of the road."

Montaigne, however, ultimately wonders what situations can truly justify the act of killing oneself. Since there are so many sudden changes in life, it is difficult to judge at what point a person is really without hope. "I have seen a hundred hares save themselves, even in the greyhounds' jaws," he wrote.

The French essayist concludes that the only acceptable justifications for suicide are unsupportable pain or a worse death.

ethics and morality of suicide   The controversy concerning the ethics of suicide has long raged not only among philosophers, but among religious disciplines as well. ALBERT CAMUS, in his *The Myth of Sysiphus,* wrote that "There is but one philosophical problem: whether or not to commit suicide." Sir Thomas Browne, in *Religio Medici* (written in 1635 and published in 1642), stated that: "Herein are they not extreme that can allow a man to be his own assassin and so highly extoll the end by suicide of CATO." The linguist, David Daube, writes in *Philosophy and Public Affairs* (1972): ". . . the history of the word 'suicide'—and a strange one it is, mirroring the flow of civilizations and ideologies as well as the vagaries of the fate and fame of individual authors." Donald Attwater, in *The Penguin Dictionary of Saints* (1965), writes about Saint Pelagia (ca. 304), a 15-year-old Christian girl who lived in Antioch during the persecution of Christians by Diocletian. When soldiers broke into her home to seize her, she eluded them and "in order to avoid outrage," she jumped to her death from the housetop. She is venerated by Catholics as a maiden martyr, an example of death before dishonor, despite once-harsh religious laws with regard to suicide.

As John L. McIntosh states in *Research on Suicide* (1985): "Recently, those controversies have been brought to the fore by many forces: changes in resuscitation and life-preserving technologies, longer life expectancies, publicized 'rational' suicides, and 'how-to' manuals (providing explicit and specific information regarding methods of suicide) which have been published in several countries."

In addition, literature and the media have provided instances concerning easy and accepted suicide.

Indeed, complex ethical, moral, and religious views on suicide, along with legal arguments, deal with topics such as the determination of the point of death and life, abortion, and EUTHANASIA. Such ethical and moral disagreements continue as both suicide *prevention* agencies and suicide *assisting* groups still exist today.

Society has not been able or willing as yet to resolve (and in certain cases even consider) these difficult ethical and moral problems as they relate to the issue of suicide. This ethical-moral-religious-social ambivalence regarding suicide stands in the way of understanding fully what Albert Camus called a "fatal game that leads from lucidity in the face of existence to flight from light."

Europe Despite striking cultural differences in suicide rates, the basic relationships of the major demographic variables for the United States are also found in most European countries. The motives and methods of suicide victims vary, as do contemporary cultural attitudes toward suicide. (Attitudes in general are more tolerant toward suicide than in the past; still, many cultures and religions continue to view self-destruction as an abomination.)

The nations of Eastern Europe have strikingly higher suicide rates than countries in the West. The highest rates occur in the Lithuania (43.7 per 100,000) followed by the RUSSIAN FEDERATION (37.1 per 100,000), BELARUS (35.5), Estonia (34.0), HUNGARY (33.9), and Latvia (32.8). Lithuanian men kill themselves at a rate of 73.8 per 100,000, closely followed by men in the Russian Federation at 62.6.

The highest rates of suicide in Western Europe are GERMANY (28.8 per 100,000), followed by FINLAND (24.2), BELGIUM (21.5), SWITZERLAND (20.4), and AUSTRIA (19.5).

Countries of Europe with the lowest alleged suicide rates include AZERBAIJAN (.65 per 100,000), ARMENIA (1.8), Tajikistan (3.4), GREECE (3.9), and Georgia (4.3). However, extremely low rates may have more to do with faulty reporting rates than actual suicide rates.

See also GLOBAL SUICIDE.

Eusebius, Bishop of Caesarea (A.D. 260–?341) Catholic bishop and historian who focused considerable attention on church martyrs. His history offers many examples treated at length, and his *Martyrs of Palestine* was written in several editions over a period of years. In *The Ecclesiastical History,* he relates tales of Christians about to be tortured who chose instead to commit suicide, "regarding death as a prize snatched from the wickedness of evil men." Voluntary martyrdom was common among the early Christians.

Eusebius also wrote a number of other works, including theological treatises and works on Christian scripture.

euthanasia Term derived from the Greek word meaning "good death" to describe a death caused by someone other than the deceased as a way of relieving suffering. Also called "mercy killing," euthanasia is an extremely controversial act still debated on religious, political, and moral grounds.

There is a difference between euthanasia and ASSISTED SUICIDE. In the former, a person other than the deceased performs an act that results in the person's death. In assisted suicide, someone helps the deceased commit suicide, but the person technically dies by his own hand. An example of assisted suicide would be a person who dies by swallowing pills supplied by a doctor for the purpose of causing death.

The law permits patients or their surrogates to withhold or withdraw unwanted medical treatment even if that increases the likelihood that the patient will die—so people cannot be hooked up to machines against their will.

In most cases, the law draws the line at actively causing a person's death. Oregon, Belgium, and the Netherlands are the only three places in the world where laws specifically permit euthanasia or assisted suicide. Oregon permits assisted suicide, whereas Belgium and the Netherlands permit both euthanasia and assisted suicide.

In 1995, Australia's Northern Territory approved a euthanasia bill that went into effect in 1996, but was overturned by the Australian Parliament in 1997. Colombia's Supreme Court ruled in 1997 that penalties for mercy killing should be removed, but the ruling does not go into effect until guidelines (still to be drafted) are approved by the Colombian Congress.

Neither suicide nor attempted suicide is criminalized anywhere in the United States or in many other countries. When penalties against attempted suicide were removed, legal scholars made it clear that this was not done for the purpose of permitting suicide. Instead, it was intended to prevent suicide. Penalties were removed so people could seek help in dealing with the problems they're facing without risk of being prosecuted if it were discovered that they had attempted suicide. Euthanasia and assisted suicide are not legal (except in Oregon) because they are not private acts. Rather, they involve one person facilitating the death of another. The concern by opponents is that assisted suicide or euthanasia could lead to abuse, exploitation, or erosion of care for the elderly or handicapped.

Two types of euthanasia are usually mentioned in professional discussions of termination of life. One is typed as "active" or direct—where life is ended by "direct" intervention, such as administering to a patient a lethal dose of a drug. The other is called "passive" or indirect—i.e., where death results from withdrawal of life-support or life-sustaining medications. Dr. Christiaan Barnard, who received international acclaim and recognition for pioneering work in heart transplant surgery, writes in *Good Life, Good Death: A Doctor's Case for Euthanasia and Suicide* that: "Indeed, even though many doctors will not admit it, passive euthanasia is accepted medical practice—a common occurrence in wards where patients live out their final hours."

The concept of "death with dignity" is today an ever-increasing focus of debate. Reasons for this concern are medical advances in technology that have brought about marked demographic changes in population(s) and a significant increase in the number of retired/aged persons.

In 1935, the British Voluntary Euthanasia Society was formed, followed by the founding in 1938 of the Euthanasia Society of America. In 1980, the World Federation of Right-to-Die Societies was founded, with 27 groups from 18 countries joining, and by the 1980s the number of pro-euthanasia groups trebled. Prominent U.S. supporters of euthanasia have included Dr. Walter C. Alvarez, Robert Frost, Dr. Henry Sloane Coffin, Dr. Harry Emerson Fosdick, and Margaret Sanger.

Euthanasia Education Council (EEC) Established in 1969, the EEC was instrumental in distributing more than a quarter of a million copies of the Living Will in an effort to ensure a patient's right to a natural death, unencumbered by heroic efforts or unnecessary resuscitation. The Euthanasia Education Council later became known as Concern for Dying; in 1991, the organization changed its name to Choice in Dying, and then to Partnership for Caring: America's Voices for the Dying.

The organization has evolved into a nonprofit organization devoted to raising expectations and increasing consumer demand for excellence in care near the end of life. The group operates the only national crisis and information hotline dealing with end-of-life issues, and provides state-specific living wills and medical powers of attorney (also called advance directives).

The group promotes accessibility to high-quality, comprehensive palliative care, including hospice care, and distributes publications and videos that offer practical information for consumers about how to get the best possible end-of-life care. The group offers education and consultation to doctors, nurses, social workers, attorneys, and clergy, and trains corporate staff to help their employees deal with end-of-life decisions.

In addition, Partnership for Caring tracks and monitors all state and federal legislation and significant court cases related to end-of-life care.

Until 1979, the Society for the Right to Die and the EEC operated as separate arms of the U.S. right-to-die movement. They shared the same offices in Manhattan and concentrated on passive EUTHANASIA, and focused its efforts on enactment of state right-to-die laws, while the nonprofit Council stressed educational and philosophical issues of "dying with dignity." The close working relationship between the two groups ended in 1979 when the EEC stopped financial support of the society, primarily because of EEC's disapproval of "indiscriminate or ill-conceived legislation." EEC became convinced that such legislation could limit rather than broaden a person's decision-making power.

For contact information, see Appendix I.

excommunication When the teachings of ST. AUGUSTINE and other early church fathers were incorporated into the laws of the ROMAN CATHOLIC CHURCH (and later the Anglican Church), suicide was declared an act inspired by the devil. Church councils proclaimed it a mortal sin, and ruled that the bodies of people who committed suicide be denied Christian burial. Even suicide attempters were excommunicated.

However, church law made a distinction between the suicides of sane and insane people, and also exempted young children from the penalties of the church laws.

These religious doctrines against the act of suicide still remain in effect in the Roman Catholic Church and in many Protestant churches, but today many priests and ministers usually are more tolerant and have found ways to modify them in most circumstances.

Increasingly, church officials are coming to recognize suicide as not only a religious question, but also a major social and medical problem. Groups such as the Anglican Church have established special commissions to consider the revision of harsh religious laws concerning suicide. The Lutheran Church in America does not view suicide as an "unforgiveable sin," and a Lutheran who commits suicide is not denied a Christian burial.

However, in ISLAM, suicide is the gravest of sins. Suicide is forbidden in the QUR'AN, which decries that taking one's own life is an act worse than homicide. Paradoxically, Muslim suicide terrorists are not uncommon in their zeal to die in a *Jihad*, or holy war. In their mind, this assures them a passport to heaven, despite the fact that the Qur'an contains nothing stating that killing guarantees a passport to heaven.

Judaism, too, considers suicide a sin. Although the Hebrew Bible did not specifically prohibit suicide, subsequent Jewish laws forbade it and denied full religious burial rites to people who took their own lives.

JEWS over the years, however, have recognized and honored "heroic" suicides—that is, self-destruction to avoid being murdered by enemies, forced into idol worship, sold into slavery, or sexually abused. In fact, dying with honor to preserve one's beliefs and affirm one's freedom to control life and death has continued throughout Jewish history, from MASADA in A.D. 73 to the Nazi concentration camp in TREBLINKA during World War II.

The Japanese at one time ritualized suicide through the ceremonial death with honor of SEPPUKU, or *hara-kiri* as practiced by the samurai, or members of the military class. *Hara-kiri* was officially outlawed in 1868, yet the tradition of suicide in the name of honor still influences certain Japanese practices. This ancient glorification of death with honor (such as the Japanese soldiers who died as KAMIKAZE PILOTS during World War II) may be responsible, at least in part, for the high rate of suicide among young Japanese today.

exile Self-imposed exile in some societies was an alternative to suicide. These voluntary exiles were socially acceptable for example, the Tixopia would set out to sea by canoe, a voyage likely to result in death.

existentialism The modern philosophical movement founded by Søren Kierkegaard, developed in GERMANY by Martin Heidegger and Karl Jaspers, and popularized after World War II by Jean Paul Sartre and ALBERT CAMUS in France.

Existentialism which embraces both religious mysticism (Kierkegaard) and atheism (Sartre), is a philosophy of crisis. It regards the whole of human and cosmic existence as a series of critical situations, each demanding the whole inner resources of the individual for its resolution; crisis follows crisis to the ultimate end in death. Despair and disillusion are the chief characteristics of existentialism. Camus saw the goal of existentialism as establishing whether suicide was necessary in a world without God.

existential suicide Completing suicide because "life isn't worth it."

EXIT Nonprofit Scottish group (formerly the Voluntary Euthanasia Society of Scotland) founded in 1935, that then broke away from the English society to become independent and to publish *How to Die with Dignity,* the first self-deliverance manual in the world. In 1993, EXIT published *Departing Drugs.* Both books are not available to the general public or minors.

From 1992 to 1995 the group sponsored research into living wills, clarifying the pros and cons of such documents, and published *Collected Living Wills,* the first such international collection.

expendable child syndrome An adolescent or child's belief that parents wish the child was dead.

explosives Most youths who complete suicide do so with guns and explosives. HANGING is the second most common method, while taking pills and poisons is the third. Young girls who kill themselves do so most often with pills and poisons, but in recent years, guns and explosives have become the second most common method. Hanging is the third method most often used by young girls.

On the other hand, young men and women who attempt suicide (but do not succeed) generally do not use such violent methods as guns, explosives, or hanging. Most attempters (without fatal results) have taken BARBITURATES or other drugs, poison or slashed their wrists—all methods that allow time for rescue.

extended family A particular way of life, in which three generations and sometimes even an aunt, uncle, and cousins in addition, lived under one roof. Many social scientists and suicidologists believe that the extended family served to protect each member from self-destructive impulses. Today, the nuclear family (with both parents working or a single-parent family) offers less support and protection.

Just how much the demise of extended families influences today's alarming rise in suicide among young people is difficult to measure.

facilitated suicide Completion of a suicide because of clinician indifference. This is also known as an "iatrogenic" suicide.

facilitating suicide The legal term for helping in a suicide completion.

Fadlan, Ibn Arab chronicler who in A.D. 921 was sent by the caliph of Baghdad with an embassy to the king of the Bulgars of the Middle Volga. Ibn Fadlan wrote an account of his journeys with the embassy, called a *Risala*. This *Risala* is of great value as a history, although it is clear in some places that inaccuracies and Ibn Fadlan's own prejudices have slanted the account.

During the course of his journey, Ibn Fadlan met a people called the Rus, a group of Swedish origin who acted as traders in the Bulgar capital. In the *Risala*, Ibn Fadlan describes a Rus funeral, which includes the suicide of a slave girl.

When a Rus chieftain died, his female slaves were asked who wanted to be buried with him. The slave girl who volunteered would then be cared for by two young women for 10 days, who watched over her and accompanied her everywhere. Garments were made for the dead chieftain as the doomed slave drank and sang every day. After the 10th day, the slave girl was killed and both the chieftain and the slave were then cremated on board a ship.

This experience is similar to other forms of institutional suicide practiced among both the Thracians and the Hindus, each with customs in which a widow or concubine offered her life when the husband or master died.

fallacies about suicide See MYTHS CONCERNING SUICIDE.

Falret, Jean-Pierre French psychiatrist who published in 1822 the first study of suicide that made use of statistical data, though admittedly on a small scale. In his *De l'hypochondrie et du suicide*, Falret classified causal factors that may lead to suicide under four headings:

1. Predisposing—heredity, temperament, climate;
2. Accidental direct—passions, domestic troubles, etc.;
3. Accidental indirect—bodily pain, illness;
4. General civilization, civil disorders, religious fanaticism.

Falret's work was yet another step in helping authorities realize that suicide resulted from the interaction of many factors.

fame During the 1830s in France, suicide actually became fashionable among young romantics. In the case of one man, charged with pushing his pregnant mistress into the Seine, he defended his action by saying, "We live in an age of suicide; this woman gave herself to death." For young poets, novelists, dramatists, painters, and members of countless suicide clubs, to die by one's own hand was a sure way to fame. In a satirical novel published in 1844, *Jerome Paturot a la recherche d'une position sociale*, the protagonist observes that "a suicide establishes a man. Alive one is nothing; dead one becomes a hero . . . All suicides are successful; the papers take them up;

people feel for them. I must decidedly make my preparations."

familicide suicide   Killing of one or more family members by a person who then goes on to commit suicide.

family therapy   A significant class of risk factors for suicide involves family problems such as poor communication, disagreements, and lack of cohesive values and goals and of common activities. Suicidal children and adolescents often feel that they are isolated within the family, show problems in independence, and view themselves as expendable to the family, a perception that is a motivating force for suicide. Family therapy with suicidal children and adolescents is an important way to treat these problems and to improve effective family problem-solving and conflict resolution, so that blame is not directed toward the suicidal child or teen.

Family therapy examines the role of the suicidal member in the overall psychological well-being of the whole family; it also examines the role of the entire family in perpetrating the problems of the suicidal person. This type of therapy can be effective because a family's patterns of behavior influences the individual, and therefore may need to be a part of the treatment plan. In family therapy, the unit of treatment isn't just the person—even if only a single person is interviewed—it is the set of relationships in which the person is imbedded.

Family therapy is brief, solution-focused, and specific, and has attainable therapeutic goals. With family therapy, suicide survivors can be taught that the future can bring resolution to what may seem an inextricable plight.

Cognitive-behavioral approaches with suicidal children and adolescents and their families try to reframe their understanding of family problems, change the family style of poor problem-solving techniques, and encourage positive family interactions. Time-limited home-based intervention to reduce suicidal thoughts in children and teens and to improve family functioning is of some help for children and adolescents without major depressive disorder. Psychoeducational approaches to reduce the extent of expressed anger may be helpful in lowering risk for suicidal behavior in children and adolescents.

Family therapy is also used to help the surviving family members of a person who has completed suicide. This type of therapy can help family members move beyond the death. With this type of treatment, family members come to see that suicide happens to people from all walks of life, to people much like themselves from families much like their own.

farmers   During late 1985 and throughout 1986, America's farm belt was being described as a "time bomb" because so many farmers were committing suicide. Debt-ridden midwestern and southern farmers were starting to feel the pressures and anxieties that accompanied low crop prices, relatively high interest rates, and low land values. These and other more subtle political factors began combining to force people off farms that, in many instances, had been in their families for generations. Land was being lost in forced sales and equipment and livestock was seized.

Farmers are not totally unique in such a situation. There is tremendous stress and pain to persons when economic and social dislocation occurs on a large scale, whether in rural or urban areas. But the farmers' predicament—which generates an additional stress element—is that in such crises they not only lose their farms, but their businesses as well. Moreover, the farmer who loses his job may lose one that was held by his father, his grandfather, and other ancestors for 100 years or more.

In mid-February 1986, more than 65,000 farmers around the country received letters from the FHA notifying them that they must restructure or renegotiate their farm loan payments or face foreclosure. The federal agency, with some 2,000 field offices in the United States, said it took the drastic action to recover $5.8 billion in delinquent loans.

As financial pressures eased somewhat among U.S. farmers into the 1990s, they worsened for British farmers, who faced continual losses from mad cow disease and then foot-and-mouth disease, followed by floods and storms of biblical proportions. By the turn of the 21st century, British farmers were committing suicide in record numbers. Registered suicides among farmers, horticulturists, and farm managers look set to be their worst for more than a decade, and were so high that more than one person a week in the industry was registered as a suicide in 1999.

fear of punishment   In some young people, the fear of punishment (real or imagined) may cause them to think obsessively of suicide as the only solution to their problems.

In families where there is little or no communication, violence sometimes becomes the only interchange between parent and child. Children who are punished regularly (and often brutally) come to think they can do nothing right. They also discover quickly that their parents are easiest to live with after they've gotten rid of their aggression through such abuse.

These child-victims sometimes become self-destructive. They anticipate their parents' abuse by punishing themselves. Then, tragically, one day they self-inflict the final, lethal punishment.

For the troubled, overly anxious or depressed young person, fear of separation can become quite morbid and totally devastating. Routine separations experienced by most of us in life, such as going to kindergarten, going off to college, breaking up with a girl- or boyfriend, moving to a new neighborhood or town—are difficult enough, but for the insecure, highly sensitive child they can prove debilitating.

Sometimes the young person affected by these fears leaves clues that indicate potential self-destructive action, such as broad hints or subtle changes in behavior.

female suicides   An American woman attempts suicide every 78 seconds, and succeeds in taking one life every 90 minutes. Although many effective treatments exist, suicide in women remains a much underrecognized, underdiagnosed, and undertreated problem.

Suicide is more common among women who are single, recently separated, divorced, or widowed, and peaks between the ages of 45 and 54, and again after age 75. The triggering life events for women who attempt suicide tend to be interpersonal losses or crises in significant social or family relationships.

Experts believe that women attempt suicide twice as much as men because of higher rates of mood disorders such as major DEPRESSION and seasonal affective disorder among women. Indeed, between 60 percent and 80 percent of women experience transient depression, and 10 to 15 percent of women develop clinical depression during the postpartum period. Experts believe women aren't as likely as men to complete the suicide attempt because women are more likely than men to have stronger social supports, to feel that their relationships are deterrents to suicide, and to seek psychiatric and medical intervention. Some researchers estimate that, among young people, as many as nine times more girls than boys attempt suicide without completing it.

Although women attempt suicide more often, men complete suicide at a rate four times that of women. The 1998 suicide rate among U.S. women was 4.4 per 100,000, compared to 18.6 for men.

Fifth Commandment   The fifth (or sixth, per the King James Version) of 10 commandments ("Thou shalt not kill") delivered by God to Moses on Mt. Sinai, according to the Old Testament of the Bible.

Organized religions were the first to condemn suicide. Christians believed life to be a gift from God, and that only God may take life away. Self-death also violated the Fifth Commandment.

However, the Judeo-Christian tradition, as well as Islamic tradition, maintains that suicide in the form of martyrdom was permissible. The Jewish religion also believes that suicide is acceptable if carried out to prevent torture, rape, or slavery. King Saul, for example, fell on his sword after defeat in battle. The mass self-destruction to prevent capture of the defenders of the MASADA, a Jewish fortress besieged by Romans in A.D. 72–73, was also considered a heroic action.

Fiji Islands   Fiji Indians have the world's highest female suicide rates, and the overall figures are among the highest anywhere as well. Most recent statistics suggest that suicide is growing fastest among adults with dependent children and among the children themselves. The latest figures show more than 100 people committed suicide in the year 2000 and more than 100 others attempted suicide, but experts say actual numbers are much higher.

There is speculation in Fiji that the high youth suicide rate is a consequence of a school examination system that discriminates against Indians (44 percent of the population) in the awarding of scholarships and places in schools.

Clinical depression associated with suicide in the Western world is mostly absent in Pacific suicides, and few of the victims are mentally unbalanced. Instead, a major cause of the rise in suicides has been the erosion of social structures and values, leaving many young people insecure.

A study in the *Journal of the American Academy of Child and Adolescent Psychiatry* noted suicide among native populations is a significant problem worldwide—but especially in the Pacific. Anthropologically, a common thread among these groups is the relatively sudden contact with Western culture, domination by the Western culture, and greater or lesser degrees of acculturative stress.

But suicide has long been a part of the Fiji culture. Early Fiji Islanders forced the many wives of a tribal chieftain to kill themselves when he died.

The women would actually compete with one another in the rush to destroy themselves, believing that the first to die would become the chieftain's favorite wife in "the world of the spirits."

See also SOUTH PACIFIC ISLANDS AND SUICIDE; SUTTEE.

filicide-suicide   Killing one or more offspring by a person who then commits suicide.

Final Exit: The Practicalities of Self-Deliverance and Assisted Suicide for the Dying
Best-selling book by DEREK HUMPHRY, founder of the HEMLOCK SOCIETY, which was published in 1991 in the face of heated controversy and national debate. *Final Exit* was written as a handbook for people who wanted to end their suffering from unbearable pain due to terminal or incurable illness. Attempts to ban the book in the United States, Australia, and New Zealand failed, but *Final Exit* remains banned in France.

The concise manual includes descriptions about:

- How to commit suicide with sleeping pills, preferably with the aid of a loved one
- a chart listing lethal doses of 14 drugs
- legal considerations, life insurance, and living wills
- finding the right doctor, hospice care, and pain control
- letters to leave behind
- how to write a self-deliverance checklist
- psychological support groups for the dying
- suicide hotlines for depression

The book sold more than a million copies worldwide, spending 18 weeks on the *New York Times*'s best-sellers list. It has since been published in translations in every major world language.

Finland   Finland has historically ranked high in both homicide and suicide among the world's cultures. WORLD HEALTH ORGANIZATION (WHO) statistics for 1998 show the country's suicide rate per 100,000 population to be 24.2. The male suicide rate was a very high 38.3, while the female rate was only 10.1. Highest among listed age groups was 45 to 54. The figures for young men who complete suicide are particularly high (one in four suicides are committed by a man under the age of 35). Nonetheless, the number of suicides, notably those of men, has been declining steadily since the peak year (1990); however, the figure for women has remained unchanged.

Because Finland had one of the highest suicide rates in the world, the country participated in a 10-year suicide prevention program with WHO help from 1986 to 1996. The project's goal was a 20 percent reduction in the incidence of suicide. The final outcome was a 9 percent reduction over the entire duration of the project (from 1987 to 1996) and an 18 percent reduction from 1990—the peak year—to 1996.

In 1996, a total of 1,247 people (956 men and 282 women) took their own lives in Finland. For every other woman and one in four men, the means of suicide was poisoning, mostly with medications.

firearms suicide   Use of a handgun, rifle, or shotgun as a way to complete suicide. Firearms are currently the method most often used to complete suicide by all groups (men, women, young, old, white, nonwhite)—and the rates are increasing. Today, firearms are used in almost 60 percent of all suicides, accounting for more than 18,000 deaths each year in the United States. Firearms are now the most common method of suicide even for women and for boys and girls age 10 to 14. More than half of the gun deaths in the United States are suicides, and more people die from firearm suicides than from homicides.

The odds that potentially suicidal adolescents will kill themselves double when a gun is kept in the home. The availability of a gun increases the likelihood of a person dying from suicide five-fold; if the gun is unlocked, sixfold, and if loaded, ninefold. The states with the highest suicide rates are Nevada, Montana, Arizona, New Mexico, and Colorado. All are states where guns are a part of the culture.

States with stricter gun control laws have lower rates of suicide. The states with the lowest suicide rates are New Jersey, New York, Massachusetts, Rhode Island, and Washington, D.C.—coincidentally, the states with some of the strictest gun laws in the country.

Although most gun owners reportedly keep a firearm in their home for protection or self-defense, 83 percent of gun-related deaths in these homes are the result of a suicide, often by someone other than the gun owner.

And yet, fewer than 10 percent of people who complete suicide buy a gun with the specific intent of killing themselves.

Emergency rooms across the nation verify that suicide attempts with firearms are almost always fatal. From 1980 to 1992, the suicide rate for 15-to-19-year-olds increased 28.3 percent, and rose among 10-to-14-year-olds by 120 percent. For black males aged 15 to 19, the suicide rate increased 165.3 percent from 1980 to 1992.

The increased rate of completed suicides may be attributed to the use of more lethal means during attempts, specifically firearms. For example, in Oregon from 1988 to 1993, 78.2 percent of suicide attempts with firearms were fatal, but only 0.4 percent of suicide attempts by drug overdose were fatal.

Flaubert, Gustave (1821–1880)   French writer whose most famous novel, *Madame Bovary* (1857), describes Emma Bovary's attempts to escape her drab existence through adultery and finally suicide. The story details the romantically motivated, marital indiscretions of a wife in a French provincial town; it is a condemnation of what he sees as the petty, drab lives of the French bourgeois class.

Flaubert confessed in his letters that as a young man "I dreamed of suicide." He wrote that he and his young provincial friends, "lived in a strange world, I assure you; we swung between madness and suicide; some of them killed themselves . . . another strangled himself with his tie, several died of debauchery in order to escape boredom; it was beautiful!"

Gustave Flaubert was a second son; his father was chief surgeon at the Hôtel-Dieu in Rouen and his mother was the daughter of a wealthy doctor. He began writing at a very early age, and published his first work when he was only 16. A solitary boy with a rich imagination, in 1841 Flaubert entered the faculty of Law in Paris. He was forced to withdraw from studies when he discovered that he was afflicted with epilepsy. Although he continued to write, none of his major works were published during this period.

He died suddenly of a stroke; his unfinished final work, *Bouvard and Pecuchet,* was posthumously published.

The famous novelist was once asked who the real-life Emma Bovary was. The author smiled wistfully and said, *"I* am Madame Bovary."

follow-up, of suicidal persons The primary goal of any suicide prevention worker is to stop the caller from killing himself. Remaking the caller's personality, curing all his troubles, no matter how serious, is not the major intention of a suicide prevention service. In fact, effective action has a limited goal, to provide an immediate, ready contact between the highly disturbed person calling a 24-hour "hotline" or "lifeline" and the community's helping agencies that are available.

Fortunately, people are not permanently suicidal. Even for the most despairing person, the suicidal mood ebbs and flows. In the majority of cases, staffers can provide the tension relief needed to ease a critical suicidal situation. They can then "arrange" things for the suicidal caller; that is, set up an interview with a staff psychiatrist, psychologist, social worker, or volunteer. Sometimes a meeting is arranged between the suicidal person and a "significant other." (The

telephone therapist determines who this might be: father, mother, wife, lover, or whoever.) The idea is to avert the critical moment that will drive the caller to the brink of self-destruction, then provide the necessary follow-up help as quickly as possible.

Each suicide prevention group necessarily tailors its service to its own needs. There is no single pattern or organization yet proved to be better or more successful than another. Some services operate autonomously; others are a unit of the community's mental health facility. A service can also be part of an emergency hospital or tied to the local university.

The majority of suicidal callers want and need help. When questioned a short time after their calls, 87 percent of the people said that they had been helped. Questioned a long time after their distress calls, 80 percent still maintained that they had been helped. Twenty-eight percent said that the service had saved their lives; 34 percent said the facility "might" have saved their lives.

The suicide prevention center must be thoughtfully created, properly administered, and generously supported in order to extend maximum understanding and assistance.

forfeiture, law of According to Henry de Bracton, legal authority of mid-13th century in England, an ordinary suicide forfeited his goods, while a person who killed himself to avoid a felony conviction forfeited both goods and land. This "law of forfeiture" remained in force throughout England into the 19th century. It was, however, often circumvented through the claim of insanity.

Forrestal, James (1892–1949) Former U.S. banker and cabinet officer in the Franklin D. Roosevelt and Harry S. Truman administrations, Forrestal left banking as America's entry into World War II loomed closer. He became undersecretary of the navy (1940–42), secretary of the navy (1942–47) and first secretary of defense (1947–49).

President Truman was unhappy with Forrestal's performance as secretary of defense, and on March 28, 1949, forced him to resign from office. Soon afterward, Forrestal, suffering from depression, was admitted to Bethesda Hospital, where he committed suicide by throwing himself out of a 16th-floor hospital window on May 22, 1949.

Foster, Vincent Walker, Jr. Deputy legal counsel for President Bill Clinton who was found dead in a roadside park from an apparently self-inflicted gunshot wound at 6 P.M. on July 20, 1993. Foster's body was found in an overgrown area at Fort Marcy, a small Civil War park across the Potomac River from Washington, D.C., in suburban Virginia. U.S. Park Police found a pistol in Foster's hand and quickly ruled the death a suicide. Reports of serious depression, together with prescriptions for antidepressants, supported that finding.

However, the nature of his death and his connection to Whitewater, Travelgate, and other political scandals set off a swirl of controversies suggesting murder and a politically motivated coverup. Rumors about his death shook the stock market and dogged the president, as Foster came to be seen by many as the key to dark secrets about some of the most powerful people in the world.

Foster was a friend of the Clinton family and former law partner of Hillary Rodham Clinton. Married and the father of three children, Foster was the number two White House lawyer. His death stunned the president's staff members, who said they were unaware of anything that might have caused Foster to take his own life.

France Official, legal and ecclesiastical attitudes toward suicide were conservative in France until well into the 18th century. Suicide was, in fact, equated with murder in various countries in Europe. In France, the corpse was treated accordingly; the body was dragged through the streets, head downward on a hurdle, and *then* hanged on a gallows.

According to the French Criminal Ordinance of August 1670 the body of a suicide was still required to be dragged through the streets and then thrown into a sewer or the town dump. Despite the law, however, many such cases were overlooked, and such severe penalties were not carried out.

In Toulouse, for example, the punishment of dragging the corpse was imposed in 1742 and again in 1768, but the suicides occurred in jail and the victims were either convicted of or indicted for a crime. Spectator revulsion against the practice ended the penalty after 1768, although burial in consecrated ground was often denied the person who committed suicide in this predominantly Catholic nation.

In 1822, studies of suicide in Paris suggested that suicide reports were probably understated for several reasons. First, relatives in certain cases tried to prevent a family disgrace by having the death attributed to some other cause, such as insanity, and, reported suicides did not consider the large number of attempted suicides.

Another extensive study concerning suicide in France was done by Brierre de Boismont, and was considered an important contribution to the problem of suicide in the mid-19th century. In his treatise *DU SUICIDE ET DE LA FOLIE SUICIDE,* published in 1856, de Boismont not only used statistics extensively, but he also questioned 265 people who had either planned or attempted suicide. On the basis of his comprehensive study, de Boismont denied that all suicides were caused by insanity. He believed other important causes included alcoholism, illness, family troubles, love problems, and poverty. His findings also brought him close to a sociological explanation of suicide. For instance, he discovered a higher proportion of unmarried persons, of old people, and of men. More generally, he saw suicide as a consequence of changes in society leading to social disorganization and to alienation for many people.

It is obvious that Brierre de Boismont and other 19th-century investigators of suicide were heading toward ÉMILE DURKHEIM's now-famous conclusion stated in *Le Suicide* in 1897: that suicide will not be widely prevalent in a society that is well-integrated politically, economically, and socially.

Recent statistics from 1997 indicate that France has a suicide rate slightly lower than that of other European countries, at 19.2 per 100,000. French men kill themselves at a rate of 28.4 per 100,000 compared to a female rate of 10.1. This total overall suicide rate is thus lower than that of GERMANY (28.8), BELGIUM (21.5), and AUSTRIA (19.5), but higher than that of ITALY (8.3), PORTUGAL (5.7), and GREECE (3.9). Statistics are provided by the World Health Organization (WHO).

French Criminal Ordinance of August 1670
This infamous law required, among other things, that the body of a person who committed suicide be dragged through the streets and then thrown into a sewer or onto the town dump. Despite the law, cases were sometimes ignored and the severe penalties were not applied. The penalty was last carried out in Toulouse, in 1768.

See also FRANCE.

Freud, Sigmund (1856–1939)
Austrian psychiatrist of Jewish descent, founder of modern psychoanalysis. Although much of Freud's work was controversial, particularly his theories about children's sexuality, his concept of the unconscious mind underlies most modern inquiries into human behavior and motives.

Concerning the act of suicide, Freud viewed the urge to kill oneself as essentially a problem within the individual. He believed that life and death forces are in constant conflict in every person, even though these conflicting forces are unconscious.

On April 27, 1910, the VIENNA PSYCHOANALYTICAL SOCIETY met for a discussion titled "Suicide in Children." Freud said then that in their desire to wean children from their early family life, schools often exposed the immature student too abruptly to the harshness of adult life. He added that too

little was known about suicide but that perhaps the self-destructive action was actually a repudiation of life because of the craving for death. This particular remark, we now know, foreshadowed Freud's later belief in a death instinct.

Sigmund Freud's paper "Beyond the Pleasure Principle" presents his later theory of suicide. He believed there are two distinct kinds of drives: One is the life instinct, or *Eros;* the other, the death, destructive and aggressive drive, or *Thanatos.* There is an ongoing, constant shifting of the balance of power between the two instincts. Eros ages, but ageless Thanatos may assert itself "until it, at length, succeeds in doing the individual to death."

Suicide, as well as homicide, is an aspect of the impulsive destructive action of Thanatos. Murder, Freud believed, is aggression turned upon another; suicide is aggression turned upon oneself. His implied value judgment is that murder should be disapproved and prevented because it is highly destructive. Suicide must also be disapproved and prevented since it is nothing less than murder "in the 180th degree."

Freud was born on May 6, 1856, in Freiberg, the son of Jacob and his third wife, Amalia. While earning his doctorate in medicine, he worked at the Institute of Physiology as a research assistant specializing in neurology. In 1896, he headed the neurological department of the First Public Children's Hospital. In 1900, he wrote *The Interpretation of Dreams,* which formed the basis of his research for the next 40 years. Freud pioneered the idea of the subconscious, and at a time when most doctors believed mental illness was caused by poor genes, Freud argued that patients could be cured of hysteria just by talking with their doctors.

Between 1921 and 1938, Freud wrote various works detailing psychoanalysis's effect on the social world. Freud fled Vienna in the 1938 invasion of Austria, moving to Paris and then to London, where he continued to write.

At the end of his life, Sigmund Freud, in terrible pain from an invasive cancerous epithelioma, murmured to his trusted doctor Max

Schur, "This makes no more sense," and so Schur injected him with a lethal dose of morphine on September 23. He was 83.

friends As they move closer to self-destruction, presuicidal persons of all ages tend to drop their close friends or deliberately to make themselves so obnoxious that the friends drop them. Suicidal patients will often become either very withdrawn or overly aggressive, an important distress signal or warning sign to parents, friends, or associates.

Once people finally decide to complete suicide, they begin to act differently.

Friendship Line for the Elderly, The A national person-to-person service based in San Francisco where trained volunteers regularly call elderly persons to offer emotional support, medication reminders, and safety checks. An offshoot of the city's suicide prevention program started in 1963, this direct service figures importantly in the suicide and mental health education of other minority groups throughout the Bay Area.

Staff members offer consultation, training, and seminars to schools, universities, hospitals, and mental health agencies. The program also includes two drug lines and a Grief Counseling Program for those who have suffered a loss by suicide or other traumatic circumstances.

The Friendship Line is the only nationwide toll-free number offering telephone support to depressed, isolated, abused, and/or suicidal older adults. It is available 24 hours a day, 365 days a year.

The toll-free national number is (800) 971-0016; in San Francisco the number is (415) 752-3778.

frustration The teenage suicide rate has risen to crisis proportions over the past 20 years, and experts believe that a combination of frustration and stress can lead a person to attempt suicide. The rising rate has been explained as a reaction to the stress inherent in adolescence compounded by increasing stress in the environment. Adolescence is a time when ordinary levels of stress are heightened by physical, psychological, emotional, and social frustrations that can lead to violence and aggression.

funerals See BURIAL (FOR SUICIDES).

Funus (The Funeral) In his 1526 colloquy, *Funus,* the Dutch scholar ERASMUS explained why God meant death to be an agony, and said that he did this "lest men far and wide commit suicide. And since, even today, we see so many do violence to themselves, what do you suppose would happen if death weren't horrible? Whenever a servant or even a young son got a thrashing, whenever a wife fell out with her husband, whenever a man lost his money, or something else occurred that upset him, off they'd rush to noose, sword, river, cliff, poison."

Yet, paradoxically, in his *The Praise of Folly* (1509), Erasmus had commended those who voluntarily killed themselves to get rid of a miserable and troublesome world. His earlier writing, *Encomium Miriae (The Praise of Folly),* was intended as a satire on the state of Europe in his time.

Furst, Sidney In a major psychoanalytic article concerning the relationship of suicide method versus motive, "The Psychodynamics of Suicide," Furst and Mortimer Ostrow suggest that the suicidal method is an expression of a sexual wish and/or punishment for a fantasized crime.

In *Suicide in America,* HERBERT HENDIN, M.D., writes: "Without psychodynamic evidence from case material, they (the team of Furst-Ostrow) maintain that male homosexuals, if suicidal, will stab or shoot themselves or arrange to be stabbed or shot as an extreme expression of their wish to be attacked by another man's penis." Hendin concludes that if these writers were correct, homosexuality would be a far more important factor in suicide in the United States than elsewhere in the world, since only in America are guns the major method of suicide.

Furst and Ostrow also regard falling from heights as an expression of sexual guilt for "phallic erection under improper circumstances." Dr. Hendin's rebuttal: "Given the alternative of such unsubstantial speculation . . . psychiatry has settled for the safe but sterile statistical approach that has dominated the subject." Hendin, along with other suicidologists, believes that "Psychodynamic study of the suicidal individual can often provide evidence of the meaning of the choice of a particular method."

Garroway, Dave The original host of TV's *The Today Show,* Garroway left the show in 1961, and was replaced briefly by John Chancellor and then by Hugh Downs. Largely forgotten by the public, Garroway committed suicide on July 21, 1982.

gas Women, more so than men, seem to prefer a passive means of self-destruction. For instance, women will more likely ingest a lethal dose of drugs, swallow pills or poison, or inhale gas rather than shoot or hang themselves. Authorities conclude this may be because women don't usually want to shed their blood or disfigure themselves.

Several types of gas can be used as a way to commit suicide, but these methods are less common than firearms. Women tend to prefer this method of suicide over more violent means. In one study of youth suicide, 78 percent of suicide attempts with firearms were fatal, as compared to 36 percent of attempts with gas poisoning.

Car Exhaust

Car exhaust is a lethal method of suicide with a large proportion of attempters dying. The active ingredient in car exhaust (carbon monoxide) is a colorless, odorless poisonous gas that is produced by the internal combustion engine. Carbon monoxide binds to hemoglobin better than oxygen, so the human body thinks it's oxygen, and breathing continues normally until the person loses consciousness. Breathing carbon monoxide fumes causes headaches, dizziness, weakness, sleepiness, nausea and vomiting, confusion and disorientation. As the level of the gas in the blood rises, the patient becomes confused and clumsy.

Loss of consciousness occurs within a few minutes, and death follows within a half hour.

Suicide by breathing car exhaust is becoming less common with the introduction of catalytic converters, which remove the carbon monoxide from the exhaust. Catalytic converters remove 90 percent of the carbon monoxide; one man survived after breathing exhaust fumes for five hours. A drop in suicides was noticed in the United States with the introduction of the catalytic converter in 1968, although they have now risen again.

Coal Gas

The detoxification of domestic gas (from coal gas with high carbon monoxide content to natural gas) might have reduced the suicide rate in nations where the switch had taken place. It has definitely reduced overall suicide rates in the UNITED KINGDOM and AUSTRALIA, although some researchers believe the reduction was temporary, and has been replaced by other methods. For example, in the 1960s when town gas was widely available in the United Kingdom, using the gas oven was the commonest method of suicide. North Sea gas, which is composed of methane, is nontoxic, and its introduction resulted in a drop in the suicide rate of one-third.

Helium

In addition to being odorless, colorless, and non-flammable, helium is also considered nontoxic, but some people use it to commit suicide. Inhaling helium leads to unconsciousness and death after a few minutes. Helium is used to inflate balloons, and is therefore inexpensive and widely available.

Nitrous Oxide (NO₂)

This method is used by Dr. JACK KEVORKIAN to help patients complete suicide. A cylinder of the deadly gas is connected by a tube to a mask over the person's nose and mouth; a valve must be released to start the gas flowing. Depending on the person's disability, a makeshift handle may be attached to the valve to make it easier to turn. By Kevorkian's estimates, this method may take 10 minutes or longer. Sometimes, patients take sedatives or muscle relaxants to keep them calm as they breathe the gas.

The poet SYLVIA PLATH, who had made several previous suicide attempts, sealed her kitchen and turned on the gas, but not before she left a note about how to reach her doctor. A series of miscalculations—her housekeeper arrived late, the door was locked, a neighbor had been knocked unconscious by the escaping gas, workmen had to force the building door open—cost Plath her life.

gatekeepers   Term used for those involved with and engaged in the educational process concerning suicide prevention, intervention, and postvention—the physicians, psychiatrists, psychologists, pyschotherapists, nurses, social workers, clergymen, lay volunteers, and others who are most likely to know of persons about to take their lives. Many of these professionals and lay volunteer workers are generally in a strategic position to identify and do something about a potentially dangerous situation.

gender differences in suicide   More than four times as many men as women die by suicide, increasing to about 10 to one in the elderly, but women attempt suicide about two or three times more often than men. Researchers aren't sure why there are such significant gender differences, but they have several possible explanations:

- aggressive behavior: Completed suicide is associated with aggressive behavior that is more common in men, and which may in turn be related to some of the biological differences identified in suicidality.
- methods: Women in all countries are more likely to ingest poisons; in countries where poisons are highly lethal and where treatment resources scarce, rescue is rare and hence female suicides outnumber males.
- help: Experts suggest women are more likely to seek help for their problems, such as DEPRESSION, whereas men are more likely to suffer in silence. In addition, women are socialized to express emotions more freely and accept a dependent position (help-accepting) more than men.

Suicide by firearm is the most common method for both men and women, accounting for 58 percent of all suicides in 1997. Seventy-two percent of all suicides were completed by white men, and 79 percent of all firearm suicides were completed by white men.

genetics and suicide   There is growing evidence that familial and genetic factors contribute to the risk for suicidal behavior. Major psychiatric illnesses (including BIPOLAR DISORDER, DEPRESSION, SCHIZOPHRENIA, ALCOHOLISM, and substance abuse) and certain personality disorders that run in families, increase the risk for suicidal behavior.

This does not mean that suicidal behavior is inevitable for individuals with this family history; it simply means that such persons may be more vulnerable and should take steps to reduce their risk, such as getting evaluation and treatment at the first sign of mental illness.

In one recent Danish study of 114 adopted boys (57 with a biological family history of suicide), boys who later completed suicide had six times more biological relatives who had killed themselves than the boys who didn't complete suicide. All of the adopted boys had been raised in families with no history of suicide.

Recently, European researchers have found a genetic mutation that appears to increase a person's odds of completing suicide more than threefold. The gene affects the levels of the chemical serotonin in the brain. The mutation reduces the ability of brain cells to absorb serotonin, a neurotransmitter related to mood, emotion, appetite, and sleep. It is well known that defects in serotonin uptake can cause depression, eating disorders, and other mental illnesses.

These genetic data are consistent with a correlation between low serotonin uptake activity and violent behavior, including violent suicidal behavior.

In the study, French and Swiss researchers compared 51 people who had attempted suicide with 139 comparable subjects who had not. They found that one mutation in the serotonin transporter gene increased a person's chances of attempting suicide by a factor of 3.63. Another less potent mutation in the same gene increased a person's risk of attempting suicide 1.72 times.

Some of the same researchers reported a relationship between variations in another serotonin-related gene, involved in synthesizing the neurotransmitter, and a person's chances of committing suicide.

Other studies have found a higher risk for suicide in identical twins compared to fraternal ones. Along a similar vein, other studies showed an increased rate of suicide in the families of psychiatric patients who committed suicide. One adoption study showed greater risk of suicide among biological than adoptive relatives. And psychiatric patients who had made a suicide attempt had higher rates of attempts in their relatives than patients who were non-attempters.

In one study of Old Order Amish, two pedigrees equally loaded for affective disorder showed one pedigree with no suicides and the other with multiple suicides.

In younger populations of suicide victims and attempters, the results are quite similar. Psychological autopsy studies reveal greater rates of sui-

cidal behavior in relatives of suicides than in controls. In psychological autopsy studies in Pittsburgh, families of suicide victims showed higher rates of suicide attempts, depression, and substance abuse in their family histories. Other studies found higher rates of suicidal behavior, substance abuse, antisocial disorder, and assaultive behavior in the relatives of prepubertal suicidal inpatients than in the relatives of nonsuicidal inpatients and normal controls.

In addition to the obvious genetic inheritance risk, studies also suggest that exposure to parental substance abuse and depression may add an environmental risk to the genetic risk for suicide. It is also true that family discord, family violence, and abuse, while not characteristic of all families with a suicide, occur more often than in other families. It is possible that some of these family difficulties might also explain the familial aggregation of suicidality.

See ABUSE, SUBSTANCE.

geographic factors   Some authorities concede that geography may influence people who live in isolated areas, in those areas where days are short and the nights long, and/or where climate is predominantly rainy or cloudy.

In the 18th century, many Europeans held the widespread notion that ENGLAND was a "land of melancholy and suicide." Natives and foreigners generally accepted the allegation that gloominess was a characteristic of the inhabitants of the British Isles, particularly the English. This melancholy was more than just a mood; it was a disease, a malady of mind and body which directly affected the imagination and was liable to end in self-destruction. The condition was linked etiologically with both the physical and social environment.

These notions of geographic (or environmental) influence have been traced back to antiquity, with roots in geography and medicine. Hippocrates perhaps started such ideas in *Airs, Waters, Places.*

During the 16th and 17th centuries, increasing significance was placed on such notions in many fields of thought, study, and practice. While considering questions of national character and cultural differences, writers and scholars discussed causal roles of such environmental aspects as air, diet, and temperature in medical and social problems.

These discussions became even more frequent in the 18th century, and the use of such ideas led many writers to oppose sanctions against suicide and to urge a less prejudiced and more tolerant view of suicide.

There does seem to be a global geographical correlation between location and suicide. Northern countries, such as Scandinavia show higher suicide rates than countries in the more tropical climates. However, other factors such as religion may also affect the rates.

There are significant geographical variations evident in America. For instance, Nevada consistently leads suicide rate statistics, followed by: Alaska, Arizona, California, Colorado, Florida, Montana, New Mexico, Oregon, Washington, and Wyoming.

Highest U.S. regional rates are generally those of the Rocky Mountain and West Coast areas, with the South showing the lowest rate, with the exception of Florida.

It was once thought that the rural suicide rate was much lower than that of urban and suburban areas; however, the rural suicide rate in the United States in recent years is very nearly that of urban areas.

See also FARMERS.

geriatric suicide   See ELDER SUICIDE.

Germany   World Health Organization (WHO) statistics for 1997 show that the total suicide rate in this country is 15.1 per 100,000. Suicide rates were highest in the over-75 age group—an astounding 45.5 per 100,000. Men in this age group committed suicide at a rate of 70.6; women over 75 had an unusually high rate of 20.5. Historically, Berlin has had one of the highest city suicide rates in the world.

gestured suicide   See SUICIDE GESTURES.

gifted children   Among the many myths of suicide is that of the stereotypical "genius" who commits suicide. In reality, every type of person, Christian or Jew, rich or poor, white or black, young or old, fat or thin, tall or short, with high or low I.Q., commits suicide. Yet it is true that many young people who attempt or complete suicide fall into the category of gifted students.

The mistake that parents of these children frequently make is assuming that intellectually precocious children are also emotionally precocious. The fourth grader who reads at the twelfth grade level is, emotionally, still in the fourth grade.

All too often, gifted children who have been moved ahead in school become loners, preferring books or special interests to friends. The more they retreat into themselves and their intellectual activities, the less chance they will ever make friends. Intellectually they are years above their peers; socially and emotionally they may be much younger. These gifted children often end up so miserable they cannot communicate with anyone, including members of their own families. Alienated, entrapped by minds that developed so much faster than their bodies, their despair leads to hopelessness and misery—and they kill themselves.

Gisu of Uganda, the   In certain societies, suicide sometimes appears to be a last resort. Among the Gisu of Uganda, suicides of the elderly sick usually took place after a variety of other means of alleviating their condition had been tried and proved ineffective.

The Gisu consider suicide as a rational act, a deliberate and logical choice between life and death, although subsidiary theories account for the fact that in the same situations, some people may choose death and others will not.

The Gisu of Uganda feel that ritual cleansing after a suicide is necessary to protect the suicide's close kin from danger and to prevent the contagion of suicide, causing the suicide of anyone passing the spot where the suicide occurred. To conceal a suicide is thus both dangerous and culpable; moreover, it is not possible to perform the necessary ritual in secret.

global suicide   About 850,000 people around the world died from suicide in the year 2000, according to the WORLD HEALTH ORGANIZATION, which represents a global mortality rate of 16 per 100,000—or one death every 40 seconds.

Moreover, over the last 45 years suicide rates have increased by 60 percent worldwide, now ranking among the three leading causes of death among men and women age 15 to 44. And suicide attempts are up to 20 times more common than completed suicides.

Although suicide rates have traditionally been highest among elderly males, rates among young people have been increasing to such an extent that they are now the group at highest risk in a third of all countries around the world.

While mental disorders (particularly DEPRESSION and substance abuse) are associated with more than 90 percent of all suicides, in fact a person's wish to die is caused by many complex sociocultural factors. Suicide is more likely to occur during periods of socioeconomic, family, and individual crisis, such as the death of a loved one, job loss, or shame.

See ABUSE, SUBSTANCE.

GLOBAL SUICIDE RATES

Suicide Rates (per 100,000)
(most recent year available, as of 2002)

Country	Year	Men	Women
Albania	1998	6.3	3.6
Antigua and Barbuda	1995	0.0	0.0
Argentina	1996	9.9	3.0
Armenia	1999	2.7	0.9
Australia	1997	22.7	6.0
Austria	1999	28.7	10.3
Azerbaijan	1999	1.1	0.2
Bahamas	1995	2.2	0.0
Barbados	1995	9.6	3.7
Belarus	1999	61.1	10.0

Country	Year	Men	Women
Bahrain	1988	4.9	0.5
Belgium	1995	31.3	11.7
Belize	1995	12.1	0.9
Brazil	1995	6.6	1.8
Bulgaria	1999	24.1	8.1
Canada	1997	19.6	5.1
Chile	1994	10.2	1.4
China (selected areas)	1998	13.4	14.8
China (Hong Kong SAR)	1996	15.9	9.1
Colombia	1994	5.5	1.5
Costa Rica	1995	9.7	2.1
Croatia	1999	32.7	11.5
Cuba	1996	24.5	12.0
Czech Republic	1999	25.7	6.2
Denmark	1996	24.3	9.8
Dominican Republic	1994	0.0	0.0
Ecuador	1995	6.4	3.2
Egypt	1987	0.1	0.0
El Salvador	1993	10.4	5.5
Estonia	1999	56.0	12.1
Finland	1998	38.3	10.1
France	1997	28.4	10.1
Georgia	1992	6.6	2.1
Germany	1998	21.5	7.3
Greece	1998	6.1	1.7
Guatemala	1984	0.9	0.1
Guyana	1994	14.6	6.5
Honduras	1978	0.0	0.0
Hungary	1999	53.1	14.8
Iceland	1996	20.8	3.7
India	1998	12.2	9.1
Iran	1991	0.3	0.1
Ireland	1996	19.2	3.5
Israel	1997	10.5	2.6
Italy	1997	12.7	3.9
Jamaica	1985	0.5	0.2
Japan	1997	26.0	11.9
Jordan	1979	0.0	0.0
Kazakhstan	1999	46.4	8.6
Kuwait	1999	2.7	1.6
Kyrgyzstan	1999	19.3	4.0
Latvia	1999	52.6	13.1
Lithuania	1999	73.8	13.6
Luxembourg	1997	29.0	9.8
Macedonia FYR	1997	11.5	4.0
Malta	1999	11.7	2.6
Mauritius	1998	21.9	7.8
Mexico	1995	5.4	1.0
Netherlands	1997	13.5	6.7
New Zealand	1998	23.7	6.9
Nicaragua	1994	4.7	2.2
Norway	1997	17.8	6.6
Panama	1987	5.6	1.9
Paraguay	1994	3.4	1.2
Peru	1989	0.6	0.4
Philippines	1993	2.5	1.7
Poland	1996	24.1	4.6
Portugal	1998	8.7	2.7
Puerto Rico	1992	16.0	1.9

GLOBAL SUICIDE RATES *(continued)*

Country	Year	Men	Women
Suicide Rates (per 100,000)			
(most recent year available, as of 2002)			
Republic of Korea	1997	17.8	8.0
Republic of Moldova	1999	27.6	5.1
Romania	1999	20.3	4.4
Russian Federation	1998	62.6	11.6
Saint Kitts and Nevis	1995	0.0	0.0
Saint Lucia	1988	9.3	5.8
St. Vincent and			
The Grenadines	1986	0.0	0.0
Sao Tome and Principe	1987	0.0	1.8
Seychelles	1987	9.1	0.0
Singapore	1998	13.9	9.5
Slovakia	1999	22.5	3.7
Slovenia	1999	47.3	13.4
Spain	1997	13.1	4.2
Sri Lanka	1991	44.6	16.8
Suriname	1992	16.6	7.2
Sweden	1996	20.0	8.5
Switzerland	1996	29.2	11.6
Syrian Arab Republic	1985	0.2	0.0
Tajikistan	1995	5.1	1.8
Thailand	1994	5.6	2.4
Trinidad and Tobago	1994	17.5	5.1
Turkmenistan	1998	13.8	3.5
Ukraine	1999	51.2	10.0
United Kingdom	1998	11.7	3.3
United States of America	1998	18.6	4.4
Uruguay	1990	16.6	4.2
Uzbekistan	1998	10.5	3.1
Venezuela	1994	8.3	1.9
Yugoslavia	1990	21.6	9.2
Zimbabwe	1990	10.6	5.2

World Health Organization, October 2001

"goal-gradient" phenomenon   Events distant in the future feel small, just as objects distant in space look small. Their prospect does not have the effect on motivational processes that it would have if it were of an event in the immediate future. Psychologists call this the "goal gradient" phenomenon. In the case of a person who has suffered some misfortune, this reduction of the motivational influence of events distant in time means that present unpleasant states weigh far more heavily than probable future pleasant ones.

Goethe, Johann Wolfgang von (1749– 1832)   German poet, novelist, playwright, and scholar who, with his good friend Friedrich Schiller, was the leading spirit in the *Sturm und Drang* period of German literature. His autobiographical novel, *The Sorrows of Young Werther (1744)*, was acclaimed throughout Europe.

Young people everywhere read and wept over Goethe's story about a young man who commits suicide after being torn apart by uncontrollable passions. Young dandies began to dress like Werther, speak like Werther, and even to destroy themselves like Werther. It became a point of status to suffer for one's genius, to struggle for art's sake, and to die young—a hero mourned by all the world. Goethe's martyr of unrequited love and unbelievably extreme sensibility created a new, idealistic, romantic style of suffering. The Romantic stance became suicidal. It was young Werther who made the act seem positively desirable to the young Romantics all over Europe.

Goethe, paradoxically, recounts how as a young man he greatly admired the Emperor Otto, who had stabbed himself. Goethe finally decided that if he were not brave enough to die in like manner, he wasn't brave enough to die at all. He wrote: "By this convection, I saved myself from the purpose, or indeed, more properly speaking, from the whim of suicide."

Goethe created an epidemic of romantic suicides throughout Europe with his novel, yet he was almost 83 years old when he died. He was buried with Schiller in a mausoleum in the ducal cemetery.

Gogh, Vincent van   See VAN GOGH, VINCENT.

Golden Gate Bridge   Famous bridge in San Francisco that is the number one spot in the world for troubled individuals to commit suicide. Since it opened in 1937, more than 1,200 people have jumped to their death from the span. (Other popular suicide spots include the Eiffel Tower, the EMPIRE STATE BUILDING, the Space Needle in Seattle, Mount Mihara in Japan, and Pasadena's Arroyo Seco Bridge.)

Cornelia Van Eirland was the first person known to have survived a jump off the bridge, on September 3, 1941. Currently, only 26 people have survived a jump off the Golden Gate Bridge; the last survival occurred in February 1995.

So great is the problem of suicides that the Golden Gate Bridge District installed telephones on the bridge for emergency purposes, one of which is to prevent suicides. There is a direct connection to the SAN FRANCISCO SUICIDE PREVENTION CENTER. In 1996, the rate dropped dramatically after the Golden Gate Bridge Patrol began monitoring the bridge as part of a $111,300 suicide prevention program. Every day, from dawn to dusk, a patrolman on a scooter drives back and forth across the bridge to stop potential jumpers before it's too late. The patrol workers study all people on the bridge, looking for clues to identify potential jumpers from among the tourists. They note the way people walk, the way they hold their heads, what they're looking at, whether they have cameras.

The Golden Gate Bridge District stopped publishing the number of suicides in June 1995 when 1,000 suicide was drawing near, but the published number of 1,200 has been documented. However, those who work closely with the bridge say the figure is much larger; some say the yearly average is close to 300.

Göring, Hermann Wilhelm (1893–1946)

German politician founder of the Nazi secret police force. Göring joined the Nazi party in 1922 at age 29 and held many important posts in Hitler's government before he became economic dictator (1937) and marshal of the Reich (1940). He was condemned to death for war crimes at the Nuremberg trials, but two hours before his scheduled hanging, he committed suicide by taking a poison capsule. On the wall of his office in Berlin, Göring a concerned wildlife preservationist, had posted this notice: "He who tortures animals wounds the feelings of the German people."

grades One of the several distress signals of the young person who may be considering suicide is a slackening interest in school attendance and school work and consequently, a decline in grades. Because school is the major activity in a child's life, it is also one of the best barometers of mental health. If a child's grades fall precipitously, chances are something is wrong. Adults should have the child talk about what's bothering him. When a child swerves from a long-established pattern, something usually is the matter.

Great Britain See ENGLAND; IRELAND; SCOTLAND; WALES.

Greece Latest suicide rates available in Greece are from 1998, in which 3.9 per 100,000 people committed suicide. This breaks down to 6.1 per 100,000 for men and 1.7 for women. This represents a light increase from the 1997 rate of 3.6 per 100,000.

Among different age groups, the highest risk occurs among the elderly Greeks over age 75; the 1997 rate is 13.6 for men and 2.6 for women in this age group.

The ancient Greeks held no clear-cut attitudes toward suicide, with Greek city-states differing markedly in their views and laws concerning self-destruction. In Thebes, for instance, suicides were condemned, and the victim was granted no funeral rites. In Athens, the law decreed that one hand of a suicide would be cut off and buried apart from the rest of the victim's body—since it was the hand that committed the dread act.

Other Greek communities established special tribunals to hear arguments of those citizens who wished to end their lives. A magistrate who was convinced by a particularly persuasive argument from an individual could grant permission for that person to kill himself. Magistrates in some areas even supplied poison hemlock to would-be suicides. Magistrates generally considered insanity, profound physical suffering, or overwhelming grief and sorrow as grounds sufficient to permit suicide.

Greek philosophers and thinkers considered the suicide phenomenon from their own points of view, in terms of ethics and morals. Perhaps the most famed suicide of ancient times was that of the Greek philosopher SOCRATES, teacher of PLATO. Socrates died by his own hand, drinking a cup of HEMLOCK, though his death in 399 B.C. was actually a form of execution that had been ordered by the rulers of Athens, who had tried him on the charge of corrupting the young people of his city-state. Plato quotes his mentor as saying before his death, "No man has the right to take his own life, but he must wait until God sends some necessity upon him, as he has now sent me." Like Socrates, Plato and his own student, Aristotle, both condemned the act of suicide. The Greek Stoic philosophers who came later held a much more lenient view of suicide. Yet both ZENO, founder of the stoic philosophy, and his successor, CLEANTHES, supposedly took their own lives.

grief, of suicide survivors   After any death of a loved person, survivors experience what professional authorities deem a "grief process." At first there is disbelief ("I can't believe she's gone"), followed by profound grief and sorrow. Survivors often weep, suffer loss of appetite, and have endless sleepless nights. They may feel anger, bitterness, outright rage. Some wonder how they can bear life without the dead loved one. At long last, sometimes months later, survivors begin to function normally and focus their thoughts on the future. This last stage is the "healing stage" in the grief process. Survivors often feel sadness and a sense of loss for years, but they are able to continue living, and generally to enjoy their lives.

In the case of suicide survivors, however, grief doesn't always resolve itself in the same manner as in other forms of death. The grief feeds on the anger and guilt and the never-to-be-answered question of "why?" And it grows and spreads under the disapproval of society, leaving survivors dragged down by a depression that may never be closed off. Sometimes the depression leads to a cycle of suicide or self-destructive acts for survivors themselves.

The grief process is especially extreme when survivors must deal with a teen or young adult suicide. Everyone involved with the suicide—parents, brothers, sisters, friends—copes with their own kind of suffering.

SIGMUND FREUD spoke of "grief work" in which there is abnormal desire for reunion with a lost loved one. Immediately after a suicide occurs, survivors need the help and intervention of others to do what is called the "mourning work" in order to continue living meaningful lives and avoid their own self-destruction.

Survivors should be encouraged to seek immediate help from a professional whom they trust: a psychiatrist, psychologist, social worker, minister, priest, rabbi, or physician; or, in the case of youngsters, a school psychologist, counselor, teacher, or administrator. Professionals can assist survivors in getting past the first stages of shock and disbelief, and then help them through the guilt and anger phases that come next.

Griffiths, Abel   The last person who committed suicide in ENGLAND to be dragged through the streets of London and buried at a crossroads. Abel Griffiths was a 22-year-old law student when he was buried in June 1823 clad only in drawers, socks, and a winding sheet at the crossroads formed by Eaton Street, Grosvenor Place, and the King's Road. Wrapped in a piece of Russian matting, his bloodied, unwashed body was quickly dropped into a hole about five feet deep. The Annual Register for that year reports that "the disgusting part of the ceremony of throwing lime over the body and driving a stake through it was dispensed with."

Superstitions and the desire to punish self-murderers were behind these burial customs. Suicides were buried at a crossroads in GREAT BRITAIN because these places represented the sign of the cross, because steady traffic over the grave could help keep the person's ghost down, and because ancient sacrificial victims had been slain at such sites. Since they were considered the ultimate sinners, people who committed suicide had been staked to prevent their restless wanderings as lost souls.

Griffiths had killed himself after having murdered his father. A chemist who knew Griffiths and who was presumably a reliable witness told the coroner's jury that he had a "DEPRESSION in the brain" and had inquired about leeching; he was certain that the man was suffering from mental disease. But the jury decided that Griffiths killed himself in a sound state of mind. (Had he been found to have been insane, his body would not have been treated with disrespect.)

Resistance to this seemingly unfair verdict was expected, and on the morning of the burial, constables and watchmen were stationed in the area to watch for protestors.

Immediately after the Griffiths burial, Parliament passed a law ordering that within 24 hours of an inquest, the corpse of a suicide must be buried privately in either a church yard or a designated burial ground. Yet because the British still believed that life was a gift from God and the taking of it was God's prerogative only, the 1823 law still contained punitive clauses. A person who committed suicide was still required to be buried at night without Christian rites, between the hours of nine and midnight, and the person's goods and chattels still had to be turned over to the Crown.

Ambivalence in this law mirrored the ambivalence of English public opinion from the late 18th century throughout much of the 19th. Forfeiture was generally waived by the Crown in cases in which a suicide was not committed in order to avoid conviction for another felony.

group conscience   ÉMILE DURKHEIM, among the first sociologists to collect data on suicide and to present the rates in tabular form, was convinced that the collective conscience of a group was a major source of control in all societal matters, including the phenomenon of suicide. He felt that every social group has set of beliefs and sentiments, a totality of social likeness. As Ronald Maris, editor of *Suicide and Life-Threatening Behavior* explains, for Durkheim the suicide rate depends upon forces external to and constraining of individuals. "To the degree that the societal groups are harmonious," Maris writes, "integrated and regulated and the individual is an active, central member of those societal groups, then the individual's suicide potential will be low and a population of such individuals will have a low suicide rate."

group therapy   A type of psychotherapy in which six to 10 clients are led by a mental health expert in discussions of mutual problems. Group therapy techniques are often used as a way of stressing that a survivor of suicide, or the friends and family of someone who has committed suicide, are not unique. Members of the group reveal their problems for the scrutiny of others, and discuss them openly as a group. This type of therapy was especially popular during the 1970s and early 1980s, but is still used today. It allows all members to benefit vicariously from resolution of another person's mutual problem.

The treatment method is similar to the various "12-step groups" used by such organizations as Alcoholics Anonymous, in which people find a way out of their dilemmas by sharing knowledge of their own triumphs and setbacks.

Guest, Judith   Author of the best-selling novel *Ordinary People,* which explores the suicide attempt of a young boy and was later made into a movie.

guns   See FIREARMS.

Hadrian (A.D. 76–138) Roman emperor who ruled from A.D. 117 until his death by suicide. His reign was considered to be a golden era of peace and prosperity for the empire.

Publius Aelius Hadrianus was born on January 24, A.D. 76, in Italica, in present-day southern Spain. His ancestors were Italian army veterans who had settled the area some 200 years before, which is the origin of his name ("Hadrian") from *Adriatic*. Historians know little of Hadrian's boyhood years, except that he was trained in the military, visited Rome, and was an enthusiastic hunter. His early career included stints as military tribune with different legions, until his guardian and uncle Trajan was adopted by the aging emperor Nerva. When in the following year Trajan succeeded him as emperor, Hadrian suddenly found himself in the inner circles of imperial power. In A.D. 100 he further secured his position by marrying Vibia Sabina, Trajan's grandniece, and by 107 he was a provincial governor. Eventually he moved to Athens, where he fell in love with the city and with Greek culture. (His enemies in Rome derided him as "the Greekling."). On August 9, 117, Hadrian learned that Trajan had adopted him, meaning he was to be Trajan's successor, and two days later the emperor died.

Hadrian was one of the greatest of the Roman emperors, and he concentrated on building up frontier defenses such as the massive Hadrian's Wall in Great Britain, but he also built roads, bridges, harbors, and aqueducts. During his reign, he made two extensive tours of the Empire, traveling to the western provinces in 121–123, and to the east in 123–126.

In 123, while traveling, Hadrian met a languid, moody boy named Antinous, and for the next seven years, he and the emperor were inseparable. Then in 130, while the two were in Egypt, Antinous drowned in the Nile River under mysterious circumstances. Some thought the boy was murdered by those jealous of his influence; others suspected that he committed suicide because of the nature of his relations with the emperor, or because he was outgrowing the age prescribed for Greek pederastic relations between the older male lover and the boy. Others think he deliberately threw himself into the river as part of some sacred sacrifice to protect the emperor's fortunes, or perhaps to cure the emperor of an illness.

What is clear is that Hadrian was devastated, ordering Antinous deified and founding the city of Antinopolis, where every year special games were held in the young god's honor. Cults of Antinous sprang up all over the empire; he was the last god of the ancient world, and much vilified by the early Christians. More than 500 statues celebrating his sensuous, melancholy beauty still survive.

Besieged by inconsolable grief, Hadrian tried to kill himself three times. He first commanded a slave to kill him with a sword, but the slave ran away, upset; then Hadrian begged a doctor in vain to poison him. Finally, Hadrian tried to stab himself to death, but was overwhelmed by his guards. At this point, he lamented that he should have the power to kill others but not himself.

Meanwhile, the summer had begun and an oppressive heat made the stay in Tibur intolerable, so Hadrian went to a seaside resort at the Gulf of Naples where he died on July 10, 138. He wrote his own epitaph whose elusive wordplay nearly defies translation:

Little soul, gentle, wandering,
Guest and friend of the body
In what place will you now abide
Pale, stark, bare,
Unable, as you used, to play.

(*Animula, blandula, vagula*
Hospes comesque corporis
Quae nunc abibis in loca
Pallidula, rigida, nudula,
Nec ut soles dabis iocos?)

hanging   Hanging is the second most common suicide method in the United States among boys and men, following firearms; and the third most common among girls and women. It is the leading method world-wide.

In 1999, 5,427 Americans killed themselves by hanging. Hanging is far more common among men than women; 19.1 percent of all suicides in men are from hanging, compared to 16.3 percent for women. Far more women kill themselves by poisons (30 percent) compared to men (7 percent).

In many societies, it is rare to find suicide by poison or drugs. Some methods such as hanging require a steadfastness of purpose that makes the labeling of death by suicide unequivocal.

Hannibal (247–183 B.C.)   Commander of the initially successful Carthaginian army against Rome during the Second Punic War (218–201 B.C.). Hannibal was forced eventually to withdraw to Africa, where he was defeated at Zama in 202 B.C. After the defeat of King Antiochus III of Syria, whom he was counseling on how to conduct his war against Rome, Hannibal fled to Asia Minor, where a detachment of Roman soldiers surrounded his hideout. Hannibal then took out the vial of poison that he always carried with him and drank it.

"Let us relieve the Romans of the fear which has so long afflicted them," he said, "since it seems to tax their patience too hard to wait for an old man's death."

hara-kiri   A ritual Japanese form of suicide (*SEPPUKU*) to expiate public shame, which is restricted to the samurai class of warriors, synonymous with its Chinese equivalent.

Hara-kiri was practiced by Japanese feudal warriors in order to prevent themselves from falling into enemy hands. In the 16th century, it became a privileged alternative to execution that was granted to warriors guilty of disloyalty to the emperor. The condemned man received a jeweled dagger from the emperor, chose a friend to be his "second," received official witnesses, and then plunged the dagger into the left side of his abdomen, drew it across to the right, and made a slight cut upward; the "second" then beheaded him with one stroke of a sword, and the dagger was returned to the emperor. By the 18th century, it became permissible to go through a semblance of disembowelment before beheading.

Voluntary hara-kiri was chosen after a private misfortune, out of loyalty to a dead master, or to protest the conduct of a living superior. Obligatory hara-kiri was abolished in 1868, but its voluntary form has persisted. It was performed by 40 military men in 1895 as a protest against the return of conquered territory to China; by General Nogi on the death of Emperor Meiji in 1912, and by many Japanese soldiers instead of surrendering during World War II.

Harvard Medical School Guide to Suicide Assessment and Intervention   A compendium of current research and thought edited by Douglas Jacobs to help health professionals determine risk and prevent suicide. The book explains methods for determining the risk level for suicidal patients, recommends a suicide assessment protocol, and provides intervention guidelines. The book discusses specific groups such as adolescents, the physically ill, and those with major mental illness, alcoholism, and borderline personality disorder.

Heaven's Gate   The CULT SUICIDE of 39 cult members in San Diego, California, in 1997, one of the largest mass suicides in U.S. history. The victims were all between 18 and 24 years old; 21 victims were women; 18 were men. The victims apparently believed their deaths would lead to a rendezvous with a UFO hiding behind Comet Hale-Bopp.

Investigators believe the 39 members of the Heaven's Gate cult drank a lethal mixture of phenobarbital and vodka and then settled to die over a three-day period. Authorities believe members mixed the drug with applesauce or pudding, then washed it down with vodka. Plastic bags may have then been placed over their heads to suffocate them.

Inside the house, investigators found a document labeled "The Routine" that outlined a process by which a group of 15 people would kill themselves, helped by eight others. Then a second group of 15 would die, also assisted by eight people. Given that 39 victims were found, that would have left a final group of nine.

The cult members had lived in a palatial home near San Diego, where they had operated a successful business designing websites for businesses. Both male and female members of the celibate Heaven's Gate group sported a unisex look, with buzz-cut hair and shapeless clothes. They had published a book in 1996 discussing a mixture of Christianity and UFO lore, posting it on their Heaven's Gate website.

According to reports, the cult's leader, Marshall Applewhite, had experienced a near death experience while being treated for heart problems during the 1970s—an experience that changed his life and led him into the cult.

Hebrew Bible   Biblical suicides are rare, with only seven instances reported in the Old Testament and one in the New Testament. Neither the Old nor the New Testament prohibits suicide, however, and suicidal behavior is not condemned. In fact, there is no specific word for the act itself.

In the Western world, the pervasive moral ideas condemning suicide are Christian, dating from the fourth century A.D., detailed by ST. AUGUSTINE (354–430) for essentially nonreligious reasons. St. Augustine was concerned primarily about the decimation of Christians by suicide and condemned suicide by Christians who chose death only for reasons of martyrdom or religious zeal hoping for immediate entrance into heaven. Old Testament figures who committed suicide include: Samson, Saul, Saul's armor bearer, Ahitophel, Zimri, Razis, and Abimelech. In the New Testament, Judas Iscariot is the only recorded suicide.

Hegesias (320–280 B.C.)   A philosopher also known as the "Death-Persuader" or the "Advocate of Death," who belonged to the Cyrenaics, one of the minor schools of Greek philosophy that flourished in the late fourth and early third century B.C. Cyrenaic philosophy taught that present individual pleasure is the highest good, and was therefore an early version of hedonism.

Hegesias, an historian in Alexandria during the reign of Ptolemy II, was far from a happy man, however. Instead, he taught that a happy life is pure illusion and that the complete suppression of pain—that is, death—is the only end worth pursuing. His lectures were so successful that many listeners actually did commit suicide after hearing him speak. Eventually, his power to induce suicide became so great that he was forbidden to speak.

help for suicidal people   Scattered throughout the United States are more than 250 suicide prevention centers accredited by the AMERICAN ASSOCIATION OF SUICIDOLOGY (AAS). Almost all of these 24-hour, seven-day-a-week crisis facilities offer emergency telephone services designed to give help quickly. Some have emergency rescue squads to assist callers *after* they have tried to commit suicide. Others are linked to hospital emergency services that can provide help as quickly as possible.

In addition, there are hundreds of self-help or mutual-aid groups in both the United States and Canada not only to help those at risk of suicide, but also to extend help to survivors of suicides.

Help is also available from professionals in private practice, in community mental health clinics, hospital emergency rooms, national agencies such as the NATIONAL INSTITUTE OF MENTAL HEALTH and the NATIONAL MENTAL HEALTH ASSOCIATION, international suicide-prevention groups such as CONTACT and the SAMARITANS, and the New York-based National-Save-A-Life League.

Canada, like the United States, has a nation-wide network of suicide hotlines. Suicidal callers should consult an updated telephone book or dial either "0" for operator information or 911. In Canada, the SALVATION ARMY operates its own suicide prevention facilities. Canada also has branches of the Samaritans and Tele-Care.

In nonemergency situations, help and advice is available to anyone through the facilities of the CANADIAN MENTAL HEALTH ASSOCIATION, which has branches countrywide. Information is also readily available from the SUICIDE INFORMATION AND EDUCATION CENTRE in Alberta.

See also AMERICAN PSYCHIATRIC ASSOCIATION; AMERICAN PSYCHOLOGICAL ASSOCIATION; INTERNATIONAL ASSOCIATION FOR SUICIDE PREVENTION; NATIONAL ASSOCIATION OF SOCIAL WORKERS.

See also Appendix I.

Hemingway, Ernest (1899–1961) U.S. writer whose longer works of fiction include *The Sun Also Rises* (1926), *For Whom the Bell Tolls* (1940), and *The Old Man and the Sea* (1952). An avowed sportsman and hunter, Hemingway extolled machismo, courage, and stoicism in his short stories and novels, which were written in a simple, terse style.

The son of a country doctor, Hemingway graduated from high school in 1917. He started working as a reporter for the *Kansas City Star*, heading to Europe during World War I, where he served as an ambulance driver in France and in the Italian infantry, getting wounded just before his 19th birthday. Soon he found himself in Paris as Toronto *Star* correspondent, where he became involved with the expatriate literary and artistic circle surrounding Gertrude Stein. During the Spanish civil war, he served as a correspondent on the loyalist side, fought in World War II, and then moved to Cuba in the 1940s. Here he bought Finca La Vigia, a bright and breezy mansion overlooking San Francisco de Paula, a village about 10 miles southeast of Havana. The writer spent most of his last 20 years in the house, the only place he said he every felt at home.

Yet much like his father, Ernest Hemingway was a tormented man, grappling with drinking, insomnia, violent outbursts, free-floating feelings of dread, and guilt over his behavior. It was at Finca that Hemingway first rehearsed his suicide in front of his friends and doctor. Seated in his armchair, he braced the barrel of his Mannlicher Schoenauer .256 against the roof of his mouth and pressed the trigger with his big toe. "The palate is the softest part of the head," he told them.

In 1954, Hemingway was awarded the Nobel Prize in literature. After Castro ejected him from Cuba, he moved to Idaho, where he was increasingly plagued by ill health, depression, and mental problems.

When Ernest Hemingway's father committed suicide in 1928, the writer had branded him a coward, but 33 years later—in July 1961—Hemingway himself swallowed the muzzle of a 12-gauge shotgun and pulled the trigger. Two of his siblings also killed themselves; a sister overdosed in 1966 and a brother shot himself in 1982.

Hemingway, Margaux (1955–1996) Model and actress who deliberately killed herself with an overdose of phenobarbital in her Santa Monica, California, apartment on July 1, 1996, according to the Los Angeles County coroner. The 41-year-old actress was the fifth person in her family to commit suicide. Her death ended a Hollywood career dogged by alcohol, epilepsy, bulimia, and life in the shadow of her more famous sister Mariel.

Santa Monica police investigators had said they found no illegal drugs or suicide note in the apartment. The final determination of death by suicide was made after toxicological tests.

Hemingway's career soared in the 1970s when she worked as a top model with companies like Fabergé, followed by a movie career. In 1976, the six-foot actress starred with her younger sister, Mariel, in the film *Lipstick,* but later movies were not critical or commercial successes.

Hemingway was the oldest granddaughter of writer Ernest Hemingway, who had used a shotgun to commit suicide nearly 35 years earlier to the day. His brother, sister, and father also killed themselves. Margaux was the fifth to kill herself out of four generations of Hemingways tormented by mental instability and manic-depression. (Margaux's older sister, Joan, whose nickname is Muffet, has been in and out of mental institutions since age 16.)

On July 6, 1996, Margaux's ashes were buried in Ketchum, Idaho, in the shadow of a memorial to her grandfather ERNEST HEMINGWAY, one of the 20th century's most celebrated literary figures.

hemlock (*Conium maculatum*)

The ancient poison drink of the Greek philosopher SOCRATES, this plant (which resembles a carrot) is rapidly fatal when ingested. Its large lacy leaves are as much as four feet long, producing a disagreeable garlicky odor when crushed. It is found in South America, northern Africa, and Asia, and in the United States and Canada. In Europe, it's called "fool's parsley." Hemlock contains coniine, a muscle relaxant similar to curare. Leaves are most toxic when the plant is flowering, but all parts of the hemlock are deadly.

The most famous suicide victim of hemlock was Socrates, who was tried on the charge of corrupting the young people of Athens. Found guilty, he was sentenced to death by drinking hemlock.

Typically, Greek city-states differed considerably in their laws about suicide. Magistrates in some areas went so far as actually to provide would-be suicides with hemlock so they could kill themselves. Typically, magistrates considered several problems to be sufficient cause for suicide, including insanity, profound physical suffering, or overwhelming sorrow.

Hemlock Society

Oldest and largest organization advocating the "right to suicide." The society has almost 25,000 members in 70 chapters across the country, who believe that people should be able to have choice and dignity at the end of life. The primary way to accomplish this is with legally prescribed medication as part of the continuum of care between a patient and a doctor. The Patients' Rights Organization (PRO-USA) is Hemlock's legislative arm working to change laws to legalize assisted suicide.

According to the society, the law they would like to enact would protect patients and doctors, allowing mentally competent patients to hasten their death with a doctor's help. Safeguards would include:

- a diagnosis of terminal or irreversible illness that severely compromises the quality of life, confirmed by two independent physicians
- an evaluation by a mental health professional if there is reason to suspect clinical depression or mental incompetence
- a written, witnessed request
- a waiting period
- voluntary assistance on the part of the doctor
- revocable by the patient at any time

- medication prescribed by the doctor and self-administered by the patient
- no criminal liability for a physician or family member who helps
- no effect on insurance
- monitoring by a state health department.

The society considers suicide only for those suffering from irreversible illnesses with unbearable suffering, who want access to a peaceful way to hasten their death. The society opposes suicide for emotional, ideological, or financial reasons, opposes violent suicide for any reason, and strongly supports suicide prevention programs. The society does not distribute the means to a peaceful death, but makes available written materials on suicide.

The society was founded in 1980 in Los Angeles by DEREK HUMPHRY and and his second wife, Ann Wickett, coauthors of *The Right to Die: Understanding Euthanasia.* The two also wrote *Jean's Way,* an account of how Humphry helped his critically ill first wife take her own life.

Humphry's first wife, Jean, was diagnosed with breast cancer and died in his arms in 1975 after she drank a cup of coffee that she knew he had laced with secobarbital and codeine to end her suffering. Less than a year later, Humphry married Ann. In the next decade they built a powerful national organization with 30,000 members and gross revenues of nearly $1 million a year, mainly from dues and book sales.

In 1989, his second wife, Ann, also was diagnosed with breast cancer. Three weeks after her surgery and four days after Ann began a regimen of radiation and chemotherapy, Derek Humphry telephoned home during a business trip to say he was leaving her. What followed was a vicious and very public battle between the two, ending in divorce in 1990 after a highly publicized bitter separation.

The next year, Humphry married Gretchen Crocker, youngest daughter of an Oregon farming family; later that year Ann traveled into the Oregon wilderness and committed suicide. At the time of her death, she was suing her former husband, charging libel and slander for comments he made about her mental state. Her suicide made headlines worldwide, in part because of her allegation in her suicide note that she was driven to kill herself by Derek.

Derek continued to serve as Hemlock's national executive director until 1992, when he retired to concentrate on writing, lecturing, and advising patients considering EUTHANASIA. He is currently president of the Euthanasia Research & Guidance Organization (ERGO!), a nonprofit group specializing in right-to-die guidelines, helping dying patients and families with information and advice, and briefing news media on end-of-life issues. He has continued to write books on the euthanasia theme, including *Dying with Dignity: Understanding Euthanasia* (1993) and *Lawful Exit: The Limits of Freedom for Help in Dying* (1994).

The Hemlock Society believes that since suicide is no longer a crime, assistance in suicide should also be decriminalized where a terminally ill or seriously incurably ill person requests this help.

The society strives to help campaign for better understanding of euthanasia and to work toward improved laws in this area. It publishes a newsletter, *Hemlock Quarterly,* that updates members on ethical, legal, and operating developments.

Hendin, Herbert   The medical director of the AMERICAN SUICIDE FOUNDATION and author of several books in the field, including *Suicide in America; Suicide and Scandinavia; Black Suicide;* and *The Age of Sensation.* He received the Louis I. Dublin award in 1982. Dr. Hendin is an international authority in the field of suicidology and has specialized in integrating the psychological and social aspects of suicide.

hereditary factors   See GENETICS AND SUICIDE.

Herodotus (ca. 484–425 B.C.)   Greek historian, born in Halicarnassus, Asia Minor. He lived for some time in Athens, then traveled in 443

B.C. as an Athenian colonist to Thurse in Italy. There he is supposed to have spent the rest of his life, writing *The Persian Wars.*

Herodotus describes the custom among Thracians of a form of institutional suicide in which a man's widows (the Thracians practiced polygamy) vied for the honor of being the one the deceased had loved most. The wife accorded this honor was then slain over the grave and buried with her husband. The Greek historian also described at length the suicide of Cleomenes, king of Sparta (end of the sixth century B.C.).

heroin and suicide   Studies suggest there is a strong association between heroin dependence and suicide. Heroin-dependent individuals are 14 times more likely than their nonaddicted peers to die by suicide. Some researchers suggest that the link between heroin and suicide indicates that some heroin overdoses may in fact be suicide attempts.

In one study, 40 percent of methadone addicts reported a history of at least one suicide attempt. Women were more likely than men to have attempted suicide (50 percent vs. 31 percent). Ten percent had attempted suicide since enrollment in their current treatment program, and 8 percent had attempted suicide in the preceding 12 months. Women also were significantly more likely than men to have attempted suicide prior to the onset of heroin addiction.

While suicide attempts among men in the study were likely to be related to the use of heroin, with most first suicide attempts occurring after the onset of heroin use, suicidal behavior among the women appeared to be related to problems of longer-standing than the use of heroin.

A deliberate heroin overdose as means of attempted suicide was reported by 10 percent of participants. Other methods used included hanging, poisoning, and gunshot. However, overdoses appeared overwhelmingly to be accidental —92 percent of those who had overdosed reported that their most recent overdose was accidental.

hidden suicide   Indirect self-harming behavior, also called subintentional suicide or indirect self-destructive behavior. This type of indirect self-harming behavior should be suspected in patients who refuse to eat, don't take prescribed medication properly, and who refuse to socialize. Older people, who may be taking medication for serious illnesses, are more likely than younger people to have the opportunity for indirect suicide.

Hippocrates (460–377 B.C.)   The central historical figure in Greek medicine considered to be the "father of medicine." The events of his life are shrouded in uncertainty, yet he provided an example of the ideal physician after which others centuries later patterned their existence.

The most famous document attributed to Hippocrates is the Hippocratic oath, which has served as a model of professional conduct and for the ethical practice of medicine ever since. In the Hippocratic oath for which he was famous, Hippocrates condemned suicide and ASSISTED SUICIDE: "I will neither give a deadly drug to anybody if asked for it, nor I will make a suggestion to this effect."

Experts believed that since most Greeks of the time practiced suicide, most likely the Hippocratic oath originated with the Pythagoreans, a school of ancient Greek philosophy that stood alone in its condemnation of suicide.

The Hippocratic oath has traditionally played an important role for physicians who are addressing end-of-life issues. Even today, many doctors struggle with the idea of assisted suicide because of the Hippocratic injunction that doctors should first do no harm. That a doctor should not be involved in suicide is very much a part of the ethics of medicine as many understand it.

Hispanics and suicide   Among Hispanics, the highest suicide rates occur among the elderly (over age 65). Still, suicide is also a problem among Hispanic youth. In 1999, the Youth Risk

Behavior Surveillance System in a nationwide survey of high school students found that in the 12 months preceding the survey, Hispanic students (12.8 percent) were significantly more likely than white, non-Hispanic or black non-Hispanic students (6.7 percent and 7.3 percent, respectively) to have reported a suicide attempt.

Among girls, Hispanic students (18.9 percent) were also significantly more likely than white non-Hispanic or black non-Hispanic students (9.0 percent and 7.5 percent, respectively) to have reported a suicide attempt.

Many Hispanic communities might well fall into high suicide risk categories because of such factors as: being socially isolated; experiencing interpersonal conflict or problems, including marital or family discord; lacking personal resources; high unemployment rate; mental disorders, especially depression, alcoholism, and schizophrenia; and physical illness.

Hispanics are the fastest-growing racial/ethnic group in the United States; in 1999, there were more than 31 million Hispanics in the United States with an average age of 28.8 years. The Hispanic population is growing several times faster than the non-Hispanic population—more than doubling between 1980 and 1999. The U.S. Census Bureau estimates that by the year 2005 Hispanics will surpass blacks as the largest minority group in the United States.

Minorities are no more likely than whites to suffer from mental illness, with the overall rate of mental disorders steady at one in five people, but various factors often keep Hispanics from getting the help they need—and when they do, the treatment may be substandard or too late. Of all the ethnic groups studied, Hispanics had the highest percentage—37 percent—without any health insurance. This group also faces major language barriers in mental health care, in which communication is especially vital to proper treatment. Few mental health providers identify themselves as Spanish-speaking, and about four in 10 Hispanics say they do not have strong English skills.

Although overall rates of mental illness among Hispanics roughly equal that of whites, young Hispanics have higher rates of depression, anxiety disorders, and suicide. The study also found that Hispanics born in the United States are more likely to suffer from mental illness than those born in Mexico or living in Puerto Rico.

Suicide risk has been found to be lower among recently immigrated Hispanics between the ages of 15 to 34 when compared with their Hispanic counterparts born in the United States.

Although rarely publicized, America's Hispanic population suffers from firearms violence at rates far greater than the U.S. population overall; about half of all suicides in the Hispanic population are completed using guns.

Hitler, Adolf (1889–1945)   German dictator, founder-leader of the National Socialist German Workers' (Nazi) Party. Austrian-born son of a customs official, he was orphaned at 15, refused admission to a Viennese art academy, lived in abject poverty, and became a violent anti-Semite. He served in the Bavarian army during World War I, received the Iron Cross and attained the rank of corporal. Hitler wrote *Mein Kampf (My Struggle)* while imprisoned in Landsberg Fortress for trying, with a group of embittered malcontents, to seize power in Bavaria in the beer hall putsch at Munich (November 8–9, 1923). Preaching Aryan supremacy and fanatic nationalism, he promised world conquest by the German "master race." Appointed chancellor by the aged President Hindenburg in 1933, and despite his own party being a minority in the Reichstag, Hitler managed to establish a dictatorship. When Hindenburg died in 1934, Hitler combined the offices of president and chancellor in the title of *Der Führer.* Thereafter, Hitler's militaristic, aggressive foreign policy led inexorably to World War II.

A carefully planned plot by leading army and civil officials to assassinate Hitler failed in July 1944, and Heinrich Himmler crushed the revolt. But when the victorious Allied armies converged on Berlin in April 1945, Hitler presumably killed himself along with his mistress-bride, Eva Braun, in a bombed steel and concrete bunker on April 30. Several other high-ranking Nazi officials also committed suicide at the fall of Berlin, including Himmler and propaganda minister Paul Joseph Goebbels.

holidays and suicide   Contrary to popular belief, suicides are not more common during the holidays. During the year, the suicide rate typically peaks in summer and again during April, May, and October. For the most recent year for which data were available (1996), November and December ranked the lowest in daily rates of suicide, according to information from the National Center for Health Statistics. Other studies have also found that the Thanksgiving and Christmas holidays have unusually low suicide rates.

holidays and survivors   Holidays can be difficult for survivors of suicide. Survivors should plan to eat well, exercise, and get plenty of sleep during these more stressful times. Holiday shopping should be finished early to eliminate unnecessary stress. Communication is important for survivors, who should decide what they can handle comfortably and confide those needs to family and friends.

Survivors should plan the holiday ahead of time, incorporating a schedule of activities to relieve tension, and making changes in holiday traditions to make things less painful. Many people find it helpful to start new traditions, such as different holiday recipes, changing the time presents are opened, altering the time and place of the holiday meal, and so on.

Survivors should plan to be with people they enjoy, and remember that tears are an honest expression of love and emotion. Some survivors say they find it easier to spend holidays away from home.

The person who has died should be included in conversations with family and friends when discussing past holidays, since some survivors experience disappointment when their loved one is excluded from holiday conversations.

Holland (Netherlands)   In Holland, where EUTHANASIA and ASSISTED SUICIDE were legalized in 2002, the suicide rate is 10.1 per 100,000. This breaks down to 13.5 per 100,000 for men and 6.7 per 100,000 women. This represents an overall decrease from the 1984 high of 12.4 per 100,000. The suicide rate decreased from the 1984 rate of 15.2 and 9.6 for women. For both sexes, the highest age group at risk for suicide were those over age 75; at this age, the suicide rate for men was 34 per 100,000 and for women, 11.5.

Dutch physicians have practiced physician-assisted suicide and euthanasia for more than two decades by following specific guidelines. Among others, these parameters require that the patient be competent, voluntarily repeating the request for death, and experiencing unbearable suffering from an irreversible illness.

One of the main reasons why the Dutch allow voluntary euthanasia is they recognize that whatever the law says, people are helped to die. Therefore, they reason, the best way to protect the vulnerable and make sure that assisted dying happens only at the request of a competent and informed terminally ill person is to regulate assisted dying.

In 2002, the Dutch Parliament approved a new law on assisted suicide, the latest stage in a regulation process that has been going on for nearly 30 years. The new law enshrines in Dutch statute the safeguards which successive court decisions have set down for regulating assisted dying. Estimates suggest that 85 percent of the Dutch public support legalized assisted dying as a choice for terminally ill people.

Under Dutch law, euthanasia and assisted suicide are no longer criminal offenses. The following criteria must be met by the doctor under the law:

• The doctor must be satisfied that the patient has made a voluntary and carefully considered request.

- The patient's suffering should be unbearable and without chance of improvement.
- The doctor must have informed the patient about his situation and prospects.
- The doctor must have come to the conclusion, together with the patient, that there is no reasonable alternative in the light of the patient's situation.
- The doctor must have consulted at least one other independent physician who must have seen the patient and given a written opinion on the due care criteria referred to above.
- The doctor must have ended the patient's life or provided assistance with suicide with due medical care and attention.

Doctors who don't make sure all the safeguards are met may be prosecuted. In practice, Dutch doctors agree to only one in three requests for assisted suicide.

Regional review committees must examine all cases of assisted dying. These committees are made up of a legal expert, a doctor, and an expert on ethical or moral issues. Any doctor who ends a patients's life at the patient's request, or assists in a suicide, is under an obligation to notify the municipal pathologist of the cause of death. The municipal pathologist refers the matter to the regional review committee, which will consider the case. If the doctor is found to have complied with the due care criteria, he or she will not be prosecuted.

homicide vs. suicide rate   The suicide rate in the United States is higher than the homicide rate. For every two people killed by homicide, three people die of suicide. And for every person who completes suicide, family and friends are left behind to deal with the pain.

homosexuality and suicide   In recent years there has been a great deal of research into the incidence of suicide among homosexuals. While the findings are inconsistent, most researchers agree that gay and lesbian people are at far higher risk of suicide than are heterosexuals.

There are many reasons for this. One is that homosexual activity is illegal or considered wrong in many countries, which can cause homosexuals to feel isolated and depressed. (It is important to remember, however, that there are millions of homosexuals all over the world living happy and fulfilled lives.)

Although most researchers agree that homosexuals are at high risk for suicide, the motives, causes, and predictability of future attempts remain as enigmatic as with other identified higher-risk populations.

There are no accurate national statistics for suicide rates among gays, lesbians, or bisexuals, since sexual orientation is not recorded on a death certificate. Because sexual orientation is a personal characteristic that people can, and often do choose to hide, in psychological autopsy studies of suicide victims where risk factors are examined, it is difficult to know for certain the victim's sexual orientation. This is particularly a problem when considering homosexual youth who may be less certain of their sexual orientation.

With regard to suicide attempts, several state and national studies have reported that high school students who report being homosexually and bisexually active have higher rates of suicide thoughts and attempts compared to heterosexuals. However, experts have not been in complete agreement about the best way to measure reports of adolescent suicide attempts, or sexual orientation, so the data are subject to question.

Because school-based suicide awareness programs have not proven effective for teenagers in general—and in some cases have caused increased distress in vulnerable youth—they are not likely to be helpful for homosexual youths either.

Risk factors that increase likelihood for suicide among gay and lesbian individuals include:

- psychiatric disorders
- substance abuses

- family problems
- depression
- harassment, violence, and gender nonconformity
- celibacy or multiple partners
- HIV and AIDS

See PSYCHOLOGICAL AUTOPSY.

honor and suicide In many early societies, either actual suicide or suicidal attempts were used to regain an individual's lost honor. Among certain African tribes, for instance, men sought revenge against their enemies by killing themselves, a practice known as "killing oneself upon the head of another." When such a suicide occurred, custom had it that the enemy responsible must, in turn, immediately kill himself in the same way. This bizarre practice continued well into modern times.

ST. AUGUSTINE formulated his prohibitions against suicide in order not only to prevent early Christians from seeking martyrdom but also to forestall young Christian girls from killing themselves in order to preserve their chastity. Lucrece, whose story is written so beautifully in a Shakespeare poem, killed herself before her family in order to affirm her honor after she was forcibly raped by Sextus Taquinius the night before.

Among the Romans, death to regain lost honor was chosen by such people as Ajax the Greater, CHARONDAS, DEMOSTHENES, CATO THE YOUNGER, and many others.

In North America, Cheyenne Indian warriors who had lost face would place themselves in life-endangering situations. If the shamed warrior acted bravely in his risk-taking venture—perhaps a buffalo hunt, a war party against another tribe, or self-inflicted pain—he won honor among his tribesmen, and thus regained lost self-esteem. If he failed and died from his actions, the tribe considered his death an honorable, face-saving one.

Lack of self-esteem without a traditional way of regaining it became a major cause for a high suicide rate among the Cheyenne in modern times. Isolated on the reservation, tribesmen suffered loss of pride, many of their traditions, and means of supporting themselves. With traditional buffalo hunts, war parties, and other methods of handling feelings of unworthiness and dishonor forbidden to them, many young men turned instead to open suicide.

Among the Chinese, suicide was the accepted way for a defeated general or deposed ruler to regain lost honor. The Japanese considered HARA-KIRI an accepted, honorable death for samurai (members of the military class). Outlawed in 1868, the ritualized hara-kiri form of suicide continued to influence Japanese practices. During World War II more than a thousand young Japanese pilots died as KAMIKAZE flyers who flew their planes at Allied warships. And in 1970, famed Japanese author YUKIO MISHIMA committed hara-kiri as a plea to his countrymen to revive old traditions and old values, including the concept of dying with honor.

The practice of dying with honor to preserve beliefs has been prevalent throughout Jewish history, as JEWS suffered persecutions and tortures in different countries in which they lived.

hopelessness There is almost always a complicated mix of feelings, attitudes, and motives involved in any suicide attempt. Suicidologist-psychologist Norman L. Farberow stresses that the suicide decision is usually not impulsive; it is, in fact, premeditated. Although it is sometimes carried out on impulse and may seem capricious, suicide is usually a decision that is given long consideration.

Many suicidal people feel hopeless. Yet despite this oppressive feeling of hopelessness, the would-be suicide usually still wishes for a last-minute solution to lifestyle problems. For many suicidal persons, there is an ambivalence, a confused tugging between loving and hating, between hope and hopelessness, between wanting to break away from family and friends while still wanting desperately to communicate with them. And all the while, there is present within the suicidal person that feeling of being without any real hope, of being entrapped in a life situation that cannot be controlled.

Hopelessness is the critical factor in suicidal behavior—even more important than depression.

hospitalization, involuntary

hospitalization, involuntary   Like alcoholics, drug abusers, or violent individuals, many suicidal individuals are caught in the web of denial and will refuse to accept any help. Often, even close family members or trusted friends fail to convince them to meet with a professional therapist or to enter a psychiatric hospital. In cases of extreme denial, when critical suicidal danger exists the patients may have to be institutionalized against their wishes.

Involuntary hospitalization is not the ideal solution to the suicidal person's problems. Most professionals in the mental health field maintain that in certain instances suicidal patients must be hospitalized for their own protection and the protection of others.

hospitals   There are usually mixed reactions among suicide attempters after they awaken in a hospital. They often deny the attempt and refuse to discuss the realities of the event. Sometimes, the patient is angry at having failed and vows secretly to succeed at self-destruction the next time. Another group of attempters admit a great feeling of relief at finding they are alive. For the latter, the suicide attempt often represents a turning point.

Whatever the attempter's attitude, however, the person must be evaluated and usually treated by a professional therapist. The success of such therapy after a suicide attempt depends to a large degree on the patient's support from family, friends, and associates. Often, the parents of a suicidal child may undergo therapy at the same time. Such therapy aims at helping parents understand what problems and pressures led to

a suicide attempt and to teach them how to prevent future crises.

Therapists show suicidal patients and parents the importance of opening up channels of communication within the family so they do not have to use suicidal acts as their means of communication.

hostile behavior   Among the various behavioral hints or warning signs is aggressive, often hostile behavior.

In one study, 60 percent of those who had attempted suicide had tried aggressive techniques as disobedience, sassiness, defiance, and rebelliousness. Less than 18 percent of nonsuicide attempters had tried such tactics.

Other aggressive patterns among suicidal youngsters have included shoplifting, joyriding in another's car, alcohol, and other drug abuse. Some run away from home, become sexually promiscuous, fight with friends and occasionally with members of their own families.

Such hostile, aggressive behavior, including physical risk-taking, may indicate what psychiatrists call "masked depression." This is behavior that generates excitement and covers up or "masks" their real feelings, which are anxious, painful, and depressive.

Hume, David (1711–1776)   Scottish philosopher and historian whose *Treatise of Human Nature* tackles major problems in human perception and existence. Hume wrote a short essay, "On Suicide," published after his death, that was quickly suppressed. In this essay, he argues against considering suicide a crime. "The life of a man," Hume wrote, "is of no greater importance to the universe than that of an oyster." The implication was that a man who kills himself does not disrupt the larger order of the universe. Moreover, says Hume, he "does no harm to society; he only ceases to do good which if it is an injury, is of the lowest kind."

Hume wrote that suicide cannot be a crime against God or the natural law because God gave humans the ability and sometimes the desire to commit suicide. It is not wrong to go against nature by building dams, diverting rivers, and so on, and it is not wrong to interfere in matters of life and death—otherwise life-saving surgery would be wrong. Hume also believed that suicide could not be a crime against the community because being a hermit is not wrong, and suicide takes this withdrawal from society just one step further. Finally, he believed that suicide cannot be a crime against the self because individuals know best what is good themselves.

humor, loss of   Among the cluster of symptoms noticeable in people who are clinically depressed is the loss of the sense of humor. They withdraw from family and friends, keeping to themselves; and they may cry for the most trivial reasons. They act sad and dejected and nothing appears humorous to them.

Humphry, Derek   Co-founder of the HEMLOCK SOCIETY with his second wife, Ann Wickett, in 1980 in Los Angeles, where the couple lived.

Humphry had been a newspaper reporter for 35 years, working for a number of British newspapers, including 14 years with the London *Sunday Times.* In 1978, he moved to the United States to work for the *Los Angeles Times.*

Humphry's first wife, Jean, was diagnosed with breast cancer, and died in his arms in 1975 after she drank a cup of coffee that she knew he had laced with secobarbital and codeine to end her suffering. Shortly thereafter, he wrote the story of his first wife death with Ann Wicett in a book called *Jean's Way.* The international acceptance of the book as a classic account of rational voluntary EUTHANASIA launched Humphry on a career campaigning for the right of what he terms "self deliverance"—the right to die.

Less than a year later, Humphry married Ann, and in the next decade they built the Hemlock Society into a powerful national organization with 30,000 members and gross revenues of

nearly $1 million a year, mainly from dues and book sales.

In 1989, Ann Humphry also was diagnosed with breast cancer. Three weeks after her surgery and four days after Ann began a regimen of radiation and chemotherapy, Derek Humphry telephoned home during a business trip to say he was leaving her. What followed was a vicious and very public battle between the two, ending in divorce in 1990 after a highly publicized bitter separation.

The next year, Humphry married Gretchen Crocker, youngest daughter of an Oregon farming family; later that year Ann traveled into the Oregon wilderness and committed suicide. At the time of her death, she was suing her former husband, charging libel and slander for comments he made about her mental state. Her suicide made headlines worldwide, in part because of her allegation in her suicide note that she was driven to kill herself by Derek.

Derek continued to serve as Hemlock's national executive director until 1992, when he retired to concentrate on writing, lecturing, and advising patients considering euthanasia. He is currently president of the Euthanasia Research & Guidance Organization (ERGO!), a nonprofit group specializing in right-to-die guidelines, helping dying patients and families with information and advice, and briefing news media on end-of-life issues. He has continued to write books on the euthanasia theme, including *Dying with Dignity: Understanding Euthanasia* (1993) and *Lawful Exit: The Limits of Freedom for Help in Dying* (1994).

Hungary   According to the World Health Organization (WHO), at least 1,000 people worldwide kill themselves each day. In recent times, when countries are ranked according to their suicide rates, Hungary is at the top year in and year out. This may say less about national characteristics than about how facts are gathered, reported, or covered up.

The reasons for the high rate of suicide in Hungary are obscure. The country enjoys one of the highest standards of living in Eastern

Europe, and has one of the least repressive regimes. Dr. Ceza Varady, director of the Institute for Mental Health in Budapest, explains that "the phenomenon reflects the Hungarian temperament, which is volatile and likes dramatic gestures."

Nearly 5,000 people complete suicide each year in Hungary, compared to a murder rate of only 300 per year. In comparisons of suicide rates in developed countries around the world, Hungary's suicide rate shows up as the highest in the world. Year after year, Hungary's suicide rate is nearly three to four times that in the United States, whereas the U.S. murder rate is more than three times that of Hungary.

Over the last 30 years, the difference between Hungary's rates and those of other countries has steadily increased. While other countries' rates have fluctuated or increased moderately, Hungary's suicide rates have skyrocketed to approximately twice the 1960 rates, which already were leading the world.

Many trace the origins of the internalized aggression reflected in these high suicide rates to Hungary's centuries-old history of being dominated—indeed, Hungarians have known only 50 years of freedom in the last 500.

In 1998, Hungary's overall suicide rate was 32.9, down from a high of 45.9 per 100,000 in 1984. Far more Hungarian men kill themselves (51.1) compared to Hungarian women (14.7).

The age group most at risk for suicide in Hungary are the elderly men and women; those over age 75 kill themselves at a rate of 90.15 per 100,000. This breaks down to 130.5 per 100,000 men, and 49.8 per 100,000 women. The next-highest risk group in men is between age 45 and 54 (92.7); the next-highest risk group in women is age 65 and 74 (24.1).

"hurried" children   Term used to describe children who are pushed by parents to grow up too fast. SIGMUND FREUD was, perhaps, the first psychiatrist to show concern about this phenomenon. In 1910, discussing suicide in children before the VIENNA PSYCHOANALYTIC SOCIETY, Freud noted that teachers, in their attempt to wean children from early family life, often rushed the immature student too abruptly into the harsh realities of adult life.

Psychology professor David Elkind wrote in *Growing Up Faster* that hurried children today are thrown into an adult world that overwhelms and terrifies them, sometimes causing self-destructive behavior patterns. Elkind, a professor of child study at Tufts University, points out that hurried adolescents frequently suffer anxiety about academic success. They then may solve this anxiety by using alcohol and other drugs as these actions make things worse, suicide may become another "adult" option.

Iceland   Iceland has one of the higher suicide rates in the world. Numerous education and media-based programs have been employed to curb this epidemic, but none of these programs have been successful. Therefore, many scientists have concluded that this high rate of suicide must be influenced by a person's genetics. Other experts believe the weather, and the long periods of darkness in winter, may influence the development of depression and suicide.

Iceland's suicide rate is 10.1 per 100,000; this translates into 16.4 for men and 3.8 for women. Unlike many other countries, the male age group most at risk for suicide is between age 25 and 34 (38.1); for women, it is over age 75 (13.3).

identity   Loss of identity or self-image leads to depression and if untreated, may push the person further into suicide.

It is during the teen years that so many changes produce extreme anxieties, tensions, and mood alterations. Teenagers become frightened, dejected, and angry at both themselves and others.

Teenagers also develop a fascination with death and dying. Many who become suicidal usually lack a true or realistic concept of the finality of death. Those teenagers who receive too little love and understanding, who feel alienated and without support, and who suffer loss of identity as a result, may become self-destructive.

Loss of identity has also been identified as one of the causes of the high suicide rate among the elderly. Loss of job, family, lifelong friends, and physical health may bring about loss of self-con-cept, loss of purpose, and feelings of meaninglessness that can lead to suicide.

Ignatius of Antioch (A.D. 50–117)   Christian bishop traditionally said to have been one of the little children whom Jesus bade the Apostles imitate. There is little doubt that he was indeed a disciple of the Twelve: His name is linked especially with those of John, Paul, and Peter.

During the period when the craving for martyrdom became almost epidemic among the early Christians, Ignatius of Antioch wrote letters, particularly those to the Christian community of Rome, that epitomized the state of zeal and mania. "I beseech you . . .," he wrote, "suffer me to be eaten by the beasts that I may be found pure bread of Christ. Rather entice the wild beasts that they may become my tomb, and leave no trace of my body, that when I fall asleep I be not burdensome to any. Then shall I be truly a disciple of Jesus Christ, when the world shall not even see my body. Beseech Christ on my behalf, that I may be found a sacrifice through these instruments."

Christians generally despised the tendency toward suicide among pagans, but premature, voluntary death as a martyr characterized large segments in the Roman Empire between the reigns of NERO and Julian (A.D 54–363).

imitation   See CLUSTER SUICIDES.

immortality   Younger children who attempt or successfully carry out suicide often do not have a true sense of mortality. To them, death represents

127

a rather vague, even romantic concept, with suicide an attractive fantasy that becomes a realistic method for testing feelings of immortality.

Most young people's experience with death is restricted to books, films, or television. Tragically for many of these children, only the harsh reality of a suicide attempt makes them realize that they are, indeed, mortal. Suicidal young people often see death as a sort of magical, mystical adventure.

impulsiveness   A personality trait that may be linked to suicide. Impulsiveness is the tendency to act without thinking through a plan or its consequences. It is a symptom of a number of mental disorders, and therefore, it has been linked to suicidal behavior usually through its association with mental disorders and/or substance abuse. A recent government study found that one in four nearly-lethal suicide attempts occurred within five minutes of the decision to attempt.

The mental disorders with impulsiveness most linked to suicide include borderline personality disorder among young women, conduct disorder among young men and antisocial behavior in adult men, and alcohol and substance abuse among young and middle-aged men. Impulsiveness appears to have a lesser role in older adult suicides.

Attention deficit hyperactivity disorder that has impulsiveness as a characteristic is not a strong risk factor for suicide by itself. Impulsiveness has been linked with aggressive and violent behaviors including homicide and suicide. However, impulsiveness without aggression or violence present has also been found to contribute to risk for suicide.

Most young people who kill themselves have trouble controlling their impulses, reacting to situations before thinking things through and/or overreacting to stimuli. An adolescent may be less depressed than an adult, but commits suicide over a trivial event because of an inability to delay self-destructive behavior.

Four out of five people who commit suicide have previously given clues—verbal, behavioral, or both—of their intent. Singly, these unexpected acts of impulsiveness may not be particularly significant, but clustered with other CLUES, they can predict potential suicide.

index suicide   The first suicide precipitating a suicide cluster.

India   The World Health Organization (WHO) has no reliable data on the rate of suicide in India, although other reports from years ago suggest the rate fluctuates from 6.3 to 8.1 per 100,000.

Nevertheless, India is notorious for a type of ritual suicide called SUTTEE, in which widows threw themselves on their husbands' funeral pyres, or drowned themselves in the Ganges River. Suttee, which was related to most Indians' strong belief in life after death, was encouraged by Hindu priests and relatives of the widow. By self-destruction, a faithful wife not only atoned for her husband's sins, but also opened the gates of paradise to him. The general populace venerated a widow who practiced suttee and condemned one who refused, sometimes actually threatening her with physical punishment. The practice of suttee continued in India for hundreds of years. It was outlawed by the British rulers of India in 1829, yet slow-changing customs saw it continue on occasion into the early 1900s.

The custom of suttee, or *sati* in India, was not indigenous to the country. It was practiced earlier by the Scythians and Thracians. The Kathei, and ancient Punjabi tribe, made *sati* a law to prevent the wife poisoning the husband. In addition, mass suicide in India (known as *jaubar*) was practiced by the women of the Rajput class to avoid molestation by victors in battles with other tribes.

Sallekhana, suicide by self-denial of food, is permissible only to ascetics, according to the Jain religion.

In India today, attempted suicide is socially unacceptable. Survivors are considered to be "tainted" and marriages in such families become difficult. When suicides do occur, the most common method is ingestion of an insecticide, a wide variety of which are easily and commonly obtainable.

indirect self-destructive behavior (ISDB) A group of behaviors that is distinguishable from overt self-destructive behavior by the criteria of time and awareness. The effect of the behaviors is long-term, and the person is usually unaware of or does not care about the effects of the behavior. These behaviors have also been called unconscious suicide.

Indirect self-destructive behaviors include self-mutilation, disregard of physicians' advice in long-term chronic illnesses, substance abuse, hyperobesity, smoking, violent crime, and compulsive gambling. Some experts also include some high-risk sports, such as mountain climbing, scuba diving, and hang gliding, when the participant exceeds the bounds of caution and begins to take unreasonable chances.

Personal characteristics of a person with ISDB include strong tendencies toward denial, a focus on the present, and a need to obtain immediate gratification from his behaviors. There seems to be a strong flavor of excitement-seeking in the activities, as if it's the stimulation of the process rather than the achievement of the goal that is most important.

It is not known whether indirect or direct suicidal behavior occurs more frequently in the same person or more generally substitute for each other. Some early research indicates it may be a factor of age, with the one substituting for the other more often in young and middle years, and the two occurring more frequently together in the older years.

indirect suicide Death as the unintended result of high-risk behavior.

See also INDIRECT SELF-DESTRUCTIVE BEHAVIOR.

inpatient suicide Completion of suicide by patient at a hospital or institution. Most inpatient suicides occur in psychiatric hospitals, followed by general hospitals and residential care facilities, according to the Joint Commission on the Accreditation of Hospitals (JCAH).

In one study of inpatient suicides, of those cases in general hospitals most occur in psychiatric units, followed by medical/surgical units and an occasional incident in an emergency room. In 75 percent of the cases, the method of suicide is hanging in a bathroom, bedroom, or closet. Twenty percent of inpatient suicides resulted from patients jumping from a roof or window.

Good patient care is the first step in preventing inpatient suicides. The root causes of inpatient suicides include having nonbreakaway bars, rods, or safety rails; lack of testing of breakaway hardware; and inadequate security. Other risks include poor patient assessment methods, such as incomplete suicide risk assessment at intake, absent or incomplete reassessment, and incomplete examination of the individual. Staff-related factors, such as insufficient orientation or training, incomplete competency review or credentialing, and inadequate staffing levels also contribute to the problem.

There are a number of ways to reduce the risk of inpatient suicides, such as improving suicide risk assessment procedures, training staff on suicide risk factors, improving patient observation, revising procedures for contraband detection, replacing nonbreakaway hardware, weight testing all breakaway hardware, and redesigning, retrofitting, or introducing security measures (such as patient monitors and alarms). The institutions should install appropriate shower heads, shower bars, and closet bars that do not easily suggest suicide methods. Staff should not leave doors open that should be closed, and should not give patients access to sharp objects and other potentially harmful items such as cleaning solvents.

Particular attention should be paid to patients who have multiple diagnoses that in combination can increase the risk of suicide (for example, a combination of depression and substance abuse). At the same time, the institution should review policies about passes and privileges for patients who are considered a suicide risk.

Organizations should assess a patient's risk of suicide at admission, and constantly observe those at highest risk. Staff members who provide any level of observation should ask at least once per shift about suicidal intent, and more often if suspicion is high. Staff should avoid relying on pacts with patients that they will not act on suicidal impulses.

inquest   A CORONER's investigation to establish cause of death. An inquest is a public hearing in which the coroner and six jurors sit in a quasi-judicial fashion to evaluate evidence presented (medical, investigative, and legal) to determine the manner, cause, and circumstances surrounding a death. An inquest is conducted on all deaths where apparent suicide, homicide, or accidents were involved in the death. Witnesses and police are subpoenaed to testify under oath to the events leading to the death. It is the sole responsibility of the jury to render a verdict (accident, suicide, homicide, natural, undetermined) and, if need be, to make recommendations or to place blame.

Inquests assist public health agencies, public and private organizations, and law enforcement agencies in their attempts to detect foul play or any existing hazardous conditions. Inquests assist insurance companies in making decisions on policy benefits for family members of the deceased and inquests help family members to learn all the facts concerning how their loved one came to die. This information helps them deal with their grief and avoid needless confusion.

insomnia   One of the symptoms of DEPRESSION that increases the individual's vulnerability to suicidal thoughts. Family members notice immediately when someone is having sleep problems. The person affected awakens much earlier than usual or else has difficulty getting to sleep at night.

For the person contemplating suicide, insomnia or excessive sleep patterns may be clues to self-destruction.

institutional suicide   Instances of suicide out of loyalty are related to RITUAL SUICIDES and are frequently described among different peoples in various historical periods.

For instance, Nicholas of Damascus, an historian in the time of Augustus, was a chieftain of a Celtic tribe, and employed a handpicked bodyguard of 600 men who were bound by a vow to live and die with him, no matter whether the chief died in battle or of a fatal disease.

Another instance of institutionalized suicide is the well-known practice whereby a widow or a concubine gives her life when the husband or master dies. HERODOTUS describes this custom among the Thracians, who practiced polygamy. When a man died, the wives vied for the honor of being judged favorite—and the woman accorded this honor was then slain over the grave and buried with her beloved husband. Analogous to this case of institutional suicide is the familiar Hindu custom of SUTTEE. Here the widow immolates herself with the husband's corpse.

Yet another example is the altruistic suicides by the Japanese KAMIKAZE PILOTS of World War II, who flew their planes at Allied warships, destroying themselves in the process.

See also HARA-KIRI; SEPPUKU.

insurance and suicide   Generally speaking, state insurance laws explicitly prohibit life insurance holders from collecting coverage in the event of suicide. Although insurers are not required to exempt suicides, it is nevertheless an almost universal practice in the insurance business.

While virtually all life insurance policies make some exclusion for death from suicide, the exclusion is often limited. After a period not to exceed two years after the policy was purchased, in most cases, death from suicide is covered on the same basis as is death from any other cause.

The theory is that individuals contemplating suicide should not be able to purchase life insurance benefits for their survivors. Not only would that be bad business for insurers, but it could conceivably serve in some cases to remove some of a person's hesitations about committing suicide. However, insurers assume that after an interval of a year or two, there is a vanishing likelihood that the person bought the policy in contemplation of suicide. In most states, life insurance policies specify that the proceeds of the policy will not be paid if the insured takes his or her own life within two years after the policy's date of issue. The suicide exclusion is only six months in Arizona, California, Connecticut, Florida, Iowa, Kentucky, Ohio, Oregon, Rhode Island, Vermont, and Virginia. There is no suicide exclusion in Maryland and Missouri.

At one time, life insurance contracts excluded the risk of suicide entirely. Today, the clause is intended to protect against adverse selection, not to exclude the risk of suicide.

The question of whether a death was suicide may be decided in court. When this happens, courts typically tend to hold for dependents. There is a legal presumption that a person *will not* take his or her own life, and this makes it difficult to prove suicide even where the facts clearly point to it. Indeed, the courts have gone to extraordinary lengths at times in holding that suicide had not been proven and in deciding that the insurance company was liable.

intent   A person's aim, purpose, or goal to die, and belief that death would follow the suicidal action. There are different degrees of intent:

- Intent, first degree: Suicide was planned by the victim.
- Intent, second degree: Suicide was impulsive and unplanned by the victim.

- Intent, third degree: Voluntary self-injury was inflicted without seriously intending suicide on the part of the attempter.

intentional underreporting   The deliberate misrepresentation of a death by suicide as due to another cause.

International Association for Suicide Prevention   Nonprofit international organization dedicated to preventing suicidal behavior, to alleviate its effects, and to provide a forum for academicians, mental health professionals, crisis workers, volunteers, and suicide survivors. The IASP tries to increase contact and collaboration between professionals, the public and a growing membership.

Founded by the late Professor Erwin Ringel in Austria in 1960, the organization since that time has grown to include professionals and volunteers from more than 50 different countries. IASP is a nongovernmental organization in official relationship with the World Health Organization. The group encourages the work of voluntary organizations, such as the network of crisis telephone services.

Apart from such efforts for suicide prevention, the IASP provides information on various other forms of crisis intervention, such as psychotherapy and drug treatment; organizes biennial world congresses on suicide prevention; and provides regional seminars. Designed to monitor the progress of suicide prevention activities on a global scale, the group also encourages the collection of valid up-to-date national data on issues of suicidal behavior and provides expertise to develop guidelines for suicide prevention programs. The IASP also tries to raise the awareness of governments, relevant international and national organizations and groups, and to the general public about issues of suicidal behavior.

Membership includes a subscription to a quarterly news bulletin, CRISIS: THE JOURNAL OF CRISIS INTERVENTION AND SUICIDE, and an information service on the Internet, including a calendar highlighting forthcoming events of relevance to the IASP community.

For contact information, see Appendix I.

International Handbook of Suicide and Attempted Suicide The standard work on suicide with a worldwide list of contributors, edited by Keith Hawton of the University of Oxford, England, and Kees van Heeringen, of the University Hospital in Ghent, Belgium.

International in scope, this authoritative text includes information on understanding, treating, and preventing suicidal behavior. It explores concepts and theories and covers key research that has supported conceptual development, preventive interventions, and clinical treatment.

international suicide rates Suicide is a major public health problem around the world, occurring in all countries that report information. Taken as an average for 53 countries for which complete data is available, the age-standardized global suicide rate is 16 per 100,000—or one suicide every 43 seconds worldwide. In the year 2000, approximately 1 million people died from suicide. The rate of suicide is almost universally higher among men compared to women by a ratio of 3.5 to 1: The rate for men was 24 per 100,000 and is 6.8 per 100,000 for women.

In the last 45 years, suicide rates have increased by 60 percent worldwide. Suicide is now among the three leading causes of death among those age 15 to 44 years (both sexes); these figures do not include suicide attempts, which are up to 20 times more frequent than completed suicide.

Rates within a country can vary quite a bit from year to year. Trends in the very largest countries of the world (those with a population of more than 100 million) are likely to provide reliable information on suicide mortality. Information is available for seven of 11 of these countries over the past 15 years. In these countries, the trends range from an almost 62 percent increase in Mexico's suicide rate to a

17-percent decrease in China, with the United States and the Russian Federation going in opposite directions by the same 5.3 percent. However, it is probably only the size of their populations that puts these countries in the same category, as they differ in almost every other aspect. Also, the magnitude of the change does not reflect the actual magnitude of suicide rates in those countries.

For example, in the most recent year for which data are available, suicide rates range from 3.4 in Mexico to 14 in China and 34 in the Russian Federation. It is very difficult to reach a common explanation for this variation from one country to the next. Although economic change is often suggested as a factor contributing to an increase in suicide rates, increases in suicide rates have been observed during periods of socioeconomic stability while stable suicide rates have been seen during periods of major socioeconomic changes.

Nevertheless, these figures may hide important differences across some population segments. For instance, a stable suicide rate may hide an increase in men's rates that is statistically compensated for by a concomitant decrease in women's rates (as occurred, for example, in Australia, Chile, Cuba, Japan, and Spain). The same would apply to extreme age groups, such as adolescents and the elderly.

While a rising unemployment rate is usually accompanied by a drop in suicide rates of the general population (for example, in Finland), it often leads to an increase in suicide rates among elderly and retired people (for example, in Switzerland).

It is well known that availability of means to complete suicide has a major impact on actual suicides in any region, such as easy access to toxic substances in China, India, and Sri Lanka, or firearms in El Salvador and the United States. This is particularly the case for firearm availability. Of all the people who died from firearm injuries in the United States in 1997, for example, more than half died by suicide.

Although traditionally suicide rates have been highest among old men, rates among young people age 15 to 34 have been increasing to such an extent that they are now the group at highest risk in a third of countries, both developed and developing. Although data on suicide attempts are available only from a few countries, figures indicate that the number of suicide attempts may be up to 20 times higher than the number of completed suicides.

Mental disorders (particularly DEPRESSION and substance abuse) are associated with more than 90 percent of all cases of suicide; in particular, high levels of alcohol consumption (such as in the Baltic States and the Russian Federation) has been linked to higher suicide rates. Most of the suicides in some countries of central and eastern Europe have recently been attributed to this problem.

However, suicide results from many complex sociocultural factors and is more likely to occur particularly during periods of socioeconomic, family, and individual crisis situations such as loss of a loved one or a job.

According to the WORLD HEALTH ORGANIZATION, which gathers global suicide statistics, the prevention of suicide has not been adequately addressed due to a lack of awareness that suicide is a major problem, and the taboo in many societies to discuss it openly. In fact, only a few countries have included "prevention of suicide" among their priorities. Reliability of suicide certification and reporting is also in great need of improvement.

See also ABUSE, SUBSTANCE; INTERNATIONAL ASSOCIATION FOR SUICIDE PREVENTION.

interpersonal suicide A suicide associated with the loss of an interpersonal relationship.

intervention The cardinal rule of suicide intervention is the same as that for prevention: *Do something.*

The following guidelines are offered by the AMERICAN ASSOCIATION OF SUICIDOLOGY (AAS).

1. Take threats seriously. Four out of five people who complete suicide have tried it or have threatened it previously. The old myth, "those who talk about it won't do it," is dangerously false. More than likely, by threatening suicide, the person is calling for help—trying to say how bad things really are.

2. Watch for clues. Most people considering suicide give clues of their intent. Look for marked changes in personality, behavior, and appearance. Watch for signs of depression, such as insomnia, loss of appetite, or continual exhaustion. Be alert when a person turns to destructive behavior patterns such as drug and alcohol abuse, especially when this behavior is unusual. A person feeling suicidal may start preparing for death. Making out a will, giving away beloved pets and valuable possessions, saving pills, or buying a gun could indicate that a person is contemplating suicide.

3. Answer cries for help. Once alerted to these clues that may constitute a "cry for help" from a loved one or friend, you can help in several ways. The most important of these is not to ignore the issue. It is better to offer help early than to regret not doing so later. The first step is to offer support, understanding, and compassion, no matter what the problems may be. The suicidal person is truly hurting.

4. Confront the problem. If you suspect that a person is suicidal, begin by asking questions such as, "Are you feeling depressed?" "Have you been thinking of hurting yourself?"—leading up to the question, "Are you thinking of killing yourself?" Be direct. Don't be afraid to discuss suicide with the person. Getting him to talk about it is a positive step. Be a good listener and a good friend. Don't make moral judgments, act shocked, or make light of the situation. Offering advice such as, "Be grateful for what you have . . . you're so much better off than most," may only deepen the sense of guilt the person probably already

feels. Discussing it may help lead the person away from actually doing it by giving him the feeling that someone cares.

5. Tell them you care. Persons who attempt suicide most often feel alone, worthless, and unloved. You can help by letting them know that they are not alone, that you are always there for them to talk to. Tell loved ones how much you care about them, and offer your support and compassion. By assuring the person that some help is available, you are literally throwing him a lifeline. Remember, although a person may think he wants to die, he has an innate will to live, and is more than likely hoping to be rescued.

6. Get professional help. The most useful thing you can do is to encourage the person who is considering suicide to get professional help. There are mental health clinics, psychiatrists, psychologists, social workers, family doctors, and members of the clergy who can help in every community. And in your community there are groups of people dedicated specifically to preventing suicide. Your ability to get professional guidance for the suicidal person may save his life.

7. Offer alternatives. Don't leave the initiative up to a suicidal person. Instead, provide him with a list of agencies in your area where he can go for help. These centers provide professional counseling to individuals and offer alternative ways to solve problems. A list of over 250 centers throughout the United States is in Appendix 1 of this work.

Once every minute of every day, someone in America attempts suicide. Official statistics show nearly 30,000 people take their own lives each year. Suicide victims come from all walks of life, from all kinds of economic and educational backgrounds. The presence of a good friend, a caring and loving family member, or involvement with helping professionals, can all lower suicide risk and can reduce the shocking statistics.

involuntary commitment   The short-term emergency hospitalization of a person deemed to be a danger to self or others, such as someone who attempts suicide. The purpose of involuntary commitment is to help a person receive necessary and appropriate mental health and/or substance abuse treatment.

"Involuntary commitment" is a legal action that begins with an appearance before a magistrate. Any person who believes an individual meets any of the criteria listed above and wishes to pursue an involuntary commitment must first appear before a magistrate to petition for an evaluation for commitment. The person who petitions does not have to be a family member, but firsthand knowledge is usually required. A petition may be filed in the county in which the person is found or in the county of residence. A petition must be based on facts to show mental illness or substance abuse and dangerousness.

If there are reasonable grounds for commitment, a custody order will be issued to have the individual placed in custody by a law enforcement officer and taken to a physician or psychologist for an examination.

When a delay would endanger life or property, a law enforcement officer may restrain a person and then take that person to an approved 24-hour facility for examination. As soon as the person is in custody, law enforcement will transport the client to a physician or psychologist who performs an examination to determine the necessity for involuntary commitment. The physician or psychologist can recommend inpatient treatment, outpatient treatment, or release.

Within 24 hours of the person's arrival at a hospital or treatment facility, a second examination to determine the necessity for involuntary commitment is completed. The examiner may again recommend inpatient treatment, outpatient treatment, or release.

If a person is held for inpatient treatment, he or she has the opportunity to appear before a District Court Judge within 10 days. The judge determines if continued involuntary commitment is appropriate. The hospital and court will notify the family and petitioner of the hearing and request their presence for input to help the judge decide whether to further hold the patient or order a release. The judge may commit the patient for inpatient treatment, outpatient treatment, a combination of inpatient and outpatient treatment, treatment at another facility, or may release the person back into the community.

See also ABUSE, SUBSTANCE.

Iran   There are no suicide rate statistics for Iran from the WORLD HEALTH ORGANIZATION. This may be related to the fact that Iran is 98 percent Muslim, with most citizens belonging to the Shia sect, a minority branch that is more conservative than the majority Sunnis.

The QUR'AN strictly prohibits suicide, promising punishment in Hell. Therefore, suicide is embarrassing and brings shame onto the family.

See also ISLAM; TERRORISM AND SUICIDE.

Ireland   Ireland ranks low among countries in its suicide rate, perhaps due to the predominant Catholic religion, which frowns on suicide. Catholics believe that suicide (under most circumstances) is a mortal sin that is punishable in the hereafter.

Death from suicide kills 11.3 Irish out of every 100,000, according to 1996 statistics from the World Health Organization. This breaks down to a much higher rate among Irish men (19.2 per 100,000) compared to Irish women (3.5).

Unlike many modern industrialized countries, suicide among the Irish occurs most often in the younger age groups; highest risk is between age 25 to 34 (34.6 per 100,000) followed by 35 to 44 age group (29.2).

irrationality   A warning sign or distress signal that could indicate a suicidal person is in danger. When a person begins to act irrationally, this may imply severe stress or mental illness, especially when the individual's behavior represents a marked and sudden change in manner.

Islam   MUSLIMS have always strongly condemned suicide. The QUR'AN, holy scriptures of Islam, expressly forbids suicide as the gravest sin, a more serious crime, in fact, than homicide. Muslims believe that each individual has his or her *Kismet*, or destiny, which is preordained by God and must not be defied.

The phenomenon of suicide missions involving Islamic terrorists would seem to contradict the historic attitude. But these are not viewed as suicide, but as *jihad*—a holy mission in which death is guaranteed to lead to paradise in the next life.

It is also true that while strong religious prohibitions have kept the reported suicide rates low, they have also suppressed the reporting of any such events by the family to avoid the shame and embarrassment that could follow.

The fundamentalist Islamic movement has strongly encouraged many Muslims to accept a theology in which under certain circumstances becoming a suicide-bomber is not considered suicide but is rather considered a form of religious "struggle" of an aspect of jihad. Therefore (in the Islamist view), a Muslim can effectively complete suicide without violating fundamental Islamic law.

Dozens of Muslims have died in this fashion over the last 20 years, mostly in Israel, although as of September 11, 2001, some have also died in the United States.

"Is Life Worth Living?"   A now-famous speech delivered by the American philosopher-psychologist WILLIAM JAMES, in 1895, to the Harvard Young Men's Christian Association. James had suffered severe clinical DEPRESSION as a young man, so was well qualified to discuss from firsthand knowledge the suicidal impulses that can overtake a person. In addressing the title question in his lecture, James's answer to the question was a resounding "yes." While it's true that none of us can prove God exists or that reason guides the course of the universe, anyone can make a positive decision to believe those things, said James. "Believe that your life is worth living," he advised, "and your belief will help to create the fact." The philosopher considered suicide a "religious disease," the cure for which is "religious faith."

isolation   A person contemplating suicide will sometimes retreat from life, withdrawing from family members and friends. In severe cases, such a person becomes suffocatingly depressed and suicidal, refusing to allow even parents or a spouse to intrude.

Whatever the reason (growing up feeling unloved, loss of a loved one, or illness) isolation is a crucial indicator of suicidal behavior.

Israel   The suicide statistics for Israel are fairly low among industrialized nations, at just 5.4 per 100,000 as of 1996 figures compiled by the WORLD HEALTH ORGANIZATION. As in most countries, more Israeli men commit suicide (8.2 per 100,000) compared to Israeli women (2.6).

To a startling degree, the population most at risk among Israelis are the aged (those over 75); they experience a risk of 40.5 per 100,000.

Although JEWS worldwide have historically had low suicide rates, the suicide rates among Jews in Israel appear to be slowly increasing.

Of the three major religions in the United States, Jews have the lowest suicide rates. However, religious statistics are difficult to compile because religion is not shown on death certificates.

The HEBREW BIBLE contains only six brief references to self-destruction, and in each case,

there are extenuating circumstances, such as the fear of being taken captive or the possibility of suffering humiliation or unbearable pain.

See also BIBLICAL SUICIDES.

Italy   Latest WORLD HEALTH ORGANIZATION statistics show this country has a suicide rate of 8.1 per 100,000; Italian men commit suicide at a rate of 12.3 per 100,000 compared to 3.9 of Italian women. The risk of suicide in Italy is very low for young children and teenagers, and increases with age for every group. Those at highest risk among Italians are the aged (over 75); 43.4 of this age group per 100,000 commit suicide.

As a predominantly Catholic country, Italy has always had relatively low rates of suicide, together with IRELAND and SPAIN.

Ixtab   Mayan goddess of the noose and the gallows, and the protector of those who committed suicide. In the Mayan culture, hanging was the only method of suicide deemed appropriate; anyone completing suicide this way was guaranteed a place in the afterlife. The Mayans believed that those who completed suicide or died by hanging (along with slain warriors, sacrificial victims, priests, and women who died in childbirth) were taken straight to paradise by Ixtab.

Ixtab, "She of the Rope," was typically depicted as hanging from a tree with a noose around her neck, her eyes closed in death, and her body partly decomposed. Due to her malevolent customs, she is also considered to be a manifestation of Cizin (the Devil).

jail suicide   Suicide that takes place in a local holding cell or detention facility. Jail suicide is the leading cause of death in such sites (usually by HANGING). Some studies have suggested that inmates at greatest risk for suicide are those housed in short-term centers (57.5 per 100,000) versus 16 to 17 per 100,000 for longer-term jails. The greatest period of risk appears to be within the first 10 days of incarceration.

High-risk inmates are young white men in their 20s who have a history of alcohol and drug abuse, a history of prior suicide attempts, but no previous mental illness. The nature of the charges is not a good indicator of suicide risk. The risk of suicide is also related to the degree of supervision provided by the correctional staff.

Incarceration seems to provide significant stress on vulnerable victims, which is aggravated by inadequate psychological care.

Jair, Eleazar ben   Zealot leader of ancient Hebrews at MASADA who became known for the most famous mass suicide in the Old World. It took place in A.D. 73 at the Fortress of Masada at the edge of the Judean Desert overlooking the Dead Sea. The Romans had overrun Judea and destroyed the Second Temple in A.D. 70, but a garrison of 1,000 men, women, and children of Eleazar ben Jair's Zealot sect held the fortress and continued to resist the Roman forces, using modern-day guerrilla war tactics. When defeat appeared certain, the Hebrew leader urged his followers to kill themselves rather than become Roman slaves.

The Jewish historian JOSEPHUS writes that the soldiers killed their wives and children, then drew lots to determine who among them would kill their companions and then take their own lives. At slaughter's end, about 960 persons had either been killed or taken their own lives. Only two women and five children had escaped the massacre, and remained alive to tell the story as recorded in *The Jewish War*, a contemporary account of the war with Rome.

James, William (1842–1910)   American philosopher and psychologist who admitted to suicidal impulses as a young man while suffering severe clinical DEPRESSION. In 1895, he delivered a now-famous address to the Harvard YMCA and spoke of those feelings and what he called "the nightmare view of life." Entitled "IS LIFE WORTH LIVING?" James's lecture was a classic example of positive thinking. He answered the title question with a resounding "Yes," and told his audience: "Believe that life is worth living and your belief will help to create the fact."

The brother of novelist Henry James, William taught at Harvard. Perhaps his most influential thesis was that faith, which had been eroded by the isolation accompanying advancing urbanization and by the individualism fostered by the teachings of Protestantism, had diminished to a dangerous degree. Among his books are *The Varieties of Religious Experience* (1902) and *Pragmatism* (1907).

Japan   The Japanese at one time ritualized suicide in what they called HARA-KIRI or SEPPUKU. Outlawed in 1868, this form of ceremonial death had been an integral part of the old moral code, going back to the days of the Samurai warrior.

The only honorable means for a disgraced warrior to redeem himself was to commit seppuku, in which he disemboweled himself with his own sword. A samurai warrior would sometimes kill himself to show allegiance to a fallen leader. Also, an emperor might order a member of the military class to commit hara-kiri to avoid the disgrace of a public execution. The ritual of seppuku sometimes took hours to complete (it was an elaborate process). Then a second person, usually the closest friend of the suicide who considered himself honored to terminate the pain and suffering, ended the ritual by beheading the suicide with a sword.

The ritual of seppuku was institutionalized during the feudal ages, from 1190 through 1867, and characterized Bushido, the moral code of the warrior class.

Even though the practice has been outlawed, the tradition of suicide with honor is still in evidence from time to time in Japan. During World War II, for example, more than 1,000 young Japanese soldiers died as KAMIKAZE PILOTS while flying their planes at Allied warships. When defeat was inevitable in that conflict, a number of prominent, high-ranking army and navy officers committed ritual hara-kiri rather than suffer the humiliation of surrender.

More recently, in 1970, the famous novelist, playwright and actor, YUKIO MISHIMA, committed ritual suicide at the age of 45. He urged his countrymen to return to old values and traditions, one of which was the ancient concept of dying with honor.

Some suicidologists speculate that the old Japanese notion of death with honor may be responsible, at least in part, for the high rate of suicide among today's young Japanese. More than twice as many Japanese young people as Americans between the ages of 15 and 24 kill themselves. This may be due in part to deep feelings of insecurity that develop in many Japanese homes, along with fierce competition in school and in the job market.

Another basic belief typical of the Japanese is the ancient Buddhist concept of *muso-kan*, a philosophy that says the human body is merely a temporary home for the soul. Thus, biological existence may not have much meaning.

WORLD HEALTH ORGANIZATION statistics for 1997 indicate that the Japanese suicide rate per 100,000 population was 18.9 (26.0 for men and 11.9 for women).

Japanese suicide   See SEPPUKU.

Jews   BIBLICAL SUICIDES among the Jews are rare; only seven instances are reported in the HEBREW BIBLE and one in the New Testament. Neither the Hebrew Bible nor the New Testament prohibits suicide, nor is suicidal behavior condemned. Even of JUDAS ISCARIOT we are told only that "he went and hanged himself" (Matthew 27:5).

The Judeo-Christian tradition (as well as ISLAM) has always held that suicide in the form of martyrdom was permissible. In fact, the most significant sanction of suicide among Jews was to avoid apostasy, the forced rejection of the Jewish faith and adoption of another religion or God. Suicide, however, was in violation of the Fifth Commandment, delivered to Moses on Sinai: Thou shalt not kill. But Jews did look at suicide as a positive act if employed to prevent torture, rape, or slavery. King Saul fell on his sword after defeat in battle, and the defenders' mass suicide at MASADA to prevent capture by the Romans was considered heroic.

In Talmudic times (A.D. 200–500) the number of recorded suicides rose. As the act became more frequent, a condemnatory tone was introduced for the first time. The Talmud decrees that a suicide is to receive no eulogy or public mourning; he is to be buried apart, in community cemeteries.

There was never universal agreement on the matter of suicide among Jews. Some authorities said relatives had a duty to the deceased regardless of the circumstances of death.

Today, although considered as a crime against God, suicide may sometimes be explained away, understood, and forgiven among Jews. This enlightened point of view has been incorporated into the approach of the three denominations of modern Judaism. A study of suicide among white adults of New York City's three major religions showed the rate for Jews higher than that for Catholics, but lower than for Protestants.

johar   A RITUAL SUICIDE by self-immolation of the widow of a man killed in battle in India.
   See also SUTTEE.

Joluo (of Kenya)   Members of this African tribe manage to keep knowledge of cases of suicide within the clan, lest the clan's prestige in the community suffer. Other clans, such as, the GISU OF UGANDA, believe that to conceal a suicide is not only dangerous, but also culpable.

Jones, Reverend Jim   See JONESTOWN MASSACRE.

Jonestown Massacre   The mass suicide-execution of followers of the Reverend Jim Jones's People's Temple cult on November 18, 1978. On that date, the Rev. Jim Jones led a mass suicide-execution of 911 of his followers of the People's Temple in the jungle of the Cooperative Republic of Guyana. On the night of the suicide, Jones ordered more than 900 of his followers to drink cyanide-poisoned punch. He told guards to shoot anyone who refused or tried to escape. Among the dead were more than 270 children.

   Only two years before, Jones (the charismatic leader of the People's Temple, an interracial helping organization) was popular among San Francisco's political circles. But after an August 1977 magazine article detailed ex-members' stories of beatings and forced donations, Jones abruptly moved his group to Jonestown, a settlement in the jungle of Guyana on South America's northern coast.

   The plan was to establish an egalitarian agricultural community, but members who worked the fields and lived mostly on rice felt it was

more like a prison. Dissent was not possible, and offenders were put into "The Box," a 6-by-4-foot underground enclosure. Misbehaving children were dangled into a well late at night. Loudspeakers broadcast Jones's voice at all hours.

   Still, the U.S. government did not intervene until November 1978, when U.S. Representative Leo Ryan decided to lead a delegation of reporters and relatives to Jonestown after being notified by people worried about their relatives in the People's Temple. Ryan's group arrived on November 17, but the mood at the compound soured after some Jonestown residents confided that they wanted to defect.

   The group was ambushed the next day as they tried to leave at a nearby airstrip, and Ryan and four others were killed. Later that night, Jones told his followers that it was time to commit suicide. He was later found shot through the head.
   See also CULT SUICIDE.

Joplin, Janis (1943–1970)   American singer-entertainer who died, some say deliberately, from an overdose of heroin in the Landmark Hotel, Los Angeles. Her road manager discovered the body the next day. Remnants of the heroin were found in a wastebasket by her bed. Joplin became known as the Queen of the Hippies.

Josephus, Flavius (A.D. 37–?95)   Jewish historian and soldier who commanded a Jewish force in Palestine in the uprising against Rome in A.D. 66. He was forced to surrender and was imprisoned in Rome by Vespasian. During the final moments of his battle with Vespasian, Josephus debated with his soldiers and offered various reasons why suicide was undesirable. He reluctantly agreed to the insistence of his soldiers that suicide was preferable to capture.

   Interestingly, following the Jewish custom of that time, each soldier slew one other soldier who was in turn killed by the next man. It ended with just Josephus and a fellow soldier remaining, and Josephus was easily able to convince the soldier to surrender along with him.

Later, he became a follower of Titus and adopted Roman citizenship. He wrote *The Jewish War,* an account of the war with Rome (A.D. 67–73); *The Jewish Antiquities,* a history of the Jews from the beginning to the outbreak of the war; and an account of his own life, defending his conduct and emphasizing his pro-Roman sentiments. He wrote sensitively about the defenders of MASADA, who ultimately killed themselves rather than surrender to the Romans.

Josephus agreed on the obligation to uphold and defend the Torah, "to sanctify the Holy Name," under all circumstances. In this cause even suicide was justified.

Joyce, James (1882–1941)   Irish novelist who left IRELAND in 1902 and spent the remainder of his life on the Continent. At the beginning of the 20th century, popular opinion generally viewed suicide as a deviation from normality. Joyce presents this attitude in an episode in his famous novel *Ulysses.* On the way to a funeral, four men discuss attempted suicide and death.

> "But the worst of all," Mr. Power said, "is the man who takes his own life." Martin Cunning-

ham drew out his watch briskly, coughed and put it back. "The greatest disgrace to have in the family," Mr. Power added. "Temporary insanity, of course," Martin Cunningham said decisively. "We must take a charitable view of it." "They say a man who does it is a coward," Mr. Dedalus said. "It is not for us to judge," Martin Cunningham said.

By the 20th century, suicide in ENGLAND was more a social disgrace than it was a sin—at least among the middle class.

Judaism and suicide   See JEWS.

Judas Iscariot   The disciple who betrayed Jesus for 30 pieces of silver. Motives given for the betrayal are greed (according to Matthew) and the power of the devil (according to John).

At the Last Supper (a Passover feast), Jesus predicted the betrayal, which Judas accomplished by leading soldiers to Jesus and identifying him with a kiss. Judas, in remorse, killed himself by hanging (Matthew 27:3–7). Aceldama, where Judas killed himself near Jerusalem, became a pauper's burial ground after it was bought by the priests with the 30 pieces of silver flung at their feet by Judas.

kamikaze pilots An example of ALTRUISTIC SUICIDE that occurs among people so dedicated to a cause or to certain values of their society that they place duty before personal needs, even before their lives. The Japanese kamikaze pilots of World War II flew their planes at Allied warships, destroying themselves in the process. More than 1,000 young Japanese died in this manner.

See also JAPAN; TERRORISM AND SUICIDE.

Kant, Immanuel (1724–1804) German transcendentalist philosopher whose most famous work is the *Critique of Pure Reason* (1781). Concerning suicide, Kant sided with the major religions, that it was morally wrong. But he took a different line of reasoning to reach that conclusion. Life, to Kant, was sacred because it was part of nature. As such, he said, each life has a place within the laws of nature, and each person must preserve his or her own life. To ignore this duty and end one's life is immoral. To Kant, true morality is rising above individual and personal feelings of despair, carrying out one's duties, and living one's life in the face of adversity. However, he did write, "It is not suicide to risk one's life against one's enemies, and even to sacrifice it, in order to preserve one's duties towards oneself."

Kawabata, Yasunari (1900–1972) Japanese novelist and winner of the Nobel Prize in literature in 1968. According to reports, he "left his home in Kamakura in the afternoon of April 16, 1972, for his workroom in nearby Zushi. There was no sign of suicidal thoughts. That evening, he was found dead with a gas conduit in his mouth in the room, which commanded magnificent views of both oceans and mountains." Kawabata was 72 years old.

Keats, John (1795–1821) British romantic poet who had studied to be a surgeon. *Lamia and Other Poems* (1820), including his great odes and narrative poems ("The Eve of St. Agnes"), secured his reputation. Keats was seriously ill with tuberculosis, a condition exacerbated by his tormented love for Fanny Brawne and which caused him to suffer deep depression and suicidal feelings. He died in Rome at age 25, convinced that true feelings cannot survive into middle age. He was idolized by the ROMANTICS of the era.

Kentucky Although suicide has never been a crime in the United States, and the property of suicides has never been confiscated, attempted suicide was at one time regarded as a felony in a few states, among them the state of Kentucky. But even in that state, attempters were almost never prosecuted. The state now rarely prosecutes persons who help others attempt or commit suicide, although this is still regarded as a criminal offense. Still, the stigma against suicide remains in the general population. Kentucky is in the South, the region with the lowest rate for suicide in the United States (with the exception of Florida).

Kevorkian, Jack (1928–) American physician known also as Doctor Death, who has

141

campaigned for the legalization of PHYSICIAN-ASSISTED SUICIDE. Taken to court many times for helping patients die, he was finally convicted in Michigan of second-degree murder and delivery of a controlled substance in the death of a patient. He was sentenced to 10 to 25 years in prison, and will be eligible for parole in 2005.

Kevorkian was born in Pontiac, Michigan, the son of Armenian immigrants, and graduated from the University of Michigan medical school with a specialty in pathology in 1952. Four years later, he published a journal article, "The Fundus Oculi and the Determination of Death," which discussed his efforts to photograph the eyes of dying patients, a practice that earned him the nickname Doctor Death. In December 1958, he presented a paper at a meeting in Washington, D.C., advocating medical experimentation on consenting convicts during executions, which prompted the University of Michigan to ask Kevorkian to leave his residency there in 1961.

He became chief pathologist at Saratoga General Hospital in Detroit in 1970, quitting his pathology career in the late 1970s to move to California. By the 1980s, he was again working in medicine, and published many articles in the German journal *Medicine and Law* outlining his ideas on EUTHANASIA and ETHICS. In 1987, he began to advertise in Detroit papers as a physician consultant for death counseling. By the next year, he published "The Last Fearsome Taboo: Medical Aspects of Planned Death," in *Medicine and Law,* which outlined his proposed system of planned deaths in suicide clinics, including medical experimentation on patients.

The next year he built his thanatron ("suicide machine") and in June 1990, he was present at the death of Janet Adkins, a 54-year-old Portland, Oregon, woman with Alzheimer's disease. She died using the suicide machine in Kevorkian's 1968 Volkswagen van.

On December 12, 1990, an Oakland County Circuit Court judge forbid Kevorkian from helping with any other suicides, and a year later murder charges against Kevorkian in the death of Adkins were dismissed in U.S. District Court.

Next, Kevorkian attended the deaths of Marjorie Wantz, a 58-year-old Sodus, Michigan, woman with pelvic pain, and Sherry Miller, a 43-year-old Roseville, Michigan, woman with multiple sclerosis. The deaths occurred at a rented state park cabin near Lake Orion, Michigan. Wantz died from the suicide machine's drugs; Miller died from carbon monoxide poisoning inhaled through a face mask. Shortly thereafter, the state board of medicine summarily revoked Kevorkian's license to practice medicine in Michigan.

Kevorkian next assisted in the suicide of Susan Williams, a 52-year-old woman with multiple sclerosis, by carbon monoxide poisoning in her home in Clawson, Michigan, in May 1992. Three months later, charges against Kevorkian in the deaths of Miller and Wantz were dismissed in Oakland County Circuit Court, but the dismissal was appealed.

Two months later, in September 1992, Lois Hawes, 52, a Michigan woman with lung and brain cancer, died from carbon monoxide poisoning at the home of Kevorkian's assistant Neal Nicol in Michigan. This was followed two months later by the suicide of Catherine Andreyev of Moon Township, Pennsylvania, who also committed suicide in Nicol's home. She was 45 and had cancer. Hers was the first of 10 deaths Kevorkian attended over the next three months; all died from inhaling carbon monoxide.

On December 3, 1992, the Michigan legislature passed a ban on assisted suicide to take effect on March 30, 1993. Shortly before the ban went into effect, Hugh Gale, a 70-year-old man with emphysema and congestive heart disease, committed suicide in his Roseville home. Prosecutors investigated after Right-to-Life advocates found papers that show Kevorkian altered his account of Gale's death, deleting a reference to a request by Gale to halt the procedure.

On February 25, 1993, Michigan governor John Engler signed the legislation banning assisted suicide, making it a felony to aid in a suicide, but allowing the law to expire after a blue-ribbon commission studied permanent legislation.

A California judge next suspended Kevorkian's medical license after a request from that state's medical board on April 27, 1993. Four months later, Thomas Hyde, a 30-year-old Novi, Michigan, man with ALS, was found dead in Kevorkian's van on Belle Isle, a Detroit park. On September 9, 1993, hours after a judge ordered him to stand trial in Hyde's death, Kevorkian was present at the death of cancer patient Donald O'Keefe, 73, in Michigan.

After refusing to post $20,000 bond in the case involving Hyde, Kevorkian began to fast in a Detroit jail from November 5 to 8, 1993. On November 29, 1993, he began to fast in Oakland County jail for refusing to post $50,000 bond after being charged in the October death of Merian Frederick, 72. On December 17, 1993, he ended his fast and left jail after an Oakland County Circuit Court judge reduced his bond to $100 in exchange for his vow not to help with any more suicides until state courts resolve the legality of his practice.

The U.S. Circuit Court dismissed charges against Kevorkian on January 27, 1994, in two deaths—becoming the fifth lower court judge in Michigan to rule that assisted suicide is a constitutional right. Four months later, a Detroit jury acquitted Kevorkian of charges he violated the state's assisted suicide ban in the death of Thomas Hyde. In further support of his position, on May 10, 1994, the Michigan Court of Appeals struck down the state's ban on assisted suicide on the grounds it was enacted unlawfully.

Oregon became the first state to legalize assisted suicide when voters passed a tightly restricted Death with Dignity Act on November 8, 1994, but legal appeals kept the law from taking effect.

Hours after Michigan's ban on assisted suicide expired on November 26, 1994, 72-year-old Margaret Garrish died of carbon monoxide poisoning in her home in Royal Oak. She had arthritis and osteoporosis. Kevorkian was not present when police arrived.

A month later, the Michigan Supreme Court upheld the constitutionality of Michigan's 1993 ban on assisted suicide, and also ruled that assisted suicide is illegal in Michigan under common law. The ruling reinstated cases against Kevorkian in four deaths.

On June 26, 1995, Kevorkian opened a "suicide clinic" in an office in Springfield Township, Michigan. Erika Garcellano, a 60-year-old Kansas City woman with ALS, was the first client. A few days later, the building's owner asked Kevorkian to leave. Kevorkian was then ordered to stand trial for assisting in the 1991 suicides of Sherry Miller and Marjorie Wantz. Shortly thereafter, a group of doctors and other medical experts in Michigan announced their support of Kevorkian, saying they would draw up a set of guiding principles for the "merciful, dignified, medically-assisted termination of life."

Further supporting Kevorkian's position, the Ninth U.S. Circuit Court of Appeals in San Francisco ruled that mentally competent, terminally ill adults have a constitutional right to help in dying from doctors, health care workers, and family members. It was the first time a federal appeals court endorsed assisted suicide. Shortly thereafter, on March 8, 1996, a jury acquitted Kevorkian in helping with two deaths.

The next month, a trial began in Kevorkian's home town of Pontiac in the deaths of Miller and Wantz. For the start of his third criminal trial, he wore colonial costume—tights, a white powdered wig, and big buckle shoes—to protest the fact that he was being tried under a centuries-old common law. He would face a maximum of five years in prison and a $10,000 fine if convicted in the deaths, but on May 14, 1996, the jury acquitted him.

Six months later, his lawyer announced a previously unreported assisted suicide of a 54-year-old woman, bringing the total number of his assisted suicides to 46 since 1990. A mistrial was declared on June 12, 1997, in what was Kevorkian's fourth trial; the case was later dropped.

Then on June 26, 1997, the U.S. Supreme Court ruled unanimously that state governments have the right to outlaw—or to approve—doctor-assisted suicide. The high court had been asked to decide whether state laws banning the practice in New York and Washington were unconstitutional.

Five months later, Oregon residents voted to uphold the state's assisted suicide law, the first of its kind in the nation. The law allows doctors to prescribe lethal doses of drugs to terminally ill patients.

On March 14, 1998, Kevorkian's 100th assisted suicide took place, involving a 66-year-old Detroit man. Six months later, Michigan's second law outlawing physician-assisted suicide went into effect. The next month, Michigan voters rejected a proposal that would have legalized physician-assisted suicide for the terminally ill.

That same month, *60 Minutes* aired a videotape showing Kevorkian giving a lethal injection to Thomas Youk, 52, who suffered from Lou Gehrig's disease. The broadcast triggered an intense debate within medical, legal, and media circles, and prompted Michigan to charge Kevorkian with first-degree murder for violating the assisted suicide law and delivering a controlled substance without a license in the death of Youk. Prosecutors later dropped the suicide charge. Kevorkian insisted on defending himself during the trial and threatened to starve himself if sent to jail. He was convicted on April 13, 1999, and sent to prison for from 10 to 25 years. On April 22, 2002, the state Supreme Court refused to hear Kevorkian's request for a new trial. In its 6–1 decision, the high court declined to review a November ruling by the Michigan Court of Appeals, which rejected Kevorkian's bid for a new trial. The state Supreme Court said it was not persuaded that the questions presented should be reviewed by the court. Kevorkian had argued that euthanasia is legal and that his conviction was unconstitutional. Kevorkian lawyer Mayer Morganroth said he planned to appeal to the federal courts and to ask the U.S. Supreme Court to consider the case.

kindling The increasing susceptibility to suicide with recurrent stress.

Klagsbrun, Francine Author-researcher who wrote the bestseller, *Too Young to Die: Youth and Suicide.* With an introduction by Harold S. Kushner, author of *When Bad Things Happen to Good People,* Klagsbrun's book has been highly acclaimed as an important work on the subject of youth and suicide.

Koestler, Arthur (1905–1983) British writer born in Vienna who in 1940 settled in Britain, where his anti-Stalinist novel *Darkness at Noon* (1940) was first published. In addition to several novels, he wrote a number of books on political and philosophical topics.

Koestler suffered in later life from Parkinson's disease, and in 1983, he and his wife Cynthia, committed suicide together. He was 78 and already dying (he had written a suicide note in June 1982), but Cynthia Koestler was only 55 and in good health.

Koestler was a vice president of the VOLUNTARY EUTHANASIA SOCIETY in London and had written an essay for the society's booklet "A Guide to Self-Deliverance."

The Koestlers' maid found a note on March 3, 1983, instructing her to ring the police and to tell them to come to the house. Police found the Koestlers sitting in their usual places, he in the armchair with an empty brandy glass in his hand; Cynthia to his left, on the sofa. They had been dead about 36 hours from an overdose of BARBITURATES. Cynthia Koestler had typed a brief footnote to her husband's suicide note: "I should have liked to finish my account of working for Arthur—a story which began when our paths happened to cross in 1949. However, I cannot live without Arthur, despite certain inner resources."

Kraepelin, Emil (1856–1926) German psychiatrist and author of *Lectures on Clinical Psychia-*

try, who expressed the belief that mental disturbances were a direct factor in at least one-third of all suicides. Many authorities disagree, stressing that such a relationship should be considered with great care because of the problems in defining mental health and mental illness. His relatively large rate figure is based on fact that the high incidence of mental illness among suicides had been previously pointed out by a number of investigators.

Kristin Brooks Hope Center A nonprofit organization founded by H. Reese Butler II, husband of the late Kristin Brooks Rossell-Butler, 28, who hanged herself April 7, 1998, after a battle with manic DEPRESSION and postpartum depression. After losing his wife, Reese founded the center to help find solutions for women who suffer from postnatal/postpartum depression and manic depression. The center also operates the first national toll-free crisis phone line, the NATIONAL HOPELINE NETWORK.

For contact information, see Appendix I.

Kübler-Ross, Elisabeth Psychiatrist and world-renowned authority on death and dying, and the author of the ground-breaking 1969 book *On Death and Dying.*

Now in her 70s, she has spent most of her life working with the dying. She was born one of triplets in Zurich, SWITZERLAND, and graduated from medical school at the University of Zurich in 1957. She came to the United States a year later, where she was appalled by the standard treatment of dying patients in New York hospitals. She completed her degree in psychiatry at the University of Colorado in 1963.

Unlike her colleagues, she made it a point to sit with terminal patients, listening as they poured out their hearts to her. She began giving lectures featuring dying patients who talked about what they were going through, and began to write the first of a series of books on the topic.

Dr. Kübler-Ross has been awarded more than 25 honorary doctorates from major universities and received the Modern Samaritan Award and the Ideal Citizen Award. Dr. Kübler-Ross founded a growth and healing center called Shanti Nilaya in Escondido, California.

In 1995, she suffered a series of major strokes, which left her paralyzed and facing her own death. While her health has stabilized, she has not completely recovered from her strokes.

"Lady Lazarus" Poem written by SYLVIA PLATH in which she all but boasted of a recent suicide attempt. She concluded the poem with:

> Dying
> Is an art, like everything else.
> I do it exceptionally well.
> I do it so it feels like hell.
> I do it so it feels real.
> I guess you could say I've a call.

On February 11, 1963, Sylvia Plath committed suicide. Her suicide attempt 10 years before had been, from all appearances, deadly serious.

Lanterman-Petrie-Short Act (LPS) Adopted in California in 1967, the act is considered a landmark in the reform of INVOLUNTARY COMMITMENT, for suicidal persons in particular and for psychiatric patients in general. In that state, prior to LPS, a person could be committed indefinitely if found to be "of such mental condition that he is in need of supervision, treatment, care or restraint," or "dangerous to himself, or to the person or property of others . . ."

Under the old system, California courts committed more than 1,000 persons a month to state institutions, often after only cursory psychiatric examination and court hearing. LPS, on the other hand, prohibits involuntary detention for longer than 72 hours. If these conditions as described by law prevails, the person can be certified for 14 days of "intensive treatment." After expiration of the 14-day certification period, suicidal persons can be confined for up to 14 addi-

tional days, if the person gives overt indication of continued danger to self or by an attempt or threat to suicide in the first 14-day period, or if he was *originally* detained for an attempt or threat and, in the judgment of the psychiatrist, continued to present that threat. (In other words, he need not have made an additional attempt or threat during the first 14 days of hospitalization.)

Unfortunately, while LPS solved one problem, it created a new one. Because inadequate provisions were made to help the suicidal person, many patients discharged after the short time span have turned up quickly in municipal hospitals or alone on the streets of cities and towns throughout the state.

Latin America Generally speaking, suicide rates per 100,000 population show that Latin American countries rank lower than most reporting nations. Authorities believe that the relative low rates in most Latin American countries may be due to the prevalence of Catholicism with its authoritarian body of common beliefs concerning suicide. It should be noted that data regarding different countries are often of questionable reliability because of varying reporting methods and criteria used by the United Nations.

Law, Liberty and Psychiatry Book by right-to-suicide advocate psychiatrist Thomas Szasz. Szasz writes: "In a free society, a person must have the right to injure or kill himself . . . there is no moral justification for depriving a person of his liberty in order to treat him." Dr. Szasz opposes involuntary hospitalization or forced treatment for suicidal persons under any circumstances. INTERVENTION, he believes, should come only when a person asks for help.

law and suicide In western European traditions, the law has traditionally not approved of suicide and, because of that, of those who expedite it. Suicide was considered to be a type of murder, and therefore a felony, according to Anglo-American law in the 17th and 18th centuries. But because the successful suicidal person escaped traditional forms of punishment by dying, the law looked elsewhere for an appropriate response. The solution, developed by both ecclesiastical and civil law, imposed burial restrictions on those who killed themselves. These laws also punished the victim's family by requiring that all the victim's assets be forfeited to the Crown, sometimes leaving the survivors destitute. By the mid-19th century these types of punishment had disappeared both in England and the United States, but suicide was still considered to be a crime.

Today, neither suicide nor attempted suicide is a crime in any state, although many jurisdictions still consider it illegal to help someone else attempt or commit suicide. PHYSICIAN-ASSISTED SUICIDE is legal in Oregon.

law enforcement officers See POLICE SUICIDE.

legal aspects of suicide Early legal aspects of suicide found civil and church law almost inseparably mixed. English law incorporated ecclesiastic canons when King Edgar adopted into civil law the punishments against the corpse (degradation) and estate (confiscation) of the suicide.

These customs were discontinued only in 1823 when the law burying the corpse at a crossroads was repealed, and in 1870 when the law forfeiting goods was erased.

Attempted suicide became a crime in ENGLAND in 1854 and continued until its repeal in 1961.

While a number of countries still retain laws making attempted suicide a crime, in most the law is used to register the attempts and to provide for treatment. In the United States, laws against completing, or attempting suicide have been repealed in each of the states. Aiding and abetting suicide remains against the law in 21 of the states.

In the courts, the attitude of the law on the case for and treatment of suicide has moved from rigid accountability for all such deaths to the principles of foreseeability and the need to take reasonable risks (within the standard of care in the community) in the treatment program in order to allow improvement.

Let Me Die Before I Wake Book written by DEREK HUMPHRY, founder of the HEMLOCK SOCIETY, and most recently published in 1984 by Hemlock/Grove. This controversial guide to "self-deliverance" for the dying person has been and still is widely debated in many professional circles and in the media. First editions of this 1981 book were sold only to members of the Hemlock Society. Public desire for more information about voluntary EUTHANASIA resulted in later extended editions.

Derek Humphry and the late Ann Wickett, his ex-wife, also wrote *The Right to Die: Understanding Euthanasia*.

Lettres Persanes In one of his *Lettres Persanes*, written in 1721 by "Usbeck" from Paris to his friend "Ibben" in Smyrna, French writer Charles de Secondat, Baron de MONTESQUIEU, ridicules the European laws on suicide and defends its practice. The French political philosopher's *The Persian Letters*, published anonymously at Amsterdam in 1721, is a bitter satire on the church and the politics of FRANCE. Defending suicide, he wrote: "Life has been given to me as a gift. I can therefore return it when this is no longer the case . . ." He added, "when I am overwhelmed by pain, poverty and scorn, why does one want to prevent me from putting an end to my troubles, and to deprive me cruelly of a remedy which is in my hands?"

Levy, Jerrold E.   Author of *Navajo Suicide* who considered that traditional modes are inadequate to maintain the relationships that are important in modern Navajo society. Navajo men, for example, are more affected than women, since they must always undertake new roles. In the matter of suicide, Levy wrote, role situations offer a better framework than relationships.

See also NATIVE AMERICANS.

life insurance   See INSURANCE AND SUICIDE.

Lifekeeper Foundation   A group formed in 1995 to promote suicide awareness, education, and prevention through art forms such as Lifekeeper Jewelry, Poetry, and the Lifekeeper National Memory Quilt project. The Lifekeeper Foundation works with national suicide and mental health organizations to continue and develop other projects and carry the message that suicide happens in good families and that it can happen to anyone.

The foundation was formed in 1995 by Sandy Martin, in memory of her only child, Tony, who killed himself at age 17, on December 16, 1988. She is the vice president of SUICIDE PREVENTION ADVOCACY NETWORK (SPAN), a board member of the AMERICAN SUICIDE FOUNDATION (ASF), and a member of AMERICAN ASSOCIATION OF SUICIDOLOGY (AAS).

For contact information, see Appendix I.

Life's Preservative against Self-Killing   Treatise written by John Sym, an English country clergyman (1581?–1637), who worried about an increase in suicide in his country. The work made available to readers his personal experiences in counseling potential suicides. Sym believed that many suicides were sick in mind and could not be held responsible for their behavior. Thus, he said, not all suicides were in a state of damnation.

He did, however, divided suicide into direct and indirect forms and condemned those types involving intemperance, gluttony, dueling, and foolhardiness. Sym's main interest, though, was in the prevention of suicide, as the book's title expresses. He describes certain premonitory and diagnostic signs, such as "unusual solitariness, neglect of one's duties, change in behavior, talking to oneself, a distracted countenance and carriage, and threatening speech and action."

Lincoln, Mary Todd (1818–1882)   The wife of President Abraham Lincoln who was assessed by the court for insanity after his assassination. Son Robert Lincoln tried to have his mother declared legally incompetent after she began to suffer hallucinations and phobias, but the law required a trial before a person could be institutionalized.

Mrs. Lincoln attempted suicide after being judged insane by the court, and she was placed in a sanitarium, where she received treatment. She improved sufficiently for yet another court to reverse the insanity verdict in 1876. She died six years later.

Lindsay, Vachel (1879–1931)   One of America's best-known poets during the early decades of the 20th century whose international fame began with the publishing of his poem, "General William Booth Enters Into Heaven," a tribute to the founder of the Salvation Army, in *Poetry* magazine in 1913.

Born Nicholas Vachel Lindsay on November 10, 1879, in Springfield, Illinois, he was the second of six children and the only son of physician Vachel Thomas Lindsay and Esther Catharine Frazee Lindsay. Vachel was taught at home by his mother until he was eight years old. After skipping seventh grade and winning writing prizes, he graduated from Stuart School in 1893.

Throughout his lifetime, Vachel detested alcohol, didn't smoke, and believed in a chaste lifestyle. Expected to become a doctor like his father, he enrolled at Hiram College as a premed student in 1897, but three years later he transferred to the Art Institute of Chicago. While he enjoyed drawing, he was unhappy at Chicago and moved to the New York School of Art, where he began to combine poetry and art.

Between 1906 and 1912, Lindsay took to wandering on foot across the country, walking penniless and stopping at farms and villages along the way to trade poetry for food and shelter. In 1920, Lindsay became the first American poet invited to recite at Oxford University and undertook his first national lecturing tour.

However, his popularity began to fade during World War I, and he began working as an English instructor at Gulf Park College in Gulf Park, Mississippi. In 1924, Lindsay was invited to Spokane, Washington, as a poet-in-residence, where the 45-year-old poet married Elizabeth Connor, a 23-year-old high school English teacher, in 1925.

By the next year, his behavior was becoming increasingly erratic, dogged by unreasonable rage and paranoia, exacerbated by diabetes and epilepsy. Lindsay began to display signs of a serious personality disorder, and recurring bouts of depression confined him to bed and blocked his writing. For most of his working life, Lindsay was tortured by doubts and fears that shattered his self-esteem, and he suffered with bouts of manic-depressive illness. In 1931, despondent, exhausted, and in substantial debt, Lindsay committed suicide by drinking Lysol. His suicide note read: "They tried to get me—I got them first!"

See MANIC DEPRESSION.

Litman, Robert E., M.D.   Founder of the Los Angeles Suicide Prevention Center and former president of the AMERICAN ASSOCIATION OF SUICIDOLOGY.

Dr. Litman is a pioneer in the area of PSYCHOLOGICAL AUTOPSIES—along with Edwin Shneidman and Norman L. Farberow—and is one of the foremost experts in suicide and the law.

Dr. Litman traced the development of SIGMUND FREUD's thoughts on suicide from 1881 to 1939, pointing out that, among other things, there is more to the psychodynamics of suicide than hostility, including rage, guilt, anxiety, and dependency, together with feelings of abandonment and of helplessness and hopelessness.

Dr. Litman has conducted many studies relating to suicide, suicidal behavior and the PREVENTION and INTERVENTION aspects of suicide.

Little Prince, The   Popular children's book published in 1943 by ANTOINE-MARIE-ROGER DE SAINT-EXUPÉRY, which describes a fantasy romanticizing suicide as a form of "going home." Saint Exupéry was an expert pilot and author of many popular books when he wrote *The Little Prince*, his most famous work.

He was 44 years old when he disappeared in his plane on July 31, 1944, after leaving Bastia in Corsica on an Allied reconnaissance mission over France. He never returned, and no trace of him or his plane was ever found. Some people are convinced the pilot-author's death was a suicide, stressing that the evening before his final flight he had prepared a letter in the form of a will. Others who saw him before he left noted that he had complained of a sleepless night and appeared restless and depressed.

Locke, John (1632–1704)   British philosopher regarded as the father of empiricism, who denied the existence of any inborn knowledge or innate ideas. Lock's theological argument against suicide had wide support in Great Britain at the time. In his *Two Treaties of Government* Locke wrote: ". . . Man being all the workmanship of one omnipotent and infinitely wise Maker; all the servants of one sovereign Master, sent into the world by His order and about His business; they are His property, whose workmanship they are made to last during His, not another's pleasure . . . Everyone . . . is bound to preserve himself, and not to quit his station wilfully . . ."

London City that had high suicide rates in areas with rooming houses and single-person dwelling units, and in areas with high rates of mobility and other signs of social disorganization, according to a study done by Peter Sainsbury in the 1980s.

Such analyses of suicide rates within small, specific geographic areas have led experts to valuable clues in the etiology of the phenomenon.

As a whole, in 1997 ENGLAND and WALES had a suicide rate of 6.6 per 100,000, considerably less than the 8.9 in 1981 and 8.6 in 1982. The suicide rate for men was also lower than in the 1980s (10.3 per 100,000) and for women it was much lower (2.9 compared to 5.9 in 1982). As in many industrialized countries, the highest suicide rate among men occurred in those over age 75. In women, the highest suicide rate was during middle age (45 to 54)—a rate of 4.4 per 100,000.

loneliness Loneliness is a state that exacerbates any other problem, disappointment, loss of job, or death in the family, and that has been closely related to hopelessness-helplessness. People thinking of suicide often feel lonely and hopeless. Life loses its value and death seems the perfect release from troubles.

Philosopher Bertrand Russell wrote of loneliness in his *Autobiography* (1967), stating: "I have sought love . . . because it relieves loneliness— that terrible loneliness in which one shivering consciousness looks over the rim of the world into the cold, unfathomable lifeless abyss . . ."

The Loneliness of Children Book by Vanderbilt University professor John Killinger, who theorized that women seeking child care must choose between their children's needs and their own. He argues that America's children must not be deprived of the parental attention that creates security and sound character. Lack of proper parental care and attention can create insecurity, anxiety, even fear—and sometimes leads to a despair that establishes a suicidal mind-set.

Los Angeles Suicide Prevention Center The first agency in the United States to establish a 24-hour suicide prevention hotline. The center was founded in 1958 by psychologists Norman L. Farberow and EDWIN S. SHNEIDMAN. They began the center with an all-professional staff but in time welcomed volunteers to the program, which includes research, prevention, and intervention aspects. Today the center is part of the Didi Hirsch Community Mental Health Center.

Shneidman and Farberow, both pioneers in the field of SUICIDOLOGY, made the Los Angeles center the prototype for prevention and crisis centers, not only in the United States, but throughout the world. Much of the research that has been done about destructive behavior, suicide, and suicide prevention has been by these two authorities at the center.

Among other things, they developed the vital research method called the PSYCHOLOGICAL AUTOPSY, a means to help medical examiners and coroners determine the cause of a death when it is not clearly indicated.

The Suicide Prevention Center operates with more than 100 volunteers who have been trained by professionals specializing in suicide prevention. Volunteers perform telephone crisis intervention, bereavement support, and community education and outreach.

For contact information, see Appendix I.

loss DEPRESSION is often caused by a person's feeling a deep sense of loss for someone or something. It may be triggered by the loss of a loved one, a job, or even the loss of a particular feeling or sense of being (such as, loss of feeling wanted or needed). This loss is so significant that it leads to overwhelming sorrow, feelings of weakness and unworthiness.

Any loss of a child, a spouse, or health can lead to severe, unrelenting depression and, subsequently, to suicidal thoughts. Young people are especially vulnerable to crippling losses.

It is no accident that the suicide rate is higher among the unmarried, the divorced, and the widowed than among the married. Similarly, those who live in anonymous urban settings are more likely candidates for suicide than those living in rural areas, where the sense of community and extended family is stronger. The individual cannot adjust to a sudden, shocking loss—of a job, a marriage, a wife, a close friend, or money. All these losses, unless help is forthcoming, may result in an ANOMIC SUICIDE. In this type of suicide, the individual's society seems to have lost its familiar structure and customary guiding organization.

LOSS (Loving Outreach to Survivors of a Suicide)
National nondenominational self-help support group for those who have experienced a death by suicide of a family member or close friend. LOSS, which is sponsored by Catholic Charities, has chapters throughout the country.

LOSS offers a safe, nonjudgmental place where group members are assisted throughout the grieving process. The support and understanding of the trained social workers coupled with the knowledge and firsthand experience of the veteran LOSS members help survivors realize they are not alone and that they will not feel the intense sadness for the rest of their lives.

Founding director of the program is the Rev. Charles T. Rubey, director of programs for Catholic Charities in Chicago.

For contact information, see Appendix I.

love
During adolescence, young people experience many emotional as well as physical changes. Often intense emotions experienced in early childhood are restimulated by adolescent changes, adding to the stresses, pressures, and problems ordinarily accompanying these years. For example, just as crippling as the actual physical loss of a parent is the sense of love lost, a feeling of not being loved or cared for. Young people who grow up feeling unloved come to think of themselves as unworthy of love. Even adults may develop a self-image of uselessness and ineptness, and they too can and do turn against themselves and others.

Young people who feel unloved by parents consider themselves "expendable." The expendable child feels his parents don't love him, feels anger but can't express it, and feels that his parents never wanted children and, thus, would be better off without him. In an effort to gain this longed-for parental love, the child turns his anger inward becoming suicidal.

Another idea that may trigger youth suicides is what some experts term the "Romeo and Juliet Factor." Even before Shakespeare wrote about these two star-crossed teenage lovers, romantic love in literature and drama had often been associated with death. Often, lovers planned to be "reunited in death." The linking of love and death can produce lethal results for romantically inclined teenagers. However, investigators have pointed out that this usually occurs only in the young person already emotionally distressed and at risk for potential suicide.

love pact suicide   See SUICIDE PACT.

Lowell, Robert (1917–1977)
American poet noted for his complex poetry and turbulent life, which was entangled with the social, political, and ideological movements in the United States during the post–World War II years. Lowell was called the father of the "confessional poets," a term used to describe JOHN BERRYMAN, SYLVIA PLATH, and ANNE HARVEY SEXTON, among others.

From 1949, Lowell, diagnosed with BIPOLAR DISORDER (manic DEPRESSION), spent periods of time in mental hospitals, drank heavily, and was married three times. During this period, he later admitted to having suicidal thoughts, and wrote about his ambivalence: "Do I deserve credit for not having tried suicide—or am I afraid the exotic act will make me blunder, not knowing error is remedied by practice . . ."

He was on his way to see his second (former) wife in New York when he died of a heart attack on September 12, 1977.

Lowry, Malcolm (1909–1957)   English novelist famous primarily for his novel *Under the Volcano,* now recognized as a masterpiece. Born in England and educated at Cambridge, he was a profoundly unhappy man. An alcoholic, Lowry confessed to thoughts of suicide to escape his isolated alcoholic hell, much like the hero of his great novel. He died in Sussex, ENGLAND, somewhat mysteriously by "misadventure." Alcohol and sodium amytal tablets were involved, leading some to suspect suicide and others to suggest murder, by his wife.

loyalty suicides   A term sometimes used to describe suicides committed out of loyalty, such as soldiers who slay themselves out of a desire to either imitate their leader's example, or simply to join their leader in the afterlife they envision.

In his account of Otho's death, the Roman writer Tacitus mentions that some of the emperor's soldiers "slew themselves near his pyre . . ." Such suicides closely parallel INSTITUTIONAL SUICIDE and RITUAL SUICIDES, such as the Hindu custom of SUTTEE, in which the widow immolates herself with the corpse of her husband. These "loyalty suicides" are also related to the concept of ALTRUISTIC SUICIDE, in which the person is "overidentified" with his society and kills him or herself out of loyalty to its expectations or demands.

LSD   Lysergic acid diethylamide (LSD) is one of a group of hallucinogenic drugs that produce psychotic symptoms and behavior. Symptoms may include hallucinations, illusions, body and time-space distortions, and, less commonly, intense panic or mystical experience. Some users attempt suicide while in an LSD-induced state.

Lucan (Marcus Annaeus Lucanus) (A.D. 39–65)   Roman poet at first a favorite of NERO who later became involved in a conspiracy against him. Upon its discovery, Lucan committed suicide. As Lucan himself said, "how simple a feat it is to escape slavery by suicide."

Lucian (ca. A.D. 125–ca. 190)   Greek satirist and teacher of rhetoric and philosophy who became prefect at Alexandria in later life. After witnessing the fiery suicide by immolation of Peregrinus, he wrote an essay, "The Death of Peregrinus," depicting the Cynic philosopher as an exhibitionist, a man with an insatiable craving for notoriety.

magical thinking and suicide A fantasy that, in relation to suicide, is associated with a feeling of power and complete control—a "You'll be sorry when I'm dead" fantasy.

An illustration of magical thinking and suicide is the old Japanese custom of killing oneself on the doorstep of someone who has caused insult or humiliation. Similar to MANIPULATIVE SUICIDE, in this case a fatal result is intended. Sometimes also called "aggressive suicide," magical thinking in a power struggle often means that if one person can't win, he or she can at least get in the last word by committing suicide.

males and suicide Generally speaking, although women attempt suicide about three times as often as men, men complete suicide about three times as often as women.

Men are at particular risk of completing suicide suddenly without warning, without being aware of the warning signs of DEPRESSION. According to the National Center for Health Statistics, white men have the highest suicide rate. In 1998, white men accounted for 73 percent of all suicides. Indeed, suicide claims more than 24,000 men's lives every year. Most younger and middle-aged men who attempt suicide share evidence of impulsivity. They are aggressive sexually, financially, and interpersonally, with a tendency to act on their feelings.

Suicide is an option that for men, climbs only more steeply with age. By age 25, men are six times as liable to take their own lives as are women; by age 85, they are 13 times more likely to kill themselves. Men accounted for 83 percent of suicides among those over age 65, and from 1980 to 1998, the largest relative increases in suicide rates occurred among those 80 to 84 years of age. The rate for men in this age group increased 17 percent (from 43.5 per 100,000 to 52). Firearms were the most common method of suicide by men over 65 in 1998, accounting for 78 percent.

Suicide rates among the elderly are highest for those men who are divorced or widowed. In 1992, the rate for divorced or widowed men over age 65 was 2.7 times that for married men, 1.4 times that for never-married men, and more than 17 times that for married women.

Young men are also at higher risk for suicide. The risk for suicide among young people is greatest among young white men, although from 1980 through 1995, suicide rates increased most rapidly among young black males.

White men have, for the past years (1950 to 1998), consistently had the highest suicide rates of any race and sex category. During this same period, men of other races had the second highest rates; white women had the third highest rates, while women of other races have consistently had the lowest rates.

Malinowski, Bronislaw (1884–1942) Polish anthropologist and author of *Crime and Custom in Savage Society,* a book presenting what has often been called "the best-known case in the history of anthropological theory," dealing with the case of suicide among the Trobriand (in the southwest Pacific). Malinowski uses his collected material to show how public disapproval of a man who had committed a major sin (in this instance, incest) acted as a legal device by prompting the offender to complete suicide. Although Malinowski's argument was concerned with the field of law, the case led anthropologists to reconsider the nature of suicide in primitive societies.

Man Against Himself Definitive work by psychiatrist KARL MENNINGER, who agrees with Freud in the existence of simultaneous contradictory drives: the life instinct (Eros) and the death instinct (Thanatos). In *Man Against Himself,* Menninger describes, analyzes, and interprets the many self-destructive acts in which people engage. He writes about different kinds of deaths that result from the interplay of the life and death instincts, which take different forms and which he calls chronic, focal, and organic suicides. Menninger believed that within the act of suicide, three elements occur in varying proportions in each suicide: (1) the wish to kill; (2) the wish to be killed; (3) the wish to die.

manic depression The informal term for BIPOLAR DISORDER characterized by swings between episodes of both mania and DEPRESSION. The illness may be subdivided into manic, depressed, or mixed types on the basis of the presenting symptoms.

In the mixed or circular type, extreme mood swings alternate from the depths of despair (lowered mood, sleep disturbance, decreased appetite, intense feelings of worthlessness) to soaring heights of euphoria (excitement, expansive or irritable mood, flights of ideas, distractibility, impaired judgment, and sometimes grandiosity). This disease often begins during adolescence or in the early 20s and may continue throughout the patient's life.

Manic depression is caused by biochemical disorders within the brain. Physicians usually treat the illness with lithium carbonate, an alkali metal to reduce the duration, intensity, and frequency of the mood swings.

As the depression phase becomes more severe, the danger of suicide becomes greater.

Patients often fall into a deep, dark despondency, and are inundated by oppressive thoughts of suicide. Family members, friends, and associates should be alert to the victim's symptoms, suicidal conversation, and overt hints of death wishes.

manipulative suicide An attempt to manipulate others by attempting suicide, usually with a nonfatal intent. Basically, the person trying to commit suicide is saying: "If you don't do what I want, I'll kill myself."

However, the word *manipulative* does not imply that a suicide attempt is not serious. Fatal attempts are often made by people who are hoping to influence the feelings of others, despite the fact that they will not be around to witness the success or failure of their efforts. Nevertheless, while people sometimes die or are injured as a result of their attempts, the intention in a manipulative suicide attempt is to cause guilt in another person. The person who attempts suicide usually does not really intend to die.

Many Faces of Suicide, The Book edited by suicide expert Norman J. Farberow, outlining the area of INDIRECT SUICIDE ("focal" or "organic" suicide), noting its characteristics and its differentiation from direct or overt suicide, especially in terms of time and the role of intention.

A number of experts contributed chapters to the book on such subjects as hyperobesity, auto accidents, heart disease, psychosomatic illnesses, malingering, gambling, and high-risk activities.

MAO inhibitors A group of antidepressant drugs that inhibit the enzyme monoamine oxidase responsible for breaking down serotonin and norepinephrine in the brain.

The main types of MAO inhibitors are isocarboxazid (Marplan), phenelaine (Nardil), and tranylepromine (Parnate). These extremely potent drugs cause frequent side effects that may be severe. Used in combination with other drugs—narcotics, stimulants, depressants—in an uncontrolled manner, the effect can be fatal. The same is true when MAO inhibitors are taken with foods that contain tyramine, such as cheese, herring, salami, and chocolate. MAO inhibitors are considered extremely dangerous drugs and are usually only administered under close medical supervision.

Marcus Aurelius (A.D. 121–180) Roman emperor and Stoic who approved of suicide only when committed on a rational basis, but not to simply express irrational ideas. As Marcus Aurelius wrote: "how admirable is the soul which is ready and resolved, if it must this moment be released from the body, to be either extinguished or scattered or to persist. This resolve too must arise from a specific decision, not out of sheer opposition like the Christians, but after reflection and with dignity, and so as to convince others, without histrionic display."

marijuana The dried tops, leaves and stems of the Indian hemp plant *Cannabis sativa,* which contain the psychoactive substance tetrahydrocannabinol (THC) and that is usually smoked in cigarettes or pipes.

Marijuana is a popular abused substance, and despite its illegal status in the United States, there are an estimated 16 million regular American users. The number of users increased each year until 1978; since that time, surveys have shown significant decline. This decrease in use is attributed to a change in attitude among young people. In 1978, 35 percent felt that regular marijuana was associated with great risk; by 1982, this figure had risen to 60 percent.

People who use marijuana are also apt to drink alcohol. When alcohol is taken with marijuana there is a greater impairment of motor and mental skills than with either drug alone. While the use of marijuana does not produce physical dependence, after long-term chronic use it does often produce psychological dependence on the euphoric and sedative effects.

A lethal dose has never been established since no deaths directly related to the action of marijuana have been reported.

Although no reliable data exists to prove or disprove effects of marijuana use on suicide rates, neither marijuana nor alcohol relieves depression.

See also DRUG ABUSE.

marital status and suicide Suicide rates are lowest among married persons. It should be noted, however, that most people who kill themselves are married simply because the majority of adults are married (though this has been changing in recent years). In other words, even though the suicide *rates* are low for married adults, the actual *number* of suicide victims among marrieds is relatively high.

According to data from the National Center for Health Statistics, age-adjusted suicide rates by marital status for white men, black men, white women, and black women show that married persons in all four race and sex groups have the lowest suicide rates. Single persons who had never married have rates twice as high as for those who are married with children. Rates are high among widowed and divorced people in almost all age groups. (Among the widowed, a spouse's death often acts as a strong precipitating factor to take their own lives.) The most astonishing feature of suicide rates by marital status is the very high rates for widowed men of both white and black races. Only among white women did divorced persons have a rate that exceeded the rate for widowed persons.

martyrdom There have been many instances in history of the phenomenon linking suicide with a desire for martyrdom. Voluntary martyrdom was common among the early Christians. As a youth, ORIGEN of ALEXANDRIA (c. A.D. 185–253/54) experienced the martyrdom of his father in 202 and wanted to suffer the same fate. However, Origen's mother prevented him from committing suicide.

Other early examples include Vibia Perpetua, a young married mother, age 22, who chose to die in the arena in the reign of Septimius Severus. EUSEBIUS, bishop of Caesarea, tells of Christians about to be tortured who chose instead suicide, regarding death as a prize snatched from the wickedness of evil men.

This type of pathological craving for martyrdom and its emotional climate characterized large groups in the Roman Empire between the reigns of Nero and Julian (A.D. 54 to 363).

Ultimately, strengthened by the increasingly important status of Christianity, both as a tolerated faith and as the state religion, voluntary martyrdom was discouraged by church leaders, and opposition to all suicide was stiffened. It was not until 563, however, at the Council of Braga, that suicide as an act was condemned by the church. This position remained canon law until 1284 when the Synod of Nimes refused burial in consecrated ground to suicides. Recent examples of voluntary martyrdom include the KAMIKAZE PILOTS of Japan in World War II and the Middle Eastern terrorists who willingly die during or as a result of their actions in behalf of *jihad* (or holy war).

Masada   A Jewish fortress besieged by the Romans in A.D. 72 to 73. The citadel was a site of the most dramatic and symbolic act in Jewish history, where rebels chose mass suicide rather than submit to Roman capture.

The Masada originally was the royal citadel of King Herod, located at the top of an isolated rock on the edge of the Judean desert and the Dead Sea valley. In 40 B.C., Herod fled from Jerusalem to Masada with his family in a moment of danger. Later, he fortified the citadel as a refuge from his enemies.

At the outbreak of the Jewish war, Menahem, son of Judah the Galilean, captured Masada at the head of a band of Zealots. After Menahem was murdered in Jerusalem by Jewish rivals, his nephew Eleazar ben Yair escaped to Masada. During these years, Masada served as a place of refuge for anyone in danger of capture. After the fall of Jerusalem in A.D. 72, Masada remained the only point of Jewish resistance. A few surviving Jewish fighters who crossed the Judean mountains joined the defenders of Masada, and it became the rebels' base for raiding operations.

In A.D. 72, the Roman governor Flavius Silva decided to uproot this outpost of resistance and marched against Masada at the head of almost 15,000 troops and Jewish war prisoners. The troops prepared for a long siege, building eight camps at the base of the Masada rock and surrounded it with a high wall, leaving no escape for rebels. As the Romans closed in, Eleazar gathered all the Masada defenders and persuaded them to kill themselves rather than fall into the hands of the Romans.

The people set fire to their personal belongings, and then 10 people chosen by a lot killed everyone else, and then completed suicide. In the morning, Romans entered a silent fortress and found some 960 dead Jews. Two women and five children survived the MASS SUICIDE by hiding in a cave, and told the story to Jewish historian and soldier Flavius Josephus (see JOSEPHUS, FLAVIUS).

See also MASS SUICIDE.

mass suicide   Suicide among a large number of people all at the same time. In the past 20 years there have been a number of notable mass suicides in the United States and other parts of the world.

In March 1997, the bodies of 39 young people who were part of the HEAVEN'S GATE religious cult died in a mansion near San Diego. The victims, who were all between 18 and 24 years old, drank a lethal mixture of phenobarbital and vodka and then settled to die over a three-day period. The victims (21 women and 18 men) apparently believed their deaths would lead to a rendezvous with a UFO hiding behind Comet Hale-Bopp.

A number of mass suicides have been linked to the SOLAR TEMPLE, an international sect that believes ritualized suicide leads to rebirth on a planet called Sirius. Mass suicides occurred on March 23, 1997, when the burned bodies of five Temple members (three women and two men) were found inside a house in Quebec. In December 1995, 16 Solar Temple members were found dead in a burned house outside Grenoble in the French Alps, and in October 1994, the burned bodies of 48 Solar Temple members were discovered in a farmhouse and three chalets in Switzerland. At the same time, five bodies (including an infant) were found in a chalet north of Montreal.

Members of another cult, known as the Branch Davidians, died on April 19, 1993, when at least 70 cult members ended their lives after fire and a shootout with police and federal agents after a 51-day siege of the compound near Waco, Texas. The sect's leader, David Koresh, who had preached a messianic gospel of sex, freedom, and revolution and told followers he was Jesus Christ, died of a gunshot wound to the head sometime during the blaze.

In October 1993, 53 Vietnamese hill tribe villagers committed mass suicide with flintlock guns and other primitive weapons in the belief they would go straight to heaven. Officials said they were the victims of a scam by a man who received cash donations for promising a speedy road to paradise.

Mexican minister Ramon Morales Almazan and 29 followers suffocated in December 1991 after he told them to keep praying and ignore toxic fumes filling their church. The year before, 12 people died in a religious ritual in Tijuana, apparently after drinking fruit punch tainted by industrial alcohol.

The Jonestown mass suicide (see JONESTOWN MASSACRE) occurred on November 18, 1978, when the Rev. Jim Jones led more than 900 followers to their deaths at the compound in Guyana, by drinking a cyanide-laced grape punch. Cult members who refused to swallow the liquid were shot.

MASADA is perhaps the best known site of mass suicides in the ancient world. An eerie parallel to Masada occurred during World War II at TREBLINKA, one of the most terrifying Nazi concentration camps. Untold thousands of Jews, mostly from Eastern Europe, were sent for extermination to Treblinka in eastern Poland. Over time, these people started to commit suicide one by one rather than submit to the horrors they were experiencing and the ultimate persecution that would end in extermination at the hands of their Nazi tormentors. Their deaths by suicide affirmed the freedom to control their own lives and deaths. These acts of suicide also led to solidarity among them, with those who remained alive helping those who wanted to kill themselves so they would die quickly.

In 17th-century Russia, the Great Schism (The Raskol) left the dissenting religious group called the Raskolniki in such despair that many followers sought death rather than wait for the end of the world (which they had predicted would occur before the end of the century). Between 1672 and 1691, more than 37 mass immolations took place in which more than 20,000 Raskolniki voluntarily burned to death. They had thought it senseless to live and risk being contaminated by heresy.

See also CULT SUICIDE.

Maximus Valerius (42 B.C.–A.D. 37)   Historian and contemporary of the Roman emperor, Tiberius who wrote that Roman suicides were not uncommon during the rule of Caesar Augustus. He recorded that in the important port city of Marseilles, the municipal senate actually supplied free HEMLOCK-laced poison to anyone who could give valid reasons for wanting to commit suicide.

McIntosh, John L.   Suicidologist and professor of psychology at Indiana University at South Bend who wrote *Suicide Among U.S. Racial Minorities, Suicide Among Children, Adolescents, and Students*, and *Suicide Among the Elderly*. He is co-editor (with Edward J. Dunne and Kaven Dunne-Maxim) of *Suicide and Its Aftermath: Understanding and Counseling the Survivors.* He also compiled *Research on Suicide: A Bibliography,* published in 1985, an important addition to the bibliographies on suicide. Professor McIntosh is a past president of the AMERICAN ASSOCIATION OF SUICIDOLOGY.

media, effects of suicide coverage   A number of suicidologists and other authorities have criticized news coverage by newspapers, magazines, television, and radio, contending that reading or hearing about a suicide victim in the news is often enough to trigger COPYCAT SUICIDES.

In 1979, sociologist David Phillips found that news stories of suicides did stimulate a wave of imitative acts. He checked Los Angeles traffic records for periods immediately following locally publicized suicides and discovered that for three days after a suicide report in the Los Angeles area, auto fatalities rose by 31 percent. He later found a similar jump in fatalities in Detroit, following front-page coverage of a suicide. (It would be impossible, of course, to prove that the auto deaths were suicides rather than accidents.)

On the other hand, studies have revealed that a drop in suicides in cities has taken place during extended newspaper blackouts, such as, when a strike has shut down the paper. On the other hand, there have been many reports of rises in the number of suicides following media coverage of a celebrity's suicide.

Most experts appear to agree that the far greater danger lies in preventing discussion and exposure of the subject of suicide. Not to report and discuss suicide simply places it back in the taboo category and promotes more myth and misinformation, which, ultimately, may cause more suicides.

Although exposure to suicides is a possible risk factor, research has not yet determined the effects of exposure to previous suicides on subsequent suicides.

medical personnel   Physicians, nurses, and ancillary medical therapists and technicians serve as a first line of defense against suicide. They are frequently called "gatekeepers" because they are often the first persons to learn of DEPRESSION or suicidal feelings, many of which are masked or disguised in physical symptoms. Medical personnel trained in interpretation of the common physical and emotional signs of depression provide the opportunity for early identification and intervention.

Medical personnel in hospital emergency rooms or serving in emergency medical services are often called on to save the life of a person who made a suicide attempt. Often the first to be greeted by an attempter on recovery, the attitude and understanding is crucial for averting further suicide attempts or subsequent suicidal behavior. Medical personnel are also important in their interaction with the families of the attempters who may be puzzled, confused, or angry.

There is an ongoing need for medical personnel to be trained in INTERVENTION, prevention, and POSTVENTION.

In addition to medical emergency services that offer help immediately in suicide crises, many communities now have mental health centers, crisis centers, suicide prevention centers, "hot lines," and walk-in services.

Menninger, Karl (1893–1990)   Psychiatrist and founder of the famed Menninger Institute in Topeka, Kansas, considered by many to be one of the foremost figures in American psychiatry. He is author of many books, including *MAN AGAINST HIMSELF,* in which he describes and interprets the many self-destructive acts in which people engage.

He summed up suicide in this way: the wish to kill, the wish to be killed, the wish to die. He said there is extreme anger against others, as well as oneself in the suicidal person. Menninger extended Sigmund Freud's concept of the death instinct (self-destruction) and its role in man's functioning, especially as it interacts with the life instinct (self-preservation) in times of stress and crisis. His book *The Vital Balance* describes five levels of personality organization from high to poor at which a person can function. Suicide, because it is self-destructive and often lethal, is listed in level 5, the lowest level.

Together with his father, Charles Frederick, Karl Menninger opened the Menninger Clinic in Topeka, Kansas, aimed at collecting many specialists in one center. In 1926, they were joined by Karl's brother William, also a psychiatrist. The Menninger Foundation, established for research, training, and public education in psychiatry, was founded in 1941 and soon became a U.S. psychiatric center.

menstruation and suicide Some experts believe that menstruation is linked to suicide attempts in some girls. Since every type of person under almost every conceivable circumstance commits suicide, it might be possible to say the menstrual cycle sometimes brings on DEPRESSION which, in turn, makes the potentially suicidal person more vulnerable. However, all victims of suicide usually show signs of intense emotional stress or mental disturbance, severe depression being only one symptom. Therefore, menstruation is more likely to be a contributing or precipitating factor than a primary cause.

mental illness Although most people who suffer from a mental illness do not die by suicide, having a mental illness does increase the likelihood of suicide. This does not mean that *every* person who is mentally ill is suicidal, or that everyone who commits suicide is mentally ill. Still, research suggests that 90 percent of suicides had a diagnosable mental disorder.

Even among mentally healthy people, a suicidal act is an abnormal reaction to stress. This is why individuals who are mentally ill—especially those suffering from a depressive illness—are usually considered to be at high risk for suicide.

Researchers suggest that about a third of all people who kill themselves are found to have been suffering from mental illness requiring treatment.

DEPRESSION is one of the highest risks for suicide, often featuring feelings of worthlessness and despair and a wish to die, and people who die by suicide are frequently suffering from undiagnosed, undertreated, or untreated depression. An estimated 2 to 14 percent of people who have been diagnosed with major depression die by suicide. Suicide risk is highest in depressed individuals who feel hopeless about the future, those who have just been discharged from the hospital, those who have a family history of suicide, and those who have made a suicide attempt in the past.

Also at high risk are individuals who suffer from depression at the same time as another mental illness. Specifically, the presence of substance abuse, anxiety disorders, SCHIZOPHRENIA, and BIPOLAR DISORDER put those with depression at greater risk for suicide.

Between 3 and 20 percent of those diagnosed with bipolar disorder (manic depression) die by suicide. Hopelessness, recent hospital discharge, family history, and prior suicide attempts all raise the risk of suicide in these patients.

Among those people who are psychotic, the rate among schizophrenics and manic depressives is disproportionately high. An estimated 6 to 15 percent of those diagnosed with schizophrenia die by suicide. In fact, suicide is the leading cause of premature death in those diagnosed with schizophrenia. Between 75 and 95 percent of these individuals are men.

People with personality disorders are approximately three times as likely to die by suicide than those without. Between 25 and 50 percent of these individuals also have a substance abuse disorder or major depressive disorder.

See ABUSE, SUBSTANCE.

mercy killing See ASSISTED SUICIDE and EUTHANASIA.

methods of suicide Firearms are the most commonly used method of suicide in the United States. The ICD (International Classification of Diseases) includes firearms and explosives in the same category, although only 1 percent of suicide deaths classified thus are due to "explosives." In 1970, 50.1 percent of the suicides in America were committed with firearms and explosives. By 1998, 60 percent of all suicides were committed with firearms and explosives.

The pattern of suicide by method doesn't vary a great deal by race, but does vary considerably by sex. Male patterns of suicide method didn't change much between 1970 and 1998. In 1970 as in 1980, firearms and explosives were the number one method of suicide for males, followed by HANGING, strangulation, suffocation, and poisoning.

There was a noticeable shift, however, between 1970 and 1980 in the most frequent suicide method employed by women. In 1970, poisoning by solids or liquids was the most frequently used method, followed by firearms (and explosives), in 1998, firearms and explosives were the methods used most frequently by women, followed by poisoning by solids and liquids. There was also an increase in the percent of suicides in which firearms and explosives were used by males and by females in both racial groups.

The choice of methods is determined by cultural factors and availability and may reflect the seriousness of intent, since some methods (such as jumping from heights) make survival virtually impossible, whereas others (such as drug overdoses) make rescue possible. However, using a method that proves not to be fatal does not necessarily imply that the intent was less serious.

Drug ingestion is the most common method used in suicide *attempts*. Use of BARBITURATES has decreased (to less than 5 percent of cases), but use of other psychoactive drugs is increasing. Use of salicylates has decreased from more than 20 percent of cases to about 10 percent, but use of acetaminophen is increasing. Although most people think of acetaminophen as a safe painkiller, an overdose can be very dangerous.

Two or more methods, or a combination of drugs, is used in about 20 percent of attempted suicides, increasing the risk of death, particularly when drugs with serious interactions are combined.

Violent methods such as shooting and hanging are uncommon among unsuccessful suicides.

Middle Ages There were varying social attitudes and practices with respect to suicide during the Middle Ages. Folk beliefs, ecclesiastical views, and medical theories considered suicide as a crime.

Antagonism to suicide and its eventual condemnation in the Holy Roman Empire were related to economics, religion, philosophy, and ultimately the law.

On the Continent, various municipal law codes did not punish suicide. The *Carolina*, the Criminal Constitution of Charles V, in 1551 confiscated the property of a suicide while the dead victim was under accusation of a felony.

In those times, the corpse of the suicide was often subjected to bizarre indignities and degradations. Most of these practices stemmed from long-standing religious and magical roots. For example, the practice of pinning down the body of a person who committed suicide predates Christianity among Europe's Germanic peoples.

In fact, legal and ecclesiastical attitudes toward suicide remained conservative until well into the 18th century; suicide was equated with murder in various parts of Europe, and the corpse was treated accordingly.

In France and England, the body was dragged through the streets, head downward on a hurdle, and then hanged on a gallows.

The three common penalties—confiscation of property, degradation of the corpse, and refusal of burial in consecrated ground—reflect attitudes toward suicide during the Middle Ages that were prevalent throughout the 18th century. It was not until the Renaissance that new attitudes toward suicide began to emerge.

Mihara-Yama volcano   Japanese volcano that in the past was a magnet for people who wanted to commit suicide. The problem began on January 7, 1933, when two young women bought steamship tickets to the Japanese island of Oshima, site of the Mihara-Yama volcano.

The women climbed to the top and stood on the lip of the boiling crater as clouds of sulfur puffed into the air. The older of the two, Mieko Ueki, 24, explained that to jump into Mihara-Yama would be a beautiful way to die, because one would instantly rise to heaven in a swirl of smoke. Then she announced her intention to do exactly that. After a mild protest from her companion, the women bowed to each other, and Mieko hurled herself into the stinking lava.

This "poetic suicide" so entranced the Japanese that 143 people later plunged to their deaths into the crater that year, including six on a single day in April. Eventually, the volcano became such a suicide magnet that the Japanese government finally closed passage to Mihara-Yama in 1935—after 804 men and 140 women had followed Mieko's volcanic leap.

Miletus, maidens of   Young Greek women in ancient times living in the now-ruined city of Miletus in western Asia Minor who were seized with the desire to die. So many young women of the city became intent on hanging themselves— for no apparent reason whatsoever—that the city fathers decided to seek legal means to stop the deaths.

The Milesians decided to pass a law requiring all maidens who hanged themselves to be carried to their graves naked except for the rope with which they had committed suicide. The vision of such a shameful, disgraceful burial was so distasteful to the young women of Miletus that the epidemic of hangings immediately ceased.

military defeat   History is filled with examples of self-destruction to escape the consequences of military defeat. Such examples go back to biblical times as exemplified by AHITOPHEL, a supporter of Absalom in his revolt against his father, King David. When Ahitopel saw that Absalom would be defeated, "he saddled his ass, and went home to his own city. And he set his house in order and hanged himself."

Vulteius, a tribune supporting Caesar in the civil war against Pompey, saw that escape was impossible and called upon his troops to die by their own hands rather than fall alive into the enemy's hands. Not one soldier survived.

The defeat of the Jewish Zealots on MASADA and their subsequent slaughter is another example, as is the defeat of Flavius Josephus that resulted in the suicide of all but one of his men and himself—and his subsequent conversion to a Roman citizen.

As recently as World War II, a number of German and Japanese military leaders chose suicide rather than surrender to Allied authorities.

See JOSEPHUS, FLAVIUS.

Mishima, Yukio (1925–1970)   Noted Japanese novelist and a candidate for the Nobel Prize in literature who committed HARA-KIRI on November 25, 1970, with one of his admirers, following the traditional SAMURAI ritual.

Mishima had been hailed as a writer of genius upon the publication of his first major work, the autobiographical *Confessions of a Mask* in 1949. He was also a playwright, a master of the ancient martial arts of karate and swordsmanship, and an actor in both his own stage plays and on the screen.

Mishima's dramatic suicide was considered not as a rash act, but as a bold gesture planned in great detail months before by a man who envisioned violent death as the ultimate assertion of self.

Mithradates (ca. 131–63 B.C.)   King of Pontus who overran Roman territories throughout

Asia Minor, and sent large armies into Greece. Sulla in Greece and Timbria in Asia defeated Mithradates, and he concluded peace, ca. 84 B.C., giving up his conquests and paying tributes. War broke out again in 74 B.C., ending in his defeat by Pompey in 66 B.C. When his plans for a new war failed, he ordered a mercenary to kill him. Mithradates had immunized himself against poisons by years of swallowing small doses. When he finally tried to commit suicide by taking poison, he failed—and then had to order a slave to kill him.

Monroe, Marilyn (1926–1962) American movie actress who died at age 36 from an apparent overdose of drugs and alcohol. Her death is still controversial, but is generally presumed to have been a suicide. Just after the movie star's death, the notes of a number of suicides linked their own deaths to Monroe's. Subsequent study noted a 12 percent rise in the number of suicides in both the United States and England following her death.

Montaigne, Michel de (1533–1592) French writer and mayor of Bordeaux, who was the first major dissenter about the sin of suicide among European writers. In a series of five essays that explored the subject of suicide, he argued that suicide should be considered a matter of personal choice, a human right that should be a rational option under some circumstances.

In his "A defense of legal suicide" (1580), he wrote: "Death is a remedy against all evils: It is a most assured haven, never to be feared, and often to be sought: All comes to one period, whether man makes an end of himself, or whether he endure it; whether he run before his day, or whether he expect it: whence soever it come, it is ever his own, where ever the thread be broken, it is all there, it's the end of the web. The voluntariest death is the fairest. Life dependeth on the will of others, death on ours."

In his writing, Montaigne broke with the Christian church in its attitude toward suicide.

While he considered suicide to be a foolish act, he did not believe it was immoral. Instead, he tried to understand and explain in his essays the various situations that might lead people to commit suicide.

Montesquieu, Charles-Louis de Secondat, baron de la Brède et de (1689–1755) French political philosopher whose first important work, *The Persian Letters,* published anonymously at Amsterdam in 1721, was a bitter satire on the church and the politics of France. His work ridiculed the barbarous and unjust European laws on suicide, a practice he defended. In one of his *Lettres Persanes,* written by "Usbek" from Paris to his friend "Ibben" in Smyrna, Montesquieu wrote: "Life has been given to me as a gift. I can therefore, return it when this is no longer the case . . ."

mood swings Four out of five people who complete suicide have previously given verbal or behavioral "clues" of their intention to do so. Among specific behavior changes are sudden mood swings that seem unpredictable. These persistent highs and lows are a warning that the person is unhappy, unstable, and increasingly sapped of both energy and emotional stability.

More, Sir Thomas (1478–1535) English author and statesman who became Lord Chancellor in 1532. On his refusal to take the oath impugning the authority of the Pope, as demanded by King Henry VIII, he was beheaded in 1535. For this martyrdom, he was canonized in 1935.

Sir Thomas More justified suicide as a form of EUTHANASIA in his *Utopia* (written in Latin, 1515 to 1516).

mortality statistics Statistics for a city, state, region, or country that are used to establish various general associations between suicide and the personal characteristics of individuals who kill themselves (age, sex, religious, or marital status), between suicide and temporal or seasonal events, and between suicide and geographic locations. It is from these general associations that experts gain clues that allow them to test specific hypotheses concerning causes.

Rates of suicide are calculated by dividing the number of persons in a group committing suicide by the total number of persons in that group. One major problem in this regard is that of obtaining valid data on completed suicides.

Rankings, such as those used by the U.S.'s Centers for Disease Control (CDC), are based on death certificate data and may represent a significant degree of misclassification and subsequent under reporting of suicide as a cause of death. According to officials at the CDC, one survey of 200 medical examiners found that more than half believed that the reported number of suicides is probably less than half the true number.

The limited accuracy and reliability of suicide statistics are, in part, attributable to the lack of a commonly accepted and applied definition of suicide, according to the CDC. Judgments by physicians, coroners, and medical examiners play a part in the process by which suicides are classified, but there are no uniform criteria for the classification of suicide to guide these judgments.

Mourning and Melancholia   Paper written by SIGMUND FREUD in 1917 that explored the individual mind for the cause of suicide, postulating that people who kill themselves are actually killing the image of the love object within them—a love object they both hate and love and with which they identify with strongly.

Freud later commented that he doubted that suicide could occur without the repressed desire for either matricide (murder of the mother) or patricide (murder of the father). Murder, he said, is aggression turned upon another; suicide is aggression turned upon the self. This is why Freud called suicide "murder in the 180th degree."

multiple suicides   See CLUSTER SUICIDE; MASS SUICIDE.

murder-suicide   Also called homicide-suicide, or dyadic death, this is a lethal event in which a perpetrator kills one or more people and then commits suicide, usually within a very short period of time. Studies have shown the perpetrators of murder-suicide have profiles that resemble individuals who commit suicide rather than those who commit homicide.

Experts aren't sure exactly how many murder-suicides occur in the United States because there is no national surveillance system to track these deaths. However, estimates suggest that murder-suicides account for up to 1,000 to 1,500 deaths each year—a mortality rate similar to meningitis or tuberculosis.

Murder-suicides are emerging as a public health problem particularly in the elderly population. One recent Florida study has shown that murder-suicide rates among people over age 55 are higher than rates in younger age groups, and that murder-suicides account for about 3 percent of all suicides and about 12 percent of all murders among the elderly. Applying these Florida figures to the country as a whole, experts estimate that about 200 murder-suicides occur every year among people 55 and older. Most of these acts involve older men killing their spouses or lovers. The Florida study also suggested that for each unsuccessful murder-suicide—that is, if one person (usually the perpetrator) survives—there are five that are successful.

Although many studies have investigated murder-suicides since 1900, it was not until 1995 that rates and clinical patterns were studied in older people. In the past, murder-suicides among the elderly were presumed to be suicide pacts, mercy killings, or altruistic actions. Although more recent research has found that men are most often the perpetrators, these murder-suicides are not mercy killings, altruistic events, or suicide pacts, and are neither acts of love nor compassionate murders. Instead, research indicates these murder-suicides are acts of desperation and DEPRESSION, other forms of psychopathology, or domestic violence.

While suicide pacts do occur among older couples, they are very rare, and make up less than one-tenth of 1 percent of all suicides in the older population. About 85 percent of murder-suicides involve spouses or partners, and the remaining victims are siblings or other family members.

Although murder-suicides are relatively rare compared to homicides and suicides, they have a dramatic, enduring impact on surviving family members and the communities in which they occur. Reports of the annual rates for homicide-suicide have been remarkably constant in the United States and other countries, ranging from 0.2 per 100,000 to 0.3 per 100,000. Murder-suicides, reported in terms of the percentage of total homicides, vary regionally in the United States from 1 percent to 20 percent, but average 5 percent.

The percentages have been reported to vary from 3 percent to 60 percent in other countries. In Canada, the only country with a national surveillance system for murder-suicide, experts report that about 10 percent of homicide offenders committed suicide.

The variation in homicide-suicide rates is related to homicide rates, i.e., the higher the homicide rate in a region, the lower the percentage of homicide-suicides. There are no national or international data for murder-suicide rates by age. This is likely due to the low base rates for all ages as well as the lack of operational definitions and surveillance systems.

Mental health experts should assess the risk for murder-suicide in all older patients in the presence of a history of thoughts about suicide or violence, or if long-married older couples both have health problems. Assessment can be complicated for many reasons, especially since the victim, rather than the perpetrator, may be the patient. The perpetrator may also resist evaluation. The strong evidence of undetected and untreated depression in older perpetrators and the existence of domestic violence in about one-third of older homicide-suicides underscores the importance of careful interviews when one or both members of an older couple present for medical appointments.

Treatment

Intensive treatment of depression and other psychiatric problems is required, together with removing guns or other lethal weapons, social support for spouses and families, and appropriate interventions to deal with marital conflict—especially where the older woman is a potential victim of aggressive, lethal behavior.

Muslims The followers of ISLAM who have always strongly condemned suicide. The QUR'AN, the holy scriptures of Islam, specifically declares that suicide is a more serious crime than homicide. Muslims believe that God is the creator, the giver of life, and He alone has the right to end it. However, some radical Muslim groups interpret their beliefs to justify TERRORISM AND SUICIDE. In committing suicide, a person violates his *kismet,* or destiny, which is preordained by God. The faithful Muslim awaits his destiny; he does not snatch it from the hands of God. While there are some suicides in Muslim countries, strong religious prohibitions have historically kept rates relatively low, or at least kept suicides from being acknowledged and recorded when they did occur.

Musset, Alfred de (1810–1857) French poet, dramatist, novelist whose only novel was *Confessions of a Child of His Age* (1835). Autobiographical in structure and content, it mirrors the disenchantment and pessimism of the young writers of the age, the *mal du siècle* ("sickness of the century"). Typical of the idealization of suicide at the time was de Musset's comment after seeing a lovely view in nature: "Ah! It would be a beautiful place in which to kill oneself." He was content, however, merely to posture—and write about it.

Myth of Sisyphus, The   Famous essay by French existentialist Albert Camus, which analyzed the problems of life, such as whether or not life is worth living. Camus wrote: "There is but one truly serious philosophical problem and that is suicide."

When he wrote *The Myth of Sisyphus* in 1940, France had just fallen to the Germans, and Camus had suffered a serious personal illness and depressive crisis—but he began his essay with suicide and ended it with an affirmation of individual life, in and for itself, as desirable because it is "absurd," with no final meaning or metaphysical justification.

myths concerning suicide   Over the years, many myths have been developed regarding suicide. In fact, like other once-taboo subjects, fallacies, myths, and misconceptions seem intrinsic to suicide. Unfortunately, they often do great damage. Several of the more prevalent and inaccurate myths surrounding the topic of suicide include:

- The person who talks a great deal about suicide won't actually attempt it.
- A person who tries and fails to commit suicide probably will not attempt suicide again.
- If a person has been very depressed for a time, says there's nothing to live for, and wants to die, then abruptly begins to act relaxed and cheerful, the suicidal thoughts have passed.
- The individual who attempts suicide has got to be crazy.
- Once someone decides to kill himself, nothing can stop him.
- Statistics indicate that suicide occurs mostly among the very wealthy because they are so jaded and bored with life.
- It cannot be suicide if the person didn't leave a note.
- They loved each other so much, they wanted to die together.

None of these popular myths about suicide is true, but each one is still widely believed by most people.

National Association of Social Workers
Professional association that is a good source of recommendations for suicide information. The group encourages the public to call for referrals, offers aid in social work, social welfare, and social services, arranges interviews, and supplies statistics, newsletter, and monthly newspaper *HASW News*.

For contact information see Appendix I.

National Center for Health Statistics (NCHS) Federal agency responsible for gathering and maintaining statistics about suicide. The NCHS is part of the Centers for Disease Control and Prevention, U.S. Department of Health and Human Services—the federal government's principal vital and health statistics agency.

Since 1960, when the National Office of Vital Statistics and the National Health Survey merged to form NCHS, the agency has provided a wide variety of data with which to monitor the nation's health. Its data systems include information on vital events as well as information on suicide, means of death, health status, lifestyle and exposure to unhealthy influences, the onset and diagnosis of illness and disability, and the use of health care.

These data are used by policymakers in government, by medical researchers, and by others in the health community. NCHS is located in Hyattsville, Maryland, with offices in Research Triangle Park, North Carolina, and with a CDC-liaison office in Atlanta, Georgia.

For contact information, see Appendix I.

National Hopeline Network A national toll-free suicide crisis hotline (1-800-SUICIDE; 1-800-784-2433) that links local centers around the country to serve the needs of the depressed and suicidal public. A call to 1-800-SUICIDE will automatically route the caller to the nearest local crisis line or mental health center. The network is managed by the KRISTIN BROOKS HOPE CENTER.

National Institute of Mental Health (NIMH) Federal institute that has been active over many years in studying the multifaceted problems relating to suicide and suicide prevention; as a division it has always been the main source of funding in research into the etiology and treatment of suicide and the dissemination of information to those involved in working with suicidal persons.

National Mental Health Association The oldest, largest nonprofit agency addressing all aspects of mental illness, including suicide. There are more than 340 affiliate groups nationwide.

For contact information see Appendix I.

National Organization of People of Color Against Suicide A nonprofit organization founded by three African-American suicide survivors designed to bring suicide and DEPRESSION awareness to minority communities that have historically been discounted from traditional awareness programs.

According to the Surgeon General's 1999 report on suicide, the rate of suicide among

African-American men increased 105 percent between 1980 and 1996. In accordance with the Surgeon General's Call to Action to Prevent Suicide, the group's objectives will be to:

- Educate those who work in the field of counseling and education
- Provide insight on depression and other brain disorders
- Share feelings and methods of coping with survivors
- Educate bereaved family members and friends
- Educate those who work with young adults on a daily basis
- Share information on suicide prevention and intervention
- Convey a message of hope

For contact information, see Appendix I.

National Self-Help Clearinghouse   Co-founded in the mid-1970s by Dr. Alan Gartner and Dr. Frank Riessman, both pioneers in the self-help field, this organization provides a complete list of self-help groups nationwide.

National Strategy for Suicide Prevention   A program that represents the combined work of advocates, clinicians, researchers, and survivors around the nation designed to prevent suicide and guide development of an array of preventive services and programs. It is designed to be a catalyst for social change with the power to transform attitudes, policies, and services.

In 1999, Surgeon General David Satcher released *A Call to Action to Prevent Suicide,* a message to the nation that included a set of recommendations derived from a national conference held in Reno, Nevada, in 1998. At that time, the *Call to Action* included 15 recommendations that provided the context for the development of the National Strategy to Prevent Suicide.

As part of his ongoing effort on the National Strategy for Suicide Prevention, on May 2, 2001, Satcher unveiled a national blueprint of goals and objectives to prevent suicide, the eighth leading cause of death in the United States. The document established 11 goals and 68 measurable objectives for public and private sector involvement to prevent suicides and attempts, as well as reduce the harmful aftereffects on families and communities.

"Suicide has stolen lives and contributed to the disability and suffering of hundreds of thousands of Americans each year," Satcher explained. "Only recently have the knowledge and tools become available to approach suicide as a preventable problem with realistic opportunities to save many live."

The public health approach laid out in his national strategy represents a rational and organized way to marshal prevention efforts and ensure that they are effective. The HHS collaborated with key advocacy groups representing clinicians, researchers, and survivors to develop the goals and objectives. The goals and objectives lay out a framework for action and guide development of an array of services and programs. It strives to provide direction to efforts to modify the social infrastructure in ways that will affect the most basic attitudes about suicide and that will also change judicial, educational, social service, and health care systems. The 68 specific objectives contained in the report include:

- Implementing integrated community-based suicide prevention programs that build life skills, beliefs, and values, and connections to family and community support known to reduce the risk of suicide
- Incorporating suicide-risk screening at the primary health care level
- Increasing the number of states that require health insurance plans to cover mental health and substance abuse care on a par with coverage for physical health care
- Providing treatment for more suicidal persons with mental health problems

- Developing technical support centers to increase the capacity of states to implement and evaluate prevention programs
- Increasing availability of comprehensive support programs for survivors of suicide
- Increasing the number of professional and volunteer groups as well as faith-based communities that integrate suicide prevention into their ongoing activities
- Improving suicide prevention education and training for health care professionals, counselors, clergy, teachers, and other key "community gatekeepers"
- Increasing the number of television programs and movies that accurately and safely depict suicide and mental illness
- Implementing a national violent death reporting system that includes suicide

Future installments of the national strategy will be released as work is completed. Currently, about 25 states have begun efforts to enact their own suicide prevention strategies.

Collaborators who developed the goals and objectives included the SUICIDE PREVENTION AND ADVOCACY NETWORK (SPAN), the AMERICAN FOUNDATION FOR SUICIDE PREVENTION, the AMERICAN ASSOCIATION OF SUICIDOLOGY, and hundreds of individuals working at state, tribal, and local levels to prevent suicide. The U.S. Air Force contributed significantly to the effort by providing a model for comprehensive community-based suicide prevention programs and its direct support of the strategy development process.

Native Americans   According to the U.S. Centers for Disease Control, suicide rates for Native Americans from 1979 to 1992 were 1.5 times higher than the national average. However, some experts question this because of the difficulty in discerning any one common Native American suicide pattern and the absence of any report of suicide incidence in many studies of Native American groups. Nevertheless, in 1972

the National Center for Health Statistics reported that the three fastest-rising causes of death among Native Americans, in order of frequency, were cirrhosis of the liver, suicide, and homicide, all of which could be traced to alcoholism. The same report estimated that the incidence of drinking among Indians was double that among the general population.

There have been numerous attempts to explain why the problem of alcoholism is so great among Native Americans, and in these attempts, there has been a tendency to ignore the diversity of the population. Native Americans in North America comprise a large number of distinct peoples with unique cultures and world views.

The major cause of drinking problems and high rates of both homicide and suicide among Native Americans in the United States and Canada is probably sociocultural stress, with a lack of identification with white society and a rejection of its goals. As Indian traditions have been weakened and family relations disturbed, Native Americans experience powerlessness and anxiety.

The most promising methods of handling problems concerning alcoholism, suicide, and homicide should include Native Americans in the planning and implementation of their own programs on a community (tribal) basis. It is important, for therapists, social workers, and counselors to be sensitive to tribal cultures and variations from tribe to tribe. Interestingly, some specifically Indian Alcoholics Anonymous groups have integrated elements of their traditional cultures into the AA format and setting, and they have achieved more success than standard AA programs.

Nazi concentration camps   Despite the heroic defense mechanisms by those imprisoned in the infamous Nazi concentration camps many prisoners committed suicide. Thousands of JEWS from Eastern Europe, for example, were sent to TREBLINKA to be exterminated. Most realized they had no hope and were destined never to leave the camp alive. Numb to everyone and everything around them, one by one they began completing suicide. Their deaths served as an affirmation of their freedom to control their own lives and deaths. These suicidal acts led to a solidarity of sorts, and those who chose to remain alive helped those who wanted to die quickly.

There are no reliable statistics available on how many people opted for suicide while subjected to the brutalities of life in the Nazi camps.

Nero (A.D. 37–68)   Roman emperor who fled Rome with enemies hard on his heels. He took refuge in a villa several miles outside the city, where four faithful servants insisted that he commit suicide honorably, rather than fall into the hands of those who had seized power in Rome.

As he watched the men prepare his funeral pyre, he muttered through tears, "Qualis artifex pereo!" ("How great an artist dies here!") Nero actually had himself killed by an attendant.

During his lifetime, he had caused several suicides, including those of his teacher SENECA, the poet LUCAN, and Petronius, thought to be the author of the *Satyricon*. These were all compulsory suicides in lieu of execution.

Netherlands   See HOLLAND.

neurobiology of suicide   The link between certain brain chemicals and suicide has been suspected for some time. In particular, the levels of serotonin—a brain neurotransmitter important in a wide range of body processes and emotions, including DEPRESSION—is considered a possible predictor of suicide. Indeed, some research has found that people with low levels of serotonin are six to 10 times more likely to commit suicide than are people with normal levels. Three different measures of serotonin function that are completely unrelated all show the same thing—a deficiency in patients with a history for more lethal suicide attempts.

Research has shown that more than 95 percent of people who committed suicide have low levels of serotonin in certain brain regions, and serotonin deficiency is characteristic of those who make the most dangerous suicide attempts. People who succeed at suicide are the ones who plan the most carefully, rather than acting impulsively—and low serotonin occurs three times more often in those who plan the most carefully.

However, simply having low levels of serotonin alone does not guarantee a person is going to attempt suicide. Instead, low levels are linked to a person's *predisposition* to commit suicide rather than definite cause that triggers suicidal behavior in every case.

Researchers aren't sure what causes serotonin levels to drop, although the condition is probably affected by a number of factors, including genetics, diet, drugs and alcohol, gender, and age.

Unfortunately, it's not possible for patients to simply go to their family doctor for a serotonin test. Further research is needed to find more direct tests of serotonin levels.

New Jersey   Among those states ranked by suicide rates per 100,000 population (1999), New Jersey, despite its dense population, was far below the national average that year, with a rate of 6.9 suicides per 100,000. The U.S. suicide rate in 1999 was 10.7 per 100,000.

New Testament   Biblical suicides are rare; there is only one instance reported in the New Testament, that being the death of JUDAS ISCARIOT, reported simply and briefly in the Book of Matthew, 27:5—"he went and hanged himself."

Nietzsche, Friedrich Wilhelm (1844–1900) German philosopher who was profoundly moral and religious. Nietzsche was regarded in his own time as an Antichrist because of his rejection of time-honored values.

He often contemplated suicide and wrote, "The thought of suicide is a strong consolation: it helps to get over many a bad night." He did not, however, advocate suicide as a solution to all life's problems, noting, "Suffering is no argument against life."

'night, Mother Marsha Norman's Pulitzer Prize–winning drama about a young woman with epilepsy who threatens suicide to her mother at the beginning of the play. She then proceeds to get her mother's life in order before she commits the act. During the tense, controversial 90-minute work, the mother, Thelma, strongly but ineffectually tries to dissuade her daughter Tessie from using the gun. The daughter is a person who has never realized any of her dreams and finds herself in a vacuum. It is a two-character close-up of suicide—not the actual act, but the motivations behind Tessie's carefully planned self-destruction.

night time and suicide Studies have linked evening hours with higher rates of suicide. Significantly more suicides do occur between noon and 6 P.M., and significantly fewer between midnight and 6 A.M. However, it is often difficult to determine precisely when a suicide actually took place. Researchers admit they must sometimes discard cases from their samples because they cannot pinpoint when a suicide occurred. For instance, if a person ingests a lethal dose of drugs at 10 A.M., but doesn't "die" until 3 P.M., when did the person commit suicide?

Nimitz, Admiral Chester W., Jr. Naval admiral who, together with his dentist wife, Joan, committed a DUAL SUICIDE on January 2, 2002. At age 86, Nimitz was described as an intelligent, decisive, confident man whose exceptional organizational and planning skills helped him to advance through naval ranks to become an admiral, as had his father before him. A submarine commander during World War II, he became chief executive for a technology company after leaving the service.

After reportedly canceling their home nursing care, Chester and Joan overdosed on sleeping pills. The contents of the suicide note, which asked that they not be resuscitated, indicated that the Nimitzes had given considerable thought to their decision and that they were not suffering from DEPRESSION or another type of MENTAL ILLNESS, but that they made the rational decision to take their lives because their health problems severely limited the quality of their lives.

No One Saw My Pain: Why Teens Kill Themselves Book about how eight families survived teenage suicide by Andrew E. Slaby, M.D., and Lili Frank Garfinkel, published by W. W. Norton & Co. (1996). In this book, Slaby, a psychiatrist specializing in DEPRESSION and crisis INTERVENTION, profiles seven families responding to the loss of a teenager and one case of failed suicide. He notes that few cries for help are followed up by doctors, teachers, suicide hotlines, or even the police, and charges that today's generation faces serious stresses in divorce, drugs, violence, and economic instability.

North Carolina In 1999, the state recorded a suicide rate per 100,000 population of 11.6.

North Dakota The state in 1999 had a 11.5 suicide rate per 100,000 population.

Norway The suicide rate in Norway is approximately one-third that of neighboring Scandinavian countries DENMARK and SWEDEN, even though all three countries are very similar ethnically, culturally, and geographically. In *Suicide in Different Cultures,* Norman Farberow argues the lower Norwegian rate is due to its more supportive family environments and childrearing practices.

According to the WORLD HEALTH ORGANIZATION (WHO) 1995 statistics, Norway has a suicide rate per 100,000 population of 12.6 (males 19.1 and females 6.2). The age group with the highest suicide rate per 100,000 population is 65–74; with a 20.6 rate.

Notebooks The French journalist, dramatist and novelist ALBERT CAMUS wrote in his *Notebooks:* "There is only one liberty, to come to terms with death. After which, everything is possible." Camus was awarded the Nobel Prize in literature in 1957. He died at age 47 in 1960, the result of an automobile accident near Sens, France.

notes, suicide See SUICIDE NOTES.

No Time to Say Goodbye: Surviving the Suicide of a Loved One Nonfiction book about surviving the suicide of a spouse by Carla Fine, whose husband killed himself in 1992. Combining her experiences, those of other survivors, and advice from mental health professionals, Fine provides a compassionate guide for dealing with the guilt, anger, and confusion after the suicide of a loved one.

Nouvelle Heloise, La Novel by the French philosopher JEAN-JACQUES ROUSSEAU in which he emphasizes the natural right people have to end their lives—as long as they cause no harm to others by doing so. He did establish one condition: People who have responsibilities to others should not commit suicide. *La Nouvelle Heloise,* published in 1761, was highly successful.

nurses Data on the relation between occupation and suicide are very sparse and tend to be mixed. In general it seems that those engaged in work giving nurturance and help to others (including nurses, social workers, physicians, police officers) tend to have higher suicide rates than most other professions or occupations.

As for their role as a key segment of the "gatekeeping" process, nurses, along with doctors, social workers, clergy, and others, have the unique opportunity of being in a position to identify and improve the potential suicide's dangerous behavior situation. The nurse, for instance, who works with a family physician is of central importance in both suicide treatment and reduction. Nurses are often in a position to establish a meaningful relationship with the distraught person. Yet, too often many nurses, not unlike doctors, are restricted by insufficient time and/or lack of suicide prevention-intervention knowledge.

obligatory suicide   Ethical concept of suicide as a personal duty.

obsession with death   A clue that a person may be at risk for suicide. Poets SYLVIA PLATH and ANNE HARVEY SEXTON, both of whom killed themselves, appeared to have a romance with death. Sexton, who committed suicide in 1974, wrote "Wanting to Die" (a poem published in 1966) in which she describes her desire to die as "the almost unnameable lust."

Newspaper columnist and author James Wechsler recalled that his son displayed suicidal gestures, such as almost walking into a moving car, driving his motor bike into a bus, and almost strangling himself on the strings of his guitar. In his book, *In a Darkness,* Wechsler says his son's death wish remained strong—until Michael did kill himself. Wechsler wrote ". . . how often we failed to say or do some things that might (or might not) have mattered."

occupation and suicide risk   The link between a person's job and risk of suicide has been controversial. Some researchers have found that the greater the responsibility, the greater the risk of suicide, but a fall in status also increases the risk. Other scientists report that professionals have the lowest suicide rate, while business and repair services, construction, agriculture, forestry and fisheries, mining, and entertainment and recreation had the highest rates.

What scientists do agree on is that work in general tends to protect against suicide, and some groups are at special risk. These special at-risk populations include psychiatrists, psychologists, ophthalmologists, anesthesiologists, physicians, musicians, dentists, law enforcement officers, lawyers, and life insurance agents.

Suicide rates are higher among the employed than the unemployed, and tends to increase during economic recessions and times of rising unemployment, and decrease in times of high employment and during wars.

See also POLICE SUICIDE.

Oklahoma   Oklahoma ranks seventh among all U.S. states by suicide rates per 100,000 population (14.7) for the year 1999.

old age and suicide   See ELDER SUICIDE.

Omega: Journal of Death and Dying   Quarterly publication, published by Baywood Publishing Company, Inc., 26 Austin Ave., Box 337, Amityville, N.Y. 11701.

This journal discusses suicide, terminal illness, the process of dying, bereavement, mourning, and funeral customs by contributions from professionals in universities, hospitals, clinics, old age homes, suicide prevention centers, funeral directors, and others concerned with THANATOLOGY and the impact of death.

Omega, a rigorously peer-reviewed journal, draws contributions from the fields of psychology, sociology, medicine, anthropology, law, education, history, and literature. The journal serves as a reliable guide for clinicians, social workers, and health professionals who must deal with problems in suicide and bereavement.

On Suicide   Essay by Scottish philosopher David Hume discussing the difficulties and contradictions in moral arguments for and against the act of suicide. The famed philosopher's essay was published following his death in 1776, but then was quickly suppressed.

The short essay argues against the position of suicide as a crime. "The life of a man," wrote Hume, "is of no greater importance to the universe than that of an oyster." The man who commits suicide, according to Hume, does not disrupt the larger order of the universe. Hume adds, that person "does no harm to society; he only ceases to do good; which if it is an injury is of the lowest kind." Other 18th-century philosophers agreed with David Hume's stance that suicide is the individual's moral right.

Oppenheim, David E.   In 1910 this prominent Viennese educator met in Vienna with members of the Vienna Psychoanalytical Society to try to discover the mysterious causes of suicide among that city's high school students. Luminaries in attendance included Alfred Adler, Wilhelm Stekel, and SIGMUND FREUD the founder of psychoanalysis. Freud later said of the April 27th meeting (formally called to discuss "Suicide in Children") that little was accomplished and indicated that much more work in this area needed to be done.

Ordinary People   Novel by Judith Guest later made into a movie, that deals with the aftermath of a teenage suicide attempt after a 17-year-old had failed in trying to save his older brother in a boating accident. No one in the upper-middle-class family talks about the accident, but young Conrad is filled with SURVIVOR GUILT. He believes that his parents, particularly his mother, blame him for not being able to save his brother. He feels his parents wish that he'd been the son to die, since his brother seemed to be the favored child.

The parents of this seemingly all-American family miss all the suicidal clues and signals.

Conrad attempts suicide with a razor blade. The turning point comes only when Conrad realizes he wasn't guilty of causing his brother's death, that nobody was guilty, and that he didn't have to be the perfect son. The novel gives readers realistic insights into the problems of the suicidal mind.

Oregon law   The state of Oregon is the only place in the United States that specifically allows PHYSICIAN-ASSISTED SUICIDE if certain stringent guidelines are met. Oregon citizens approved a law in November 1994 that would allow legalized physician-assisted suicide under limited conditions. Under the Death With Dignity law, a person who sought physician-assisted suicide would have to meet certain criteria, including:

- must have six months or less to live
- must make two oral requests for assistance in dying
- must make one written request for assistance
- must convince two physicians that he is sincere, is not acting on a whim, and that the decision is voluntary
- must not have been influenced by depression
- must be informed of "the feasible alternatives, including, but not limited to, comfort care, hospice care and pain control"
- must wait for 15 days between the request and the act

Patients who meet all these requirements could receive a prescription of a BARBITURATE that would be enough to cause death. Mercy killings by a family member or friend would not be allowed, and assisted suicides like those performed by Dr. JACK KEVORKIAN would not be allowed. Physicians would be prohibited from inducing death by injection or carbon monoxide.

The National Right to Life Committee, supported by the ROMAN CATHOLIC CHURCH, obtained a court injunction to delay implementation of the measure, and the law became stalled in the appeals process. In the meantime, the measure was not enacted. The Oregon Medical Association originally took no stand on the matter, but later objected to it because of what it considers legal flaws.

In the first full year after assisted suicide became legal in Oregon, relatively few people requested help in dying. Only 23 actually obtained medication to induce their death, and at least six of these patients never used the pills, but died a natural death.

In 1997, conservatives within the Oregon government forced approval in early June 1997 of a second public referendum. This mail-in ballot procedure was held from October 15 through November 4, 1997. But in a surprising development, an employee of the state attorney general's office said on November 4, 1997, that the law had cleared all of the court appeals on October 27, and was actually in force. Within 24 hours of the announcement of the results, state officials started to prepare forms for physicians to record instances of assisted suicide, which were later distributed to physicians in the state.

The "Request for Medication to End my Life in a Humane and Dignified Manner" form required two doctors to record:

- the patient's medical diagnosis
- the prognosis
- the date of the first request for suicide assistance
- an assessment that the patient is capable, fully informed, and acting voluntarily
- that the patient is aware of risks associated with the medication
- that the patient has been informed of alternatives, such as hospice and pain management, and that the patient can withdraw the request at any time

Immediately after the law was affirmed, Thomas Constantine, the administrator of the federal Drug Enforcement Administration (DEA) announced that prescribing drugs to help termi-

nally ill patients kill themselves would be a violation of the Controlled Substances Act, and was not a legitimate medical use under the federal drug laws. He warned that the government would impose severe sanctions on any doctor who wrote a prescription for lethal doses of medicine for a patient.

On March 26, 1998, a woman in her mid-80s died from a lethal dose of barbiturates which had been prescribed by her doctor under this law. She was the first person to publicly make use of physician-assisted suicide in Oregon. She had been fighting breast cancer for 20 years and recently had been told by her doctor that she had less than two months to live. She had been experiencing increased difficulty breathing. She made a tape recording in which she said that she was "looking forward to" death because she would "be relieved of all the stress I have." Her personal doctor would not help her end her life, so she turned to an advocacy group called Compassion in Dying, who found a doctor to help her. She fell into a deep sleep about five minutes after taking the lethal dose of pills, and died peacefully about 25 minutes later.

By mid-1988, Attorney General Janet Reno reversed Constantine's earlier ruling and stated that doctors who use the law to prescribe lethal drugs to terminally ill patients will not be prosecuted. She further noted that "there was no evidence that Congress meant for the DEA to have the novel role of resolving the profound moral and ethical questions involved in the [physician-assisted suicide] issue . . . the drug laws were intended to block illegal trafficking in drugs and did not cover situations like the Oregon suicide law."

By the end of 1998, only about one Oregonian per month had chosen to commit physician-assisted suicide. Although many people thought large numbers of terminally ill patients would take advantage of the law, the U.S. Centers for Disease Control found that during the calendar year 1998, only 23 patients sought help to die during 1998. Of the 23, 15 committed suicide, usually within a day of receiving the prescription. Six died from their illnesses without using the medication, and two remained alive at the end of 1998. Further, the CDC found that gender, education, and health insurance status, or fear of pain did not play an influential role in prompting a person to seek help in dying. The CDC compared these 15 patients with 43 others with similar fatal diseases but who elected to not seek help, and found a number of determining factors that led people to seek help in dying.

These factors included concern about loss of autonomy or control of bodily functions, never having married, being divorced and having led an independent life. Six of the 15 had to change doctors at least once to find one willing to write a prescription. Of the 15 who committed suicide, all were white; eight were male, with a median age of 68 years.

Doctors usually prescribed a fatal dose of Secobarbital, along with an antivomiting medicine so that the barbiturate would be properly adsorbed. Everyone who committed suicide became unconscious within five minutes, and most were dead within an hour.

During the year 2001, 21 Oregonians ended their lives with the help of the assisted suicide law (six fewer than in the previous years). Over the first three years that the law has been in place the number of patients choosing legal PAS has remained stable, at about six per 10,000 deaths. College-educated patients were much more likely to choose physician-assisted suicide than were those with less than a high school diploma, by a factor of 12 or more.

On November 5, 2001, Attorney General John Ashcroft wrote a letter to Asa Hutchinson, chief of the Drug Enforcement Administration, declaring that assisting a terminally ill patient to commit suicide is not a "legitimate medical purpose" for federally controlled drugs. He said that any physicians who use drugs to help patients die face suspension or revocation of their licenses to prescribe federally controlled drugs. This reversed an earlier order in June 1998 by his predecessor, Janet Reno.

The attorney general of Oregon, Hardy Myers, quickly initiated a lawsuit to have Ashcroft's directive declared unconstitutional. A doctor, pharmacist, and three people who may want to kill themselves with a doctor's help were plaintiffs. The federal district court in Oregon issued a temporary injunction to prevent the federal government from enforcing Ashcroft's interpretation of the Controlled Substances Act (CSA).

In April 2002, a federal judge upheld Oregon's law allowing physician-assisted suicide, ruling that the Justice Department does not have the authority to overturn it.

The U.S. Supreme Court unanimously ruled (on June 26, 1997) that the average American has no constitutional right to a physician-assisted suicide, which means that New York and Washington laws banning such suicides are constitutional. On the other hand, the court implied that there is no constitutional bar that would prevent a state from passing a law permitting physician-assisted suicide, which is what Oregon did. This means that the legality of physician-assisted suicide must be fought on a state-by-state basis. Chief Justice Rehnquist wrote: "Throughout the nation, Americans are engaged in an earnest and profound debate about the morality, legality and practicality of physician-assisted suicide. Our holding permits this debate to continue, as it should in a democratic society."

The Supreme Court decision was very narrow, ruling only on whether the public had a general right to assisted suicide. The case was originally brought by six terminally ill individuals in intractable pain who wanted access to assisted suicide, but by the time the court heard legal arguments, all six had died. Because the court was unable to rule on whether terminally ill individuals should have a right to assisted suicide, they made a decision on whether citizens generally had that right.

Many of the justices indicated that certain groups within society might have a constitutional right to access to suicide (such as people who are terminally ill and in intractable pain). If a case were brought by such a person, the court might find in that person's favor. The problem will be to find a person who can survive a terminal illness long enough for the case to make it to the Supreme Court.

organic suicide   A suicide attempt at a response to serious physical illness or pain.

Origen of Alexandria (ca. A.D. 185–ca. 254)
As a youth, Origen experienced the martyrdom of his father in A.D. 202 and was possessed by a desire to suffer the same fate. His mother prevented him from self-destruction, but he still victimized himself through self-castration—to become a eunuch for the kingdom of heaven. As historian George Rosen notes: "Perhaps his self-castration . . . may be interpreted as a symbolic surrogate for voluntary death." After years of teaching in Caesarea in Palestine, he died as a result of tortures inflicted during the Decian persecution.

Osbourne, Ozzy (1948–   )   Former leader of the rock group Black Sabbath who produced the album "Speak to the Devil" and a macabre song called "Suicide Solution," which contains such lines as, "Suicide is the only way out; don't you know what it's really about?"

In October 1984, John McCollum, 19, a fan of Osbourne's, put on the album and shot himself in the head with his father's pistol. Osbourne and CBS Records were sued in Los Angeles Superior Court by the boy's parents.

Osbourne, 37, said his lyrics were misinterpreted, that "They're really anti-suicide, anti-drink and drugs." McCollum's father, Jack, charged that the music was an "invocation to the devil." On August 7, 1986, Judge John Cole dismissed the lawsuit, saying that the McCollum attorney failed to show why Osbourne's songs should not be provided First Amendment protection. Judge Cole was quoted by the wire services as saying: "Trash can be given First Amendment protection, too."

other-driven suicide   Completion of suicide that is impelled by another person.

Otto, Emperor   German emperor referred to by JOHANN WOLFGANG VON GOETHE as the one person who, in the writer's youth, he had so admired. Since the Emperor Otto had stabbed himself, Goethe decided that if he were not brave enough to die in such a manner, he wasn't brave enough to die at all. Goethe wrote: "By this conviction, I saved myself from the purpose, or indeed, more properly speaking, from the whim of suicide." Goethe, who wrote the auto-biographical novel *The Sorrows of Young Werther* —acclaimed all over Europe, with its themes of martyrdom, unrequited love, and excessive sensibility—died at the age of 83, asking for more light.

paraquat A deadly poisonous insecticide first synthesized in 1882, but only recognized as an herbicide in 1955 by ICI (now Zeneca). Its extreme toxicity and its involvement in suicide around the world (700 cases in 10 years in Malaysia alone, for example) has led to bans and strict controls. Poisoning by paraquat causes death within several hours to a few days as a result of multiple organ failure. There is no antidote.

parasuicide A nonfatal act in which a person deliberately causes self-injury or ingests a substance in excess of any prescribed dosage. The term was suggested as a replacement for the phrase ATTEMPTED SUICIDE, which was often hard to decide in terms of intention, consciousness, extent of injury, extent of effort to injure, differentiation from substance abuse, and other factors, but is now out of vogue.

The term was introduced in 1969 by psychiatrist Norman Kreitman of the Royal Edinburgh Hospital as a word that described the action without having to decide a person's intent. Parasuicide may be a genuine attempt by persons to kill themselves, or it has been suggested that it can be a cry for help, as the only way that distress is recognized.

See ABUSE, SUBSTANCE.

parents of suicides While a suicide almost always concerns several other people, parents usually feel most responsible. This is especially true when a teenager or young adult commits suicide; parents blame themselves regardless of what may have caused the tragic action.

SURVIVOR GUILT is also usually strong in the case of surviving parents. While nobody can minimize the impact of a suicide and nobody can wholly free survivor parents of the anger, guilt, remorse, and pain they feel, there are today a number of self-help groups nationwide that are set up to help parents (as well as other survivors) mourn and heal. Edwin S. Shneidman coined the term POSTVENTION to describe this help, which means giving survivors the kind of support they need immediately after a suicide and, in time, assisting them in coming to terms with the tragedy.

Aside from professional help provided by doctors, psychiatrists, and psychologists, surviving parents need the sharing, caring, and understanding of others in a similar situation. They need to be able to talk with other people who will not judge them, not patronize them, but through their own experiences know how to listen intelligently.

partial suicide Nonfatal self-destructive act sometimes called self-mutilation. This is, properly speaking, a "quasi-suicidal attempt."

passive euthanasia Intentionally not preventing death in those who suffer from a terminal condition. Passive EUTHANASIA involves letting someone die from a disease or injury, whereas active euthanasia involves taking active steps to kill a person. For example, passive euthanasia includes removing life support equipment (such as turning off a respirator), stopping medical procedures or medications, stopping food and water and allowing the person to dehydrate or starve to death, or not performing cardio-pulmonary resuscitation (CPR) and allowing a person whose heart has stopped to die.

Perhaps the most common form of passive euthanasia is to give a patient large doses of morphine to control pain, in spite of the likelihood that the painkiller will suppress respiration and cause death earlier than it would otherwise have happened. Such doses of painkillers have a dual effect of relieving pain and hastening death. Administering such medication is regarded as ethical in most political jurisdictions and by most medical societies.

These procedures are performed (or not performed) on terminally ill, suffering persons and on individuals with massive brain damage who are in a coma from which they cannot possibly regain consciousness.

Peau de Chagrin, La Essay written by French author HONORÉ DE BALZAC in 1831 to support the romantic dogma that the intense, true feeling of life does not survive into one's middle years. Balzac said the alternatives were "To kill the emotions and so live on to old age, or to accept the martyrdom of our passions and die young . . ." Interestingly, Balzac died in 1850 at age 51.

penacide Completion of suicide to end intense pain.

Penitentials A code of penalties for moral offenses written by Egbert, archbishop of York. The *Penitentials* appeared in the mid-eighth century, and made an exception to the church position refusing burial in consecrated ground to suicides if the person was insane. There was, throughout the medieval period, a growing recognition that mental and emotional disorder may lead to suicide.

Peri parthenion Fragmentary Hippocratic work (*On the Diseases of Maidens*) that comments

on mental symptoms, including suicidal tendencies, to which young girls are prone if they suffer menstrual problems. These symptoms, particularly as related to suicidal behavior, have been interpreted as an example of psychopathic collective behavior.

See also MILETUS, THE MAIDENS OF.

Perlin, Seymour, M.D. Editor of the definitive collection, *A Handbook for the Study of Suicide*. Dr. Perlin is emeritus professor of psychiatry and behavioral science, Department of Psychiatry, George Washington University Medical Center in Washington, D.C. He is also founder and past president of the AMERICAN ASSOCIATION OF SUICIDOLOGY.

personality A number of studies have shown that a large percentage of young suicidal people—both attempters and completers—have come from disrupted or disturbed home environments, lacking in stability and support. For instance, parents may be divorced, constantly quarreling, or one or both parents absent because of death or desertion. Sometimes a parent is alcoholic, or a child abuser. Children who grow up in these kinds of unstable or broken homes can feel abandoned and lonely, filled with resentment and anger at both the parent(s) who have hurt them and at themselves.

In addition, some PERSONALITY DISORDERS, resulting in serious mental illnesses, are traceable to chemical changes in the brain. One major danger signal of possible suicide is a change in personality or behavior, such as a tendency for a person to become uncommunicative and to isolate him- or herself. There is a noticeable loss of interest in friends, family, and activities and decreased sexual desire.

Studies show an affective disorder is one of the most important factors that promoted risk for suicidal behavior in adults and children.

personality disorders Persons with personality disorders are prone to ATTEMPTED SUICIDE—

especially emotionally immature people with borderline personality disorder or antisocial personality disorder, who tolerate frustration poorly and react to stress impetuously with violence and aggression.

Psychological autopsies found that between 31 and 57 percent of completed suicides were diagnosed as having a personality disorder. Moreover, 71 percent of personality-disordered inpatients had a history of suicidal behavior.

Some people with personality disorders have a history of excessive alcohol consumption, drug abuse, or criminal behavior. An inability to form mature, lasting relationships typical of these disorder may lead to reduced social opportunity, loneliness, and depression. This may account for the large number of attempted suicides among separated or divorced people.

philosophers and suicide Throughout history the concept of suicide has fascinated philosophers, who influenced peoples and societies.

For example, Greek and Roman philosophers discussed suicide and usually endorsed it within specific limitations. The STOICS were perhaps staunchest of the pro-suicide group, led by their founder ZENO. The EPICUREANS considered that one's destiny was a personal choice. CATO, Pliny and SENECA all thought the choice of suicide was acceptable. However, there have been many dissenters among philosophers. PLATO, for one, strongly opposed suicide, as did Virgil, Ovid and Cicero.

As time went on, new views of suicide became popular. JOHN DONNE reacted against the existing attitudes of the church toward suicide and viewed the act as neither a violation of the law nor against reason (though he considered it contrary to the law of self-preservation). Other 17th-century philosophers and secular writers echoed Donne's position, including DAVID HUME, Baron de Montesquieu, Voltaire, and JEAN-JACQUES ROUSSEAU defended suicide under certain conditions.

In more recent times, Immanuel Kant called suicide "an insult to humanity." Dietrich Bonhoeffer viewed suicide as a sin in that it represented a denial of God.

Modern-day attitudes toward suicide are no less complex and controversial than those of earlier times.

physical health, loss of It is not uncommon for someone who gets sick to view him- or herself as being less than a complete person. This can often lead to serious DEPRESSION and, ultimately, suicidal thoughts. Loss of physical health can be as psychologically damaging or devastating as a loss of identity. However, no studies are available to indicate what percent of suicides result from loss of physical health. So many other psychological and social factors affect such suicides that no single causal force can be pinpointed.

physician-assisted suicide Suicide in which a doctor helps a person to kill himself. Some people who decide that they wish to complete suicide are physically unable to accomplish the act, and would need assistance from their physician.

In a physician-assisted suicide, a doctor supplies information or the means of complete suicide (such as a prescription for a lethal dose of sleeping pills, or a supply of carbon monoxide gas) to a patient so that they can commit suicide.

Throughout North America, completing suicide or attempting to commit suicide is not a legal offense. However, helping another person commit suicide is a criminal act. The only exception is Oregon which—under severe restrictions—allows people who are terminally ill and in intractable pain to get a lethal prescription from their physician. Physician-assisted suicide is not specifically mentioned in the laws of North Carolina, Utah, and Wyoming. In Canada, physician-assisted suicide is illegal throughout the country.

Oregon citizens approved a law in November 1994 that would allow legalized physician-assisted suicide under limited conditions. Under the Death with Dignity law, a person who sought physician-assisted suicide would have to meet certain criteria, including:

- must have six months or less to live
- must make two oral requests for assistance in dying
- must make one written request for assistance
- must convince two physicians that he is sincere, is not acting on a whim, and that the decision is voluntary
- must not have been influenced by depression
- must be informed of "the feasible alternatives, including, but not limited to, comfort care, hospice care, and pain control"
- must wait for 15 days between the request and the act

Patients who meet all these requirements could receive a prescription of a BARBITURATE that would be enough to cause death. Mercy killings by a family member or friend would not be allowed, and assisted suicides like those performed by Dr. JACK KEVORKIAN would not be allowed. Physicians would be prohibited from inducing death by injection or carbon monoxide.

The National Right to Life Committee, supported by the ROMAN CATHOLIC CHURCH, obtained a court injunction to delay implementation of the measure, and the law became stalled in the appeals process. In the meantime, the measure was not enacted. The Oregon Medical Association originally took no stand on the matter but later objected to it because of what it considers legal flaws.

In the first full year after assisted suicide became legal in Oregon, relatively few people requested help in dying. Only 23 actually obtained medication to induce their death, and at least six of these patients never used the pills, but died a natural death.

The most famous example of a physician-assisted suicide is that advocated by Dr. Kevork-

ian, who has promoted this type of intervention, and assisted at the deaths of hundreds of patients. Originally, he hooked his patients up to a machine that delivered measured overdoses of medications after the patient pushed a button to initiate the sequence. More recently, he provided carbon monoxide and a face mask so that his patient could trigger the flow of gas.

According to a recent decision by the U.S. Supreme Court, which reversed the decisions rendered in two lower courts, the justices found no constitutionally protected right to physician-assisted suicide. More than 50 health care groups had signed an amicus ("friend of the court") brief opposing physician-assisted suicide. The high court had accepted two cases from the Ninth and Second U.S. Circuit Courts of Appeals, both of which raised the question of whether a constitutional right exists to physician-assisted suicide. The two circuit courts had found that the state laws banning physician-assisted suicide in Washington and in New York violated the protections of the 14th Amendment of the Constitution. The Supreme Court's decision acknowledges that a constitutional right to physician-assisted suicide does not exist.

The issue of assisted suicide has highlighted the deficits in care of the dying and focused attention on the preeminent obligation of health care professionals to provide responsible, respectful, appropriate, and ethically sound care. The AMERICAN MEDICAL ASSOCIATION and the American Nurses Association believes that doctors and nurses (respectively) should not participate in assisted suicide, since this violates ethical traditions of these professions.

See OREGON LAW.

physicians Medical doctors have one of the highest suicide rates of any professional group. The number of doctors who commit suicide in the United States each year—between 100 and 150—is more than the size of an entire graduating class from an average-size medical school. More doctors die by suicide each year than from drownings, plane crashes, accidents, and homicides combined.

Unlike the general population, medical doctors are much more likely to use drugs, not guns, to kill themselves, and they tend to do so during the most productive years (the mean age is 48). The suicide rate for male physicians is estimated at 1.15 times greater than the expected rate of the general male population (some studies indicate the rate is double.) For women physicians, the rate is three times higher than the expected rate of the female population. In the 25 to 39 age group, 26 percent of all physicians' deaths are attributed to suicide.

pills, as suicide method   In the past, the most common method of suicide for women was poisoning by solids or liquids (36.7 percent), followed by firearms (and explosives) (30.2 percent). By 1980, firearms and explosives were the methods most often used by women (38.6 percent), followed by poisoning by solids, including pills, and liquids (26.9 percent).

Historically, suicidal women seemed to prefer ingesting a lethal dose of drugs, swallowing pills or poison, or inhaling gas. The speculation was that women didn't want to shed their blood or disfigure themselves, thus they would choose a more passive means of self-destruction. Others theorized that women opted for using a passive method, such as pills, because they really didn't want death by suicide, rather they were "crying out for help," calling attention to an intolerable situation. This increase in firearms as a method among female suicides indicates a move toward more lethal methods, say authorities—that is, methods with less chance for intervention or rescue.

As of 1999, both men and women still killed themselves with firearms more often than any other method; 61.7 percent of men used this method, as did 36.9 percent of women. For women, the next most common method was by ingesting solid and liquid poisons and pills (30 percent); the next most common method for men was HANGING/strangling/suffocation (19.1 percent). Solid and liquid poisons was the third most common method for men (7 percent).

Plath, Sylvia (1932–1963)   American poet and novelist whose best-known work is the novel *The Bell Jar*, first published pseudonymously in England in 1962. A semi-autobiographical work, the novel is about a woman caught up in a crisis so severe that she attempts suicide. It recounts the heroine's rebellion against the constricting forces of society and her emotional and psychological conflicts resulting from family tensions. Similar themes may be found in Sylvia Plath's poetry.

Sylvia's surface perfection masked grave personal problems, some of which may have begun with the death of her college professor father when she was eight. During the summer following her junior year at Smith, after returning from a stay in New York City, where she had been a student "guest editor" at *Mademoiselle* magazine, Sylvia nearly succeeded in killing herself by swallowing sleeping pills. She later described this experience in *The Bell Jar*.

After a period of recovery involving electroshock and counseling, Plath resumed her academic and literary efforts, graduating from Smith summa cum laude in 1955 and awarded a Fulbright scholarship to study at Cambridge, England. It was in England where she met and married Ted Hughes.

In 1959, after suffering one nervous breakdown and suicide attempt, from which Plath recovered, and after a brief teaching stint at Smith, she and her husband and two children moved to England. Her marriage to English poet Ted Hughes subsequently ended.

On February 11, 1963, on her third attempt, Sylvia Plath killed herself with cooking gas at the age of 30. Poems that were collected after her suicide ensured her posthumous reputation as a major poet. These poems, a haunting record of her encroaching mental illness, include the volumes *Ariel, Crossing the Water,* and *Winter Trees.*

Plato (ca. 428–ca. 348 B.C.) Greek philosopher who founded the famous Academy at Athens, whose writings include *The Apology, Phaedo* and *The Republic.* His great teacher, SOCRATES, was one of the most notable suicides of ancient times. Plato quoted Socrates as saying before his death (which was really a form of execution ordered by the rulers of Athens), "No man has the right to take his own life, but he must wait until God sends some necessity upon him, as he has now sent me."

Plato, and his own student, ARISTOTLE, both disapproved of suicide. Plato looked upon people as the "chattels" of God, and, as such, they had no right to destroy themselves. ALFRED ALVAREZ, in *The Savage God,* tells us that Plato used the simile of the soldier on guard duty who must not desert his post, and also that of man as the property of the gods, who are as angry at our suicide as we would be if our chattels destroyed themselves. Life itself was the discipline of the gods.

Plato, Dana Former child star whose drug-overdose death was ruled a suicide. The 34-year-old former star of the NBC sitcom *Diff'rent Strokes* died May 8, 1999, while visiting her fiancé's parents in Oklahoma.

Police initially said she died of an accidental overdose of a painkiller and VALIUM, but the state later found that she had fatal concentrations of the muscle relaxant Soma and a generic form of the painkiller Lortab in her body, together with the equivalent of seven tablets of the muscle relaxant in her stomach. The death was ruled a suicide because of the high level of drugs and her history of suicidal tendencies, although she did not leave a suicide note.

Plato had been prescribed both drugs, according to her fiancé, for back injuries she suffered in a car accident.

Her life became less successful after her TV show was canceled in 1984. She was arrested seven years later for robbing a Las Vegas video store and placed on five years' probation. A year later, she was given another five years' probation for forging prescriptions for Valium. The day before her death, Plato went on the Howard Stern radio show in New York to deny a former roommate's claims that she was taking drugs. Plato insisted she had been sober for about 10 years, but said she had taken painkillers when her wisdom teeth were removed four months earlier.

poets Throughout the years, there has been a seemingly endless number of poet-suicides. Toward the end of the 18th century, the romantics made suicide a major theme and preoccupation, if not obsession. In the Middle Ages, the church's influence was so powerful and pervasive that suicide was simply not a possible subject. It was during the Renaissance and Reformation that the religious taboos begin to lose their power so that poets could again discuss suicide. JOHN DONNE wrote the first book in English on the subject, *BIATHANATOS* (not published, however, in his lifetime).

It was after the rationalists, such as VOLTAIRE and DAVID HUME, attacked the suicide taboos, superstitions, and primitive punishments, that the laws were slowly changed; along with shifting emotional attitudes, the stage was set for the romantic era with its sublime agony.

Since then the world has witnessed poet-suicides who include: THOMAS CHATTERTON, Gerard de Nerval, VIRGINIA WOOLF, HART CRANE, DYLAN THOMAS, Delmore Schwartz, MALCOLM LOWRY, JOHN BERRYMAN, Cesare Pavese, Randall Jarrell, SYLVIA PLATH, ANNE HARVEY SEXTON, and the Russian poets Mayakovsky, Yesenin, and Tsvetayeva. There have been countless others.

poison, as suicide method Among the five most popular or preferred methods used to commit suicide, poison ranks second among women and third among men.

The U.S. Centers for Disease Control uses the classifications "poisoning by solids or liquids," which includes poisoning by drugs or pills.

See also PILLS, AS SUICIDE METHOD.

Pokorny, Alex D. Author-psychiatrist, whose contributions to the literature of suicide includes "Suicide Rates in Various Psychiatric Disorders," *Journal of Nervous Mental Disorders* (1964) 139:499–506. He investigated the suicide rate among former patients of a psychiatric service of a Veteran's Hospital (in Texas) over a 15-year period and calculated the suicide rates on the basis of 100,000 such patients per year as follows: DEPRESSION, 566; SCHIZOPHRENIA, 167; neurosis, 119; PERSONALITY DISORDER, 130; ALCOHOLISM, 133; and organic brain syndrome, 78. He noted that, as a subgroup, manic-depressive patients had the highest rate.

police suicide Law enforcement officers represent a career that carries one of the highest risks for suicide of all. Every 24 hours, one police officer commits suicide, and a third of all active duty and retired officers suffer from post-traumatic stress syndrome (PTSD). In fact, twice as many police officers (about 300 each year) commit suicide as are killed in the line of duty, according to a study by the National Association of Police Chiefs.

Undiagnosed PTSD leads to feelings of hopelessness, despair, and after many years, suicide. One recent study revealed that New York City officers kill themselves at a rate of 29 per 100,000 a year—more than double the national suicide rate of the general U.S. population (12 per 100,000). Most of the victims of police suicide are young men with no record of misconduct, who shoot themselves while off duty.

While there are no government statistics on the suicide rate of police officers, the Occupational Safety and Health Administration reports that the police have a life span eight to 11 years shorter than other Americans. The high-stress dynamics of the job sometimes lead officers to take their own lives, and the fact that officers walk around each day with a weapon handy at all times also plays a role. Alcohol is also often a factor, along with troubled marriages or relationships. As problems and stress mount, many

police officers say they are reluctant to tell superiors they are having problems for fear it may destroy their careers. Instead, they try to solve their problems by themselves, which often leads to alcohol or substance abuse and suicide.

Experts suspect that many suicides by police go unreported to avoid stigmatizing families and to allow them to collect insurance claims and other compensation.

Typically, the officer who commits suicide is a young white man working patrol, abusing alcohol, separated or seeking a divorce, and experiencing a recent loss or disappointment. Often he is coping with a domestic dispute, and 90 percent of the time the officer is drinking heavily when he shoots himself.

See ABUSE, SUBSTANCE.

politics There have been a number of studies on the link between presidential elections and suicide. The various studies, while generally inconclusive in their results, indicate that there is usually a slight drop in deaths by suicide prior to U.S. presidential elections—and a slight increase in the number of deaths by suicide following such elections. There was a noticeable increase in suicides in the United States following the assassination of President John F. Kennedy in 1963.

Pollock, Jackson (1912–1956) American painter who died on August 11, 1956, in East Hampton, New York, in an auto accident believed to have been deliberate. Many authorities called the accident "autocide." Pollock, an alcoholic, was filled with self-doubt and anxiety.

pontifex maximus The highest priest of Roman religion and official head of the college of pontifices. As the chief administrator of religious affairs, he regulated the conduct of religious ceremonies, consecrated temples and other holy places, and controlled the calendar. During the time of the Roman empire and until

Christianity became firmly established, the emperor was designated pontifex maximus. After the supremacy of Christianity, the popes assumed the title.

In Rome, a suicide by HANGING was refused an honorable burial according to that part of the civil law administered by the pontifex maximus. This practice was continued into the Imperial period, and was a vestige of earlier religious views. However, suicide was never a penal offense in Rome and in time there were, for all practical purposes, no penalties.

Portwood, Doris   A EUTHANASIA pioneer and author of the 1978 groundbreaking book, *COMMON SENSE SUICIDE: THE FINAL RIGHT*, a thoughtful and honest examination of suicide. In this work, she addressed the audience of which she was a member—the aging—urging a reappraisal of current attitudes toward suicide in the context of the elderly. She wrote: "Today, the needs of the individual and those of the social community appear to merge, in an economic sense, on the question of old-age suicide. A planned departure that serves oneself, one's family, and also the state surely is worthy of decent consideration."

Portwood was the author of two books for children on Chinese subjects, and had worked as an editor in the U.S. Office of War Information in India during World War II.

At age 82 and suffering from Parkinson's disease, she took BARBITURATES in the presence of two close friends and died quietly in her home outside Portland, Oregon.

postvention   Term coined by suicide expert EDWIN S. SHNEIDMAN, to describe the intervention of others needed by all survivors of suicide (attempters, families of suicides, friends, associates, and so on).

Postvention means extending to suicide survivors the caring support they need immediately after a suicide and, in time, assisting them to come to terms with the tragedy.

potential suicides   Almost every type of person, young or old, poor or rich, white or black, educated or illiterate, Christian or Jew, completes suicide. But the person most likely to attempt or commit suicide is one who has previously tried or threatened suicide; experienced chronic illness and/or isolation; suffered extreme financial stress resulting from joblessness or bankruptcy (or both); suffered a recent death in the family; experienced acute domestic troubles (such as, divorce, separation, or a broken home); experienced severe DEPRESSION; been psychotic and exhibited withdrawal and confusion; been an active alcoholic for a number of years; chronically abused or misused addictive drugs; or has had a history of suicide in the family.

Most potential suicides leave clues to their imminent action. Sometimes these warning signs are broad hints, sometimes only subtle changes in behavior.

However, suicide is usually premeditated—a decision that has come only after long consideration. While it might seem impulsive or capricious, the decision is *not* impulsive. It is possible, therefore, to spot a potential suicide if others know what to look for.

See also CLUES OF SUICIDE.

poverty   In Europe during the mid-19th century, numerous authors who wrote about suicide related the action to poverty, and believed that for this reason, suicide occurred more often among the laboring poor in urban settings.

Today, while poverty is certainly a public problem, it is only one of the many more serious risk factors behind the overall rate of suicide increases in the United States.

Poverty would not explain the marked increase in the contribution of young men and women suicides since the 1950s.

Although the potential for the act of suicide is universal, there are many complex cultural, economic, and social experiences that affect and shape the overall dynamics of the suicide phenomenon. Poverty alone cannot adequately explain how suicide has grown to its present proportions in our modern society.

prediction of suicide At the current time there is no definitive way to predict suicidal behavior. Although researchers have identified factors that place individuals at higher risk for suicide, very few people with these risk factors will actually kill themselves. These risk factors include MENTAL ILL-NESS, substance abuse, previous suicide attempts, a family history of suicide or of sexual abuse, and impulsive or aggressive tendencies.

While many people have at least one of these risk factors, most of them will not complete suicide. Moreover, suicide is a relatively rare event and it is therefore difficult to predict which persons with these risk factors will ultimately complete suicide.

See ABUSE, SUBSTANCE.

pregnancy and suicide While there have been cases where pregnant adult and teenage women have committed suicide, there is no indication that pregnancy is a key motivator for self-destruction. Everybody gets depressed from time to time, and certainly pregnant women—especially those who did not want to have a child—are no exception. They may experience profound feelings of worthlessness and lack of self-esteem (which lie at the base of many severe DEPRESSIONS); they sometimes take a negative view of both themselves and their relation to the world around them; and in extreme cases, depressed pregnant women have a negative view of the future. If their depression grows and becomes too deep, they may give up all hope. These painful feelings sometimes cause depressed persons to blame themselves for their condition, and they want to punish themselves in various ways for the personal failings they believe they have. Sometimes the punishment takes the form of suicide.

prevention (of suicide) The best way to prevent suicide is to learn what is causing the distress, the tension, and anguish—and then work to treat these emotions within the suicidal person. Practical measures for helping highly suicidal persons include: reduce the pain; fill the frustrated needs; provide a viable answer to the question of life's worth; indicate alternatives in life; give transfusions of hope; play for time; increase the options; listen; involve others; block the exit (for action on the suicidal person's part); and, invoke precious positive patterns of successful coping.

Prevention resources include psychotherapy, counseling, outreach groups, and private as well as federal agencies. Most recently, the federal government developed the NATIONAL STRATEGY FOR SUICIDE PREVENTION, a program that represents the combined work of advocates, clinicians, researchers, and survivors around the nation designed to prevent suicide and guide development of an array of preventive services and programs. It is designed to be a catalyst for social change with the power to transform attitudes, policies, and services.

In 1999, Surgeon General David Satcher released *A Call to Action to Prevent Suicide,* a message to the nation that included a set of recommendations derived from a national conference held in Reno, Nevada, in 1998. At that time, the Call to Action included 15 recommendations that provided the context for the development of the National Strategy for Suicide Prevention.

As part of his ongoing effort on the National Strategy for Suicide Prevention, on May 2, 2001, Satcher unveiled a national blueprint of goals and objectives to prevent suicide, the eighth leading cause of death in the United States. The document established 11 goals and 68 measurable objectives for public and private sector involvement to prevent suicides and attempts, as well as reduce the harmful after effects on families and communities.

"Suicide has stolen lives and contributed to the disability and suffering of hundreds of thousands of Americans each year," Satcher explained. "Only recently have the knowledge and tools become available to approach suicide as a preventable problem with realistic opportunities to save many lives."

The public health approach laid out in his National Strategy represents a rational and organized way to marshal prevention efforts and ensure that they are effective. The HHS collaborated with key advocacy groups representing clinicians, researchers, and survivors to develop the goals and objectives. The goals and objectives lay out a framework for action and guide development of an array of services and programs. It strives to provide direction to efforts to modify the social infrastructure in ways that will affect the most basic attitudes about suicide and that will also change judicial, educational, social service, and health care systems. The 68 specific objectives contained in the report include:

- Implementing integrated community-based suicide prevention programs that build life skills, beliefs and values, and connections to family and community support known to reduce the risk of suicide
- Incorporating suicide-risk screening at the primary health care level
- Increasing the number of states that require health insurance plans to cover mental health and substance abuse care on a par with coverage for physical health care
- Providing treatment for more suicidal persons with mental health problems
- Developing technical support centers to increase the capacity of states to implement and evaluate prevention programs
- Increasing availability of comprehensive support programs for survivors of suicide
- Increasing the number of professional and volunteer groups as well as faith-based communities that integrate suicide prevention into their ongoing activities
- Improving suicide prevention education and training for health care professionals, counselors, clergy, teachers, and other key "community gatekeepers"

- Increasing the number of television programs and movies that accurately and safely depict suicide and mental illness
- Implementing a national violent death reporting system that includes suicide.

Future installments of the national strategy will be released as work is completed. Currently, about 25 states have begun efforts to enact their own suicide prevention strategies.

Collaborators who developed the goals and objectives included the SUICIDE PREVENTION AND ADVOCACY NETWORK (SPAN), the Association for Suicide Prevention, the AMERICAN ASSOCIATION OF SUICIDOLOGY, and hundreds of individuals working at state, tribal and local levels to prevent suicide. The U.S. Air Force contributed significantly to the effort by providing a model for comprehensive community-based suicide prevention programs and its direct support of the strategy development process.

primitive societies   Suicide is an act whose primary aim is the intentional and deliberate taking of one's own life. Ruth S. Cavan, writing in *Suicide,* postulates that suicides are of two types: conventional and personal. Conventional suicide occurs as a result of tradition plus the force of public opinion. That is why, among some tradition-bound peoples, within certain situations, suicide is demanded. Notable examples include SEPPUKU, the ritualistic suicide of a Japanese man of rank faced with disgrace or humiliation; the SUTTEE of the Indian widow who was forced to self-immolation (by cremation) on her husband's funeral pyre; and in certain primitive tribes, exposure to the elements of the old and infirm and their abandonment—as among primitive Eskimos. "Such conventional suicides," wrote Cavan, "are typical of societies in which most problem situations are solved by strongly held customs."

These types of suicides were also traditional among several widely scattered primitive tribes. Early records show that widows committed suicide in northwest Europe immediately after the husband's death. More recent anthropological studies of certain African tribes indicate that their frequency of suicide was comparable to that of European countries with relatively low suicide rates and that suicide among the tribes was considered evil. Erwin Stengel, author of *Suicide and Attempted Suicide,* explains:

> Physical contact with the body of a suicide is feared to have disastrous effects, such as illness or suicide among one's kin. The tree on which a person hanged himself is felled and burned. The ancestors have to be placated by sacrifices. The place where the suicide happened is believed to be a haunt of evil spirits. Suicide is dreaded in the community, and a threat of suicide is sometimes used to exert pressure on the family.

In Tikopia, a small island in the western Pacific where pagan ideology lingers, suicide is looked at with wild disapproval. The gods will receive the souls of the dead, it is believed, but not of suicides. Their souls are destined to wander aimlessly until their ancestral spirits find them. Yet the spirits have no objection to the man who commits suicide by going off to sea in a canoe, or the woman who swims out to sea. These suicide methods are admired. The Christian Tikopians believe that a suicide's soul goes not to paradise, but to Satan.

Among the GISU OF UGANDA, suicides of the aged and infirm usually took place after all means of alleviating their condition had been tried and found ineffective. In some primitive societies, suicide was an act of last resort. The Joluo of Kenya, who hold attitudes toward suicide not unlike the Gisu, manage to keep knowledge of a suicide within the clan, to protect the community's prestige. The Tiv of Nigeria appear to have the lowest incidence of suicide yet recorded; so few, it seems, that one anthropologist-researcher was unable to document cases of Tiv suicide.

Prinze, Freddie (1954–1977)   American comedian-actor who killed himself in January, 1977, at the age of 23. Friends and business associates told authorities that Prinze was despondent about the breakup of his marriage, which may have been caused by a desire for too much love. Despite his early success in show business, the young comedian, co-star of the TV series *Chico and the Man,* seemed never to have developed an internal feeling of competence and self-confidence. In his suicide note, Prinze wrote: "I must end it. There's no hope left. I'll be at peace. No one had anything to do with this. My decision totally."

prisoners   While many people kill themselves while in jails and state prisons, there are no reliable data on rates as compared to suicides in the general population. Among those prisoners of institutions who do commit suicide, the majority hang themselves. Also, there appears to be a complexity of motivations along with a mix of conflicting tendencies underlying prisoners' suicidal acts. There is also the tendency, at times, on the part of prison or jail authorities to protect the particular institution's reputation and/or record by concealing the suicidal acts of prisoners. Some prisons put on a special "suicide watch" for prisoners convicted of especially heinous crimes.

A lack of uniformity of search procedures and criteria of categorization, not to mention comparability of data, have made studies to date unreliable.

See also JAIL SUICIDE.

Protestants   In the United States, Catholics appear to have suicide rates that are higher than rates for JEWS, but lower than the rates for Protestants. This same relationship occurs in most countries where the major religious groups are Jews, Catholics, and Protestants. An exception is Austria, primarily a Catholic country, yet with a suicide rate that has consistently ranked as one of the highest in the world.

Generally speaking, the highest suicide rates—relating suicide to religious groups—are found among the multidenominational, loosely federated Protestants. Suicide rates among Jews in the United States, and in Israel, appear to be gradually increasing. Experts suspect that Protestantism contributed to suicide by favoring individualism, free thought, and free inquiry, leading people more easily to doubt and despair.

However, there is a need for caution in the comparison and evaluation of rate differences relating religion and suicide. The World Health Organization warns: "The true incidence of suicide is hard to ascertain. Varying methods of certifying causes of death, different registration and coding procedures, and other factors affect the extent and completeness of coverage, making international comparisons impracticable."

While the attitude of most Protestant factions remains one of general condemnation of suicide, the specific sanctions are not as equally severe as in the past—or in all denominations. The funeral rites accorded people who committed suicide still differ in many cases from the rites of those who have died a natural death. Also, exemption from sanctions on the ground of mental instability or disturbance is usually more readily granted than in the past.

Overall, there seems to be a greater willingness to understand rather than to condemn suicide. However, the tendency to conceal suicidal acts still persists, but that may well be primarily out of a sense of guilt felt by those who feel they could have prevented the act.

Prozac and suicide   Prozac is one of the world's most popular antidepressants, one of a new class of drugs with fewer side effects than older drugs. Yet some critics continue to charge that Prozac makes a few patients more likely to complete suicide. These accusations have persisted despite repeated and categorical rebuttals by the drug's manufacturer, Eli Lilly, which points out that patients who are depressed enough to need medication are also frequently suicidal. For every accusation of suicide, there are thousands of other, formerly depressed

patients who insist their lives were saved by the drug. So far Lilly has won every Prozac-related civil suit—more than 100 in all.

Still, critics worry that for a very small minority of patients, Prozac and other drugs in its class appear to trigger suicidal thoughts.

Prozac's manufacturers insist that there is no scientific evidence to establish a link between Prozac and suicide, and cite a 1991 study by a U.S. Food and Drug Administration (FDA) advisory panel that unanimously agreed there was no credible evidence of a causal link between the use of antidepressants, including Prozac, and violent behavior. Even the drug's critics agree that the effect (which the company says does not exist) occurs in only a small number of cases—fewer than 1 percent.

But critics insist that even though the incidence seems very low, when it happens it is such a serious matter that doctors should be very careful in prescribing Prozac. Critics say the danger is greatest during the first week or two of Prozac use, when some patients who were already at risk for suicide have a rare reaction that makes them feel energized and more ready to act on their self-destructive impulses. A second period of increased risk occurs when a patient, who had been virtually immobilized by deep DEPRESSION, still entertains suicidal thoughts. At this point, critics say, the drug has eased their depression enough so they have the energy to carry out these thoughts.

Some researchers insist that a direct link exists between SSRIs and the emergence of suicidal thinking in people who had never had such thoughts. Dr. Martin Teicher of Harvard Medical School reported in 1990 that he and his colleagues had observed suicidal thoughts emerging in six patients who were taking Prozac. Other researchers and clinicians began reporting that they saw it, too.

Serotonin is a chemical vital to the brain's regulation of a wide variety of body functions, including sleep, appetite, breathing, and blood circulation. Low serotonin levels have been blamed for many mental and physical problems, including depression, obsessive-compulsive disorder, and panic disorder. Prozac and the other SSRIs have been prescribed for all those problems, and have produced dramatic improvement in most cases.

Experts suggest that until more research has been done, doctors should be much more careful about prescribing SSRIs, investigating the patient's history to uncover any previous indications of suicidal thought or other instability.

Because any physician can prescribe Prozac—not just psychiatrists—general practitioners, primary care doctors, and specialists in other areas might not be as alert for danger signs as a psychiatrist might be.

According to the Boston *Globe,* internal Lilly documents show that in 1990, corporate executives pressured Lilly scientists to alter records on physicians' experiences with Prozac. They changed mentions of suicide attempts to "overdose" and of suicidal thoughts to "depression." Some of Lilly's own studies were cited by the German equivalent of the Food and Drug Administration, delaying Prozac's approval there. They showed that previously nonsuicidal patients who took the drug had five times the rate of suicide or suicide attempts as patients who took older antidepressants. When the drug was finally approved for sale in Germany, the manufacturer was required to add a label warning that the drug's use carried a risk of suicide, and recommended that sedatives be given along with it.

The *Globe* reported that figures in Lilly internal documents showed that in early clinical trials, one in 100 previously nonsuicidal patients who took Prozac became anxious and agitated, and either attempted or committed suicide during the studies. Some of the previously unknown information that Eli Lilly possessed about the drug has come to light during civil trials in which the company was sued for wrongful deaths following suicides, or during criminal trials in which defense lawyers argued that Prozac caused a defendant's violent and homicidal behavior.

A patent has been granted for Prozac's successor, R-fluoxetine, which the company says will decrease side effects such as headaches, anxiety, and insomnia, and also "inner restlessness (AKATHISIA), suicidal thoughts and self-mutilation." Akathisia, an overwhelming physical and mental restlessness, has been cited by physicians and researchers as a frequent side effect in the cases in which they believe Prozac is causing violent, impulsive, and sometimes suicidal behavior.

pseudocide   Pseudo-suicide; faked suicide.

psychic blow   An event that threatens a person's acceptable life circumstances that may lead to suicide.

psychic homicide   Suicide by the children of abusive or hostile parents.

psychic suicide   Willing oneself to die without any external physical action.

psychodynamic theory   The branch of psychology that investigates motivation and emotional processes—in this instance, how psychic, social, and cultural factors are interwoven to produce suicidal behavior in individuals from very different backgrounds. It is the systematized knowledge and theory of human behaviors and motivation in which the role of emotions is of special significance.

Psychodynamics incorporates the role of unconscious motivation, as well as conscious, and assumes that behavior is determined by past experience, genetic endowment, and current reality.

psychological autopsy   A method by which coroners and medical examiners are helped in efforts to determine the cause of a death in a case of suspected suicide, when a cause is not clearly indicated.

In performing a psychological autopsy, members of the investigative team interview friends, relatives, associates, teachers, and any other significant associates who might have played a role in the person's life. The victim's routine for several days and hours before the death is examined. Team members then try to paint an overall picture of the person's character, personality, and state of mind. On the strength and significance of the data, team members try to judge whether the person's death was suicide or not. The team then reports its findings to the coroner or medical examiner, who includes this with the postmortem investigation and determines whether to list the death as a "suicide," "homicide," "accident," "natural," or "undetermined."

The idea of psychological autopsy was created by psychologists Edwin S. Shneidman and Norman L. Farberow, cofounders in 1958 of the LOS ANGELES SUICIDE PREVENTION CENTER.

Psychological autopsies are also used in forensic investigations and legal cases where insurance payouts have been denied because of suicide (and the estate challenges the determination). PAs are also used to explain why a suicide occurred and in developing an epidemiological database for preventive interventions.

psychosis   A major mental disorder of organic or emotional origin involving a person's ability to think, respond emotionally, remember, communicate, interpret reality, and behave appropriately. It is characterized by impairment sufficient enough to interfere grossly with the capacity to meet the ordinary demands of life. Disturbances may appear in the form of aggressive behavior and diminished impulse control, along with delusions and hallucinations.

psychotherapy   The application of specialized counseling techniques to the treatment of mental disorders or to the problems of everyday adjustments. In a more specific sense, the term includes only those techniques (such as psycho-analysis, nondirective or directive counseling, psychodrama) utilized by specialists.

Ultimately, the objective of any and all forms of psychotherapy is to relieve symptoms or to resolve problems in living or to seek personal growth.

psychotic suicide   Most people who commit suicide do not suffer from psychotic illness; usually, suicidal behavior stems from deep DEPRESSION and, at times, from neurotic disturbances that are less severe or intense than psychoses. Some suicides, however, are related to psychotic illnesses. In this case, the victim suffers a break with reality, loses the ability to distinguish what is occurring and what is imagined. The patient acts out fantasies, not understanding that the behavior seems weird and disorganized to other people. Most psychotics have periods of lucidity, and many are able to live relatively normal lives until something triggers a break with reality.

Authorities say some psychotic illnesses are caused by a physical problem; some result from biochemical imbalances in the body that may be hereditary. Still others have deep-seated psychological or emotional causes that result from unstable or disruptive family relationships.

Psychotic illnesses are usually treated with drugs, often in tandem with psychotherapy, and with family therapy that involves parents, siblings, and other relatives.

Psychotic illness may lead to suicidal thoughts and actions before family members or friends realize that the patient is deeply disturbed. Usually, this is because the psychotic person won't acknowledge the severity of the illness.

punishment, suicide as   One reason for suicide is a wish to punish—either the self or someone else. Psychologists usually understand and explain suicide in terms of various levels of pressure on the individual, which may parlay into killing oneself.

SIGMUND FREUD implied that murder is aggression turned upon another; suicide is aggression turned upon the self. Suicide, in other words, becomes "murder in the 180th degree."

Sometimes, confused suicidal persons, especially the very young, view killing themselves as a way to "punish" others, to make someone close to them show more respect or love for them. They view themselves as being present to enjoy the punishment their death has inflicted or the belated love it has generated.

If the suicidal person feels he or she has disappointed a loved one or a close friend by not living up to their expectations, the punishment that is suicide is turned inward.

Dr. KARL MENNINGER, in MAN AGAINST HIMSELF, writes that everyone who attempts or completes suicide is driven (consciously and unconsciously) by three motives: the wish to kill, the wish to be killed, and the wish to die.

Quinlan, Karen Ann (1954–1985) The first modern icon of the right-to-die debate. After the 21-year-old Quinlan collapsed after swallowing alcohol and tranquilizers at a party in 1975, doctors saved her life, but the young woman suffered brain damage and lapsed into a persistent vegetative state. Her family waged a much-publicized legal battle for the right to remove her life support machinery.

Although she did not commit suicide, the case of Karen Ann Quinlan laid the groundwork for legislation granting terminally ill people and their families the right to authorize withdrawal of life-sustaining procedures when death is believed imminent. The problem posed by the 21-year-old woman from Morris County, New Jersey, as she lay breathing mechanically day after day in a fixed death-in-life situation sparked new and enlightening discussions on the definition of death.

Quinlan's parents went to court for permission to remove her life support and lost; the New Jersey Supreme Court overturned the lower court ruling, a major concern being Karen's right to privacy, which was asserted in her behalf by her family.

As a result of the successful appeal, she was weaned from the respirator. She did not die as expected, however, and was transferred from the hospital to a nursing home, where she remained in a coma, fed through tubes, until she died 10 years later in July 1985. Before Karen Ann Quinlan's tragic case came to light, right-to-die legislation had been introduced in only five states. Shortly afterward, 50 bills were introduced in 38 states.

In the years after the Quinlan case, health care directives have become popular. Now every state has a law allowing some sort of health care directive. In late 1991, the federal Patient Self Determination Act took effect, requiring that any facility receiving Medicare or Medicaid funds must discuss health care directives with their new patients. Because nearly every hospital receives Medicare or Medicaid funds, patients should now be given a written explanation of their state's law on health care directives and the hospital's policies regarding health care directives upon admission to a hospital. The law also requires health care facilities to make a record of each patient's health care directives as part of their medical records.

Qur'an, the Sacred scripture of the MUSLIMS, comprising 114 *suras* (chapters) of unequal length, nearly all of which are supposedly of divine revelation—Allah speaking directly through the angel Gabriel to Mohammed. The holy scriptures of ISLAM expressly declared suicide to be a more serious crime than homicide. Muslim belief explains this attitude: Each person has his or her *kismet,* or destiny, which is foreordained by Allah, or God, and must not be defied. Some suicides do take place in Muslim countries; however, strong religious restrictions keep rates relatively low.

race Although there are reputedly a few isolated parts of the world where no suicides are committed—or at least none are reported (such as, several small South Sea islands and the Hindu Kush Mountains of India)—no race or ethnic group is exempt from the suicidal potential.

Among the world's nations, the countries usually high on the scale in terms of suicide rates per 100,000 population are: HUNGARY, DENMARK, FINLAND, AUSTRIA, GERMANY, SWEDEN, SWITZERLAND, and JAPAN. Countries on the low end of the suicide rate charts include: the Philippines, Angola, Jamaica, Mexico, the Bahamas, Kuwait, Jordan, Kenya, and EGYPT.

Within the United States, the suicide rate for African Americans is lower than the rate for Caucasians. However, the figures for both groups are considerably closer in urban areas, and in certain metropolitan areas, the rate for African Americans is higher than it is for whites living in other sections of the city. Also, the rate is higher for young blacks than it is for whites. Ethnic groups with predominantly Catholic members appear to have suicide rates that are higher than the rate for JEWS, but lower than the rates for ethnic members of predominantly PROTESTANT faiths.

A very high risk group in the United States is the Native American. Many believe such causal factors as isolation, alienation, poverty, hopelessness, and drugs and alcohol play a major role in the native suicide rate.

Raskolniki A dissenting religious group of 17th-century Russia in such despair that many of its members sought death rather than wait for the end of the world, which they had predicted would occur before century's end. Between 1672 and 1691, some 37 mass immolations took place, as more than 20,000 Raskolniki voluntarily burned to death. By these MASS SUICIDES, they confirmed their belief that it was senseless to remain on Earth and risk contamination by heresy.

rates, suicide Suicide deaths are compiled by the National Center for Health Statistics (NCHS) and published yearly. Variables on each suicide included: age, race, sex, place of residence, place of occurrence, date of death, cause of death.

Special estimates (prepared by the U.S. Bureau of Census) were used to compute rates for the years 1970 to 1980. Unpublished population statistics of U.S. residents provided by NCHS were used to compute rates for 1979 and 1980. Updated population estimates for the intercensal years are based on the previous U.S. Census. Because suicide varies by age, age-adjusted suicide rates are presented in some sections in this work to allow for comparison of rates between populations without concern for different age structures in the populations being compared.

Data on suicide deaths for various countries are compiled by the World Health Organization. Unfortunately, not all countries disclose such information and other countries lag behind in providing mortality data, so a listing by country is not exhaustive.

rational suicide Some right-to-die advocacy groups promote the idea that suicide, including

ASSISTED SUICIDE, can be a rational decision. Others have argued that suicide is never a rational decision and that it is the result of DEPRESSION, anxiety, and fear of being dependent or a burden.

The term *rational suicide* was coined by Manhattan artist and former social worker Jo Roman, who advocated choosing the time of one's own death—which she did at age 62 in 1979 before taking a fatal overdose of pills. She had been diagnosed as having a breast tumor that would have been treatable by mastectomy, but she rejected the operation. Roman called her friends in to say good-bye, had the group's conversation taped, then spent the evening with her husband and a close friend before ingesting the pills. Her videotapes on advocacy of self-termination were subsequently shown in an educational television documentary.

Surveys of terminally ill people indicate that very few consider taking their own life, and when they do, it is usually related to their depression. Attitude surveys suggest that assisted suicide is more acceptable by the public and health providers for the old who are ill or disabled, compared to the young who are ill or disabled.

At this time, there is limited research on how often people who are terminally ill are depressed or have suicidal thoughts, whether they would consider assisted suicide, the characteristics of such people, and the context of their depression and suicidal thoughts. Neither is it yet clear what effects other factors, such as the availability of social support, access to care, and pain relief may have on end-of-life preferences.

rationalists, the   A group of early to mid-18th century, writers, philosophers, and thinkers who steadily hammered away at the suicide taboos, superstitions, and the primitive, punishments still being meted out for suicide. As a result, strict laws about suicide were gradually changed, along with a corresponding shift in society's emotional attitudes.

razor blades, as suicide weapon   Though razor blades are not a frequently used method of suicide (based on those deaths identified according to cause of death codes established by International Classification of Disease, or ICD), any person—family member, friend, acquaintance—who has doubts about a suicidal individual's intentions should check for any possible lethal weapon, including razor blades. Young people, especially, have used this method of suicide attempt or suicide.

Rebel without a Cause   A 1950s film starring actor James Dean, who was killed on September 30, 1955, in a car accident in California (many experts called his death "AUTOCIDE"). Dean, who in real life appeared to live the characters he played on the screen, played the angry young *Rebel without a Cause* who plays "chicken" with another teenager as their cars race toward each other along the edge of a high cliff. Tens of thousands of teenage fans identified with the complex actor's personal rebelliousness and his open defiance of the adult establishment.

reckless driving, as suicide clue   Risky behaviors, including reckless driving, are considered to be a warning sign of potential suicidal behavior. In one study, about 25 percent of accident victims were depressed people with feelings of helplessness and a sense of loss typical of suicidal persons. Those studied had experienced fantasies and dreams of death and self-destruction shortly before their accidents. Experts believe the serious accidents the victims suffered could well have resulted from underlying wishes to kill themselves.

Dr. Karl Menninger interpreted most accidents as the result of unconscious self-destructive drives. Dr. Alfred L. Moseley of the Harvard Medical School concludes that suicides are a "significant though unknown" proportion of the rising number of annual auto deaths in the U.S.

AUTOCIDE occurs when a car is used as a method of self-imposed death.

recognition of suicide potential   See CLUES OF SUICIDE.

Reformation   The religious reform movements of the 1500s in Western Europe, which had as their object the correction of abuses that had arisen in the Western Catholic Church. Those movements resulted in the disunity of that church and the foundation of Protestant churches. Martin Luther's teachings gave impetus to the Reformation, which began in Germany in 1515 with his thesis against the sale of indulgences. It was during the Renaissance and Reformation that the churchly taboos against suicide began gradually to lose their power. Sir Thomas More justified suicide as a form of EUTHANASIA in his *Utopia*.

religion   See CLERGY AND SUICIDE PREVENTION.

Renaissance   Time of the great revival of art, letters, and learning in Europe from the 14th through the 16th centuries, marking the transition from the medieval to the modern world.

With regard to suicide, new and less stringent attitudes toward suicide began to gradually emerge during the Renaissance. These more lenient, understanding attitudes finally came out into the open in the 18th century, as churchly taboos began to lose their power.

Research on Suicide: A Bibliography   Comprehensive bibliography compiled by John L. McIntosh, assistant professor of psychology at Indiana University at South Bend, and published by the Greenwood Press, Westport, Connecticut, in 1985.

reserpine   Drug commonly used for treatment of high blood pressure. Extensive clinical use revealed that it caused as many as 15 percent of patients to become depressed in a fashion indistinguishable from endogenous DEPRESSION.

Reserpine depression was discovered by a cardiovascular researcher who noted an astoundingly high incidence of suicide in patients receiving this drug.

revenge suicide   Spite as the motivation behind suicide is particularly common among children under age 13. Notes left by some suicidal patients indicate that the message behind the act is: "It's your fault" or "Now we're even!" While an adult who feels unloved might confront a spouse with his fears, suspicions, and anger, a young person might make a point by committing suicide.

The youngster's view of death usually includes the notion that after the act of suicide, he or she will remain behind, hovering invisibly over the funeral scene, taking pleasure in witnessing the parents' and friends' grief.

"right to die" movement   See EUTHANASIA; HEMLOCK SOCIETY.

"right to suicide"   Every society throughout recorded history has had to contend with this complex issue. Each has had to determine when, if ever, suicide is justifiable, and when, if ever, it might be permitted. No society can survive if it allows widespread suicide among its members. And in most cultures and most times in history, people have feared, forbidden, and condemned suicide. But at certain times, and under certain conditions, they have not only tolerated, but also encouraged it.

risk of suicide   There are a number of risk factors for suicidal behavior, including gender, age, race, religion, marital status, occupation, physical health, mental health, and previous suicidal behavior.

Gender
Men commit suicide more than three times as often as do women in all age groups. Women,

however, are more likely to attempt suicide than are men. This means that while fewer men attempt suicide, more of them succeed.

Age

Suicide rates increase with age and underscore the significance of the midlife crisis. Among men, suicides peak after the age of 45. Among women, the greatest number of completed suicides occur after age 55. Older people attempt suicide less often than do younger people, but they are often more successful.

While the elderly make up only about 10 percent of the population, older people account for one quarter of all U.S. suicides. The rate for those above age 75 is three times as much as for younger people.

However, the suicide rate is rising most rapidly among young people, particularly among men age 15 to 24. In this age group, the rate for women is increasing at a lower rate, but it is increasing.

Race

Two of every three completed suicides are committed by white men; the risk of suicide among whites is nearly twice that of all other groups. However, this general rule is changing, as the suicide rate among blacks (especially African American men) is rising. Among young people who live in inner cities, and certain Native American and Inuit groups, suicide rates have greatly exceeded the national rate. Suicide rates among immigrants are higher than for the native-born population.

Religion

Historically the suicide rates among Roman Catholics has been lower than among JEWS and PROTESTANTS, but a person's degree of involvement in the church may be a more accurate measure of risk than simple religious affiliation.

Marital Status

Marriage and children significantly lessens the risk of suicide; single, never-married individuals have suicide rates twice as high as for those who are married and have children. Losing a spouse, however, is worse than never getting married when it comes to suicide—previously married people have much higher suicide rates than do the never-married. Sometimes, people will commit anniversary suicides on the day that a loved one died.

Occupation

The higher a person's social status, the greater the risk of suicide, but a fall in status also increases the risk. Work, in general, tends to protect against suicide. Special at-risk populations include: psychiatrists, psychologists, ophthalmologists, anesthesiologists, physicians, musicians, dentists, law enforcement officers, lawyers, and life insurance agents. Suicide rates also are higher among those without a job, and the rate increases during recessions and times of rising unemployment, and decreases during times of high employment and during wars.

Climate

No significant seasonal correlation with suicide has been found. Suicides decrease slightly in winter.

Physical Health

Not surprisingly, there is a relationship between poor physical health and suicide. Postmortem studies have found that people who commit suicide are physically ill between 25 percent and 75 percent of the time. It is estimated that a physical illness is a significant factor in up to half of all suicides. As many as 70 percent of suicide victims have some form of cancer.

In addition, seven diseases of the central nervous system—all of which are associated with DEPRESSION—increase the risk of suicide: epilepsy, multiple sclerosis, head injury, cardiovascular disease (stroke), Huntington's disease, dementia, and AIDS. Some endocrine diseases also are linked with a higher suicide risk, including Cushing's disease, Klinefelter's syndrome, and porphyria. Both peptic ulcers and cirrhosis of the liver are also linked to suicide risk. Benign prostatic hypertrophy (BPH) treated with prostate removal, and kidney disease treated with hemodialysis, are both linked to suicide; mood disorders may occur in both conditions.

There are several reasons why some illnesses may contribute to a higher risk of suicide. Diseases that cause loss of mobility, disfigurement (particularly among women), and chronic intractable pain can be difficult to bear. In addition to the direct effects of illness on risk, secondary effects (such as disrupted relationships and job loss) increase the risk of suicide.

In addition, certain medications can produce depression, which may lead to suicide in some cases. Some of these drugs include RESERPINE (Serpasil), corticosteroids, high blood pressure medication, and some chemotherapy drugs.

Mental Health

It's clear that MENTAL ILLNESS plays a part in many suicides—especially substance abuse (see ABUSE, SUBSTANCE), depression, and SCHIZOPHRENIA. As many as 95 percent of all people who attempt or complete suicide have a diagnosed mental disorder, and depression accounts for about 80 percent of this figure. Schizophrenia accounts for about 10 percent, and dementia or delirium accounts for 5 percent. Among all people with mental disorders, 25 percent are alcohol dependent. The suicide risk in people with depressive disorders is about 15 percent, and 25 percent of everyone with a history of impulsive or violent acts are also at high risk of suicide.

Previous psychiatric hospitalization for any reason increases the risk of suicide. The suicide risk for psychiatric patients is three to 12 times higher than for nonpatients, although the degree of risk varies according to age, sex, diagnosis, and inpatient or outpatient status.

Psychiatric patients who commit suicide tend to be relatively young, which may be partly because two early-onset disorders (schizophrenia and recurrent major depression) account for just over half of all these suicides, and reflect an age and diagnostic pattern found in most studies

of psychiatric patient suicides. Patients with panic disorder also are at increased risk for suicide.

Previous Suicidal Behavior

A past suicide attempt is possibly the best indicator that a patient is at greater risk for suicide. Some 40 percent of depressed patients who attempt suicide have made a previous attempt. The risk of a second attempt is highest within three months of the first attempt.

ritual suicide   Various cultures over the years have endorsed, even encouraged, ritual suicides.
See also SEPPUKU; SUTTEE; GISU OF UGANDA.

Rollin, Betty   Former television reporter for ABC and NBC, and author of the book, *Last Wish*, wherein Rollin admits that she secretly helped her terminally ill mother, Ida, commit suicide in 1983. In the book, the author reveals that her mother expressed the desire to end her own life after months of torturous and apparently futile chemotherapy for inoperable ovarian cancer. Rollin maintains that her role in the drug overdose of 75-year-old Ida Rollin in her Manhattan apartment did not violate a New York State law against "promoting suicide."

"I did not directly help my mother to commit suicide," Rollin told reporters. "If I did, I would not have written a book about it." She said she "did research and gave my mother the information." Under New York state law, "promoting suicide" is a felony, punishable by up to four years in prison. Some legal authorities said such cases pose difficult problems. Rollin was not indicted by the state for any wrongdoing, and *Last Wish* went on to make several best-seller lists.

Roman Catholic Church   By the end of the fourth century, ST. AUGUSTINE had established rules against suicide that would provide the basis for Christian doctrine through the ages. He argued that suicide allowed no opportunity for repentance and branded all suicides as crimes.

St. Augustine's teachings and those of other early church authorities were incorporated into the laws of the Roman Catholic Church and, later, the Anglican Church, in which suicide was seen as an act inspired by the devil and was a mortal sin. Bodies of those who committed suicide were denied Christian burial, and even attempters of suicide were excommunicated.

Church laws did make an exception in the case of "insane" people, and also exempted young children from the severe penalties of law. These religious laws against suicide have remained in effect in the Roman Catholic Church (and in many PROTESTANT churches, as well).

Today, however, many priests and ministers appear inclined to find ways in which church laws can be altered toward leniency in special circumstances.

romance, breakup of   Some people, especially young people, suffer deep DEPRESSION and feelings of worthlessness following the breakup of a romance. Such persons have been known to think and even talk about suicide—which is one clue to look for in people who have been affected by a romantic loss.

romantics, the   A group of artists and writers— led by THOMAS CHATTERTON who killed himself in 1770 at the age of 17—thought of death as "the great inspirer" and "great consoler." It was they who made suicide fashionable, and during the epidemic in France in the 1830s, practiced it as one of the most elegant of sports. For the young would-be poets, novelists, dramatists, painters, and members of countless suicide clubs, to die by suicide was a short and sure way to fame.

The epidemic never quite took hold in England, although it started there with Chatterton's suicide. As the 19th century wore on, romanticism gradually dissipated and along with it faded the idealization of death.

Romeo and Juliet   Play written ca. 1595 by William Shakespeare, this tragedy was based on a poem by Arthur Brooke which in turn was taken from a romance by Bendello.

In the story, the Montagues and the Capulets, two powerful families in Verona, have an ancient grudge. A byzantine story line filled with twists and turns, plus one of the most beautiful love scenes in the English language, culminates in the deaths by suicide of both young lovers, Romeo and Juliet, he by poison and she by Romeo's dagger. The alarm is spread and the feuding Montagues and Capulets meet at the tomb. The families are reconciled by the tragedy their feud had caused.

ropes, as suicide weapon   Hanging, strangulation, and suffocation—closely related enough to be regarded as a single means of self-destruction—is today the second most common method of suicide among men. It was second in popularity only to firearms and explosives.

Rothko, Mark (1903–1970)   Russian-born American painter who was originally a figurative painter, but whose later abstract works are his most famous. Always melancholy, Rothko said he painted "tragedy, ecstasy, doom, and so on." As he became more famous his depression deepened. Rothko committed suicide in New York City, on February 25, 1970, at age 67.

Rousseau, Jean-Jacques (1712–1778)   French philosopher, political thinker, and novelist, who was born in Geneva, the son of a watchmaker. It was in his novel *La Nouvelle Heloise* (1769), a famous and influential work, that he emphasized a person's natural right to complete suicide as long as no one else is harmed by doing so. Rousseau established one condition, however: People who have responsibilities to others should not commit suicide.

His notion that the "natural," or primitive, man ("the noble savage") was inherently good, and that evil arose from the distortions of society, was enormously influential in the rise of romanticism in literature and music, and is still a powerful force, in education especially.

See also ROMANTICS, THE.

Russian Federation The suicide rate for the federation in 1997 was a whooping 39.3 per 100,000, much higher than the international average, but fairly typical among eastern European countries. This represents a stunning average for men who kill themselves at a rate of 66.4 per 100,000, compared to a woman's average of 12.3.

When broken down by age, the highest rate for men is middle age, from 45 to 54—a rate of 100 per 100,000. For Russian women, the highest suicide rate is over age 75 (32.7 per 100,000).

While the suicide rate for Russian children age 14 and below is not high, the rate jumps alarmingly in the 15-to-25 age group, to 53 per 100,000 among young Russian men and 80.3 for men aged 25 to 34.

In the past, Russians as part of the Soviet Union refused to provide data to the World Health Organization in Geneva, insisting that suicide was a bourgeois activity that did not occur in the Soviet Union.

Ryder, Hugh (fl. 1664–1693) Surgeon to King James II, who tells of "A young woman who had been at a Meetinghouse . . . in a great discontent went home and fell into such despair, that being melancholy by herself in her chamber, with a knife cut her throat . . ." The wound proved not to be lethal and under Ryder's care, the woman recovered. This account of a published case history served to reinforce the view of suicide being the result of a mental disorder.

Saint-Exupéry, Antoine-Marie-Roger de (1900–1944) French writer and aviator who was obsessed with aviation from an early age. He joined the French Army Air Force in 1921, then became a commercial pilot five years later. Throughout his career, he wrote popular books —many were fantasies for children—about flying. He celebrated his faith in man and life, in his philosophical and mystical books, yet, all the while, he seemed preoccupied with thoughts of death. His father died when Saint-Exupéry was only four years old, and a brother died when he was 17.

His best-known fantasy for young readers, *Le Petit Prince* (*The Little Prince*, 1943), romanticized suicide as a way of "going home," and depicted death as a painless process whereby one simply shed the body like "an old abandoned shell" after which the freed soul would soar into the skies.

In 1944, while making a reconnaissance flight during World War II over southern France, Saint-Exupéry disappeared. His *Citadelle* was published posthumously in 1948, with an English-language edition, *The Wisdom of the Sands,* in 1950.

Authorities never determined what happened to Saint-Exupéry's plane. Fellow pilots who saw him before he took off on his final mission said that he complained of a sleepless night and appeared restless and depressed, and, the evening before the flight he had prepared a letter to serve as a last will. It is not known whether his death was a suicide or an accident.

See LITTLE PRINCE, THE.

Salvation Army A religious organization that is part of the Christian church, following main-stream Christian beliefs and its articles of faith, emphasizing God's saving purposes. The Army's objects are the advancement of the Christian religion, education, and relieving poverty. The Army also is interested in preventing suicides, operating numerous suicide prevention centers in the United States and Canada. The Salvation Army's night patrols, rescue and anti-suicide missions helped more than 220,000 suicidal people in 2001.

The movement was founded in 1865 by William Booth, spreading from London to many parts of the world, including the United States and Canada. The rapid deployment of the first Salvationists was boosted by the adoption of a quasi-military command structure in 1878 with the title of "Salvation Army."

Adhering to the idea of spiritual warfare, the Army uses certain soldierly features such as uniforms, flags, and ranks to identify and inspire followers. Salvation Army officers have the status of ordained ministers and are employed by the Army in a professional capacity and on a full-time basis. They are members of the Salvation Army who have committed their lives to doing God's will and serving others.

Samaritans A nonreligious, nonprofit volunteer organization whose sole purpose is to provide support to individuals in crisis, who have lost someone to suicide, or who are feeling suicidal. The group was founded in London in 1953 by the Rev. CHAD VARAH who wanted to "befriend" suicidal people. Today the international humanitarian movement maintains more than 400 branches in 32 countries, including the United States.

All of the workers are volunteers, themselves former suicide attempters, who work with suicidal people in much the same way that recovering alcoholics in Alcoholics Anonymous work with new members. Samaritan volunteers are caring individuals of every age and walk of life who go through intensive training.

Typically, the Samaritans offer a hotline staffed by trained volunteers who are good listeners and are available 24 hours a day for anyone who is depressed, in crisis, or suicidal. The Samaritan's philosophy, known as "befriending," provides an empathetic response to every person who calls no matter what the problem. Samaritans volunteers do not express personal judgments or values and, instead, focus on the callers' emotions and state of mind.

The Samaritans gain their name from the parable of the Good Samaritan; their approach is always secular, practical, and non-sectarian.

See also BEFRIENDERS INTERNATIONAL.

"Samsonic" suicides Samson's destruction of the Philistines in the Temple of Dagon was an act of vengeance, but it was also suicidal. Samson prayed, "Let me die with the Philistines," and his wish was granted (Judges 16:23–31). This is probably the earliest historical description of a revenge type of suicide. Over the years, some have described revenge suicides as "Samsonic."

samurai Members of the military class in feudal Japan who performed a ritualized suicide in the form of HARA-KIRI. This was an elaborate ceremonial death for the samurai warrior who had in some way humiliated or disgraced himself, and thus his family. Often, after a chieftain had died, the warrior would kill himself as a show of allegiance. Sometimes an emperor would order a samurai warrior to commit *hara-kiri* to avoid the disgrace of a public execution.

Hara-kiri is an example of an ALTRUISTIC SUICIDE, in which self-inflicted death was considered honorable; to continue living would have been an act of ignominy.

See also SEPPUKU.

San Francisco Suicide Prevention (SFSP) One of the oldest volunteer crisis line in the United States, founded in 1963 as a way to provide telephone intervention to people experiencing suicidal crisis. Over the years, the focus of the agency has shifted from strictly suicide prevention to more general counseling services, which are provided 24 hours a day by more than 150 trained volunteers. Today SFSP is divided into four program areas that operate eight hotlines.

The suicidal crisis line was the first service offered by SFSP. Today, 100 trained volunteers answer more than 200 calls every day from people who need emotional support, with suicide prevention volunteers saving thousands of lives. Volunteers also provide emotional support on a daily basis to regular callers with chronic mental illness.

The newest program is the Survivors of Suicide group designed to help family or friends who lost someone to suicide.

For contact information, see Appendix I.

Savage God, The: A Study of Suicide Nonfiction book by ALFRED ALVAREZ, published in the United States by Random House in 1972. This book is an account of poet SYLVIA PLATH's suicide and an investigation into motives for suicide, with particular emphasis on people in the arts—writers and poets, as well as philosophers. Alvarez, born in London in 1929, returns in the last section of the book to a very personal view of suicide as he chronicles his own suicide attempt. The title comes from William Butler Yeats' "After Us the Savage God."

Scandinavia Among the three western Scandinavian countries (DENMARK, NORWAY, SWEDEN), Denmark has the highest suicide rate per 100,000 population, according to World Health

Organization (WHO) statistics, with a 1996 rate of 17 suicides per 100,000 (all ages, both sexes). Sweden is in the middle with a 1996 rate of 14.2 per 100,000; Norway is third with a 1995 rate per 100,000 population of 12.6. Denmark and Norway have both shown rate increases in the last decade, while Sweden's rate has shown a slight decline. Denmark's suicide rate in recent years has placed it in the top countries for highest rates per 100,000 population.

schizophrenia   General name for a group of psychotic reactions characterized by withdrawal, disturbances in emotional and affective life and, depending upon the type, the presence of hallucinations, delusions, negativistic behavior; and progressive deterioration. The search for underlying causes has centered on both functional and organic factors. Suicide has become the leading cause of death for people with schizophrenia. In fact, some experts believe the rate of suicide among these troubled patients ranges between 10 percent and 13 percent. Young white men who functioned well before becoming ill, and who have high expectations of themselves, are most at risk.

In chronic schizophrenia, suicide may result from the episodes of DEPRESSION to which these patients are prone. The suicide method is usually bizarre and often violent.

Attempted suicide is uncommon, although it may be the first gross sign of psychiatric disturbance, occurring early in schizophrenia, possibly when the patient becomes aware of the disorganization of thought and volitional processes.

However, the cause or causes of schizophrenia are still obscure and may well be the result of the interaction of two or more factors. A better understanding of the complex disorder depends, of course, on the results of ongoing research.

Schizophrenia often strikes patients during the early or mid-teen years and at first may be hardly noticeable. However, as the disorder progresses, schizophrenics may develop strong suicidal tendencies. The break with reality,

sometimes mixed with deep depression, occasionally leads to complex mixes of beliefs and fantasies that can bring about self-destruction. There have been cases, through relatively rare, where schizophrenics have attacked or killed others and then committed suicide.

school violence and suicide   While incidents of fatal multiple-victim violence in schools is rising, few teenage killers complete suicide at the site of their attacks. The most famous three incidents in recent history in which teens killed students and teachers before committing suicide occurred at a high school in Erfurt, Germany, on April 26, 2002; at Columbine High School in Littleton, Colorado, in April 1999; and at an elementary school in Dunblane, Scotland, in 1996.

The murder-suicides at Columbine High School were carried out by Eric Harris, 18, and Dylan Klebold, 17, two angry students who killed 12 other students, one teacher, and themselves. The young German student singled out teachers at his school, killing 14 adults and three students before turning the gun on himself. In Dunblane, Scotland, a man opened fire on a class of primary school students, killing 16 students, all but one of them younger than seven, a teacher, and himself.

There are far more incidents of school violence that do not involve suicide; for example, there were 220 violent incidents in American schools between July 1, 1994, and June 30, 1999. Most of these incidents were homicides and involved the use of firearms. Although the total number of events has decreased steadily since the 1992–93 school year, the total number of multiple-victim events appears to have increased. During the school years from August 1995 through June 1999, there were an average of four multiple-victim events a year, compared to an average of one multiple-victim event per year in the three years from August 1992 through July 1995. Thus, while the total number of events of school-associated violent deaths have decreased, the total number of multiple-victim events appears to have increased.

Nevertheless, according to the journal *Criminal Justice Ethics*, it is still true that more than 99.99 percent of U.S. public schools have never had a homicide or suicide on school grounds, let alone a mass killing.

Nevertheless, in the wake of the Columbine killings, the culture of high schools is changing as some teenagers identify with the killers and yearn for attention, making lists of their enemies and warning that they will "pull a Columbine." A much larger group of teens has become more watchful and ready to report any threat, no matter how unlikely.

Erfurt, Germany

In a rampage shooting eerily evoking the likes of Columbine but even more deadly, a recently expelled student in Erfurt, Germany, entered his former school, killing 17 people as he went room to room with a shotgun and a handgun before turning one on himself. It was one of the worst school killings of its type. It was even more disturbing that it took place in a country with gun-control laws so stringent that the number of shooting deaths each year in the entire country is barely half that of New York. In fact, in Germany—a country of nearly 80 million people—only 15,000 private citizens have the right to even own a gun for security reasons. To get permission, a person has to persuade the government that he or she faces a threat and can pass tests to properly handle a gun.

The massacre began as students were finishing their end-of-year exams at Gutenberg High School in Erfurt, a city of about 200,000 in eastern Germany. According to students, Robert Steinhaeuser, 19, who had been expelled several months before, entered a mathematics classroom about 11 A.M. wearing black clothes and a black mask. Pulling out a shotgun and handgun, he shot the teacher in front of other students and then went from room to room, shooting as many teachers as he could find. A janitor called the police, but the student shot and killed one

officer as he tried to enter the building. When police were finally able to enter, they found 17 dead victims and Steinhaeuser, who had committed suicide.

Columbine

Angry, disenfranchised students Eric Harris, 18, and Dylan Klebold, 17, went on a rampage at Columbine High School in April 1999, killing 12 classmates and a teacher. Although they used guns for the murders, more than 50 homemade explosive devices were also found in and around the school. Harris and Klebold shot themselves in the school library as police ringed the school.

Dunblane, Scotland

Thomas Hamilton, 43, was a gun collector and disgraced scoutmaster who was known as "Mr. Creepy" by local boys in Dunblane, a little Highlands village 40 miles from Edinburgh. Disliked by his neighbors, Hamilton reportedly had never gotten over his fury at being fired as a scoutmaster because of his fixation with young boys. Still seething with rage 20 years after being fired from the scouting position, a week before his rampage he wrote to Queen Elizabeth complaining about a campaign to ruin his reputation. On March 13, 1996, he walked to the Dunblane Primary School with four guns, burst into a gymnasium where 29 children were in class, and slaughtered 16 children, their teacher, and then himself. Another teacher and 12 other students were wounded. After the slayings and suicide, Great Britain banned private possession of handguns.

Schopenhauer, Arthur (1788–1860) German philosopher who formulated a philosophy of pessimism: Discord or strife is the central feature of all existence, both within the individual and in the universe at large, with frustration and pain as the inevitable products, and resignation, or negation of the will, as by the saint or ascetic, as the only solution. In his basic work, *The World as Will and Idea* (1818), Schopenhauer postulates that the world is the expression of the individual's idea, and especially his will, which is, basically, an expression of a universal, blind impulse to exist. Art, he says, is both a means of understanding existence and of escape from the senseless strife.

Schopenhauer wrote; "It will generally be found that as soon as the terrors of life reach the point where they outweigh the terrors of death, a man will put an end to his life." He also believed that suicide may be regarded as an experiment—but "a clumsy experiment to make, for it involves the destruction of the very consciousness which puts the question and awaits the answer."

Scotland   Northern country of Great Britain with a suicide rate of 11.9 per 100,000 (18.2 for men and 5.6 for women). Among Scots, the age group for both men and women at highest risk for suicide is not old age but young adulthood: Scottish men aged 25 to 34 have a suicide rate of 34.2 per 100,000; Scottish women of the same age group have a rate of 9.4.

second attempts (among suicidal persons)   Simply because a person shows improvement after a suicidal crisis doesn't mean that the suicidal risk is over. In fact, most suicides occur within about three months following the beginning of "improvement," when the individual has the energy to put morbid thoughts and feelings into effect. Many of the tens of thousands who attempt suicide will try again and four out of five people who commit suicide have attempted to kill themselves at least once previously.

Seduced by Death: Doctors, Patients and Assisted Suicide   Investigation into how the Netherlands is coping with the legalization of EUTHANASIA, by HERBERT HENDIN, M.D., medical director of the AMERICAN SUICIDE FOUNDATION, and professor of psychiatry at New York Medical College in Valhalla.

In this book, published in 1998 by W. W. Norton & Co., Hendin investigates how euthanasia is working in the Netherlands, looking at the issue from ethical, political, and practical viewpoints. He also explores why the United States could possibly be the next country to legalize euthanasia.

See also SUICIDE IN AMERICA.

self-destructive behavior   Behavior aimed at harming the self. Self-destructive behavior may be direct, which usually includes suicidal thoughts, attempted suicides, and completed suicides. Or this behavior may be indirect, characterized by taking a life-threatening risk without intending to die, generally repeatedly and often unconsciously, with consequences that are ultimately self-destructive. Examples of indirect self-destructive behavior are excessive drinking and drug use, heavy smoking, overeating, neglect of one's health, self-mutilation, hunger strikes, criminal behavior, and reckless driving.

self-immolation   Suicide by setting oneself on fire. Self-inflicted burn injuries make up only a small percentage of the patients seen in burn centers, and self-immolation is only a fraction of that population.

Persons who commit self-immolation have many motives, including suicide, impulsive behavior, various psychological illnesses, sacrificial religious rituals, and political protest. The incidence of self-inflicted burns ranges from less than 1 to 9 percent of patients admitted to burn care facilities. More than half of these patients have had previous psychiatric hospitalizations.

People who burn themselves are among the most difficult patients to treat because of the combination of major medical trauma and psychiatric problems. These patients have a higher-than-average incidence of MENTAL ILLNESS, substance abuse, family problems, poor judgment, and poor coping skills. Preexisting psychiatric diagnoses typically include major

DEPRESSION, SCHIZOPHRENIA, PSYCHOSIS, schizoaffective disorder, and BIPOLAR DISORDER (manic depression).

Self-immolation has been recorded throughout history. In A.D. 165, the Cynic philosopher Peregrinus Proteus cremated himself on a pyre. SUTTEE, a form of self-immolation popular in India until outlawed in 1829, is reportedly still practiced in remote parts of the country. The practice of suttee requires a widow of an Indian husband to throw herself on her husband's burning funeral pyre as his body is cremated.

Self-immolation as a political act has also practiced through the centuries, including protest of the Nazi concentration camps, the conditions of terror in Russian gulags, and the Chinese political system. This type of self-immolation could be considered ALTRUISTIC SUICIDE, in which the group's authority over the individual is so pronounced that the individual loses his or her own personal identity, and wishes to die for the community.

See ABUSE, SUBSTANCE.

Seneca, Lucius Annaeus (ca. 3 B.C.–A.D. 65)

Son of the rhetorician of the same name, Seneca became entrusted with the education of NERO, later became consul, was charged with plotting against Nero, and ultimately was forced to commit suicide to avoid the emperor's vengeance. After he stabbed himself, Seneca's wife, Paulina, not wishing to be left behind, also killed herself in the same way.

Seneca was a major representative of Roman Stoicism; his philosophy is contained in his *Moral Essays* and other works.

seppuku

In JAPAN, when suicide was still an integral part of the samurai warrior's moral code, the only honorable means for a disgraced warrior to redeem himself was to commit *seppuku,* or ritual suicide, in which he disemboweled himself with his own sword. The elaborate procedure often took hours to complete; a sec-

ond person ended the ceremonial death by cutting off the warrior's head.

Although Japan outlawed *seppuku* in 1868, the tradition of honorable suicide continues to influence Japanese practice. During World War II, for instance, more than 1,000 young Japanese soldiers served as KAMIKAZE PILOTS who flew their planes at enemy warships and certain death. Near the end of the war and shortly before Japan's defeat, a number of military officers committed ritual seppuku rather than accept the humiliation of surrender. As recently as 1970, the internationally famous author YUKIO MISHIMA committed *seppuku* as a plea to the people of his country for the return of old values and old traditions in Japan—one of which was the concept of dying with honor.

The word *seppuku* comes from the Japanese rendering of two Chinese characters meaning "cutting of the stomach." The same two characters in reverse order can also be pronounced *hara-kiri,* which became much more common, though considered vulgar, in spoken Japanese.

sex differences, suicide rates

Traditionally, women and young girls are the major suicide attempters in modern society; an estimated three to four times as many women as men attempt suicide every year, but roughly three times as many men as women complete suicide. Some experts estimate that, among young people, as many as nine times more girls than boys attempt suicide unsuccessfully.

Suicide is still more prevalent among eld-erly men than among elderly women (65 and over). In the United States, in 1997, for instance, the suicide rate per 100,000 population for men 75 and over was 44.7; for their female counterparts—same age group—the rate was 5.1.

Suicide involves so many variables that it is impossible to arrive at simple or definitive answers as to how patterns change or why they differ among the sexes.

Sexton, Anne Harvey (1928–1974)   American poet and good friend of SYLVIA PLATH, both of whom killed themselves.

Anne Gray Harvey was born in Newton, Massachusetts, in 1928. After attending Garland Junior College for one year, she married Alfred Muller Sexton II at age 19, and six years later she gave birth to a daughter. Shortly thereafter, she was diagnosed with postpartum DEPRESSION, suffered her first mental breakdown, and was admitted to Westwood Lodge, a neuropsychiatric hospital to which she would repeatedly return for help. Following the birth of her second daughter in 1955, Sexton suffered another breakdown and was rehospitalized. Her children were sent to live with her husband's parents, and that same year she attempted suicide on her birthday. It was her doctor who first encouraged her to pursue an interest in writing poetry.

Like other confessional poets, Sexton offered her readers an insider's view of her emotional anguish, making the experience of being a woman a central issue in her poetry. Sexton wrote a poem titled "Wanting to Die" (1966), in which she describes her desire as "the almost unnameable lust." She wrote in a memoir of her poet friend Plath, "We talked of death, and this was life to us." It is said that the two brilliant young poets spent many hours together going over details of their suicide attempts. In the end, both finally succeeded.

Sexton is the author of *Live or Die,* which includes the poem "Wanting to Die." The collection won the 1967 Pulitzer Prize for poetry.

Shneidman, Edwin S.   One of the foremost authorities in the field of suicidology and professor emeritus of THANATOLOGY and suicidology at the UCLA School of Medicine. Shneidman, author and editor of numerous books on suicide (including *Definition of Suicide*), was cofounder and codirector—with Dr. Norman L. Farberow—of the LOS ANGELES SUICIDE PREVENTION CENTER. He was charter director of the Center for the Study of Suicide Prevention at the National Institute of Mental Health, Bethesda, Maryland. He has been a Public Health Service special research fellow and visiting professor at Harvard, visiting professor at the Ben Gurion University of the Negev, clinical associate at the Massachusetts General Hospital and the Karlinska (Stockholm) Hospital, and a fellow at the Center for Advanced Study in the Behavioral Sciences (at Stanford).

Dr. Shneidman has been president of the Clinical and Public Service Divisions of the AMERICAN PSYCHOLOGICAL ASSOCIATION and founder-president of the AMERICAN ASSOCIATION OF SUICIDOLOGY (Denver). His book, *Death of Man,* was nominated for a National Book Award. Dr. Shneidman has contributed chapters on suicide to a number of anthologies and other publications, including the *Encyclopaedia Britannica* (1973), *Comprehensive Textbook of Psychiatry* (1975) and *Encyclopaedia of Psychology* (1984).

Dr. Edwin S. Shneidman has devoted a lifetime of work to the field of suicidology and has made a major contribution to the thinking of members in all disciplines who are still trying to prevent suicides and help suicidal persons discover less drastic alternatives to life's problems.

siblings, grief after suicide   The suicide of a brother or sister, whether older or younger, often produces not only grief but also fear, confusion, and often guilt in surviving siblings. Although almost every youngster has wished during a time of anger, envy, or jealousy for the death of a brother or sister, if death actually occurs, the youngster is stricken with complex feelings of anguish and guilt.

When the death is caused by suicide, the fear, confusion, and guilt feelings sometimes become unbearable. Parents will often try to hide the facts of a suicide from surviving children in a family, which can only add to the child's fears and confused grief. Sibling guilt and desolation are only made worse by half-truths, conspiracies of silence, and implications of stigma. Survivor brothers and sisters then suffer feelings of blame, wondering how they might have prevented the suicide, or in what ways they might unwittingly have contributed to their siblings' self-destructive decision.

silent suicide The hidden intention to complete suicide by nonviolent means through self-starvation or not complying with essential medical treatment. Silent suicide often is missed, especially in the face of an undiagnosed DEPRESSION.

Family members often think that elderly people who commit silent suicide are making rational end-of-life decisions. However, the elderly committing silent suicide is different from terminally ill patients who refuse further treatment in order not to prolong the act of dying.

sin, concept of While a few societies and religions have tolerated or even looked with favor on suicide, it has usually been regarded with repulsion. ST. AUGUSTINE regarded suicide as a sin, and a number of church councils denied religious rites to anyone who committed suicide.

Jewish law and the QUR'AN, the sacred text of Islam, denounced it, and medieval law decreed that a suicide victim's property be confiscated and the body desecrated by being dragged by the heels through the streets, face downward, or buried at a crossroads with a stake through the heart.

It was St. Augustine's denouncement of suicide as a sin that created an official church position against an act, which, he asserted, "precluded the possibility of repentance." He called it a form of homicide and thus a violation of the Decalogue Article, "Thou shalt not kill."

sleeplessness Often one of the several symptoms of clinical DEPRESSION. Severely depressed people may have trouble sleeping, and wake up in the middle of the night or the early morning hours. The opposite may be the case, as well; they often sleep all the time, dozing off in midday or early evening. Both types, the sleepless

person and the constant dozer, will usually begin to lose their appetites, eat little or nothing, and become lifeless and gaunt.

People who cannot sleep are not all victims of clinical depression. But if this is a reaction noticeable with a cluster of other symptoms, such as loss of appetite, loneliness, unusual silence and withdrawal from family and friends, then the individual may need help in the form of professional treatment. If such symptoms go unnoticed or unattended, the depressed person sometimes retreats further into himself, and suicide may begin to seem a real alternative to a life of despair and misery.

See also INSOMNIA.

Socrates (ca. 470–399 B.C.) Greek philosopher who broke with earlier philosophical traditions and laid the foundations for the development of both ethics and logic. Although he wrote nothing himself, his ideas survive in the writings of PLATO and XENOPHON. Refusing to bow to tyranny, whether imposed by the mob or by oligarchs, Socrates was tried on the charge of corrupting the young people of Athens and sentenced to death by drinking HEMLOCK.

Solar Temple, Order of the An international sect that believes ritualized suicide leads to rebirth on a planet called Sirius. On March 23, 1997, the charred bodies of three women and two men were found inside a house in Saint Casimir, Quebec. All were members of the Solar Temple. Two years earlier, 16 Solar Temple members were found dead in a burned house outside Grenoble, in the French Alps. In 1994, the burned bodies of 48 Solar Temple members were discovered in a farmhouse and three chalets in Switzerland. At the same time, five bodies, including that of an infant, were found half a world away in a chalet north of Montreal.

The Temple was founded by Luc Jouret and Joseph Di Mambro in 1984. At its height of popularity in January 1989, there were 442 members, 90 in Switzerland, 187 in France, 86 in

Canada, 53 in Martinique, 16 in the United States, and 10 in Spain. However, membership had been declining around the time of the mass suicide in 1994.

See also CULT SUICIDE.

SOLES (Survivors of Law Enforcement Suicide)   A nonprofit group focusing on support and outreach to anyone who is grieving the loss of a loved one's suicide. The group sponsors a website with numerous online mail lists, chats, and links, together with a photo memorial page.

For contact information, see Appendix 1.

Sorrows of Young Werther, The   Sensational novel by JOHANN WOLFGANG VON GOETHE, German poet, dramatist, and novelist. This romantic narrative (German title: *Die Leiden des jungen Werthers,* published in 1774) describes a young man who kills himself. It had a startlingly strong influence on young people of the time. Men began to dress like Werther, speak like Goethe's protagonist, and dream of killing themselves like Werther. The whole Werther phenomenon touched off a wave of romantic notions about suffering for one's genius, struggling for art, and dying young while the world mourned its idealistic heroes.

South Carolina   The state's rate per 100,000 population of suicide has remained fairly stable since 1970, when it was 10.9, and in 1999 stood at 10.8. The state's rate per 100,000 population ranks it 24th in the nation.

South Dakota   South Dakota in 1999 had a suicide rate of 14 per 100,000 population. South Dakota is tied with Maine for the 10th highest suicide rate in the country.

South Pacific Islands and suicide   The South Pacific might look like a paradise, but suicide is its dark secret, and anecdotal evidence suggests a resurgence after suicide rates dropped in the 1990s. PARAQUAT, a cause of painful, inevitable death, is the islanders' method of choice.

Samoans and Fiji Indians have the world's highest female suicide rates. Among the overall figures for the Federated States of Micronesia (FSM), the rate for the Marshall Islands, Samoa, and Fiji are among the highest anywhere. Even French Polynesia, among the most developed island countries, is experiencing high rates, while New Zealand, with a heavy Polynesian population, has some of the highest suicide levels among youths in the developed world. Also, indigenous Hawaiians have much higher suicide rates than others in the state.

In Fiji, experts speculate that the high youth suicide rate is a consequence of a school examination system that discriminates against Indians (44 percent of the population) in awarding of scholarships and school placements. Some residents claim that Fiji students are being terrorized by annual make-it-or-break-it exams between the ages of 11 and 18.

Paraquat was first produced in 1882, but recognized as a herbicide in 1955. Its extreme toxicity led to its popularity as a suicide method around the world (there were 700 cases in 10 years in Malaysia alone, for example), despite bans and strict controls.

One study found that the 2000 Fiji coup had driven suicide rates to their highest ever levels, with a 200 percent jump in the last two years. Suicides in FSM, Marshalls, and Palau have increased from about 10 a year during the 1960s to about 40 a year in 2001.

Clinical DEPRESSION associated with suicide in the Western world is not usually a factor in Pacific suicides, and few of the victims are mentally unbalanced. Instead, experts believe that a major cause for the rise in the suicide rate has been the erosion of social structures and values, leaving many young people vulnerable to suicide. This is exacerbated by the relatively sudden contact with and domination by the Western world to the detriment of their own culture.

In Samoa, where 70 percent of suicides are among men, experts also blame authoritarian child rearing and the traditional view that youths are expected to serve and obey. They are not consulted until they become *matai* (chiefs or family heads), a status most Samoan men achieve in their 30s, but most women never achieve. Studies in Micronesia show most suicides are among boys and men between 15 and 24 who hang themselves after fights with their parents.

Soylent Green A 1973 movie starring Charlton Heston and Edward G. Robinson that featured an overpopulated world in which people were encouraged to go to special suicide centers to be assisted in dying. The film was similar to Kurt Vonnegut's short story, "Welcome to the Monkey House."

state-by-state suicide rates Western states have the highest rate of suicide per 100,000 than any other area in the country, according to the latest statistics available (1999). The state with the highest suicide rate is Nevada, at 22.3 per 100,000, more than double the country-wide average of 10.7. This is followed by Wyoming (20.4), Montana (18.4), New Mexico (18.3), and Arizona (16).

The states with five lowest suicide rates per 100,000 are all in the Northeast, headed by Washington, D.C. (5.8 per 100,000). These are followed by New York (6.6), New Jersey (6.9), Massachusetts (7), and Connecticut (8.3).

The breakdown, which changes each year, is as follows:

Alabama: 12.7
Arizona: 16
Arkansas: 13.2
California: 9.3
Colorado: 14.2
Connecticut: 8.3
Delaware: 11.4
District of Columbia: 5.8
Florida: 13.4

Georgia: 11.2
Hawaii: 11.5
Idaho: 14.5
Illinois: 8.4
Indiana: 10.6
Iowa: 10.6
Kansas: 11.3
Kentucky: 11.9
Louisiana: 11.8
Maine: 14
Maryland: 8.4
Massachusetts: 7
Michigan: 9.9
Minnesota: 9.2
Mississippi: 11
Missouri: 12.8
Montana: 18.4
Nebraska: 10.6
Nevada: 22.3
New Hampshire: 11.4
New Jersey: 6.9
New Mexico: 18.3
New York: 6.6
North Carolina: 11.6
North Dakota: 11.5
Ohio: 9.8
Oklahoma: 14.7
Oregon: 14.4
Pennsylvania: 10.7
Rhode Island: 9.7
South Carolina: 10.8
South Dakota: 14
Tennessee: 13.2
Texas: 10
Utah: 13.2
Vermont: 10.6
Virginia: 11.5
Washington: 14.2
West Virginia: 12.7
Wisconsin: 11.3
Wyoming: 20.4

status loss and suicide When image is so important, loss of status or identity can prove devastating. This is especially true for young people.

If youngsters do find an identity and that identity is suddenly stripped from them for some reason before they feel secure and worthwhile, suicide may be the means they choose for coping with the loss.

In certain cases, loss of status or identity may be the crucial indicator of imminent suicide.

stock market crash, 1929, and suicides   On October 29, 1929, post–World War I prosperity came to a startling end as stock prices plummeted. Stock losses for the period from 1929 to 1931 were estimated at $50 billion, and the result was the worst depression in U.S. history. A number of businessmen lost everything in the precipitous crash and killed themselves, some by jumping from tall office buildings in Manhattan. No accurate data exist as to how many suicides were completed as a direct result of the crash.

Stoics   Disciples of a Greek philosopher named ZENO. Stoic philosophy was similar to the Taoist philosophy of China, both of which teach followers to attune with their inner nature—what the Romans called "reason," the Chinese the *Tao*, and the Greeks the *Logos*. Stoics encourage simple living and contentment with one's present state of being.

The Roman Stoic who determined that he had enough of life had his veins severed by trained technicians of the day. SENECA, one of the leaders of the Roman Stoics, wrote that, "If life please you, live. If not, you have a right to return whence you came." He and his fellow Stoics did not, however, advocate suicide merely to escape from everyday life. They were concerned with people living good and rational lives, free of serious sickness, debilitating disease, or political oppression. They urged people to think very carefully before completing suicide, and to allow themselves to suffer before impulsively destroying themselves.

The Stoic philosophy started in Greece, where advocates adopted a lenient view of suicide as a result of their opinion that death is a release from the sufferings of life. Suicide to them was not so much a matter of right and wrong as it was determining the most logical way to act in a given situation. Legend says that Zeno, founder of the Stoic philosophy, killed himself after breaking his toe. He decided that God had sent his broken toe as a sign that he had lived long enough—he was 98 years old at the time.

Zeno's successor, CLEANTHES, is thought to have completed suicide, too. He had developed a boil on his gum and was advised by a doctor to abstain from eating for a couple of days, thus allowing time for the boil to heal. Instead, Cleanthes continued to starve himself after the sore had healed. He argued that having gone so far on the path to death, he might as well complete the act.

"Stoicism" gets its name from the Stoa (porch) in Athens where Zeno taught.

"Stormy Monday"   According to questionable suicide statistics, "Stormy Monday" is the favored day for self-destruction. For example, in 1979 (an "average" year), about 82 suicides occurred nationwide every Monday. By contrast, Saturday statistics showed an average of 71 suicides, the lowest rate among days of the week. Interestingly, Saturday saw the most deaths by auto accident and homicide that particular year.

stress as suicide clue   Stressful behavior— where a person acts nervously, irrationally, peculiarly, "differently"—is one crucial indicator of possible suicidal thoughts and/or intentions. Coupled or clustered with other verbal or behavioral clues, this often signals imminent suicide.

The unbelievable stress placed on Japanese teenagers during examinations is one of the factors that contributes to the high teen suicide rate in Japan—one of the highest in the world. The examination system is referred to as "Examination Hell."

See also CLUES OF SUICIDE.

suicidal crisis, acute   See ACUTE SUICIDES.

suicidal crisis, how to help   Suicidal crises usually concern two people: the suicidal person and the "significant other." The latter may be a parent, lover, associate, or friend. This "significant other" must be advised immediately of the situation, and, where possible, become involved in life-saving efforts.

How quickly others intervene in a suicidal crisis is crucial. If someone suspects suicidal behavior, quick action is vital. Parents, friends, doctors, teachers, ministers, or any key people in the person's life should be told immediately. The worst that will happen is that the person might feel foolish for stirring up a suicide scare where none exists. But experts say it is far better to err in the direction of overcaution than to ignore the signals and take a chance on losing a life.

Trained professional or volunteer staff members of any accredited suicide prevention and crisis center can predict a suicide with a fair degree of accuracy. Active, increasingly effective suicide prevention services can offer a suicidal person a fresh outlook on life.

suicidal ideation   Having thoughts about completing suicide. Authorities say it is not abnormal to have such thoughts at one time or another during the course of a lifetime. A healthy, well-integrated personality, however, quickly dismisses such destructive thoughts as an unacceptable alternative to life.

Suicidal Ideation Questionnaire (SIQ)   Psychological test that measures suicidal thoughts in adolescents. The SIQ is a supplement to the Reynolds Adolescent Depression Scale. The SIQ–JR is a specialized version of the SIQ that was developed for use with adolescents in junior high school. Both versions may be administered in individual or small group settings.

Suicide, Le   First scientific study of suicide, by noted French sociologist ÉMILE DURKHEIM. Originally published in 1897 and published in this country in 1951 as *Suicide,* the historical, groundbreaking work has had a continuing and pervasive impact on subsequent work in the field of suicidology.

suicide, preteen   The very young—children as young as two—are also trying to commit suicide in increasing numbers.

Yet the National Center for Health Statistics still does not compute suicide data for children under age 10. There is a belief that experts now know is false—that suicide in children under 10 is so rare as to be unmeasurable. Thus, no reliable data exist for suicides of youngsters under 10. In one study of 127 Pittsburgh elementary school children, 41 percent admitted to having suicidal thoughts.

Suicide and Life Threatening Behavior
Quarterly journal of the AMERICAN ASSOCIATION OF SUICIDOLOGY.

suicide attempts   There may be as many as 20 to 25 attempted suicides for every one completed suicide; the ratio is higher for women and youth, and lower for men and the elderly.

Risk factors for attempted suicide in adults include DEPRESSION, alcohol abuse, cocaine use, and separation or divorce. Risk factors for attempted suicide in youth include depression, alcohol or other drug use disorder, physical or sexual abuse, and aggressive or disruptive behaviors.

Most suicide attempts are expressions of extreme distress, and are not just harmless bids for attention. A suicidal person should not be left alone and needs immediate mental health treatment.

Suicide Awareness/Voices of Education (SAVE)   A nonprofit support group composed mostly of suicide survivors. SAVE was started in 1989 by six suicide survivors; until early 1998, the organization operated solely on the efforts of volunteers.

SAVE is committed to the education of the general public about the depressive brain diseases such as clinical DEPRESSION and BIPOLAR DISORDER that can result in suicide if left untreated.

The organization offers information, a speaker's bureau, and school-based suicide prevention programs. Each spring, preceding National Mental Health Month, SAVE sponsors a Suicide Awareness and Memorial Day (SAMD).

suicide bombers   See TERRORISM AND SUICIDE.

suicide by cop   A situation in which an individual who wishes to die uses the police to complete suicide. Typically, the person acts in such a way as to force the police to use their weapons. By initiating an assault or otherwise provoking a police officer, suicide-prone individuals achieve their goals without losing self-esteem. Suicide by cop is a relatively new term to describe "victim-precipitated homicide."

Studies suggest that police may confront shootings motivated by suicidal subjects more often than reports indicate. In one case, an adult male drove his car onto the front lawn of police headquarters in downtown Detroit. He got out of his car, took out a handgun, and began shooting at the building. Several police officers returned fire until they killed the subject. In another case, Philadelphia police responded to a burglary-in-progress call at a local school. Upon arrival, the suspect fired twice at the police. A subsequent chase through the school corridors followed. A police dog eventually cornered the subject, and as the officers approached, they found the subject crouched and pointing a gun at them. Police fired, killing the subject. Police later found that the subject's gun was a starter pistol, incapable of firing live rounds. Furthermore, family members later identified the subject's voice on police

tapes as the person who placed the initial burglary call to police. Police later learned that the subject had been hospitalized as the result of a suicide attempt.

suicide career   An individual pattern of multiple suicide attempts.

suicide contagion   The exposure to suicide or suicidal behaviors within the family, peer group, or through media reports of suicide that triggers an increase in other suicides or suicidal behavior. Direct and indirect exposure to suicidal behavior has been shown to trigger an increase in suicidal behavior in those at risk for suicide, especially in adolescents and young adults.

The risk of suicide contagion as a result of media reporting can be minimized by factual and concise media reports of suicide. Prolonged exposure to reports of suicide also can increase the likelihood of suicide contagion.

Because suicide is caused by many complex factors, experts stress that media coverage should not:

- report oversimplified explanations such as recent negative life events or acute stressors
- divulge detailed descriptions of the method used to avoid possible duplication or to glorify the victim
- imply that suicide was effective in achieving a personal goal such as gaining media attention.

Anyone who has been exposed to suicide or suicidal behaviors within the family or among the peer group should be evaluated by a mental health professional in order to minimize the risk of suicide. Those deemed at risk for suicide should then be referred for additional mental health services.

suicide gestures   Initiating suicidal acts at a low level of lethality, such as ingesting just a few over-the-counter medications. No matter how unlikely they are to result in death, suicide gestures should not be dismissed lightly, since they are pleas for help that require thorough evaluation and treatment to prevent repeated attempts. This is especially true given that 20 percent of people who attempt suicide try again within one year; 10 percent finally succeed.

suicide "how to" manuals   Books and articles that give explicit instructions on how to complete suicide. Several controversial types of these manuals have been published over the years. LET ME DIE BEFORE I WAKE: Hemlock's Book of Self-Deliverance for the Dying was written by DEREK HUMPHRY in 1981. First editions were sold only to HEMLOCK SOCIETY members; a third edition was published in 1984 by the society and distributed by the Grove Press in New York. The book addresses the option of "rational suicide" only for a person in advanced terminal illness or serious incurable physical illness.

Jean's Way was written by Humphry and his second wife, Ann Wickett, published in 1978 and again in 1981. This book described the suicide of Humphry's first wife, Jean, who was suffering with cancer. It is considered a classic account of what the authors call rational voluntary EUTHANASIA.

FINAL EXIT: THE PRACTICALITIES OF SELF-DELIVERANCE AND ASSISTED SUICIDE FOR THE DYING was written by Humphry and translated into 12 major languages. The book was a New York Times best-seller in 1991, and in the updated 1997 edition (Dell paperback) sells consistently every year.

Humphry's Supplement to Final Exit published in 2000, provides new information to bring Final Exit up to date politically, legally, and ethically. The book includes an explicit chapter on how to take one's life with helium gas.

Exit: A Guide to Self Deliverance was published by Arthur Koestler in London in 1981 and sold only to members of the British Voluntary Euthanasia Society who were over age 25.

Suicide in America   Book by psychiatrist-author Herbert Hendin, M.D., internationally known authority on the subject of suicide. The book examines the personal and social factors contributing to suicide among different groups of people, including the young, in America; published in 1982 by W. W. Norton. In 1982, Dr. Hendin received the Louis I. Dublin award of the AMERICAN ASSOCIATION OF SUICIDOLOGY. His other books include: The Age of Sensation; Black Suicide; Suicide and Scandinavia; Seduced by Death: Doctors, Patients and Assisted Suicide.

Suicide Information and Education Centre (SIEC)   Established in 1982, SIEC is a special library and resource center providing information on suicide and suicidal behavior. The Suicide Prevention Training Programs (SPTP) provide caregiver training in suicide INTERVENTION, awareness, bereavement, crisis management, and related topics.

For contact information, see Appendix I.

"Suicide Is Painless"   Song also known as the theme song for "M*A*S*H," long-running television series starring Alan Alda taken from the 1970 motion picture of the same name.

The words are by Mike Altman, music is by Johnny Mandell.

suicide notes   Between 10 percent and 35 percent of people who complete suicide leave a note behind, often including concrete instructions to survivors and using specific names of people, places, and things. The notes appear to serve as a way of reaching out to specific individuals, trying to influence and even control them after the writer's death.

Notes left by elderly people often express concern for those left behind, whereas those of younger people may express anger or vindictiveness. The content may indicate the mental disorder that led to the suicidal act. Often, suicide notes are mundane lists of instructions, final wishes, and so on.

In attempted suicides, a note is less common; it indicates premeditation and a high risk of repeated attempts and completed suicide.

Many notes are destroyed by families who fear stigmatization. One study by psychologists Edwin Shneidman and Norman L. Farberow found that it is possible to distinguish between genuine and simulated (fake) notes—and that the genuine notes included more angry feelings and more expressions of revenge than the simulated notes (which were composed by carefully selected people asked to think as if they were about to kill themselves). Most genuine suicide notes are specific as to instructions to survivors, very decisive; they give little evidence of thinking about suicide *per se,* and more evidence of self-blame and hostility.

suicide pacts   Part of a larger phenomenon known as DUAL SUICIDE, this involves the death of two or more people who intentionally complete suicide at the same time and place. Suicide pacts (also called "love-pact suicide") also include MURDER-SUICIDE between lovers in which both people agree to die at the same time and place, but instead of a double suicide, one kills the other and then completes suicide.

One highly publicized suicide pact between two teenagers resulted in the book *CRAIG AND JOAN.* In 1969, Joan Fox and Craig Badiali, both 17, killed themselves by asphyxiation. The two New Jersey teens left 24 suicide notes between them protesting the Vietnam War.

On March 10, 1987, four Bergenfield, New Jersey, teenagers—two boys and two girls—decided to complete suicide together by sitting in a car with the motor running inside a locked garage. Thomas Rizzo, 19; Thomas Olton, 18; and sisters Lisa and Cheryl Burress, 16 and 17, were discovered dead in the locked car on the morning of March 11, victims of carbon monoxide poisoning; estimated time of death was between 3:30 and 4:00 A.M. The four young people were reportedly distraught over the death of a friend, Joe Major, who had lost his life

in a fall from the Palisades in Fort Lee, New Jersey, in September 1986.

Two days after the Bergenfield tragedy, another suicide pact cost the lives of teenagers Karen Logan, 17, and Nancy Grannan, in Alsip, Illinois. They had apparently killed themselves in a garage full of auto exhaust, and police said they had probably been influenced by the news of the joint suicides of the four New Jersey young people.

While suicide pacts do occur among older couples, they are very rare, and make up less than one-tenth of one percent of all suicides in the older population.

Suicide Prevention Advocacy Network   A nonprofit organization that links the energy of those bereaved by suicide with the expertise of leaders in science, business, government, and public service to achieve the goal of significantly reducing the national rate of suicide by the year 2010.

SPAN was founded by the parents of Teri Ann Weyrauch, M.D., who committed suicide on June 17, 1987, at age 34. Filled with grief, the Weyrauchs volunteered with many local and national suicide prevention efforts until they decided to launch an organization to give suicide survivors and their supporters the chance to help create political will and bring suicide prevention to its rightful place in the forefront of the American consciousness.

For contact information, see Appendix I.

suicide threats   Any and all suicide threats, whether said seriously or jokingly, should be taken seriously.

It is a myth and misconception that people who talk about suicide don't follow through with their threat. All threats must be taken as a serious warning.

The slightest thing can sometimes turn the thought into reality. For instance, refusing to take a suicide threat seriously can be the triggering factor. To the suicidal person, it confirms that nobody cares or understands, and may serve as the catalyst to attempt suicide.

A suicide or suicide attempt has often been recognized by experts as a "cry for help." Most suicides are ambivalent; there's an urge to die as expressed in the threat, but there's also an urge to live.

superstition Superstition concerning the act of suicide was common during the Middle Ages, when suicides were relatively rare (as a result of strict church rules). Because of superstitious fears, the victim's body was degraded and often was dragged through the streets and spat on or hung on public gallows. Victims were sometimes buried on the spot where the act took place; at other times, the body was left unburied in an area set aside for public executions. Often a suicide's corpse was superstitiously buried at a crossroads with a stake driven through its heart and a heavy stone placed on its face to prevent the dead person's spirit from rising.

In England as late as 1823, the body of a man known as Mr. ABEL GRIFFITHS was dragged through London's streets and buried at a crossroads. His was the last such suicide to be treated in that manner.

survivor guilt After a suicide, the emotions of the survivors are often as intense and unbearable as were those of the person who completed the act. Those left behind experience the pain of sudden loss, but they also have exaggerated feelings of shame, guilt, and self-blame. The suicide itself immediately raises obvious questions, such as "Why?" and "What could I have done to prevent it?" As Rabbi Earl A. Grollman writes in *Suicide: Prevention, Intervention, Postvention*: "Death is a robber. Death by suicide brings the greatest of all affronts to those who remain."

Survivors who have experienced the loss of a loved one through suicide need meaningful support in what experts call "postvention"—self-help groups and neighborhood support.

The survivor family is at high risk until proven otherwise. Most communities today have mental health centers where active, effective survivor assistance services offer the victims of a loved one's self-destruction a fresh grasp on life.

Survivors of Loved Ones Suicide (SOLOS)
Nonprofit self-help organization for relatives and friends of those who have completed suicide. The group provides support to survivors through outreach and education to help people deal effectively with their loss. The group tries to ensure better access to existing resources, provide forums for mutual support and information, promote research, and help educate the public.

For contact information, see Appendix I.

suttee A practice in ancient India in which widows, motivated by the pressure from society, threw themselves on their dead husband's funeral pyre or drowned themselves in the holy Ganges River.

They were encouraged to do this by Hindu priests and their own relatives. The widows were taught that a faithful wife could atone for her husband's sins on earth and open to him the gates of paradise.

Women who practiced suttee were venerated by the populace. Those who refused were not only condemned but also often threatened with harsh physical punishment.

The Mahasati (the great suttee) or the Sahagamana (joint departure) system of a cremating the woman alive on the death of her husband is an ancient custom in India. Scholars of the Puranas trace the origins to the suicide of Satidevi in the sacrificial fireplace of Lord Brahma, while a few attribute it to the pre-caste Vedic system of Indian society. In the Indian mythology of the Mahabharat, there is the instance of Madri dying on the funeral pyre of husband Pandu, leaving the children to the care of the first wife, Kunti.

Feminists proclaim the suttee system as a cruel institution established by men against the women, while the lower caste in India have felt it as another means of torture placed on them by upper-caste Brahmins.

There is no simple answer as to how the suttee system originated. In a time when people believed that a woman's path to heaven is through her character and devotion to her husband, it was perhaps thought that a woman's life served no purpose after the death of her husband. The practice might have come into practice as a family conspiracy against the widow to benefit from her assets. Moreover, the life of a widow was so bad, the women perhaps favored death to humiliation. In addition, women who participated in suttee were glorified, and so the attraction of instant fame and immortality were also important.

Some women believed that if they died with their husband, they would be united with him in heaven in an eternal marriage.

The ancient practice continued in India for hundreds of years. Even after suttee was outlawed in 1829 by the British rulers of the country, slow-changing customs kept it going well into the 1900s.

Switzerland Tiny, peace-loving Switzerland has one of the highest suicide rates per 100,000 population in the world. In 1996, World Health Organization statistics revealed that the total suicide rate for all ages was 20.4; the male rate was 29.2; the female rate was 11.6.

The highest rate among men was from ages 75 and up, with a rate of 80.2. For women, those over 75 also had the highest rate per 100,000 population, with 23.5.

Synod of Nîmes Voluntary martyrdom among Christians was discouraged by church leaders as Christianity spread and became tolerated as a recognized state religion in the Roman Empire. However, it was not until the Council of Braga in A.D. 563 that voluntary martyrdom and suicide as an act were condemned by the church. This position was confirmed by the Councils of Auxerre (578) and Antisidor (590) and remained the canon law until 1284, when the Synod of Nîmes refused burial in consecrated ground to suicides.

Tabachnick, Norman Psychiatrist who, with colleagues at the LOS ANGELES SUICIDE PREVENTION CENTER, studied the psychology of fatal accidents. The researchers learned that roughly 25 percent of accident victims among those studied were depressed and had feelings of helplessness and a sense of loss similar to that in suicidal people. The subjects admitted to fantasies and dreams of death and self-destruction just prior to their accidents. Researchers concluded that the serious accidents may have resulted from unconscious desires to destroy themselves.

Opposite traits characterized the remaining 75 percent of accident cases studied. These people were self-reliant and thought of themselves as strong and forceful. Under pressure, they reacted to difficulty quickly and impulsively, and gave little or no thought to the consequences of their actions.

Other studies into teenagers' driving habits have confirmed the combined role of personality traits and emotions in influencing serious accidents.

taboos It is because suicide is still such a taboo topic—one that stigmatizes not only the suicidal victim but the survivors as well—that so many people have difficulty discussing it openly and honestly. Religions condemn it as a sin, and for years law books listed it as a crime. Long ago, courts actually punished the families of suicides, and rulers confiscated all the victim's property. Churches denied suicides burial in consecrated sites.

Today, for the most part, such arcane laws and church practices have disappeared.

Fortunately, there is evidence in recent years that ancient myths and misconceptions are slowly being removed as more people come to understand suicide.

Tacitus, Publius Cornelius (ca. A.D. 55– ca. 120) Roman historian and a distinguished lawyer. Best known for such historical works as the *Historiae*, in which he gives an account of Otho's death and how some soldiers killed themselves near his pyre, prompted by a desire to imitate his "glorious example and moved by affection for their emperor." Tacitus explains that after this many of every rank chose suicide at Bedriacum, Placentia, and other camps as well.

It was Tacitus who reported, also, the ancient practice of bog burials—of pinning down the body of suicides. The practice antedates Christianity among the Germanic peoples of Europe. This was done to prevent the spirits of the dead from returning to haunt or do harm to the living.

teachers, role in suicide prevention Because they usually spend more hours with the child than do most parents, teachers are in a position to observe and be aware of what the individual child's life is really like. They can spot drug users, loners, depressed students, mood swings, and those who cut classes or are disruptive. All these are possible red flags that should alert teachers that something could be wrong.

In some communities across the United States, teachers undergo training on how to recognize early warning signs, how to approach the suicidal child, and how to assess his/her potential to complete suicide. School counselors and nurses are usually included in the training courses. Teachers, properly trained to the clues of suicide, can be a valuable pipeline to students because young people reveal their despair and anguish in their school work.

Teasdale, Sara (1884–1933) American poet famous for works of delicate and personal lyrics, this extraordinarily sensitive, almost reclusive woman eventually became despondent and completed suicide at the age of 48.

Sara Trevor Teasdale was born in St. Louis, Missouri, into an old established devout family who taught her at home until she was nine. Upon graduation from high school, between 1904 and 1907 Teasdale and a group of friends published a monthly literary magazine called *The Potter's Wheel.* As she grew older, she traveled often to Chicago, where she joined the circle of writers surrounding *Poetry* magazine and wrote several well-received books, including *Helen of Troy and Other Poems* (1911) and *Rivers to the Sea* (1915).

After rejecting the poet Vachel Lindsay and several other men as suitors, she married St. Louis businessman Ernst Filsinger in 1914.

In 1918, she won the Columbia University Poetry Society Prize (which became the Pulitzer Prize for poetry) and the Poetry Society of America Prize for *Love Songs,* which had appeared in 1917. She published three more volumes of poetry during her lifetime: *Flame and Shadow* (1920), *Dark of the Moon* (1926), and *Stars Tonight* (1930).

Teasdale's work was praised for its classic simplicity and clarity, in addition to her passionate subject matter. These later books trace her growing finesse and poetic subtlety.

She divorced in 1929 (against her husband's will) and lived the rest of her life as a semi-invalid. Weakened after a difficult bout with pneumonia and increasingly depressed and reclusive, Teasdale completed suicide on January 29, 1933, with an overdose of sleeping pills. Her final collection, *Strange Victory,* appeared posthumously that same year.

She left a suicide note in the form of a poem to a lover who had left her:

> When I am dead, and over me bright April
> Shakes out her rain drenched hair,
> Tho you should lean above me broken hearted,
> I shall not care.
> For I shall have peace.
> As leafy trees are peaceful
> When rain bends down the bough.
> And I shall be more silent and cold hearted
> Than you are now.

teenage suicide Over the last several decades, the suicide rate in adolescents has increased dramatically, until by 1997 suicide was the third leading cause of death for 15- to 24-year-olds (11.4 of every 100,000 persons) following unintentional injuries and homicide. Suicide also was the third leading cause of death for 10- to 14-year-olds, with 303 deaths among 19,097,000 children in this age group. In 1998, among youth ages 10 to 19, there were 2,054 suicides. For those age 15 to 19, there were 1,802 suicide deaths among 19,146,000 teens.

Although the overall suicide rate has declined over the past 20 years, from 12.1 per 100,000 in 1979 to 11.3 per 100,000 in 1998, the suicide rate for teens 15 to 19 years old has increased by 6 percent. For adolescents 10 to 14 years old, the suicide rate increased by more than 100 percent over that time period. And while youth suicide rates did decrease significantly between 1993 and 1998, suicide was still the third leading cause of death for young people 10 to 19 years old in 1998. More teenagers died from suicide than from cancer, heart disease, AIDS, birth defects, stroke, pneumonia and influenza, and chronic lung disease combined.

Gender Issues

Teenage boys are about four times more likely to kill themselves than are teenage girls. Among young people 20 to 24 years of age, there were 2,384 suicide deaths among 17,488,000 people in this age group, and the gender ratio in this age range was about six boys to every one girl.

But while more boys die from suicide, more girls attempt suicide and report higher rates of DEPRESSION. Experts believe the gender difference in suicide completion is most likely due to the differences in suicide methods, since boys are more likely to use firearms, which are more likely to lead to a fatal outcome.

Culture Issues

In 1998, white boys accounted for 61 percent of all suicides among youth age 10 to 19, and white boys and girls together accounted for more than 84 percent of all youth suicides. However, the suicide rate among Native American teenage boys is exceedingly high in comparison with the overall rate for boys age 10 to 19 (19.3 per 100,000 vs. 8.5 per 100,000).

The suicide rate has been increasing most rapidly among African-American boys age 10 to 19—more than doubling from 2.9 per 100,000 to 6.1 per 100,000 from 1981 to 1998. On the other hand, a 1999 national survey of high school students found that Hispanic boys and girls were significantly more likely than white students to have reported a suicide attempt (12.8 percent vs. 6.7 percent). Among Hispanic students, girls (18.9 percent) were almost three times more likely than boys (6.6 percent) to have reported a suicide attempt. The most likely explanation for ethnic rate differences are variations in cultural factors that promote or inhibit suicide.

Homosexuality

It has been widely reported in the media that gay and lesbian youth are at higher risk to complete suicide than other youth and that a significant percent of all attempted or completed youth suicides are related to issues of sexual identity. However, there are no national statistics for suicide completion rates among gay, lesbian, or bisexual persons, and in the few studies examin-

ing risk factors for suicide completion where an attempt was made to assess sexual orientation, the risk for gay or lesbian persons did not appear any greater than among heterosexuals, once mental and substance abuse disorders were taken into account.

Several state and national studies have reported that high school students who report homosexual or bisexual activity have higher rates of suicide thoughts and attempts compared to youth with heterosexual experience. Experts do not agree about the best way to measure reports of adolescent suicide attempts on sexual orientation, however, so the data are subject to question.

See ABUSE, SUBSTANCE.

Suicide Attempts

A far greater number of youths attempt suicide each year. Suicide attempts are difficult to count because many may not be treated in a hospital or may not be recorded as self-inflicted injury. Survey data from 1999 indicate that 19.3 percent of high school students had seriously considered attempting suicide, 14.5 percent had made plans to attempt suicide, and 8.3 percent had made a suicide attempt during the year preceding the survey. All suicide attempts should be taken seriously.

Warning Signs

The challenge for family and friends of teens is to be able to tell the difference between normal teen angst and actual despair. Luckily, many experts agree that there are recognizable warning signs. Sixty percent of suicidal teens are depressed, and depression tends to cause certain types of behavioral changes—a cluster of changes in behavior and mood, in sleep and eating patterns, and energy level. Other warning signs of depression include dramatic changes in behavior or appearance, in weight, or in performance in school. Any talk about wanting to die or complete suicide should be seen as a real risk factor. Another strong signal is continuing alcohol or drug use because one of the first things troubled teens try to do is to medicate themselves by drinking or taking drugs instead of seeking psychological help.

Risk Factors

Suicide is a complex behavior that is usually caused by a combination of factors. Researchers have identified a number of risk factors associated with a higher risk for suicide, and factors that may reduce the likelihood of suicidal behavior. It is important to note, however, that the importance of risk and protective factors can vary by age, gender, and ethnicity.

Previous attempts   If a teen has attempted suicide in the past, there is a higher chance of recurrence in the future. If a teenage boy has attempted suicide in the past, he is more than 30 times more likely to complete suicide, while a female with a past attempt has about three times the risk. About a third of teenage suicide victims have made a previous suicide attempt.

Mental disorders or substance abuse   Research shows that more than 90 percent of teenagers who complete suicide have a mental or substance abuse disorder or both, and that most are depressed. In a 10- to 15-year study of 73 adolescents diagnosed with major depression, 7 percent of the adolescents had completed suicide sometime later. The depressed adolescents were five times more likely to have attempted suicide as well, compared with a control group of age peers without depression.

Almost half of teenagers who complete suicide have been seen by a mental health professional. In addition, aggressive, disruptive, and impulsive behavior is common in youth of both sexes who complete suicide.

Family history   A high proportion of suicides and attempters have had a close family member who attempted or completed suicide, which may be either linked to imitation or genetics. Many of the mental illnesses which contribute to suicide risk appear to have a genetic component.

Stressful life event or loss   Stressful life events often precede a suicide or suicide attempt, such as trouble at school or with the

police, fighting, or breaking up with a friend. Rarely a sufficient cause of suicide, these events may act as precipitating factors in young people.

Gun access   There is a direct link between the accessibility and availability of firearms in the home and the risk for youth suicide. The more guns there are and the easier they are to retrieve, the higher the risk.

Exposure to suicidal behavior   Whether a real or fictional account of suicide, research suggests this can trigger suicide in vulnerable teens. In addition, local epidemics of suicide have a contagious influence. Suicide clusters nearly always involve previously disturbed young people who knew about each other's death but rarely knew the other victims personally.

Incarceration   Data suggest a high prevalence of suicidal behavior in juvenile correctional facilities. One study found that suicide in juvenile detention and correctional facilities was more than four times greater than youth suicide overall. According to another recent study, more than 11,000 juveniles engage in more than 17,000 incidents of suicidal behavior in juvenile facilities each year.

Other identified risk factors include a family history of mental or substance abuse disorders, a history of physical and/or sexual abuse, low levels of communication with parents, the possession of certain cultural and religious beliefs about suicide (for instance, the belief that suicide is a noble resolution of a personal dilemma), and lack of access or an unwillingness to seek mental health treatment.

The impact of some risk factors can be reduced by INTERVENTIONS (such as providing effective treatments for depressive illness). Those risks factors that cannot be changed (such as a previous suicide attempt) can alert others to the heightened risk of suicide during periods of the recurrence of a mental or substance abuse disorder, or following a significant stressful life event.

Protective Factors

Factors that protect against suicide include a teen's genetic or neurobiological makeup, attitude and behavior characteristics, and environment. Problem-solving skills, impulse control, conflict resolution, and nonviolent handling of disputes all help reduce risk, together with family and community support, access to effective mental health care and support, restricted access to guns, and cultural and religious beliefs that discourage suicide and support self-preservation instincts.

Measures that enhance resilience or protective factors are as essential as risk reduction in preventing suicide. Positive resistance to suicide is not permanent, so programs that support and maintain protection against suicide should be ongoing.

Methods

Firearms are the most common method of suicide by both boys and girls, and younger and older teens for all races. More than 60 percent of youth suicides between the ages of 10 and 19 in 1998 were firearm related. The rate of youth suicides involving a firearm increased 38 percent between 1981 and 1994, and although firearm-involved suicides declined more than 20 percent from 1994 to 1998, these numbers are still high.

Prevention

Despite this very real threat during the teen years, many families feel uncomfortable about discussing the topic with their children, fearing that if they bring up the subject it will plant a suggestion where none before existed. In fact, talking with a teenager about their negative feelings can help ease the sense of hopelessness the child may have.

Parents who worry that their child might be suicidal should seek help from a mental health professional (either a psychologist, psychiatrist, psychiatric nurse, school counselor, religious counselor, or social worker). Pediatricians and family doctors also can help, although they may have less training in suicidal crises. In case of a suicide emergency, parents can call 911 or take the child to a hospital emergency room.

Although it's not possible to prevent every case of suicide, parents who closely watch their teenagers and work hard at maintaining communication have the best chance of saving their child's life.

A relatively recent phenomenon has been the so-called CLUSTER SUICIDES, surges of copycat self-destruction. Since 1982, clusters of suicides among teens have occurred in Omaha, Nebraska; Cheyenne, Wyoming; three cities in Texas—Plano, Clear Lake City, and Richardson; and Westchester County, New York. In Bergenfield, New Jersey, a middle-class suburb 10 miles west of New York City, two teenage boys and two teenage sisters sat together in an idling car while it filled a garage with lethal carbon monoxide. The day after the quartet's suicide pact, two depressed teenage girls in Alsip, Illinois, killed themselves in much the same way, their bodies recovered in an exhaust-filled garage.

telephone intervention Telephone crisis intervention service usually staffed 24 hours a day to counsel suicidal callers.

The first phone interview is crucial and often spells the difference between life and death. The caller *must* be made to feel he is being interviewed by an empathetic, knowledgeable authority who not only wants to but *can* help.

The AMERICAN ASSOCIATION OF SUICIDOLOGY and the NATIONAL COMMITTEE ON YOUTH SUICIDE PREVENTION both publish suicide prevention and crisis center listings of hotlines and counseling services.

television, effect on suicide Many experts believe that TV watching may be a catalyst for suicide on the part of some impressionable young people who see news stories concerning teenage suicides. Others believe that incidents directly linked to TV are isolated cases.

The medium of television is often accused of exacerbating the problem and effects of teen suicide by publicizing and sometimes sensationalizing the facts. While this may be true in certain cases, someone doesn't become suicidal just by watching TV and seeing that someone else has done it. Experts agree that the suicide decision is not impulsive; it is, in fact, usually premeditated. While it might be done on impulse, generally suicide is an action that is given long consideration.

A far greater danger than television lies in *preventing* discussion of the subject of suicide. In fact, the element of candid discussion—educational, factual, informational—is the best weapon available to combat teenage self-destruction. Television, properly done, provides that vital, valuable forum.

temporal factors   The idea that suicide occurs more often during certain times of day or season.

One California study showed that about 14 percent of suicides occur between 9 A.M. and 10 A.M., while 13 percent take place from 1 P.M. to 2 P.M. Others have found that more suicides occur between noon and 6 P.M. and that fewer happened between midnight and 6 A.M.

As for the relation of suicide to seasons, spring is traditionally the most suicidal time of year. Some authorities think that because spring is a time of "rebirth" and most people feel happier, the suicidal person may regress and feel more depressed *because* he sees others being more cheerful—and such feelings may lead to suicide. According to suicide rates from 1980 to 2000, April is the peak month for suicides in general, February is the month when SUICIDE CLUSTERS peak.

The suicide rate among the general population reaches a low point in November and December. Clearly, suicide does not peak during the holidays.

Monday appears to be the day on which most suicides occur. In an average year, an estimated 82 suicides take place nationwide every Monday. Saturday statistics, by contrast, showed an average of 71 suicides, the lowest rate among days of the week.

Weather, holidays, phases of the moon, and the occurrence of sunspots seem not to affect suicidal tendencies. While the word *lunacy* derives from the Latin word for "moon," no reliable evidence exists to indicate that more suicides than usual occur during a full moon. On the other hand, some believe there is a global geographical correlation: Northerly places, such as Scandinavia, show higher suicide rates than do more tropical countries. In the United States, the Rocky Mountain region has the highest suicide rate, while New England has the lowest rate per 100,000 population.

terminal illness   See EUTHANASIA; HEMLOCK SOCIETY.

terrorism and suicide   An age-old tactic in which the very act of the attack is dependent upon the death of the perpetrator. In suicide terrorism, the terrorist fully understands that if he does not kill himself, the planned attack will not be implemented. Terrorists use suicide attacks to instill a feeling of helplessness in a population—the idea that there is no way of protecting themselves against attack, creating fear and panic.

As many terrorist groups in the 20th century conquered their inhibitions about killing large numbers of innocent victims indiscriminately, suicide terrorism has reemerged in the last two decades as a favored tactic of certain terrorist groups because of the fear it generates and the ability to execute accurate, large-scale attacks without sophisticated technology.

The largest number of suicide terrorist attacks in recent years have come from the Liberation Tigers of Tamil Eelam (LTTE, or Tamil Tigers), a separatist group fighting the government of Sri Lanka. Using suicide attackers, the Tigers managed to kill two heads of state, Indian Prime Minister Rajiv Gandhi, in 1991, and Sri Lankan President Ranasinghe Premadasa, in 1993. Other groups using suicide terrorism include the Kurdistan Workers' Party (PKK), a Kurdish, Marxist separatist group fighting the government of

Turkey; Hezbollah, an Iranian-backed group of Shiite Islamists based in Lebanon; and al-Qaeda, Osama bin Laden's network of radical Sunni Islamists.

While not technically terrorism, the kamikaze attacks of Japanese pilots during World War II also showed a willingness to use suicide as a weapon. This indicates that the concept of self-sacrifice is not specific to any given culture, but it is becoming more common.

The most recent wave of suicide terrorism began with attacks by Hezbollah in Lebanon in 1983. The tactic was adopted by the Tamil Tigers in Sri Lanka in 1987, by the Palestinian Islamist group Hamas in Israel in 1994, and by the PKK in Turkey in 1996. Al-Qaeda embraced suicide terrorism in the mid-1990s when the network began planning the 1998 bombings of the U.S. embassies in Kenya and Tanzania, and the 2001 attack on the World Trade Center and the Pentagon. The second Palestinian *intifada* (uprising), which began in 2000, has featured numerous suicide attacks from both religious and secular Palestinian terrorist groups. In May 2002, FBI director Robert S. Mueller III said future suicide attacks on American soil are "inevitable."

The Islamist movement has strongly encouraged many Muslims to accept a theology in which becoming a suicide bomber is not considered suicide, but instead is a form of religious "struggle." Therefore, in the view of some Islamists, a Muslim can effectively commit suicide without violating Islamic law. Dozens of Muslims have died in this fashion over the last 20 years.

Among the Hamas, an organization that has carried out a number of suicide attacks against Israeli buses, markets, and other civilian targets, the perpetrator of a suicide attack is not considered to have completed suicide. Instead, he is rather perceived to be a *shahid*—a martyr who died while fulfilling a religious command, the jihad or "holy war."

Suicide attacks may provide the *shahid* and his family with substantial rewards. Most *shahids* are poor, and his actions will improve his social sta-

tus after death. The family of the *shahid* is honored and paid a financial reward for the attack. In addition to the religious mission and the family rewards, the *shahid* also receives some personal benefits, including eternal life in paradise, the chance to see the face of Allah, the loving kindness of 72 virgins who will serve him in heaven, and a chance to promise a life in heaven to 70 of his relatives.

The typical suicide bomber is young (usually between 18 to 27), unmarried, unemployed, and poor. He has usually completed high school, usually becoming a student at Islamic fundamentalist education centers. Most *shahids* complete a suicide attack because of a combination of religious fanaticism and nationalist extremism—a wish for revenge, not personal despair.

Usually a *shahid* does not volunteer for his missions, but is selected by his Islamic religious teacher after a close examination by the teachers over a long period of time. After he is selected, he usually participates in long training sessions in order to test his attitudes and performance under pressure and in life-threatening situations. Only the best trainees subsequently disappear from home, beginning several days of intensive training in order to understand all operational aspects of his mission and to learn how to deal with the explosive device. At this time the *shahid* also undergoes a process of physical and mental purification.

Suicides are generally thought of as self-inflicted death to escape a painful or unbearable life. Individuals who are highly suicidal have reached a point where death my be perceived as preferable to a continued existence. Although the term *suicidal* is currently being used to describe the individuals responsible for the recent tragedies in New York, Washington, and Pennsylvania, it is important to remember that the vast majority of suicidal persons are no threat to others.

Terrorists who kill themselves in fulfillment of their mission are not primarily suicidal, but may be willing to sacrifice their lives for a cause, to advance an ideology, or to martyr themselves in service to a charismatic leader against a perceived enemy, such as the terrorist attacks on September 11, 2001. In these cases, individuals who take their lives and the lives of others are not necessarily suffering from mental illness.

thanatology Study of death and dying. Thanatos is the Greek name for a mythical personification of death, borrowed by SIGMUND FREUD to represent the death instinct. In New York City, there is a Foundation of Thanatology.

Thanatos Ancient Greek personification of death. Thanatos, the son of Nyx, was often accompanied his twin brother, Hypnos; the two lived in a cave along the river Lethe. When the Fates cut the thread of a person's life, Thanatos would claim the spirit as his own. In art, he was pictured as a young winged man with a sword and an extinguished or inversed torch.

Psychoanalyst SIGMUND FREUD adopted this term to describe the death, destructive, and aggressive drive—the opposite of the life instinct, which Freud called Eros. Freud believed that there is a constant shift between the power of the Eros and Thanatos in every person. Eros ages, he believed, while ageless Thanatos may assert itself "until it, at length, succeeds in doing the individual to death."

See also THANATOLOGY.

Thebes In ancient Greece, capital of Boeotia, and scene of many legends, such as those of Cadmus and Oedipus. People in Thebes openly condemned a person who completed suicide, and refused to allow that person funeral rites.

theological views on suicide See listings dealing with specific major religions; SAINT AUGUSTINE.

Thomas, Dylan (1914–1953) British poet and prose writer born in Swansea, South Wales, who drank himself to death before his 40th birthday. He exhibited death-oriented behavior much of his life by engaging in what many experts deemed "life-shortening activities." Thomas's compulsive drinking, and his entire lifestyle, appeared to involve an inexorable movement, whether intentioned or subintentioned, toward the brink of self-destruction.

One of his most famous works, "Do Not Go Gentle Into That Good Night" (1952) was written for his father. Thomas died in New York while directing the final production of *Under Milk Wood*, which he described as a "play for voices." He is generally considered one of the finest English-speaking poets of the 20th century.

Thracians Natives of ancient Thrace who practiced polygamy. After the man's death, his wives vied for the honor of being judged the one he loved most. The wife accorded this honor was slain over the grave and buried with her husband.

This is a form of what experts call INSTITUTIONAL SUICIDE, analogous to the Hindu custom of SUTTEE, in which the widow immolated herself with the corpse of her husband.

time of day See TEMPORAL FACTORS.

Tiv of Nigeria African people who appear to have the lowest incidence of suicide yet recorded. So few, in fact, that an expert was unable to document cases of Tiv suicide. Yet they realize that it is something that does sometimes happen and they discussed the means by which it is typically accomplished.

Tojo, Hideki (1885–1948) Japanese general and prime minister from 1941 to 1944 who attempted suicide prior to his execution as a war criminal. Tojo was instrumental in planning the December 7, 1941, attack on Pearl Harbor.

Tom Sawyer   Mark Twain's famous novel (1876) in which he showed a clear understanding of the childhood fantasy of making a point by killing oneself.

Frustrated by his Aunt Polly, Tom found comfort in the fantasy of drowning himself in the nearby Mississippi. He imagined with relish his limp body being brought to his aunt and her saying, "Oh, if I had only loved him more. How differently I would have treated him if we had only known." The vision brought tears of self-pity to his eyes.

Too Young to Die: Youth and Suicide   One of the truly important works dealing with the subject of adolescent and teenage suicide, by Francine Klagsbrun. Elisabeth Kübler-Ross, M.D., calls Klagsbrun's book "an important work . . . Let us hope that parents and counselors, teachers and ministers will read this book in order to understand the cry for help that so many children send out, before their despair exceeds their wish to live." Mrs. Klagsbrun's husband, Dr. Samuel C. Klagsbrun, was an advisor for the NATIONAL COMMITTEE ON YOUTH SUICIDE PREVENTION.

Toronto Distress Centre   One of several key centers in Canada's nationwide network of suicide prevention and crisis hotlines that service large population areas. Other centers are found in Montreal, Quebec, and Vancouver, British Columbia.

traffic accidents   Authorities say that many deaths recorded by medical examiners as accidents are actually suicides in disguise. In fact, many coroners routinely list the death as an accident when the cause of death is not known. The Federal Center for Studies of Suicide Prevention, Bethesda, Maryland, states that many reckless, speeding drivers are playing unconscious roles in hastening their own deaths.

Some experts believe that fully 25 percent of the drivers who die in auto accidents cause them subintentionally by careless, excessive risk-taking.

See also AUTOCIDE.

tranquilizers   A group of depressant drugs that act selectively on the brain and spinal cord. They are not unlike BARBITURATES in many ways, especially in their sedative effect, but in normal doses they do not induce sleep or cause drowsiness.

Tranquilizers are divided into two classes—major and minor. The major tranquilizers (also called neuroleptics), include haloperidol and chlorpromazine, and are used to treat serious mental illness. Minor tranquilizers, which include meprobamate (Miltown), chlordiazepoxide (Librium) and diazepam (VALIUM), can produce euphoria and are all too often abused or misused—not only for their own effects, but also to offset the effects of alcohol, amphetamines, and other drugs.

The minor tranquilizers have been used in a number of suicide attempts, especially by females—both adult and teenager—but fatalities are rare when used alone. Successful suicides are generally the result of a synergistic effect between the tranquilizer and another drug such as alcohol. Combining tranquilizers with alcohol or other depressant drugs is dangerous since each drug increases the effect of the other so that the combined effect is more powerful than the effect of either alone. In addition, tolerance can develop with regular prolonged use and increased doses may be needed to produce the original tranquilizing effects. Long-term heavy use can result in psychological and even physical dependence, although physical dependence is infrequent when one considers the large number of people who use tranquilizers. They are legally available only on prescription.

treatment   See COUNSELING; POSTVENTION.

Treblinka   One of the most notorious World War II Nazi concentration camps, located in Poland, where thousands of Jews were exterminated. Many chose to kill themselves as an affirmation of the freedom to control their own destiny. These suicidal acts, closely paralleling the situation at MASADA in A.D. 73, sparked the start of a rebellion that ultimately became an open revolt, one of the few such revolts that took place in a Nazi concentration camp. The courageous action was in keeping with the theme of death with honor to preserve one's beliefs prevalent throughout the long history of the Jewish people.

Trosse, George (1631–1713) British clergyman who suffered a psychotic breakdown in the mid-17th century. His autobiography, published after his death, contains a vivid account of his experiences, including strong suicidal impulses.

U

Ulysses See JOYCE, JAMES.

unemployment and suicide Suicide rates increase when unemployment is high. Psychologists have postulated possible reasons for such increases. They include: DEPRESSION among those unable to get work; tendency toward abuse of family members; dissolution of the family; increased abusive drinking and drug use; increased anguish and anxiety; and cultural frustration described generally as loss—loss of family love, loss of control over one's own destiny, loss of identity (alienation), loss of self-esteem, and, in general, loss of meaning in life.

While social disorganization, which greatly impressed French sociologist ÉMILE DURKHEIM has an important bearing on suicide rates, psychic aspects must also be considered. Unfortunately, the manner in which these processes operate is not all that clear. What is clear is that suicide is such a complex of causes—social, psychological, family interactions—that no single theory is sufficient to account for the intricacies of the suicide act.

Unfinished Business: Pressure Points in the Lives of Women A study of women and DEPRESSION by noted American writer Maggie Scarf. Scarf won a Niéman Fellowship at Harvard University and was twice a Fellow at the Center for Advanced Study in the Behavioral Sciences at Stanford University.

unintentional death Accidental death from suicidal attempt.

The poet SYLVIA PLATH is a well-known example of an unfortunate and tragic death that many experts think resulted accidentally—unintentionally—from a suicide attempt. Until he or she dies, experts believe a suicide is pleading to be saved.

United Kingdom See ENGLAND; IRELAND; SCOTLAND; WALES.

unmarried, singles See MARITAL STATUS AND SUICIDE.

unusual methods of suicide While most people kill themselves by using guns, HANGING, or poisoning, there are occasionally quite unusual ways of completing suicide.

People have ended their lives by swallowing poisonous spiders, by power-drilling holes in their heads, by sticking hot pokers down their throats, by choking on underwear, by injecting peanut butter into their veins, by crushing their necks in vises, and by hurling themselves into vats of beer.

urban suicide The state with the highest suicide rate is a western state, relatively low in population density: Nevada (1999 rate was 22.3 per 100,000 while the U.S. rate that year was 12 per 100,000). Other states with the highest suicide rates are: Arizona, Colorado, Idaho, Montana, New Mexico, Oklahoma, Oregon, and Wyoming. In 1999, the state with the lowest suicide rate was New York, at only 6.6 per 100,000.

Highest U.S. regional rates are those of the West Coast and the Rocky Mountain areas. The region with the lowest rate is the northeast.

It was felt for several decades in the 20th century that the rural suicide rate was much lower than that of urban areas. In recent years, since the decline of the nation's small- and medium-sized farms and the rise of corporate agribusinesses, it appears that the rural suicide rate in the U.S. is now on a level with the urban rate.

Additionally, however, the suicide rates have been found to be positively correlated with these factors: male gender, increasing age, widowhood, single and divorced status, childlessness, high density of population, residence in big towns, a high standard of living, economic crisis, drug and alcohol consumption, history of a broken home in childhood, mental disorder and physical illness. Again, many authorities say the validity of statistical data concerning suicide and the correlation of suicide rates to geographical area and other related factors are questionable and ought not to be generalized.

Uses of Enchantment, The   Nonfiction work by BRUNO BETTELHEIM in which he explains the unbridled power that fairy tales and myths have over children. Bettelheim's contention: that children love them so because the stories embody their strongest hopes and fears. One almost universal fear in fairy tales is the fear of being separated from one's parents. Called separation anxiety; the younger we are, the more excruciating is our anxiety when we feel deserted, for the young child actually perishes when not adequately protected.

Experts say that the typical suicidal adolescent is likely to be a teenager who quite early in his life was literally separated from vital relationships or who never experienced a real trusting relationship.

U.S. law   See LAW AND SUICIDE; LEGAL ASPECTS OF SUICIDE.

U.S. suicide statistics   The most up-to-date and reliable suicide statistics available to researchers and others interested in the field of suicidology come from the Centers for Disease Control (CDC) in Atlanta. They analyze vital statistics from the National Center for Health Statistics for use by clinicians, health planners and evaluators, and other public health professionals interested in the number and characteristics of suicide, both among youths and adults.

The suicide data specified in the national vital statistics reflects the judgments and professional opinions of the physicians, coroners, or medical examiners who certify the medical/legal cause of death on the death certificate. Most authorities are of the opinion that suicide statistics based on death certificates probably *understate* the true number of suicides for several reasons:

1. Inadequate information on which to make a determination of suicide as the cause of death.
2. Certifier bias or error.
3. No death certificate filed on the victim.

Utopia   Book written by English author and statesman SIR THOMAS MORE (1478–1535), depicting an ideal commonwealth. In the work, More justified suicide as a form of EUTHANASIA. More was beheaded in 1535 by command of Henry VIII for refusing to take an oath impugning the authority of the pope (for which martyrdom he was canonized in 1935).

Valium   Trade name for diazepam, a TRANQUIL-IZER and sedative hypnotic used to treat tension, anxiety, and alcohol withdrawal. It is also a common method for committing suicide.

Users can develop tolerance along with a potential for physical and psychological dependence. Valium, or diazepam, is one of the most widely prescribed drugs in the United States, and has a significant potential for abuse when taken with alcohol or other central nervous system depressants.

Vancouver Crisis Centre   One of Canada's established "distress centres" that serves large population areas with suicide prevention hotlines.

van Gogh, Vincent (1853–1890)   Dutch painter and one of the world's great pre-modernists, who killed himself at age 37. Vincent van Gogh was born near Brabant, the son of a minister. Largely self-taught, he became one of the elemental forces of impressionist art.

Originally intending to enter the ministry, most of his life was characterized by restlessness. His move to Paris in 1886 brought van Gogh into contact with Paul Gauguin, Camille Pissarro, Georges Seurat, and Henri de Toulouse-Lautrec. Two years later, he moved to Arles, in the south of France, hoping to establish an artists' colony there. He was joined briefly by Gauguin in October 1888, but the visit was not a success. A final argument led to the infamous episode in which van Gogh cut off his ear. Although he experienced his first attack of insanity in Arles, he painted every day and produced an astonishing amount of marvelous work, such as the sunflower series.

In 1889, he became a voluntary patient at the St. Remy asylum, where he continued to paint, often making copies of artists he admired. As he descended into madness, his brushwork became increasingly agitated, the dashes constructed into swirling, twisted shapes. He moved to Auvers, to be closer to his brother, Theo, in 1890, and his last 70 days were spent in a hectic program of painting. He left the asylum in May 1890 to stay a short time with his brother in Paris, and then went to stay with a friend of Cezanne and Gauguin. Two months later, he shot himself and died sometime thereafter.

Varah, Chad (1911–   )   British clergyman who founded the SAMARITANS in 1953. Born in 1911, Varah was ordained as Anglican clergyman in 1936. One of his first duties was to officiate at the funeral of a 14-year-old girl who had completed suicide when she became shocked at the first visible signs of puberty. Because she had nobody with whom she could discuss these symptoms, she became convinced she was suffering from an incurable illness and taking her own life seemed the only way out.

Varah was profoundly shocked at this tragedy, and from that day onward he resolved to eliminate the taboo against public discussion of sexuality and bodily functions. It was as a sex therapist that he first offered the Samaritans telephone counseling service, recognizing that in 1953 a great deal of human misery could be linked to problems with sexuality and sexual relationships. The telephone service began with just a single telephone, but within 10 years there were 41 branches of the Samaritans in the United Kingdom. Just three years later, in 1966, there were 6,537 Samaritan volunteers based in 80 branches. In 1974, Chad founded BEFRIENDERS INTERNATIONAL, the worldwide body of Samaritans branches that spread across the globe. By 1993, there were more than 18,000 volunteers counseling suicidal callers. Calls to the Samaritans have continued to go up every year, and there are now 203 branches around the world, including the United States.

Throughout his long life, Varah has campaigned tirelessly for a more rational, humane society, without sacrificing his deep religious principles. In his 80s, he began a campaign to discourage East African immigrants from continuing their tradition of female genital mutilation and was able to note several successes achieved not by political action but by actually going to the homes of the families and explaining how the lives of their daughters would be more fulfilled and happy if they were not subjected to this practice.

Vatel (ca. 1622–1671) The *maître d'hôtel* of Louis II de Bourbon, prince de Condé, Vatel killed himself out of shame when a dinner and entertainment for Louis XIV apparently turned out badly. It seems Vatel misunderstood a fishmonger concerning the quantity of fish available for his use.

"I cannot endure the disgrace," he cried. Going to his room, he fixed his sword to the door and ran upon the point. Vatel was highly praised for his courage and resolution, even though the praise was mingled somewhat with reproach.

"victim-precipitated" murders When victims, appear to deliberately provoke others into killing them, sometimes flashing knives or wielding guns or goading others with threats of violence. The theory is that many men consider suicide as a weak, cowardly way out of their problems. Rather than self-inflicted destruction,

some young men aggressively create violence, hurt others in the process, but manage to get themselves killed—dying as heroes, preserving their definition of masculinity.

See also SUICIDE BY COP.

Vienna Psychoanalytical Society Members of this group met on April 27, 1910, in Vienna, Austria, to try to learn more about the mysterious causes of suicide among that famed city's high school students. Leading psychoanalysts met with educators to discuss the problem. It was SIGMUND FREUD, the father of psychoanalysis, who came away from the historic meeting admitting that they had accomplished very little, and that much more work was necessary in this area of concern. He said too little was known about suicide, but that perhaps the act was a repudiation of life because of the craving for death. This observation foreshadowed Freud's ultimate belief in a death instinct—a theory of suicide still accepted by many scholars—as set forth in his later paper, *Mourning and Melancholia.*

Vigne, Pier delle (1190–1249) Longtime chief counselor of Emperor Friedrich II Hohenstaufen who was accused of treachery by conspiring against his lord in 1247 and was imprisoned and blinded. In despair, and to avoid further torture, delle Vigne took his own life.

His suicide is significant in history primarily because it is the one suicide to which DANTE refers specifically. Dante, in fact, actually talked with Pier delle Vigne.

Villechaize, Hervé (1943–1993) Actor best known for playing Tattoo on *Fantasy Island*, who was despondent over his health when he shot himself to death in 1993. Villechaize stopped growing very early in life, but despite the efforts of his surgeon father to find a cure, none was possible—so the boy had to live with his small height and undersized lungs.

Villechaize studied at the Beaux-Arts School in Paris and exhibited his own paintings, which were well received. At 21 he left France for the United States, where he continued to paint, take photos, and started acting. He was quickly offered several roles for plays and films. His first big success was as a killer in *The Man with the Golden Gun* (1974). This was followed by his role on the successful TV series *Fantasy Island* (1978), in which he played Tattoo, the faithful servant of Mr. Roarke (Ricardo Montalban).

However, he was fired in 1983 after arguments about his salary, and he subsequently lost his model-actress wife. The series continued without him but was canceled a year after he left. At this point, Villechaize became depressed, began drinking, and was beset by health problems; he nearly died of pneumonia in 1992. A year later, after watching a movie, he wrote a farewell note, made a tape recording, and shot himself in his backyard. His common-law wife, Kathy Self, discovered his body and called the ambulance, but he later died at the hospital. Hervé Villechaize was cremated, and his ashes were scattered off Point Fermin, in Los Angeles.

Vivienne: The Life and Suicide of an Adolescent Girl

Book by authors John E. Mack and Holly Hickler that describes in detail the months leading to Vivienne's suicide by HANGING. While the signals and clues to her suicidal thinking and behavior were evident, nobody noticed or did anything to help the young girl. She was crying out for help—but her cries proved to be in vain.

Voltaire (François-Marie Arouet) (1694–1778)

French philosopher, writer, and wit whose inquiring mind and skeptical views, particularly on matters of religion, epitomize the French Enlightenment. One of the leaders of the Enlightenment, along with d'Holbach, Hume, Rousseau, and Beccaria, Voltaire condemned the existing conventional treatment of suicides. He steadily attacked the taboos, superstitions, and primitive punishments still being imposed for suicide victims. As a result, he and others laid the foundation for a secular approach to the problem of suicide; saw laws slowly changed; and were instrumental in a gradual shift in society's emotional attitudes.

Volteius

A Roman tribune who, with his friends, found themselves surrounded by Pompeian troops in their attempt to cross the Adriatic. They had defended themselves courageously, but realized that escape was impossible. Vulteius thus called upon his men to die by their own hands rather than to fall alive into the enemy's hands. Not one soldier survived to become a prisoner of Pompey. As Lucan noted in *The Civil War*, "How simple a feat it is to escape slavery by suicide."

Voluntary Euthanasia Society

A nonprofit group organized in 1935, by a group of doctors, lawyers, and clergymen. It was followed in 1938 by Euthanasia Society of America. The society is seeking to make it legal for competent adults, who are suffering unbearably from a terminal illness, to be allowed to request medical help to die at their own informed and persistent request. Today, a number of countries have such societies, including Australia, South Africa, and the Netherlands.

volunteers

Ideally, suicide prevention and crisis centers will be staffed with at least one, or perhaps two professionals, such as psychiatrists, psychologists, or psychiatric social workers. The remainder of the staff are usually nonprofessional volunteers. Experts believe lay volunteers can be very effective staff members *if* they are *carefully selected* and *rigorously trained*.

Many experts believe it may not be a good idea to select people who have suffered psychotic breakdowns or who themselves at one time attempted suicide, or who appear overly interested in suicide.

An efficient suicide prevention service relies heavily on volunteer staff members who offer consultation, training, and seminars to high schools, universities, hospitals, and mental health agencies. Their direct, person-to-person services are the foundation for suicide intervention and prevention programs available at centers across the country. They provide a ready contact between the community's disturbed, suicidal persons and the many helping agencies that are available to them. And they often spell the difference between life and death.

Vonnegut, Kurt, Jr. (1922–) American author of numerous novels, who wrote in *God Bless You, Mr. Rosewater,* "Sons of suicides seldom do well." In fact, both sons and daughters of suicides have a higher than average rate of suicide themselves. Experts believe this is not due to any genetic inheritance factors, but because they grow up in an environment of guilt, anger, and with a sense of low self-esteem.

vulnerability   See CLUES OF SUICIDE.

Wales   The World Health Center (WHO) statistics combine suicide rate numbers for ENGLAND and Wales. The suicide rate per 100,000 totals for the two United Kingdom countries in 1997 was 6.6 among males, the rate was 10.3; for women, 2.9. The age groups with the highest total suicide rate were over age 75, with a total rate of 10.4 per 100,000; suicide rate for men in this age bracket was 16.9, and for women was 3.9. However, the second-highest age group was slightly skewed in 1997 by the incredibly high suicide rate among young men in England and Wales (15.7 per 100,000) for a total rate for the 25–34 age group of 9.4 per 100,000.

Wallace, Samuel E.   In his book, *After Suicide,* sociologist Samuel Wallace explains the vital need suicide survivors have for the sympathetic understanding of friends, associates, and relatives. "Listening to someone else talk. How simple," writes Wallace, "and how few do it." He conducted in-depth interviews with 12 widows of suicides over a one-year period after their spouses' deaths. The interviewers taped the widows' words, saying little themselves. After the study, the survivor women agreed that just being able to talk out their feelings had helped them enormously. One woman observed that, "It saves your life, really."

war, effect on suicide rate   Ironically, suicide rates tend to drop in time of war. During World War I, for example, suicide rates dropped in Europe both in the countries involved (such as, FRANCE, GERMANY, BELGIUM) and in countries that were neutral (such as SWITZERLAND). Following the armistice, the suicide rates began to return to prewar levels. As noted British clergyman and author William Ralph Inge observed: "The statistics of suicide show that, for non-combatants at least, life is more interesting in war than in peace."

warning signs   See CLUES OF SUICIDE.

Washington   According to Centers for Disease Control (CDC) statistics, Washington's suicide rate per 100,000 rose from 13.3 in 1980 to 14.2 in 1997. The 1997 suicide rate for the state was higher than the U.S. rate of 12 per 100,000.

weather   Studies have shown that oppressive weather has little to do with causing suicide. The same studies indicate that suicide rates tend to rise during the spring months, reaching a peak in April, June, and July, then falling back during winter months, with low points during December and January.

However, suicide "clusters" (where several persons, usually teens, kill themselves in a relatively short time frame) tend to peak in February.

Experts suspect that the notion of dull, dismal, inclement weather causing suicides goes back to the superstition that suicide is a dark and mysterious, devil-inspired act.

See also GEOGRAPHIC FACTORS; TEMPORAL FACTORS.

will, loss of   One of several distress signals or warning signs is a sudden loss or lack of the will or desire to do anything, such as go to school or work, be with friends or family, any activity. Suicidal people often suffer a lethargic feeling. Life becomes a useless struggle, they can't get moving, they feel everything is too much trouble, and there's not that much worth doing.

withdrawal   Another warning signal that something is wrong and suicide may be impending. This clue usually follows periods of uncharacteristic irritability, fighting, then DEPRESSION. Along with withdrawal come other suicidal telltales, such as loss of will, sudden lack of interest in appearance, and irregular sleeping habits.

women   Women attempt suicide about three times as often as men, but men complete suicide about three times as often as do women. This has been the case ever since suicide records have been kept. In 1980, the *highest* rate of suicide for women was in the age group 30 to 34; the suicide rate for the same year was 10.3 in the age group 50 to 54. The suicide rate per 100,000 dropped for women from 6.5 in 1979 to 5.9 in 1980, lowest in the past decade. Men in the United States have a markedly higher risk of suicide than do women, and the differential between men and women rates is widening even more.

Woolf, Virginia (1882–1941)   Gifted English writer who killed herself after struggling all her life with recurrent bouts of severe BIPOLAR DISORDER (manic depression). Woolf was born in London on January 25, 1882, to statesman Leslie Stephen and Julia Duckworth Stephen. She was homeschooled by her parents until her mother died and her father went into deep mourning; at this point Woolf had her first severe mental breakdown. In 1904, Woolf's father died, and she had a second mental breakdown, attempting suicide by jumping out of a window.

Eight years later, she married writer and editor Leonard Woolf, after which she had a third mental breakdown that lasted for three years. During this time she completed a novel, *The Voyage Out,* but its publication was delayed by her breakdown and World War I. It was finally published in 1915 by her half brother, Gerald Duckworth.

When World War II was declared, the Woolfs prepared to complete suicide if England was invaded. During the Battle of Britain, her London home was destroyed by bombs. Depressed and hearing voices, she feared she was going mad again and that this time she would not recover. She could not concentrate, read, or write, and despairing, she filled her pockets with stones and drowned herself in the River Ouse on March 28, 1941, leaving suicide notes for her husband and sister. The notes read in part: "I feel certain that I'm going mad again. I feel we can't go thru another of those terrible times. And I shan't recover this time. I begin to hear voices . . ."

After her death, her husband, Leonard, published various essays, short stories, letters, and diaries, as well as several volumes of autobiography that detail their life together.

Woolf had a convincing life history of bipolar disorder, culminating in suicide at the age of 59, and including a suicidal attempt in her 30s that was almost successful. She had her first breakdown at the age of 13, and others when she was 22, 28, and 30. From 1913 to 1915, from the age of 31 to 33, she was ill so often and for so long that permanent insanity was feared. These attacks were severe, requiring many weeks of medical treatment and bed rest. During the rest of her life she had milder mood swings.

Her mental problems were almost certainly genetic. For generations her family history is filled with gloomy men and eccentric women. The family was also very creative, not only in literature.

Her brother Thoby was an emotionally disturbed child, and her sister, Vanessa, experienced an episode of DEPRESSION in her 30s after a miscarriage. The attack lasted two years, and was regarded by the family as similar to Virginia's depressions. Her brother Adrian also suffered from episodes of nervousness and depression. Likewise, her father was a gloomy man who experienced two mild attacks of depression, and her grandfather had three serious depressions that affected his career. Her first cousin developed severe mania in his 20s and died within a few years in an asylum.

World Health Organization (WHO) International organization headquartered in Geneva, SWITZERLAND, that was founded in 1948. The WHO gathers suicide statistics from around the globe.

wrist-slashing Both men and women who attempt suicide without fatal results usually do not use such violent methods as guns and HANGING. Most, it appears, will take pills or poisons, or slash their wrists with ordinary razor blades—all methods that generally allow time for rescue. In fact, the Centers for Disease Control includes this method in the classification "all other means" in its surveillance methods.

Xenophon (ca. 430–ca. 355 B.C.) Athenian soldier, historian and wealthy disciple of SOCRATES whose principal historical work was the *Anabasis*. His other writings included *Memorabilia*, a defense of Socrates, and *Hellenica*, a history of Greece. According to Xenophon, HEMLOCK—the poison drunk by Socrates—was introduced in 403 B.C.

Xerxes I (ca. 519–465 B.C.) Son of Darius I and King of Persia, 486–465 B.C., he conquered Egypt and invaded Greece over a bridge of boats at the Hellespont. Victorious at Thermopylae, Xerxes pillaged Athens, but retired to Asia when his fleet was destroyed at Salamis, in 480 B.C. His army, under Mardonius, was defeated at Plataea, 479 B.C. On his retreat from Greece, a number of his men threw themselves overboard to lighten the overloaded vessel and the ship came safely to harbor.

After he landed, Xerxes ordered that a golden crown be presented to the pilot for saving the king's life. He also commanded that the man's head be cut off, as he had caused the loss of so many Persian lives.

Yeats, William Butler (1865–1939) Irish poet, one of the great writers of modern times, who won the Nobel Prize in literature in 1923. It was Yeats who penned the line, "After us the Savage God"—from whence ALFRED ALVAREZ got the title for his well-known book, THE SAVAGE GOD: A STUDY OF SUICIDE. Yeats meant that the ultimate concern of art was, inevitably, the end of self-death.

Young, Gig (1913–1978) Oscar-winning actor who was an insecure alcoholic when he married for the fifth time in 1978, taking as his bride Kim Schmidt, a German actress 33 years his junior, whom he met in Hong Kong while filming *The Game of Death*. Three weeks after the wedding, at their New York apartment, Young shot his bride in the head with a .38 and then turned the gun on himself.

The Game of Death was Young's last film, and also that of its star, Bruce Lee. (Young had been cast to play the Waco kid in *Blazing Saddles;* after his death, he was replaced by Gene Wilder.)

youth and the very young See CHILDREN AND SUICIDE.

Yuit Eskimos Among the Yuit Eskimos, an individual may decide to die in order for his spirit to be able to save the life of a close relative—or to earn the prestige that this society affords the person who "honorably" ends his life while still at the peak of his powers. His death is a public ceremonial with the actual act being performed by his closest kinsman, who is ritually purified afterwards.

According to anthropologist Jean La Fontaine, "In this society the decision to die and its implementation are separate acts, but the man who deals the death blow is an agent of his victim, which makes a public performance essential to demonstrate this." Dr. La Fontaine explains: "The Eskimo case thus comes under the definition of suicide that is usually recognized by anthropologists: a death for which responsibility is socially attributed to the dead person."

Zealots   See JAIR, ELEAZAR BEN; MASADA.

Zeno (of Citium) (ca. 363–264 B.C.)   Greek philosopher born at Citium, Cyprus, who trained at Athens under Cynic teachers and later founded the school of Stoicism around 300 B.C. Legend has it that Zeno committed suicide after breaking his toe. He was 98 years old at the time and decided that God had sent the broken toe as a sign that he had lived long enough.

Zilboorg, Gregory (1890–1959)   Psychiatrist-in-chief of the United Nations who stated that every suicidal case contained not only unconscious hostility but also an unusual lack of capacity to love others. This is a refinement of KARL MENNINGER's assertion that the drives in suicide are made up of the wish to kill; the wish to be killed; and the wish to die.

Dr. Zilboorg once wrote, "Statistical data on suicides as compiled today deserve little credence. All too many suicides are not reported as such."

Zimri   General who usurped the throne of Israel in 876 B.C. for a few days. After the capture of the city of Tirzah, Zimri realized the hopelessness of his situation and this led him to seek death. "He went into the citadel of the king's house and burned the king's house over him with fire, and died" (I Kings 16:18).

APPENDIXES

I. National Associations, Institutions,
Organizations, and
Government Agencies

II. Suicide Prevention and Crisis
Intervention Agencies in the
United States

III. International Suicide Rates Per 100,000

APPENDIX I
NATIONAL ASSOCIATIONS, INSTITUTIONS, ORGANIZATIONS, AND GOVERNMENT AGENCIES

American Association of Suicidology
2459 South Ash Street
Denver, CO 80222
(303) 692-0985 or (202) 237-2280
http://www.suicidology.org
Website provides information on current research, prevention, ways to help a suicidal person, and surviving suicide. A list of crisis centers is also included.

American Foundation for Suicide Prevention
120 Wall Street
22nd Floor
New York, New York 10005
(888) 333-AFSP; (212) 363-3500
http://www.afsp.org
Their website provides research, education, and current statistics regarding suicide; links to other suicide and mental health sites are offered. Information and help is also available by calling 1-888-333-AFSP (2377).

American Foundation for Suicide Prevention/Canada
Halifax Chapter
Jennifer Langille
Nova Scotia Hospital

P.O. Box 1004-300 Pleasant Street
Dartmouth, Nova Scotia
Canada B2Y 2Z9
(902) 426-4959

American Psychiatric Association
1400 K Street, NW
Washington, DC 20005
(888) 357-7924 or (202) 682-6000
http://www.psych.org
Call for information and referrals to psychiatrists in your area, or visit their website.

American Psychological Association (APA)
750 First Street, NE
Washington, DC 20002
(202) 336-5500
http://www.apa.org
APA's website provides information about who is at risk, suicide warning signs, and steps toward suicide prevention. Call APA if you have questions about their website or any other mental health issues.

American Sociological Association
1722 North Street, NW
Washington, DC 20036

Association for Death Education & Counseling
342 North Main Street
West Hartford, CT 06117-2507
(860) 586-7503
http://www.adec.org

Boys Town
(800) 448-3000 (crisis hotline) or (800) 545-5771
http://www.boystown.org
An organization that cares for troubled children—both boys and girls—and for families in crisis. Their hotline staff is trained to handle calls and questions about violence and suicide.

Canadian Association for Suicide Prevention
c/o The Support Network
11456 Jasper Avenue
#301
Edmonton, Alberta T5K 0M1
(780) 482-0198
www.suicideprevention.ca

Center for Suicide Research and Prevention
Rush-Presbyterian-St. Luke's Medical Center
1753 West Congress Parkway
Chicago, IL 60612
(312) 942-7208

Center for Thanatology Research & Education, Inc.
391 Atlantic Avenue
Brooklyn, NY 11217
(718) 858-3026
http://www.thanatology.org

Compassionate Friends
P.O. Box 3696
Oak Brook, IL 60522-3696
(630) 990-0010
http://www.compassionate-friends.org
Nonprofit self-help organization to counsel families of those who have died.

CONTACT USA
4 North Circle Drive
Harrisburg, PA 17110
(717) 232-3501
http://www.contactusa.org

Dying With Dignity
55 Eglinton Avenue East
Suite 705
Toronto, Ontario M4P 1G8
  CANADA
(416) 486-3998 or (800) 495-6156
http://www.web.apc.org

Foundation for Thanatology
630 West 168th Street
New York, NY 10032
(212) 928-2006

Kristin Brooks Hope Center
609 East Main Street
Unit 112
Purcellville, VA 20132
(540) 338-5756
www.livewithdepression.org

Lifekeeper Foundation
3740 Crestcliff Court
Tucker, GA 30084
(678) 937-9297
http://www.lifekeeper.org

National Alliance for the Mentally Ill (NAMI)
(800) 950-NAMI (6264)

http://www.nami.org
Group provides information about family support and self-help groups. Their website includes links to information about teen suicide, child suicide, brain biology, and suicide, as well as general suicide information links.

National Mental Health Association (NMHA)
(800) 228-1114 or (800) 969-NMHA (6642); (800) 433-5959 (TTY)
http://www.nmha.org
Organization that provides information on depression and its treatment, and for referrals to local screening sites.

National Mental Illness Screening Project/Suicide Division
(800) 573-4433
http://www.nmisp.org
Hotline counselors can help callers locate a free, local confidential screening.

National Organization of People of Color Against Suicide
http://www.nopcas.com

National Suicide Hotline
800-SUICIDE

Parents Anonymous, Inc.
675 West Foothill Boulevard
Suite 220
Claremont, CA 91711
(909) 621-6184
http://www.parentsanonymous.org

Partnership for Caring: America's Voices for the Dying
1620 I Street NW
Suite 202
Washington, DC 20006

(202) 296-8071 or (800) 989-9455 (Hotline)
http://www.partnershipforcaring.org

San Francisco Suicide Prevention Center
(415) 781-0500 (crisis line)

Suicide Awareness-Voices of Education (SA\VE)
(612) 946-7998
http://www.save.org
Website provides suicide education, facts, and statistics on suicide and depression. It links to information on warning signs of suicide and the role a friend or family member can play in helping a suicidal person.

Suicide Information & Education Centre (SIEC)
1615-10th Avenue SW
#201
Calgary, Alberta Canada T3C 0J7
(403) 245-3900
http://www.siec.ca or http://www.suicideinfo.ca/siec.htm
A special library and resource center providing information on suicide and suicidal behavior.

Suicide Prevention Advocacy Network (SPANUSA)
5034 Odins Way
Marietta, GA 30068
(770) 998-8819 or (888) 649-1366
http://www.spanusa.org
A nonprofit organization dedicated to creating an effective national suicide prevention strategy. SPAN links the energy of those bereaved by suicide with the expertise of leaders in science, business, government, and public service to significantly reduce the national suicide rate by the year 2010.

Survivors of Loved Ones Suicides (SOLOS)
P.O. Box 592
Dumfries, VA 22026
(703) 580-8958
http://www.solos.org

Tears of a Cop
http://www.tearsofacop.com
Website designed to promote awareness of suicide and PTSD in police work.

U.S. Centers for Disease Control and Prevention
National Center for Injury Prevention and Control
Division of Violence Prevention
Mailstop K65
4770 Buford Highway, NE
Atlanta GA 30341
(770) 488-4362
http://www.cdc.gov/ncipc/
Visit their website for links to suicide statistics, the SafeUSA website, and safety information.

World Health Organization
Avenue Appia 20
1211 Geneva 27
Switzerland
(+00 41 22) 791 21 11
http://www.who.int

Yellow Ribbon Suicide Prevention Program
P.O. Box 644
Westminster, CO 80036-0644
(303) 429-3530
http://www.yellowribbon.org

APPENDIX II
SUICIDE PREVENTION AND CRISIS INTERVENTION AGENCIES IN THE UNITED STATES

* Member, American Association of Suicidology

ALABAMA

Auburn

Crisis Center of E. Alabama, Inc.
P.O. Box 1053
Auburn, AL 36831
Crisis Phone 1: (334) 821-8600
Business Phone: (334) 821-8600

Birmingham

* Crisis Center, Inc.
3600 8th Avenue S.
Suite 501
Birmingham, AL 55512
Crisis Center: (205) 323-7777
http://www.crisiscenterbham.com
Hrs Avail: 24

Decatur

Mental Health of North Central Alabama
4110 Highway 31 South
Decatur, AL 35603
Crisis Phone 1: (256) 355-5904
Business Phone: (256) 355-6091
http://www.mhcnca.org

Gadsden

Thirteenth Place, Inc.
405 South 12th Street
Gadsden, AL 35901

Crisis Phone 1: (256) 547-9505
Business Phone: (256) 547-8971
Hrs Avail: 24

Huntsville

Crisis Services of N. Alabama, Inc.
P.O. Box 368
Huntsville, AL 35804
Crisis Phone 1: (800) 691-8426;
   (256) 716-1000
Business Phone: (256) 716-4052
http://www.CSNA.org
Hrs Avail: 24

Mobile

Contact Mobile Helpline, Inc.
P.O. Box 66608
Mobile, AL 36660
Crisis Phone 1: (334) 431-5111;
   (800) 239-1117
Business Phone: (334) 431-5100
http://www.helpline_ir.org
Hrs Avail: 24

Tuscaloosa

Indian River Mental Health Center
Tuscaloosa Crisis Line
P.O. Box 2190
Tuscaloosa, AL 35401
Crisis Phone 1: (205) 345-1600
   (after 5 P.M.)
Business Phone: (205) 345-1600

ALASKA

Anchorage

South Central Counseling Center
4020 Folker Street
Anchorage, AK 99508
Crisis Phone 1: (907) 563-3200
Business Phone: (907) 563-1000
Hrs Avail: 24

Fairbanks

* Fairbanks Crisis Line
P.O. Box 70908
Fairbanks, AK 99707
Crisis Phone 1: (907) 452-4357;
   (800) 898-5463
Business Phone: (907) 451-8600
Hrs Avail: 24

Kenai

Central Peninsula Counseling Services
506 Lake Street
Kenai, AK 99611
Crisis Phone 1: (907) 283-7511
Business Phone: (907) 283-7501
Hrs Avail: 24

Ketchikan

Center for Human Services
3050 5th Avenue
Ketchikan, AK 99901
Crisis Phone 1: (907) 225-4135;
   (907) 225-5170; (907) 225-2802

Business Phone: (907) 225-4135
http://www.city.ketchikan.ak.us
Hrs Avail: 24

Wasilla

Life Quest
P.O. Box 873388
230 E. Paulson
Suite 68
Wasilla, AK 99654
Crisis Phone 1: (800) 478-2410;
(907) 225-5170
Business Phone: (907) 376-
2411
Hrs Avail: 24

ARIZONA

Phoenix

*** Alternative Behavioral
Services of Arizona**
444 N. 44th Street
Suite 400
Phoenix, AZ 85008
Crisis Phone 1: (602) 222-9444;
(800) 631-1314
Business Phone: (602) 685-
3881
Hrs Avail: 24

SW Behavioral Health Center
3707 North 7th Street
Suite 100
Phoenix, AZ 85014
Crisis Phone 1: (602) 222-9444
Business Phone: (602) 257-
9339
Hrs Avail: 24

Safford

Safford Crisis Line
P.O. Box 956
Safford, AZ 85546
Crisis Phone 1: (602) 428-4550
Business Phone: (602) 428-
4550
Hrs Avail: 24

Springdale

* NW Arkansas Crisis Intervention Center
614 E. Emma
Suite 213
Springdale, AR 72764
Crisis Phone 1: (800) 798-8336
(teen line)
Crisis Phone 2: (888) 274-7472
(adults)
Crisis Phone 3: (888) 723-3225
(latchkey/youth)
Business Phone: (501) 756-1995

Tucson

*** Southern Arizona Mental
Health Corp.**
1930 E. 6 Street
Tucson, AZ 85719
Crisis Phone 1: (520) 662-6000
Business Phone: (520) 617-
0043
Hrs Avail: 24

ARKANSAS

Hot Springs

**Community Counseling
Services**
505 W. Grand Avenue
Hot Springs, AR 71902
Crisis Phone 1: (501) 624-7111;
(800) 264-2410
Business Phone: (501) 623-
5510
Hrs Avail: 24

CALIFORNIA

Berkeley

**Crisis Support Services of
Alameda County**
P.O. Box 9102
Berkeley, CA 94709
Crisis Phone 1: (510) 849-2212
Crisis Phone 2: (510) 889-1333
Business Phone: (510) 848-1515

http://www.crisissupport.org
Hrs Avail: 24

Burlingame

Crisis Intervention and Suicide Prevention Center
1860 El Camino Real
Suite 400
Burlingame, CA 94010
Crisis Phone 1: (650) 368-6655
Crisis Phone 2: (650) 692-6655
Crisis Phone 3: (650) 726-6655
Business Phone: (650) 692-6662
http://www.YFA.org
Hrs Avail: 24

Capitola

SPS of Santa Cruz County
P.O. Box 1222
Capitola, CA 95010
Crisis Phone 1: (831) 458-5300
Crisis Phone 2: (831) 649-8008
Business Phone: (831) 459-
9373
Hrs Avail: 24

Culver City

*** Suicide Prevention Center,
Didi Hirsch Community
Mental Health Center**
4760 S. Sepulveda Boulevard
Culver City, CA 90230
Crisis Phone 1: (877) 7CRISIS
Crisis Phone 2: (310) 391-1253
Business Phone: (310) 751-5373
http://www.suicidecrisisline.org
Hrs Avail: 24

Davis

*** Suicide Prevention of Yolo
County**
P.O. Box 622
Davis, CA 95617
Crisis Phone 1: (530) 756-5000
Crisis Phone 2: (530) 753-0797
Crisis Phone 3: (530) 666-7778
Crisis Phone 4: (530) 668-8445

Crisis Phone 5: (916) 371-3779
Crisis Phone 6: (916) 372-6565
Business Phone: (530) 756-7542
Hrs Avail: 24

Fairfield

Suicide Prevention/Crisis Line of Volunteer
210 Courage Drive
Fairfield, CA 94533
Crisis Phone 1: (707) 428-1131
Business Phone: (707) 435-2080
Hrs Avail: 24

Garden Grove

New Hope Teen Line
12141 Lewis Street
Garden Grove, CA 92840
Crisis Phone 1: (714) 639-8336
Crisis Phone 2: (714) 441-2099
http://www.newhopeonline.org
http://www.newhopenow.org
http://www.teenline.org
Business Phone: (714) 441-2099
Hrs Avail: 24

Lafayette

CONTACT Care Center
P.O. Box 901
Lafayette, CA 94549
Crisis Phone 1: (925) 284-2273
Crisis Phone 2: (925) 235-5244
Crisis Phone 3: (925) 837-1181
Crisis Phone 4: (925) 284-2350
Crisis Phone 5: (925) 284-2274
Crisis Phone 6: (925) 754-8111
Crisis Phone 7: (925) 945-8336
Business Phone: (925) 284-2207
http://www.contactcare.net
Hrs Avail: 24

Los Alamitos

Hotline of Southern California
P.O. Box 32
Los Alamitos, CA 90720

Crisis Phone 1: (562) 596-5548
Crisis Phone 2: (714) 894-4242
Business Phone: (323) 594-0960
Hrs Avail: 8 A.M.–midnight

Los Angeles

Foundation for Religious Freedom
1680 North Vine
Los Angeles, CA 90028
Crisis Phone 1: (800) 556-3055
Business Phone: (323) 468-0567
http://www.
Hrs Avail: 9–5 P.M.; 24 hr voice mail

Psychological Trauma Center
8730 Alden Drive
Room C-212
Los Angeles, CA 90048
Crisis Phone 1: (310) 423-3514
Business Phone: (310) 423-3506
http://www.ptcweb.org
Hrs Avail: 8 A.M.–5:30 P.M.

Teen Line
P.O. Box 48750
Los Angeles, CA 90048
Crisis Phone 1: (800) 852-8336
Crisis Phone 2: (310) 855-4673
Business Phone: (310) 423-0456
http://www.teenlineonline.org
Hrs Avail: 24

Modesto

Stanislaus Co. Behavioral Health & Recovery Center
1501 Claus Road
Modesto, CA 95355
Crisis Phone 1: (209) 558-4600
Crisis Phone 2: (209) 525-6225
Business Phone: (209) 558-4700

Newark

Second Chance, Inc.
P.O. Box 643
Newark, CA 94560
Crisis Phone 1: (510) 792-4357
Business Phone: (510) 792-4357
Hrs Avail: 24

Pacific Grove

Family Service Agency of the Central Coast
P.O. Box 52078
Pacific Grove, CA 03950
Crisis Phone 1: (831) 649-8008
Business Phone: (831) 375-6966
Hrs Avail: 24

Pasadena

* Kaiser Permanente Behavioral Healthcare Helpline
393 East Walnut Street
Pasadena, CA 91188
Crisis Phone 1: (800) 900-3277
Business Phone: (626) 405-5669
http://www.kp.org
Hrs Avail: 24

Pasadena

Pasadena Mental Health Center
1495 North Lake
Pasadena, CA 91104
Crisis Phone 1: (213) 798-0907
Business Phone: (213) 681-1381
Hrs Avail: 9 A.M.–12 A.M.

Redding

* Help, Inc.
P.O. Box 992498
Redding, CA 96099
Crisis Phone 1: (530) 225-5255
Business Phone: (530) 225-5255
Hrs Avail: 24

Sacramento

* Suicide Prevention/Crisis Services
8912 Volunteer Lane
Sacramento, CA 95826
Crisis Phone 1: (916) 368-3111
Crisis Phone 2: (916) 773-3111
Crisis Phone 3: (916) 885-2300
Crisis Phone 4: (916) 645-8866
Business Phone: (916) 368-3118
Hrs Avail: 24

San Bernardino

Family Helpline Service Agency
1669 North E Street
San Bernardino, CA 92405
Crisis Phone 1: (909) 886-4889
Crisis Phone 2: (909) 475-5200
Crisis Phone 3: (800) 832-9119
Crisis Phone 4: (866) 475-1411
Business Phone: (909) 886-6737
Hrs Avail: 24

San Diego

United Behavioral Health Access and Crisis Line
P.O. Box 1370
San Diego, CA 92160
Crisis Phone 1: (619) 641-6890
Crisis Phone 2: (800) 479-3339
Business Phone: (619) 641-6889
Hrs Avail: 24

San Francisco

* San Francisco Suicide Prevention
P.O. Box 191350
San Francisco, CA 94119
Crisis Phone 1: (415) 362-3400
Crisis Phone 2: (415) 781-0500
Crisis Phone 3: (845) 485-9700
Crisis Phone 4: (845) 486-2866
Business Phone: (845) 486-2705

http://www.sfsuicide.org
Hrs Avail: 24

Center for Elderly Suicide Prevention and Grief
3626 Geary Boulevard
San Francisco, CA 94118
Crisis Phone 1: (415) 752-2314 (geriatrics)
Crisis Phone 2: (415) 752-3778 (elderly)
Business Phone: (415) 750-4180
http://www.gioa.org
Hrs Avail: 24

San Joaquin

San Joaquin Co. Mental Health
1212 North California
Stockton, CA 95202
Crisis Phone 1: (209) 468-8686
Business Phone: (209) 468-8700
http://www.healthcareservices.com
Hrs Avail: 24

San Jose

Contact Santa Clara Co.
P.O. Box 8021
San Jose, CA 95155
Crisis Phone 1: (408) 279-0111
Crisis Phone 2: (408) 279-8228
Crisis Phone 3: (888) 247-7717
Business Phone: (408) 275-6176
http://www.contactcares.org
Hrs Avail: 24

* Santa Clara Suicide & Crisis Service
2221 Enborg Lane
San Jose, CA 95128
Crisis Phone 1: (408) 279-3312
Crisis Phone 2: (408) 633-2482
Crisis Phone 3: (408) 885-6250
Business Phone: (408) 885-6250

http://www.sccsacs.org
Hrs Avail: 24

San Luis Obispo

Hotline of San Luis Obispo County
P.O. Box 5456
San Luis Obispo, CA 93403
Crisis Phone 1: (805) 544-6065
Crisis Phone 2: (805) 549-8989
Crisis Phone 3: (800) 549-8989
Crisis Phone 4: (805) 544-0566
Business Phone: (805) 544-6016
http://slohotline.org
Hrs Avail: 24

San Rafael

Suicide Prevention & Comm. Counseling Service of Marin
P.O. Box 4369
San Rafael, CA 94913-4369
Crisis Phone 1: (415) 499-1100
Business Phone: (415) 499-1193
Hrs Avail: 24

Santa Cruz

Suicide Prevention Service of the Central Coast
P.O. Box 1222
Santa Cruz, CA 95061
Crisis Phone 1: (831) 458-5300
Crisis Phone 2: (831) 649-8008
Business Phone: (831) 459-9373

Stockton

San Joaquin Co. Mental Health
1212 North California
Stockton, CA 95202
Crisis Phone 1: (209) 468-8686
Business Phone: (209) 468-2399
http://www.healthcareservices.com
Hrs Avail: 24

Ventura

* Behavioral Health Crisis Team
200 North Hillmont Avenue
Ventura, CA 93003
Crisis Phone 1: (805) 652-6727 (mobile team)
Crisis Phone 2: (805) 371-8375
Business Phone: (805) 652-6565
Hrs Avail: 24

Walnut Creek

* Contra Costa Crisis Center
P.O. Box 3364
Walnut Creek, CA 94598
Crisis Phone 1: (800) 718-4357
Business Phone: (925) 939-1916
http://www.crisis-center.org
Hrs Avail: 24

Yuba City

Sutter-Yuba MH Crisis Clinic
1965 Live Oak Boulevard
Yuba City, CA 95991
Crisis Phone 1: (530) 673-8255
Crisis Phone 2: (888) 923-3800
Business Phone: (530) 822-7200
http://www.co.sutter.ca.us
Hrs Avail: 24

COLORADO

Arvada

Jefferson Center for Mental Health
5265 Vance Street
Arvada, CO 80002
Crisis Phone 1: (303) 452-0300
Business Phone: (303) 425-0300
www.jeffersonmentalhealth.org
Hrs Avail: 24

Aurora

Comitis Crisis Center
9840 East 17th Avenue

P.O. Box 913
Aurora, CO 80040
Crisis Phone 1: (303) 343-9890
Business Phone: (303) 341-9160
Hrs Avail: 24

Boulder

Mental Health Center of Boulder
1333 Iris Avenue
Boulder, CO 80304
Crisis Phone 1: (303) 447-1665
Business Phone: (303) 447-1665
www.mhcbc.org
Hrs Avail: 24

Colorado Springs

Pikes Peak Mental Health Center
115 South Park Side
Colorado Springs, CO 80905
Crisis Phone 1: (719) 596-5433
Business Phone: (719) 572-6250
Hrs Avail: 24

Suicide Prevention Partnership
3595 East Fountain Boulevard
Suite J-1
Colorado Springs, CO 80910
Crisis Phone 1: (719) 596-5433
Crisis Phone 2: (719) 596-2575
Business Phone: (719) 573-7447
http://www.codenet.net/suicideprevention
Hrs Avail: 24

Greely

* North Range Behavioral Health
1306 11th Avenue
Greely, CO 80631
Crisis Phone 1: (888) 296-5827
Business Phone: (970) 353-3686

Littleton

Living Support Network
P.O. Box 170
Littleton, CO 80160
Crisis Phone 1: (303) 894-9000 (teenline)
Crisis Phone 2: (303) 860-1200
Business Phone: (303) 861-4262
http://www.livingsupportnetwork.org

Pueblo

* Pueblo Suicide Prevention Center, Inc.
1925 East Orman
Suite G-25
Pueblo, CO 81004
Crisis Phone 1: (719) 544-1133
Crisis Phone 2: (719) 564-5566
Business Phone: (719) 564-6642
Hrs Avail: 24

CONNECTICUT

Derby

Griffin Hospital-Psychiatric Crisis Team
130 Division Street
Derby, CT 06418
Crisis Phone 1: (203) 732-7550
Business Phone: (203) 735-7421
http://www.griffinhealth.org
Hrs Avail: 24

Hartford

* The Samaritans of the Capital Region
P.O. Box 12004
Hartford, CT 06112
Crisis Phone 1: (860) 232-2121
Business Phone: (860) 232-9559
Hrs Avail: 24

Meriden

Midstate Behavioral Health System
883 Paddock Avenue
Meriden, CT 06450
Crisis Phone 1: (203) 630-5309
Crisis Phone 2: (203) 630-5308
Crisis Phone 3: (800) 567-0902 (toll free)
Business Phone: (203) 630-5305
Hrs Avail: 24

Middletown

Middlesex Hospital-Crisis Assessment and Triage Service
28 Crescent Street
Middletown, CT 06457
Crisis Phone 1: (860) 344-6496
Crisis Phone 2: (860) 344-7047
Business Phone: (860) 344-6765
Hrs Avail: 24

River Valley Services Mobile Crisis Team
P.O. Box 351 Silver Street
Middletown, CT 06457
Crisis Phone 1: (860) 344-2100
Crisis Phone 2: (860) 388-0668
Business Phone: (860) 262-5218
Hrs Avail: 24

New Haven

Clifford W. Beers Guidance Clinic-CAMPES
93 Edwards Street
New Haven, CT 06511
Crisis Phone 1: (888) 979-6884
Crisis Phone 2: (888) 97-YOUTH
Business Phone: (203) 772-1270
Hrs Avail: 24

Conn. Mental Health Center-Acute Care Services
34 Park Street
New Haven, CT 06519

Crisis Phone 1: (203) 974-7713
Business Phone: (203) 974-7713
Hrs Avail: M-F 9 A.M.–10 P.M.; S-S 9 A.M.–8 P.M.

New London

Contact of Southeast Connecticut
2 Union Plaza
Suite 300
New London, CT 06320
Crisis Phone 1: (860) 848-1281
Crisis Phone 2: (860) 433-8697
Crisis Phone 3: (860) 848-1282
Business Phone: (860) 447-1126
Hrs Avail: 24

Plainville

* The Wheeler Clinic Emergency Service
91 Northwest Drive
Plainville, CT 06062
Crisis Phone 1: (860) 747-3434 (TTY)
Crisis Phone 2: (860) 747-8719
Business Phone: (860) 747-3434
http://www.wheelerclinic.org
Hrs Avail: 24

Rocky Hill

* United Way of Connecticut/INFOLINE
1344 Silas Deane Highway
Rocky Hill, CT 06067
Crisis Phone 1: (800) 203-1234
Crisis Phone 2: (860) 522-4636
Business Phone: (860) 571-7500
http://www.ctunitedway.org
Hrs Avail: 24

Waterbury

Waterbury Hospital Psychiatric Center
64 Robin Street
Waterbury, CT 06708

Crisis Phone 1: (203) 573-6500
Business Phone: (203) 573-6500
http://waterburyhospital.org

DELAWARE

Milford

* Kent/Sussex Community Mental Health Services
P.O. Box 912
Milford, DE 19963
Crisis Phone 1: (800) 345-6785
Business Phone: (302) 422-1133
Hrs Avail: 24

Wilmington

* CONTACT Delaware, Inc.
P.O. Box 9525
Wilmington, DE 19809
Crisis Phone 1: (302) 761-9100
Deaf Contact: (302) 761-9700
Business Phone: (302) 761-9800
www.contactdelaware.org
Hrs Avail: 24

Mobile Crisis Intervention Service
809 Washington Street
Wilmington, DE 19801
Crisis Phone 1: (800) 345-6785
Crisis Phone 2: (302) 577-2484
Crisis Phone 3: (800) 652-2929
Business Phone: (302) 577-2484
Hrs Avail: 24

Tressler Brandywine Program Center of Delaware
240 North James Street
Suite 200
Wilmington, DE 19804-3132
Crisis Phone 1: (302) 633-5128
Business Phone: (302) 995-2002
Hrs Avail: 24

WASHINGTON, DC

Comprehensive Psychiatric Emergency Program-Commission on Mental Health Services
1905 E Street, SE
Building 14
Washington, DC 20003
Crisis Phone 1: (888) 793-4357
Crisis Phone 2: (202) 561-7000
Business Phone: (202) 673-9307

FLORIDA

Bartow

Peace River Center Crisis Line
1255 Golf View Avenue
Bartow, FL 33830
Crisis Phone 1: (863) 519-3744
Crisis Phone 2: (863) 519-3745
Business Phone: (863) 519-3747
Hrs Avail: 24

Bradenton

Manatee Glens Corp.
391 6th Avenue
Bradenton, FL 34205
Crisis Phone 1: (948) 741-3117
Business Phone: (941) 741-3111
www.manateeglens.com
Hrs Avail: 24

Cocoa

Crisis Services of Brevard, Inc.
P.O. Box 417
Cocoa, FL 32923-0417
Crisis Phone 1: (321) 632-6688
Crisis Phone 2: (321) 631-8944 211
Business Phone: (321) 631-9290
http://www.crisis-services.org
Hrs Avail: M-F 8 A.M.–5 P.M.

Daytona Beach

ACT Corp.
1220 Willis Avenue
Daytona Beach, FL 32114
Crisis Phone 1: (800) 539-4228
Business Phone: (904) 947-4270
http://www.actcorp.org
Hrs Avail: 24

De Funiak Springs

Cope Center
3686 Highway 31 South
De Funiak Springs, FL 32433
Crisis Phone 1: (850) 892-4357
Business Phone: (850) 892-8045
www.copecenter.org
Hrs Avail: 24

Fort Lauderdale

First Call for Help/Broward Co.
16 Southeast 13th Street
Fort Lauderdale, FL 33316
Crisis Phone 1: (954) 467-6333
Business Phone: (954) 524-8371
Hrs Avail: 24

Ft. Myers

Ruth Cooper Center
2789 Ortiz Avenue SE
Ft. Myers, FL 33905
Crisis Phone 1: (941) 275-4242
Business Phone: (941) 275-3222
Hrs Avail: 24

Ft. Pierce

New Horizons of the Treasure Coast
4500 West Midway Road
Ft. Pierce, FL 34981
Crisis Phone 1: (561) 468-5600
Crisis Phone 2: (888) 468-5600
Business Phone: (561) 468-5600
Hrs Avail: 24

Ft. Walton Beach

Crisis Line/Bridgeway Center, Inc.
137 Hospital Drive
Ft. Walton Beach, FL 32548
Crisis Phone 1: (850) 244-9191
Crisis Phone 2: (850) 682-0101
Business Phone: (850) 833-9204
Hrs Avail: 24

Gainesville

* Alachua County Crisis Center
218 Southeast 24th Street
Gainesville, FL 32641
Crisis Phone 1: (352) 264-6789
Business Phone: (352) 264-6777
Hrs Avail: 24

Meridian Behavioral Healthcare
P.O. Box 2818
Gainesville, FL 32641
Crisis Phone 1: (800) 330-5615
Crisis Phone 2: (800) 732-0315
Business Phone: (904) 758-0670
Hrs Avail: 24

Jacksonville

First Call for Help
P.O. Box 41428
Jacksonville, FL 32203
Crisis Phone 1: (904) 632-0600
Crisis Phone 2: (800) 346-6185
Business Phone: (904) 387-5641
www.NEFLSurvivors.org
Hrs Avail: 24

Key West/Monroe County

Helpline, Inc.
P.O. Box 2186
Key West, FL 33045
Crisis Phone 1: (305) 296-4357
Crisis Phone 2: (800) 273-4558
Crisis Phone 3: (305) 292-8440

Business Phone: (305) 292-8445
Hrs Avail: 24

Lantana

* Center for Information & Crisis Services-Crisis Line
P.O. Box 3588
Lantana, FL 33465
Crisis Phone 1: (561) 930-1234
Crisis Phone 2: (561) 930-TEEN
Crisis Phone 3: (561) 930-5040 (Elder Help)
Business Phone: (561) 547-8637 x1071
Hrs Avail: 24

Maitland

Central Florida Helpline
P.O. Box 941524
Maitland, FL 32794-1524
Crisis Phone 1: (407) 740-7477
Crisis Phone 2: (407) 740-TALK
Business Phone: (407) 740-7408
www.centralfloridahelpline.org
Hrs Avail: M-F 10 A.M.–4 P.M.

Miami

Metro Dade Advocates for Victims
P.O. Box 380817
Miami, FL 33238-0817
Crisis Phone 1: (305) 758-2546
Business Phone: (305) 758-2804
Hrs Avail: 24

Switchboard of Miami, Inc.
701 SW 27th Avenue
Suite 1000
Miami, FL 33135
Crisis Phone 1: (305) 358-4357
Business Phone: (305) 358-1640
www.switchboardmiami.org
Hrs Avail: M-F 9 A.M.–5 P.M.

Middleburg

Clay County Behavioral Health Center-Access Team
3292 County Road 220
Middleburg, FL 32068
Crisis Phone 1: (904) 291-5290
Business Phone: (904) 291-5290
Hrs Avail: 8 A.M.–4:30 P.M.

Naples

Hotline & Referral/Project Help, Inc.
P.O. Box 7804
Naples, FL 34101
Crisis Phone 1: (941) 262-7227
Business Phone: (941) 649-5660
Hrs Avail: 24

New Port Richey

The Harbor Behavioral Health Care
P.O. Box 428
New Port Richey, FL 34656
Crisis Phone 1: (727) 849-9988
Business Phone: (727) 841-4455 x417
Hrs Avail: 24

Ocala

Marion-Citrus Mental Health Center
P.O. Box 771942
Ocala, FL 34478
Crisis Phone 1: (352) 629-9595
Crisis Phone 2: (352) 726-7155
Crisis Phone 3: (352) 629-6586
Business Phone: (352) 620-7300
Hrs Avail: 24

Orlando

* We Care Crisis Center, Inc.
112 Pasadena Place
Orlando, FL 32803
Crisis Phone 1: (407) 425-2624
Business Phone: (407) 425-5201 x124
www.wecarecrisiscenter.org
Hrs Avail: 24

Panama City

Panama City Crisis Line
Life Management Center
Panama City, FL 32405
Crisis Phone 1: (850) 769-9481
Business Phone: (850) 769-9481
Hrs Avail: 24

Pensacola

Pensacola Help Line-Lakeview Center, Inc.
1221 West Lakeview Street
Pensacola, FL 32501
Crisis Phone 1: (850) 438-1617
Business Phone: (850) 432-8336
Hrs Avail: 24

Pinellas Park

* Personal Enrichment Through MHS, Inc.
11254 58th Street North
Pinellas Park, FL 33782
Crisis Phone 1: (727) 541-4658
Crisis Phone 2: (727) 791-3131
Business Phone: (727) 545-6477
http://www.pemhs.org
Hrs Avail: 24

Rockledge

Circles of Care, Inc.
1770 Cedar Street
Rockledge, FL 32956
Crisis Phone 1: (321) 722-5257
Business Phone: (321) 722-5200
www.circlesofcare.org
Hrs Avail: 24

Starke

Meridian Behavioral Healthcare, Inc.
945 Grand Street
Starke, FL 32091
Crisis Phone 1: (904) 964-8382
Crisis Phone 2: (800) 330-5615 (toll free)
Business Phone: (904) 964-8382
http://www.meridian-healthcare.org
Hrs Avail: 24

St. Petersburg

Pinellas Care-Family Resources Inc.
P.O. Box 11538
St. Petersburg, FL 33733
Crisis Phone 1: (727) 344-5555
Business Phone: (727) 550-4052
www.pinellascares.org
Hrs Avail: 24

Tallahassee

* Telephone Counsel. & Referral Serv.
P.O. Box 10950
Tallahassee, FL 32302
Crisis Phone 1: (850) 224-6333
Business Phone: (850) 681-9131
www.tcrs211.org
Hrs Avail: M-F 9 A.M.–5 P.M.

Tampa

* Hillsborough County Crisis Center, Inc. of Tampa Bay
Crisis Center Plaza
Tampa, FL 33613
Crisis Phone 1: (813) 236-TEEN
Business Phone: (813) 964-1964
www.crisiscenter.com
Hrs Avail: 24

Tampa Help Line/Christian Helpline
P.O. Box 9565
Tampa, FL 33674
Crisis Phone 1: (813) 286-7064
Business Phone: (813) 286-7064
Hrs Avail: 24

Vero Beach

Mental Health Association Crisis Line
2001 9th Avenue
Suite 301
Vero Beach, FL 32960-3431
Crisis Phone 1: (561) 562-2000
Business Phone: (561) 569-9788
Hrs Avail: 24

GEORGIA

Atlanta

Emergency Mental Health Services
141 Pryor Street, SW
Suite 4035
Atlanta, GA 30303
Crisis Phone 1: (404) 730-1600
Business Phone: (404) 730-1600
Hrs Avail: 24

Augusta

Access Center-Integrated Health Resources
945 Broad Street 400
Augusta, GA 30901
Crisis Phone 1: (706) 560-2943
Business Phone: (706) 826-4677
Hrs Avail: 24

Columbus

* Contact Helpline Chattahoochee Valley
P.O. Box 12002
Columbus, GA 31917
Crisis Phone 1: (706) 327-3999

Business Phone: (706) 327-0199
www.contact211.org
Hrs Avail: 24

Decatur

Central Access
445 Winn Way
Decatur, GA 30034
Crisis Phone 1: (404) 892-4646
Business Phone: (404) 294-0499
Hrs Avail: 24

Jonesboro

Clayton County Mental Health Center
853 Battlecreek
Jonesboro, GA 30236
Crisis Phone 1: (770) 996-4357
Crisis Phone 2: (770) 994-1064
Business Phone: (770) 478-2280
Hrs Avail: 24

Marietta

Cobb-Douglas Counties Commission
Services Board
361 North Marietta Parkway
Marietta, GA 30060
Crisis Phone 1: (770) 422-0202
Business Phone: (770) 429-5014
Hrs Avail: 24

Warner Robins

Helpline Georgia
2762 Watson Boulevard
Warner Robins, GA 31093
Crisis Phone 1: (800) 338-6745
Business Phone: (912) 953-5675
Hrs Avail: 24

HAWAII

Honolulu

* Helping Hands Hawaii
2100 North Nimitz Highway
Honolulu, HI 96819
Crisis Phone 1: (808) 521-4556
Crisis Phone 2: (808) 521-4555
Business Phone: (808) 536-7234
Hrs Avail: 24

Wailuku

* Maui Kokua Services, Inc.
P.O. Box 1237
Wailuku, HI 96793
Crisis Phone 1: (808) 244-7407
Business Phone: (808) 244-7405
Hrs Avail: 24

IDAHO

Boise

Emergency Line Region IV Services/Mental Health Center
1720 Westgate Drive
Boise, ID 83704
Crisis Phone 1: (208) 334-0808
Business Phone: (208) 334-0808
Hrs Avail: 24

* Idaho Suicide Prevention Hotline
1810 West State Street, 122
Boise, ID 83702
Crisis Phone 1: (800) 526-2120
Business Phone: (208) 426-3532
Hrs Avail: 24

Bonners Ferry

Boundary County Youth Crisis and Domestic Violence Hotline
P.O. Box 633
Bonners Ferry, ID 83805

Crisis Phone 1: (208) 267-5211
Business Phone: (208) 267-5211
Hrs Avail: 24

Idaho Falls

Region VII Mental Health
150 Shoup
Suite 19
Idaho Falls, ID 83402
Crisis Phone 1: (800) 708-3474
Business Phone: (208) 528-5700
Hrs Avail: 24

Lewiston

YWCA Crisis Services
300 Main Street
Lewiston, ID 83501
Crisis Phone 1: (208) 746-9655
Business Phone: (208) 743-1535
Hrs Avail: 24

Sandpoint

Region I Mental Health
1717 West Ontario
Sandpoint, ID 83864
Crisis Phone 1: (888) 769-1405
Crisis Phone 2: (208) 265-4535 (weekdays 8–5)
Business Phone: (208) 265-4535
Hrs Avail: 24

Twin Falls

Twin Falls Emergency Services
Region 5 Mental Health
823 Harrison
Twin Falls, ID 83301
Crisis Phone 1: (208) 734-4000
Business Phone: (208) 736-2177
Hrs Avail: M-F 5 P.M.–8 A.M.; S-S 24 hrs.

ILLINOIS

Anna

Union County Counseling Service
204 South Street, Box 248
Anna, IL 62906
Crisis Phone 1: (618) 833-8551
Business Phone: (618) 833-8551
www.uccounseling.org
Hrs Avail: 24

Batavia

* Suicide Prevention Service/Crisis Line of The Fox Valley
528 S. Batavia Avenue
Batavia, IL 60510
Crisis Phone 1: (630) 482-9696
Crisis Phone 2: (630) 482-9393
Crisis Phone 3: (630) 482-9595 (teen line)
Business Phone: (630) 482-9185
http://www.spsfv.org
Hrs Avail: 24

Bloomington

Emergency Crisis Intervention Team
108 West Market Street
Bloomington, IL 61701
Crisis Phone 1: (309) 827-4005
Crisis Phone 2: (800) 570-PATH
Business Phone: (309) 827-5351
Hrs Avail: 24

PATH-Providing Access To Help
201 East Grove
Bloomington, IL 61701
Crisis Phone 1: (309) 827-4005
Crisis Phone 2: (800) 570-7284
Business Phone: (309) 828-1022
Hrs Avail: 24

Carbondale

South Illinois Regional Social Services
604 East College
Suite 101
Carbondale, IL 62901-3399
Crisis Phone 1: (618) 549-3351
Crisis Phone 2: (618) 985-3313
Crisis Phone 3: (618) 549-3352
Crisis Phone 4: (618) 457-7814 (TDD/TTY)
Crisis Phone 5: (800) 269-9981 (toll free Frank./Will. Co.)
Business Phone: (618) 457-6703
http://www.sirss.org
Hrs Avail: 24

Champaign

* Center of Champaign Mental Health
202 W. Park Avenue
Champaign, IL 61820
Crisis Phone 1: (217) 359-4141
Business Phone: (217) 373-2430
Hrs Avail: 24

Chicago, North

Connection Resource Services
3001 Greenbay Road
Chicago, IL 60064
Crisis Phone 1: (800) 310-1234
Business Phone: (847) 689-4357
Hrs Avail: 24

Chicago

In Touch Helpline
University of Illinois
2010 Student Service Building
Chicago, IL 60607
Crisis Phone 1: (312) 996-5535
Business Phone: (312) 996-3490
Hrs Avail: M-F 9 A.M.–5 P.M.

Clinton

Dewitt City Human Resource Center
P.O. Box 616
Clinton, IL 61727
Crisis Phone 1: (217) 935-9496
Business Phone: (217) 935-9496
Hrs Avail: 24

Du Quoin

Perry County Counseling Center
1016 South Madison Street
Suite A
Du Quoin, IL 62832
Crisis Phone 1: (618) 542-4357
Business Phone: (618) 542-4357
Hrs Avail: 24

Edgemont

Call for Help, Suicide & Crisis Intervention
9400 Lebanon Road
Edgemont, IL 62203
Crisis Phone 1: (618) 397-0992
Crisis Phone 2: (618) 397-0963
Business Phone: (618) 397-0968
Hrs Avail: 24

Elgin

Ecker Center for Mental Health
1845 Grandstand Place
Elgin, IL 60123
Crisis Phone 1: (847) 888-2211
Business Phone: (847) 695-0484
Hrs Avail: 24

Freeport

Contact Stephenson Co.
P.O. Box 83
Freeport, IL 61032
Crisis Phone 1: (815) 233-4357
Business Phone: (815) 233-4402
Hrs Avail: 24

Galesburg

Bridgeway, Inc.
2323 Windish Drive
Galesburg, IL 61401
Crisis Phone 1: (800) 322-7143
Business Phone: (309) 344-2323
Hrs Avail: 24

Hillsboro

Montgomery Co. Health Dept.
11191 Illinois Route 185
Hillsboro, IL 62049
Crisis Phone 1: (888) 324-5052
Business Phone: (217) 532-2001
Hrs Avail: 24

Joliet

Will County Mental Health Center
501 Ella Avenue
Joliet, IL 60433
Crisis Phone 1: (815) 727-8512
Business Phone: (815) 727-8512
www.willcountyhealth.org
Hrs Avail: 24

Lincoln

Lincoln Crisis Clinic/Logan-Mason Mental Health Center
304 8th Street
Lincoln, IL 62656
Crisis Phone 1: (217) 732-3600
Business Phone: (217) 732-2161
Hrs Avail: 24

Lombard

Dupage County Health Dept. MH Division-Access & Crisis Center
440 South Finley Road
Lombard, IL 60148
Crisis Phone 1: (630) 627-1700
Crisis Phone 2: (630) 932-1447 (TTY)

Business Phone: (630) 627-1700
Hrs avail: 24

Mattoon

Coles County Mental Health Center
P.O. Box 1307
Mattoon, IL 61938-1307
Crisis Phone 1: (217) 234-6405
Crisis Phone 2: (217) 234-6421 (TTY)
Business Phone: (217) 234-6405
Hrs Avail: 24

Moline

The Robert Young Center
4600 3rd Street
Moline, IL 61265
Crisis Phone 1: (800) 322-1431 (toll free)
Crisis Phone 2: (309) 779-2999
Business Phone: (309) 779-2043
Hrs Avail: 24

Mt. Vernon

Mt. Vernon Crisis Line
Comprehensive Services
P.O. Box 428
Mt. Vernon, IL 62864
Crisis Phone 1: (618) 242-1512
Business Phone: (618) 242-1510
Hrs Avail: 24

Paris

Human Resources Center
P.O. Box 1118
Paris, IL 61944
(217) 465-4141
Business Phone: (217) 465-4118
www.hrcec.org
Hrs Avail: 24

Peoria

Mental Health Assn. of Illinois Valley
5407 North University
Peoria, IL 61614
Crisis Phone 1: (309) 673-7373
Business Phone: (309) 692-1766
http://www.mhaiv.org
Hrs Avail: 24

Quincy

Transitions of Western Illinois
4409 Maine
Quincy, IL 62301
Crisis Phone 1: (217) 222-1166
Business Phone: (217) 223-0413
www.twi.org
Hrs Avail: 24

Rockford

Contact of Rockford
P.O. Box 1976
Rockford, IL 61110
Crisis Phone 1: (815) 636-5000
Business Phone: (815) 636-5001
Hrs Avail: 24

Sullivan

Sullivan Crisis Line
Moultree Co. Counseling Center
2 West Adams
Sullivan, IL 61951
Crisis Phone 1: (217) 728-7611
Business Phone: (217) 728-4358
Hrs Avail: 24

Taylorville

Taylorville Helpline—Christian Co. Mental Health Center
730 North Pawnee
Taylorville, IL 62568
Crisis Phone 1: (217) 824-4905
Crisis Phone 2: (217) 824-3335

Business Phone: (217) 824-4905
Hrs Avail: 24

Woodstock

McHenry County Crisis Program
P.O. Box 1990
Woodstock, IL 60098
Crisis Phone 1: (800) 892-8900
Business Phone: (815) 338-2910
http://www.mchenry-crisis.org

INDIANA

Anderson

Contact/Help of Madison County
P.O. Box 303
Anderson, IN 46015
Crisis Phone 1: (765) 649-5211
Business Phone: (765) 649-4939
Hrs Avail: 24

Evansville

* Southwestern Indiana MHC, Inc.
415 Mulberry
Evansville, IN 47713
Crisis Phone 1: (812) 423-7791
Business Phone: (812) 423-7791
Hrs Avail: 24

Gary

Rape Line—Crisis Center
101 North Montgomery
Gary, IN 46403
Crisis Phone 1: (219) 938-0900
Business Phone: (219) 938-7070
Hrs Avail: 24

Greenwood

Valle Vista Hospital Access Center
898 East Main Street
Greenwood, IN 46143

Crisis Phone 1: (317) 887-1348
Business Phone: (317) 887-
1348
www.bhcvallevista.com
Hrs Avail: 24

Indianapolis

Custer Center-Tri Meridian
P.O. Box 44757
Indianapolis, IN 46208
Crisis Phone 1: (877)
NOGAMBLE
Business Phone: (317) 929-
1010
www.trimeridian.com
Hrs Avail: 24

**Indianapolis Community
Hospital, Inc. Access
Services**
7150 Clearvista Drive
Indianapolis, IN 46256
Crisis Phone 1: (317) 621-5700
Crisis Phone 2: (800) 662-3445
(toll free)
Business Phone: (317) 621-
5100
www.commhospiny.org
Hrs Avail: 24

*** Mental Health Assoc. of
Marion Co.**
Crisis & Suicide Intervention
Service
2506 Willowbrook Parkway 100
Indianapolis, IN 46205
Crisis Phone 1: (317) 251-7575
Business Phone: (317) 251-
0005
www.MCMHA.org
Hrs Avail: 24

Lafayette

* Lafayette Crisis Center
1244 North 15th Street
Lafayette, IN 47904
Crisis Phone 1: (765) 742-0244
Business Phone: (765) 742-0247

www.indy.net/~Lafcc
Hrs Avail: 24

Lawrenceburg

**Community Mental Health
Center**
285 Bielby Road
Lawrenceburg, IN 47025
Crisis Phone 1: (812) 537-1302
Crisis Phone 2: (877) 849-1248
(toll free)
Business Phone: (812) 537-1302
www.CMHCINC.org
Hrs Avail: 24

Lebanon

**Mental Health Assoc. in
Boone County**
227 W. Main Street
Suite 314
Lebanon, IN 46052
Crisis Phone 1: (765) 482-1599
Business Phone: (765) 482-3020
Hrs Avail: 24

Merrillville

**Contact—Cares of NW
Indiana**
P.O. Box 10247
Merrillville, IN 46411
Crisis Phone 1: (219) 769-3141
Business Phone: (219) 769-0611
Hrs Avail: 24

Monticello

Twin Lakes Contact—Help
P.O. Box 67
Monticello, IN 47960
Crisis Phone 1: (219) 583-4357
Business Phone: (219) 583-
4357
Hrs Avail: 24

Terre Haute

Vigo Co. Lifeline Inc.
P.O. Box 1017
Terre Haute, IN 47808-1017

Crisis Phone 1: (812) 235-8333
Crisis Phone 2: (877) 377-5433
(toll free)
Crisis Phone 3: (812) 234-5672
(teen line)
Business Phone: (812) 238-
2620
Hrs Avail: 24

IOWA

Cedar Rapids

* Foundation 2, Crisis Center
1540 2nd Avenue
Cedar Rapids, IA 52403
Crisis Phone 1: (319) 362-2174
Business Phone: (319) 362-
2176
Hrs Avail: M-F 8 A.M.–6 P.M.

Davenport

Genesis Medical Center
1227 East Rusholme
Davenport, IA 52803
Crisis Phone 1: (563) 421-2975
Business Phone: (563) 421-
2948
Hrs Avail: 24

Des Moines

*** Community Telephone
Service Crisis Line**
Service of the Amer. Red Cross
2116 Grand Avenue
Des Moines, IA 50312
Crisis Phone 1: (515) 244-1000
Crisis Phone 2: (800) 244-7431
Business Phone: (515) 244-
6700
Hrs Avail: 24

Dubuque

Phone A Friend Crisis Line
3505 Stoneman Road
Suite 5
Dubuque, IA 52002
Crisis Phone 1: (319) 588-4016

Business Phone: (319) 557-
8331
Hrs Avail: 24

Iowa City

Iowa City Crisis Center
1121 Gilbert Court
Iowa City, IA 52240
Crisis Phone 1: (319) 351-0140
Business Phone: (319) 351-
2726
www.johnsoncountycrisiscenter.
org
Hrs Avail: 24

Sioux City

Aid Center
715 Douglas Street
Sioux City, IA 51101
Crisis Phone 1: (712) 252-5000
Business Phone: (712) 252-
1861
Hrs Avail: 24

Waterloo

**Family Service League Crisis
Service**
3830 West 9th Street
Waterloo, IA 50702
Crisis Phone 1: (319) 233-8484
Business Phone: (319) 233-
8484
Hrs Avail: 24

KANSAS

Emporia

Emporia Emergency Services
MH Center of E. Central Kansas
1000 Lincoln
Emporia, KS 66801
Crisis Phone 1: (316) 343-
2626
Business Phone: (316) 342-
0548
www.MHCECK.org
Hrs Avail: 24

Garden City

Garden City Area MHC
11111 East Spruce
Garden City, KS 67846
Crisis Phone 1: (316) 276-7689
Business Phone: (316) 276-
7689
www.amhc.org
Hrs Avail: 24

Humboldt

SE Kansas MHS Emer. Line
1106 South 9th Street
Humboldt, KS 66748
Crisis Phone 1: (316) 223-5030
Crisis Phone 2: (316) 431-7890
Business Phone: (316) 473-
2241
Hrs Avail: 24

Kansas City

**The Mental Health Assoc. of
the Heartland**
739 Minnesota Avenue
Kansas City, KS 66101-2703
Crisis Phone 1: (913) 281-1234
Crisis Phone 2: (913) 281-2299
(teen line)
Business Phone: (913) 981-
2221
Hrs Avail: 9 A.M.–9 P.M.

**Wyandotte Mental Health
Center**
36th and Eaton
Kansas City, KS 66103
Crisis Phone 1: (913) 831-1773
Business Phone: (913) 831-
9500
www.WMHCI.org
Hrs Avail: 24

Lawrence

*** Headquarters Counseling
Center**
P.O. Box 999
Lawrence, KS 66044

Crisis Phone 1: (785) 841-
2345
Business Phone: (785) 841-
2345
www.hqcc.lawrence.ks.us
Hrs Avail: 24

Salina

**Hotline Crisis Info. &
Referral**
227 North Sante Fe
Suite 203
Salina, KS 67401
Crisis Phone 1: (785) 827-4747
Business Phone: (785) 827-
4803
Hrs Avail: 24

Scott City

**Scott City Area Mental
Health Center**
210 West 4th
Scott City, KS 67871
Crisis Phone 1: (316) 334-5619
Business Phone: (316) 872-
5338
Hrs Avail: 24

Topeka

The Consortium Inc.
534 S. Kansas Avenue
Suite 600
Topeka, KS 66603
Crisis Phone 1: (866) NOBETOO
Business Phone: (785) 232-
1196
Hrs Avail: 24

Ulysses

**Ulysses Area Mental Health
Center**
P.O. Box 757
Ulysses, KS 67880
Crisis Phone 1: (316) 356-3198
Business Phone: (316) 356-
3198
Hrs Avail: 24

Wichita

COMCARE of Sedgwick Co.
934 North Water
Wichita, KS 67203
Crisis Phone 1: (316) 356-3198
Business Phone: (316) 356-3198
Hrs Avail: 24

KENTUCKY

Ashland

Pathways Inc. of Ashland
P.O. Box 790
Ashland, KY 41144
Crisis Phone 1: (608) 324-1141
Business Phone: (608) 324-1141
Hrs Avail: 24

Bowling Green

* Life Skills Helpline
707 East Main Street
Bowling Green, KY 42101
Crisis Phone 1: (270) 843-4357
Business Phone: (270) 843-4357
Hrs Avail: 24

Corbin

Cumberland River Comprehensive Care Center
P.O. Box 568
Corbin, KY 40702
Crisis Phone 1: (606) 528-7010
Business Phone: (606) 528-7010
Hrs Avail: 8 A.M.–4:30 P.M.

Elizabethtown

Elizabethtown Crisis Line
1311 North Dixie
Elizabethtown, KY 42701
Crisis Phone 1: (270) 769-1304
Business Phone: (270) 765-2605
Hrs Avail: 24

Hopkinsville

Hopkinsville Crisis Line—Pennyroyal Regional Mental Health
735 North Drive
Hopkinsville, KY 42240
Crisis Phone 1: (270) 881-9551
Business Phone: (270) 886-5163
Hrs Avail: 24

Jackson

Kentucky River Community Care
3775 Highway 15 South
Jackson, KY 41339
Crisis Phone 1: (800) 262-7491
Business Phone: (606) 666-9278
Hrs Avail: 24

Lexington

Bluegrass Regional MH
201 Mechanic Street
Lexington, KY 40507
Crisis Phone 1: (800) 928-8000
Business Phone: (859) 253-2737
Hrs Avail: 24

Louisville

Crisis & Information Center
101 West Muhammad Ali Boulevard
Louisville, KY 40202
Crisis Phone 1: (502) 568-2325
Business Phone: (502) 589-8630
www.sevencounties.org
Hrs Avail: 24

Owensboro

River Valley Behavioral Health
1100 Walnut Street
Owensboro, KY 42301
Crisis Phone 1: (270) 684-9466

Business Phone: (270) 689-6500
www.rvbh.com
Hrs Avail: 24

Prestonsburg

Mountain Comprehensive Care Center
150 South Front Avenue
Prestonsburg, KY 41653
Crisis Phone 1: (800) 422-1060
Business Phone: (606) 886-8572
Hrs Avail: 24

LOUISIANA

Baton Rouge

* Baton Rouge Crisis Intervention Center
4837 Revere Avenue
Baton Rouge, LA 70808
Crisis Phone 1: (225) 924-3900
Business Phone: (225) 924-1431
www.brcic.org
Hrs Avail: 24

De Ridder

Beauregard De Ridder Community Help-line
P.O. Box 815
De Ridder, LA 70634
Crisis Phone 1: (337) 462-0609
Crisis Phone 2: (800) 54 ABUSE
Business Phone: (337) 462-1452
Hrs Avail: 24

Monroe

Mainline
P.O. Box 1322
Monroe, LA 71210
Crisis Phone 1: (318) 387-5683
Business Phone: (318) 343-3585
Hrs Avail: 6 P.M.–6 A.M.

Young Womens Christian Association (YWCA)
1515 Jackson Street
Monroe, LA 71202

Crisis Phone 1: (318) 323-4112
Crisis Phone 2: (318) 323-1505
Crisis Phone 3: (318) 325-3611
Crisis Phone 4: (318) 323-9034
  (teen line)
Business Phone: (318) 323-
  1505
http://www.ywcanela.org
Hrs Avail: 8 A.M.–5 P.M.

New Orleans

*** River Oaks Admission and
  Referral**
1525 River Oaks Road West
New Orleans, LA 70123
Crisis Phone 1: (504) 734-1740
Crisis Phone 2: (800) 366-1740
Business Phone: (504) 734-
  2199
www.riveroakshospital.com
Hrs Avail: 24

* VIA LINK
928 Calhoun Street
New Orleans, LA 70118
Crisis Phone 1: (504) 895-5502
Business Phone: (504) 895-
  5550
Hrs Avail: M-F 8 A.M.–5 P.M.

MAINE

Augusta

**Kennebec Somerset Crisis
  Response**
32 Wintrap Street
Augusta, ME 04330
Crisis Phone 1: (888) 568-1112
Business Phone: (207) 626-
  3448
Hrs Avail: 24

Biddeford

* Crisis Response Services
4201 Connecticut Avenue, NW
Suite 408
Biddeford, ME 04005
Crisis Phone 1: (207) 282-6136

Crisis Phone 2: (800) 660-8500
  (toll free)
Crisis Phone 3: (888) 568-1112
  (toll free)
Business Phone: (202) 237-
  2280
http://www.suicidology.org
Hrs Avail: 24

Farmington

*** Evergreen Behavioral
  Services**
RR4 Box 5122A
Farmington, ME 04938
Crisis Phone 1: (800) 394-1900
Business Phone: (207) 778-0035
http://www.fchn.org

Lewiston

**Tri Co. MH Service, Crisis
  Intervention Unit**
484 Main Street
Lewiston, ME 04240-2008
Crisis Phone 1: (888) 568-1112
Crisis Phone 2: (207) 783-4680
Crisis Phone 3: (207) 783-4681
Crisis Phone 4: (207) 783-4682
Crisis Phone 5: (207) 783-4696
Business Phone: (207) 783-
  4695
Hrs Avail: 24

Machias

**Northeast Crisis
  Service/Phone Help**
P.O. Box 29
Machias, ME 04654-0558
Crisis Phone 1: (888) 568-1112
Business Phone: (207) 255-
  6904
www.wcpa.net
Hrs Avail: 24

Portland

* Ingraham
P.O. Box 1868
Portland, ME 04104

Crisis Phone 1: (207) 774-4357
Crisis Phone 2: (888) 568-1112
Business Phone: (207) 874-
  1055
www.ingraham.org
Hrs Avail: M-F 8 A.M.–5 P.M.

Rumford

*** GRAMI-Oxford County
  MH**
150 Congress Street
Rumford, ME 04276
Crisis Phone 1: (207) 364-3030
Crisis Phone 2: (800) 335-9999
  (toll free)
Crisis Phone 3: (888) 568-1112
  (toll free)
Business Phone: (207) 364-
  3549
http://www.grami.org
Hrs Avail: 24

Saco

*** Cumberland County Crisis
  Response Inc.**
50 Moody Street
Saco, ME 04072
Crisis Phone 1: (207) 774-4357
Crisis Phone 2: (207) 282-6136
Business Phone: (207) 284-5981
www.ingraham.org
Hrs Avail: 24

Skowhegan

* Crisis Stabilization Unit
P.O. Box 588
Skowhegan, ME 04976
Crisis Phone 1: (207) 474-2506
Crisis Phone 2: (888) 568-1112
Business Phone: (207) 474-2564
Hrs Avail: 24

Waterville

*** Kennebec Valley Mental
  Health Center**
67 Eustis Parkway
Waterville, ME 04901

Crisis Phone 1: (888) 568-1112
Crisis Phone 2: (207) 873-2136
  (weekdays only)
Business Phone: (207) 873-
  2136
Hrs Avail: 24

MARYLAND

Baltimore

* First Step
8303 Liberty Road
Baltimore, MD 21244
Crisis Phone 1: (410) 521-3800
Business Phone: (410) 628-6120
http://www.firststepmd.org
Hrs Avail: M-Th 9 A.M.–9 P.M.; F
  9 A.M.–4 P.M.; S 9 A.M.–1 P.M.

Baltimore Crisis Line
Sinai Hospital
Belvedere and Greenspring
  Avenue
Baltimore, MD 21215
Weekdays: (410) 601-5457
Evenings & Weekends: (410)
  601-5902
Business Phone: (410) 601-5457
Hrs Avail: 24

*** Baltimore Crisis Response,
  Inc.**
1105 Light Street
Baltimore, MD 21230
Crisis Phone 1: (410) 752-2272
Business Phone: (410) 576-
  5097 x310
Hrs Avail: 24

Columbia

*** Grassroots Crisis
  Intervention Center**
6700 Freetown Road
Columbia, MD 21044
Crisis Phone 1: (410) 531-6677
Business Phone: (410) 531-6006
www.grassrootscrisis.org
Hrs Avail: 24

Easton

For All Seasons, Inc.
300 Talbot Street
Easton, MD 21601
Crisis Phone 1: (410) 820-5600
Crisis Phone 2: (800) 310-7273
Business Phone: (410) 822-
  1018
Hrs Avail: 24

Frederick

* Frederick County Hotline
263 West Patrick Street
Frederick, MD 21701
Crisis Phone 1: (301) 662-2255
Crisis Phone 2: (800) 422-0009
  (youth crisis)
Crisis Phone 3: (301) 694-8255
Crisis Phone 4: (301) 662-2255
Business Phone: (301) 663-0011
Hrs Avail: 24

Glen Burnie

**Anne Arundel Co. Crisis
  Response System**
7493 Baltimore-Annapolis
  Boulevard
Glen Burnie, MD 21061
Crisis Phone 1: (410) 768-5522
Business Phone: (410) 768-
  1875
http://www.thesantegroup.org
Hrs Avail: 24

Hyattsville

*** Prince Georges County
  Hotline & Suicide
  Prevention Center**
P.O. Box 149
Hyattsville, MD 20781-0149
Crisis Phone 1: (301) 864-7130
  (teens)
Crisis Phone 2: (800) 422-0009
Crisis Phone 3: (301) 864-7130
Crisis Phone 4: (301) 864-7161
Crisis Phone 5: (301) 927-4500

Business Phone: (301) 864-7095
http://www.pghotline.org
Hrs Avail: 24

Lanham

*** Prince Georges Co. Crisis
  Response Team/Affiliated
  Sante Group**
8200 Corporate Drive
Lanham, MD 20785
Crisis Phone 1: (410) 768-5522
Business Phone: (301) 429-
  2181
http://www.thesantegroup.org
Hrs Avail: 24

Rockville

*** Montgomery County Hot-
  line c/o MH Association**
1000 Twinbrook Parkway
Rockville, MD 20851
Crisis Phone 1: (301) 424-CALL
Crisis Phone 2: (301) 738-9697
  (teen line)
Business Phone: (301) 424-
  0656
http://www.mhamc.org
Hrs Avail: 24

Salisbury

Life Crisis Center
P.O. Box 387
Salisbury, MD 21803
Crisis Phone 1: (410) 749-4357
Crisis Phone 2: (410) 749-4363
Crisis Phone 3: (410) 749-0688
  (TTY)
Crisis Phone 4: (800) 422-0009
  (toll free)
Business Phone: (410) 749-0632
Hrs Avail: 24

Waldorf

Center for Abused Persons
2670 Crane Highway
Suite 303
Waldorf, MD 20601

Crisis Phone 1: (301) 843-1110
(DC metro line)
Crisis Phone 2: (301) 645-3337
Crisis Phone 3: (301) 645-3336
Crisis Phone 4: (301) 645-9389
(teen line)
Business Phone: (301) 645-
8994
Hrs Avail: 24

White Marsh

**Baltimore Co. Crisis
Response System**
7939 Honeygo Boulevard
White Marsh, MD 21236
Crisis Phone 1: (410) 931-2214
Crisis Phone 2: (410) 931-2116
Business Phone: (410) 931-
2116
http://www.thesantegroup.org
Hrs Avail: 24

MASSACHUSETTS

Attleboro

New Hope/Attleboro
140 Park Street
Attleboro, MA 02703
Crisis Phone 1: (800) 323-4673
Business Phone: (508) 226-
4015
www.new-hope.org
Hrs Avail: 24

Boston

* The Samaritans of Boston
654 Beacon Street
Boston, MA 02215
Crisis Phone 1: (617) 247-0220
Business Phone: (617) 536-
2460
Hrs Avail: 24

Fall River

*** Samaritans of Fall River-
New Bedford, Inc.**
P.O. Box 9642
Fall River, MA 02720

Crisis Phone 1: (508) 999-7267
Business Phone: (508) 679-
9777
Hrs Avail: 8 A.M.–11 P.M.

Falmouth

*** Samaritans on Cape Cod
and the Islands, Inc.**
P.O. Box 65
Falmouth, MA 02541
Crisis Phone 1: (508) 548-8900
Crisis Phone 2: (800) 893-9900
Business Phone: (508) 548-
7999
www.capesamaritans.org
Hrs Avail: 24

Framingham

* Samaritans Suburban West
235 Walnut Street
Framingham, MA 01702
Crisis Phone 1: (877) 875-4500
Business Phone: (508) 872-
1780
Hrs Avail: M-F 9 A.M.–5 P.M.

Haverhill

**N. Essex MH Center-Crisis
Service & Central Intake**
60 Merrimack Street
Haverhill, MA 01830
Crisis Phone 1: (978) 521-7763
Crisis Phone 2: (800) 281-3223
Business Phone: (978) 521-
7777
http://www.hes.com
Hrs Avail: 24

Holyoke

**Mt. Tom Mental Health
Center**
40 Bobala Road
Holyoke, MA 01040
Crisis Phone 1: (413) 536-2251
Business Phone: (413) 536-
5473
Hrs Avail: 24

Methuen

*** Samaritans of Merrimack
Valley**
169 East Street
Methuen, MA 01844
Crisis Phone 1: (888) 767-8336
(teen line)
Crisis Phone 2: (978) 452-6733
Crisis Phone 3: (978) 465-6100
Crisis Phone 4: (978) 372-7200
Crisis Phone 5: (978) 688-6607
Business Phone: (978) 688-0030
Hrs Avail: 24

Northampton

**Service Net-Emergency
Services of Northampton**
129 King Street
Northampton, MA 01702
Crisis Phone 1: (413) 586-5555
Business Phone: (413) 586-
5555
Hrs Avail: 24

Norwood

* Riverside Community Care
190 Lenox Street
Norwood, MA 02062
Crisis Phone 1: (781) 769-8674
Business Phone: (781) 769-8670
www.riversidecc.com
Hrs Avail: 24

Southbridge

Y.O.U. Inc. Family Services
52 Charlton Street
Southbridge, MA 01550
Crisis Phone 1: (800) 435-9990
Business Phone: (508) 765-
9101
http://www.youinc.org
Hrs Avail: 24

Springfield

Psychiatric Crisis Services
503 State Street
Springfield, MA 01109

Crisis Phone 1: (413) 733-6661
Business Phone: (413) 746-
3758
Hrs Avail: 24

Westfield

Westfield Crisis Team
77 Mill Street
Westfield, MA 01085
Crisis Phone 1: (413) 568-6386
(TTY)
Hrs Avail: 24

Worcester

Crisis Center Y.O.U. Inc.
81 Plantation Street
Worcester, MA 01604
Crisis Phone 1: (508) 791-6562
Business Phone: (508) 849-
5600
www.youinc.org
Hrs Avail: 24

MICHIGAN

Ann Arbor

**University of Michigan
Health Systems**
1500 East Medical Center Drive
Ann Arbor, MI 48109
Crisis Phone 1: (734) 996-4747
Business Phone: (734) 936-
5900
Hrs Avail: 24

Bloomfield Hill

Common Ground Sanctuary
1410 South Telegraph
Bloomfield Hills, MI 48302
Crisis Phone 1: (800) 231-1127
(toll free)
Crisis Phone 2: (248) 456-0909
Crisis Phone 3: (248) 292-0194
Business Phone: (248) 456-8150
www.commongroundsanctu-
ary.org
Hrs Avail: 24

Cadillac

**North Central Community
M.H.**
527 Cobbs
Cadillac, MI 49601
Crisis Phone 1: (231) 775-3463
Crisis Phone 2: (800) 492-5742
Crisis Phone 3: (800) 442-7315
Business Phone: (231) 775-
3463
Hrs Avail: 24

Coldwater

**Pines Behavioral Health
Services**
200 Orleans Boulevard
Coldwater, MI 49036
Crisis Phone 1: (517) 279-1193
Crisis Phone 2: (888) 725-7534
Business Phone: (517) 279-8404
http://www.pinesbhs.org
Hrs Avail: 24

Detroit

*** Neighborhood Service
Organization**
220 Bagley
Suite 200
Detroit, MI 48226
Crisis Phone 1: (313) 224-7000
Crisis Phone 2: (800) 241-4949
Business Phone: (313) 961-1060
Hrs Avail: 24

East Lansing

**Gateway Community
Services**
910 Abbott Road
Suite 100
East Lansing, MI 48823
Crisis Phone 1: (800) 292-4517
Crisis Phone 2: (800) 292-4357
(parent helpline)
Business Phone: (517) 351-4000
http://www.gatewayservices.org
Hrs Avail: 24

The Listening Ear, Inc.
1017 East Grand River
East Lansing, MI 48823
Crisis Phone 1: (517) 337-1717
Business Phone: (517) 337-
1728
Hrs Avail: 24

Flint

**Mental Health Crisis Clinic—
Genesee Co. Mental Health**
918 Patrick Street
Flint, MI 48503
Crisis Phone 1: (810) 257-3740
Business Phone: (810) 232-
5850
www.gencmh.org
Hrs Avail: 24

Holland

Ottawa County Helpline
12265 James Street
Holland, MI 49424
Crisis Phone 1: (616) 396-4357
Crisis Phone 2: (616) 393-4357
(TTY)
Business Phone: (616) 392-
1873
Hrs Avail: 24

Kalamazoo

* Gryphon Place
1104 South Westnedge
Kalamazoo, MI 49008
Crisis Phone 1: (616) 381-4357
Business Phone: (616) 381-
1510
www.gryphon.org
Hrs Avail: 24

Lapeer

Lapeer Co. Comm. MHC
1570 Suncrest Drive
Lapeer, MI 48446
Crisis Phone 1: (888) 225-4447
Business Phone: (810) 667-0500
Hrs Avail: 24

Mt. Pleasant

Listening Ear Crisis Center, Inc.
P.O. Box 800
Mt. Pleasant, MI 48804
Crisis Phone 1: (989) 772-2918
Business Phone: (989) 773-6904
Hrs Avail: 24

Muskegon

Comm. MH Services of Muskegon Co.
376 East Apple
Muskegon, MI 49442
Crisis Phone 1: (231) 720-3200
Business Phone: (231) 720-3200
Hrs Avail: 24

Port Huron

* St. Clair County Community MH Services
1007 Military Street
Port Huron, MI 48060
Crisis Phone 1: (810) 987-6911
Business Phone: (810) 987-7050
www.scccmh.org
Hrs Avail: 24

Saginaw

Crisis Intervention Services- Saginaw City MH Center
500 Hancock
Saginaw, MI 48602
Crisis Phone 1: (517) 792-9732
Crisis Phone 2: (800) 233-0022
Business Phone: (517) 797-3400
Hrs Avail: 24

St. Joseph

The Link Crisis Intervention Center
2002 South State Street
St. Joseph, MI 49085

Crisis Phone 1: (616) 983-0430
Crisis Phone 2: (800) 312-5454
Business Phone: (616) 983-5465
www.link4teens.org
Hrs Avail: 24

Three Rivers

St. Joseph County CMH
210 South Main Street
Three Rivers, MI 49093
Crisis Phone 1: (616) 273-2000
Crisis Phone 2: (800) 622-3967
Business Phone: (616) 273-5000
Hrs Avail: 24

Traverse City

* Third Level Crisis Center
P.O. Box 1035
Traverse City, MI 49685
Crisis Phone 1: (231) 922-4800
Crisis Phone 2: (800) 442-7315
Business Phone: (231) 922-4802
Hrs Avail: 24

Ypsilanti

SOS Crisis Center
101 South Huron
Ypsilanti, MI 48197
Crisis Phone 1: (734) 485-3222
Business Phone: (734) 485-8730
Hrs Avail: 24

MINNESOTA

Alexandria

Listening Ear Crisis Center
700 Cedar Street
Suite 266
Alexandria, MN 56308
Crisis Phone 1: (320) 763-6638
Business Phone: (320) 763-6638
Hrs Avail: 24

Apple Valley

Dakota County Crisis Response Unit
14955 Galaxie Avenue
Apple Valley, MN 55124
Crisis Phone 1: (952) 891-7171
Business Phone: (952) 891-7171
Hrs Avail: 24

Austin

Crime Victims Resource Center
101 14th Street, NW
Suite 5
Austin, MN 55912
Crisis Phone 1: (507) 437-6680
Business Phone: (507) 437-6680
Hrs Avail: 24

Brainerd

Crisis Line & Referral Service
P.O. Box 192
Brainerd, MN 56401
Crisis Phone 1: (218) 828-4357
Crisis Phone 2: (800) 462-5525
Business Phone: (218) 828-4515
Hrs Avail: 24

Grand Rapids

Northland Recovery Center
1215 South East 7th Avenue
Grand Rapids, MN 55744
Crisis Phone 1: (800) 652-9025
Business Phone: (218) 327-1026
Hrs Avail: 24

Minneapolis

Crisis Connection
P.O. Box 19550
Minneapolis, MN 55419
Crisis Phone 1: (612) 379-6363
Business Phone: (612) 379-6369
Hrs Avail: 24

*** Hennepin County Crisis
    Intervention Center**
701 Park Avenue South
Minneapolis, MN 55415
Suicide: (612) 347-2222
Business Phone: (612) 347-3164
Hrs Avail: 24

Owatonna

**Owatonna—Steele Co. Con-
    tact**
P.O. Box 524
Owatonna, MN 55060
Crisis Phone 1: (507) 451-9100
Business Phone: (507) 451-1897
Hrs Avail: 24

St. Paul

**Ramsey County Adult Crisis
    Center**
1919 University
St. Paul, MN 55101
Crisis Phone 1: (651) 523-7900
Business Phone: (651) 523-7999
http://www.co.ramsey.mn.us/
Hrs Avail: 24

MISSISSIPPI

Jackson

* Contact Crisis Line
P.O. Box 5192
Jackson, MS 39296
Crisis Phone 1: (601) 713-HELP
Business Phone: (601) 713-4099
Hrs Avail: 24

MISSOURI

Cape Girardeau

**Community Counseling
    Center**
402 South Silver Springs Road
Cape Girardeau, MO 63703
Crisis Phone 1: (800) 356-5395
Business Phone: (573) 334-
    1100
Hrs Avail: 24

Maryland Heights

*** Behavioral Health
    Response**
P.O. Box 1125
Maryland Heights, MO 63043-
    9881
Crisis Phone 1: (314) 469-6644
    (St. Louis)
Crisis Phone 2: (800) 811-4760
Crisis Phone 3: (800) 811-4760
Business Phone: (877) 469-
    4908
http://www.bhrstl.org
Hrs Avail: 24

Springfield

*** Burrell Center, Inc./Crisis
    Assist Team**
930 South Robberson
Springfield, MO 65807
Crisis Phone 1: (417) 862-6555
Crisis Phone 2: (800) 494-7355
Business Phone: (417) 269-
    5400
Hrs Avail: 24

St. Joseph

**Family Guidance Center for
    Behavioral Health Care**
510 Francis Street
Suite 200
St. Joseph, MO 64501
Crisis Phone 1: (888) 279-8188
Business Phone: (816) 364-1501
Hrs Avail: 24

St. Louis

* Kids Under Twenty One
2718 South Brentwood
St. Louis, MO 63144
Crisis Phone 1: (314) 644-KUTO
Business Phone: (314) 963-
    7571
http://www.KUTO.org
Hrs Avail: Su-Th 4 P.M.–10 P.M.;
    F-Sa 4 P.M.–12 A.M.

* Life Crisis Services, Inc.
1423 South Big Bend Boulevard
St. Louis, MO 63117
Crisis Phone 1: (314) 647-4357
Business Phone: (314) 647-
    3100
www.lifecrisis.org
Hrs Avail: 24

MONTANA

Billings

Mental Health Center
1245 North 29th Street
Billings, MT 59103
Crisis Phone 1: (406) 252-5658
Business Phone: (406) 252-
    5658
Hrs Avail: 24

Bozeman

Bozeman Help Center
421 East Peach
Bozeman, MT 59715
Crisis Phone 1: (406) 586-3333
Business Phone: (406) 587-
    7511
www.bozemanhelpcenter.com
Hrs Avail: 24

Great Falls

Crisis Line-Voices of Hope
P.O. Box 6644
Great Falls, MT 59405
Crisis Phone 1: (406) 453-4357
Business Phone: (406) 771-
    8648x3336
Hrs Avail: 24

Helena

**Golden Triangle Community
    MH Center**
1101 Missoula
Helena, MT 59601
Crisis Phone 1: (406) 443-5353
Business Phone: (406) 443-4922
Hrs Avail: 24

Kalispell

Lamplighter Health
860 North Meridian
Kalispell, MT 59901
Crisis Phone 1: (406) 752-6262
Business Phone: (406) 257-1336
Hrs Avail: 24

NEBRASKA

Boys Town

Girls & Boys Town National Hotline
13940 Gutowski Road
Boys Town, NE 68010
Crisis Phone 1: (800) 448-3000
(national hotline)
Crisis Phone 2: (800) 448-1833
(national TDD)
Business Phone: (402) 498-1831
http://www.boystown.org
Hrs Avail: 24

Lincoln

Community Mental Health
2200 St. Marys
Lincoln, NE 68502
Crisis Phone 1: (402) 441-7940
Business Phone: (402) 441-7940
Hrs Avail: 24

North Platte

Heartland Counseling and Consulting Clinic
110 North Bailey
North Platte, NE 69103
Crisis Phone 1: (308) 534-6963
Business Phone: (308) 534-6029
Hrs Avail: 24

NEVADA

Reno

* Crisis Call Center
P.O. Box 8016
Reno, NV 89507
Crisis Phone 1: (877) 885-HOPE
Business Phone: (775) 784-8085
Hrs Avail: 24

NEW HAMPSHIRE

Berlin

Berlin Mental Health Center
3 12th Street
Berlin, NH 03570
Crisis Phone 1: (603) 752-7404
Business Phone: (603) 752-7404
http://www.nnhmhds.org
Hrs Avail: 24

Concord

* Riverbend Community MH services
P.O. Box 2032
Concord, NH 03302
Crisis Phone 1: (603) 226-0817
Business Phone: (603) 226-0817
www.riverbendcmhc.org
Hrs Avail: 24

Conway

Carroll Co. MH
25 West Main Street
Conway, NH 3818
Crisis Phone 1: (603) 447-2111
Business Phone: (603) 447-2111
Hrs Avail: 9 A.M.–5 P.M.

Northern New Hampshire MH & Development
87 Washington Street
Conway, NH 03818
Crisis Phone 1: (603) 447-2111
(Carroll Co.)
Crisis Phone 2: (603) 237-4955
(Colbrook)
Crisis Phone 3: (603) 752-7404
(Aderscogen Valley)
Crisis Phone 4: (603) 636-2555
(Groveton)

Business Phone: (603) 447-3347
http://www.nnhmhds.org
Hrs Avail: 24

Dairy

* CLM Behavioral Health Systems
43 Birch Street
Dairy, NH 03038
Crisis Phone 1: (603) 434-1577
(after 5pm)
Crisis Phone 2: (800) 762-8191
(toll free)
Business Phone: (603) 434-1577
Hrs Avail: 24

Dover

* Strafford Guidance Center, Inc.
Emergency Crisis Team
103 Central Avenue
Dover, NH 03820
Crisis Phone 1: (603) 742-0630
Business Phone: (603) 742-0630
Hrs Avail: 24

Keene

* The Samaritans of the Monadnock Region
103 Roxbury Street
Suite 304
Keene, NH 03431
Crisis Phone 1: (603) 357-5505
Business Phone: (603) 357-5510
Hrs Avail: 24

Laconia

* Genesis—The Counseling Group
111 Church Street
Laconia, NH 03246
Crisis Phone 1: (603) 528-0305
Business Phone: (603) 528-0305
Hrs Avail: 5 P.M.–8 A.M.

Lebanon

* Headrest, Inc.
P.O. Box 247
Lebanon, NH 03766
Crisis Phone 1: (603) 448-4400
Business Phone: (603) 448-4872
www.headrest.org
Hrs Avail: 24

Manchester

* MHC of Greater Manchester
401 Cypress Street
Manchester, NH 03103
Crisis Phone 1: (603) 668-4111 (TTY)
Business Phone: (603) 668-4111
Hrs Avail: 24

Pembroke

Community Services Council of NH
P.O. Box 2338
Pembroke, NH 03275
Crisis Phone 1: (603) 225-9000
Crisis Phone 2: (800) 852- 3388
Business Phone: (603) 225-9694
http://www.nhhelpline.org
Hrs Avail: 24

Portsmouth

Seacoast Mental Health Services
1145 Sagamore Avenue
Portsmouth, NH 03801
Crisis Phone 1: (603) 431-6703
Business Phone: (603) 431-6703
Hrs Avail: 24

NEW JERSEY

Atlantic City

Psychiatric Intervention Program

Atlantic City Medical Center
1941 Pacific Avenue
Atlantic City, NJ 08401
Crisis Phone 1: (609) 344-1118
Business Phone: (609) 344-1118x2883
Hrs Avail: 24

Bridgeton

Crisis Hotline-Cumberland Co. Guidance Center
333 Irving Avenue
Bridgeton, NJ 08302
Crisis Phone 1: (856) 455-5555
Crisis Phone 2: (856) 455-7621 (TTY)
Business Phone: (856) 455-5555
Hrs Avail: 24

Ewing

Contact Mercer Co.
1985 Pennington Road
Ewing, NJ 8618
Crisis Phone 1: (609) 896-2120
Business Phone: (609) 883-2880
Hrs Avail: 24

Flemington

Hunterdon Helpline
P.O. Box 246
Flemington, NJ 08822
Crisis Phone 1: (908) 782-4357
Business Phone: (908) 735-4357
Hrs Avail: 24

Glassboro

Center for Family Services
250 S. Delsea Drive
Glassboro, NJ 08028
Crisis Phone 1: (856) 728-1085
Business Phone: (856) 728-7045
Hrs Avail: 24

Hoboken

St. Marys Community MH
506 3rd Street
Hoboken, NJ 07030
Crisis Phone 1: (201) 795-5505
Business Phone: (201) 792-8200
Hrs Avail: 24

Lyndhurst

Comprehensive Behavioral Healthcare Inc.
516 Valley Brook Avenue
Lyndhurst, NJ 07071
Crisis Phone 1: (201) 935-3322
Crisis Phone 2: (201) 646-0333
Business Phone: (201) 935-3322
http://www.comcare.org
Hrs Avail: M-Th 9 A.M.–9 P.M.; F 9 A.M.–5 P.M.

Morrestown

Contact Burlington Co.
P.O. Box 333
Moorestown, NJ 08057
Crisis Phone 1: (609) 234-8888
Business Phone: (856) 234-5484
www.contactburlco.org
Hrs Avail: 24

Morristown

Crisis Hotline
100 Madison Avenue
Morristown, NJ 07962
Crisis Phone 1: (973) 540-0100
Business Phone: (973) 540-0100
Hrs Avail: 24

Mt. Holly

Screening and Crisis Interv. Program
Co. Memorial Hospital
175 Madison Avenue
Mt. Holly, NJ 08060

Crisis Phone 1: (609) 261-8000
Business Phone: (609) 261-
8000
Hrs Avail: 24

Newark

**Emergency Psychiatric
Services**
100 Bergen Street
Newark, NJ 07103
Crisis Phone 1: (973) 623-2323
Business Phone: (973) 972-
0480
Hrs Avail: 24

Paramus

**262 Help County Crisis
Hotline**
610 Industrial Boulevard
Paramus, NJ 07652
Crisis Phone 1: (201) 262-4357
Crisis Phone 2: (201) 795-5505
Crisis Phone 3: (201) 262-7462
Business Phone: (201) 262-
7108
http://www.careplusnj.org
Hrs Avail: 24

Pequannock

Contact Hotline
P.O. Box 219
Pequannock, NJ 07440
Crisis Phone 1: (973) 831-1870
Business Phone: (973) 831-
1879
Hrs Avail: 24

Red Bank

Helpline-Crisis Unit
Riverview Medical Center
1 Riverview Plaza
Red Bank, NJ 07701
Crisis Phone 1: (732) 219-5325
Business Phone: (732) 530-
2438
www.meridianhealth.com
Hrs Avail: 24

Scotch Plains

* Contact We Care, Inc.
P.O. Box 952
Scotch Plains, NJ 07076
Crisis Phone 1: (908) 232-3333
Crisis Phone 2: (908) 232-2880
Business Phone: (908) 490-
1480
http://www.contactwecare.org
Hrs Avail: 24

Somers Point

Contact Cape Atlantic
P.O. Box 296
Somers Point, NJ 08244
Crisis Phone 1: (609) 646-6616
(Atlantic Co.)
Crisis Phone 2: (609) 390-3333
(Cape May Co.)
Crisis Phone 3: (609) 266-8228
(Atlantic Co.)
Crisis Phone 4: (609) 823-2109
(Reassurance Contact)
Business Phone: (609) 823-
1850
Hrs Avail: 24

Voorhees

**Contact Community
Helpline**
P.O. Box 714
Voorhees, NJ 08043
Crisis Phone 1: (856) 795-2155
(voice/TDD)
Crisis Phone 2: (856) 935-4357
(Cumberland)
Crisis Phone 3: (856) 795-2119
(M-F 9-5 (Sept-June))
Crisis Phone 4: (888) 375-TEEN
Crisis Phone 5: (856) 765-1991
Crisis Phone 6: (856) 881-6200
(Salem)
Business Phone: (856) 795-
5073
http://www.snj.com/contact
Hrs Avail: 24

NEW MEXICO

Albuquerque

AGORA
The Univ. of New Mexico Crisis
Center
Student Union, SUB 105
P.O. Box 29
Albuquerque, NM 87131
Crisis Phone 1: (505) 277-3013
Business Phone: (505) 277-
3013
Hrs Avail: 9 A.M.–midnight

Portales

**Mental Health Resources,
Inc.**
300 East First Street
Portales, NM 88130
Crisis Phone 1: (505) 359-1221
(8 A.M.–6 P.M.)
Crisis Phone 2: (800) 432-2159
(toll free 6 P.M.–8 A.M., M-F 5
P.M.–8 A.M.)
Business Phone: (505) 359-1221

Santa Fe

Crisis Response of Santa Fe
P.O. Box 2267
Santa Fe, NM 87504-2267
Crisis Phone 1: (800) 477-7633
Crisis Phone 2: (505) 820-6333
Business Phone: (505) 982-
5565
http://www.pmsnet.org
Hrs Avail: 24

NEW YORK

Albany

**Capitol Dist. Psychiatric
Center**
75 New Scotland Avenue
Albany, NY 12208
Crisis Phone 1: (518) 447-9650
Business Phone: (518) 447-9611
Hrs Avail: 24

Batavia

* Regional Action Phone, Inc.
P.O. Box 281
Batavia, NY 14021
Crisis Phone 1: (716) 343-1212
Crisis Phone 2: (716) 345-9406
Crisis Phone 3: (800) 889-1903
   (Orleans Co.)
Crisis Phone 4: (800) 359-5722
   (Genisee)
Business Phone: (716) 343-1212
Hrs Avail: 24

Buffalo

* Crisis Services, Inc.
2669 Main Street
Buffalo, NY 14214
Crisis Phone 1: (716) 834-3131
Business Phone: (716) 834-2310
Hrs Avail: 24

Elmsford

**Sterling Center of the MHA
of Westchester Co.**
2269 Saw Mill River Road
Elmsford, NY 10523
Crisis Phone 1: (914) 347-6400
Business Phone: (914) 345-5900
Hrs Avail: 24

Goshen

Orange County Help Line
Mental Health in Orange
   County Inc.
20 Walker Street
Goshen, NY 10924
Crisis Phone 1: (845) 294-9355
Crisis Phone 2: (800) 832-1200
Business Phone: (845) 294-7411
Hrs Avail: 24

Ithaca

*** Suicide Prevention & Crisis
Service**
P.O. Box 312
Ithaca, NY 14851

Crisis Phone 1: (607) 272-1616
Business Phone: (607) 272-
1505
Hrs Avail: 24

Jamestown

**Jamestown Crisis Line-Jones
Memorial Health Center**
57 Glasgow Avenue
Jamestown, NY 14701
Crisis Phone 1: (716) 484-1314
Business Phone: (716) 664-
8326
Hrs Avail: 24

New Paltz

Family of New Paltz
51 North Chesnut Street
New Paltz, NY 12561
Crisis Phone 1: (845) 255-8801
Business Phone: (845) 255-8801
Hrs Avail: 24

**Psychological Counseling
Center**
VLC 10 State Univ. College
New Paltz, NY 12561
Crisis Phone 1: (845) 257-4945
Business Phone: (845) 257-2920
Hrs Avail: 24

New York City

Covenant House Nineline
346 West 17th Street
New York, NY 10011
Crisis Phone 1: (800) 999-9999
   (toll free)
Crisis Phone 2: (800) 999-9915
   (TTY)
Business Phone: (212) 727-
4021
http://www.covenanthouse.org
Hrs Avail: 24

Help-Line Telephone Services
3 West 19th Street
10th floor
New York, NY 10001

Crisis Phone 1: (212) 532-2400
Business Phone: (212) 684-
4480
Hrs Avail: M-F 9 A.M.–6 P.M.

* Samaritans of NYC
P.O. Box 1259-Madison Square
   Garden
New York, NY 10159
Crisis Phone 1: (212) 673-3000
Crisis Phone 2: (877) SUICIDE
Business Phone: (212) 677-
3009
http://www.samaritansnyc.org
Hrs Avail: 9 A.M.–6 P.M.

North Bellmore

Long Island Crisis Center
2740 Martin Avenue
North Bellmore, NY 11710
Crisis Phone 1: (877) 796-4673
   (children of hope)
Crisis Phone 2: (516) 549-8700
Crisis Phone 3: (516) 679-1111
Crisis Phone 4: (516) 679-1113
Crisis Phone 5: (516) 679-1112
Business Phone: (516) 826-0244
http://www.
longislandcrisiscenter.org
Hrs. Avail: 24

Plattsburgh

*** Crisis Center of Clinton,
Essex and Franklin
Counties**
36 Brinkerhoff Street
Plattsburgh, NY 12901
Crisis Phone 1: (518) 561-2330
Business Phone: (518) 561-
2330
Hrs Avail: 24

Potsdam

*** REACHOUT of St.
Lawrence County, Inc.**
P.O. Box 5051
Potsdam, NY 13676

Crisis Phone 1: (315) 265-2422
Business Phone: (315) 265-2422
Hrs Avail: 24

Poughkeepsie

The Dutchess County Department of Mental Hygiene
230 North Road
Poughkeepsie, NY 12601
Crisis Phone 1: (518) 462-0181
Crisis Phone 2: (845) 485-9700
Crisis Phone 3: (845) 486-2866
Business Phone: (845) 486-2705
http://www.timesunion.com/
    communities/samaritans
Hrs Avail: 24

* Dutchess County HELPLINE
230 North Road
Poughkeepsie, NY 12601-1328
Crisis Phone 1: (845) 485-9700
Crisis Phone 2: (845) 485-9700
Crisis Phone 3: (877) 485-9000
Crisis Phone 4: (845) 486-2866
    (TTY)
Business Phone: (845) 486-2750
Hrs Avail: 24

Rochester

* Lifeline/Health Assn. of Rochester
1 Mt. Hope Avenue
Rochester, NY 14620
Crisis Phone 1: (716) 275-5151
Business Phone: (716) 423-9490
Hrs Avail: 24

Rockport

Niagara Co. MH Hotline & Crisis Intv.-Troll Access Center
5467 Upper Mountain Road
    Shaw Building-Mt. View
    Campus
Rockport, NY 14094

Crisis Phone 1: (716) 285-3515
Business Phone: (716) 285-3519
Hrs Avail: 24

Stony Brook

* Response of Suffolk Co., Inc.
P.O. Box 300
Stony Brook, NY 11790
Crisis Phone 1: (631) 751-7500
Business Phone: (631) 751-7620
www.responsehotline.org
Hrs Avail: 24

Utica

Crisis Evaluation Team-St. Elizabeth Medical Center
2209 Genesee Street
Utica, NY 13501
Crisis Phone 1: (315) 734-3456
Crisis Phone 2: (315) 732-0473
Business Phone: (315) 734-3456
Hrs Avail: 24

Valhalla

Crisis Intervention Unit
Westchester Country Medical
    Center
Grasslands Road
Valhalla, NY 10595
Crisis Phone 1: (914) 493-7075
Business Phone: (914) 493-7075
Hrs Avail: 24

Woodstock

Family of Woodstock
16 Rock City Road
Woodstock, NY 12498
Crisis Phone 1: (914) 338-2370
Business Phone: (914) 331-7080
www.familyofwoodstockinc.org
Hrs Avail: 24

NORTH CAROLINA

Ahoskie

Roanoke-Chowan Human Service Center
144 Community College Road
Ahoskie, NC 27910
Crisis Phone 1: (252) 332-4442
Crisis Phone 2: (877) 685-2415
Business Phone: (252) 332-4137
Hrs Avail: 24

Asheboro

Randolph Helpline
P.O. Box 4397
Asheboro, NC 27203
Crisis Phone 1: (336) 633-7209
Crisis Phone 2: (800) 742-2572
Business Phone: (336) 633-7223
Hrs Avail: 24

Burlington

* Suicide & Crisis Serv/Alamance Co.
P.O. Box 2573
Burlington, NC 27215
Crisis Phone 1: (336) 227-6220
Business Phone: (336) 228-1720
Hrs Avail: 24

Chapel Hill

Crisis Central
412a Caldwell Street
Chapel Hill, NC 27516
Crisis Phone 1: (800) 974-0479
Business Phone: (919) 913-4000
Hrs Avail: 24

Charlotte

The Relatives, Inc.
P.O. Box 30186
Charlotte, NC 28203
Crisis Phone 1: (704) 377-0602

Business Phone: (704) 335-0203
Hrs Avail: 24

Clyde

* Parents Against Teen Suicide/T.E.A.C.H.
P.O. BOX 129
Clyde, NC 28721
Crisis Phone 1: (800) 367-7287
Business Phone: (828) 627-1001
http://www.teachhotline.org
Hrs Avail: 24

Durham

CONTACT Helpline
2706 North Roxboro Road
Durham, NC 27704
Crisis Phone 1: (919) 683-1595
Business Phone: (919) 220-2534
Hrs Avail: 24

Durham Center Hotline
501 Willard Street
Durham, NC 27701
Crisis Phone 1: (919) 560-7100
Business Phone: (919) 560-7100
Hrs Avail: 24

Fayetteville

Contact of Fayetteville, Inc.
509 Person Street
Fayetteville, NC 28301
Crisis Phone 1: (910) 485-4134
Business Phone: (910) 483-8970
Hrs Avail: 24

Goldsboro

Wayne Co. MHC Hotline
301 North Herman Street
Goldsboro, NC 27530
Crisis Phone 1: (919) 735-4357
Business Phone: (919) 731-1133
Hrs Avail: 24

Greensboro

Switchboard Crisis Center
330 South Greene
Greensboro, NC 27402
Crisis Phone 1: (919) 275-0896
Business Phone: (919) 275-9341
Hrs Avail: 24

Teen Crisis Line
301 East Washington Street
Suite 201
Greensboro, NC 27401
Crisis Phone 1: (336) 387-6161
Business Phone: (336) 333-6853
Hrs Avail: 4 P.M.–midnight

Greenville

REAL Crisis Intervention, Inc.
600 East 11th Street
Greenville, NC 27858
Crisis Phone 1: (252) 758-4357 (TTY)
Crisis Phone 2: (252) 758-1976 (teens)
Business Phone: (252) 758-4357
Hrs Avail: 24

Lexington

Hope Helpline Ministries
21 Sunrise Avenue
Lexington, NC 27292
Crisis Phone 1: (336) 249-8974
Business Phone: (336) 249-8824
Hrs Avail: 24

Manteo

Outer Banks Hotline
602 Amadas Street
Manteo, NC 27954
Crisis Phone 1: (252) 473-3366
Business Phone: (252) 473-5121
Hrs Avail: 24

Morehead

Helpline Carteret County
209 North 35th Street
Morehead, NC 28557
Crisis Phone 1: (252) 247-3023
Business Phone: (252) 240-0540
Hrs Avail: 24

Raleigh

Hopeline, Inc.
P.O. Box 10490
Raleigh, NC 27605
Crisis Phone 1: (919) 231-4525
Business Phone: (919) 832-3326
Hrs Avail: 24

Roanoke Rapids

Riverstone Counseling
210 Smith Church Road
Roanoke Rapids, NC 27870
Crisis Phone 1: (252) 537-2909
Business Phone: (252) 537-6174
Hrs Avail: 24

Salisbury

Piedmont Behavioral Healthcare
1807 East Innes Street
Salisbury, NC 28146
Crisis Phone 1: (704) 633-3616
Business Phone: (704) 633-3616
Hrs Avail: 24

Sanford

Lee County MH Crisis Line
130 Carbonton Road
Sanford, NC 27330
Crisis Phone 1: (919) 774-4520
Business Phone: (919) 774-6521
Hrs Avail: 24

Smithfield

Contact Johnston Co.
140 Market Street
Smithfield, NC 27577
Crisis Phone 1: (919) 934-6161
Business Phone: (919) 934-
6979
Hrs Avail: 24

Statesville

The Counseling Center of Iredell
125 West Bell Street
Statesville, NC 28677
Crisis Phone 1: (704) 872-7638
Business Phone: (704) 872-
7638
Hrs Avail: 24

Wilmington

* Crisis Line/Open House of Coastal Horizons Center
3333 Wrightsville Avenue
Suite 102
Wilmington, NC 28403
Crisis Phone 1: (910) 392-7408
Business Phone: (910) 343-
0145
www.coastalhorizons.org
Hrs Avail: 24

Wilson

Wilson Crisis Center
P.O. Box 8026
Wilson, NC 27894
Crisis Phone 1: (252) 237-5156
Business Phone: (252) 237-
5156
Hrs Avail: 24

NORTH DAKOTA

Bismarck

* Helpline
P.O. Box 160
Bismarck, ND 58503
Crisis Phone 1: (800) 472-2911

Business Phone: (701) 255-3692
Hrs Avail: 24

West Central Human Service Center
600 South 2nd Street
Suite 5
Bismarck, ND 58504-5731
Crisis Phone 1: (701) 328-8899
Crisis Phone 2: (888) 328-2112
(toll free-Bismarck)
Crisis Phone 3: (800) 366-6888
(TDD & TTY)
Crisis Phone 4: (800) 366-6889
(TDD)
Business Phone: (701) 328-8888
http://www.discovernd.com
Hrs Avail: 24

Lake Region Human Service Center
200 Highway 2, SW
Devils Lake, ND 58301
Crisis Phone 1: (701) 665-211
(TDD & TTY)
Crisis Phone 2: (800) 755-2745
(toll free)
Crisis Phone 3: (701) 662-5050
Business Phone: (701) 665-2200
Hrs Avail: 24

Dickenson

Badlands Human Service Center
200 Pulver Hall
Dickenson, ND 58601-4857
Crisis Phone 1: (701) 227-7574
(TTY & TDD)
Crisis Phone 2: (888) 227-7525
(toll free)
Crisis Phone 3: (888) 225-5009
Business Phone: (701) 227-7500
Hrs Avail: 24

Fargo

* Firstlink Hotline
P.O. Box 447
Fargo, ND 58107

Crisis Phone 1: (701) 235-7335
Crisis Phone 2: (701) 232-4357
Business Phone: (701) 293-
6462
Hrs Avail: 24

South East Human Service Center
2624 9th Avenue SW
Fargo, ND 58103-2350
Crisis Phone 1: (701) 298-4450
(TTY)
Crisis Phone 2: (888) 342-4900
(toll free)
Business Phone: (701) 298-4500
Hrs Avail: 24

Grand Forks

Northeast Human Service Center
151 South 4th Street
Suite 401
Grand Forks, ND 58201
Crisis Phone 1: (701) 775-0525
Business Phone: (701) 795-3000
Hrs Avail: 24

Jamestown

South Central Human Service Center
520 3rd Street, NW
Jamestown, ND 58402
Crisis Phone 1: (701) 253-6304
Crisis Phone 2: (800) 260-1310
(toll free)
Business Phone: (701) 253-6300
Hrs Avail: 24

Minot

Minot Suicide Prevention Service-Unimed Medical Ctr.
407 3rd Street, NE
Minot, ND 58701
Crisis Phone 1: (701) 857-2700
Business Phone: (701) 857-
2000
Hrs Avail: 24

North Central Human Service Center

400 22nd Avenue NW
Minot, ND 58703
Crisis Phone 1: (701) 857-8666
    (TDD)
Crisis Phone 2: (888) 470-6968
    (toll free)
Business Phone: (701) 857-
8500
Hrs Avail: 24

Williston

NW Human Service Center
316 2nd Avenue West
Williston, ND 58802
Crisis Phone 1: (701) 774-4692
    (TDD)
Crisis Phone 2: (800) 231-7724
    (toll free)
Crisis Phone 3: (701) 572-9111
Business Phone: (701) 774-
4600
Hrs Avail: 24

OHIO

Akron

* Portage Path Community MH Center

10 Penfield
Akron, OH 44310
Crisis Phone 1: (330) 434-9144
Business Phone: (330) 434-
1214
Hrs Avail: 24

Athens

Tri-County Mental Health and Counseling Services

90 Hospital Drive
Athens, OH 45701
Crisis Phone 1: (740) 593-3344
    (TDD)
Business Phone: (740) 592-
3091
Hrs Avail: 24

Bowling Green

The Link of Behavioral Connections

315 Thurstin Avenue
Bowling Green, OH 43402
Crisis Phone 1: (419) 352-1545
Crisis Phone 2: (800) 472-9411
Business Phone: (419) 352-5387
Hrs Avail: 24

Bucyrus

CONTACT Crawford Co.

P.O. Box 631
Bucyrus, OH 44820
Crisis Phone 1: (419) 562-9010
Crisis Phone 2: (419) 468-9081
Business Phone: (419) 562-
9099
Hrs Avail: 24

Canton

* Crisis Intervention Center of Stark Co.

2421 13th Street, NW
Canton, OH 44708
Crisis Phone 1: (330) 452-6000
Business Phone: (330) 452-9812
Hrs Avail: 24

Chillicothe

Chillicothe Crisis Center

4449 State Route 159
Chillicothe, OH 45601
Crisis Phone 1: (740) 773-4357
Business Phone: (740) 773-
4357
Hrs Avail: 24

Cincinnati

* 281-CARE/Crisis Care Center

3891 Reading Road
Cincinnati, OH 45229
Crisis Phone 1: (513) 281-2273
Business Phone: (513) 281-2866
Hrs Avail: 24

Cleveland

Mental Health Services, Inc.

1736 Superior Avenue
Cleveland, OH 44114
Crisis Phone 1: (216) 623-6888
Business Phone: (216) 623-
6555
Hrs Avail: 24

Columbus

* Suicide Prevention Services

1301 North High Street
Columbus, OH 43201
Crisis Phone 1: (614) 221-5445
Business Phone: (614) 299-
6600
Hrs Avail: 24

Dayton

* Suicide Prevention Center, Inc.

P.O. Box 1393
Dayton, OH 45401
Crisis Phone 1: (800) 320-4357
Business Phone: (937) 226-
0818
Hrs Avail: 24

Delaware

* Helpline of Delaware & Morrow Counties

11 North Franklin Street
Delaware, OH 43015
Crisis Phone 1: (740) 369-3316
Crisis Phone 2: (800) 684-2324
Business Phone: (740) 363-1835
Hrs Avail: 24

Kent

Townhall II Helpline

155 North Water Street
Kent, OH 44240
Crisis Phone 1: (330) 678-4357
Business Phone: (330) 678-3006
Hrs Avail: 24

Lancaster

Info. & Crisis Serv. Info. & Referral
P.O. Box 1054
Lancaster, OH 43130
Crisis Phone 1: (710) 687-0500
Business Phone: (740) 687-0500
Hrs Avail: 24

Mansfield

Help Line/Adapt
741 Sholl Road
Mansfield, OH 44907
Crisis Phone 1: (419) 522-4357
Business Phone: (419) 756-1717
Hrs Avail: 24

Marion

CONTACT Care Line-Marion Area
320 Executive Drive
Marion, OH 43302
Crisis Phone 1: (740) 383-2273
Business Phone: (740) 387-5210
Hrs Avail: 24

Martins Ferry

Hillcrest of Ohio Valley Medical Center
9090 North Fourth Street
Martins Ferry, OH 43935
Crisis Phone 1: (304) 242-2908
Hrs Avail: 24

Medina

* Alternative Paths, Inc.
246 Northland Drive
Suite 200A
Medina, OH 44256
Crisis Phone 1: (330) 725-9195
Business Phone: (330) 725-9195
www.alternativepaths.org
Hrs Avail: 24

Mt. Gilead

* Helpline of Delaware & Morrow Counties
950 Meadown Drive
Suite B
Mt. Gilead, OH 43338
Crisis Phone 1: (419) 947-2520
Business Phone: (419) 946-1350
Hrs Avail: 24

Napoleon

* First Call for Help, Inc.
1330-A North Scott Street
Napoleon, OH 43545
Crisis Phone 1: (877) 419-7233 (teen line)
Crisis Phone 2: (877) 419-7233
Crisis Phone 3: (800) 468-4357
Business Phone: (419) 599-1660
http://www.firstcallnwo.org
Hrs Avail: 24

New Philadelphia

Cornerstone Support Services
344 West High Avenue
New Philadelphia, OH 44663
Crisis Phone 1: (330) 343-1811
Crisis Phone 2: (330) 627-5240 (Carroll Co.)
Crisis Phone 3: (330) 254-4530 (Tuscarawas Co.)
Business Phone: (300) 339-7850
Hrs Avail: 24

Oxford

Community Counseling and Crisis Center
110 South College Avenue
Oxford, OH 45056
Crisis Phone 1: (513) 523-4149
Business Phone: (513) 523-4146
Hrs Avail: 24

Toledo

* Rescue Mental Health Services
3350 Collingwood Boulevard
Toledo, OH 43610
Crisis Phone 1: (419) 255-9585
Business Phone: (419) 255-9585
Hrs Avail: 24

Warren

* CONTACT Community Connection
1569 Woodland NE
Suite 10
Warren, OH 44483
Crisis Phone 1: (330) 393-1565
Crisis Phone 2: (330) 545-4371
Business Phone: (330) 395-5255
Hrs Avail: 24

Xenia

Greene County Crisis Services
452 West Market
Xenia, OH 45385
Crisis Phone 1: (937) 426-2302
Crisis Phone 2: (937) 376-8702 (TTY)
Business Phone: (937) 376-8701
Hrs Avail: 24

Youngstown

* Help Hotline Crisis Center, Inc.
P.O. Box 46
Youngstown, OH 44501
Crisis Phone 1: (330) 747-2696
Crisis Phone 2: (800) 427-3606
Crisis Phone 3: (330) 747-2697
Business Phone: (330) 747-2696
Hrs Avail: 24

Zanesville

* Six County, Inc. Crisis Hotline
3405 Dillon Acres Road
Zanesville, OH 43701

Crisis Phone 1: (800) 344-5818
Business Phone: (740) 455-5755
Hrs Avail: 24

OKLAHOMA

Lawton

United Way Helpline
P.O. Box 66
Lawton, OK 73502
Crisis Phone 1: (580) 355-7575
Business Phone: (580) 355-7575
Hrs Avail: 24

Oklahoma City

* Contact Telephone Hotline
P.O. Box 12832
Oklahoma City, OK 73157
Crisis Phone 1: (405) 848-2273
Business Phone: (405) 840-9396
Hrs Avail: M-F 8 A.M.–5 P.M.

Ponca City

Helpline/Ponca City
P.O. Box 375
Ponca City, OK 74602
Crisis Phone 1: (740) 765-5552
Business Phone: (740) 765-5552
Hrs Avail: 24

Tulsa

Tulsa Helpline
P.O. Box 52847
Tulsa, OK 74152
Crisis Phone 1: (918) 836-4357
Business Phone: (918) 838-0698x2
Hrs Avail: M-F 8 A.M.–6 P.M.;
   Sat 9 A.M.–5 P.M.

OREGON

Coos Bay

Helpline of the South Coast
365 D Street
Coos Bay, OR 97420

Crisis Phone 1: (541) 888-5911
Crisis Phone 2: (541) 828-6728
Business Phone: (541) 266-0250
Hrs Avail: 24

Eugene

Whitebird Clinic
341 East 12th Avenue
Eugene, OR 97401
Crisis Phone 1: (541) 687-4000
Business Phone: (541) 342-8255
Hrs Avail: 24

Grants Pass

RSVP of Josephine County
1505 Northwest Washington
   Boulevard
Grants Pass, OR 97526
Crisis Phone 1: (541) 479-help
Business Phone: (541) 955-5547
www.rsvpjoco.org
Hrs Avail: 24

Medford

Community Works Helpline
900 East Main Street
Medford, OR 97504
Crisis Phone 1: (541) 779-4357
Business Phone: (541) 779-2393
Hrs Avail: 24

Salem

Northwest Human Services, Inc.
1049 Oak Street, SE
Salem, OR 97303
Crisis Phone 1: (503) 581-5535
Business Phone: (503) 588-5822
www.open.org/chl
Hrs Avail: 24

PENNSYLVANIA

Allentown

Warmline
P.O. Box 4116
Allentown, PA 18105
Crisis Phone 1: (610) 820-8451
Business Phone: (610) 435-9651
Hrs Avail: 24

Altoona

Altoona Hospital Center for Mental Health Services
620 Howard Avenue
Altoona, PA 16601-4899
Crisis Phone 1: (814) 946-2279
Business Phone: (814) 946-2141
Hrs Avail: 24

Contact Altoona
P.O. Box 11
Altoona, PA 16603
Crisis Phone 1: (814) 946-9050
Business Phone: (814) 946-0531
Hrs Avail: 24

Bala Cynwyd

Contact Careline for Greater Philadelphia
P.O. Box 2516
Bala Cynwyd, PA 19004-6516
Crisis Phone 1: (610) 649-5250
Crisis Phone 2: (215) 877-9099
Crisis Phone 3: (215) 877-2140
Crisis Phone 4: (215) 879-4402
Crisis Phone 5: (215) 879-8887
Business Phone: (215) 877-9099
http://www.contactcareline.org
Hrs Avail: 11 A.M.–7 P.M.

Beaver

CONTACT Beaver Valley
P.O. Box 584
Beaver, PA 15009

Crisis Phone 1: (724) 728-3650
Crisis Phone 2: (724) 728-6878
Business Phone: (724) 728-9511
http://www.teenhelpline.org
http://www.call-contact.org
Hrs Avail: M-F 9 A.M.–4 P.M.

Butler

* Irene Stacy Community Mental Health Center
112 Hillvue Drive
Butler, PA 16001
Crisis Phone 1: (724) 287-0440
Business Phone: (800) 292-3866
Hrs Avail: M-Th 9 A.M.–9 P.M.

Camp Hill

Community Mental Health Center
503 North 21st Street
Camp Hill, PA 17011
Crisis Phone 1: (717) 763-2222
Crisis Phone 2: (800) 722-5385 (toll free teen line)
Crisis Phone 3: (717) 763-2345 (teen line)
Business Phone: (717) 763-2219
Hrs Avail: 24

Easton

Northampton County Crisis Intervention
45 North 2nd Street
Easton, PA 18042
Crisis Phone 1: (610) 252-9060
Business Phone: (610) 252-9060
Hrs Avail: 24

Erie

Erie Hotline, Inc.
P.O. Box 6556
Erie, PA 16512
Erie Hotline: (814) 453-5656

Business Phone: (814) 453-5656
Hrs Avail: 24

Gettysburg

Adams/Hanover Counseling Service
44 South Franklin Street
Gettysburg, PA 17325
Crisis Phone 1: (717) 334-2121
Business Phone: (717) 334-9111
Hrs Avail: 24

Hanover

Adams/Hanover Counsel Service
625 West Elm Avenue
Hanover, PA 17331
Crisis Phone 1: (717) 632-4900
Crisis Phone 2: (717) 637-3711 (Hanover Hospital)
Crisis Phone 3: (717) 334-0468 (9 A.M.–5 P.M.)
Crisis Phone 4: (717) 334-2121 (Gettysburg Hospital)
Crisis Phone 5: (800) 673-2426
Business Phone: (717) 632-4900
Hrs Avail: 24

Harrisburg

Contact Helpline
P.O. Box 90035
Harrisburg, PA 17109
Crisis Phone 1: (717) 652-4400
Business Phone: (717) 652-4987
www.contacthelpline.org
Hrs Avail: 24

* Dauphin County Crisis Intervention
100 Chestnut Street
Harrisburg, PA 17101
Crisis Phone 1: (717) 232-7511
Crisis Phone 2: (888) 596-4447
Business Phone: (717) 255-2705
Hrs Avail: 24

Indiana

The Open Door
20 South Sixth Street
Indiana, PA 15701
Crisis Phone 1: (724) 465-2605
Business Phone: (724) 456-2605
www.theopendoor.org
Hrs Avail: 24

Johnstown

Contact Community Telephone Helpline
P.O. Box 5086
Johnstown, PA 15909
Crisis Phone 1: (800) 307-1177 (toll free)
Business Phone: (814) 534-3889

Lancaster

Contact Lancaster Helpline
447 East King Street
Lancaster, PA 17602
Crisis Phone 1: (717) 299-4855
Business Phone: (717) 291-2261
www.contactlancaster.org
Hrs Avail: 24

Lancaster County Helpline
1120 Francis Avenue
Lancaster, PA 17601
Crisis Phone 1: (717) 394-2631
Crisis Phone 2: (717) 399-7417 (TTY)
Business Phone: (717) 394-2631
Hrs Avail: 24

New Castle

Contact E.A.R.S. Helpline
P.O. Box 7804
New Castle, PA 16107
Crisis Phone 1: (724) 658-5529
Business Phone: (724) 652-0333
Hrs Avail: 24

Norristown

Montgomery Co. Emerg. Serv. Inc.
50 Beech Drive
Norristown, PA 19401
Crisis Phone 1: (610) 279-6100
Business Phone: (610) 279-6100
Hrs Avail: 24

Philadelphia

Contact Philadelphia
P.O. Box 12586
Philadelphia, PA 19151
Crisis Phone 1: (215) 879-4402
Business Phone: (215) 877-9099
Hrs Avail: 24

Philadelphia Suicide & Crisis Center
1101 Market, 7th Floor
Philadelphia, PA 19107
Crisis Phone 1: (215) 686-4420
Business Phone: (215) 685-6440
Hrs Avail: 24

Pittsburgh

* Contact Pittsburgh, Inc.
P.O. Box 111294
Pittsburgh, PA 15238-0694
Crisis Phone 1: (412) 820-4357
Crisis Phone 2: (412) 469-9999
Crisis Phone 3: (412) 361-8336 (teen line)
Crisis Phone 4: (412) 864-4357
Crisis Phone 5: (800) 578-5100
Crisis Phone 6: (412) 373-4357
Crisis Phone 7: (412) 787-4357
Crisis Phone 8: (412) 343-4357
Business Phone: (412) 820-0100
Hrs Avail: 24

Helpline
P.O. Box 111249
Pittsburgh, PA 15238
Crisis Phone 1: (412) 255-1155
Business Phone: (412) 578-2450
www.unitedwaypittsburgh.org
Hrs Avail: 24

Plaines

Helpline
1095 Highway, 315
Plaines, PA 18705
Crisis Phone 1: (570) 829-1341
Business Phone: (570) 829-1341
Hrs Avail: 24

Richboro

Contact Bucks County
P.O. Box 167
Richboro, PA 18954-0167
Crisis Phone 1: (215) 547-1889 (Lower Bucks Co.)
Crisis Phone 2: (215) 536-0911 (Upper Bucks Co.)
Crisis Phone 3: (215) 340-1998 (Central Bucks Co.)
Crisis Phone 4: (215) 355-6000
Business Phone: (215) 355-6611
Hrs Avail: 24

Scranton

Voluntary Action Center of Northeastern Pennsylvania
538 Spruce Street
Suite 420
Scranton, PA 18503
Crisis Phone 1: (570) 961-1234
Business Phone: (570) 347-5616
Hrs Avail: 24

Upland

Delaware County Crisis Intervention
Crozer Medical Center-Access Center
Upland, PA 19013

Crisis Phone 1: (610) 447-7600
Business Phone: (610) 565-6000
http://www.cgrc.com

West Chester

Chester County Mental Health-Crisis Intervention Services
222 North Walnut Street
West Chester, PA 19380
Crisis Phone 1: (610) 918-2100
Crisis Phone 2: (879) 918-2100 (toll free)
Business Phone: (610) 918-2100
Hrs Avail: 24

Wilkes Barre

Community Counseling Service of Northeastern Pennsylvania
110 South Pennsylvania Avenue
Wilkes Barre, PA 18701
Crisis Phone 1: (570) 823-2155
Business Phone: (570) 552-6000
Hrs Avail: 24

Williamsport

Williamsport YWCA Helpline
815 West 4th Street
Williamsport, PA 17701
Crisis Phone 1: (570) 327-2870
Crisis Phone 2: (800) 326-9577
Business Phone: (570) 323-8555
Hrs Avail: 24

York

CONTACT York
P.O. Box 1865
York, PA 17405-5802
Crisis Phone 1: (717) 757-0733
Crisis Phone 2: (717) 757-0739
Crisis Phone 3: (800) 826-3277 (toll free)
Business Phone: (717) 854-5802
Hrs Avail: 24

Crisis Intervention-York Hospital
1001 South George Street
York, PA 17405
Crisis Phone 1: (717) 851-5320
Business Phone: (717) 851-3500
www.wellspan.org
Hrs Avail: 24

RHODE ISLAND

Providence

* The Samaritans of Rhode Island
2 Magee Street
Providence, RI 02906
Crisis Phone 1: (401) 272-4044
Business Phone: (401) 272-4243
Hrs Avail: 24

Wakefield

Sympatico/Phoenix House of New England
1058 Kingstown Road
Wakefield, RI 02879
Crisis Phone 1: (401) 539-7474
Business Phone: (401) 783-0782
Hrs Avail: 24

SOUTH CAROLINA

Aiken

Aiken County Help Line, Inc.
P.O. Box 2712
Aiken, SC 29802
Crisis Phone 1: (803) 648-9900
Business Phone: (803) 641-4143
Hrs Avail: Sa-S 9 A.M.–5 P.M.

Andersen

Crisis Ministries
P.O. Box 1925
Andersen, SC 29622

Crisis Phone 1: (864) 226-0297
Crisis Phone 2: (800) 868-4870
Business Phone: (864) 226-0297
Hrs Avail: 24

Columbia

* Helpline of the Midlands Inc.
P.O. Box 152
Columbia, SC 29202
Crisis Phone 1: (803) 790-4357
Business Phone: (803) 733-5448
www.uway.org
Hrs Avail: 24

Gaffney

Helpline
P.O. Box 1231
Gaffney, SC 29342
Crisis Phone 1: (864) 487-4357
Business Phone: (864) 487-4357
Hrs Avail: 24

Greenville

Mental Health Association of Greenville Co.
301 University Ridge
Greenville, SC 29601
Crisis Phone 1: (864) 582-1100
Business Phone: (864) 271-8888
Hrs Avail: 24

N. Charleston

* Hotline
P.O. Box 71583
N. Charleston, SC 29415-1583
Crisis Phone 1: (843) 744-4357
Crisis Phone 2: (843) 747-8336
Crisis Phone 3: (800) 922-2283
Crisis Phone 4: (800) 922-2283
Crisis Phone 5: (800) 273-TALK (teen line)
Business Phone: (843) 747-3007

http://www.lowcountryhelp.org
Hrs Avail: 24

SOUTH DAKOTA

Sioux Falls

* HELP!line Center
1000 West Avenue
Suite 310
Sioux Falls, SD 57104
Crisis Phone 1: (605) 339-4357
Business Phone: (605) 334-6646
www.helplinecenter.org
Hrs Avail: 24

TENNESSEE

Athens

McMinn/Meigs Monroe CONTACT
P.O. Box 69
Athens, TN 37371
Crisis Phone 1: (423) 337-3800
Business Phone: (423) 745-1042
Hrs Avail: 24

Chattanooga

Contact of Chattanooga
6221 Vance Road
Chattanooga, TN 37421
Crisis Phone 1: (423) 266-8228
Crisis Phone 2: (423) 266-4862
Business Phone: (423) 629-0039
Hrs Avail: 24

Clarksville

Clarksville/Montgomery Co. Crisis Intervention Center
P.O. Box 212
Clarksville, TN 37041
Crisis Phone 1: (931) 648-1000
Crisis Phone 2: (931) 552-4636 (info line)
Business Phone: (931) 647-8099
Hrs Avail: 24

Johnson City

Contact Ministries
P.O. Box 1403
Johnson City, TN 37605
Crisis Phone 1: (423) 926-1044
Business Phone: (423) 926-0145
Hrs Avail: 24

Kingsport

CONTACT-CONCERN of Northeast
P.O. Box 3336
Kingsport, TN 37664
Crisis Phone 1: (423) 246-2273
Business Phone: (423) 246-2273
www.contactconcern.org
Hrs Avail: M-F 8 A.M.–5 P.M.

Knoxville

Contact Helpline of Knoxville
P.O. Box 11234
Knoxville, TN 37939-1234
Crisis Phone 1: (865) 523-9124
Business Phone: (865) 523-9108
www.Korrnet.org/helpline/
Hrs Avail: 24

Kelen Ross McNabb Center
1520 Cherokee Trail
Knoxville, TN 37920
Crisis Phone 1: (865) 637-9711
Business Phone: (865) 637-9711
Hrs Avail: 24

Overlook Mobile Crisis Unit
6800 Baum Drive
Knoxville, TN 37919
Crisis Phone 1: (865) 539-2409
Business Phone: (865) 539-2409
http://www.covenanthealth.com

Memphis

* The Crisis Center
P.O. Box 40068
Memphis, TN 38174
Crisis Phone 1: (901) 274-7477
Business Phone: (901) 276-1111
Hrs Avail: M-F 9 A.M.–5 P.M.

Lakeside Behavioral System
2911 Brunswick Road
Memphis, TN 38133
Crisis Phone 1: (901) 377-4733
Crisis Phone 2: (800) 232-5253
Business Phone: (901) 377-4700
Hrs Avail: 24

Nashville

* Centerstone Community Health Centers, Inc.
P.O. Box 40406
Nashville, TN 37204
Crisis Phone 1: (800) 681-7444
Business Phone: (615) 463-6600
www.centerstonecmhc.org
Hrs Avail: M-F 8 A.M.–5 P.M.

* Crisis Intervention Center, Inc.
P.O. Box 40752
Nashville, TN 37204-0752
Crisis Phone 1: (615) 269-4357 (helpline)
Crisis Phone 2: (615) 244-7444
Business Phone: (615) 298-3359
http://www.crisisinterventioncenter.org
Hrs Avail: 24

Oak Ridge

CONTACT Helpline
P.O. Box 4641
Oak Ridge, TN 37831
Crisis Phone 1: (865) 482-4949
Business Phone: (865) 482-5040

www.Korrnet.org/orhelp
Hrs Avail: 24

Tullahoma

Contact-Life Line of the Highland Rim
P.O. Box 1614
Tullahoma, TN 37388
Coffee County: (931) 455-7133
Franklin Co.: (931) 967-7133
Bedford Co.: (931) 684-7133
Moore Co.: (931) 759-7133
Business Phone: (931) 455-7150
www.centerstonecmhc.org
Hrs Avail: 24

TEXAS

Abilene

Mental Health Assoc. in Abilene
3305 North 3rd Street
Suite 302
Abilene, TX 79608
Crisis Phone 1: (915) 677-7773
Business Phone: (915) 673-2300
http://www.abilenementalhealth.org
Hrs Avail: 24

Amarillo

* Texas Panhandle MH Authority
P.O. Box 3250
Amarillo, TX 79116
Crisis Phone 1: (806) 359-6699
Toll Free In-State: (800) 692-4039
Business Phone: (806) 359-2025
www.tpmhmr.org
Hrs Avail: 24

Austin

* Hotline to Help
P.O. Box 3548
Austin, TX 78705

Crisis Phone 1: (512) 472-4357
Business Phone: (512) 703-
1332
Hrs Avail: 24

Texas Youth Hotline
P.O. Box 149030
Austin, TX 78714-9030
Crisis Phone 1: (888) 580-4357
Crisis Phone 2: (800) 210-2278
Business Phone: (512) 833-
3477
http://www.texasyouth.org
Hrs Avail: 24

Beaumont

* Life Resources Community
2750 South 8th Street
Building C
Beaumont, TX 77701
Crisis Phone 1: (409) 838-1818
Business Phone: (409) 839-
1080
Hrs Avail: 24

*** Rape & Suicide Crisis of
Southeast Texas**
P.O. Box 3208
Beaumont, TX 77704
Crisis Phone 1: (409) 835-
3355
Business Phone: (409) 832-
6530
Hrs Avail: 24

Dallas

*** Contact Counseling and
Crisis Line**
P.O. Box 800742
Dallas, TX 75380-0742
Crisis Phone 1: (972) 233-2233
Crisis Phone 2: (972) 233-8336
(teen line)
Business Phone: (972) 233-
0866
http://www.teencontact.com
http://www.contactdallas.org
Hrs Avail: 24

* Suicide & Crisis Center
2808 Swiss Avenue
Dallas, TX 75204
Crisis Phone 1: (214) 828-1000
Business Phone: (214) 824-7020
www.sccenter.org
Hrs Avail: M-F 9 A.M.–5 P.M.

Ft. Worth

*** Family Service
Intervention**
1424 Hemphill
Ft. Worth, TX 76104
Crisis Phone 1: (817) 927-5544
Business Phone: (817) 927-
8884x274
Hrs Avail: 24

Houston

*** Crisis Intervention of
Houston, Inc.**
3015 Richmond Avenue
Suite 120
Houston, TX 77098
Crisis Phone 1: (281) 461-9992
Crisis Phone 2: (713) 468-5463
Business Phone: (713) 527-
9864
www.crisishotline.org
Hrs Avail: M-F 9 A.M.–5 P.M.

Cypress Creek Hospital
17750 Cali
Houston, TX 77090
Crisis Phone 1: (800) 666-3878
Business Phone: (281) 586-7600
Hrs Avail: 24

Intracare Hospital
7601 Fannin
Houston, TX 77054
Crisis Phone 1: (713) 790-0949
Crisis Phone 2: (713) 222-2121
Hrs Avail: 24

**NeuroPsychiatric Center of
MHMRA of Harris Cty**
1502 Taub Loop
Houston, TX 77030

Crisis Phone 1: (713) 970-7070
Business Phone: (713) 970-
4600
Hrs Avail: 24

West Oaks Hospital
6500 Hornwood
Houston, TX 77074
Crisis Phone 1: (713) 995-0909
Crisis Phone 2: (713) 778-5250
Crisis Phone 3: (800) 777-7160
Business Phone: (713) 995-
0909
http://www.brownschools.com
Hrs Avail: 24

Laredo

* Lifeline of Laredo, Inc.
1803 Juarez Avenue
Laredo, TX 78040
Crisis Phone 1: (956) 722-5433
Business Phone: (956) 722-5433
Hrs Avail: 24

Lubbock

Contact Lubbock
P.O. Box 6477
Lubbock, TX 79493-6477
Crisis Phone 1: (806) 765-
8393
Teen Line: (806) 765-7272
Business Phone: (806) 765-
7272
www.contactlubbock.org
Hrs Avail: 24

Midland

**Permian Basin Comm.
Centers**
401 East Illinois
Suite 403
Midland, TX 79701
Crisis Phone 1: (915) 570-3300
(Midland Co.)
Crisis Phone 2: (877) 475-7322
(Pecos Co.)
Crisis Phone 3: (915) 333-3265
(Ector Co.)

Crisis Phone 4: (800) 542-4005
(Big Bend Area)
Business Phone: (915) 570-3333
http://www.pbmhmr.com
Hrs Avail: 24

Richmond

Fort Bend County Womens Center
P.O. Box 183
Richmond, TX 77406-0183
Crisis Phone 1: (281) 342-4357
Business Phone: (281) 342-0251
http://www.fortbendwomen-scenter.org
Hrs Avail: 24

San Angelo

* Concho Valley Crisis Hotline
244 North Magdalen
San Angelo, TX 76903
Crisis Phone 1: (915) 655-5933
Business Phone: (915) 655-8965
Hrs Avail: 24

San Antonio

* United Way Help Line
700 South Alamo
San Antonio, TX 78293-0898
Crisis Phone 1: (210) 227-4357
Business Phone: (210) 352-7000
www.unitedwaysatx.org
Hrs Avail: 24

Victoria

Hope of South Texas
314 East Rio Grande
Victoria, TX 77901
Crisis Phone 1: (361) 573-3600
Crisis Phone 2: (800) 365-7345
Business Phone: (361) 573-5868
Hrs Avail: M-F 8 A.M.–5 P.M.

Wichita Falls

Concern, Inc.
P.O. Box 1945
Wichita Falls, TX 76307
Crisis Phone 1: (940) 723-0821
Business Phone: (940) 723-8231
Hrs Avail: 24

UTAH

Salt Lake City

Valley Mental Health Crisis Service
1228 South 900 East
Salt Lake City, UT 84105
Crisis Phone 1: (801) 483-5444
Business Phone: (801) 483-5444
www.VMH.com
Hrs Avail: 24

VERMONT

Brattleboro

Healthcare and Rehabilitation Service of Southeast Vermont
4 High Street
Suite 5
Brattleboro, VT 05301
Crisis Phone 1: (802) 257-7989
Business Phone: (802) 257-4011
www.unitedwaywindham.org
Hrs Avail: 9 A.M.–5 P.M.

Randolph

Clara Martin Center
P.O. Box G
Randolph, VT 05060
Crisis Phone 1: (800) 639-6360
Business Phone: (802) 728-4466
Hrs Avail: 24

St. Albans

St. Albans Emer. & Crisis Service
107 Fisher Pond Road
St. Albans, VT 05478

Crisis Phone 1: (802) 524-6554
Business Phone: (802) 524-6554
Hrs Avail: 24

VIRGINIA

Arlington

* CrisisLink
Administrative Office
Arlington, VA 22207
Crisis Phone 1: (703) 527-4077
(TTY & TTD)
Business Phone: (703) 527-6603
www.crisislink.org
Hrs Avail: M-F 9 A.M.–5 P.M.

Blacksburg

New River Valley Community
700 University City Boulevard
Blacksburg, VA 24060
Crisis Phone 1: (540) 961-8400
Business Phone: (540) 961-8400
Hrs Avail: 24

Bristol

Bristol Crisis Center
P.O. Box 642
Bristol, VA 24203-0642
Crisis Phone 1: (540) 466-2312
Crisis Phone 2: (540) 628-7731
(Washington Co.)
Business Phone: (540) 466-2218
Hrs Avail: 24

Charlottesville

Madison House
170 Rugby Road
Charlottesville, VA 22903
Crisis Phone 1: (804) 295-8255
Business Phone: (804) 977-7051
Hrs Avail: 24

Danville

Contact Crisis Line
P.O. Box 41
Danville, VA 24543
Danville: (804) 792-4357
Business Phone: (804) 793-4940
Hrs Avail: 8 A.M.–10 P.M.

Dumfries

* ACTS Helpline
P.O. Box 74
Dumfries, VA 22026
Crisis Phone 1: (703) 368-4141
Crisis Phone 2: (703) 368-6544
   (Spanish M-F 6 P.M.–10 P.M.)
Crisis Phone 3: (703) 368-8069
   (teen line)
Business Phone: (703) 368-
   4141
Hrs Avail: 24

Glenn Allen

Henrico Mental Health
10299 Woodman Road
Glenn Allen, VA 23060
Crisis Phone 1: (804) 261-8484
   (Henrico Co.)
Crisis Phone 2: (804) 748-6356
   (Chesterfield Co.)
Crisis Phone 3: (804) 556-3716
   (Goochland Co.)
Crisis Phone 4: (804) 752-4200
   (Hanover Co.)
Crisis Phone 5: (804) 598-2697
   (Powattan Co.)
Business Phone: (804) 261-
   8500
Hrs Avail: 24

Lynchburg

**Crisis Line of Central
   Virginia**
P.O. Box 3074
Lynchburg, VA 24503
Crisis Phone 1: (804) 947-4357
Business Phone: (804) 947-5921
Hrs Avail: 24

Martinsville

**Contact Martinsville-Henry
   Co.**
P.O. Box 1287
Martinsville, VA 24114
Crisis Phone 1: (540) 632-7295
Business Phone: (540) 638-
   8980
Hrs Avail: 24

Newport News

Contact Peninsula
P.O. Box 1006
Newport News, VA 23601
Crisis Phone 1: (757) 245-0041
Business Phone: (757) 244-
   0594
Hrs Avail: 24

Norfolk

*** The Crisis Line of the
   Planning Counsel**
P.O. Box 3278
Norfolk, VA 23514-3278
Crisis Phone 1: (757) 622-1126
Business Phone: (757) 622-1309
Hrs Avail: 24

Richmond

**Richmond Behavioral
   Healthcare Authority**
107 South 5th Street
Richmond, VA 23219
Crisis Phone 1: (804) 819-4100
Business Phone: (804) 819-
   4000
Hrs Avail: 24

Roanoke

**Trust: Crisis Hotline &
   Shelter**
404 Elm Avenue
Roanoke, VA 24016
Crisis Phone 1: (540) 344-1948
Crisis Phone 2: (540) 982-8336
   (teen line 6 P.M.–10 P.M.)

Business Phone: (540) 344-4691
Hrs Avail: 24

Winchester

Concern Hotline, Inc.
P.O. Box 2032
Winchester, VA 22601
Winchester: (540) 667-0145
Warren County: (540) 635-
   4357
Shenandoah County: (540)
   459-4742
Business Phone: (540) 667-
   8208
Hrs Avail: 24

WASHINGTON

Bremerton

Crisis Clinic of Penninsulas
5455 Almira Drive, NE
Bremerton, WA 98311
Crisis Phone 1: (360) 479-3033
Business Phone: (360) 415-
   5816
Hrs Avail: 24

Kitsap MH Services
5455 Almira Drive, NE
Bremerton, WA 98311
Crisis Phone 1: (360) 479-3033
Crisis Phone 2: (360) 373-
   3425
Crisis Phone 3: (800) 843-
   4793
Business Phone: (360) 373-
   5031
http://www.kitsapmentalhealth.
   org
Hrs Avail: 24

Cathlamet

**Wahkiakum County Mental
   Health**
42 Elochoman Valley Road
Cathlamet, WA 98612
Crisis Phone 1: (360) 795-8630
Crisis Phone 2: (800) 635-5989

Business Phone: (360) 795-8630
Hrs Avail: M-S 7 A.M.–6 P.M.

Clarkston

* Rogers Counseling Center
900 7th Street
Clarkston, WA 99403
Crisis Phone 1: (509) 758-4665
Crisis Phone 2: (509) 758-3341
Business Phone: (509) 758-3341
Hrs Avail: M-F 8:30 A.M.–5:30 P.M.

Colville

Stevens County Counseling Services
165 East Hawthorne
Colville, WA 99114
Crisis Phone 1: (509) 684-4597 (8 A.M.–4:30 P.M.)
Crisis Phone 2: (800) 767-6081 (weekends/after hrs.)
Business Phone: (509) 684-4597
Hrs Avail: 24

Coupeville

* Island Mental Health
P.O. Box 160
Coupeville, WA 98239
Crisis Phone 1: (800) 584-3578
http://www.voa.org
Hrs Avail: 24

Davenport

* Lincoln County Counseling Center
1211 Merriam
Davenport, WA 99122
Crisis Phone 1: (800) 767-6081
Crisis Phone 2: (509) 725-3001
Business Phone: (509) 725-3001
Hrs Avail: M-F 8 A.M.–5 P.M.

Dayton

* Columbia County Services
P.O. Box 30
Dayton, WA 99328

Crisis Phone 1: (509) 382-2527
Business Phone: (509) 382-2527
Hrs Avail: 24

Ellensburg

* Crisis Line of Kittitas County
110 West 6th Avenue
Ellensburg, WA 98926
Crisis Phone 1: (509) 925-4168
Business Phone: (509) 925-2166
Hrs Avail: 24

Everett

* Volunteers of America/Care-Crisis Response Services
P.O. Box 839
Everett, WA 98206
Crisis Phone 1: (425) 258-4357
Business Phone: (425) 259-3191
Hrs Avail: 24

Friday Harbor

* North Islands Mental Health
P.O. Box 247
Friday Harbor, WA 98250
Crisis Phone 1: (800) 584-3578
Business Phone: (360) 378-2669
Hrs Avail: M-F 8 A.M.–5 P.M.

Hoquiam

* Evergreen Counseling Center
615 8th Street
Hoquiam, WA 98550
Crisis Phone 1: (800) 685-6556
Crisis Phone 2: (360) 538-5327
Crisis Phone 3: (360) 538-2889
Business Phone: (360) 538-2889
Hrs Avail: 24

Kennewick

B-F Counties Crisis Response
2635 West Deschutes
Kennewick, WA 99336
Crisis Phone 1: (800) 548-8761
Business Phone: (509) 783-0500
Hrs Avail: 24

Long Beach

Willapa Counseling Center
P.O. Box 863
Long Beach, WA 98631
Crisis Phone 1: (800) 884-2298
Business Phone: (360) 642-3787
Hrs Avail: 24

Longview

* Lower Columbia Mental Health
1538 11th Avenue
Longview, WA 98632
Crisis Phone 1: (360) 425-6064
Crisis Phone 2: (360) 423-5380
http://www.peachealth.org
Hrs Avail: 24

Moses Lake

* Grant Mental Healthcare
P.O. Box 1057
Moses Lake, WA 98837
Crisis Phone 1: (509) 765-1717
Business Phone: (509) 765-9239
Hrs Avail: M-F 8 A.M.–5 P.M.

Mt. Vernon

* Community Mental Health
208 West Kincaid Street
Mt. Vernon, WA 98273
Crisis Phone 1: (800) 584-3578
Business Phone: (360) 416-7500
Hrs Avail: 24

Newport

*** Pend Oreille County
Mental Health**
P.O. Box 5055
Newport, WA 99156
Crisis Phone 1: (800) 404-5151
Business Phone: (509) 447-
5651
Hrs Avail: 24

Olympia

*** Crisis Clinic Resource
Network**
P.O. Box 2463
Olympia, WA 98506
Crisis Phone 1: (360) 586-2800
Business Phone: (360) 586-2888
www.crisis-clinic.org
Hrs Avail: 24

Omak

*** Okanogan County
Counseling Service**
P.O. Box 3208
Omak, WA 98841
Crisis Phone 1: (509) 826-6191
Crisis Phone 2: (866) 826-6191
Business Phone: (509) 826-6191
Hrs Avail: 24

Othello

*** Community Counseling
Services of Adams County**
165 North 1st Street
Othello, WA 99344
Crisis Phone 1: (509) 659-4357
Crisis Phone 2: (509) 488-5611
(teen line)
Business Phone: (509) 488-5611
Hrs Avail: 24

Port Angeles

*** Peninsula Community
Mental Health Center**
118 East 8th
Port Angeles, WA 98362

Crisis Phone 1: (360) 452-
4500
Business Phone: (360) 457-
0431
Hrs Avail: M-F 8 A.M.–5 P.M.

Port Townsend

*** Jefferson MH-Community
Counseling Service**
P.O. Box 565
Port Townsend, WA 98368
Crisis Phone 1: (360) 385-0321
Crisis Phone 2: (800) 659-0321
Business Phone: (360) 385-
0321
http://www.jmhs.org
Hrs Avail: 24

Pullman

**The Palouse Regional Crisis
Line/Nightline**
340 Northeast Maple
Suite 1
Pullman, WA 99163
Crisis Phone 1: (509) 332-1505
Business Phone: (509) 332-
1505
Hrs Avail: 24

Republic

*** Ferry County Community
Services**
42 Klondike Road
Republic, WA 99166
Crisis Phone 1: (800) 269-2380
Business Phone: (509) 775-
3341
Hrs Avail: 24

Richland

* Contact Tri-Cities
P.O. Box 684
Richland, WA 99352
Crisis Phone 1: (509) 943-6606
Business Phone: (509) 943-
9017
Hrs Avail: 24

Seattle

*** Crisis Clinic of King
County**
1515 Dexter Avenue North
Suite 300
Seattle, WA 98109
Crisis Phone 1: (800) 244-5756
Business Phone: (206) 461-
3210
www.crisisclinic.org
Hrs Avail: 24

**Seattle Counseling Service
for Sexual Minorities**
112 East Broadway Avenue
Seattle, WA 98102
Crisis Phone 1: (206) 461-3222
Business Phone: (206) 323-
1768
Hrs Avail: M-F 9 A.M.–5 P.M.

Spokane

* First Call for Help
107 South Division
Spokane, WA 99202
Crisis Phone 1: (509) 838-4428
Business Phone: (509) 838-
4651
Hrs Avail: 24

Stevenson

**Skamania County
Counseling Center**
P.O. Box 790
Stevenson, WA 98648
Crisis Phone 1: (509) 427-9488
Business Phone: (509) 427-
9488
Hrs Avail: 24

Tacoma

* Crisis Clinic of Pierce
1201 South Proctor
Tacoma, WA 98405
Crisis Phone 1: (253) 272-9882
Business Phone: (253) 404-
3503

www.compmh.org
Hrs Avail: 24

Walla Walla

* Inland Counseling Center
209 South Second Street
Walla Walla, WA 99362
Crisis Phone 1: (509) 522-4278
Business Phone: (509) 525-0241
Hrs Avail: 24

Wenatchee

* Chelan-Douglas Behavioral Health Clinic
701 North Miller Street
Wenatchee, WA 98801
Crisis Phone 1: (509) 662-7105
Crisis Phone 2: (800) 852-2923
Business Phone: (509) 662-7195
Hrs Avail: 24

Yakima

Behavioral Health Services
918 East Mead Avenue
Yakima, WA 98903
Crisis Phone 1: (509) 576-0934
Statewide Toll Free: (800) 572-8122
Business Phone: (509) 453-1344
Hrs Avail: 24

* Central WA Comprehensive Mental Health-Open Line
P.O. Box 959
Yakima, WA 98907
Crisis Phone 1: (509) 575-42002
Business Phone: (509) 576-4084
http://www.cwcmh.org
Hrs Avail: 24

WEST VIRGINIA

Huntington

Contact Huntington, Inc.
P.O. Box 2963
Huntington, WV 25728
Crisis Phone 1: (304) 523-3448
Business Phone: (304) 523-3447
www.CONTACTHUNTINGTON.com
Hrs Avail: 24

Lewisburg

Seneca Health Services
100 Church Street
Lewisburg, WV 24901
Crisis Phone 1: (304) 645-3319
Business Phone: (304) 645-3319
www.SHSINC.org
Hrs Avail: 24

Oak Hill

Contact-Care of Southern WV
P.O. Box 581
Oak Hill, WV 25901
Crisis Phone 1: (304) 877-3535
Business Phone: (304) 877-3535
Hrs Avail: 24

Wheeling

Hillcrest of Ohio Valley Medical
111 Parkview Lane
Wheeling, WV 43935
Crisis Phone 1: (304) 242-2908
Business Phone: (304) 242-2908
Hrs Avail: 24

WISCONSIN

Appleton

Appleton County Crisis Intervention Center
401 Elm Street
Appleton, WI 54911

Crisis Phone 1: (920) 832-4646
Business Phone: (920) 832-4646
Hrs Avail: 24

Cedarburg

Cope Ozaukee County Hotline
P.O. Box 723
Cedarburg, WI 53012
Crisis Phone 1: (414) 377-2673
Crisis Phone 2: (414) 377-2673
Business Phone: (414) 377-1477
http://www.coperesources.net
Hrs Avail: 24

Eau Claire

* Omni Clinic
221 West Madison Street
Eau Claire, WI 54703
Crisis Phone 1: (715) 832-5030
Business Phone: (715) 832-5030
Hrs Avail: 24

Elkhorn

Walworth Co. Dept. of Human Services
P.O. Box 1005 W4051
Elkhorn, WI 53121
Crisis Phone 1: (262) 741-3200
Business Phone: (262) 741-3200
Hrs Avail: 24

Fond Du Lac

CIC/Fond Du Lac County Health Center
459 East 1st Street
Fond Du Lac, WI 54935
Crisis Phone 1: (920) 929-3535
Business Phone: (920) 929-3500
Hrs Avail: 24

Grafton

The County Hotline of Cope Ozaukee
885 Badger Circle
Grafton, WI 53024
Crisis Phone 1: (262) 377-2673
Crisis Phone 2: (262) 377-7786
  (teen line/senior support)
Business Phone: (262) 377-1477
http://www.coperesources.net
Hrs Avail: 24

Green Bay

* Family Services of Northeast Wisconsin, Inc.
P.O. Box 22308
Green Bay, WI 54305
Crisis Phone 1: (920) 436-8888
Business Phone: (920) 436-6813
www.familyservicesnew.org
Hrs Avail: 24

La Crosse

First Call For Help
1910 South Avenue
La Crosse, WI 54601
Crisis Phone 1: (608) 791-4344
Crisis Phone 2: (800) 362-8255
Business Phone: (608) 791-6335
Hrs Avail: 24

Madison

* Emergency Services MHC of Dane County
625 West Washington Avenue
Madison, WI 53703
Crisis Phone 1: (608) 280-2600
Business Phone: (608) 280-2700
Hrs Avail: 24

Milwaukee

Psychiatric Crisis Service
9499 West Watertown Plank Road
Milwaukee, WI 53226

Crisis Phone 1: (414) 257-7222
Business Phone: (414) 257-7260
Hrs Avail: 24

Sturgeon Bay

HELP of Door County, Inc.
332 Pennsylvania Avenue
Sturgeon Bay, WI 54235
Crisis Phone 1: (920) 743-8818
Business Phone: (920) 743-8785
www.helpofdoorcounty.org
Hrs Avail: 24

Waukesha

MHA in Waukesha Co., Inc. c/o First Call for Help
S22 West 22660 Broadway
Suite 5S
Waukesha, WI 53186-8199
Crisis Phone 1: (262) 547-3388 (TTY)
Business Phone: (262) 547-0769
http://www.mhawauk.org
Hrs Avail: 24

WYOMING

Cheyenne

Cheyenne Helpline
P.O. Box 404
Cheyenne, WY 82003
Crisis Phone 1: (307) 634-4469
Business Phone: (307) 632-4132
Hrs Avail: 24

Worland

Victims of Violence Center
101 North 19th Street
Worland, WY 82401
Crisis Phone 1: (307) 347-4991
Business Phone: (307) 347-4992
Hrs Avail: 24

CANADA
PROVINCIAL AND TERRITORIAL AGENCIES

ALBERTA

Canadian MH ASSN
723 14th Street NW
Suite 103
Calgary, Alberta T2N 2A4
Tel: (403) 266-1605

Distress Centre
112 11th Avenue SE
Calgary, Alberta T2G 0X5
Tel: (403) 264-8336

PACE
201 10118-101 Avenue
Grand Prairie, Alberta T8V 0Y2
Tel: (780) 539-6666

Salvation Army Suicide Prevention Bureau
9620-101A Avenue
Edmonton, Alberta T5H 0C7
Tel: (780) 428-TEEN

Samaritans of Southern Alberta
P.O. Box 939
Lethbridge, Alberta T1J 3Z1
Tel: (403) 320-1212

Suicide Prevention Program
9912 Manning Avenue
Fort McMurray, Alberta T9H 2B9
Tel: (780) 743-4357

BRITISH COLUMBIA

The Crisis Center
763 East Broadway
Vancouver, British Columbia V5T 1X8
Tel: (604) 872-1811

MANITOBA

Klinic Community Health Centre, Inc.
870 Portage Avenue
Winnipeg, Manitoba R3G OP1
Tel: (888) 322-3019

NEW BRUNSWICK

Chimo Help Line
P.O. Box 1033
Fredericton, New Brunswick
E3B 5C2
Tel: (506) 450-4357

NOVA SCOTIA

Help Line
5670 Spring Garden Road
Halifax, Nova Scotia B3J 1H6
Tel: (902) 421-1188

ONTARIO

Canadian Medical Association
P.O. Box 8650
Ottawa, Ontario K1G 0G8
Tel: (613) 731-9331

Distress Centre # 1 Toronto
P.O. Box 243
Toronto, Ontario M5C 2J4
Tel: (416) 598-1121

Distress Centre # 2 Toronto
P.O. Box 243
Toronto, Ontario M5C 2J4
Tel: (416) 486-6766

Distress Centre Ottawa
160 Elgin Street
Ottawa, Ontario K2P 2M3
Tel: (613) 238-1089

Distress Centre Windsor
P.O. Box 2025
Windsor, Ontario N8Y 4R5
Tel: (519) 256-5009

Toronto East General Hospital
825 Coxwell Avenue
Toronto, Ontario M4C 3E7
Tel: (416) 469-6286

QUEBEC

Centre De Prevention Du Suicide
1535 Chemin Ste. Foy
Suite 100
Quebec, P.Q. G15 2P1
Tel: (418) 683-0933

Suicide Action
2345 Belangereast
Montreal, Quebec H2G 1C9
Tel: (514) 723-3594

SASKATCHEWAN

Saskatoon Crisis Intervention Services
1410 20th Street West
Saskatoon, Saskatchewan
S7M 024
Tel: (306) 933-6200

APPENDIX III
INTERNATIONAL SUICIDE RATES PER 100,000

Country	Year	Men	Women	Total	Country	Year	Men	Women	Total
Albania	1998	6.3	3.6	4.9	Kuwait	1999	2.7	1.6	2.1
Argentina	1996	9.9	3.0	6.4	Kyrgyzstan	1999	19.3	4.0	11.6
Armenia	1999	2.7	0.9	1.8	Latvia	1999	52.6	13.1	32.8
Australia	1997	22.7	6.0	14.3	Lithuania	1999	73.8	13.6	43.7
Austria	1999	28.7	10.3	19.5	Luxembourg	1997	29.0	9.8	19.4
Azerbaijan	1999	1.1	0.2	0.65	Macedonia FYR	1997	11.5	4.0	7.7
Bahamas	1995	2.2	0.0	1.1	Malta	1999	11.7	2.6	7.1
Bahrain	1988	4.9	0.5	2.7	Mauritius	1998	21.9	7.8	14.8
Barbados	1995	9.6	3.7	6.6	Mexico	1995	5.4	1.0	3.2
Belarus	1999	61.1	10.0	35.5	Mexico	1995	5.4	1.0	3.2
Belgium	1995	31.3	11.7	21.5	Netherlands	1997	13.5	6.7	10.1
Belize	1995	12.1	0.9	6.5	New Zealand	1998	23.7	6.9	15.3
Brazil	1995	6.6	1.8	8.4	Nicaragua	1994	4.7	2.2	3.4
Bulgaria	1999	24.1	8.1	16.1	Norway	1997	17.8	6.6	12.2
Canada	1997	19.6	5.1	12.3	Paraguay	1994	3.4	1.2	2.3
Chile	1994	10.2	1.4	5.8	Philippines	1993	2.5	1.7	2.1
China (partial)	1998	13.4	14.8	14.1	Poland	1996	24.1	4.6	14.3
Hong Kong SAR	1996	15.9	9.1	12.5	Portugal	1998	8.7	2.7	5.7
Colombia	1994	5.5	1.5	3.5	Puerto Rico	1992	16	1.9	8.9
Costa Rica	1995	9.7	2.1	5.9	Republic of Korea	1997	17.8	8.0	12.9
Croatia	1999	32.7	11.5	22.1	Republic of Moldova	1999	27.6	5.1	16.3
Cuba	1996	24.5	12.0	18.2	Romania	1999	20.3	4.4	12.3
Czech Republic	1999	25.7	6.2	15.9	Russian Federation	1998	62.6	11.6	37.1
Denmark	1996	24.3	9.8	17.0	Singapore	1998	13.9	9.5	11.7
Ecuador	1995	6.4	3.2	4.8	Slovakia	1999	22.5	3.7	13.1
Egypt	1987	0.1	0.0	0.1	Slovenia	1999	47.3	13.4	30.3
El Salvador	1993	10.4	5.5	7.9	Spain	1997	13.1	4.2	8.6
Estonia	1999	56.0	12.1	34.0	Sri Lanka	1991	44.6	16.8	30.7
Finland	1998	38.3	10.1	24.2	Surinam	1992	16.6	7.2	11.9
France	1997	28.4	10.1	19.2	Sweden	1996	20.0	8.5	14.2
Georgia	1992	6.6	2.1	4.3	Switzerland	1996	29.2	11.6	20.4
Germany	1998	21.5	7.3	28.8	Tajikistan	1995	5.1	1.8	3.4
Greece	1998	6.1	1.7	3.9	Thailand	1994	5.6	2.4	4
Guatemala	1984	0.9	0.1	0.5	Trinidad/Tobago	1994	17.5	5.1	11.3
Guyana	1994	14.6	6.5	10.5	Turkmenistan	1998	13.8	3.5	8.6
Hungary	1999	53.1	14.8	33.9	Ukraine	1999	51.2	10.0	30.6
Iceland	1996	20.8	3.7	12.2	United Kingdom	1998	11.7	3.3	7.5
India	1998	12.2	9.1	10.6	USA	1998	18.6	4.4	11.2
Iran	1991	0.3	0.1	0.2	Uruguay	1990	16.6	4.2	10.4
Ireland	1996	19.2	3.5	11.3	Uzbekistan	1998	10.5	3.1	6.8
Israel	1997	10.5	2.6	6.5	Venezuela	1994	8.3	1.9	5.1
Italy	1997	12.7	3.9	8.3	Yugoslavia	1990	21.6	9.2	15.4
Japan	1997	26.0	11.9	18.9	Zimbabwe	1990	10.6	5.2	7.9
Kazakhstan	1999	46.4	8.6	27.5					

BIBLIOGRAPHY

Apter, et al. "Correlation of suicidal and violent behavior in different diagnostic categories in hospitalized adolescent patients," *Journal of the American Academy of Child and Adolescent Psychiatry.* 34 (1995): 7–11.

Balak, A., Cornelius, J., Thase, M., and Salloum, I. "Cocaine use associated with increased suicidal behavior in depressed alcoholics," *Addictive Behaviors.* 23/1 (1998): 119–121.

Blumenthal, S. J. "Suicide: A guide to risk factors, assessment, and treatment of suicidal patients," *Medical Clinics of North America.* 72(4) (1998): 937–71.

Blumenthal, S. J., and Kupfer, D. J., eds. *Suicide over the life cycle: Risk factors, assessment, and treatment of suicidal patients.* Washington, D.C.: American Psychiatric Press, 1990.

Brent, D. A., et al. "Long-term impact of exposure to suicide: A three-year controlled follow-up," *Journal of the American Academy of Child and Adolescent Psychiatry.* 35 (1996): 5–13.

Breton, J. J., Tousignant, M., Bergeron, L., Berthiaume, C. "Informant-specific correlates of suicidal behavior in a community survey of 12- to 14-year-olds." *Journal of the American Academy of Child and Adolescent Psychiatry.* 41/6 (June 2002): 723–30.

Cohen, D. "Homicide-suicide in older people," *Psychiatric Times.* 17/1 (2000): 49–52.

———. "Homicide-suicide in the aged: A growing public health problem," *Journal of Mental Health and Aging.* 1/2 (1995): 83–84.

Cohen, D. and Wareham, J. "An analysis of contemporary state statutes about assisted suicide," *Journal of Mental Health and Aging.* 4/1 (1998): 4–8.

Cohen, D., Llorente, M., Eisdorfer, C. "Homicide-suicide in older persons," *American Journal of Psychiatry.* 155/3 (1998): 390–396.

Conwell, Y., Brent, D. "Suicide and aging: Patterns of psychiatric diagnosis," *International Psychogeriatrics.* 7/2 (1995): 149–64.

Conwell, Y. "Suicide in elderly patients." In Schneider, L. S., Reynolds, C. F. III, Lebowitz, B. D., Friedhoff, A. J., eds. *Diagnosis and Treatment of Depression in Late Life.* Washington, D.C.: American Psychiatric Press, 1994.

Cordaro, J. "Who defers to whom? The Attorney General targets Oregon's Death with Dignity Act," *Fordham Law Review.* 70/6 (May 2002): 2477–514.

Desjarlais, R., Eisenberg, L., Good, B., Kleinman, A., eds. *World Mental Health: Problems and Priorities in Low-Income Countries.* New York: Oxford University Press, 1996.

Driessen, M., John, U., Veltrup, C., and Weber, J. "Psychiatric comorbidity, suicidal behavior, and suicidal ideation in alcoholics seeking treatment," *Addiction.* 93/6 (1998): 889–894.

Du L., Bakish, D., et al. "Association of polymorphism of serotonin 2A receptor gene with suicidal ideation in major depressive disorder," *American Journal of Medical Genetics.* 96/1 (February 2000): 56–60.

Fedden, H. R. *Suicide: A Social and Historical Study.* London: Peter Davies, 1938.

Fergusson, D. M., Horwood, L. J., Lynskey, M. T. "Childhood sexual abuse and psychiatric disorder in young adulthood, II: psychiatric outcomes of childhood sexual abuse," *Journal of the American Academy of Child and Adolescent Psychiatry.* 35/10 (1996): 1365–74.

Gould, M. S., King, R., Greenwald, S., et al. "Psychopathology associated with suicidal ideation and attempts among children and adolescents," *Journal of the American Academy of Child and Adolescent Psychiatry.* 37/9 (1998): 915–23.

Hankoff, L. D. "Ancient Egyptian Attitudes toward Death and Suicide" *Pharos* (April 1975): 60–64, 75.

Hazen, P. G., Carney, J. F., Walker, A. E., Stewart, J. J. "Depression—a side effect of 13-cis-retinoic acid therapy," *Journal of the American Academy of Dermatology.* 9 (1983): 278–279.

Heckman, T. G., et al. "Thoughts of suicide among HIV-infected rural persons enrolled in a telephone-delivered mental health intervention," *Annals of Behavioral Medicine.* 24/2 (Spring 2002): 141–8.

Hillbrand, Marc and Spitz, Reuben T., eds. *Lipids, Health, and Behavior.* Washington, D.C.: American Psychological Association, 1997.

Horgan, John. "Right to Die," *Scientific American* (May 1996). Available online at: http://www.sciam.com/0596issue/0596infocus.html

Hoyert, D. L., Arias, E., Smith, B. L., Murphy, S. L., and Kochanek, K. D. "Deaths: Final data for 1999," *National Vital Statistics Report.* 49/8 (2001). DHHS Publication No. (PHS) 2001–1120.

Hughs, D. H. "Can the clinician predict suicide?" *Psychiatric Services.* 46 (1995): 5–13.

Jacobs, D., ed. *The Harvard Medical School Guide to Suicide Assessment and Intervention.* San Francisco, Calif.: Jossey-Bass, 1999.

Jiwanlal, S. S. and Weitzel, C. "The suicide myth," *RN.* 64/1 (January 2001): 33–7.

Khan, A., Leventhal, R. M., Khan, S., Brown, W. A. "Suicide risk in patients with anxiety disorders: a meta-analysis of the FDA database," *Journal of Affective Disorders.* 68/2–3 (April 2002): 183–90.

Kaplan, S. J., Pelcovitz, D., Salzinger, S., et al. "Adolescent physical abuse and suicide attempts," *Journal of the American Academy of Child and Adolescent Psychiatry.* 36/6 (1997): 799–808.

Kessler, R. C., Borges, G., Walters, E. E. "Prevalence of and risk factors for lifetime suicide attempts in the National Comorbidity Survey," *Archives of General Psychiatry.* 56/7 (1999): 617–26.

Kyba, F. C. "Legal and ethical issues in end-of-life care," *Critical Care Nursing Clin North America.* 14/2 (June 2002): 141–55, vii.

Kleinman, A. and Cohen, A. "Psychiatry's global challenge. *Scientific American.* (March 1997): 86–89.

Lee, S. and Kleinman, A. "Mental illness and social change in China,"

Harvard Review of Psychiatry. 5/1 (1997): 43–46.

Lindberg, G., Bingefors, K., Roenstam, J. et al. "Use of calcium channel blockers and risk of suicide: Ecological findings confirmed in population based cohort study," *British Medical Journal.* 316 (1998): 741.

Lipschitz, A. "College suicide: A review monograph," New York: *American Foundation for Suicide Prevention.* 1990.

Loh, Jules, "The man with a gun is a cop; The gun is in his mouth," *The Oregonian.* (January 30, 1994): A24.

Luoma, J. B., Martin, C. E., Pearson, J. L. "Contact with mental health and primary care providers before suicide: a review of the evidence," *American Journal of Psychiatry.* 159/6 (June 2002): 909–16.

Main, Carla T. "Dying for an Injunction: The debate over Oregon," *National Review Online.* http://www.nationalreview.com

Malphurs, J. E. and Cohen, D. "A newspaper surveillance study of homicide-suicide in the United States," *American Journal of Forensic Medicine Pathology.* 23/2 (June 2002): 142–8.

Mann, J., McBride, A., Brown, R., et al. "Relationship between central and peripheral serotonin indexes in depressed and suicidal psychiatric inpatients," *Archives of General Psychiatry.* 49 (1992): 442–446.

Mann, J. J., Oquendo, M., Underwood, M. D. et al. "The neurobiology of suicide risk: a review for the clinician," *Journal of Clinical Psychiatry.* 1999; 60 (Supplement 2) (1999): 7–11.

Matas, Robert. "Oregon Reconsiders Death-With-Dignity Law, *The Globe and Mail* (November 3, 1997): A1.

McCraig, L. F., Stussman, B. J. "National Hospital Ambulatory Care Survey: 1996. Emergency

department summary." *Advance Data from Vital and Health Statistics, no. 293.* Hyattsville, Md.: National Center for Health Statistics, 1997. http://www.cdc.gov/nchs/data/ad293.pdf

McCue, J. D. and Cohen, L. M. "Freud's physician-assisted death," *Archives of Internal Medicine.* 159 (1999): 1521–1525.

McIntosh, J. L., Santos, J. F., Hubberd, R. W., eds. *Elder Suicide: Research, Theory, and Treatment.* Washington, D.C.: American Psychological Association, 1995.

Morbidity and Mortality Weekly Report, "Nonfatal self-inflicted injuries treated in hospital emergency departments —United States, 2000," *MMWR Morbidity and Mortality Weekly Report.* 24; 51 (20) (May 2002): 436–8.

National Center for Injury Prevention and Control. *Fact Book for the Year 2000: Suicide and Suicide Behavior.* http://www.cdc.gov/ncipc/ pubres/FactBook/suicide.htm

———. "Suicide deaths and rates per 100,000: United States 1994–1997." http://www.cdc.gov/ncipc/data/us9794/Suic.htm

Neutel, C. and Patten, S. "Risk of suicide attempts after benzodiazepine and/or antidepressant use," *Annals of Epidemiology.* 7/8 (1997): 568–574.

"Cop suicides listed at 300 for this year," *New York Newsday* (December 31, 1994): A7.

Nilsson, L., Ahlbom, A., Farahmand, B. Y., Asberg, M., Tomson, T. "Risk factors for suicide in epilepsy: a case control study," *Epilepsia.* 43/6 (June 2002): 644–51.

Noah, L. "Attorney General's intrusion into clinical practice," *New England Journal of Medicine.* 346/24 (June 13, 2002): 1918–19.

Oregon Health Division. "Oregon's Death with Dignity Act: Annual

Report 2000." http://www.ohd.hr.state.or.us/chs/pas/ar-disc.htm

Petronis, K. R., Samuels, J. F., Moscicki, E. K., et al. "An epidemiologic investigation of potential risk factors for suicide attempts," *Social Psychiatry and Psychiatric Epidemiology.* 25/4 (1990): 193–9.

Pfleger, Katherine. "Ashcroft to Pursue Suicide Doctors," *Washington Post,* http://www.washingtonpost.com/wp-srv

Piven, J. "Narcissistic revenge and suicide: the case of Yukio Mishima." Part II. *Psychoanalytic Review.* 89/1 (February 2002): 49–77.

Quillen, T. "Palliative sedation vs. assisted suicide," *Nursing.* 32/5 (May 2002): 12.

Rotheram-Borus, M., Piacentini, J., Miller, S., Graae, F., and Castro-Blanco, D., "Brief cognitive-behavioral treatment for adolescent suicide attempters and their families," *Journal of the American Academy of Child and Adolescent Psychiatry.* 33 (1994): 508–517.

Shaffer, D., Gould, M. and Hicks, R. "Worsening suicide rate in black teenagers," *American Journal of Psychiatry.* 151/12 (1994): 1810–1812.

Vieland, V., Whittle, B., Garland, A., et al. "The impact of curriculum-based suicide prevention programs for teenagers: an 18-month follow-up," *Journal of the American Academy of Child and Adolescent Psychiatry.* 30/5 (1991): 811–5.

Volanti, John, "The mystery within, understanding police suicide," *FBI Law Enforcement Bulletin.* (February 1995): 19–23.

————. *Police Suicide: Epidemic in Blue.* Springfield, Ill.: Charles C. Thomas, 1996.

Waern, M., et al. "Burden of illness and suicide in elderly people: case-control study," *British Medical Journal.* 324/7350 (June 8, 2002): 1355.

Weissman, M. M., Bland, R. C., Canino, G. J., et al. "Prevalence of suicide ideation and suicide attempts in nine countries," *Psychological Medicine.* 29 (1) (1999): 9–17.

Weitoft, G. R., Haglund, B., Hjern, A., Rosen, M. "Mortality, severe morbidity and injury among long-term lone mothers in Sweden," *International Journal of Epidemiology.* 31/3 (June 2002): 573–580.

Wirthwein, D. P., Barnard, J. J., Prahlow, J. A. "Suicide by drowning: a 20-year review," *Journal of Forensic Science.* 47/1 (January 2002): 131–136.

World Health Organization, "WHO Statistics: Numbers of Deaths and Death Rates," American Foundation for Suicide Prevention. http://www.afsp.org/index1.htm

Yamey, Gavin. "Suicide rate is decreasing in England and Wales," *British Medical Journal.* 320 (January 8, 2000): 75.

INDEX

David of Augsburg **64**
DEA. *See* Drug Enforcement
  Administration
Dean, James B. **64–65,** 200
Death: The Final Stage of Growth
  (Kübler-Ross) 43
death certificates 57, **65,** 165
death education 17–18, **65**
Death of Man (Shneidman) 213
Death of Peregrinis, The (Lucian)
  65–66, 153
death wish **66**
"death with dignity" 90
Death with Dignity law. *See* Ore-
  gon law
"Death-Persuader" 115
Decalogue Article 20, **66**
Decius the Younger xix
Deer Hunter, The (film) 56
"Defense of legal suicide, A"
  (Montaigne) 164
Definition of Suicide (Shneidman)
  66
"Dejection: An Ode" (Coleridge)
  66–67
Delaware 216
delle Vigne, Pier. *See* Vigne, Pier
  delle
Democritus xx
Demosthenes xix, **67**
Denmark **67,** 107, 208–209
Dentist Well-Being Program 68
dentists and suicide **67–68**
departing drugs **68**
Departing Drugs (EXIT publication) 92
depression **68–69,** 161, 203
  Accutane and 2–3
  in alcoholics 7, 8
  and attempted suicide 18
  in bipolar disorder 27, 68,
    156
  breakup of romance and 204
  bulimia in 30
  calcium channel blockers and
    33
  in cancer patients 35

cause of 69
in children 40
cholesterol and 44
cocaine and 51
in college students 51
crying in 60
electroconvulsive treatment
  for 80–81
in epilepsy 86
gender and 68
insomnia in 130, 214
loss of humor in 125
"masked" 124
melatonin and 81
neurobiology of 172
reserpine and 201
in schizophrenia 209
sense of loss in 151
serotonin and 44
in teenagers 227, 228
treatment of 69. *See also*
  antidepressants
in unemployed 235
in victims of bullying 30
warning signs of 68
withdrawal in 242
in women 95, 235
diabetes **69**
*Dialogue of a Misanthrope with His
  Own Soul, A* (ancient papyrus)
  xvi
Diary of a Writer, The (Dostoevsky) 72
diazepam 233, 237
dichotomous thinking **69**
Dictionnaire de Trevoux xv
Dido xix
"dignity, death with" 90
Diogenes 12, **69**
direct and indirect self-destructive behavior (ISDB) **69,** 87,
  119, 129, 211
direct communication 52
direct euthanasia 90
*Directory of Suicide Prevention and
  Crisis Intervention Agencies in the
  U.S.* 9

disbelief stage of grief process
  110
Dispossessed, The (Berryman) 25
Dispute over Suicide, A (ancient
  papyrus) xvi
distress centres (Canada)
  69–70, 233, 237
distress signals 49–50, **70.** *See
  also* risk of suicide
  abnormal coping mechanisms
    as 57
  acting out as 3
  in adults 4
  aggressive behavior as 6
  in alcoholics 6
  attempted suicide as. *See*
    attempted suicide
  change in eating habits as 78
  in children 41–42
  communication of suicidal
    intent as 52–53
  crying as 60
  death wish as 66
  decline in grades as 109
  in doctors 71
  in elderly 80
  irrationality as 135
  isolation as 136
  loss of concentration as 56
  loss of will as 241–242
  mood swings as 164
  obsession with death as 175
  reckless driving as 200
  stress as 217
  substance abuse and 2
  teachers recognizing
    225–226
  in teenagers 227–228
  watching for 133
  withdrawal as 242
District of Columbia 216
Divine Comedy (Dante) xxiii
divorce and suicide **70,** 157
"Do Not Go Gentle Into That
  Good Night" (Thomas) 232
Doctor Death. *See* Kevorkian,
  Jack

"love-pact suicide" 221
Loving Outreach to Survivors of
a Suicide (LOSS) 58, **152**
Lowell, Robert **152**
low-frequency electromagnetic
fields 81
Lowry, Malcolm **153**
loyalty suicides 55, 130, **153**.
See also altruistic suicide
LPS. *See* Lanterman-Petrie-Short
Act
LSD 73, **153**
LTTE. *See* Liberation Tigers of
Tamil Eelam
Lucan (Marcus Annaeus
Lucanus) xxi, **153,** 172, 239
Lucian 65–66, **153**
Lucrece xxi, 123
Lucretius 86
lunar changes, and suicide
84–85, 230
Lutheran Church xxiv, 58, 91
Luxembourg 107
lysergic acid diethylamide. *See*
LSD

M

Macedonia 107
Mack, John E. 239
Madame Bovary (Flaubert) 97
magical thinking and suicide
155
Mahasati 222
Mahayana 30
Maine
suicide rate for 216
voting on assisted suicide 15
Major, Joe 221
major tranquilizers 233
male suicides 4, 104, **155,**
201–202, 212
in African Americans 4–5
aggressive behavior and 104
in Apaches 13
in Canada 34
cancer and 35

in children 41
depression and 68
divorce and 70
in doctors 71, 185
economic cycles and 82
in elderly 79
in England 83
honor and 123
and methods of suicide 92,
104, 114, 155, 162, 185
in teenagers 226–227
Malinowski, Bronislaw 4,
155–156
Malta 107
Man Against Himself (Menninger)
46, **156,** 160, 195
Mandell, Johnny 220
mania 27, 156
manic depression 27, **156,** 161
in college students 51
depression in 27, 68, 156
manipulative suicide **156**
Many Faces of Suicide, The (Farberow) **156**
MAO inhibitors **156–157**
Marcus Aurelius **157**
marijuana **157**
Maris, Ronald W. 55, 111
marital status and suicide 70,
157, 202
Marplan 156
Marr, Neil 30
Marshall Islands 215
Martin, Sandy 149
martyrdom 96, **157–158.** *See
also* kamikaze pilots; terrorism
and suicide
of Donatists 71–72
of early Christians xxi, 44
Eusebius on 45, 89
Ignatius on 45, 127
Synod of Nîmes on 223
Martyrs of Palestine (Eusebius)
89
Maryland 216
Masada xviii, 91, 96, 137, 138,
140, **158,** 159, 163

Masaryk, Thomas G. xxix
*M*A*S*H* (television series) 220
"masked depression" 124
mass suicide **158–159**. *See also*
cult suicide; Masada; Treblinka
in India 128
in Middle Ages xxiii
Massachusetts 216
matai 216
Mauritius 107
Maximus Valerius **159**
Mayan culture 136
McClure, Guy 83
McCollum, John 179
McIntosh, John L. 88, **159–160,**
201
media, effects of suicide coverage 53, **160,** 219, 229–230
medical personnel **160**
Mein Kampf (Hitler) 120
melancholy 11, 32, 64, 84, 105
melatonin 81
Memorabilia (Xenophon) 245
Menninger, Karl xxx–xxxi,
160–161
on accidents 200
on chronic suicide xxxi, 46,.
64
on drives of suicide
xxx–xxxi, 249
Man Against Himself by 46,
156, 160, 195
The Vital Balance by 161
Menninger Clinic 161
menstruation and suicide **161**
mental illness **161**. *See also specific illness*
in alcoholics 7
in college students 51
in Hispanic Americans 120
with impulsiveness 128
and suicide risk 203
in teenagers 228
meprobamata 233
mercy killing. *See* euthanasia
methadone 119
methane 103

profiles of 173–174, 233
protective factors of
228–229
rates of 226
risk factors of 228
status loss and 217
stress and 101, 228
and suicide notes 220
warning signs of 227–228
Teicher, Martin 192
telephone intervention **229**. *See also* crisis hotlines
television, effect on suicide 53, 160, 219, **229–230**
temporal factors 85, **230**
"Ten Commandments of Suicide" 66
Tennessee 216
terrorism and suicide 91, 135, 166, **230–232**
tetrahydrocannabinol 157
Texas 216
Thailand 108
thanatology **232**
Thanatos xxx, **232**
thanatron 142
THC 157
Thebes **232**
Theognis of Megara xx
Theseus xix
third degree intent 131
Thomas, Dylan **232**
Thracians **232**
threats, suicide **221–222**
Thucydides xix
Tijuana Cult 61
Tikopia xv, 191
time of day, and suicide 85, 230
Tiv of Nigeria 191, **232**
Tojo, General Hideki **232**
Toledo, Council of xxii
Tom Sawyer **233**
Too Young to Die: Youth and Suicide (Klagsbrun) 144, **233**
Torah xvii
Toronto Distress Centre **233**

traffic accidents **233**. *See also* autocide
tranquilizers **233,** 237
tranylepromine 156
Treatise of Human Nature (Hume) 124
treatment. *See* counseling; postvention
Treblinka 91, 159, **233–234**
tricyclic antidepressants 74, 78–79
Trinidad and Tobago 108
Trobriand Islanders xv, xvi, 55
Trosse, George **234**
Troyes, Council of xxii
Truman, Harry S. 98–99
Tuinal 24
Turkmenistan 108
Twain, Mark 233
twin studies of suicide 105
Two Treaties of Government (Locke) 150
tyramine 157

U

Ukraine 108
Ulysses (Joyce) 140
Under Milk Wood (Thomas) 232
Under the Volcano (Lowry) 153
unemployment and suicide 132, 175, **235**
Unfinished Business: Pressure Points in the Lives of Women (Scarf) **235**
unintentional death **235**
United Kingdom. *See* England; Scotland; Wales
unusual methods of suicide **235**
urban suicide **235–236**
Uruguay 108
U.S. suicide statistics 108, 132, **236**
state-by-state **216**
Uses of Enchantment, The (Bettelheim) 26, **236**

Utah 216
Utopia (More) xxiv, 201, **236**
Uzbekistan 108

V

Valence, Council of xxii
Valium 233, **237**
Van Dusen, Henry Pitney 46
Van Eirland, Corlenia 109
Vancouver Crisis Centre **237**
Varady, Geza 62, 126
Varah, Chad 48, 207, **237–238**
Vatel **238**
Venezuela 108
verbal direct communication 52
verbal indirect communication 52
Vermont 216
"victim-precipitated" murders 219, **238**
Vienna Psychoanalytical Society 76, 100, 126, 176, **238**
Vietnamese Suicide 61, 159
Vigne, Pier delle **228**
Villechaize, Herve **238–239**
Virginia 216
Vital Balance, The (Menninger) 161
Vivienne: The Life and Suicide of an Adolescent Girl (Mack and Hickler) **239**
Voltaire (François-Marie Arouet) xxvi, 45, 186, **239**
Volteius **239**
Voluntary Euthanasia Society 90, 144, **239**
Voluntary Euthanasia Society of Scotland. *See* EXIT
volunteers **239–240**
of Befrienders International 24
clergy 48
at crisis hotlines 56, 98, 101, 207–208, 239
in support groups 219
Vonnegut, Kurt, Jr. **240**